A History of QST
Volume 1: Amateur Radio Technology
1915-2013

Edited by **Ward Silver, NØAX**

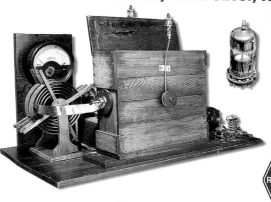

ARRL 100 YEARS

Contributors
Jim Breakall, WA3FET
Tim Duffy, K3LR
Hal Kennedy, N4GG
Phil Karn, KA9Q
Jan King, W3GEY
Dave Leeson, W6NL
Carl Luetzelschwab, K9LA
John Stanley, K4ERO

Cover Design
Sue Fagan, KB1OKW

Production—Design and Layout
Michelle Bloom, WB1ENT

Copyright © 2013 by
The American Radio Relay League, Inc.

Copyright secured under the Pan-American Convention

International copyright secured.

All rights reserved. No part of this work may be reproduced in any form except by written permission of the publisher. All rights of translation are reserved.

Printed in the USA

Quedan reservados todos los derechos

ISBN: 978-1-62595-003-1

First Edition
First Printing

Please e-mail us at **pubsfdbk@arrl.org** (publications feedback) to give us your comments on this book and what you would like to see in future editions. Please include your name, call, e-mail address and the book title, edition and printing in the body of your message. Also indicate whether or not you are an ARRL member.

Table of Contents

Foreword

About This Book

Contributor Biographies

About the ARRL

Amateur Radio in the Spark Era
"Operation of a Non-Synchronous Rotating Gap" by A.S. Blatterman
"Applications of the Audion" by Paul F. Godley
"Transatlantic Amateur Communication Accomplished!" by K.B. Warner, 1BHW

Amateur Radio's Contributions to Propagation Science
"The Reflection of Short Waves" by John Reinartz, 1XAM
"The Status of 28,000-kc. Communication" by Ross Hull
"Practical Communication on the 224-Mc Band" by Ross Hull
"Transequatorial Propagation of VHF Signals" by R.G. Cracknell, ZE2JV
"Observations on Long-Delay Echoes" by J.H. Dellinger
"Lunar DX on 144 Mc.!" By Ed Tilton, W1HDQ
"MINIMUF: A Simplified MUF-Prediction Program for Microcomputers"
    by Robert Rose, K6GKU

Amateur Radio's Collaboration with the Scientific Community
"The Bureau of Standards – A.R.R.L. Tests of Short Wave Radio Signal Fading" by S. Kruse
"MacMillan Expedition Nears Arctic Daybreak" by K. B. Warner, 1BHW
"Radio Astronomy" by Byron Goodman, W1DX
"ARRL-IGY Propagation Research Project" by Mason Southworth, W1VLH

Amateur Radio's Contributions to Antenna Design
"The Wave Antenna for 200-Meter Reception" by Harold H. Beverage, 2BML
"A 14-Mc. Rotary Beam Antenna for Transmitting and Receiving" by John Shanklin, W3CIJ
"Directional Antennas with Closely-Spaced Elements" by John D. Kraus, W8JK
"The T-matched Antenna" by John D. Kraus, W8JK
"The 'Quad' Antenna" by George Grammer, W1DF
"The Multimatch Antenna System" by Chester Buchanan, W3DZZ
"Yagi Antenna Design" by Jim Lawson, W2PV
"Transmission Line Transformers" by Jerry Sevick, W2FMI
"*MININEC*: The Other Edge of the Sword" by Roy Lewallen, W7EL
"A Receiving Antenna that Rejects Local Noise" by Brian Beezley, K6STI

Amateur Radio and Radio Circuit Design
"The One-Control Superheterodyne" by James McLaughlin
"Short-Wave Receiver Selectivity to Match Present Conditions"
    by James Lamb, W1CEI (later W1AL)
"2, 6, and 10 with Crystal Control" by James Millen, W1HRX
"Experimental Parametric Amplifiers" by Frank Jones, W6AJF
"Defining and Measuring Receiver Dynamic Range" by Wes Hayward, W7ZOI

Amateur Radio, Modes, and Networks
"What Is Single-Sideband Telephony?" by Byron Goodman, W1DX
"A New Narrow-Band Image Transmission System" by Copthorne MacDonald, W4ZII/2
    (WA2BCW, VY2CM)
"The Making of an Amateur Packet-Radio Network" by David Borden, K8MMO, and
    Paul Rinaldo, W4RI
"Automatic Packet-Radio Location System (APLS) Proposal" by Bob Bruninga, WB4APR
"PACTOR — Radioteletype with Memory ARQ and Data Compression"
    by Hans-Peter Helfert, DL6MAA, and Ulrich Strate, KF4KV
"*APLINK*: The Delivery Systems" by Jim Mortenson, N2HOS
"Toward New Link-Layer Protocols" by Phil Karn, KA9Q
"PSK31: A New Radio-Teletype Mode" by Peter Martinez, G3PLX
"*WSJT*: New Software for VHF Meteor-Scatter Communication" by Joe Taylor, K1JT

Amateur Radio in Orbit
"The Oscar Satellite" by Harley Gabrielson, W6HEK
"Making Use of the Oscar III Telemetry Signals" by Arthur Walters, W6DKH
"OSCAR at 25: The Amateur Space Program Comes of Age" by Jan King, W3GEY,
    Vern Riportella, WA2LQQ and Ralph Wallio, WØRPK
"OSCAR at 25: Beginning of a New Era" by Jan King, W3GEY, Vern Riportella, WA2LQQ
    and Ralph Wallio, WØRPK
"AMSAT's MICROSAT/PACSAT Program" by Tom Clark, W3IWI

Appendix: References

Foreword

There can be no separation between the story of Amateur Radio and the technology that sustains and facilitates it. As Marconi famously said, "We are all amateurs," meaning that in those early days of wireless discovery, there was little to distinguish the amateur experimenters making discoveries on the workbench or in the radio shack from the professionals working in a laboratory. Today, a century removed from those first hesitant steps into the wireless world, technology continues its headlong rush into the future of Amateur Radio.

This book chronicles some of the most important technological advances by amateurs as reported in the ARRL literature as articles in *QST* and later *QEX*, as well as books and conference proceedings published by the ARRL. The stories span the entire range of innovation from pure, raw invention based on first principles to adaptations of existing technologies into wholly new systems.

Beginning with the earliest days of spark and coherers, the story progresses to the contributions Amateur Radio has made to understanding the science of radio propagation, supporting the work of scientists and engineers. The creation of antennas and circuits advanced that work to push the capabilities of stations ever further into the hiss and crackle of the ionosphere and beyond. As computer technology blossomed, amateurs were quick to adapt it to radio communications, building their own planet-wide networks from protocols and systems they designed themselves. Even reaching into space, amateurs built and launched their own satellites on a shoestring, relative to commercial and government projects, showing what could be accomplished in a fraction of the size and weight of the "big birds."

These innovations have nourished the Amateur Service since before there was a formal recognition of Amateur Radio. Our Basis and Purpose (Part 97.1), written into law in 1934, places a strong emphasis on technical innovation, recognizing that a vibrant community of amateurs will advance the radio and communications arts and train generations of operators and technicians who can then fulfill our commitment to provide emergency communications and enhance goodwill around the world.

All of these efforts continue today as amateurs invent circuits, antennas, and protocols, only to find these lead to new modes of propagation and operation. In turn, those new discoveries and inventions lead back to the world of design and the cycle begins again. Always, there is another amateur to be contacted, another opening to be discovered, another means of modulation, or another way to operate, build or even launch a station.

Time and again, we find that innovation in the amateur community is quickly recognized and turned to the advantage of their fellow citizens. In many cases, inventions made by amateurs are at the headwaters of companies and organizations that then serve people around the world. The cycle shows no sign of slowing down!

In a quotation attributed to Isaac Newton, he explains that, "If I have seen farther it is by standing on the shoulders of giants." All amateurs should be intensely proud of the accomplishments of the many amateurs who have expanded our knowledge and capabilities over this first century of Amateur Radio and of those who are innovating today and who will continue the tradition tomorrow, giants all.

David Sumner, K1ZZ
Executive Vice President
Newington, Connecticut
November 2013

About this Book

Each section of this book contains selected articles that present or describe a significant advance of Amateur Radio technology, 43 in all. Each article is prefaced by a short introduction that presents some context for the article — technical, historical, or both. The article is then presented exactly as it appeared in the original publication. The articles are organized in chronological order within the section.

Of course, no book can capture all of the advances. Some are inevitably omitted and it is not for lack of appreciation. In recognition, many other articles and books are listed in a table of references as an appendix. It is regrettable that not all could be reproduced here, but we hope that this collection can be considered a representative sampling of supporting and related publications.

The reference table, along with a selection of additional articles which can be downloaded as PDF files, is also available online at **www.arrl.org/history-of-qst**. You'll find a web page for the companion volume of *QST* advertisements there, too.

The ARRL wishes to extend its gratitude to the volunteers making up the group of experts who recommended, selected, and in many cases, contributed an introduction to the sections and individual articles. Biographies for each are presented following this introduction. Each of them has made significant contributions in their own right and we are honored to include their perspectives and thankful for their time.

Contributor Biographies

Jim Breakall, WA3FET

An ARRL Life Member, Jim was first licensed as WN3FET in 1965. He received BS and MS degrees in Electrical Engineering from Penn State University and a PhD in Electrical Engineering and Applied Physics from Case Western Reserve University, Cleveland, Ohio, and has more than 40 years of experience in numerical electromagnetics and antennas. He was a Project Engineer at the Lawrence Livermore National Laboratory (LLNL), Livermore, California, and an Associate Professor at the Naval Postgraduate School (NPGS), Monterey, California. Presently he is a Full Professor of Electrical Engineering at Penn State. Dr Breakall began his career in both theoretical and experimental research as a graduate student at the Arecibo Observatory in Puerto Rico, working on antenna analysis and radar probing of the ionosphere. At LLNL, he and his group worked on the development of the *Numerical Electromagnetics Code* (*NEC*), the first sophisticated antenna modeling program.

Dr Breakall is also a member of the IEEE Antennas and Propagation Society, IEEE Broadcast Technology Society, Eta Kappa Nu, International Union of Radio Science Commission B, IEEE Wave Propagation and Standards Committee, has been an Associate Editor for the *Radio Science* journal, and served as an Arecibo Observatory Users and Scientific Advising Committee Member. He has been a frequent speaker at the Dayton Hamvention Antenna Forum and has built two major contest superstations, K3CR and KC3R, near Penn State, and WP3R, on his farm in Puerto Rico near the big Arecibo dish.

Tim Duffy, K3LR

Tim was first licensed in 1972 as WN3SZX. He has been involved in most facets of Amateur Radio, from building and operating an extensive VHF repeater network, to emergency communications, to contesting. Tim has operated most of the major contests as a single-operator, and for the past 20 years has grown his Western Pennsylvania station and team of operators to become one of the top contest stations in the world. He has competed in the World Radiosport Team Championship (WRTC) four times, is a member of the CQ World Wide Contest Committee, a past Chairman of the ARRL Contest Advisory Committee (CAC), is Vice Chairman of the World Wide Radio Operators Foundation (WWROF), and is Chairman of Contest University, Inc (CTU). He was inducted into the CQ Contest Hall of Fame in 2006 and serves as Vice President for the Radio Club of America (RCA)

Before graduating with a BSEE degree from Pennsylvania State University, his professional career began as a broadcast engineer while still in high school, expanding to Chief Engineer positions. He became the Director of Engineering for SYGNET, building the first Cellular One networks in the Western Pennsylvania area. He then moved to Dobson Communications as Chief Technical Officer (CTO) and Senior Vice President before becoming Senior Vice President for Networks at AT&T and CTO for Stelera Wireless. He holds nine patents for E911 technology and is on the board of directors for the Atlantic Tower Company. Tim is currently the Chief Marketing Officer and General Manager at DX Engineering in Tallmadge, Ohio.

Hal Kennedy, N4GG

Harold (Hal) has been continuously active in Amateur Radio for 52 years. He was first licensed in 1961 and was issued the call sign N4GG in 1977. Hal holds a BSEE from Lafayette College and an MS-Management from the Sloan School at MIT, where he attended as an Alfred P. Sloan Fellow. Hal's first career was predominantly in the aerospace and defense industry, where he spent more than 30 years in technical and management positions of increasing responsibility. He has been an Amateur Extra licensee since age 14. Hal has authored numerous *NCJ* and *QST* articles and has contributed to the *ARRL Handbook* and *ARRL Antenna Book*.

Ham radio was passed down to Hal — his father was a ship's operator in the days of spark and obtained the call 2NJ in 1916. In 2010 Hal completed building "Blue Lightning," an authentic to the era ½-kW synchronous rotary spark gap transmitter. In addition to writing and on-the-air activities, he gives demonstrations of Blue Lightning and continues to speak on the subjects of the "early days" of Amateur Radio as well as on antenna design and analysis.

Phil Karn, KA9Q

Phil has been a licensed ham since 1971 and has a BSEE from Cornell University and an MSEE from Carnegie Mellon University. In the early 1980s, he worked at Bell Labs in Naperville, Illinois, and Murray Hill, New Jersey. Since 1991, he has worked at Qualcomm in San Diego, California, and is well-known for his contributions to wireless data networking protocols, network and data security, and cryptography.

Phil has been an AMSAT technical volunteer since 1980. He designed and implemented software modems for three amateur spacecraft (AO-40, ARISSat-1, Fox-1) and two deep-space research spacecraft (ACE, STEREO). He was also an important contributor to the development of packet radio, working on the AX.25 protocol, TCP/IP (both amateur and Internet use), and he devised the Multiple-Access, Collision-Avoidance (MACA) scheme now integral to IEEE 802.11 (a.k.a. "WiFi"). He is now mostly retired and living in San Diego.

Jan King, W3GEY

Jan has a distinguished record within the small satellite and launch vehicle communities, with more than 44 years of experience in the field. During this time he has been associated with the design and development of 18 small spacecraft and 12 larger spacecraft, as well as one launch vehicle. He has worked in the aerospace field in government, industry and academia. In addition, at the request of the United States government, he served as a member of the US Delegation to the ITU 1987 Mobile WARC in Geneva and a member of the US Delegation to the Future Air Navigation Systems Committee of ICAO in 1985-86. For the 1997-98 academic year, he was the Schriever Chair professor in the Department of Astronautics, United States Air Force Academy. He was the co-recipient of the National Medal of Technology for the year 1991. This award was presented to the Pegasus Launch Vehicle Development Team of OSC by the President of the United States.

In parallel to his professional career he is one of the founding members of AMSAT (the Radio Amateur Satellite Corporation) and has been the project manager for many of that organization's successful space projects. The organization has been a leading force in the small satellite technology arena since 1969.

Dave Leeson, W6NL

Dave has been licensed over 60 years and has a special interest in Amateur Radio technology, antennas and HF contesting. He has held the calls W6QHS, P40Q and HC8L, and is the trustee for W6WX and W6YX. Including P40V, EA9UK and HC8N, stations operated and/or engineered by Dave with other colleagues have won some 50 international contests and numerous domestic competitions over the years. He is the author of a number of *QST* articles, Dayton presentations, and the ARRL book *Physical Design of Yagi Antennas*. Dave's other hobby was auto racing, from which he retired after back-to-back sports car national championships. He and his wife Barbara, K6BL, live in the Santa Cruz Mountains near Los Gatos, California.

Professionally, Dr Leeson received degrees from Caltech, MIT and Stanford. From 1968-1993 he was the founding CEO and Chairman of California Microwave, Inc. In 1994 he returned to Stanford as a Consulting Professor. He is the author of a number of academic papers, including a widely cited reference on oscillator phase noise, and is currently working on new papers and books on microwave engineering and history. He offers his students these lessons learned: "Experiment trumps theory;" "Don't change plugs between practice and the race;" "Every five minute job takes twenty-four hours;" "If something stops working, it was the last thing you touched;" and "Never say no to adventure."

Carl Luetzelschwab, K9LA

Carl received his Novice license in October 1961. He selected K9LA in the mid 1970s when the FCC offered 1×2s to Extras. Carl's interests in Amateur Radio include propagation (he writes a monthly column about solar and propagation topics, and contributes similar articles to various Amateur Radio publications), DXing (he's on the Top of the Honor Roll), contesting (he was Editor of the *National Contest Journal* from 2002 thru 2007), and experimenting with antennas.

Carl received a Master's degree in Electrical Engineering from Purdue University and began his career in 1974 with Motorola in Schaumburg, Illinois, and later in Fort Worth, Texas, as an RF design engineer. In 1988 he joined Magnavox in Fort Wayne, Indiana (now Raytheon), and continued RF design work — mostly designing RF power amplifiers for commercial and military applications. He retired in early October 2013 and now has more time to work on his vintage equipment.

John Stanley, K4ERO

John got his Novice call, KN4ERO, in 1955 as a high school freshman. He became K4ERO a year later and operated as K4ERO/1 while earning his BSEE at Massachusetts Institute of Technology. While working at HCJB in Quito, Ecuador he was HC1JX. John used a dozen other DX calls during a 45-year career as a shortwave broadcast engineering consultant. He and Ruth, WB4LUA, are now retired and living in Rising Fawn, Georgia. Both have Amateur Extra licenses.

John has taught at four universities and trained engineering staff at many broadcast organizations worldwide. He has also designed and overseen construction of many broadcast antennas and transmitters, including site selection and propagation studies for a number of shortwave, AM and FM stations. He designed RF-related equipment for Texas Instruments and the UCLA ionospheric lab in Alaska.

Ward Silver, N0AX, Editor

Ward has been a ham since 1972 when he earned his Novice license (WN0GQP). His experiences in ham radio led him first to graduate with a BSEE from the Missouri University of Science and Technology and then to a 20-year career as an electrical engineer, designing microprocessor-based products and medical devices. In 2000, he began a second career as a teacher and writer, leading to his receiving the 2003 Bill Orr Technical Writing Award. He is a founder of the World Radiosport Team Championships and is President of the YASME Foundation.

Ward is Lead Editor of the two primary Amateur Radio technical references published by the American Radio Relay League — the *ARRL Handbook* and the *ARRL Antenna Book*. He is the author of all three ARRL licensing study guides and writes the popular *QST* magazine column "Hands-On Radio." His email newsletter *The ARRL Contest Update* reaches more than 25,000 readers twice a month. He has written several titles in the "For Dummies" series by Wiley Publishing: *Ham Radio for Dummies* (now in its 2nd Edition), *Two-Way Radios and Scanners for Dummies*, and *Circuitbuilding Do-It-Yourself for Dummies*.

About the ARRL

The seed for Amateur Radio was planted in the 1890s, when Guglielmo Marconi began his experiments in wireless telegraphy. Soon he was joined by dozens, then hundreds, of others who were enthusiastic about sending and receiving messages through the air—some with a commercial interest, but others solely out of a love for this new communications medium. The United States government began licensing Amateur Radio operators in 1912.

By 1914, there were thousands of Amateur Radio operators—hams—in the United States. Hiram Percy Maxim, a leading Hartford, Connecticut inventor and industrialist, saw the need for an organization to band together this fledgling group of radio experimenters. In May 1914 he founded the American Radio Relay League (ARRL) to meet that need.

Today ARRL, with approximately 155,000 members, is the largest organization of radio amateurs in the United States. The ARRL is a not-for-profit organization that:
- promotes interest in Amateur Radio communications and experimentation
- represents US radio amateurs in legislative matters, and
- maintains fraternalism and a high standard of conduct among Amateur Radio operators.

At ARRL headquarters in the Hartford suburb of Newington, the staff helps serve the needs of members. ARRL is also International Secretariat for the International Amateur Radio Union, which is made up of similar societies in 150 countries around the world.

ARRL publishes the monthly journal *QST* and an interactive digital version of *QST*, as well as newsletters and many publications covering all aspects of Amateur Radio. Its headquarters station, W1AW, transmits bulletins of interest to radio amateurs and Morse code practice sessions. The ARRL also coordinates an extensive field organization, which includes volunteers who provide technical information and other support services for radio amateurs as well as communications for public-service activities. In addition, ARRL represents US amateurs with the Federal Communications Commission and other government agencies in the US and abroad.

Membership in ARRL means much more than receiving *QST* each month. In addition to the services already described, ARRL offers membership services on a personal level, such as the Technical Information Service—where members can get answers by phone, email or the ARRL website, to all their technical and operating questions.

Full ARRL membership (available only to licensed radio amateurs) gives you a voice in how the affairs of the organization are governed. ARRL policy is set by a Board of Directors (one from each of 15 Divisions). Each year, one-third of the ARRL Board of Directors stands for election by the full members they represent. The day-to-day operation of ARRL HQ is managed by an Executive Vice President and his staff.

No matter what aspect of Amateur Radio attracts you, ARRL membership is relevant and important. There would be no Amateur Radio as we know it today were it not for the ARRL. We would be happy to welcome you as a member! (An Amateur Radio license is not required for Associate Membership.) For more information about ARRL and answers to any questions you may have about Amateur Radio, write or call:

ARRL—the national association for Amateur Radio®
225 Main Street
Newington CT 06111-1494
Voice: 860-594-0200
Fax: 860-594-0259
E-mail: **hq@arrl.org**
Internet: **www.arrl.org**

Prospective new amateurs call (toll-free):
800-32-NEW HAM (800-326-3942)
You can also contact us via e-mail at **newham@arrl.org**
or check out the ARRL website at **www.arrl.org**

Amateur Radio in the Spark Era

By Hal Kennedy, N4GG, Carl Luetzelschwab, K9LA and Ward Silver, NØAX

Although there were many experiments with electricity and magnetism in the 1800s and Michael Faraday demonstrated wireless transfer of energy via induction in 1831, it wasn't until 1864 that James Clerk Maxwell predicted the existence of electromagnetic waves mathematically. His work, further refined by Oliver Heaviside and now known as Maxwell's equations, spurred Heinrich Hertz to begin his studies, finally verifying experimentally the existence of electromagnetic waves in 1886 and 1887.

In 1895, Guglielmo Marconi successfully transmitted signals up to distances of 2.4 km and in 1899 his transmissions spanned the English Channel. Finally, or perhaps at last, in December 1901 Marconi succeeded in receiving the letter "S" in Morse code from Poldhu, England, at a lonely receiving station in St John's, Newfoundland. Around this time, in 1900-1901 the amateurs hit the airwaves.

In that era, experimentation was the order of the day and the design of spark transmitters and antenna systems quickly underwent major improvements based on empirical trial and error. At the same time, the first dreadfully insensitive receivers also quickly evolved as the vacuum tube replaced magnetic coherers beginning in 1908. As a result, the range of amateur stations increased rapidly, with state-of-the-art stations eventually spanning hundreds of miles on a routine basis.

The line between amateur and commercial and scientific development was often blurred as innovations and inventions were quickly passed among the burgeoning wireless community. Individual amateurs often participated in all three aspects, carrying the news through hand-written letters, magazines, professional journals and even newspaper articles.

The limited resources available to amateurs may have been a "silver lining," however. For the commercial services, the problem of distance was usually solved by increasing power and size. Some of the early commercial spark stations had gargantuan alternator-based transmitters of 50 kW, 100 kW and more. Antenna systems were thousands of feet across and often hundreds of feet high. Amateurs, however, had to make do with much less, turning instead to optimizing their far-smaller stations and honing their technique.

And so you see that DXing, the quest for spanning longer and longer distances, has been with Amateur Radio since its very earliest days, driving the development and adaptation of wireless technology and operating improvements. The three articles reproduced here illustrate two examples of the state of the amateur art and their culmination in truly long-distance, two-way communication around the world.

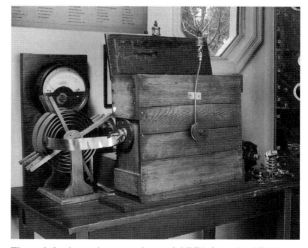

The original spark transmitter of ARRL founder Hiram Percy Maxim, W1AW. The antenna tuning coil is visible at left in front of a large meter that measures antenna current. The rotary spark gap (and a bearing oiler) is inside the wooden box for safety and noise reduction. The key is visible just to the right of the spark gap.

"Operation of a Non-Synchronous Rotating Gap" by A.S. Blatterman

By Hal Kennedy, N4GG

A quick look at the schematic below shows us what appears to be a very simple transmitter made of a step-up transformer, capacitor, rotary spark gap and output transformer. It looks easy to design and tune up, right? Wrong!

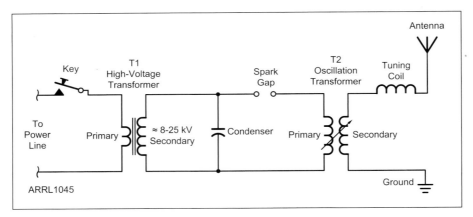

A modern car uses the *exact* components found in a 1900 spark transmitter: a battery, an induction coil to step up to high voltage (ignition coil), a spark gap (spark plug) and an antenna (ignition wiring). All that's missing is a telegraph key. If we grounded the car's chassis, connected an antenna directly to the ignition coil's high-voltage output and added a telegraph key in series with the ignition coil primary, we would have a complete 1900-era spark gap transmitter.

Using Morse code, the signal from this transmitter had a range of about 10 miles, with the emission occupying a *huge* amount of spectrum that was centered on a frequency determined by the L-C resonance of the antenna's series inductance and parallel capacitance to ground. If that was where spark transmitter design stopped, so too would have Amateur Radio from sheer lack of range.

(A detailed article by N4GG that gives the reader a working knowledge of a spark transmitter and the accompanying jargon is available on this book's website — **www.arrl.org/history-of-QST**. Reading this article will greatly enhance appreciation of Blatterman's article and the challenges that faced radio amateurs one hundred years ago as they attempted to span greater and greater distances.)

The introduction of the high-voltage capacitor across the gap (labeled "Condenser" in the figure above) greatly increased output power and narrowed radiated bandwidth. Both improved efficiency. Spark transmitter output had moved from low power white noise to higher power narrow-band quasi-sine waves. This modification alone pushed spark transmission well beyond 10 miles. It also left both amateurs and commercial interests such as those of Marconi with the idea that from here forward, more powerful sparks and higher antennas were *all* that was needed to extend range. This viewpoint persists today and, when viewed from the broader perspective of communications technology, is just as incorrect now as it was then.

The addition of an output coil in series with the antenna provided crude selection of operating frequency, reduced bandwidth, and removed up to 10,000 volts from the antenna. The tuning coil was the earliest instantiation of what we today call an "antenna tuner." It was the first device to roughly match the impedance of the antenna to that of the transmitter, although it was not understood as such until years later. The coil further increased antenna current — another step forward.

The last major technical advances were the introduction of rotary gaps, both synchronous and non-synchronous types, and air-coupled output transformers that were known at the time as "oscillation transformers." These improvements appeared on the air between 1910 and 1915, and greatly extended range again. It's worth noting that even from 1900 to 1915, range was being extended more through technical improvements than through increasing power and antenna height.

Optimization of the transmitter's tuning components and controls was complicated by the fact that in a spark transmitter, nearly everything affects nearly everything else. Also, what should be optimized? Output power? Tone (spark rate)? Efficiency? Output bandwidth? Optimizing for one thing usually adversely affected something else. The amateur of 1915 addressed these issues through trial and error, rules of thumb and folklore.

By this time, available options had moved beyond empirical methods. Additional complications were imposed by the Radio Act of 1912 which required the operating wavelength be below 200 meters where spark rigs were difficult to tune. Also mandated was good "decrement" (< 0.2). Today we use "Q" in place of decrement; both define the damping of an electromagnetic wave. Like it or not, the transmitter needed to be reasonably spectrally pure — something that never mattered much before!

The ARRL was founded in mid-1914, and shortly thereafter Blatterman's article changed the approach to spark transmitters from empirical to analytical. Blatterman presented formulas, graphs and tables to support the construction and tuning of an efficient and spectrally pure (as much as a spark rig could be) transmitter. From this point in 1916 until the end of amateur spark in 1923, there were no additional "breakthrough" changes to spark transmitter design. Instead the technology was perfected, culminating in the transatlantic tests of 1921. There, despite CW having been perfected by then, and judged to be superior to spark, the first amateur transmissions heard across the Atlantic were those of "King Spark."

Operation of a Non-Synchronous Rotating Gap

By A. S. Blatterman

Radio Laboratory, Washington University, St. Louis, Mo.

RESULTS OF PRELIMINARY INVESTIGATIONS TO DETERMINE CORRECT CONDENSER CAPACITY FOR USE WITH ROTARY GAPS AND THE EFFECT OF SPARK RATE ON POWER AND TONE OF WIRELESS OUTFITS

Reprinted with permission from the Electrical World, September 16, 1916

SEVERAL interesting articles have appeared recently* dealing with the rotating gap, and the writer would hesitate to bring up the subject again if it were not for the fact that in studying the literature on the subject little data is discovered bearing directly on the operating features. This is particularly true of the non-synchronous type of gap as affected by changes in the size of the condenser and in the spark rate. General experience has shown that the correct value of capacity is considerably less for a given transformer when a rotary gap is employed than when a plain stationary gap is used, and the spark rate effects both the tone and the amount of power utilized. The efficiency is also involved here. In attempting to study the problem analytically, it appears that the relations between both these factors, capacity and spark rate, and the power and high-fre-

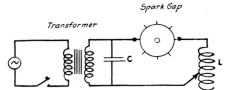

Fig. 1—A Common Form and Arrangement of Spark Gap

quency currents in the condenser and antenna circuits are very complex. An investigation of the subject is now under way and it is the results of the first set of experiments which have been carried out in this connection which form the basis of this article.

Where the cycle of primary current is of

---

*"Theory and Design of Radio Transformers," F. Cutting, Proc. I. R. E., April, 1916.

"Design of the Audio Frequency Circuit," J. Weinberger, Proc. I. R. E., December, 1915.

"Resonance in Transformer," L. B. Turner, Electrician, Aug. 2, 1912.

"'Hytone' Radio Transmitter," M. Eastham, Proc. I. R. E., December, 1914.

"Resonance Phenomena in Low Frequency Circuit of Radio Transmitter," H. E. Hallborg, Proc. I. R. E., June, 1915.

low frequency, that is, 25 to 133 cycles, the advantages of a high spark rate with musical tone can be achieved by using for the spark gap a device which breaks up the wave of voltage from the inductor or transformer into several sparks per alternation. A common form of spark gap for this purpose consists of a metal disk, rotated at high speed, which carries a number of equally spaced studs or spokes about its periphery and which revolves between stationary electrodes. The familiar arrangement of the gap and its arrangement in the circuits is shown in Fig. 1.

Construction of Synchronous Rotating Gap

The device differs in its operation and to some extent in its purpose from the so-called synchronous rotating gap. In the latter the disk is rotated at a particular speed such that the r.p.s. multiplied into the number of studs on the disk is equal to the number of alternations per second of the primary alternating wave. The stationary electrodes are mounted on a frame so that they can be rotated about the disk after the manner of the brush-rocker on a dynamo, and thus cause stationary and revolving electrodes to come opposite each other for sparking at the instant when the alternating wave is passing through its maximum. Thus, one spark is obtained in each alternation of the voltage cycle, and it can be made to take place at the maximum value of voltage in the cycle. To secure and maintain the synchronous relation of spark disk to primary wave the disk is mounted on the shaft of the generator which supplies power to the transformer. To secure the desired high spark tone the spark gap, transformer and generator are designed for a primary wave of high-fequency, commonly 240 or 500 cycles, which give respectively spark rates of 480 and 1,000 per second. The transformer is adjusted (approximately) to the condenser so as to produce a condition of resonance for the frequency employed. That is, if L represents the inductance of the transformer in henries, and C the capacity of the condenser in farads, then, roughly, adjustments are made to make

$$2\pi f L = \frac{1}{2\pi f C}$$

In practice the adjustment is made for a condition of 15 or 20 per cent off resonance. Thus, if resonance is obtainable at a speed of 1,500 r.p.m. the operating speed will be set at, say 1,300 r.p.m.

Construction of Non-Synchronous Rotating Gap

With the non-synchronous rotating gap, on the other hand, the disk is revolved at high speed, generally without regard to the primary frequency, and instead of obtaining one spark per alternation at a constant voltage, the voltage wave is broken up into several sparks occurring at no very clearly defined instants during the alternation, though one particular condition may be that shown in Fig 2, where 1, 2, 3, 4, 5, 6, 7, 8, 9, 10 indicate instants of sparking.

The condition for sparking is that the instantaneous value of voltage in the wave shall be sufficient to break down the gap between the stationary and moving electrodes when these come opposite each other. If, as is entirely possible, a pair of moving electrodes come opposite the side electrodes at an instant in the alternating wave when the voltage is not sufficient to break down the gap or when the voltage is passing through its zero value, then the regular sequence of sparking will be broken, and one, two, three or more studs may pass the stationary side electrodes before the voltage has reached a value sufficient to cause a spark. Important factors are the number of studs on the disk, the rotative speed, the length of the spark gap between the moving and stationary studs, the size of the condenser.

If the spark gap is made long by drawing the side electrodes back from the disk then a considerable voltage will be required to produce sparking, and thus only a few sparks will be obtained during an alternation. Some of the moving studs will come opposite the stationary studs without sparking, because they do come opposite at instants in the alternating wave when the voltage is too low to bridge the gap. The greater the number of moving studs or the greater the rotative speed of the disk the greater will be the number of inactive studs during the cycle. If, however, the gap is made very short, as short as is mechanically possible, then a very low voltage is all that is required to break down the gap, and hence the condition may exist that sparking takes place to every movable stud as each pair in turn is presented to the stationary electrodes.

Limitations of Spark Length

The maximum possible spark length, to take the case which is shown in Fig. 2, which can be used and still permit sparking to each stud, is that corresponding to the voltage at instants 1, 5, 6, 10, where now the division points 1, 2, 3, 4, etc., must be interpreted as denoting instants when moving and stationary studs come opposite one another in a position suitable for sparking.

When the gap length is longer than this every stud will not yield a spark. When it is shorter each stud may still yield a spark. When the gap is set at the critical length every stud will yield a spark only when moving studs are presented to stationary studs at instants which divides the alternation symmetrically, as shown in Fig. 1. For if the instants of opposite position, which will hereafter be called the sparking position, of moving and stationary studs are displaced along the cycle as shown in Fig. 3, then at instants 5 and 10 there is available only a potential 5-5' (=10-10') to break down a gap whose length is set for the potential 5-5 (=10-10), see Fig. 2, and hence instead of five sparks per alternation there will be only four. One stud has become inactive. If the gap is shortened to allow discharge at voltage 5-5', then all studs will again yield sparks; and the shorter the gap is made the greater is the permissible displacement of instants 1, 2, 3, 4, 5, etc., along the cycle. When the displacement is such that the instants 5 and 10 of the representative case coincide with instants of zero voltage in the wave, then, of course, one stud will be inactive. This is shown in Fig 4.

If the above reasoning is correct we must conclude that when the spark gap is very short there are two ways in which sparking may occur.

1. In every alternation each stud may yield a spark, in which case the sparks will follow each other at equal intervals.

2. In every alternation each stud but one may yield a spark, in which case sparks will occur in groups, the time interval between groups being twice as great as that between sparks in a group.

If sparking occurs in either the first or second way just described, it may be expected that the length of the gap must be less as the speed of the disk is increased,

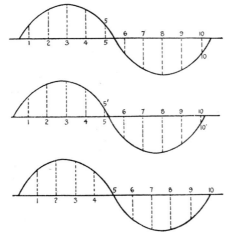

Figs. 2, 3 and 4—Cycles of Transformer Voltage Showing Sparking Positions of Gaps

In Fig 2 sparking positions of gap are shown as symmetrically placed in the low frequency cycle. In Fig. 4 a particular case is shown of certain sparking positions occurring at instant of zero voltage in wave.

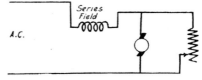

Fig. 5. Connections for Reducing Speed of Series Motor

while at lower speeds it should be possible to use longer spark gaps. Experience has shown that these effects do exist. When the disk is rotated at high speed the spark gap must be made very short to produce anything like a smooth tone; and lengthening the gap by as little as 1/100 in. is often found to give the spark tone a very ragged quality, apparently indicating that a number of studs miss spark. On the other hand, when the disk is rotated at low speed the allowable spark gap is found to be much longer.

Effect of Gap Speed on Power and Aerial Current

General experience has also shown that the rotative speed of the gap as well as the size of the condenser has important effects on the power and the aerial current, and in order to investigate this the following experiments were carried out.

For the first experiments a small 60-cycle, 5000-volt transformer was used. The spark gap was of a common type carrying eighteen studs. The motor was an a.c. series motor whose speed could be varied through a range of 500 r.p.m. to 5,000 r.p.m., the lower speeds being obtained by adjusting a water resistance placed in shunt with the armature, as shown in Fig. 5. The higher speeds were obtained by giving the brushes a considerable lead. Instantaneous values of speed were read from a tachometer. In this way the speed could be kept quite constant for any set of readings.

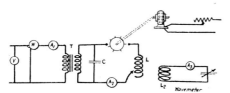

Fig. 6. Connections of Apparatus for Spark Gap Experiments

An adjustable glass plate condenser of maximum capacity, 0.01 mf., was used. The high-frequency inductance was of copper strip wound in a flat spiral. The set-up is shown in Fig. 6. An ammeter A, voltmeter V and wattmeter W were placed in the primary side of the transformer. In the high-frequency circuit was placed a hot-wire ammeter. As the maximum range of this meter was only 8 amp., it had to be used with a shunt and calibrated for the wave length used. The calibration was effected by sending with reduced power and observing the reading of the meter without the shunt and then with the shunt connected. The ratio of the two readings then gave the multiplying value of the shunt. For observing wave length and decrement in the high-frequency circuit the wavemeter inductance L was loosely coupled with the condenser circuit, and observations taken by means of the hot-wire milliammeter in the wavemeter circuit in the usual way.

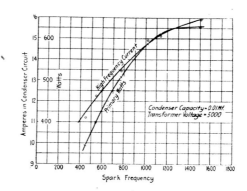

Fig. 7. High-Frequency Current in Condenser Circuit and Watts in Primary of Transformer as Functions of Spark Frequency

A preliminary set of readings (Table 1) were obtained with the speed as independent variable.

Current in the condenser circuit and power in watts in the primary of the transformer were plotted against spark frequency, as in Fig. 7. It was found that with the higher spark rates the condenser current and power increased at a slower and slower rate toward what appeared to be a maximum.

This was interesting, and steps were at once taken to ascertain if the curves did pass through a maximum and then fall as the motor speed was carried to very high values.

The 5,000-volt transformer was replaced by one wound for 13,000 volts, and a new spark gap installed having twelve points, whose speed could be accurately controlled from 200 r.p.m. to 12,000 r.p.m.

The effect of disk speed was examined first. The motor speed was varied for different values of the capacity in the condenser and readings taken of speed, high-frequency current, watts input to the transformer, primary voltage and primary current. Table 2 and curves of Figs. 8, 9 and 10 show results with condenser capacities of 0.005 mf., 0.01 mf. and 0.02 mf. respectively.

All three of these curves exhibit distinct maxima of current in the high-frequency circuit corresponding to certain critical motor speeds.

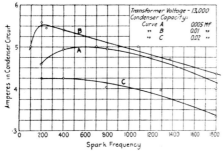

Figs. 8, 9 and 10. Current in the Spark Circuit as a Function of Spark Frequency with Different Condenser Capacities

The power in the condenser circuit, which if this circuit were coupled to an aerial, would, of course, determine the aerial current, is

$$P = I^2 R, \text{ watts},$$

R being the high-frequency resistance of the circuit and equal to

$$R = \frac{1}{300\pi^2} \frac{\lambda\delta}{C}$$

where
- λ = wave length in meters
- C = capacity in microfarads
- δ = logarithmic decrement (semi-period).

Decrement determinations made at different speeds showed some variation in the high-frequency resistance of the spark circuit. This is probably due to a change in the effective length of the spark with change in speed, this being greater at the low speeds. It is also probably due in part to a quenching effect at high speeds. This method of determining the resistance of a spark circuit by the usual methods of measuring decrement and substitution in the above formula cannot be applied when the spark is quenched or when its resistance is comparable with the resistance of the rest of the circuit. Under this condition the damping is linear and not logarithmic.*

The important thing to know, however, is that as the spark frequency is continuously decreased from a high value, the high-frequency current at first increases, reaches a maximum, and then decreases. This result had been anticipated, and in the theory proposed to account for it, it seemed that similar effect might be produced by changing the size of the condenser. Accordingly, a set of readings were taken at different speeds, the speed being held constant and the condenser varied in steps from 0.005 mf. to 0.02 mf. The results are given in Table 3. The curves of Fig. 11 drawn from this data show that for any given speed the current in the condenser circuit is maximum for a certain value of capacity and any change from this critical capacity is accompanied by a decrease in current.

The curves of high-frequency current in the above figures may be taken to indicate in a comparative way the variation of power in the condenser circuit. The power is, of course, proportional to the current squared, provided the resistance of the cir-

Table 1—Effect of Variations of Spark Frequency on Primary Watts and High Frequency Current

Motor Speed, r.p.m.	Spark Freq. N	Primary Watts	H. F. Current, Amps.
1500	450	345	11.2
1800	540	400	12.2
2600	780	510	13.4
3400	1020	590	14.9
3800	1140	610	15.2
5000	1500	630	15.9

*J. Stone Stone, "The Electrician," Sept. 18, 1914, Proc. I. R. E., December, 1914.

Table II—Effects of Variations of Condenser Capacity and Gap Speed on Primary Watts and High Frequency Current

Capacity of Condenser in mf.	Motor Speed r.p.m.	H. F. AMPS.	Watts	Prim., Amps.	Prim., Volts
0.005	12,000	3.6	115	5.1	108
	6,900	4.7	140	5.2	108
	4,000	4.9	150	5.2	108
	2,000	4.9	173	5.3	108
	1,000	4.46	185	5.4	108
0.010	12,000	4.0	110	5.3	108
	5,400	5.0	125	5.3	108
	3,500	5.0	130	5.2	108
	2,000	5.4	140	5.3	108
	1,220	5.5	150	5.4	108
	1,000	5.6	165	5.6	108
	500	5.0	175	5.8	108
0.020	12,000	3.0	96	5.3	108
	6,400	4.0	115	5.4	108
	4,000	4.0	115	5.4	108
	2,000	4.5	124	5.4	108
	1,000	4.5	135	5.5	108

cuit does not change, but in a qualitative way, the plot of current also shows the changes in power. In this connection, Table 2 shows that the efficiency as determined by the ratio output to input, reaches a maximum for a certain spark frequency. This is evident because the primary watts continue to increase after the current in the condenser circuit begins to fall off.

Results similar to the above have been obtained with an actual transmitter, the readings of the aerial ammeter being kept under observation while the spark frequency and condenser were varied, care being taken in the latter case to keep the wave length constant by compensating changes in closed circuit inductance. This procedure kept the radiated wave length the same and thus avoided the possibility of changing aerial resistance with changing wave lengths.

It would appear, offhand, that with a given transformer potential, an increase in either spark frequency or in the size of the condenser would be accompanied by an increase in power, in accordance with the formula, $\frac{1}{2}CV^2N$. The frequency observed increase in power with decrease in spark frequency and condenser, therefore, leads to the hypothethis that the average value of V is affected by these factors, and entering as the square in the determination of power, overbalances opposing changes in either C or N.

Table III—Results with Constant Gap Speed and Variable Condenser Capacity

C in mf.	Amperes in Condenser Circuit			
	N=360	N=1000	N=1800	N=2400
0.005	4.9	4.8	4.1	3.6
0.0075	....	5.3	5.0	4.3
0.01	5.5	5.0	4.4	4.0
0.02	4.25	4.0	3.4	3.0

Consider, first, the case in which capacity is changed and N remains fixed. When the condenser is reduced the potential to which

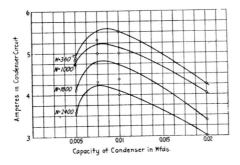

it is charged in a given short interval of time is greater than when a larger condenser is used. The condenser charges in the time interval between successive sparking positions of the disk electrodes, and hence, if in this interval the potential is increased, even though it be at the expense of decreased capacity, the energy per spark may be increased because **this varies with the square of the spark voltage and only according to the first power of capacity**.

Limit to Changes in Condenser Capacity

There is evidently a limit to which this automatic adjustment of spark voltage through changes in condenser capacity can be carried. There soon comes a point beyond which the potential, for a given transformer winding, cannot be further increased, and hence at this point it is disadvantageous to use smaller condensers.

We are not dealing here with the resonance effects producable through the proper balancing of capacity against the inductance of the transformer, although the curves of Figs. 8, 9, 10, 11 do undoubtedly show that for the particular transformer used in these tests a capacity in the neighborhood of 0.01 mf. is best, and it may be that a condenser of this value is that required for resonance. The effects described, however, are believed to be due to the inherent regulation of spark potential in the manner described. In fact, the building up of potential through resonance in the usual way does not take place when discharges occur, as they do here, several times in each alternation.

An explanation similar to the above also explains the results obtained by varying the spark frequency, either by changing the speed of the disk or the number of studs thereon. It was found, starting with a very high spark frequency, that decreasing the motor speed while the condenser remained unchanged, caused at first an increase in oscillatory power which continued up to a maximum value corresponding to a certain critical motor speed, beyond which (i. e., lower speed) the power fell off. As in the previous case of variable capacity and constant speed, it is believed that the effect is due to the fact that down to a certain speed corresponding to a certain spark frequency the condenser potential reaches a higher value due to the longer interval of charging between studs so that even though the spark frequency is decreased the average value of the squared voltages increases at a more rapid rate and hence more power is utilized.

This theory is roughly checked by the fact that when a non-synchronous gap is rotated at low speed and with small condensers the spark does not spring radially from the moving electrodes, but anticipates the exact diametrical position of moving and stationary studs and leads to the advancing electrodes as they approach successively into sparking position. At high speeds and with large condensers this effect is not nearly so pronounced.

It is also important to note that these experiments show that as the speed decreases the condenser required for maximum high-frequency current increases, and bear out the statement made in the opening paragraph of this paper that smaller condensers must be used with rotary gaps than with stationary ones.

In regard to the readings of the hot-wire ammeter in the condenser circuit it must be understood that these are the summation effects of a high and a low-frequency current, the former being that of the oscillatory condenser discharge while the latter is the current sent through the condenser at line frequency by the transformer. This

Continued on Page 354

Synchronous Gap. Cont. from page 332
low frequency charging current, however, is very small, being, in these experiments, of the order of ¼ of 1 per cent. of the total indication and can therefore be neglected. Errors of observation of speed and meter readings probably amount to 2 per cent or 3 per cent, the latter due primarily to slight variations in the spark.

"Applications of the Audion" by Paul F. Godley

By Hal Kennedy, N4GG

Paul Godley, later to become famous for the transatlantic tests of 1921, provided a summary of known Audion circuits and applications for the amateur to the Radio Club of America (RCA) in 1916. No doubt publication of some of this material predates the first regular issue of *QST*, published in late 1915.

Receiver detectors moved from the Branly coherer, to a magnetic coupler (the "Maggie" by Marconi), to solid state (galena and other salts/crystals) from the late 1890s through around 1908.

The two-element tube (a diode) was patented by De Forest in 1906 and the first triode was patented by De Forest in 1908. Circuits appeared quickly showing how the vacuum tube could replace galena as a much improved detector.

Godley describes the application of the Audion to audio amplification, oscillators, regenerative reception and heterodyne reception methods. The conversion to vacuum tube technology was well under way by 1916. The ramifications are obvious to us today and reliable long-distance communication on short waves only became possible with the advent of vacuum tube amplification.

Shortly after publication, amateurs started transmitting with Audion oscillators, followed by more power from Audions in parallel. This was the beginning of the end of spark. Spark and CW went head to head in the transatlantic tests of 1921, with CW the clear winner. The end of the spark era occurred between 1922 and 1924. Finally, spark was outlawed in 1929.

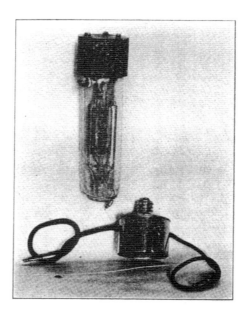

A Navy-type Audion with a new high-reliability spiral filament. Below the tube is a brass cap with terminals that makes connection with the tube electrodes — an early example of what would evolve into the tube socket. Note that what we would call the tube's base today was considered the cap at the time.

Applications of the Audion

By Paul F. Godley
Copyright, 1916, by The Radio Club of America.

THE popularity of the **audion** as a detector and amplifier is unquestioned. Yet there seems to be a general lack of familiarity among a great many amateurs with the audion and its operation, to say nothing of misunderstandings concerning its value as a detector. The misunderstandings are due in the majority of cases to lack of knowledge and to the attempts on the part of manufacturers of other detect-

on the market, unfortunately, poor audions just as there are poor crystals of galena or silicon, but, notwithstanding, due to its inherent properties, the audion is, and probably will remain, the detector superior.

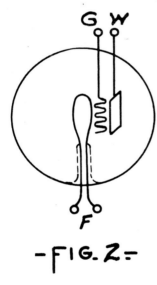

-FIG. 2-

The audion consists of a filament, a "grid," and a plate or "wing" enclosed in a bulb from which to a degree the air has been exhausted. (Figure 2) Figure 3 shows the simple audion circuit, and we have here the **combined action of rectification** and **amplification**, and it is because of this relay action that a properly constructed audion must of necessity excel any simple rectifier.

The audion is a voltage operated device. That is, the greater the potential of the charges applied to the grid, the greater will be the corresponding change in the wing

*Presented before The Radio Club of

circuit, or telephone currents, so that the first thing which concerns us in the selection of apparatus suitable for application in conjunction with the audion is how we

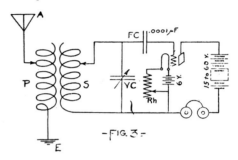

-FIG. 3-

may insure at all times under given conditions maximums of potential at the grid. In this connection it will be well to look for a moment at a certain relationship existing between the electromotive force and capacity in any oscillatory circuit.

Every electrical conductor has a certain capacity depending upon its size, its shape, and surrounding conductors. The larger this conductor, the greater the charge required to bring it to a certain potential. Hence the potential is directly proportional to the charge and inversely proportional to the capacity, or $E = Q/C$ where E is the E. M. F., Q the quantity, and C the capacity. Therefore if we have a closed oscillatory circuit in resonance with an exciting circuit and we decrease the amount of variable capacity, in order to maintain resonance we may increase the amount of in-

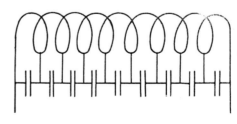

-FIG. 4-

ductance and by so doing we increase the E. M. F. Inasmuch as all coils have more or less distributed capacity it would be ad-

America, June 9th, 1916.

vantageous to eliminate entirely the variable capacity providing we could adopt some suitable means of continuously varying the inductance. The distributed capacity of any coil **may** be considered as in Figure 4. It will be noticed that the capacities between turns appear as in series with each other as far as the coil as a whole is concerned and it is therefore apparent that, providing the coil consists of sufficient turns, the value of the capacity as compared to the inductance will have fallen to a relatively small value. Mr. H. E. Hallborg, in the Proceedings of The Institute of Radio Engineers (Vol. 1, Part 2), in discussing the paper read before that body by Mr. F. A. Kolster on "The Effects of Distributed Capacity of Coils used in Radiotelegraphic Circuits" says, "The distributed capacity of two similar coils is half that of one, obeying the same law as condensers in series; and when connected in parallel, double." The exact value varies with the degree of coupling, as Mr. Kolster has stated. Hence, with a straight coil of considerable length, the distributed capacity of the coil as a whole falls off in definite proportion to the increase in coil length or number of turns." With reference to Figure 4 we see therefore that the shorter the length of the wave to be received the more important becomes the consideration of distributed capacity because of the few number of turns in the inductance. Distributed capacity effects may depend upon **the cross-section of the wire used, the specific inductive capacity and thickness of the insulation, the diameter of the coil, length of tap leads, or the design and disposition of switch points.** In this connection the following will be of interest. A coil 3¼" in diameter consisting of 167 turns of No. 26 D.C.C. magnet wire had a natural wave length of 148 meters. After being shellaced, its natural wave length was found to be 186 meters. Twelve taps were taken off to switch points, and the natural wave length was found to be 222 meters. The coil was mounted as the secondary of a tuning transformer, the carrying rods being used to bring out connections, and the natural wave length had increased to 268 meters. It is quite apparent that better signals would have been obtained with this

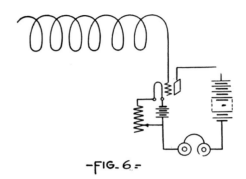

-FIG. 6.-

coil in conjunction with the audion had the coil been taken in its original form and sufficient winding added if necessary to bring its natural wave length up to the desired value. By the addition of this disadvantageous capacity the natural wave length of this coil has been raised to the point where other serious losses begin to occur when this coil is used in the reception of wave lengths in the neighborhood of the final natural wave length of the coil. These losses are known as end-turn losses and will be referred to later.

Again referring to coil design, the following may also be of interest. 118 feet of No. 28 D.C.C. magnet wire were wound on a tube 3 1-16" in diameter, and had a natural wave length of 148 meters. The same wire wound on a tube 5½" in diameter was found to have a natural wave length

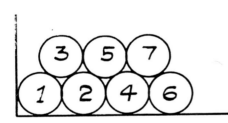

-FIG. 5.-

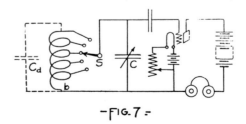

-FIG. 7.-

of 180 meters, and when this same wire was wound on a tube 9" in diameter it was found to have a natural wave length of 244 meters.

	Diameter in inches	Length in inches	Number of turns	Measured Natural Wave Length in Meters	Calculated Inductance in Microhenries	Calculated Capacity in Microfarads
(1)	3 1-16	3.13	150	148	1520	.00000406
(2)	5½	1.67	80	180	1850	.00000493
(3)	9	1.08	50	244	1675	.00000997

No. 28 D.C.C. Magnet Wire — 48 turns per inch

$$L = \frac{2\pi^2 A^2 N^2}{BK}$$

A = Radius
N = Number of turns
B = Length
K = A Constant

Values of K
Coil (1) 711
Coil (2) 414
Coil (3) 230

It might be well to add that multilayer coils, that is, coils of more than one layer of wire, are entirely out of the question for short wave work, and usually should not be used in any case unless some special means is taken to reduce the capacity effects encountered. Figure 5 shows a method sometimes employed when multilayer coils are desired for their economy of space.

In general, for the best results it is far better to use separate pieces of apparatus than to attempt the assembly of a complete receiver in a small cabinet. Such a compact arrangement usually entails a maze of connections, braces of conducting material, various complicated mechanisms, etc., etc., all of which tend to decrease the efficiency due to counter inductive effects, resistance losses at various switch points, and above all losses resulting from undesirable capacity, for even the mere presence of conducting bodies in proximity to the audion circuits may result in a surprisingly great decrease in signal strength.

It is readily seen that the more sensitive the detector, the more apparent becomes a given percentage of lost energy and the more apt is the presence of lost energy to become noticeable. Using an audion it is a very easy matter to show the marked presence of high frequency resistance losses, leakage due to poor insulation, and above all, end turn losses in about 99% of the radio apparatus manufactured, and especially that on the market for amateur use. In many cases those losses aggregate apparently as high as 80% on certain wave lengths, and on wave lengths usually used for amateur communication, 50% loss appears to be quite the rule. Inasmuch as the restrictions to which amateurs are subject in the operation of transmitting apparatus limit to a very great degree the range to be covered with a given power, the importance of loss elimination in the receiver can not be overestimated. The radio frequency dealt with on a wave length of 200 meters is 1,500,000 cycles per second. Ten meters of No. 22 copper wire has a resistance of .431 ohms for direct current, but for an oscillatory current of a frequency of 1,500,000 cycles the resistance of this same length of wire has increased approximately ten times due to the fact that the "skin effect" which takes place in the wire allows the passage of the high frequency current on, or very near, the surface of the wire only. The high frequency resistance of a wire may be decreased by increasing the amount of surface, and this may be done without necessarily increasing the diameter by the use of a stranded wire, or a strand of wires wherein each wire is insulated from its neighbors. Such a conductor consisting of fine enamelled wires is known as "Litzendraht" and may be used to advantage on waves above 700 or 800 meters but recent developments tend to show that stranded conductors are of questionable advantage in connection with the higher frequencies. "Litzendraht" may be purchased on the market, or those to whom the price seems prohibitive may do well to purchase D.C.C. magnet wire, say No. 36 or No. 38, and braid or twist it themselves. This may be done quite conveniently by stretching 30 or 40 wires between two supports, and twisting them by the use of an eye-bolt secured in the chuck of a small hand drill.

Resistance leakages are encountered in coils used for receivers due to the coloring matter used in insulations or to the presence of moisture in the insulation. Wire having colored insulation may be avoided to distinct advantages and every effort should be made to exclude all moisture from windings and their supports. When paper or cardboard tubes are used in the construction of inductances, they should be thoroughly dried out by placing them in a warm, dry room for several days or, baked in an oven at not too high a temperature. The tube should then be well shellaced. It is advisable to purchase shellac in bulk and mix with 95% alcohol as the lower grades of alcohol contain a great percentage of water. After the tube is thoroughly dried and wound, care should be taken that all the moisture which may possibly be in the insulation of the wire is expelled, after which the whole coil is covered with a thin coat of shellac; a second coat being added later if desired.

The natural wave length of any coil of wire may be determined by connecting as in Figure 6 and exciting the coil with a wave meter. It will be found that the wave length at which the greatest response is obtained is quite sharply defined. Due to the distributed capacity of the coil it is in itself an oscillatory circuit and acts as such immediately upon its excitation by a circuit with which it is in resonance.

Take the coil mentioned in connection with the discussion of distributed capacity and utilize it in a receiver, as in Figure 7. It is desired to tune to an incoming signal at a wave length of 275 meters. It is possible to use less than half of the coil for this purpose and, as a result, **two** oscillatory circuits exist—the circuit comprised by the inductance b to s and the condenser C responding to 275 meters, and the circuit comprised by the entire inductance and the capacity Cd (distributed capacity) responding to 268 meters. Due to the slight difference between their periods of vibration a division of the energy between the two circuits is unavoidable, the energy loss to the detector being governed by the percentage of difference between the periods of the two circuits. It will also be quite apparent that, since circuits having two distinct periods of freedom are here dealt with, the damping of the receiver at a switching device so arranged as to connect or disconnect the sections automatically as required. (See Figure 4, page 160, July 1916 Number of "QST"). It should be remembered that the arrangement of these sections must be such that the natural periods of vibration of the coil or coils present are at all times well removed from the wave length being received regardless of the value of such wave length. In the construction of a receiving tuner of sufficient size to properly cover wave lengths between say 200 and 3000 meters, it is hardly practicable to divide the coils into small sections such that the natural wave length of each section is well below 200 meters. It is possible however to cut the number of divisions down to five or six with careful study and painstaking experimental work with the wave meter. It might be well to call attention to the fact that end-losses may occur in both the primary and secondary coils of the receiving tuner and that, where a series condenser is used in the primary circuit, it should always be placed between the antenna and the receiving transformer since otherwise the natural wave length of the primary inductance in conjunction with the

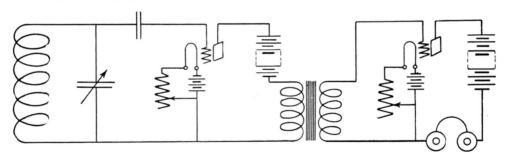

-FIG 9-

will result. Short circuiting is however detrimental under certain conditions and for the best work should not be depended upon. In case it is desirable to utilize this method means should be provided for shortcircuiting the overhanging turns when their number is great, the "short" to be lifted as soon as their number falls below say one quarter of the total turns in the coil.

The simplest method of eliminating this "end-loss effect" is to short circuit the unused portions of the receiving coils. A marked improvement of signals in the neighborhood of the affected wave lengths certain wave lengths will be extremely great and hence, the selectivity of the system as a whole quite materially lessened.

A second method of eliminating the end-turn losses lies in the provision of means for a division of the coil into sections and antenna may easily exceed the safe limit.

A very simple method of preventing end-turn losses is one wherein separate inductances are employed for different ranges of wave length. The proper size of these coils may be very easily determined by means of a wave meter.

These inductances may take the form of variometers and to a decided advantage for, in this form, no necessity is found for tap off connections and since a continuously variable inductance is had the variable capacity element may also be eliminated from the circuit. For short wave reception the variometer, once used, will be found to be indispensible, inasmuch as capacity loss due to decreased voltage and end-turn losses have been eliminated as far as it is possible to do so in a practicable manner.

One very interesting application of the audion is found in the form of the Audion Amplifier (Figure 9) wherein the audion is used as a relay. A step-up transformer is provided, the primary of which is substituted for the telephones in the circuit of the first detector, the outside end of the secondary being connected directly to the grid of the amplifier audion. The filament of this audion is then connected to the primary of the transformer, or if two audions are being used and both lighted from the same battery, no connection at all need be pro-

from the next by a layer of paper .005" thick. On top of the primary wind sufficient good quality paper to form a layer .025" thick. The secondary should consist of 50 layers of No. 38 S.S.C. magnet wire, each layer having the same separating paper as the primary layers. It is important that the leads from the two windings be brought out at the proper places. Care should be taken to connect the coil in properly as the primary of the coil can not be used as the secondary with any degree of success."

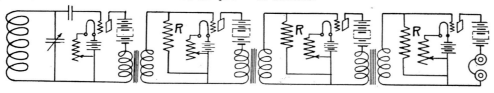

-FIG. 10-

vided at this point. It is possible to go further and use a second and third step (Figure 10) in the process of amplification. It will be found disadvantageous however to go further than a third step because of the interactions between the amplifier circuits resulting in a continuous whistling sound in the telephones. Resistances marked R in Figure 10 may consist of a few lead pencil marks on pieces of paper, the weight of the marks being varied as desired. This high resistance leak tends to prevent the whistling sound mentioned above.

The construction of a very good step-up transformer for this purpose is described by Stanley and Camp in the 1916 Year Book of The Radio Club of America as follows. "Assemble in a fibre tube six inches long,

Figure 11 shows an arrangement of audion detectors originated by Professor G. W. Pierce of Harvard University. An audion amplifying transformer as described above is used between the detector and the first amplifier audion. The battery current in the wing circuits of the remaining audions is increased until ionization of the gases in the bulbs occurs, i.e., until the blue glow appears. A very careful adjustment of this arrangement will give wonderful amplification, probably somewhere in the neighborhood of 1,000 times. This adjustment is difficult however and the critical condition of the audions comparatively hard to maintain especially, when less than three steps are employed, although the writer has occasionally secured excellent results with but two steps.

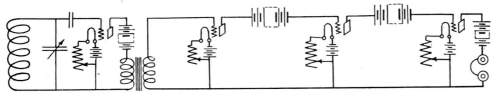

-FIG. 11-

one inch outside diameter and seven-eighths of an inch inside diameter, a bundle of number 22 or smaller, double annealed iron wire. If the wires are all cut the length of the fibre tube and packed in as tightly as possible a good core will be had upon which should be pressed two fibre heads, each 3¾" square and ½" thick. These heads must be so placed that there will remain a clear winding space of 4¾". In this space is wound a primary which will consist of 36 layers of No. 34 S.S.C. magnet wire, each layer being separated

If the wing circuit of an audion is sufficiently coupled either electro-magnetically or electro-statically to the grid, or closed oscillatory circuit of the audion, and if a charge is placed on the grid thereby interrupting the existing flow between the filament and the plate, the resulting pulse of current in the wing circuit will be repeated by means of the coupling back into the grid circuit. The grid condenser will then again receive a charge, which it delivers to the grid and the phenomenon again takes place, and will, providing the adjustments are proper, continue to do so indefinitely, and at a frequency usually dependent upon the time period of the closed oscillatory circuit. If the closed oscillatory circuit is tuned to an antenna, and this system placed in resonance with an incoming wave, it is readily seen that, inasmuch as the resultant pulse of current in the wing circuit is many times greater than the initial charge thrown on the grid, and since the wing circuit current may be repeated back into the grid circuit in exact phase with the incoming oscillations, a reinforcement or amplification of the received signal may result, the degree of amplification depending upon the radio frequency of the received wave. In this condition the audion is oscillating or generating a continuous oscillation.

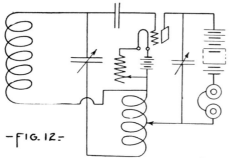

-FIG. 12-

It is impossible to receive a continuous oscillation with a plain rectifier due to the fact that the received currents are of such frequency as to be inaudible to the human ear. However, inasmuch as a generator of continuous oscillations is had at the receiving station advantage may be taken of the "heterodyne" method of reception for undamped waves. Reception by this method is accomplished by the production of beats at an audible frequency between the wave being received and the wave generated at the receiving station. For example, assume that an incoming wave has a frequency of 200,000 cycles per second. Now there is

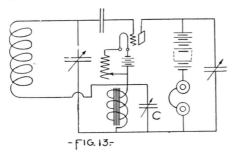

-FIG. 13-

produced in the receiving circuit an alternating current with a frequency of, say, 199,000 cycles. The result is a "beat" frequency, dependent upon the difference between the two frequencies present, which in this case is 1,000 cycles per second, an audible note. Since the audion then acts as a generator, rectifier, and amplifier, by

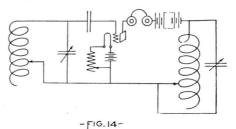

-FIG. 14-

its use, either damped or undamped waves may be received and amplified.

Figures 12 and 13, respectively, show electro-magnetic and electro-static coupling between the grid and wing circuits. In Figure 12 the coupling consists of an auto-transformer. It may consist of an **inductively** coupled transformer and, as is apparent, the proper degree of coupling between the two circuits may be obtained by variation. In Figure 13 the coupling consists of the condenser C, shunted by an iron core choke coil, which permits the passage of direct current only. This is the so-called "ultraudion." Figure 14 shows an oscillating system wherein no coupling is provided other than the small amount offered by the audion itself. Here the wing circuit is tuned to resonance with the grid circuit, the energy being transferred as above suggested through the coupling provided by the audion. This elimination of external coupling however often renders the circuit difficult of operation especially on the longer wave lengths. The writer prefers the method as shown in Figure 15. Coils a, b, and e are so arranged that e slides into b, and b into a. Their length may be of the order of 8" and their diameter about 4" or 5". They should be wound with No. 28 S.S.C. magnet wire. Taps are provided a cut every ¾" and a loading coil and suitable variometer should be used in conjunction with coil a for tuning the antenna. The loading coil (not shown) should consist of a tube 6" in diameter and 14" in length wound with No. 28 D.S.C. magnet wire. The condensers C1, C2, and C4 should have a capacity of about .001 microfarads. C3 is comparatively very small, its maximum capacity being that of C1 with pointer on 10° scale mark.

A simple and very good method is shown in Figure 16. Here S may be a tube 7" in diameter and 14" in length wound with No. 28 D. S. C. magnet wire. P may be a coil 6" in diameter and 8" in length wound with No. 24 D.S.C. magnet wire. On coil S taps should be taken off every ¾" to accommodate switch No. 1, and about every ¼" for a distance of 3" from the lower end of the coil for the accommodation of switch No. 2. The range of this system will lie between approximately 2,000 and 15,000 meters phones. This sound may be quite loud and disagreeable. The common inductance should then be decreased until this sound

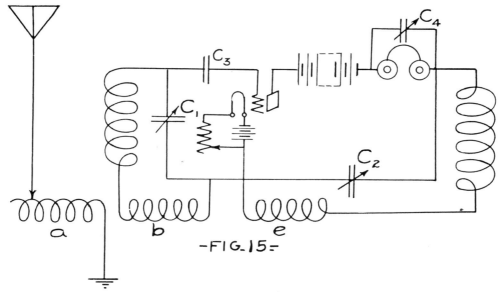

-FIG. 15-

where the capacity of C is of a maximum value of .001 microfarads.

Inasmuch as the peculiarities of operation of these arrangements are the same throughout, an outline of the procedure with reference to Figure 16 will suffice for all. The value of inductance and capacity in the grid or closed oscillatory circuit of Figure 16 is set at random. The amount of inductance common to both the wing and grid circuits is increased at switch No. 2 until a howling noise is heard in the telephones.

ceases, at which time the audion should be oscillating. By adjusting the antenna inductances, a point will be found where a hiss is heard and reaches a maximum. At this point the entire system is in resonance. This hissing sound is due to the shock excitation of the system by infinitesimally small atmospheric disturbances or stray damped waves. If the adjustment of the secondary tuning condenser now be varied, it will be found that the oscillations of the audion may be stopped or started at will

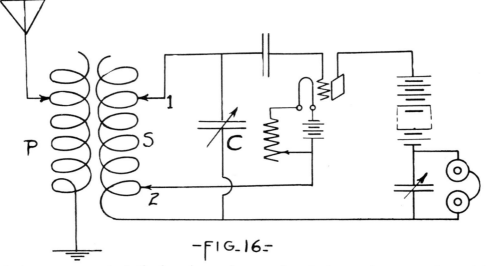

-FIG. 16-

and that their stoppage is accompanied by a rather muffled click in the telephones. The system as a whole may be gradually swung from 2,000 to 15,000 meters and kept at all times in resonance. Hence, any stations which happen to be working within range may be logged for future reference. Both damped and undamped waves may be received on these systems. The damped (spark) waves however, will come in with a hiss, that is, their natural spark tune will not be apparent. By decreasing the amount of wire common to the wing and grid circuits, a point will be reached where the audion ceases to generate, and at this point the natural spark tone of the station will be apparent. However, in this condition the audion still continues the repeating action and amplification results. Close adjustment of grid-wing circuit coupling is necessary for the best results.

Figure 17 shows a circuit applicable to the shorter wave lengths, that is, below 2,000 meters. It will here be noticed that the secondary tuning condenser has been dispensed with, all the tuning of the secondary or closed oscillatory circuit being accomplished by the variometer. It will be necessary to provide at least three variometers, each wound with different sizes of wire, to cover the range from 200 to 2,000 meters. The secondary circuit is coupled to the antenna circuit by means of the coil which may consist of 50 turns of No. 22 magnet wire wound on a tube 4" in diameter. The two coils comprising the coupler M, for coupling the wing and grid circuits, may also be approximately this size, except that one should slide within the other. Direct coupling may be used at this point, but with a smaller measure of success due to the impossibility of getting as close an adjustment of the coupling, and it may also be found advantageous at certain wave lengths to resort to tuning the wing circuit by the insertion of variometers. Great pains should be taken in the assembly of apparatus for the reception of shorter wave lengths by these methods and care should be taken to eliminate all end-turn and similar effects, inasmuch as the presence of additional frequencies due to overhanging ends or nearby oscillators may make these circuits at the higher frequencies absolutely inoperative.

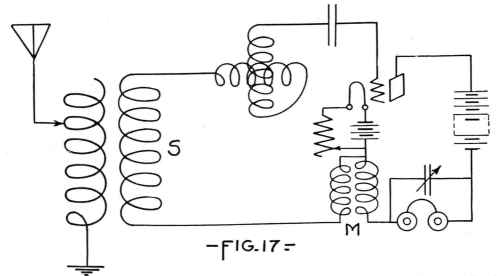

– FIG. 17 –

"Transatlantic Amateur Communication Accomplished!" by K.B. Warner, 1BHW

By Ward Silver, N0AX

The objective of 20 years of experimentation and step-by-step improvements was transoceanic contact between amateurs — the DX urge was paramount especially in those early days! Before the formal tests were conducted, there were many examples reported of amateur signals being received around the globe across great distances. Marconi's spark stations were in regular contact with Europe but with power of 37 kW. What could amateurs accomplish?

US amateur signals were regularly received in New Zealand and Australia, for example, some with low power CW signals that would be considered QRPp (super low power) even today. While it may have been clear that signals could span the oceans, two-way contact had thus far proved elusive — it was time to muster all the technology Amateur Radio had to make the contact. The story is set up marvelously by these excerpts from Clinton De Soto in *Two Hundred Meters and Down*…

[During the second transatlantic] it will be remembered, one of the three European stations reliably reported heard in the United States was French 8AB, at Nice, France…The owner of 8AB was Léon Deloy. During the summer of 1923 Deloy visited the United States to study American amateur methods, with the avowed determination to be the first to span the Atlantic.

Returning home to France in early autumn, he applied all of the information he had received, completed his new station and tested with British 2OD in October, and in November cabled A.R.R.L. Traffic Manager Schnell that he would transmit on 100 meters from 9 to 10 p.m., starting November 25th.

From the very first, 8AB and the identifying cipher group "GSJTP" were audible in Hartford. The next night, the 26th, Deloy transmitted again and, having been advised by cable that he was being heard, sent two messages, which were copied not only by Schnell and K. B. Warner at 1MO, but also by Reinartz at 1XAM [including] a schedule for an attempt at two-way work the following night.

The night of November 27, 1923, Both Schnell and Reinartz were on the air. Schnell had secured special permission from the Supervisor of Radio at Boston to use the 100-meter wavelength, and everything was in readiness. At the stroke of 9:30 the strangely-stirring 25-cycle gargle from 8AB came on the air. For an hour he called America, then sent two more messages. At 10:30 he signed off, asking for an acknowledgement. Long calls from 1MO and 1XAM and then…

Let's let K.B. Warner, 1BHW, himself finish the story, shall we?

Transatlantic Amateur Communication Accomplished!

1MO and 1XAM Work French 8AB When Two-Way Amateur Contact is Established Across Ocean for First Time; 1MO Wins QST's Brown Derby for Feat; One Hundred Meters Does the Trick

THE Atlantic Ocean was bridged in two-way amateur operation for the first time in history when Station 1MO in West Hartford, Conn., communicated for almost two hours on the night of November 17th with French Station 8AB, operated by Leon Deloy in Nice, France. Later that same night Station 1XAM, sometime 1QP, in South Manchester, Conn., also worked 8AB.

For years we have dreamed of this; for over a year we have seen it coming; for weeks we have been sure that winter weather would see the thing accomplished. It has been done, fellows; we are actually in back-and-forth contact with Europe over our amateur sets. For the first time in history we have worked a European amateur, and for the first time the amateurs of distant foreign countries have sat by their respective firesides and talked to each other with ease.

The story of how it was done goes back to this summer when Mr. Deloy, the leading French amateur, visited this country to study American amateur methods with the avowed intention of "working" us this winter. Hundreds of our fellows met him at the A.R.R.L. Convention in Chicago this fall. Returning home, Deloy applied the "dope" he had collected here and built a short-wave transmitter and when all was in readiness cabled Traffic Manager Schnell that he would transmit on 100 meters from 9 P.M. to 10 P.M. starting Nov. 25th. This news was spread immediately by broadcast and many stations commenced listening. Schnell built a special short-wave tuner for the job and at 9 P.M. on the 25th was tuned to 100 meters and waiting. Promptly at 9 o'clock Deloy started up, and from the very first word he was copied by 1MO. Altho Deloy has been heard in America before, this was in itself an achievement. For an hour he called "ARRL" and sent the cypher group "GSJTP" for identification purposes. The next night, No. 26th, Deloy again transmitted and, having been advised by cable that he was QRK, sent two messages, which were copied not only by 1MO but by 1QP. One of these, the first amateur message ever sent from France, read as follows:

NICE FRANCE
A.R.R.L.
WANT THIS FIRST TRANSATLANTIC MESSAGE TO CONVEY MOST HEARTY GREETINGS OF FRENCH TO AMERICAN AMATEURS.
LEON DELOY

GRATULATIONS THIS IS FINE DAY MIM PSE QSL NR 1 2.

Then Schnell asked him if he would take some messages, and greetings were sent to General Ferrie, director of French military radio, and to Dr. Pierre Corret, president of the French Joint Transatlantic Committee. Meanwhile 1XAM (1QP on special

THE TRANSMITTER AT 1MO-1BHW which, under the call 1MO and on a wavelength of 110 meters, was the first American amateur station to connect with a European amateur. This set was built in accordance with the scheme outlined by John L. Reinartz, of 1QP-1XAM, in another article in this issue, which every transmitting amateur should read.

The other message made a further schedule and proposed listening for a reply on about the same wave. Meanwhile 1MO got permission from the Supervisor of Radio to test on the short wave, and the following night, the 27th, was in readiness. Deloy

1MO And His "Hay-Wire" Receiver With Which He Worked F8AB. (Photo by Foto Topics, Inc.)

came on at 9:30 and for an hour called America and sent two more messages. At 10:30 he signed off, asking for a QSL, 1MO gave him a long call on 110 meters, and European and American amateurs were working for the first time, for Deloy came right back! It brought the thrill that comes but once in a lifetime. Deloy's first words were:

R R QRK UR SIGS QSA VY ONE FOOT FROM PHONES ON GREBE FB OM HEARTY CON-

license) called 8AB on 115 meters simultaneously with 1MO and Deloy acknowledged receipt, asking him to QRX. The Editor took the key at 1MO for a few minutes and exchanged compliments with Deloy, and then Schnell asked 8AB for a message from French amateurs for WNP, the MacMillan Arctic Expedition's "Bowdoin." This message Deloy sent, expressing the hope that they might soon work Mix; but a couple of words were missed at 1MO and a repeat was asked for. Reinartz had copied it solid, however, and acknowledged it to 8AB, who then shifted to his wave and chewed the rag with him for several minutes. Then 1MO and 8AB connected again, Deloy repeated the WNP message to Schnell, but shortly after developed some sort of transmitter trouble and signed off rather hurriedly at 12:28 A.M.

For two hours these two American stations had worked the French station and in this space but one repeat in each country was necessary. At 1MO, 8AB was audible 25 ft. from a loud-speaker working on one audio step, and 1XAM used loud-speaker thruout too. Deloy reported 1MO "a foot from fones," using a Grebe CR-13.

Not only was the ocean spanned but new records were made for 100-meter operation; in fact, we believe we can say it was the short wave that made the accomplishment possible. It is interesting to note that all three stations in this communication used the same circuit arrangement, a Hartley with modification originated by Reinartz and described in detail elsewhere in this issue. Deloy visited Reinartz while here this past fall and was so interested in the possibilities of the short-wave set that he resolved to build one, with the results already reported.

The next night after this work, Nov. 28th, was a bad one, with plenty of static and noise. 1MO had a schedule with 8AB at midnight; they exchanged calls but that was all. 8AB changed wave length and apparently had trouble. His note was poor and he faded badly. 1BGF in Hartford, listening on a Grebe CR-13, and 1XAM also heard him.

Thanksgiving night, the 29th, 1XAM again worked F8AB for a few minutes. 8AB was right on KDKA's short concert wave, about 103 meters, and could be heard only when KDKA was idling. 1XAM heard him at 8, 8:30 and 9 P.M., and connected with him at 10:40 P.M., asking him to shift wave length. This he apparently did but nothing more was heard of him. 1MO had had a schedule at 6 P.M. but 8AB was not heard.

On the night of Nov. 30th 1MO had 8AB on from 10:58 P.M. until 1:17 A.M., signals very QSA but decent copying utterly impossible because of terrific squeals from several local receivers, to say nothing of heavy static. Four long messages were sent to 8AB and acknowledged. He sent two to 1MO which were copied complete by 1XAM who, fortunately, was free from "listener QRM." 8AB was also heard by 2CQZ, 1BGF, 1ANA, and 1XAQ.

At this writing, the first of the month, a very determined little group of amateurs is hard at the job, resolved that 8AB shall be kept in nightly contact with this country.

Schnell Wins the Brown Derby

It is going to be hard to explain to you fellows, we know, how an A.R.R.L. officer happened to win the Brown Derby offered by the Editor of *QST* as a trophy to the first ham to work to Europe. We hear agonized yells of "Collusion!" We're helpless, tho. Schnell vowed his determination to win the lid, he got busy and did it—and there's nothing else to do, he has won it.

IN the first transatlantic operation between U1MO and F8AB, a message of greetings was sent to the renowned General Ferrié, director of French military radio, reading as follows:

HARTFORD, CONN.
GENERAL FERRIE,
PARIS, FRANCE.
AMERICA GREETS YOU FOR THE FIRST TIME BY AMATEUR RADIO ACROSS THE ATLANTIC OCEAN ON 100 METERS.
AMERICAN RADIO RELAY LEAGUE.

The answer was received on the morning of Dec. 2d when F8AB sent his Nr. 9 to U1MO:

PARIS,
AMERICAN RADIO RELAY LEAGUE,
HARTFORD, CONN.
REMERCIE ET MAGNIFIQUES FELICITATIONS RESULTATS OBTENUS AVEC ONDE 100 METRES QUI ONT PERMIS ETABLIR NOUVELLE LIAISON ENTRE FRANCE ET ETATS UNIS.
GENERAL FERRIE.

Translated, this reads:

AMERICAN RADIO RELAY LEAGUE,
HARTFORD, CONN.
MANY THANKS AND MOST HEARTY CONGRATULATIONS ON THE RESULTS OBTAINED WITH 100 METER WAVE, WHICH HAVE PERMITTED THE ESTABLISHMENT OF A NEW BOND BETWEEN FRANCE AND THE UNITED STATES.
GENERAL FERRIE.

(Jealous of our high British hat, we think, and wanted something to wear himself. Hi!). We're going to hand-paint this derby until O.M. Stetson himself won't know what it is—watch FS's smoke!

The Stations

We have no particulars on M. Deloy's transmitter, but imagine his power was close to a kilowatt, for which he is licensed, as he certainly had a mean signal. The note, by the way, is 25-cycle unrectified, and the signal was strong enough to receive non-oscillating, merely regenerating on the 25-cycle modulation! His receiver is a new short-wave Grebe. 1XAM used the transmitter described elsewhere in this issue, with 3.1 amps. in the antenna on 115 meters; he of course used a Reinartz tuner for reception, with a 2-step. The sender at 1MO is of the same type but is a full-wave self-rectifying circuit using two UV-203-A's on each side of the cycle. The antenna current on 110 meters is about 1.5 amperes. The power at both 1MO and 1XAM is under a half kilowatt. 1MO's receiver was at best a pile of junk, just a couple of cardboard tubes with a few turns of wire in the ordinary tickler circuit, a 4-plate variable condenser, and a junk detector-onestep. Not a thing extraordinary, in other words, about any of the stations—*the accomplishment is merely a demonstration, more effective than all our talk, of the efficacy of the*

shorter waves. Deloy recognized this too. In his conversation with the Editor via radio he said: "This is...a great moment in my life, for which I have been working several years. Hearty congratulations to you both and to League for great development of short wave work."

The distance covered by these tests, some 3400 miles, is not remarkable, for western

amateurs dump signals to New Zealand over much vaster distances as a matter of course, nor does it compare with the WNP-6CEU record for two-way communication. But it was over an area confessedly much more difficult to cover, it is the first two-way transocean contact with any foreign country, and it is the most important achievement of Amateur Radio in years in that it definitely links us with our European cousins.

Beating the Tests

It seems assured that this is but the forerunner of regular transatlantic operation. European amateurs of course continue to log large numbers of American hams regularly. On the night of Nov. 24th 1AWW in Springfield, Mass., and 8BOY and 3BVA at State College, Pa., copied 6NI in Liverpool, England, calling "Test" on D.C.C.W., signals QSA, wave between 225 and 250 meters, 10:20 to 10:30 P.M. E.S.T. Altho we imagine 6NI is a broadcasting station, this was in good Continental. British 2AW and Dutch PA9 solicit special 100-meter tests with American amateurs—the Traffic Manager is arranging schedules. PA9, by the way, is the first authorized amateur transmitter in the Netherlands, especially licensed to the Dutch amateur transatlantic committee at Delft for the 1923-24 tests. There is some activity in Italy and ACD is ready with 200 watts, waiting for his license. Belgium shows signs of life and before long there will be amateur transmitters there. In France and England of course they are ready for us this winter by the dozens, but they will have to step some to keep up with F8AB.

To Deloy and 1MO and 1XAM, our hearty congratulations. You have started a great winter!

—K.B.W.

Amateur Radio's Contributions to Propagation Science

By Carl Luetzelschwab, K9LA and Dave Leeson, W6NL

In 1902, Arthur E. Kennelly (an American) and Oliver Heaviside (a British subject) independently postulated that Marconi's success could be explained by reflection from an electrically conducting layer in the Earth's upper atmosphere. Although many experiments were undertaken, little was understood about the Kennelly-Heaviside layer except for some fundamental observations that night time was better for the longer wavelengths and shorter wavelengths traveled farther.

Forced to fend for ourselves in the "wasteland" below 200 meters by the Radio Act of 1912 that moved amateurs out of the "prime" 1000 to 200 meter wavelengths, we soon discovered the value of the new spectrum. Thus, our exile inadvertently provided us with new ground to cover and new discoveries to make. All it took was a "we'll show them" spirit and soon Amateur Radio operators did just that.

This seeming banishment ushered in one of the most interesting periods in Amateur Radio as ionospheric propagation was being discovered. One big problem hindering propagation studies was that the measuring equipment was extremely crude. For example, received signal strength was measured with an RF ammeter in the antenna lead and the use of the broad spark waveform didn't help, either. In essence, the in-depth study of the Kennelly-Heaviside layer had to wait for continuous wave (CW) signals and better transmitting/receiving equipment.

The saga included the discovery of skip zone by A. Hoyt Taylor of the Naval Research Laboratory (NRL), amateur transatlantic tests and the first QSOs with Leon Deloy, F8AB, the struggle with the Navy for control of the spectrum, and the beginnings of international call signs. It culminated in the 1927 International Radiotelegraph Conference that solidified the amateur claim to bands we still occupy today. This is all covered in Clinton Desoto's book *200 Meters and Down*, still in print via the ARRL and great reading!

Amateur Radio and the Short Waves

Beginning in February 1921, the first Transatlantic Sending Tests produced no results, but there were other circumstances that prevented US amateurs from being heard in Europe. In December 1921, the second Transatlantic Sending Tests produced positive results — 30 or so US amateurs were heard on the other side of the Atlantic. And in September 1922, an amateur worked all nine US districts in one night (there were only nine districts then, not ten as we have today).

In November 1923, the first transatlantic QSO between the US and Europe was completed. Also in this month the first US to Japan QSO was completed. In summary, all these tests showed everyone that wavelengths below 200 meters were not useless. There was much interest in trying to understand how these receptions and QSOs took place — in other words, how did signals propagate from the US to Europe and Japan?

The earliest comment in *QST* about propagation on the "short waves" appears in the January 1924 issue, in which Editor K. B. Warner, 1BHW, stated that "the accomplishment is merely a demonstration, more effective than all our talk, of the efficiency of the shorter waves." This certainly wasn't a technical explanation, but it was an omen of the contributions to understanding propagation to come from Amateur Radio.

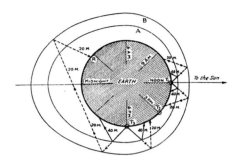

And the contributions to understanding propagation did come. As illustrated above, we gained a basic explanation in April 1925 of how an ionospheric "layer" (the term "ionosphere" wasn't used until 1929) provided long distance QSOs on these short wavelengths. Also in early 1925, amateurs discovered a "dead belt" in the distances covered by these short waves, and eventually in October 1925 we were talking about "skipped distance" and ultimately the "skip zone."

A great summary of the whole story has been written by C-P Yeang, "Characterizing Radio Channels: The Science and Technology of Propagation and Interference, 1900-1935." Yeang is also the author of the very well written "When Hobbyist were Experts: The U.S. Radio Amateurs' Long-Range Short-Wave Experiments Circa 1920." Yeang is currently at the University of Toronto. (**www.hps.utoronto.ca/people/yeang.htm**)

In August 1947, Amateur Radio operators reported what was to become known as transequatorial propagation at VHF. From earlier work performed by amateurs with the US Army Signal Corps, two amateurs successfully bounced signals off the Moon on 2 meters in January 1953. In May 1969 we saw reports of long-delayed echoes by amateurs that contributed to the database of recorded instances of this fascinating phenomenon. And in December 1982 we were introduced to the first HF propagation prediction program to be run on a PC.

Onward and Upward

Contributions continue to be made today. Every time you encounter an unexpected or unexplained opening, you may be experiencing some phenomenon that is yet to be explained — or even fully discovered. Experienced amateurs know of and use HF band openings not predicted even by the best propagation models. VHF and UHF operators make contacts all the time using sporadic E propagation that has yet to be fully characterized. At the other end of the spectrum, on 160 meters there are "spotlight" DX openings between small regions — thought to be created by duct-like structures in the lower ionosphere —that move about throughout an evening.

Amateurs are making use of improved solar and geomagnetic field measurements, both terrestrial and satellite. Improvements in equipment, coordination and reporting over the Internet, better visualization techniques, and use of databases to track contacts all multiply the power of the amateur to observe and contribute to the understanding of propagation.

Tomorrow's amateur will likely have access to a wider range of frequencies than at any time in the previous century. New VLF, LF, and MF allocations are all under consideration. Additional bands or channels in the HF range have been proposed. Continuing advances in semiconductors are enabling amateurs to communicate over longer and longer distances at microwave and mm-wave frequencies previously unattainable. There are entire decades of spectrum between 100 GHz and light that are *terra incognita* to the communications field.

As amateurs have always found, moving to new frequency ranges results in new discoveries about propagation. Given the tools, techniques, and time we will no doubt continue to see a steady stream of experimenters scouting out the skies in search of contacts and understanding.

"The Reflection of Short Waves" by John Reinartz, 1XAM

By Carl Luetzelschwab, K9LA

Not long after Marconi claimed his reception (there still are those who believe this never really happened), theorists were already working on this interesting topic. In the March 15, 1902, issue of *Electrical World and Engineer*, A. E. Kennelly hypothesized "It may be safe to infer, however, that at an elevation of about 80 kilometers, or 50 miles, a rarefaction exists which, at ordinary temperatures, accompanies a conductivity to low-frequency alternating currents about 20 times as great as that of ocean water." Kennelly further hypothesized "There is well-known evidence that the waves of wireless telegraphy, propagated through the ether and atmosphere over the surface of the ocean, are reflected by that electrically-conducting surface."

Later that same year, Dr. Oliver Heaviside hypothesized in the Telegraphy section of the Encyclopedia Britannica (published December 19, 1902): "There is another consideration. There may possibly be a sufficiently conducting layer in the upper air." This became known as the Heaviside layer and later, the Kennelly-Heaviside layer, acknowledging the contribution of both. The term "ionosphere" came later, and has been attributed to Sir Robert Watson-Watt.

With respect to Amateur Radio contributions in understanding propagation, we find that John L. Reinartz, 1XAM, undertook a year-long study of the propagation of short waves in 1924. He received some 5000 reports of his 1XAM transmissions on different frequencies from Europe (five observers) and North America (18 observers). The full details of this work were published in *Radio News*, and a summary appeared in the following article.

Reinartz's Amateur Radio work between 20 meters and 60 meters resulted in several important observations in the following article that certainly helped advance the theory of propagation. Out of these observations, it was found that in daylight the signals could be heard throughout only a very small territory right around the transmitter, beyond which there was a broad belt in which no signals were heard. After this, the signals could be heard again for a very great distance. Reinartz reported that the size of this "dead belt" (it wasn't called "skip zone" yet) was independent of the transmitter power.

In the May 1925 issue of the *Proceedings of the Institute of Radio Engineers* (IRE), Dr. A. Hoyt Taylor of the Naval Research Laboratory reported on their extensive experiments taken enroute on a ship from New York to Panama on various frequencies. In this paper, the terms "skip region" and "miss region" were used.

A follow-up article in the October 1925 *QST* by Dr. Taylor and Dr. E. O Hulburt (Dr. Hulburt was also with the Naval Research Laboratory) discussed many aspect of the Kennelly-Heaviside layer — ionization, de-ionization, absorption, the "skipped distance," reflection versus refraction, seasonal effects, day and night effects, and extreme distances. Note that the term "skipped distance" was introduced, and this took favor over the "dead belt," and this led to the term "skip zone."

In summary, Amateur Radio played an important role in early investigations of the Kennelly-Heaviside layer, with the concept of a skip zone being one of the more ubiquitous. Although the precise theory of propagation put forth by Reinartz had some problems, there's no doubt that his Amateur Radio experimental work contributed ultimately to understanding propagation.

John L. Reinartz, 1XAM, in his favorite corner waiting for the cameraman's powder to flash. If you look closely you will note that he is using a Reinartz receiver, for which we don't blame him.

The Reflection of Short Waves
By John L. Reinartz, 1XAM

> Again it is QST's privilege to present an article of the first importance in radio affairs; this time from that tireless experimenter, John L. Reinartz. We consider this article one of the most important contributions made to radio literature.

REFLECTION plays an important part in the use of the shorter radio waves. This became apparent during a series of experiments which I undertook early in 1924 and which lasted throughout that year. The details of these experiments will not be given here since they are fully recorded in a series of articles which begin in the April issue of Radio News. In the very first of these tests, when very short waves were used, the signals became *weaker after sunset* instead of becoming stronger as is expected of wavelengths above 100 meters. Also, as more and more observers entered the test, it was discovered that the signals were *stronger at a great distance* than they were nearby. Thus it became clear that the short wavelengths acted quite differently from those of 100 meters and above. In fact, it is not an exaggeration to say that an entirely new field of possibilities was opened.

The reflection of radio waves is nothing new. Many authors have presented the idea of the Heaviside layer in a variety of different ways so as to account for such things as fading, extreme ranges at night, and so on. The Heaviside layer, it will be remembered, is a theory devised by the late Oliver Heaviside. This theory assumes that as one goes up through the earth's atmos-

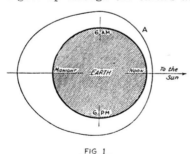

FIG. 1

phere one finally gets to a point at which the gas pressure is so small that the atmosphere becomes a good electrical conductor. Since a good conductor is also a good reflector of radio waves, we have thereby surrounded the earth with a reflecting shell. Nearer the earth is more air which is a conductor during the daytime but an insulator at night. The reason for this change is that the sun's rays ionize the air in the daytime. This amounts to an extension downward of the reflecting shell, therefore the reflector is always nearer the earth's surface on the sunny side of the earth than it is at the dark side of the earth. Some time after the sun sets, de-ionization occurs in all the lower atmosphere and there is left the upper layer we have described before. See Fig. 1. The Heaviside theory assumes that radio waves

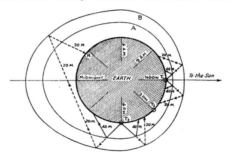

FIG. 2

glide along the inside of this shell for great distances with very little loss. The irregularities of reception are accounted for by irregularities in the Heaviside layer. Changes in signal strength at a given point are accounted for by saying that the Heaviside layer is agitated and therefor reflects in a fashion that changes from minute to minute.

During the very extensive tests made throughout 1924, many effects were met which suggest a modified theory. A few of these effects are:

1. In tests at noon there was a minimum wavelength that could be heard by the receiving operator. A shorter wavelength would not answer, no matter how much power was used. At 50 meters the difference between a wave which would give very strong signals and a wave which would give no signals at all was less than one meter. At the same time one could not go up on the wavelengths very high until the signals again failed to come through. There was then a very narrow band of wavelength which would work at this time of the day. Later in the after-

noon this band would move upward somewhat.

2. It was found that in daylight transmission the signals could be heard through only a very small territory right around the station, after which there was a broad belt in which no signals at all could be heard. After this the signals could be heard again for a very great distance. See Fig. 4. The small territory around the station is not of much use; in fact it may be less than a quarter of a mile across. Therefore we are interested in the distance at which signals can *again* be heard. During the forenoon this distance is less toward the East than toward the West. At noon it is the same in both directions and during the afternoon it is less toward the West than toward the East.

3. The general effect of the shifting of the useful waveband was that during the

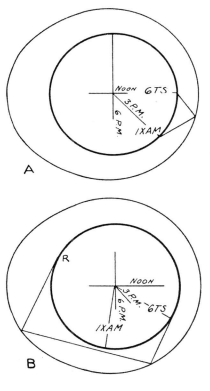

FIG. 3

forenoon, contact between two stations could be maintained by gradually shortening the wavelength in steps of a few meters at a time until noon. As the afternoon progressed the wave would again gradually have to be made longer in similar steps. The rate at which the waveband shifted was greatest around sunrise, least at noon and again rapid around sunset.

4. As the waveband shifted it was found that when a certain receiving station had just lost the signals other receiving stations further off could still hear them.

5. In afternoon operation, if communication was first established on the shortest wavelengths that would work, signals would gain slowly in strength and then drop off very quickly to zero. In forenoon operation signals would be stronger when communication was first established and then would fall off slowly. This would be expected from the different rate at which the waveband was shifting.

6. The size of the "dead belt" was independent of the power of the transmitter but outside of that belt the range of the transmitter depended upon the power used.

During 1924 some 5000 reports on the transmission of 1XAM were received from 5 observers in Europe and 18 in North America.[1] Inspection of these reports suggested that different frequencies are reflected from different heights above the earth's surface. They also suggested that this height (for a given wavelength) varies with the time of the day and with the seasons. It then occurred to me that the sun might be the determining factor and might account for the effects mentioned. We have said that the sun causes ionization of our atmosphere and that this effect is greatest at noon and least at midnight. Therefore the inside of the reflecting shell we have been talking about will be nearer to the earth on the sunny side than on the dark side. This was shown in Fig. 1. This figure fits in with some of the things that have been observed and mentioned. Looking at it one would naturally expect that at noon reflection would be the same to the West and East. One would also expect that in the forenoon the waves would come to earth at a greater distance to the West than to the East and finally one would expect the reverse in the afternoon.

The figure just drawn does not account for another thing, the fact that different wavelenghs *are not reflected to the same distance*. If we agree that short waves will penetrate further up into the Heaviside layer before being reflected down again, then we will account for this also. This idea is shown in Figure 2. In this drawing A is the same layer that was shown in Figure 1. The solid arrows from

---

[1]—During the course of his various tests Mr. Reinartz has held two-way daylight conversation with 6TS, 6AGK, 6GM, 6ARX and 7GS. His signals at waves between 18 and 42 meters have been copied many times by French 8BF and also less often by British 5LF, 2LZ and 5GL.

the transmitters T1 and T3 show how a wavelength such as 40 meters will be reflected. It is seen that these waves all come down rather close to the transmitter and no particularly great ranges result. Now if 20 meter waves penetrate further upward before being reflected they must be reflected from a second layer B somewhat higher up. Naturally this will cause them to come down much further from the transmitting station as can be seen easily enough by following the dotted arrows. In this figure we have followed only those waves which started upward at an angle of 45 degrees. There are things which make one suspect that this is the most effective reflecting angle.

If Figure 2 is correct some of the other things spoken of can also be accounted for. The reason that there was always a shortest wavelength that could be heard by the observers in the 1XAM tests was because any wavelength still shorter would go too far up in the Heaviside layer and would be reflected down at a very great distance, passing entirely over the receiving station. These things can be cured by going to a longer wavelength which comes down sooner.

Figure 3 also attempts to represent the actual results of tests between station 6TS (station of Paul Willis at Santa Monica, California) and 1XAM (South Manchester, Conn.) The distance between the two stations is about three hours in time.

When 6TS is transmitting on 20 meters at noon Pacific Time (Fig. 3a) he can just barely be heard at 1XAM. By 3 P.M. Pacific Time, the signals are no longer audible at 1XAM. Figure 3b shows why—the waves are being reflected from such an altitude that they miss the earth. Possibly if there were an observer on the earth at the point marked R 6TS's signals would be found to be coming in splendidly there. When 6TS is transmitting on 40 meters at noon Pacific Time, his signals are reflected to earth much too close to him to be heard on the east coast. During midwinter these signals commence to come in at 1XAM

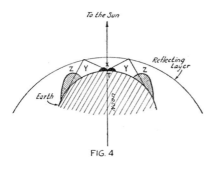

FIG. 4

about 4:30 P.M. Pacific Time, and are good for about two hours, when they too are reflected from such a height as to miss 1XAM. Then the 75-meter band is used, with good results until dawn.

In Figure 4 is shown approximately the way in which the audibility of the received

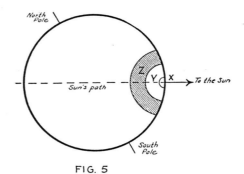

FIG. 5

signal changes with distance from the transmitter. This figure will stand a bit of explaining. X is the small region in which the station can be heard directly. Y is the dead belt in which nothing can be heard and Z is the belt in which the signal will be heard strongly. Of course these territories have only been shown edgewise in Figure 3 and are really shaped somewhat as shown in Figures 5 and 6 for different locations. When it is noon at the sending station and the sun is overhead the areas are circular with their centers at the sending station. Reflection occurs equally in all directions. See Fig. 5. For any other time of the day and for any location where the sun does not shine directly downward at noon the belts are not truly circular. See Fig. 6.

The work referred to has been based on experiments with waves between 20 and 60 meters. On wavelengths above 60 meters the effects were not noticeable and during daylight the effective range of the wavelengths above 60 meters did not compare favorably with their night range. One can go further and say that the daylight range of wavelengths above 60 meters was not found to be equal even to the range which they gave at night with unreflected (gliding wave) transmission.

I hope that this work will lead to the accumulation of actual figures that will be of practical assistance in choosing the best wavelength for any given operation condition. We should not be content to try to reach the receiving station by direct (unreflected) transmission because this takes too much power. With one kilowatt input the range by direct transmission is but 10% of that obtained with reflected waves of a length between 20 and 40 meters. If we are willing to choose the wavelength for each particular distance and each particular time of day it is possible to put the region of strongest signal right on the receiving station and to obtain communica-

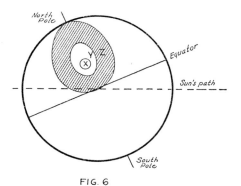

FIG. 6

tion with strong signals but small input power. The advantage of the short wave is not that it is radiated more effectively but that it is reflected to points further away with the result just the same as if it had been bundled up and delivered intact at the receiving station.

1925 will see direct international contact on waves below 1 meter and even now the American Radio Relay League is asking its government for a band at or around that wavelength. The problem is by no means solved; rather this is just a beginning. There is no place on earth that harbors an amateur who cannot be of service in this work. There is much work yet to do, so much that I ask all amateurs to co-ordinate their work with that of others who are working at the same problem. Who will help during 1925 to add to the information now at hand?

Acknowledgment

The information leading to this article was obtained through co-operation of the amateurs of the world and from my own observations of the behavior of signals from America, Europe and Australia. I am very grateful to those who have actively co-operated with me and to those who have contributed without knowing it.

Editor's Notes

[The thought that high-frequency wave motion will penetrate the Heaviside layer to a greater elevation than longer waves is rather in opposition to our generally accepted beliefs on such matters and may deserve further investigation.

The apparent best angle of reflection may be accounted for by considering the layer as a diffuse reflector. In the figure herewith the energy following path 1 straight upward from the transmitter can be supposed (after it strikes the Heaviside layer) to spread like a jet of water from a fountain. The energy would then wander off in the diffuse reflector and become lost. Energy leaving by path 2 would be reflected fairly effectively to some moderately distant point. At some still flatter angle as the one followed by path 3 the reflection will be very effective indeed. These changes will be understood by remembering the way sunlight is reflected from the clouds. It looks as if the reflection should become better and better as the angle grows flatter. This may be true but there is suggested the possibility that energy started at such a low angle as that following path 4 is compelled to struggle through too

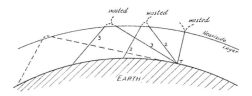

many obstructions and therefore never gets clear of the earth. It seems reasonable to assume that solid obstruction on the earth's surface such as houses, trees and particularly electric wiring systems might prove effective barriers to the short waves.— Tech. Ed.]

Movies!

THOSE who have to do with planning a convention or get-together in the near future will be interested in hearing of a letter we have just received from Mr. J. L. Bernard, Publicity Manager of the Radio Corporation. He says that they have prepared a two-reel film on the Radio Corporation Trans-Atlantic work, with scenes at Rocky Point, Riverhead, Broad Street, and many other stations over here and abroad. This sounds as though it might make a most interesting addition to any program. And the best part of all is that the Radio Corporation is distributing the film free. For details, write them, attention of Mr. Bernard, at 233 Broadway, New York City.

R. Saraiva, an A.R.R.L. member at Macao, China, reports that 6CMU and 6AWT are only U.S. stations to be heard in China.

"The Status of 28,000-kc. Communication" and "Practical Communication on the 224-Mc Band" by Ross Hull

By Ward Silver, N0AX

Ross Hull was the author of many early *QST* articles describing new modes of propagation, reporting on scientific studies, and summarizing practical techniques for constructing and using equipment and antennas on new bands. Licensed in Australia as 3JU, Hull never had an American call sign as US licenses were available only to citizens at the time. Even though he was unable to transmit here in North America, he contributed greatly to advancements in Amateur Radio as the Associate *QST* Editor. His untimely death from electrocution in 1938 provided impetus for the "Switch to Safety" campaign that continues to this day.

This section of the book includes two samples of Hull's many articles on topics from the theoretical to the applied. During the period of 1925 through the late 1930s, amateurs were expanding their capabilities to frequency ranges well above the early "short wave" bands to the "ultra-highs" — what are known as the VHF and UHF bands today.

Amateur experimentation in these unknown regions began in the mid-1920s with the December 1924 *QST* article describing 9APW's simple receiver and transmitter for the 5 meter band. At the time, there was no understanding of the effects of the sunspot cycle and little of the seasonal variations that play such a big role in the type and availability of propagation.

The long history of Amateur Radio's discoveries and contributions to expanding our understanding and abilities at 30 MHz and above are summarized very well in Emil Pocock, W3EP's book, *Beyond Line of Sight — A History of VHF Propagation from the pages of QST*. (While no longer in print, used copies are available.) The book captures a number of firsts, including the following table of the first contacts and *QST* report on many types of VHF propagation:

Major VHF Propagation Modes

Mode	First Contact	Earliest QST Article
Tropospheric scatter	c. 1931	February 1951
Tropospheric refraction	c. 1934	June 1935
Sporadic E	1935	August 1938
Aurora	1939	June 1951
Meteor Scatter	1946	January 1946
F Layer	1946	December 1947
Transequatorial	1947	August 1957
Ionospheric scatter	c. 1947	August 1957
Earth-Moon-Earth	1953	May 1946
Auroral E	c. 1958	November 1970
Transequatorial FAI		October 1978
Field-aligned Irregularities	1978	January 1982

The first of the two articles by Hull included here describes the opening of the 10 meter band to amateurs in March of 1928 during the peak of sunspot Cycle 16. The solar equinox is generally a time of good HF propagation and coast-to-coast coverage was quickly established as "Many amateurs claimed immediately that the new band was more satisfactory than any other." Even then, there was "No meters like 10 meters!" The article is also noteworthy in discussing the reflecting ability of the ionosphere in terms of the reflecting layer's equivalent height as was the convention at the time. In addition, a reversible beam antenna design is provided based on Uda and Yagi's design, only recently introduced in October 1928 *QST*.

In the second of Hull's articles, practical direction is provided for building equipment using the new "acorn" tube and highly directional wooden-boom Yagi antennas that were just coming into wide use in amateur stations. Propagation is favorably compared to that of the 56 Mc band as the signals seem to "soak into valleys and cover the landscape more effectively" than on the lower band. A sidebar to the article also notes that distance records on 56 Mc were being "smashed" as directive antennas allowed hams to take advantage of the new and unknown propagation modes.

The mid-1930s, in summary, were an exciting and groundbreaking time for Amateur Radio as the reach of hams was extended to the upper regions of the HF spectrum and into the entirely new VHF bands. The equipment was simple, if touchy, and the easily-constructed Yagi antennas brought much more area within the reach of an average station. *QST* articles such as this pair by Hull were instrumental in both bringing professional and academic advances to amateurs and in contributing the observations of hams to the various scientific research programs.

The Status of 28,000-kc. Communication

A Review of Results Attained, a Discussion of Seeming Discrepancies With Present Theories and a Presentation of Some Practical Suggestions

By Ross A. Hull*

IN addition to being of very considerable importance, the present development of the 28,000-kc. band is at once the most engaging and most baffling problem that the amateur has faced for many years. Of course any problem is, to the amateur, engaging if it is baffling but this one would seem to possess a rare combination of the expected and the unexpected which makes it of particular appeal to the imaginative or experimentally inclined individual. The possibilities of the new band have so far been exploited in only a fragmentary and superficial manner but at this stage it is considered that sufficient evidence has been accumulated to indicate many apparent discrepancies between practical performances a l the predictions of scientists and engineers.

W6UF
The station which participated with W1CCZ in the experimental work with high angle radiations described in the text. The transmitter comprises a UX-112 crystal oscillator, a UX-112 and two UX-210's as intermediate amplifiers, and a UX-852 as the final amplifier. The two last amplifiers both operate on the output frequency and the UX-852 is therefore neutralized. The receiver is of conventional type employing a UX-199 tube as detector and UX-201-A as amplifier.

It is this condition which has prompted us to write of the work which has been accomplished in the hope of providing the incentive for a much larger group of amateurs to experiment in fields to be outlined. It is this condition, also, which has impelled us to place on record the performances which appear to be at variance with present theory, hoping earnestly that those scientists who have conducted the past brilliant researches in the characteristics of the upper atmosphere will be incited to come to our aid and level off the seeming incongruities with which we cannot help being concerned.

In March of last year the band of frequencies between 28,000 and 30,000 kc. was thrown open to the amateurs of this country. Before the end of that month several stations had become active and communication across the continent had been established. Many amateurs claimed immediately that the new band was more satisfactory than any other. Amateurs familiar with the present theories of high-frequency transmission phenomena admired the enthusiasm of the leaders in this new exploration, felt pleased that the Kennelly-Heaviside "layer" should have come low enough to have permitted such an auspicious opening, but hinted knowingly that the "layer" would soon rise to its normal heights, when contact would fail. That some such change in the equivalent layer height has taken place at intervals during the year is evident from an examination of the results which have been obtained. The extent of these changes and their frequency, however, differ so from what one would have been led to expect from the present knowledge of the upper atmosphere that they are thought to constitute one of the discordant notes on which we hope to play at some length.

It must be admitted that the presentation of this estimate of the status of 28,000-kc. communication is handicapped seriously by the fact that it is based on the observations of amateurs only (whose activity in the daylight hours is, with very few exceptions, limited to the week-ends) and that these observations and reports of contact cover an unknown fraction of recent amateur activity throughout the world. In consequence, our data consist chiefly of smatterings of observations taken during the daylight hours of most week-ends during the last eight months. If we were more daring, or if it was not our object to present a strictly conservative report, we would hazard a guess at the possible performances during the entire period, hoping that we would not be overlooking some theory which presupposed a week-end trip on the part of the ionized regions to locations nearer earth.

---
*Associate Technical Editor, QST. In charge A.R.R.L. Technical Development Program.

After the first successes in late March and early April, when communication was established across this continent, between the Atlantic coast and France, and from both the Atlantic and Pacific coasts to the middle-western States, it became evident that the equivalent layer must be lower, on the basis of present theories, than had been anticipated for that time of year. Furthermore it seemed apparent that the equivalent layer was maintaining this low position with unexpected consistency, for of the first seven week-ends since the opening of activity six of them had been known to provide conditions permitting satisfactory communication. Without making allowances for imperfections in transmission and reception equipment—which undoubtedly influenced the results—the general impression was created that communication on the new band, when both transmitter and receiver were in full daylight, was quite the equal of that on the 14,000-kc. band. Signal strengths in most cases were of a high order, though it was thought at the time the periods of severe fading were more frequent than on the lower-frequency band.

These results, together with the prediction that the equivalent layer probably would be at its lowest during the summer months,[1] led many to decide then and there that the 28,000-kc. band, presented to the amateur as interesting but worthless territory at the International Radiotelegraph Conference, was, in a considerable measure, the solution to our congestion problem. The free electrons in the upper atmosphere, however, were already starting on a vile move upwards to spite us.

During the months of May, June and July, when, if at any time, 28,000-kc. communication should have been successful, according to present ideas of the behaviour of the ionized regions, the contacts were wiped almost into oblivion. On only four week-ends of the thirteen in these three months was any communication reported. It is clear, however, that the satisfactory week-ends in this period were quite the equal of any in the previous period, R7 and R8 signals of particular steadiness being common even in contacts between the coasts and central States. Of course, we must admit a weakness in the evidence which leads us to deduce that the equivalent layer height was greater during the week-ends of May, June and July than during those of March and April. In the first place, it is certain that amateur activity is at its lowest ebb during the summer week-ends when vacations and automobile trips are of greater appeal than the contortions of a mere ionized atmosphere. Further, it is conceivable that 28,000-kc. activity was at a lower ebb even than that on other frequency bands as the combined result of the psychological effect of the first successes and the temptations of the great outdoors. If only amateurs could be made to appreciate the significance of their efforts!

Early August gave indications of a return toward civilization on the part of both the amateurs and the free electrons, for at that time satisfactory contacts were reported in increasing numbers. And as the season progressed and the days became shorter, communication became even more satisfactory and more wide-spread, whereas, if the equivalent layer had behaved as current hypotheses would seem to dictate, it should have migrated to higher regions from which the 28,000-kc. signals would never have returned to earth.[2] During this period also, our concept of the performance in general may be distorted somewhat by the fact that the number of amateurs and their experimental activity was definitely on the increase. However, there should be some significance in the statement, based on reports received, that satisfactory communication over distances up to 100 miles and over 1,000 miles was established during all of the fifteen week-ends between that of August 12th, and that of the last reports to hand—November 18th.

Nor was this communication limited to the Northern Hemisphere. During September, for instance, the first Australian successes in communication across Australia and between Australia and New Zealand occurred at a period when communication in this country was being maintained, and when the first signals from the United States were being copied in New Zealand. Through October and November, to the week-end of our most recent reports, activity increased steadily and for every week-end the upper atmosphere continued to prove equal to all the demands that the 28,000-kc. band of frequencies made upon it. As the result of possible improvements in the apparatus used, or on account of still further changed conditions, communication during the seven week-ends ending November 18th, became definitely more consistent and more reliable. By this time contact had been established between England and both the Atlantic and Pacific Coasts, between Hawaii and both the Pacific Coast and the central States, and, on November 9th, between the Pacific Coast and New Zealand. The reports, though dealing more with new contacts made than with the reliability of any one of them, indicated that signals of the order of R7 and R8 were general over distances beyond the skip-distance, even from transmitters with an

---

1. A. Hoyt Taylor, *Proceedings of Institute of Radio Engineers*, August, 1926, makes one of many such predictions.

2. A. Hoyt Taylor, *Proceedings of the I.R.E.*, August, 1926, as one example.

input as low at 10 watts. Reports from the few amateurs who caught on to the idea that it was the characteristics of any one prolonged contact and not the news of the momentary first linking of some two stations which was of greatest importance, served to create the impression that whenever communication was established it was usually with signals of greater intensity and steadiness than those found on the 14,000-kc. band, and that fading, when not substantially absent, was at a very low period. At times, it would seem, the only audible fading was at such a low period that it could be detected only after prolonged contact, when the signals would have been observed to vary a point or two in audibility from one transmission to the next.

Since the development of the 28,000-kc. band was one of the activities in which the Technical Development Program was scheduled to take a part, we had been observing the progress of affairs with particular interest. Toward the end of October the results had wandered so far from our expectations that we made hurried plans to conduct a week of intensive observation, hoping that we would be in time to take advantage of the continued apparent abnormalities of the ionized regions and possibly to take observations during the expected period when they would return to the condition which we had come to regard as normal for that time of year. Our hopes in the case of the latter possibility were to be in vain! In general, we had been completely baffled by the consistency and effectiveness of the communication reported and we had found it impossible to reconcile the results with our interpretation of the current hypotheses regarding the conditions in the upper atmosphere. We were determined to see for ourselves how effective and how consistent communication could be and to make quite certain that the equivalent layer was not fooling us by breezing down to lower levels just for the week-ends. In addition we hoped to be able to duplicate and possibly check the experiments[3] of Meissner, conducted on 27,000 kc., in which, contrary to reasonable expectations, some higher angles of radiation were found to be much more effective than radiations at low angles or at the tangent of the earth's surface.

But in order to make clear this, to us, important objective it will be necessary to digress in order to discuss some of the present views concerning the nature of the ionized regions and the possible behavior of frequencies of the order of 28,000-kc. in them. We might point out at this moment that it would appear as though many amateurs regard the problems of communication on the new band merely as those of the transmitter or receiver circuit. Some of their chief worries, it would seem, are whether the Hartley is better than the Ultraudion on that frequency and whether the tuned-grid tuned-plate can be made to oscillate with equivalent ease. It must be admitted that such considerations are properly a phase of the problem but it is certain that they do not compare either in interest or importance with that essential and elusive part of the communication system which extends a few hundred miles above our heads. In all earnestness we plead for a greater appreciation of this point on the part of amateurs engaged in experiment on the new band.

It is well known to all amateurs that long distance, high frequency communication is made possible by the existence of a condition of ionization in the atmosphere which produces a refraction or bending of the waves leaving the surface of the earth, causing them to come down again at distant

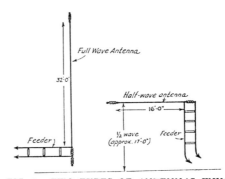

FIG. 1. TWO TYPES OF ANTENNAS WHICH SHOULD BE PARTICULARLY EFFECTIVE FOR OPERATION ON THE 28,000-KC. BAND

The antenna dimensions given were calculated for a frequency of 28,846 kc. No feeder lengths are provided since they will be dependent upon the location of the transmitter with respect to the antenna. They can be determined, however, by reference to the Sept. 1928 QST on page 35.

points, the locations of which are dependent upon the conditions in the ionized atmosphere and upon the frequency being used for the transmission. We will not attempt a detailed explanation of the influences by which the atmosphere is considered to be ionized, since this has already been treated in great detail in *QST* by Taylor and Hulburt and, more recently, by Rice. A brilliant array of more comprehensive articles on the subject is also available in other technical publications.[4] We might state, however, that the ionization responsible for the refraction can be considered as the

---

3. A. Meissner, *Proceedings of the I.R.E.*, November, 1927.

4. *Proc. I.R.E.; Bell. Tech. Journal; Physical Review;* and many foreign publications.

breaking up of neutral gas molecules of the upper atmosphere into their negative constituents—electrons—and their positive constituents—ions. The most important agency, causing this ionization or freeing of electrons is considered to be sunlight. In consequence the ionization experiences a daily variation due to the rotation of the earth and a seasonal change as a result of the inclination of the earth's axis to the orbit. A common miscon-

THE 28,000-KC. EQUIPMENT AT W1CCZ

The 28,000-kc. transmitter used for the tests is on the table at the right, above it being the feeder-tuning apparatus. Two UX-852 tubes, with their grids and plates connected, were used as rectifiers in the plate-supply system. A UX-204-A was operated as the oscillator. The main receiver, at the extreme left, employs a UX-222 in a stage of tuned radio frequency amplification. The apparatus at the upper center is an auxiliary 14,000-kc. and 7,000-kc. transmitter. This apparatus is located in a small shack about a quarter of a mile from the main W1CCZ station.

ception on the part of amateurs is that the ionization is in the form of a relatively thin layer which exists at 100, 120 or perhaps 400 miles above the earth's surface depending upon the time of the day or year. In actuality, it would seem, the ionization exists from the surface of the earth to the outermost limit of our atmosphere. The ionization is not, of course, constant, but extends upwards in an irregular gradient to a height of maximum intensity at, possibly, a point between 150 and 600 miles above the surface of the earth, after which it tapers off in another irregular gradient to the limit of the atmosphere. In order to avoid the complexities of reference to this gradient quantitatively the practice has been adopted in some scientific circles of speaking in terms of "the height of the layer"[5] or "the equivalent layer height." The gradient of ionization which would cause a 14,000-kc. wave to be bent in such a manner as first to reach the earth again at a distance of 1,000 miles would be termed "an equivalent height of so many miles," the term being intended to suggest that if a

---

5. We are inclined to think that the use of such terminology, though possibly convenient, is quite confusing. Amateurs need hardly be warned that the constant visualization of such "layers" is likely to result in false concepts

reflecting medium was placed at the "so many" miles height, and that should the waves travel to and from it in straight lines, they would reach the earth for the first time at the same 1,000-mile point. In short, the "equivalent layer height" already mentioned many times in this paper refers to the height of an imaginary reflecting surface which would cause the same skip distance as that resulting from the particular ionization gradient being considered. The important thing is to avoid the temptation to think of the ionized regions as a "ceiling" of a definite height—instead to keep in mind the fact that any heights mentioned are only those of an imaginary equivalent reflector.

The gradient of the ionization or, more correctly, the gradient of the free electron density, is the factor actually responsible for the bending or refraction of the waves. The speed of travel of the waves is increased by an increase in the number of free electrons in their path and consequently when any two adjacent rays, for example, are projected into the regions of the atmosphere where free electrons exist in increasingly greater numbers, the higher of the two rays meets more free electrons than the lower. The higher ray therefore travels faster than the lower and the beam of rays is bent.[6] If the ray beam starts out at a low angle it possibly will be bent only slightly and will return to earth nearer and nearer to the transmitter until a critical angle is reached from which the beam will return at the nearest possible point to the transmitter. At some higher angles the beams are considered to be bent in such a manner as to go out into space without ever returning to earth.

Aside from the gradient of the free electron density, another factor enters into the process of refraction. It is the frequency of the transmitted signal. The degree of refraction is decreased as the frequency is increased and hence the angles of the radiated rays which are bent away from the earth and lost become lower as the frequency goes up. By making a number of assumptions it has been calculated[7] with an equivalent layer height of 100 miles (a "measured" average height over this country during several days in August, 1927) that on a frequency of about 20,000-kc. all rays radiated at angles greater than 10.8 degrees from the tangent of the earth's surface are bent off into space and wasted as far as long distance communication is concerned. Further, with the same equivalent layer height, and on the same assumptions, it has been shown that only the lowest rays would ever come to earth when a frequency of 26,090-kc. was used and that this, in con-

---

6. Rice, *QST*, July and August, 1927.
7. Taylor, *Proc. I.R.E.*, August, 1926.

sequence, is the highest frequency on which communication could be had between two distant points on this earth. From this we would be led to expect communication with frequencies between 28,000- and 30,000-kc. only when the equivalent layer height was in the vicinity of about 75 miles and then only by utilizing the tangent ray or rays radiated at very small angles to it.

We realize fully that this has been but a pitifully crude and abbreviated statement of the generalities of some existing hypotheses but it will have served its purpose if it has indicated to amateurs not yet familiar with them these two facts—that they require an equivalent layer height of the order of 75 miles if reliable long-distance 30,000-kc. communication is to be had, and that they assume all rays radiated at angles greater than a few degrees above the tangent ray to be lost in space for all time. In reconciling these same hypotheses with the long studied performances on the lower frequencies, however, it would seem that the equivalent layer height must be assumed to be at least 100 miles in the summer days, except on rare occasions, and that its height at other seasons must be still greater. And measurements[8] of its height, taken in various ingenious fashions and on the basis of some assumptions, have tended to check these figures. As a result of which we felt justified in wondering whether the equivalent layer had been extraordinarily low during many portions of the last eight months, whether frequencies of the order of 30,000-kc. were refracted in just the manner that had been visualized or if the free electron density gradient (and perhaps the ionization gradient in general) differed in some strange fashion from the character which we understood to be in order.

The anticipated loss of all rays except those radiated at very low angles also concerned us greatly—as it has concerned many others—for the Meissner experiments had appeared to prove that the 27,270-kc. radiated at angles of 38 degrees and others at 80 degrees from the tangent ray were vastly superior to those of the low angles for communication between Nauen and Buenos Aires. Meissner's published results[3] were limited to the behavior of that frequency only over that particular distance and it was hoped in our week of experiment to see which, if any, of the upper angles were effective on 28,000-kc., and to discover whether the most effective angles for one distance were also the best for all other distances beyond the skip.

The station at which the experimental work was conducted was W1CCZ at Wianno on Cape Cod. The apparatus and the special beam antenna[9] had been built some months previously at the summer home of Mr. E. C. Crossett for experiment on the 28,000-kc. band but activity had ceased when Mr. Crossett moved to his Chicago home in September. At our request the station was reopened and placed at our disposal for the test week.

The antenna system consisted of a horizontal fundamental Hertz antenna fed at one end through a tuned two-wire feeder

THE OPERATING SHACK AND ANTENNA AT W1CCZ

system. A reflector wire was located one-quarter wavelength behind this antenna and two other reflectors were supported one-half wavelength on either side of the antenna. At a point three quarter-waves in front of the antenna a single director was mounted, the whole arrangement being similar to the system suggested by Uda[10] and Yagi.[11] The mechanical arrangement of the system was such that it could be adjusted to any angle above the horizontal in either a westerly or easterly direction, the exact orientation being on a line running 14 degrees north of west, corresponding to the Great Circle between Wianno and Eastern Australia. The transmitter used to excite the antenna consisted of a UX-204-A tube arranged in a self-excited circuit and operated with an input of approximately 400 watts.

The chief difficulty in our way was that of obtaining observers who were free enough to give us their entire interest during the days of the test. We were extremely fortunate in finding two amateurs "on the air" who threw themselves into the work with apparently limitless enthusiasm and stood watch for us during almost the entire full daylight hours of the week. The amateurs were Mr. William Eitel of W6UF and Mr. Ivan O'Meara of ZL2AC. Without the coöperation of these two gentlemen our ob-

---

8. Briet and Tuve, *Phys. Rev.*, Sept., 1926. Taylor and Hulbert, *Phys. Rev.*, Feb., 1926, R. A. Heising, *Proc. I.R.E.*, Jan., 1928. Dahl and Gebhardt, *Proc. I. R. E.*, March, 1928. Breit, Tuve and Dahl, *Proc. I.R.E.*, Sept., 1928, Schelling, *Proc. I.R.E.*, November, 1928.

9. *QST*, October, 1928.
10. Uda, *Proc. I.R.E.*, May, 1927.
11. Yagi, *Proc. I.R.E.*, June, 1928.

jectives undoubtedly would not have been reached. We would place on record our appreciation of the splendid spirit and keen understanding shown by them.

Activities opened on November 1st at 2:00 p.m. E.S.T. It was planned to transmit for the first half hour of every hour of the week during which any communication conceivably could be possible. This first

THE 28,000-KC. TRANSMITTER AT W6TS
This station also was active in observing the special test transmissions and has played an important part in recent work with Reinartz of W1XAM. 1XAM and 6TS, it will be remembered, were pioneers in the activity on the old 40- and 20-meter bands.

transmission was therefore of one-half hour duration. At the termination of the period W6UF was heard calling W1CCZ and soon afterwards communication was established with that station. The beam at this time was adjusted at an angle of 60 degrees to the horizontal facing west. W6UF at Los Gatos, Cal., reported the signals a steady R5 and, after being told the nature of the tests in progress, immediately agreed to stand by for the entire week. His signals were R5 with slight fading. Without delay the beam was adjusted to a sequence of angles between 80 degrees and the horizontal position and Eitel reported definite consequent changes in signal intensity. A further immediate observation on his part, and one of probable great significance was that fading was influenced definitely by the changes in beam angle. With the beam changed to 30 degrees to the horizontal, the signal strength was reported to have increased from R5 to R9 and the fading which was severe at some angles, was observed to have disappeared almost completely. Eitel picturesquely qualified the increase in signal strength at the 30-degree angle by stating "My father sitting in a chair six feet from me can hear signals distinctly at all times when angle is changed to 30 degrees."

As we afterwards discovered, O'Meara of ZL2AC at Gisborne, New Zealand, was listening to these same transmissions and, to our surprise, also reported that the 30-degree angle was greatly superior to any other. The signals were first heard by him at 7:45 a.m. New Zealand time (3:15 p.m. E.S.T.) when they were reported R3 to R4 with slight fading. At about the same time O'Meara heard the harmonic of WIK at R4. During the progress of the test the signals from W1CCZ varied between R3 and R5 at various beam angles but increased whenever the 30-degree angle was used. A signal's strength of R6 to R7 was given for transmission at this angle. At the end of the first hour the WIK harmonic was reported to have faded to R1 while the signals from W1CCZ maintained a strength of between R5 and R7 until the transmitter was closed down at 6:00 p.m. E.S.T. (10:30 a.m. N.Z.T.)

Out of the kindness of our hearts we had made a schedule with W6UF for the following days no earlier than noon E.S.T. (9 a.m. P.S.T.). Communication was again established at this time, W6UF's signals being R4. At this time the beam was adjusted at 60 degrees east (having been left at that angle after a previous test transmission) and the W1CCZ signals were reported R4 also. The beam was immediately changed to 30 degrees west, when the signal strength jumped to R8-R9 as on the previous day. ZL2AC also followed the transmissions on this second afternoon and apparently on all succeeding days, but unfortunately his full report on the remaining receptions has not, at this moment, been received.

Contact with W6UF was continued until 5 p.m. E.S.T. when the last of several attempts that day was made to communicate with the New Zealand station. ZL2AC was being heard at R4 by W6UF but no trace of his signals was evident at W1CCZ.

With the exception of one day, when Eitel was obliged to be away from his home, daily communication was maintained with him for the seven days. At no time were the signals from W1CCZ reported by him to be of an audibility of less than R8 when the beam angle was at 30 degrees. It would appear that the signals made their first appearance suddenly at almost full strength and, as darkness extended beyond the transmitter, disappeared with similar rapidity. The W1CCZ signals were first evident at Los Gatos at about 7:45 a.m. P.S.T. (10:45 a.m. E.S.T.) The signals from W6UF, however, were not heard at Wianno until 10:30 E.S.T. After this hour thoroughly consistent signals could be exchanged until about 6 p.m. E.S.T. when the W6UF signals usually would drop out. On only one afternoon did they disappear before this—at 5:35 p.m. E.S.T. The W1CCZ signals, though, did not drop out until between 6:30 and 6:45 p.m. E.S.T. when the beam was adjusted to the 30-degree angle. On the last evening of the test period, when the reflectors and director had been removed, the signals at W6UF went out almost an hour earlier. In general, the signals from W1CCZ could be received across the continent approximately an hour earlier and an hour later than the signals of W6UF. The antenna used at W6UF was a full-wave "Zeppelin" fed Hertz operated at heights varying from 10 to 25 feet above ground.

Experiment, with different beam angles and with the director and some or all of the reflectors removed, was made, extending over almost the entire hours when communication was possible. Code letters were sent to designate the different settings of the beam and in this way Eitel selected the most effective setting without a knowledge of the angle. Many splendid checks were obtained of the improved signal intensity and greatly reduced fading at beam angles within a few degrees of 30 degree. In contrast to Meissner's results no particularly effective angles above this were evidenced. The removal of the director made it clear that it was of very slight benefit. Also, experiment in the removal of the side reflectors made it appear that they were not of appreciable importance. The rear reflector, it seemed, was performing most of the work by itself. When it also was removed, leaving the antenna system as a simple horizontal fundamental Hertz approximately one wavelength above ground, the signal strength immediately dropped from the normal R8-R9 to R4-R5 and fading became pronounced.

It is unfortunate that conditions were such that similar signals were received from stations using ordinary antennas during the entire week. It had been hoped that at some time of the test period the usual signals would disappear, so making it possible to determine whether or not the signals from the beam failed in the same manner.

As the result of our observations of the 28,000-kc. work in general and of this test week in particular we find our mind filled with what appear to be important questions —problems to which we have not, as yet, found any solutions. We feel that we might well state them in the hope that other experimenters will come forward with suggestions. They include:

(a) With the knowledge that 25 of the 36 week-ends including and preceding that of November 18th were satisfactory for communication in the 28,000-kc. band and that such communication was maintained on every day of the first week of November, are we to believe that the conditions in the upper atmosphere at those times were as unusual as present hypotheses would demand?

(b) If the conditions during the last nine months should be considered normal, why is it that such frequent and such satisfactory communication has been possible on the 28,-000-kc. band when the hypotheses concerning the behavior of such frequencies would not seem to permit it?

(c) Can we assume that the high-angle rays actually are increased in amplitude when a beam antenna, such as that used, is tilted at high angles?

(d) If this is so, and if the gradient of ionization in the atmosphere is such that only the lowest rays ever return to earth, why is it that the rays radiated at relatively high angles to the earth's tangent appear to be much more effective than those radi-

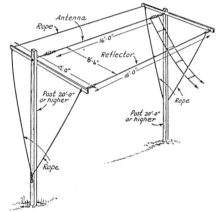

FIG. 2. ONE PRACTICAL ARRANGEMENT FOR AN ANTENNA AND ADJUSTABLE REFLECTOR

The cross pieces supporting the reflector wire could be pivoted on the upright poles with iron bolts. Then, by adjusting the tie ropes, the angle could be varied. If transmission in the opposite direction is to be attempted the reflector could be pulled over to the other side of the antenna by means of the ropes. The dimensions of the antenna and reflector are given in this case also for 28,846-kc.

ated at low angles? Why is it that the radiation at higher angles provides, at various distances, not only definitely higher signal intensities but also a marked reduction in fading and an increased period of reception during any one day?

As a further result of our observations we are able to present some odd suggestions regarding equipment and experimental possibilities which may be of interest to amateurs who are to undertake operation on the 28,000-kc. band. They are concerned chiefly with antennas which, it would seem, have a very important influence over the results obtained.

Vertical half-wave antennas suspended at heights above ground less than their length, and horizontal antennas at heights greater than one wavelength, it would appear, radiate strongly at low angles. In the light of our experience, therefore, they would not seem particularly effective on the 28,000-kc. band. Full-wave vertical antennas suspended near the ground and horizontal antennas strung at a height of one-half wavelength are considered to radiate strongly at angles between 20 and 40 degrees. They probably would be more satisfactory than simple antennas arranged in other fashions. The low heights make it possible that the antenna will be drastically screened in some loca-

ANOTHER VIEW OF THE W1CCZ ANTENNA

tions and every endeavor should be made to erect it in an open area well clear of trees or buildings.

The experiences with the W1CCZ beam antenna have made it evident that any such system can be made much simpler than was first thought. In its most practical form the system would consist of a half-wave antenna mounted centrally between two reflector wires one wavelength apart. A quarter wave behind the antenna the third reflector would be mounted, the four wires being supported in some wooden structure which would permit the angle to be varied. The exact form of the supporting frame is not of particular importance and the amateur can be depended upon to design some assembly which is most suited to his facilities.

Another highly satisfactory and still simpler system would consist of a horizontal half-wave antenna with a single reflector wire behind it. The reflector could be tied into place with ropes and made adjustable in the manner shown in Figure 2.

The length of the antennas for a given frequency can be determined in the usual manner.[12] The reflector wire or wires should

---

12. J. J. Lamb, *QST*, Oct., 1928.

be made approximately nine-eighths the length of the antenna.

The apparatus or circuit used in the transmitter itself need not differ from those used on the other high frequencies. Particular attention should be given to the tank-circuit constants, the plate supply system and the mechanical construction in accordance with what are at present considered good practices, and special care must be taken in the tuning adjustments if a clean and steady signal is to be obtained. It is, perhaps, more important on this band than on any other to maintain the input to the tube at or below the rated value.

The best modern practice for the lower-frequency bands can well be followed in the 28,000-kc. receiver also. The only possible necessary change, beyond that of the tuning-circuit constants, will be the detector plate voltage. In most receivers, an increase in this voltage over that used on other bands will be found necessary to provide a satisfactory condition of oscillation.

With a good 28,000-kc. transmitter and receiver and a suitable antenna (preferably one equipped with one or more adjustable reflectors) a magnificent field for communication and experiment is opened up to the amateur. The chief thing is to realize that communication can be expected only when the two stations are separated by a region of daylight and that contact is likely to fail completely at some times.

What is most needed at the present time is the complete and accurate record of performances obtained, particularly with regard to the date, times and consistency of *prolonged* and frequent contacts. Amateurs will therefore contribute definitely to the development of the band if they will make a practice of noting the details of such contacts and sending their observations to Headquarters. Another urgent need, of course, is some variation of existing hypotheses which will account for the results being obtained!

Some day, we believe, the new band will be found to comprise frequencies of untold worth.

Strays

W9DJK suggests that the CQ parrot owned by a fifth district ham really ought to have an operator's license to avoid complications with the Radio Commission. If apprehended it is thought said parrot could ask for nothing better than solitary confinement on a diet of crackers and water.

Clipping from the humor column of the Duluth (Minn.) *Herald:*

"A professional radio operator seems to be one who connects with lost explorers after amateurs show him how."

Practical Communication on the 224-Mc. Band

The New Tube and Directive Antennas Reveal a World of Possibilities

By Ross A. Hull*

TWENTY-FOUR hours after we had obtained delivery of one of the new acorn type tubes, we had a duplex 35-mile communication circuit in operation using 56 mc. one way and 224 mc. the other. Directive antennas were used for both bands at the home station and plain antennas at the mobile station. Signals were maximum strength at both ends of the circuit. We thought we had had our full share of thrills

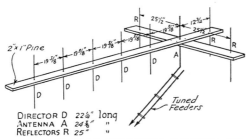

FIG. 1—THE YAGI DIRECTIVE ANTENNA OPERATED AT W1AL ON 130 CENTIMETERS (ABOUT 230 MC.)

The antenna, director and reflector are made of ⅛-inch brass rod pushed through holes in the wooden structure, the latter being thoroughly soaked with hot paraffin. The feeders are cut approximately to an odd number of quarter wavelengths and tuned with series condensers in the conventional Zepp fashion. The supporting structure can be arranged in any one of a hundred ways—our next one will be on a rotatable pole hitched up to a brass wheel alongside the operating table!

during the recent work with directive antennas on 56 mc. But here was another one, fast on the heels of our recent fulsome dose. 224-mc. band signals that would just about burst the diaphragm of anybody's speaker—signals which appeared to have all the desirable characteristics of the 56-mc. ones (if not more).

During the few days since then we have built a couple of extra receivers and made a very sketchy preliminary survey of the manner in which a 130-centimeter wave from a directive antenna pokes its way through the Connecticut hills. The data at hand are far too meagre to allow any emphatic statement comparing 56 and 224 mc. but it is our impression that the signals on the new band soak into valleys and generally cover the landscape more effectively than our 56-mc. signals have done. At the moment we are

* Associate Editor, *QST*.

getting geared up for an attempt at contact between Hartford and Boston on 130 centimeters and enthusiasm in these parts is running very high. The reception of strong signals in an automobile over a 50-mile path blocked by hills 1200 feet high leads us to suspect very strongly that all sorts of surprising distances will be possible just as soon as we fit out the necessary directive antennas for reception and transmission at both ends of the circuit.

The tremendous advantage of operation on the extremely high frequencies is not in the novelty of the work but in the possibility of fitting out a highly effective directive antenna while still keeping it small enough to pick up and cart around. It takes a fair amount of space to fit out an antenna with a power gain of twenty on 56 mc. but there is no conceivable location in which there would not be room for a dozen such antenna systems suited for the 224-mc. band. The "signal squirter" with a brass wheel controlling its direc-

FIG. 2—THE LIGHT IN THE WINDOW—THE 130 CENTIMETER TRANSMITTER AT W1AL

Mounted right in the window frame, this simple transmitter pushes large chunks of juice to the directive antenna on the veranda roof. The antenna, in turn, squirts this at the moment, in a northeasterly direction.

tion alongside the ham operating position is no dream of the distant future. If we can afford the brass wheel we will build one just as soon as we finish writing this article.

Before describing the equipment which has worked out so nicely in our case, we might mention the considerations involved in deciding upon 224 mc. as the band on which to start this ultra-ultra-high-frequency work. The acorn tube is thoroughly satisfactory for operation down to about half a meter. In other words, there would be no serious tube problem in reception on any of the wavelengths under consideration. Operation at wavelengths below about 125 centimeters, however, would mean that the only available tube for transmission (using conventional circuits) would be the "acorn." Since we wanted to be able to use higher powered transmitters than would be provided by the new tube, we decided that the band from 224 to 240 mc. (about 134 to 125 centimeters) would be the ideal spot. The W.E. 304A or the 800 are capable of splendid operation in that territory and provide all the steam one would want.[1] The 224-mc. band was selected in preference to the 112-mc. band for the very simple reason that the directive antenna could then be kept down to the point where even

[1] Other circuit and tube combinations were discussed in "Firing Up on the Newly-Opened Ultra-High Frequencies," *QST*, September, 1934.

a highly directive system would be small enough to fit in any attic or on any porch roof.

The antenna chosen for our first work is of the "Yagi" type. In this system, a single half-wave antenna is used, backed by one or more reflectors and fitted with a series of directors strung out in

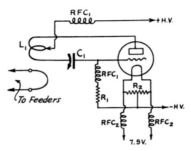

FIG. 3—CIRCUIT OF THE 130-CENTIMETER (224-MC. BAND) TRANSMITTER

C_1—National Type NC800 condenser.
L_1—Single turn tank coil of very small copper tubing or No. 12 gauge wire. Actual length of conductor is 7 inches—the turn 1-inch diameter.
R_1—20,000 10-watt resistor.
R_2—50- or 100-ohm center-tapped resistor.
RFC_1—15 turns of No. 18 wire wound on a pencil—the turns being pulled apart slightly.
RFC_2—About 10 turns of the filament leads wound on a pencil (see Fig. 2).

The new W.E. 304A is now used in this circuit at AL. The 800 shown in Fig. 2 was also satisfactory.

Five-Meter Performance Hits New Levels

Directive Antennas Permit Smashing All Records:
Activities at High Pitch

WAS it freaky weather, never to be duplicated? Was the location just one in a million? Has anyone else been able to duplicate it?—These were the questions aired freely when Ross Hull revealed the amazing effectiveness of the directive antenna he had strung up at W1AL. Months of continuous communication, observation, and comparison are needed before the final answers can be made, but at this stage it certainly looks as though we can rule out all thoughts of freakiness. With Headquarters ops taking shifts, AL has been kept on the air every night (six weeks of it at this writing) and for schedules each morning. Ninety-seven out of an even hundred schedules with W1HRX have resulted in satisfactory communication. Every day since October *QST* went to press with Hull's story, Hartford-Boston contact has been had. Signals are, of course, not always the same strength. Dizzy cycles of good and bad weather follow each other at intervals of a few days with steady R9 signals one night and severe fading the next. But communication holds up just the same.

And that isn't all! AL was heard strongly by Mr. H. S. Shaw, of General Radio, 292 miles along the line of the beam at Mt. Desert Island, Me. Wow! Then, a four-hour continuous contact was had with W1XR at Mt. Washington (190 miles) using a second antenna pointed in that direction. Many excellent contacts have been had with Dr. G. W. Pickard, W1XZ, at Seabrook, N. H. (127 miles, with XZ located on the beach within a stone's-throw of the sea) and as many as 13 consecutive QSO's with Boston area hams have been had after a single CQ.

In short, an ultra-high frequency directive antenna does things!

The response to Hull's article has been perfectly swell. We gain the impression, from telegrams, radiograms and letters, that directive antennas are sprouting like mushrooms over the whole countryside. The first new one heard at AL was W1ZO at Medford, Mass. With a 200-volt plate supply, ZO handed us an R9 signal if ever there was one.

Watch the coming issues of *QST* for further dope on directive systems and for reports of the experiences at other stations.

—EDITOR

November, 1934

front of the antenna along the line of transmission. The antenna has the merits of being very simple to construct and infinitely simpler to adjust than any system in which several antennas have to be fed in phase or with some particular phase relationship. Fig. 1 gives full details of the antenna and the wooden frame upon which its elements were mounted. In the installation at W1AL this frame was in turn supported on a tripod arrangement made of 2" x 1" pieces. The wooden elements through which the antennas, directors, and reflectors were pushed, were well painted with hot paraffin.

FIG. 4—THE LAST OF THREE 224-MC. BAND RECEIVERS
Though having the appearance of a permanent assembly, this receiver is nevertheless capable of easy modification. The detector equipment is mounted on its own small copper plate base and can be removed as a unit in quick time. The audio tube is "sunk-mounted" in order to conserve panel height

TRANSMITTER

The transmitter used at AL employs the circuit given in Fig. 3. This is just about the simplest circuit one could imagine but, with a 304A or 800 tube, proved capable of delivering substantial power—enough, at least, to permit checking the operation of the antenna with a neon bulb. The input power was held down to about 40 watts (70 ma. at something under 600 volts). The transmitter was set on the desired frequency first by making a check with a Lecher wire system (to be described) and then by listening to the signal in a 56-mc. receiver. With the transmitter set on 130 centimeters, a harmonic of the 5-meter receiver provided a signal at approximately 57 mc. The Zepp feeders were then cut to approximately an odd number of quarter waves, hitched to the antenna of the Yagi system and tuned with the conventional series condensers at the station end. These condensers happened to be Cardwell neutralizing condensers. Any two or three-plate midgets would serve the purpose.

CHECKING FREQUENCY

Since some difficulties have been reported by ultra-high frequency enthusiasts using the Lecher wire arrangement for checking wavelength we will describe the actual layout used in our work. The wires themselves are of No. 18 bare copper wire strung two inches apart between stand-off insulators along an eight-foot length of board. One end of the wires remains free, the other ends being connected to a one-turn coupling coil located near the transmitter tank circuit. In operation, a sliding bridge—consisting of a piece of stiff bare wire on the end of a two-foot wooden dowel—is run slowly down the length of the wires until a point is reached where the oscillator plate current makes a sudden fluctuation. The point is marked. The bridge is then moved farther down the wires until a second node is located. This also is marked. The same procedure is then followed to locate a third node. At this stage, the distance between each pair of marks is measured. If the Lecher system is operating correctly and if it is mounted well clear of surrounding objects, the distances will all be the same and will represent quite accurately one half of the wavelength being measured. An alternative sliding bridge—useful when the oscillator has plenty of output—is a flashlamp bulb with wires soldered to its contacts. These wires are hooked over the wires of the Lecher system and the lamp

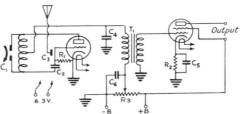

FIG. 5—CIRCUIT OF THE SIMPLE 224-MC. BAND RECEIVER

C_1—*Special split-stator tuning condenser (see text). Since the photographs were taken it has been found desirable to use two pairs of stator plates instead of one in order to give ample extra frequency coverage.*
C_2—*Very small grid condenser (see text).*
C_3—*Brass strip 3/16 inch wide mounted close to the exposed surface of C_2 (see Fig. 6).*
C_4—*.002 μfd. fixed condenser.*
C_5—*2 μfd. or more.*
C_6—*1 μfd.*
R_1—*1.5 megohm, half-watt resistor.*
R_2—*1200 ohm, one-watt resistor.*
R_3—*100,000 ohm potentiometer. Note that this resistor is across plate supply and that, if batteries are used, the supply should therefore be disconnected when switching off set.*

A 41 tube is used as the audio amplifier and allows speaker operation. A transformer or choke-condenser coupling unit must be used with this tube. For headphone work, a 37 audio tube would probably be more appropriate.

The coil is described in the text.

moved along until the various points are located at which the lamp lights brightest. The points will be extremely critical.

RECEIVERS

Three different receivers have been built for this experimental work during the last three days. The gadget illustrated in Figs. 4, 5 and 6 is No. 3 of the series. Its circuit arrangement, shown in Fig. 5, is the simplest of the lot. In operation, the set is just about as smooth as one could imagine. The first of our receivers was an elaborate affair in which the most profound precautions were taken in the layout of the detector circuit, in the provision of by-passing and in the fitting of some means of adjustment for almost everything in the circuit. Our experience with this receiver and with No. 2 of the series served to reveal many of the beautiful features of the new tube. We were afraid of it at first but we soon learned that, given half a chance, the tube will perform on, say, 130 centimeters, in just about the way one would expect a 37 to handle on 75 meters.

The key unit in the new receiver is the detector assembly. It is built on a heavy copper plate, measuring two inches by four inches. The assembly includes the tube socket and the tuned circuit components and therefore constitutes a complete oscillator which could be fitted into almost any type of receiver or low-powered transmitter. In this particular instance, we attached the copper plate to the channel of a receiver chassis, hitched a pentode audio amplifier and—presto—acquired a complete super-regenerative receiver. The detector is, of course, of the self-quenching type. A separate interruption oscillator was used in the first two receivers but, for reasons yet to be discovered, it did not seem to justify its existence.

FIG. 6—THE "ACORN" DETECTOR TUBE AND ITS TUNING EQUIPMENT

The tuning condenser shown with two rotor plates and one pair of stator plates (a single stator plate split) has since been provided with another pair of stators to give ample tuning range on either side of the 224-mc. band. The grid condenser may be seen immediately to the right of the coil. The brass strip of the antenna coupling condenser can be seen apparently touching the right-hand coil connection.

Since the most important part of the receiver is the input to the detector, we will discuss it in some detail. The tube socket is made from two strips of "Victron." These could be obtained from a sheet of the raw material or cut from a National Victron transposition insulator. Any other high-grade insulating material could, of course, be used. These two strips, fitted with the lugs that come with the tube, are supported slightly above the copper base in order to avoid the necessity for drilling the copper to accommodate the bottom of the tube. Our first receiver had a hole cut in the copper plate in the manner suggested in the instruction sheet for the 955. We deviated from that procedure in this case with the idea of avoiding structural complications. Since the smallest midget condenser did not appear to be satisfactory for the grid condenser C_2, we proceeded to build one from two pieces of brass, measuring ¾ by ⅜ inch. Each piece was folded in two and the pieces were then interleaved, the plates being kept apart by thin pieces of mica. The whole assembly was drenched with Duco cement and then squeezed in a vice. A lead was then soldered to each of the brass elements. Another item which had to be "homebrewed" was the tuning condenser. Believing that the normal midget condenser has an excessively large path between its terminals, we cooked up a special condenser shown clearly in Fig. 6. It consists of a three-plate Cardwell Trim-air midget with the one stator plate sawn down the middle. In this way a split stator condenser is obtained—one having an extremely low minimum capacity and a short path between one terminal and the other. It

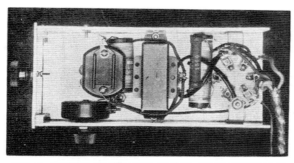

FIG. 7—UNDERNEATH THE 224-MC. BAND RECEIVER

All the gadgets not above the chassis channel can be spotted in this photograph. The location of the detector voltage control potentiometer is perhaps unconventional but certainly convenient in operation.

(Continued on page 66)

November, 1934

Practical Communication on the 224-Mc. Band

(Continued from page 11)

is very important, with this type of condenser, to insulate the rotor from ground. The inductance, supported between the two lugs of the tuning condenser, consists of five turns of No. 18 wire, wound on an ordinary round pencil (about 5/16" diameter), the turns being spaced approximately the diameter of the wire. The tap is located on the third turn from the plate end of the coil.

The remaining features of the receiver are perfectly conventional and can be followed from the circuit and photographs. It might be mentioned that the channel on which the receiver is assembled measures $7\frac{1}{2}$ inches by $3\frac{1}{4}$ inches by 2 inches deep. A Lecher system again could be used to check the frequency of the receiver and the check might well be followed by listening to the harmonic produced by small 5-meter transmitter or a 5-meter receiver oscillating but not super-regenerating. The harmonics so obtained will, of course, appear as dead spots in the 224-mc. receiver and in our case they were very well defined and permitted a splendid check of the calibration obtained with the Lecher system.

If a Lecher system has not been used to check the frequency of the receiver (or if the receiver has not been checked against a "Lecher-checked" transmitter) there is some danger of mistaking the third harmonic from a 56-mc. oscillator for the fourth. Any possible doubt can be cleared up by setting the "five-meter" oscillator on 60 mc., then finding what appears to be its fourth harmonic on the new receiver. If it really is the fourth harmonic, another harmonic (the fifth) will be obtained by tuning the "five-meter" oscillator to 48 mc. Since a suitable frequency meter may not be available for this test, we suggest dependence on the Lecher method.

The general procedure in tuning the transmitting antenna and in coupling the receiver to its antenna follow exactly along the lines observed in 56-mc. working.

The purpose of presenting this sketchy description of a transmitter and receiver for the new band is to provide some basis on which to start actual communication. Several stations in the New England area are all set to make new records on 224 mc. and we anticipate that activity on this band will soon be giving 56 mc. a tough run.

Plunk down your vest-pocket directive antennas, gang, and let's find out just how much fun we have been missing—it's plenty.

"Transequatorial Propagation of VHF Signals" by R.G. Cracknell, ZE2JV

By Carl Luetzelschwab, K9LA

One of the finest examples of Amateur Radio's contributions to propagation was the discovery and use of transequatorial VHF propagation (TEP). It was in August 1947 when XE1KE began working Argentine stations, notably LU6DO at first, quite regularly on 50 MHz. These QSOs occurred in the late afternoon and early evening, well after the expected times based on the normal mid-day peak of the F_2 region.

QST reported many more similar QSOs in the next several years (during the maximum of Cycle 18). There was little transequatorial propagation observed in the sunspot minimum period between Cycle 18 and 19, but TEP reappeared in 1955 and throughout the maximum years of Cycle 19.

The first theoretical explanation of TEP in an Amateur Radio publication was by R. G. Cracknell, ZE2JV, in the following article that proposed northern and southern zones for the TEP he observed. Of course there are two other TEP zones in the world — between Central America/Caribbean and South America, and between Australia and Japan.

One of ZE2JV's partners in TEP research was R. A. Whiting, 5B4WR, who subsequently published an article in the April 1963 *QST* titled "How Does TE Work?" Whiting's article went a bit farther with the theory and included the figure below that showed the tell-tale ionospheric signature of TEP — areas of high electron density on either side of the geomagnetic equator — and it included a conceptual ray trace from Salisbury, Southern Rhodesia (now Harare, Zimbabwe) to Limassol, Cyprus as shown in the figure. Thus TEP was discovered by Amateur Radio operators and included their inputs and ideas to describe the physics of it.

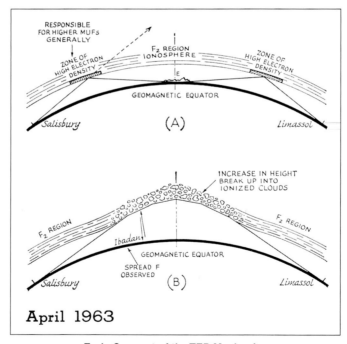

Early Concept of the TEP Mechanism

Transequatorial Propagation of V.H.F. Signals

A Study of North-South V.H.F. Propagation
Based on the work of F9BG, G4LX,
ZC4IP, ZC4WR and ZE2JV

BY R. G. CRACKNELL,* ZE2JV

DURING the years since the end of World War II increasing use of the 50-Mc. band by amateurs in areas adjacent to the tropics has revealed the existence of radio propagation in the v.h.f. region, up to at least 80 Mc., that cannot be explained by conventional theories. Peculiarities of the earth's magnetic equator,[1] about which this mode of propagation occurs, give Southern Rhodesia a most favorable position from which to observe *TE* effects. For this reason study of transequatorial propagation was chosen as a project for the International Geophysical Year.

Commercial and other use of the 30-80-Mc. portion of the spectrum is mainly restricted to short-range "groundwave" services, such as television broadcasting and mobile communication. Results of amateur observations indicate, however, that for the areas of the world where *TE* propagation is encountered it represents an opportunity for long-distance communication having a high degree of reliability for certain hours and seasons.

In general, the *TE* path is between areas on either side of the geomagnetic equator[1] and 1500 to 2500 miles away from it. It is effective during the hours of darkness, and on frequencies up to 1.5 times the observed daytime maximum usable frequency for F-layer propagation. Optimum propagation conditions occur at the time of the equinox, between points in the same longitude, located about 2000 miles from the geomagnetic equator.

The *TE* mode may be usable between locations where the direct line between the two stations cuts the geomagnetic equator at an angle as low as 45 degrees, and beyond the distance limits mentioned above, but moving away from the most favorable spots causes both the reliability and the maximum usable frequency to drop off. The quality of the modulation on a *TE*-propagated signal is often distorted by a characteristic flutter fading. The signal is good enough for communication purposes, but the mode is unlikely to be of value for broadcasting or television. The transmitter power required to produce an intelligible signal is small. A few watts of r.f. in a vertical quarter-wave aerial may induce a signal of one microvolt or more in a similar aerial located 4000 miles away in the opposite *TE* zone.

> In 1947 a form of long-distance propagation of 50-Mc. signals hitherto unknown was discovered when XE1KE began working Argentine stations on 50 Mc. in the afternoon and evening hours. In recent years this transequatorial propagation has received much attention in scientific as well as amateur circles. Detailed here are the results of a remarkable series of observations by competent v.h.f. enthusiasts bearing on this as yet little-understood phenomenon.

Transequatorial propagation is by no means limited to the hours of darkness. At the peak of solar activity, daytime signals above 50 Mc. were weak and infrequent at Salisbury, but in 1959, probably due to decreased ionization at the lower levels, signals from the *TE* area around the Mediterranean have been received at ZE2JV very regularly, and at great strength on frequencies up to 56 Mc., throughout the day.

Examination of Fig. 1 shows that the geomagnetic equator traverses Africa in an arc approximately centered on Victoria Falls, and having a radius of about 2000 miles. The effect of this curvature is to give places in southern Africa lying within the *TE* belt an abnormally large zone into which *TE* propagation takes place, and from which interference and noise can be received.

The density of ionization is affected by the angle of the sun. Across Africa the geomagnetic equator lies well to the north of the geographical equator. Hence Southern Rhodesia and its neighbors experience *TE* propagation effects together with a higher density of ionization than is generally experienced elsewhere.

---
* Salisbury, Southern Rhodesia.
[1] Southworth, "A Look Back and Ahead at PRP," *QST*, June, 1959, page 48.

The Experimental Program

An automatically keyed c.w. transmitter delivering 60 watts to a 4-element array has been in operation from the author's location in Salisbury, Southern Rhodesia, since September, 1957. Its transmissions on 50.04 Mc. have been received with varying degrees of consistency in Poona, Bahrein, Israel, Cyprus, Libya, Switzerland, Morocco, France, Portugal, Madeira Islands, England and North America. Two-way contacts were made with all of these countries where operation on 50 Mc. is permitted. Crossband work was done with the others, 50–28 Mc.

Jean Garat, F9BG, Toulon, France, George Barrett, ZC4IP, and R. A. Whiting, ZC4WR, Limassol, Cyprus, accurately recorded the time of arrival, variations in signal strength, and peculiarities of the propagation of these signals throughout the evening, over long periods. It was found impractical to record the time of closure of the propagation path, it being in the early morning hours ordinarily. Gordon Spencer, G4LX, Newcastle, England, undertook similar thorough observation of the 50-Mc. signals, though he received them for much shorter periods and with considerably reduced regularity. From February 1959 on, L. S. Cole, ZS6IG, Johannesburg, South Africa, transmitted twice each evening, for regular observation on Cyprus. Regular reception of European television signals in Salisbury was of interest, but multiple use of the same frequencies, especially 48.25, 49.75 and 53.25 Mc., was confusing.

An estimate of the m.u.f. was made regularly in Salisbury by tuning a receiver over the range of 30 to 75 Mc. Television signals and harmonics of commercial stations in southern Europe and the Middle East countries were sufficient for reasonable accuracy. It is probable that the m.u.f. actually rose above 75 Mc. many times. However, resonant beam antennas are necessary for effective reception at these frequencies, and for practical reasons these were limited to the amateur bands at 28, 50, 72 and 144 Mc. From March through May, 1958, F9BG made three transmissions nightly on 72.025 Mc. His signal was never positively identified in Salisbury, but this may have been due to strong interference on this frequency from Beirut, Lebanon.

ZC4WR, who conducted the experimental work on the characteristics of *TE*, developed a technique for photographing the received signal, as displayed on an oscilloscope. The receiver was operated without a.v.c., and the signal voltage was taken from the a.m. diode detector and fed to the oscilloscope amplifier. Though the technique was later improved, the pictures were taken with a time-base duration of 0.08 to 0.1 second. First exposures were 0.1 second at f.2. Pulses of 0.03 and 0.02 second were transmitted, and photographs were made of signals received during various kinds of propagation. Normal 28-Mc. signals were also photographed for comparison purposes.

As the directional properties of the antennas appeared to vary from day to day, and even from hour to hour, tests were made to determine the degree of scatter, and to investigate possible correlations between this and the percentage of flutter, and extensions of the *TE* zone. The Yagi array at ZE2JV was aimed first north, then east and then south, while signal levels and characteristics were recorded at Cyprus. The tabulated observations showed very marked differences in both scatter and degree of signal flutter, but there was no significant correlation between the two. The strength of signals received in Cyprus from Johannesburg was found to vary directly with the degree of scatter. The scatter indication was also high when the ZE2JV signal was heard in England by *TE*, and when direct contact was possible on 50 Mc. between Salisbury and Kenya-Uganda.

An attempt was made to determine the effect of vertical directivity. The 4-element Yagi (low-angle radiator) was compared with a half-wave dipole mounted ¾ wavelength above ground (high-angle radiator). These tests showed a fairly constant gain of about 6 db. for the Yagi, but the percentage of flutter was always higher with the dipole.

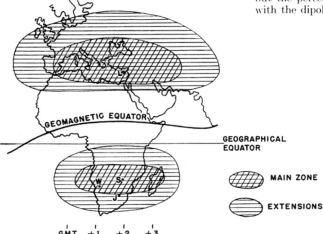

Fig. 1—Northern and southern *TE* zones, as indicated by amateur experience. The curve in the Geomagnetic Equator as it crosses Africa appears to have a focussing effect on *TE* propagation. The cities of Windhoek, Salisbury, Limassol and Johannesburg are indicated by their initial letters.

Results

Extent of Zones: The northern and southern *TE* zones, as indicated by our observations, are shown in Fig. 1. The extent of the northern zone is based on reports of reception of the 50-Mc. transmissions made from ZE2JV, and from reception of television and other signals in the v.h.f. range at Salisbury. The southern zone outlines are based on the reception of amateur 50-Mc. signals in Limassol, Cyprus. At frequencies higher than the 50-Mc. band, the zones are more limited in geographical extent, but extensions at lower frequencies were of no significance.

To avoid complication of the results by the possibility of confusion between normal F_2 and *TE* propagation, no account has been taken of the reception of signals lower in frequency than 50 Mc. Reports from England showed that our 50-Mc. signals were received there frequently for two brief evening periods, 1700 to 1715 GMT, usually showing a "clean" signal, and 1900 to 1930, always showing flutter fading that is characteristic of *TE* propagation. (Local time in Southern Rhodesia is GMT plus two hours.)

The 1700-to-1715 period was discounted, as F_2 propagation may have been responsible, but F_2 propagation during the later period appeared unlikely. Tests on 52.5 Mc. in the other direction bore this out. Transmissions on this frequency by G4LX were received in Salisbury (though very weakly) in the later period, but only one 5-second burst was heard during the 1700 to 1715 period in three months of testing.

There are some 500 television stations in Europe and the Middle East. With the majority of them in the 40-to-70-Mc. range there is no way of telling with any degree of certainty the origin of the mass of TV signals received at Salisbury in this frequency band. It was assumed, for example, that a very strong video signal on 49.75 Mc., heard from 1000 to 2200 daily for 6 months of the year, and less consistently the rest of the year, was from Odessa. Published data indicated that all Russian stations used this frequency (video 49.75 Mc., audio 56.25 Mc.), but an Odessa amateur told us that the video of that station had been shifted to 97 Mc., and that the only Russian video on 49.75 Mc. after early 1959 was the 100-kw. station in Moscow. If this information is accurate, the reception of strong signals on this frequency consistently is of considerable significance.

A graph of the m.u.f. as observed at 1830 GMT for an entire year is given in Fig. 3. Typical m.u.f. for the evenings of April, 1958, is shown in Fig. 4.

Extensions of the southern zone over Africa were observable with greater accuracy, since they were based on the reception of amateur signals in Cyprus. The geographical location and power limitations of these stations are, of course, readily ascertained, but it is by no means certain that a 100-kw. TV signal comes by direct path. Test transmissions from Jinji, Uganda, beamed at Cyprus, were not received there, but Uganda

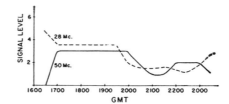

Fig. 2—Signal levels during a long evening contact, October 18, 1957. ZC4IP, Limassol, Cyprus, was on 28 Mc. and ZE2JV, Salisbury, Southern Rhodesia, on 50 Mc.

stations have been heard in Cyprus when they were beamed south, into the region where backscatter can carry them back north across the equator. Test transmissions from Johannesburg showed clearly that this city is at or just outside the main *TE* zone.

It would appear that Newcastle, England, is situated near the northern limit of *TE*, and that Capetown, South Africa, is near the southern limit. From this it would appear to be possible that reception of TV from the north of England on 48.75 Mc. in Capetown is the longest "one-hop" propagation that has been experienced.

Seasonal Effects: The principal effects of the position of the sun are discussed later, but it may be mentioned here that there tend to be more frequent and longer extensions to the south in the southern summer, and to the north in the

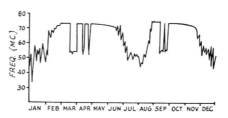

Fig. 3—Maximum usable frequency at Salisbury, Southern Rhodesia, at 1830 GMT. Two major *TE* seasons are clearly indicated.

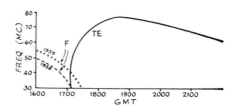

Fig. 4—Hourly curve of the m.u.f. as observed by ZE2JV in April, 1958. F_2-layer curves for 1958 and 1959 are given at the left.

northern summer. These are most noticeable a month or so each side of the respective solstice. The line joining locations most favorably situated with respect to each other appears to veer away from the line of longitude between an equinox and a solstice. This can possibly be explained by a tendency for conditions to be optimum when the

December 1959

time of sunset approximates. Thus, from Southern Rhodesia there is an extension to the east in the southern winter, and to the west in summer.

Scatter and seasonal extensions of the *TE* zone do not appear to be entirely independent. The longest scatter extensions to the north take place in the northern summer, and vice versa.

Extension of the range by other forms of propagation was experienced in February and November to North America (northwest) and in May to Japan (northeast). In order that this may occur at 50 Mc. the m.u.f. at the point of the second reflection must be high enough to propagate the wave at the angle at which it was propagated by *TE*. These openings were of a sporadic nature, but they seemed to occur 48 to 60 hours after an outburst of fairly high sunspot activity. The distance was always in the region of 8000 miles. No east-west DX was worked, except by back-scatter or tropospheric propagation.

Reliability

September–November, 1957: Although the equipment used by ZC4IP for this period was not as good as that employed subsequently, and his antenna was merely an indoor dipole in a built-up area of Limassol, he received signals from ZE2JV on 50 Mc. 58 evenings out of 63 on which tests were made. Frequently conditions were good enough for duplex telephony, using 50 and 28 Mc. An attempt to determine the time of closure of the path was made on the night of October 18–19, but it was abandoned at 0135 local time, with both bands still open. Communication had been maintained crossband since 1830. Fig. 2 shows the signal levels on both bands during this 5-hour contact.

March–July, 1958 F9BG, Toulon, had coöperated in many tests since September, 1957. From September to November he received the ZE2JV 50-Mc. transmissions less regularly, and for shorter periods, than they were received at Cyprus. In March, 1958, he erected a 3-element Yagi on the top of a building overlooking the Mediterranean, and thereafter failed to hear the transmissions on only four evenings, testing 4 or 5 evenings each week. Many of the transmissions were received with considerable strength.

Though commercial transmissions on 70 to 71 Mc. from Cyprus and f.m. and other signals up to 74 Mc. were frequently received at Salisbury in March and April, the 72-Mc. transmissions of F9BG were never positively identified.

September, 1958: G4LX, Newcastle, England, reported reception of the ZE2JV tests several times in May, 1958. In the fall he had permission for operation on 52.5 Mc. He made tests every evening in September, and at noontime (at the midpoint) on Sundays only. The evening tests were received at Salisbury 3 evenings out of 29 tried in September, though European television interference made reception very difficult. G4LX, on the other hand, heard ZE2JV 15 evenings out of 29 tried, and heard noontime tests on 2 out of 4 tries.

September–December, 1958: ZC4WR, also of Limassol, Cyprus, listened to the 50-Mc. tests in 1957. He was then using a single 6J6 converter and a vertical wire of random length. Even so, he heard the 50-Mc. signals every day in October that tests were made by ZE2JV (all but two days). In 1958 he erected a 4-element Yagi on the top of a block of flats, 100 feet above ground, and employed a crystal-controlled converter of modern design. The signal levels during October and November, 1957, and September and October, 1958, are shown graphically in Fig. 5.

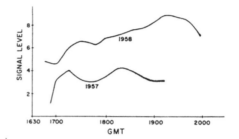

Fig. 5—Average 50-Mc. signal level of ZE2JV, as observed by ZC4WR during 20 days in October and November, 1957, and September and October, 1958. Higher levels in 1958 were due in part to improved equipment at the Cyprus end.

Looking at TE Signals

The first photograph shows an unmodulated signal from ZE2JV as received on Cyprus. This and subsequent photographs were made with an exposure of .08 second at f.4, from a short-persistance cathode-ray tube. The time base was truly one-shot, in that opening the camera shutter triggered the time base, which gave a single sweep. Fly-back could not occur until the shutter was closed. Examination of *TE* signals is still in progress, but it seems safe to assume that the received energy consists of components arriving so that they differ in phase or frequency. Oscillograms of this nature do not appear continuously, but rather at five times per second, or thereabouts, at irregular intervals. The rest of the time the carrier is relatively "clean."

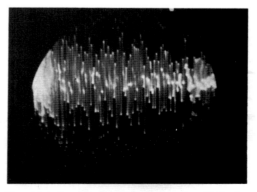

Unmodulated carrier of ZE2JV, as received on 50 Mc. by ZC4WR by *TE* propagation.

Flutter is usually of a complex nature. Phase distortion can make amplitude modulation unintelligible, and amplitude variations can "key" a signal so that even the slowest code is difficult to copy. These effects can appear simultaneously, each in varying degrees, but extremes of flutter are experienced only with simple antennas. Never, when low-angle antenna systems have been in use at both ends, has the degree of flutter been sufficient to destroy intelligibility. A.m. signals appear to be demodulated. More speech clipping than would normally be tolerated, and modulation depth in excess of 100 per cent (with suitable precautions to prevent carrier splitting) are helpful under conditions of severe flutter.

Flutter is not an essential feature of *TE* propagation, though it is normally present in the late evening. It may appear over the whole band of *TE*-propagated signals, or only over a segment of it. Generally signals within a few kilocycles of the m.u.f. show little or no flutter.

Types of Evening Propagation

Most evenings showed propagation similar to that of the early-evening part of Fig. 2. The 50-Mc. signal appeared about 1900 local time (1700 GMT), building up to moderate strength with only minor variations. Flutter fade was present after about the first hour, and beam tests would show a moderate degree of scatter. Fig. 6 shows an average of three such evenings in September and October, 1958.

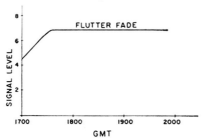

Fig. 6—Average of three typical evenings of *TE* propagation. Signal levels build up to moderate levels around 1900 local time, and thereafter show only minor variations. *TE* flutter appears after the first hour.

On abnormal evenings following high daytime m.u.f., signals of *F*-type characteristics may last as late as 2100 local time. When this happens, the fadeout affects all frequencies from 28 to 56 Mc. simultaneously. Fadeout is not necessarily rapid, and signals from high-powered TV stations (at the high end of the range) may last for 30 minutes after weaker signals have faded out. *TE* propagation has not been observed after these occurrences, but this is not proof that it did not occur later at night. No flutter appeared on these signals, but beam tests indicate that the degree of scatter may be very high.

More frequently *F*-type signals would not appear until late afternoon, and in these cases fadeout occurred earlier in the evening, to be followed by the return of a signal showing *TE* characteristics, but with exceptional strength.

Fig. 7 shows a graph of signal strengths on two such evenings. Photographs of the received signals show the characteristics of *F* and *TE* propa-

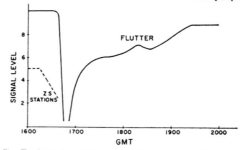

Fig. 7—Both *F* and *TE* propagation appear in this graph for September 26 and October 7, 1958. Solid line is the ZE2JV signal. Farther south ZS signals are shown in broken line at the left.

gation. Still another type, Fig. 8, shows no fadeout in the period of transition from *F* to *TE*. Photographs made of this (not reproduced here) show a mixture of the two types of propagation.

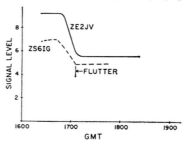

Fig. 8—Gradual transition from *F* to *TE* reception at ZC4WR, September 18, 1958. ZS6IG, Johannesburg, South Africa, is shown in dashed line.

There were few evenings when propagation was not in one of the categories described above. Ionospheric storms apparently had little effect. Disturbed conditions are of two types, as shown in Figs. 9 and 10. Of the two, the first occurred more often, and was probably due to late-persisting ionization in the lower levels. The second shows sporadic signals observed, and it would appear that late-evening *F*-type signals were being cut off by sporadic-*E*.

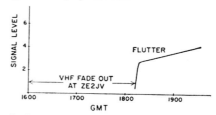

Fig. 9—ZE2JV signal during disturbed conditions, September 9. The v.h.f. range was devoid of signals from the north at ZE2JV, between 1800 and 2000 local time.

Noise Levels

Noise measurements made in Salisbury show the level to be high through the *TE* seasons.

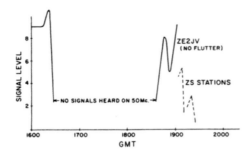

Fig. 10—Another type of disturbed conditions, September 30, showed the ZE2JV signal hitting a high level in the early evening at Cyprus, followed by a 2-hour fadeout and subsequent *TE* propagation from ZE and ZS.

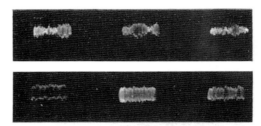

Periods of unmodulated carrier showing the complex fading pattern of *TE* propagation (upper three examples) in comparison with the steadier F_2 signal in the lower row.

There is a marked drop in midsummer and midwinter, when receiving on frequencies above the m.u.f. At these times the noise level is comparable with that experienced in temperate zones. Noise level during the *TE* seasons stays high through the day, and often does not appear to vary with propagation conditions. It does vary directly with the degree of scatter, however.

Observations on Cyprus were quite different. There the noise level rose with propagation conditions. A belt of severe thunderstorms across the Rhodesias gave an S-unit increase in noise level at the Cyprus end of the path. Apparent contradictions in these noise observations can be explained by two factors: The *TE* zone as seen from Salisbury is larger, and the geomagnetic equator crosses Africa well to the north of the geographical equator.

The tropical convergence zone can be considered as a vast noise generator. This zone remaining approximately in the subsolar region is substantially in the southern *TE* belt. North of the geographical equator (Kenya-Uganda, from where 50-Mc. signals scatter back into Rhodesia with great strength) desert conditions are rapidly approached. Noise from the tropical convergence zone can, therefore, be received in Cyprus only by *TE* propagation, whereas in Rhodesia noise from the zone can be received by direct scatter and back-scatter propagation. This is consistent with the fact that noise is received throughout the day up to the highest frequency reached by *TE* propagation.

Echoes

Occasionally echoes indicating a ⅙-second delay appear on *TE* signals. Unfortunately, these have not yet been photographed. Such echoes were prevalent on the 40-Mc. signals of Sputnik I as it travelled over the *TE* zones during the evening.

The delay suggests that these echoes may be circumterrestrial. It is difficult to imagine how this can happen when east-west work within the *TE* belts has not been possible. (IGY beacon stations in South America, just below 50 Mc., were never received.) Unconfirmed evidence has suggested that signals may be propagated to east and west by beaming a powerful signal away from the equator. If, as seems likely, ionization at the lower levels is the main barrier to east-west work, it would appear possible for such propagation to take place.

Echoes of even longer delay have been reported.

Back-Scatter

Contacts on 50 Mc. with Kenya and Uganda were commonplace in the evening hours. Signals usually had *TE* characteristics, but when these East African stations work farther south into Johannesburg and Windhoek their signals are often without flutter. Such contacts took place only when the indication of scatter was high.

Back-scatter from other Rhodesian amateurs is common on 28 Mc. when both stations beam north. Signals are the flutter type, but remarkably constant day and night. The level is just sufficient for readability on a.m. with 100-watt stations. Back-scatter is not so consistent on 50 Mc., but the lower level of activity, lower power, and frequent interference from DX television are limiting factors.

50-Mc. pulses from ZE2JV, recorded when flutter was relatively severe and beam tests showed a high degree of scatter.

A portable station on a 5,200-foot elevation near Umtali provided round-the-clock communication on 50 Mc. with Salisbury, a 160-mile path. During the evening its back-scatter signal from the north was of good strength. The same transmitter working from the town itself was never heard, despite numerous tests.

Only once was a sporadic-*E* signal heard on 50 Mc. This was from Windhoek, Southwest Africa. Lack of sporadic-*E* signals otherwise is in part due to low activity, as there are few stations within the usual range for this type of propagation.

Split pulses from ZE2JV recorded during October, 1958 — Such pulses appeared only occasionally, in a string of normal ones. Breaks in the continuity of the signal in this way occasionally make keyed signals difficult to copy.

Conclusions

For purposes of this account, *TE* propagation is definited as v.h.f. propagation between points on opposite sides of the geomagnetic equator, and at least 1000 miles from it, without intermediate reflection from the surface of the earth. It will be noted that the term "*TE* scatter" is avoided. This term is thought unsuitable, as scatter appears to play a part only in certain circumstances.

The differences in signal characteristics at various times might suggest entirely different modes of propagation, but the writer feels that the mode is substantially similar for each type mentioned, and that all are merely variations of the same basic mode. The regions of the ionosphere between the temperate zones and the geomagnetic equator have been said to exhibit a tilt, and would appear to be regions of flux and turbulence. A wave transmitted toward the geomagnetic equator, striking the tilted ionosphere, could be projected forward to take a similar deflection at the region of tilt on the other side of the geomagnetic equator before being returned to earth. This low angle of strike at both points would enable higher frequencies to be propagated by the F_2-layer than would normally be possible.

There would appear to be no reason why a signal so propagated should have characteristics widely different from those propagated in the normal manner. However, a wave reflected from a moving medium will show a frequency shift (Doppler effect) and should the ionosphere in these regions be turbulent it would seem likely that characteristics similar to those observed would be imparted to the signal.

The effect of lower-level ionization in the *E* and *D* regions appears to be the controlling factor, in daytime, of the maximum usable frequency. Late persistence of lower-level ionization may delay the appearance of *TE*, and sporadic-*E* may occasionally obstruct propagation. The possibility of propagation from the top of lower-level ionization in the subsolar region is not entirely rejected as a possible explanation for long-persisting *F*-type propagation. Duct propagation conceivably could support circumterrestrial propagation around the equator.

All types of propagation observed exhibit certain features in common. The zone into which signals propagate remains substantially the same irrespective of the type of propagation (two-hop propagation excluded.) All types of propagation are observed over a wide band of frequencies. Scatter readings do not vary with different types of propagation observed on the Salisbury-Cyprus path.

Carrier photographs show that the types of propagation tend to mix, even when this is not apparent in listening to the received signals.

The possibility of propagation outside the F_2-layer is discounted by the similarity of conditions over the range from 18 to 72 Mc.

Pulse tests and carrier photography, and the lack of connection between scatter tests and the degree of flutter, indicate that the flutter is caused by the state of the ionosphere at the regions of refraction. The presence of identical flutter on signals from East Africa, and the sharp directivity of beams on this path, confirm this opinion.

Acknowledgments

The help and information supplied by the Propagation Research Project of The American Radio Relay League was responsible for the beginning, and to a large degree, the continuation of this project across the African continent. The willing cooperation of amateurs in many countries, who supplied data upon which this account is based, and the work of R. A. Whiting, ZC4WR, who played a major part in the experiments, are gratefully acknowledged.

Strays

Here's another neat console, this one the pride and joy at W7CQK. It is a home-built job, and certainly no wife could ever object to such a handsome piece of furniture. Incidentally, that map in the background is made up from two of the United Airlines maps that are found at the seat of each airline passenger. Pasted together at the center (they are in register) you end up with a fine relief map of the country. Back to the console—it's made up of hardboard (perforated in the lower sections, for ventilation) fastened to a wooden frame, and finished off with a smooth-as-glass top.

"Observations on Long-Delay Radio Echoes" by J.H. Dellinger

By Carl Luetzelschwab, K9LA

In the November 3, 1928, issue of the scientific publication *Nature*, Professor Carl Størmer reported on a letter he had received at the end of the summer of 1927 from Jørgen Hals, an engineer in Oslo (Norway). Jørgen repeatedly heard echoes of the Dutch shortwave transmitter station PCJJ in Eindhoven. The shorter echoes were from the round-the-world signal (delayed about 1/7 of a second), but the longer echoes were delayed about 3 seconds.

Størmer postulated that the long delays were the result of the wave taking an extra-terrestrial path following the Earth's magnetic field. This idea came from Birkeland's earlier experimental work with cathode rays directed towards a magnetic sphere.

Størmer then went on to organize a long series of observations of PJCC on 31.4 meters wavelength (9.55 MHz) in October 1928. During this campaign, echoes from 3 to 15 seconds were heard, with most of them around 8 seconds.

Dr. Van der Pol provided details of these observations in the December 8, 1928, issue of *Nature*. The accompanying illustration shows this original data. Note that delays up to 30 seconds were observed. Dr. van der Pol suggested the mechanism was the extremely slow group velocity of the wave when the operating frequency was near the Kennelly-Heaviside (early name for the ionosphere) plasma frequency.

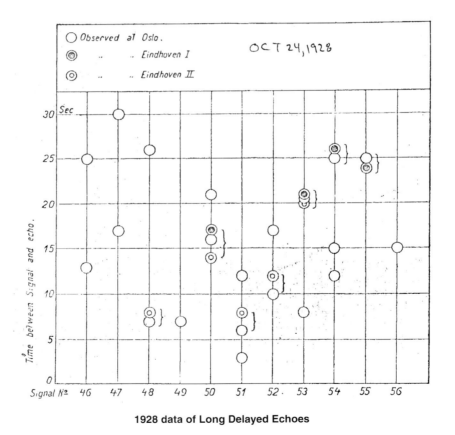

1928 data of Long Delayed Echoes

Long-delayed echoes first showed up in the Amateur Radio literature in the August 1934 issue of *QST*. J. H. Dellinger (then Chief of the Radio Section at the US Bureau of Standards in Washington, DC) requested cooperation from Amateur Radio operators — he was looking for reception reports of special transmissions from transmitter GSB in England (on 9.51 MHz) and transmitter HBL in Switzerland (on 6.675 MHz). Any reports of long delayed echoes would be forwarded to British authorities, who were coordinating the investigation for the world as a whole.

The next instance of long delayed echoes in an Amateur Radio publication was in 1956. Bill Holcomb, W9SDP, requested hearing from others who had experienced the "long-delayed echo" phenomenon in the Strays column in the July 1956 *QST*.

Discussion of long-delayed echoes was somewhat sparse until the seminal article by Villard, W6QYT (head of the Radioscience Laboratory at Stanford University); Graf, W5LFM; and Lomasney, WA6NIL in the May 1969 *QST*. In this article, the history of long-delayed echoes was reviewed, including descriptions of the original transmitting stations, signal intensity versus time recordings of possible echoes, reports of LDEs gathered from Northern and Southern California DX clubs as shown in the accompanying figure, a theoretical discussion of recent plasma theory, and a request to gather more reports from Amateur Radio operators.

Summary of LDE Reports

Date	Call	Band, MHz.	Approx. duration, seconds	Time, GMT	Phone/ c.w.	Audible on Own/Other
Oct. 16, 1932	W6ADP	28	18	≈1800	c.w.	Own
Winter, 1950–51	W5LUU	7	5	≈0300	c.w.	Own
Winter, 1965	K6EV	14	3–4	0600–0700	s.s.b.	Own
Dec. 2, 1967	W5VY	28	3	1328	s.s.b.	Own
Jan. 27, 1968	W5LFM	10	½	1400–1430	Time Ticks	Station RID
Dec. 18, 1968	W6KPC	28	1	≈2000	s.s.b.	Other
Jan. 21, 1969	W6OL	14	6–10	1536	c.w.	Other
Feb. 17, 1969	K6CAZ	2	≈2	1430–1500	s.s.b.	Own and Other

Early LDE Reports from Amateurs

A follow-up article by Villard, Graf, and Lomasney appeared in the February 1970 *QST*, the result of the request in the May 1969 *QST*. In addition to more theoretical discussions, it also presented two pages of long delayed echo reports from amateurs all over the continental US (and even a couple from overseas reports) on all the HF bands at the time (80, 40, 20, 15 and 10 meters).

Although the first observations of long delayed echoes occurred outside the Amateur Radio community, amateurs contributed heavily to the database of LDEs. There are subsequent *QST* articles about LDEs, but the articles mentioned here were the beginning.

Observations on Long-Delay Radio Echoes

An Opportunity for Amateur Coöperation

By J. H. Dellinger*

SPECIAL signals are being transmitted from two European stations for the study of long-delay echoes. The signals and the whole undertaking are adapted to the participation of persons all over the world who have high-frequency receiving sets, no technical training being required.

Long-delay echoes are a most surprising and baffling phenomenon. Mr. J. Hals was listening in Norway, one day in 1927, to telegraphic signals from station PCJJ in Holland on a frequency of about 9600 kc. Some of the signals were followed, after about 3 seconds, by a faint echo or reproduction. Echo signals occurring one-seventh of a second after an emitted signal had been well known, being due to the reception of waves that had travelled all the way around the earth. But the discovery of echoes after a materially greater interval than a seventh of a second immediately raised the puzzling question of where such an echo could come from.

The phenomenon has been verified in a few scattered observations by Dutch, British, and French engineers. Echoes have been heard from 1 to 30 seconds after the emitted signal. Not enough is known, however, to determine what causes the echo signals nor how they are propagated. Two theories have been proposed. One, by Dr. C. Stormer of Norway, considers that there are streams of electrons in space some hundreds of thousands of miles out from the earth's equator, converging in a vast toroid upon the magnetic poles of the earth, and accounting for the aurora borealis or northern lights. Dr. Stormer supposes that the signals are reflected from these electron streams in space. The other theory, by Dr. B. Van der Pol and Professor E. V. Appleton, considers that these echoes are due to a slowing up and reflection of the waves by a peculiar distribution of ionization in the very high levels of the ionosphere (that portion of the atmosphere, 65 miles and more above the surface of the earth, which is responsible for all long-distance radio transmission).

The British Broadcasting Corporation through its magazine, *World-Radio*, and with the aid of Professor Appleton, has just inaugurated a world-wide endeavor to learn more about these long-delay echoes. Special emissions are provided from two high-power high-frequency stations to facilitate observations by anyone who cares to listen with a high-frequency receiving set. Listeners in all parts of the world have been enrolled in the endeavor, over 10,000 of them in Great Britain. It seems likely that information of unique value to science will result, and an orderly explanation of the curious phenomenon developed, when definite data are secured on the frequencies and the times of day and season at which these echoes occur, their intensities, the area over which a given echo is heard, their relation to magnetic storms, sunspots, etc.

THE SPECIAL TRANSMISSIONS

The stations transmitting the special signals are GSB, Daventry, England, and HBL, Geneva, Switzerland (the League of Nations station). The GSB signals are transmitted on 9510 kc., with a tone or modulation of 1000 cycles per second, each Sunday, Tuesday, and Thursday, from 3:25 to 3:55 a.m., Eastern Standard Time. The HBL signals are transmitted on 6675 kc., modulated continuous waves, each Sunday, Wednesday and Friday, from 6:00 to 6:30 a.m., E.S.T. Each transmission consists of a five-minute adjusting period (GSB using phonograph music, and HBL using its call letters in code repeated) followed by the letters of the alphabet in code, spaced a minute apart. Thus, for instance, GSB transmits the letter "A" in code at 3:30, and after a minute of silence the letter "B" at 3:31, then the letter "C" at 3:32, etc., finishing with letter "Z" at 3:55. During the one-minute intervals between signals the observers listen for echoes and observe the elapsed time in seconds with a watch having a second hand. It should be noted that the GSB signals are receivable with a receiving set as used for receiving broadcast programs, but the HBL signals are unmodulated c.w. and, therefore, require an oscillating receiving set.

I would be very glad to have any successful reception of long-delay echoes in the United States reported to me, and will relay the information to the British authorities who are coördinating the investigation for the world as a whole. Observers should give the identifying letter of the signal observed, the time to the nearest second at which the direct signal was heard, the time to the nearest second at which the echo was heard, an estimate of the relative intensities of direct signal and echo, a description of the sharpness or apparent shape of the echo, and any pertinent information on interference, fading of signals, etc.

(Continued on page 83)

---

*Chief, Radio Section, U. S. Bureau of Standards, Washington, D. C.

Observations on Long-Delay Radio Echoes

(Continued from page 42)

I would be interested also in receiving reports of reception of long-delay echoes on any other stations, especially high-frequency stations of this country. It may, on the other hand, be difficult to be certain of any echoes observed because of the lack of silent periods as in the special signals from the two European stations.

Summaries of the results of this investigation will be made available later in publications in this country. Persons desiring to keep in touch with all details of the project meanwhile can do so by consulting the weekly issues of *World-Radio*, published by Broadcasting House, London, W. 1, England.

"Lunar DX on 144 Mc.!" by Ed Tilton, W1HDQ

By Carl Luetzelschwab, K9LA

Prior to World War II, John H. DeWitt, Jr, W4ERI, was the chief engineer of WSM in Nashville, Tennessee. With typical amateur inquisitiveness, he thought about receiving echoes from the Moon. His early experiments failed due to equipment limitations. The idea remained with him all during World War II, but higher priorities as director of the Evans Signal Laboratory (a forerunner to the US Army Signal Corps) fielding radar equipment to the troops made it impossible for him to try again.

After the war, W4ERI (still director of the Labs) issued instructions to modify certain standard radar equipment for the Moon investigation. Longer pulses were incorporated, the transmitter was driven harder for more output power, and a telegraph key was used to turn the RF on and off.

Immediate success was not in the cards. The transmit/receive circuit (gas tubes that ionize in transmit to protect the receiver) was not functioning properly and this circuit had to be redesigned to a mechanical circuit. The antenna was doubled in size (offering 6 dB more gain in a two-way system) under the direction of E. K. Stodola, W3IYF. The bandwidth of the receiver was reduced (to 50 Hz), an electronic keyer replaced the telegraph key, and a sweep generator was implemented to operate a nine-inch cathode ray oscilloscope.

The measured receiver sensitivity at 111.5 MHz was 0.04 microvolts in the 50 Hz bandwidth (that equates to –135 dBm, typical of today's receivers but many times more sensitive than a typical ham receiver of the day). The transmitter input power was 8000 watts, and its 50% efficiency gave 4000 watts output to the antenna. With the antenna gain of 23 dB, calculations said the received signal bounced off the Moon would be about 16 dB above the noise back on Earth.

The first faint echo was heard on January 10, 1946, as described in May 1946 *QST*. Subsequent to that feat, plans were implemented for a transmitter with higher output power (which was worked on by Clarence Holritz, W9BBD). The expectation of these tests was to gather much useful information about wave propagation — information that someday might be useful to the amateur. It was also hoped to study propagation at other frequencies.

The success of the military in bouncing signals off the Moon encouraged amateurs to attempt this feat. The military tests were high-power projects and the slim margin of success indicated that lunar DX for amateurs was a very low probability. The best available information for a shot at 144 MHz moonbounce indicated it would take the legal power limit (which was one kilowatt input — that means the higher the efficiency of the power amplifier, the more output power), an antenna gain of at least 20 dB, and a receiver noise figure (sensitivity) at the forefront of technology (around 5 dB at that time).

Bill Smith, W3GKP, and Ross Bateman, W4AO, took up this challenge. On January 15, 1950, they heard what sounded like an echo. Being just one tiny beep, W3GKP and W4AO wanted more solid proof, so work was done for more output power and more antenna gain. A move by W3GKP to a new home location delayed further testing until late 1952 when everything was again set up. The first positive results occurred on January 23, 1953, and further results the next day provided irrefutable evidence that amateur moonbounce was possible. The article here from March 1953 *QST* elaborates on this feat.

As part of the Project Vanguard program, hams who received echoes from moonbounce experiments received this QSL card.

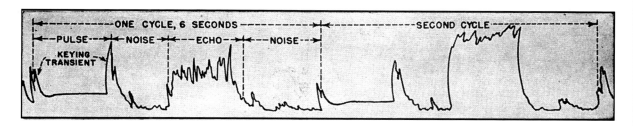

Lunar DX on 144 Mc.!

W4AO and W3GKP Bounce 2-Meter Signals Off the Moon

LISTENING to the wire recording from which the above graph was made, it doesn't sound like much; a one-second beep, an interval of receiver noise, then a wavering trailing bee-e-e-e-p barely discernible in the midst of the slightly musical rushing sound that is characteristic of high-selectivity reception. You wouldn't be impressed if you happened to hear it casually, but to Ross Bateman, W4AO, and Bill Smith, W3GKP, it was music of the sweetest sort; evidence that more years of thinking, figuring, building, rebuilding and testing were not in vain. An amateur signal had been sent to the moon and back, at last!

Bouncing signals off the moon is not new, of course. It was done on 110 Mc. by the Signal Corps back in 1946 [1] and something approximating intelligence was sent from Cedar Rapids, Iowa, to Washington, D. C., on 400 Mc. more recently,[2] using the moon as a reflector. These were high-power projects, however, and their slim margin of success indicated that lunar DX for amateurs was a long-chance proposition. It was an end that just might be achieved, but only after the most painstaking effort, if at all.

The best available information indicated that it would take the level amateur power limit, pushed to the last watt. An antenna gain of at least 20 db. was required, and a degree of receiver performance to tax the ingenuity of the best engineers in the business was called for. Obviously, a 144-Mc. WAS, lunar style, was a long way off, but it was a challenge that a few enterprising and infinitely patient hams were bound to accept.

One such ham was Bill Smith, W3GKP, then of Silver Spring, Maryland. Smitty knew what he was about, and he went at the job with no illusions about aiming his beam at the rising moon

[1] Kaufman, "A DX Record: To the Moon and Back," *QST*, May, 1946.
[2] Sulzer, Montgomery, and Gerks, "An U.H.F. Moon Relay," *Proc. IRE*, March, 1951, p. 361.

◆

Ross Bateman, W4AO, *left*, and Bill Smith, W3GKP, smile happily over the success of *Project Moonbeam*, after three years of trying. The high-power stages of the 1-kw. 2-meter transmitter are in the left-hand rack, as are crystal-controlled converters for 144 and 50 Mc. The large cabinet houses power supplies, modulator and control circuits.

some night and then sitting back to listen to the W6s. He knew the requirements, in a general way, and he felt sure that the trick could be turned, eventually. The first step was to find a co-worker, so that the burden of equipment development and construction could be shared. A ham with a kilowatt rig and a big beam for 144 Mc. would be a fine start. Several prospects were lined up, and early in 1950 a few transmitting tests were made, while W3GKP worked on his receiving gear, but none of the prospects had sufficiently good equipment to make reception possible at that stage of the game.

Other amateurs, among them W4AO, Falls Church, Va., had been working along similar lines. Learning of W3GKP's interest, Ross joined forces with Smitty, and *Project Moonbeam* was on its way in earnest. Ross brought to the operation the technical know-how and the enthusiasm and perseverance Smitty had been looking for, and he had a 2-meter rig capable of a full and efficient kilowatt, a 32-element array, a low-noise receiver and a quiet suburban location. After many evenings of discussion, planning and construction, the stage was set for a series of tests with a set-up that appeared to have some chance of succeeding.

The rig at W4AO was maintained on frequency precisely, and keyed in one-second pulses.

March 1953

The required separation in frequency between the transmitter and receiver frequencies (to take care of Doppler effects resulting from movements of the earth and moon) had been calculated, and the receiver frequency set with elaborate stability precautions. A wire recorder was connected to the receiver output, to catch as permanent evidence any sign of a returned signal. The system was put in operation whenever the moon was in the right place, and no minor considerations like eating or sleeping were allowed to interfere.

At long last, at 5:03 A.M. on July 15, 1950, came something that sounded like an echo. It was faint and indefinite, but it started at the right time and it sounded like the real thing. What was more important, it was caught on the wire recorder. It was just one tiny beep after a long series of transmitter pulses, but it was enough to keep enthusiasm going.

Workers of lesser stature might have called in the press and announced their results to the world, but Ross and Smitty wanted something more solid than a single faint and somewhat dubious return on which to rest their case. Copies of the recording were mailed out to a few interested parties who could be trusted to say nothing until given the word, and *Moonbeam* went on and on. (A wire copy of that first success has rested in the desk of *QST*'s V.H.F. Editor for nearly three years.)

Test after test piled failure on failure, but still the beeps were sent. An infinitesimal improvement in receiver noise figure, another decibel of antenna gain, a correction of a degree of antenna aiming error, an improved method of "reading"

OUR COVER

Aiming an antenna at the moon is an exacting proposition. Our cover shows W4AO, *left*, and W3GKP checking the alignment of the 20-wavelength stacked rhombics used for *Project Moonbeam*.

signals inaudible in the noise; any or all of these might tip the balance. Methods that were tried and found wanting will not be recounted here, but they were many.

Moving to a new home location necessitated the dismantling of the receiving set-up at W3GKP, so *Moonbeam* moved its entire facilities to the basement at W4AO. In November, 1952, a huge stacked rhombic was erected and tested, and it showed a gratifying improvement over the 32-element array. A system had been devised to tie in transmitter and receiver frequencies together accurately. A new receiver front end brought the noise figure down under 4 db.

Tests on November 30th and December 3rd brought no results, so a slight modification was made in the rhombic design, to radiate maximum signal at 2 degrees above the horizon, in readiness for the next round December 27th. There were some very faint returns this time, but nothing tangible on the 30th and 31st.

Meanwhile, the staff of *Moonbeam* had been augmented by the addition of Ted Tuckerman, W3LZD, of Dunmore, Penna., who erected a 30-wavelength rhombic array in time for tests

(Continued on page 116)

Part of the equipment used in *Project Moonbeam*, as it operates in the basement at W4AO, Falls Church, Va. At the control position is the Super-Pro receiver, flanked by microphone preamplifier and beam direction indicator. The rolling table, *center*, carries frequency-checking gear. On the workbench at the right are the frequency control units and exciter. The high-power stages of the transmitter are out of sight at the right, in racks that also house the crystal-controlled converters for the v.h.f. bands.

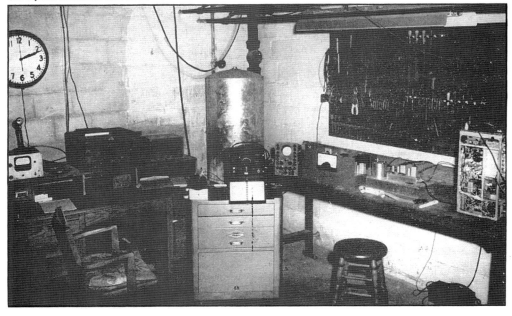

Lunar DX

(Continued from page 12)

in late January. The receiver bandwidth at W4AO was shaved another notch for this try, too.

Ted arranged to listen for the ground-wave signal with his normal 2-meter array aimed at W4AO, and then switch to the moon rhombic to try for the echo. His low-noise crystal-controlled converter and communications receiver were equipped with a super-selective 50-kc. i.f. system built by W3LCK. On January 23rd, this combination produced its first positive results, and a series of weak echoes was received at W3LZD, at a time when nothing was detected by the set-up at W4AO.

Tests the following afternoon produced nothing, but beginning at 1533 EST on the 27th, a whole series of echoes was recorded at W4AO, two cycles of which are reproduced at the start of this article. Success, at last, and in sufficient quantity and quality to provide irrefutable evidence!

The equipment used in this and earlier stages of *Moonbeam* will be described by W4AO and W3GKP in a subsequent issue of *QST*. Now the question is, "Where do we go from here?" As Smitty puts it, "This is the end of Phase A — we've got an echo. Phase B will be to transmit intelligence to another station. Phase C will be to work somebody, two-way. Phase D will be to break the 2-meter record. Phases E, F ———— well, can go on almost indefinitely. After three years we're just getting started!"

— *E. P. T.*

"MINIMUF: A Simplified MUF-Prediction Program for Microcomputers" by Robert Rose, K6GKU

By Carl Luetzelschwab, K9LA and Ward Silver, N0AX

If you were active in Amateur Radio prior to 1982, you may remember doing propagation predictions manually. To do manual predictions, we used a modified cylindrical projection map of the world, great circle paths for the cylindrical projection map, worldwide maps of F_2 region MUFs (maximum useable frequencies), and data to estimate the E region MUF. The first presentation of this manual effort was by William Foley, K4FEC, in the February 1946 *QST*. A second similar article by Franklin Moore, WB9GCC, appeared in the August 1971 *QST*. Over the years we progressed from monthly publications with monthly data to three books with data for three levels of solar activity.

In the 1960s and 1970s, large-scale numerical codes (such as *IONCAP*, *ITS-78*, and *SKYWAVE*) were developed to replace the manual method of propagation predictions. These were run on large computers (of course "large" is relative — these early computers that ran these codes would be considered small today).

To make propagation predictions more available, a simple model of the F_2 region of the ionosphere was developed to show the dynamics of the MUF and how its sensitivity to solar activity varies. This new model consisted of 80 BASIC program steps, and was called *MINIMUF*. The initial introduction of *MINIMUF* to the Amateur Radio community was done by Robert B. Rose, K6GKU, in the December 1982 *QST* article that follows. Bob was the head of the Ionospheric Assessment Systems Branch at the Naval Ocean Systems Center in San Diego.

MINIMUF was small enough to fit on a Texas Instrument TI-59 calculator or on a Radio Shack TRS-80 microcomputer. Getting it small enough to fit on a small personal computer (the acronym PC would evolve later) meant some compromises were accepted. For example, the F_2 region of the ionosphere was ordered about geographic coordinates — not geomagnetic coordinates as is the real ionosphere. It also had a problem with polar paths in the summer. Its accuracy was pegged at an RMS error of ±3.8 MHz.

Yes, *MINIMUF* was crude at the time. But it allowed Amateur Radio operators (and many others) to predict when specific paths were likely to be open. And it jump-started the transition to improved ionosphere models and improved propagation prediction techniques, which eventually evolved to ray tracing including the Earth's magnetic field and collisions between electrons and neutral atmospheric constituents.

WA3MXJ

LONG DISTANCE H. F. PROPAGATION PREDICTION CHART

Terminal A: IOWA
Terminal B: HEARD ISLAND
Short/Long Path: SHORT
Path Length: 18,300 KM

Month, Year: MARCH, 1969
Sunspot Number: 99
Prepared By: F. MOORE
Date: 10 MARCH 1969

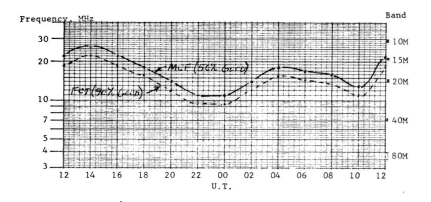

U.T.	F2(4000)MUF A"	B"	Solar Zenith Angle A'	B'	E(2000)MUF A'	B'	Terminal MUF A	B	Path MUF	F2(4000)FOT A"	B"	Terminal FOT A	B	Path FOT
00	31	11	93°	165°	7	–	31	11	11	26	9.3	26	9.3	9.3
02	23	14	–	81°	–	9.1	23	14	14	19.5	12	19.5	12	12
04	19	18	–	73°	–	17.9	19	18	18	16	15.3	16	15.3	15.3
06	17	23	–	66°	–	15.2	17	23	17	14.5	19.5	14.5	19.5	14.5
08	16	28	–	55°	–	16	16	28	16	13.6	24	13.6	24	13.6
10	13	28	–	66°	–	15.2	13	28	13	11	24	11	24	11
12	22	28	86°	72°	4.3	15.1	22	28	22	18.7	24	18.7	24	18.7
14	35	26	66°	88°	14.2	8.8	35	26	26	30	22	30	22	22
16	37	22	45°	165°	17.1	–	37	22	22	31.5	18.7	31.5	18.7	18.7
18	38	18	35°	–	12.9	–	38	18	18	32	15.8	32	15.8	15.8
20	37	14	48°	–	16.7	–	37	14	14	31.5	12	31.5	12	12
22	36	11	70°	–	13.5	–	36	11	11	30.5	9.3	30.5	9.3	9.3

Terminal MUF is the higher of the "E" and "F2" MUF's. Path MUF is the lower of the terminal MUF's. The terminal FOT is the higher of the "F2-FOT" and the "E-MUF". Path FOT is the lower of the terminal FOT's.

Manual propagation prediction was a very tedious job. The process shown here was developed by Franklin Moore, WB9GCC, based on a table of the expected monthly median MUF for each increment of time; 2 hours in this sample manual prediction from 1969 between Indiana and Heard Island, VKØ/H. Moore described the process in August 1971 *QST***.**

MINIMUF: A Simplified MUF-Prediction Program for Microcomputers

On which band and at what time should you expect propagation to Pakistan or Pennsylvania? Use this computer model of muf and prepare your own up-to-the-minute predictions.

By Robert B. Rose,* K6GKU

In the mid 1970s, Navy engineers were working to utilize the explosion in microprocessor computing technology to improve the timeliness and accuracy of hf-propagation predictions. The primary emphasis was directed toward allowing hf users in the field to assess current propagation conditions. Up to that time, hf-prediction codes were long, complex programs requiring large computers. The user in the field depended on long-term predictions based on years of historical observations. This method often lacked the ability to reflect current solar activity and any changes in the operating scenario. The Navy work was directed toward developing a simplified hf-prediction system that was adaptable to almost any micro or minicomputer using the BASIC language. Further, it was desired that the user be able to enter current solar/geophysical parameters, such as solar flux. This provided more accurate predictions.

The hf sky-wave channel, shown in Fig. 1, is generally described as being bounded by the maximum usable frequency (muf) and by the lowest usable frequency (luf). The luf is an absorptive function, and is controlled by power, signal-to-noise requirements and other such system gain functions. It is a fuzzy boundary, and, as far as amateur operation is concerned, frequencies near the luf are the least efficient part of the spectrum. Most hf users know that the closer to the muf one operates, the more efficient the communications channel becomes. DXers are particularly interested in the muf characteristics of certain paths. The muf is a physical boundary that is controlled by the level of solar activity and solar illumination on the path. It is a concise constraint that the hf user cannot overcome with power, antenna or other mechanical means. Because it does vary on a day-to-day basis, and because sometimes it is vastly different than long-term predictions would show, it seemed that a simplified muf-prediction algorithm would be a very useful tool. In the mid 1970s, scientists at the Naval Ocean System Center predicted that the peak of solar cycle 21, 1978 to 1982, would be higher than initially expected, further motivating the project.[1]

Traditionally, the prediction of muf was done by a large, complex computer model, nominally consisting of 150,000 to 200,000 bytes of computer code. In 1977, a simple model was developed to show the dynamics of the muf and how its sensitivity to solar activity varies.[2] "Simple" is an understatement; the new model consisted of 80 BASIC program steps! Many military, industrial and commercial hf users have implemented and tested MINIMUF.

The initial verification was done by comparing the predictions with oblique-incidence-sounder data, which is the only way to observe the actual muf boundary. The original sounder data base encompassed 196 path months (4704 test points) of observed maximum usable frequencies measured over 23 different hf-sounder paths. MINIMUF was found to have an rms error of ±3.8 MHz. Current users find it useful from 2 to 50 MHz for muf predictions out to 6000 miles.[3] However, accuracy degrades for ranges of less than 250 miles.

As one can imagine, anything as simple as MINIMUF invites "tinkering." Over the past three years, numerous experimenters have made attempts to improve the model with such features as adding an E and F_1 region (MINIMUF is a single-layer F-region model), changing constants to reflect local conditions and giving it more diurnal variation. All of these revisions, when compared against oblique-sounder data, degraded the accuracy and made the program more complicated. These exercises only served to prove the old adage, "If it works, don't fix it." The ver-

*Head, Ionospheric Assessment Systems Branch, Naval Ocean Systems Center, San Diego, CA 92152

[1]Notes appear on page 38.

sion of MINIMUF described in this article was first published in 1978,[4] and is still the principal version in use.

Application Tips

With increasing solar activity, user interest in updating MINIMUF to reflect current conditions also increased. The updating method found to be most effective was to vary the sunspot-number input parameter as a function of the 10.7-cm solar flux. Because of the lag in F-region response to a rapid increase in solar activity, it is best to use either a 5-day, 15-day or 90-day running average of the 10.7-cm flux. The type of application will determine which is best. The 5-day mean is a short-term, more dynamic input, while the 90-day mean is more applicable for long-term planning. These flux values can be acquired from the U.S. Department of Commerce, National Oceanic and Atmospheric Administration, Environmental Research Laboratories, Boulder, CO 80303 or from WWV transmissions at 18 minutes after each hour. The conversion from 10.7-cm flux to sunspot number is accomplished by the graph shown in Fig. 2.

Two other points are borne out by field testing. First, MINIMUF is an F-region approximation. Any intervention by E-region modes of propagation, either as multiple E or EF complex modes, is not predictable by MINIMUF. Such operational situations, however, are proving to represent only a small percentage of the total. Second, MINIMUF has the greatest accuracy within the one- and three-hop ranges, between about 250 and 6000 miles. Predictions for transmission paths longer than this should be used with some caution. Fig. 3 is a sample output listing that users may find helpful in getting their version of MINIMUF working.

Conclusion

MINIMUF is simple, and it works. It is expected to be particularly useful during the next solar-minimum period, in the mid 1980s, for operation in the new WARC bands.

It is emphasized that MINIMUF is not designed to replace the current large-scale numerical codes such as IONCAP, ITS-78, SKYWAVE, and the like. If you have ready access to a large computer, use the large codes. If you are limited to a Texas Instruments TI-59® calculator, Radio Shack TRS-80® microcomputer, or similar micro-based systems, MINIMUF was designed for you. It is conceivable that in the future MINIMUF will be resident in a read-only memory (ROM) in a microprocessor controlled transceiver. If the operator enters the desired end points, date, time and solar flux, he or she could quickly determine whether a frequency band was open in the desired direction. Technically, it is feasible now.

The author wishes to acknowledge the contributions of Dr. Paul Levine of Megatek Corporation, who produced the original MINIMUF concept, and Messrs. J. N. Martin and D. B. Sailors of the

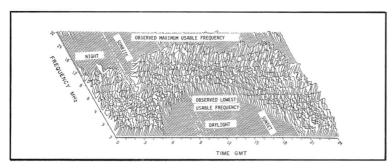

Fig. 1 — A typical 24-hour plot of the hf sky wave channel.

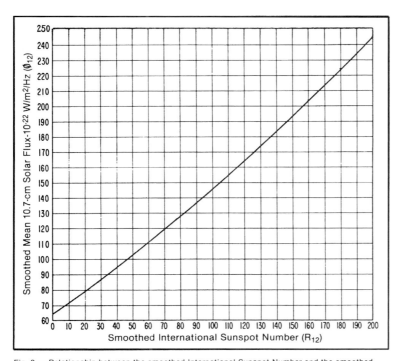

Fig. 2 — Relationship between the smoothed International Sunspot Number and the smoothed mean 10.7-cm Solar Flux.

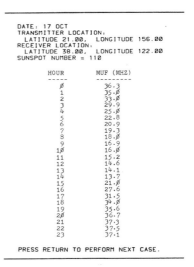

Fig. 3 — Example of a 24-hour muf listing from MINIMUF-3.5. Times given are in UTC.

December 1982 37

Naval Ocean Systems Center, San Diego, California, for their work in the mathematical and software development of MINIMUF, and also for the extensive accuracy verifications they performed.

APPENDIX — MINIMUF BASIC PROGRAM

A listing of the MINIMUF-3.5 program is included. Lines 100 through 720 contain a small driver, which allows the model to be exercised. The actual MINIMUF program starts at line 1000.

The input variables for the MINIMUF program are as follows:

L1 — Transmitter latitude ($-90° \leq L1 \leq 90°$)
W1 — Transmitter west longitude ($-360° \leq W1 \leq 360°$)
L2 — Receiver latitude ($-90° \leq L2 \leq 90°$)
W2 — Receiver west longitude ($-360° \leq W2 \leq 360°$)
M0 — Month ($1 \leq M0 \leq 12$)
D6 — Day ($1 \leq D6 \leq 31$)
T5 — Time (UT), hours ($0.0 \leq T5 \leq 24.0$)
J9 — Output muf, MHz
S9 — Sunspot number
PI — 3.141593
P0 — 1.570796

[Editor's Note: This program listing is from a Tektronix computer. You may have to change some statements for the version of BASIC used by your computer. For example, this computer has a function, PI, which returns the value for π. Some versions of BASIC do not have the ACS (arc cosine) function, and it must be derived. The statement $-ATN(X/SQR(-X*X+1))+1.5708$ will work in place of ACS(X).]

Notes

[1] P. E. Argo, J. R. Hill, R. B. Rose and M. P. Gannis, "Radio Propagation and Solar Activity," *QST*, Feb. 1977, pp. 24-27.
[2] R. B. Rose, J. N. Martin and P. H. Levine, "MINIMUF-3: A Simplified HF MUF Prediction Algorithm," Naval Oceam Systems Center Technical Report TR-186, Feb. 1, 1978.
[3] km = miles × 1.6093.
[4] R. B. Rose and J. N. Martin, "MINIMUF-3.5: An Improved Version of MINIMUF-3," Naval Ocean Systems Center Technical Document TD-201, Oct. 26, 1978.

```
1 REM - SAMPLE DRIVER FOR MINIMUF 3.5
100 INIT
110 DIM M$(37),A$(4),M(12)
120 DATA 31,28,31,30,31,30,31,31,30,31,30,31
130 READ M
140 M$="JANFEBMARAPRMAYJUNJULAUGSEPOCTNOVDEC"
150 R0=PI/180
155 P1=2*PI
160 R1=180/PI
170 P0=PI/2
180 PAGE
190 PRINT "TRANSMITTER LAT, LON = ";
200 INPUT L1,W1
210 IF L1=>-90 AND L1<=90 THEN 240
220 PRINT "INVALID LATITUDE.  MUST BE IN RANGE (-90,+90)."
230 GO TO 190
240 IF -360<=W1 AND W1<=360 THEN 270
250 PRINT "INVALID LONGITUDE.  MUST BE IN RANGE (-360,+360)."
260 GO TO 190
270 PRINT "RECEIVER LAT, LON = ";
280 INPUT L2,W2
290 IF -90<=L2 AND L2<=90 THEN 320
300 PRINT "INVALID LATITUDE.  MUST BE IN RANGE (-90,+90)."
310 GO TO 270
320 IF -360<=W2 AND W2<=360 THEN 350
330 PRINT "INVALID LONGITUDE.  MUST BE IN RANGE (-360,+360)."
340 GO TO 270
350 PRINT "DATE (DAY,MONTH) = ";
360 INPUT D6,M0
370 IF 1<=M0 AND M0<=12 THEN 400
380 PRINT "INVALID MONTH.  MUST BE IN RANGE (1,12)."
390 GO TO 350
400 IF 1<=D6 AND D6<=M(M0) THEN 430
410 PRINT USING 420:M(M0)
420 IMAGE "INVALID DAY.  MUST BE IN RANGE (1,",FD,")."
425 GO TO 350
430 PRINT "SUNSPOT NUMBER = ";
440 INPUT S9
450 IF S9>0 THEN 480
460 PRINT "INVALID SUNSPOT NUMBER.  MUST BE NON-NEGATIVE."
470 GO TO 430
480 PAGE
490 A$=SEG(M$,3*M0-2,3)
500 PRINT USING """DATE: "",FD,1X,FA":D6,A$
510 PRINT "TRANSMITTER LOCATION: ";
520 PRINT USING 530:L1,W1
530 IMAGE "LATITUDE ",FD.2D,", LONGITUDE ",FD.2D
540 PRINT "RECEIVER LOCATION: ";
550 PRINT USING 530:L2,W2
560 PRINT USING """SUNSPOT NUMBER = "",FD":S9
570 PRINT
580 PRINT "    HOUR     MUF(MHZ)"
590 PRINT
600 L1=L1*R0
610 W1=W1*R0
620 L2=L2*R0
630 W2=W2*R0
640 FOR T5=0 TO 23
650 GOSUB 1000
660 PRINT USING 670:T5,J9
670 IMAGE 5X,2D,7X,2D.D
680 NEXT T5
690 PRINT
700 PRINT "PRESS RETURN TO PERFORM NEXT CASE.";
710 INPUT A$
720 GO TO 180
1000 REM - MINIMUF 3.5
1010 K7=SIN(L1)*SIN(L2)+COS(L1)*COS(L2)*COS(W2-W1)
1020 IF K7=>-1 THEN 1050
1030 K7=-1
1040 GO TO 1070
1050 IF K7<=1 THEN 1070
1060 K7=1
1070 G1=ACS(K7)
1080 K6=1.59*G1
1090 IF K6>=1 THEN 1110
1100 K6=1
1110 K5=1/K6
1120 J9=100
1130 FOR K1=1/(2*K6) TO 1-1/(2*K6) STEP 0.9999-1/K6
1140 IF K5=1 THEN 1160
1150 K5=0.5
1160 P=SIN(L2)
1170 O=COS(L2)
1180 A=(SIN(L1)-P*COS(G1))/(O*SIN(G1))
1190 B=G1*K1
1200 C=P*COS(B)+O*SIN(B)*A
1210 D=(COS(B)-C*P)/(O*SQR(1-C↑2))
1220 IF D=>-1 THEN 1250
1230 D=-1
1240 GO TO 1270
1250 IF D<=1 THEN 1270
1260 D=1
1270 D=ACS(D)
1280 W0=W2+SGN(SIN(W1-W2))*D
1290 IF W0=>0 THEN 1310
1300 W0=W0+P1
1310 IF W0<=P THEN 1330
1320 W0=W0-P1
1330 IF C=>-1 THEN 1360
1340 C=-1
1350 GO TO 1380
1360 IF C<=1 THEN 1380
1370 C=1
1380 L0=P0-ACS(C)
1390 Y1=0.0172*(10+(M0-1)*30.4+D6)
1400 Y2=0.409*COS(Y1)
1410 K8=3.82*W0+12+0.13*(SIN(Y1)+1.2*SIN(2*Y1))
1420 K8=K8-12*(1+SGN(K8-24))*SGN(ABS(K8-24))
1430 IF COS(L0+Y2)=>-0.26 THEN 1520
1440 K9=0
1450 G0=0
1460 M9=2.5*G1*K5
1470 IF M9<=P0 THEN 1490
1480 M9=P0
1490 M9=SIN(M9)
1500 M9=1+2.5*M9*SQR(M9)
1510 GO TO 1770
1520 K9=(-0.26+SIN(Y2)*SIN(L0))/(COS(Y2)*COS(L0)+1.0E-3)
1530 K9=12-ATN(K9/SQR(ABS(1-K9*K9)))*7.639437
1540 T=K8-K9/2+12*(1-SGN(K8-K9/2))*SGN(ABS(K8-K9/2))
1550 T4=K8+K9/2-12*(1+SGN(K8+K9/2-24))*SGN(ABS(K8+K9/2-24))
1560 C0=ABS(COS(L0+Y2))
1570 M9=9.7*C0↑9.6
1580 IF T9>0.1 THEN 1600
1590 T9=0.1
1600 M9=2.5*G1*K5
1610 IF M9<=P0 THEN 1630
1620 M9=P0
1630 M9=SIN(M9)
1640 M9=1+2.5*M9*SQR(M9)
1650 IF T4<T THEN 1680
1660 IF (T5-T)*(T4-T5)>0 THEN 1690
1670 GO TO 1820
1680 IF (T5-T4)*(T-T5)>0 THEN 1820
1690 T6=T5+12*(1+SGN(T-T5))*SGN(ABS(T-T5))
1700 G9=PI*(T6-T)/K9
1710 G8=PI*T9/K9
1720 U=(T-T6)/T9
1730 G0=C0*(SIN(G9)+G8*(EXP(U)-COS(G9)))/(1+G8*G8)
1740 G7=C0*(G8*(EXP(-K9/T9)+1))*EXP((K9-24)/2)/(1+G8*G8)
1750 IF G0=>G7 THEN 1770
1760 G0=G7
1770 G2=(1+S9/250)*M9*SQR(6+58*SQR(G0))
1780 G2=G2*(1-0.1*EXP((K9-24)/3))
1790 G2=G2*(1+(1-SGN(L2))*0.1)
1800 G2=G2*(1-0.1*(1+SGN(ABS(SIN(L0))-COS(L0))))
1810 GO TO 1880
1820 T6=T5+12*(1+SGN(T4-T5))*SGN(ABS(T4-T5))
1830 G8=PI*T9/K9
1840 U=(T4-T6)/2
1850 U1=-K9/T9
1860 G0=C0*(G8*(EXP(U1)+1))*EXP(U)/(1+G8*G8)
1870 GO TO 1770
1880 IF G2>J9 THEN 1900
1890 J9=G2
1900 NEXT K1
1910 RETURN
```

Amateur Radio's Collaboration with the Scientific Community

By Ward Silver, N0AX

In the beginning, the distinction between the scientific and amateur communities didn't exist. One of the first "amateurs" in our family tree, the self-taught Michael Faraday, discovered electromagnetic induction and mutual induction in the 1830s and later predicted the existence of electromagnetic waves. James Clerk Maxwell then integrated the work of Faraday and others into what became known as Maxwell's equations, establishing the theoretical basis of electromagnetism. It was not until 1886-1887 that Professor Heinrich Hertz demonstrated the existence of electromagnetic waves, using the first dipole and loop antennas to transmit VHF and UHF radio waves across his laboratory. The phenomenon of radio had begun.

The names associated with early wireless are numerous and legendary — Marconi, Fessenden, Tesla, Braun and many more worked tirelessly to establish practical systems of transmitting information with the new waves. As workable systems were developed, descriptions of them were published in the popular magazines and newspapers of the day. This led interested members of the public to build their own transmitters and receivers, using whatever materials they had on hand or could "re-purpose" from other devices and appliances.

Within a very short time after Marconi's initial success, what we can truly call Amateur Radio got its start, as described in the section "Amateur Radio in the Spark Era." Even though commercial and military professionals had begun to develop wireless technology in earnest, there was still plenty to be learned, and amateurs proved to be very capable at experimentation and observation.

These abilities and the amateurs' enthusiastic willingness to volunteer their services was quickly discovered by the research community, which began to make use of the increasingly widespread networks to collect and report data. Early propagation experiments, such as the National Bureau of Standards fading tests, relied heavily on amateurs to develop a data set from which the existence of the ionosphere as a reflecting medium could be deduced. Later, amateurs jumped into service in support of observation programs during the International Geophysical Year of 1957-1958. As a result of these efforts, propagation modes previously unknown to science (although not entirely unknown to amateurs) were studied and characterized.

The amateur's tenacity and know-how was also discovered and utilized by the expeditioners and explorers who were busily investigating the remaining untraveled regions on the surface of the Earth. On occasion, an amateur would travel with the expedition, such as the MacMillan expedition described in the *QST* article reproduced here, or the Gatti-Hallicrafters expedition to Africa after World War II. More frequently, amateurs would be put into service as receiving, relay or backup stations for the expedition's radio communications, such as during the polar expeditions of Admiral Byrd.

Amateurs even did original scientific work on their own, such as the groundbreaking radio astronomy of Grote Reber, W9GFZ. In this case, the entire field was literally invented by Reber, who combined his interest in astronomy with his Amateur Radio skills. During the 1930s, he was literally the only person on Earth listening to the radio sky! Amateur Radio also played a big part in Dr. Joe Taylor, K1JT's interest in radio astronomy, leading directly from a hobby to a Nobel Prize for his research on binary pulsars.

In November 1947, Bob Leo, W6PBV (now W7LR, standing) and Bill Snyder, W0LHS, were just getting familiar with the state-of-the-art Hallicrafters equipment before leaving on the 6-month Gatti-Hallicrafters expedition to Africa. [photo courtesy Bill Snyder, W0LHS]

While the scientific community has not engaged the amateur with the same vigor in recent years that it did decades ago, there have been recent experiments that involved our participation. For example, the listening tests conducted during March 1997 by the High Frequency Active Auroral Research Program (HAARP) facility (now mothballed) in Alaska received many high-quality reception reports from amateurs regarding signals transmitted near the 80 and 40 meter bands. For many years, amateur observers helped biologists track the burrowing owls on their annual migrations by listening for signals from miniature transmitters attached to the birds. There is no reason programs such as these could not continue to be conducted!

Is There Any Science Left for Amateurs?

Surely, with all of the resources and effort being expended around the globe, there can't be much place for the amateur in scientific discovery, can there? One can only be reminded of the consensus among scientists of the late 1800s that pretty much everything was understood, and once the nature of radioactivity and quantized energy were explored, all that remained would be to add significant digits to the appropriate physical constants! Now, as then, there remains plenty for the amateur to do, particularly in support of scientific research. For example, in the field of propagation, there remain significant questions as to how sporadic E propagation occurs. The ARRL's Logbook Of The World (**www.arrl.org/lotw**) is the world's largest database of validated point-to-point contacts in the MF, HF, VHF and UHF spectrum. As amateur equipment improves and automated monitoring networks continue to spread, more unexplained phenomena can be investigated with real data: spotlight propagation and the dawn enhancement in the upper medium frequency (MF) range, to name two.

Mark Spencer, WA8SME, constructed this sea-state monitoring buoy that logs air and sea temperature, air pressure, salinity and wave action along with GPS position data, transmitting it back to shore using APRS.

Direct collaboration between researchers and amateurs may take on additional importance in an age of reduced budgets and increasing sophistication of "civilian" equipment. Numerous amateur astronomers conduct regular monitoring of variable stars, so the process of integrating amateur data into professional experimentation is hardly new. What's needed is an active effort to provide a liaison to the research community, both to publicize amateur capabilities and to define and coordinate amateur participation.

A new application of Amateur Radio to scientific experimentation has "ballooned" in recent years, as well, as remote sensing and video or still images are transmitted from high-altitude balloons that travel to the edge of space. Some balloons have travelled across North America, and the Atlantic Ocean has even been spanned. Other vehicles such as remotely-piloted model aircraft and model rockets are also carrying Amateur Radio as part of their payloads. Marine platforms such as buoys are being outfitted with amateur transmitters to relay telemetry back to shore. This type of activity, leveraging the power of microcontrollers and digital protocols, is sure to continue its rapid advance.

Finally, it should be noted that while most early amateurs did not have access to the industrial-scale resources of the professionals and academics, they possessed two critical attributes in abundance: time and curiosity. This is as true today as it was a century ago. The amateur is free to spend as much time as is available investigating, observing, refining, speculating and considering. The amateur is similarly free of the imperative to produce practical results or discoveries in order to justify continued employment or funding. The amateur of the 21st century has the additional benefit of Internet access to a great deal of historic and current literature, continuous connections to a worldwide community of like-minded individuals, and computing resources that put the mainframes of the 20th century to shame. All this can be brought to bear on the interesting problems of the day. Even better, new questions can be asked, and that, perhaps, is the greatest value of all — to ponder entirely unconsidered areas of investigation. The physical world has many secrets yet to be discovered and there is no reason that the amateur should not participate in the grand hunt for them.

"The Bureau of Standards – A.R.R.L. Tests of Short Wave Radio Signal Fading" by S. Kruse

By Carl Luetzelschwab, K9LA

As the wavelengths used became shorter, fading became more severe. This was not just an Amateur Radio problem — wireless telegraph operators also experienced problems when fading was rapid and intensive. In the April 1920 issue of *QST*, Traffic Manager J. O. Smith requested reports from amateurs in an attempt to better understand fading so as to improve message handling.

Around this time, the Bureau of Standards realized the importance of understanding fading with respect to military and commercial applications and also realized that Amateur Radio offered a large database from which to draw. Bureau personnel met with the ARRL to come up with a joint proposal for fading tests in the summer of 1920 as reported in *QST* for July 1920.

S. Kruse (an Assistant Electrical Engineer at the Bureau of Standards) discussed the results of these tests in the November and December 1920 issues of *QST*. The six transmitting stations (five were amateurs) were 1AW in West Hartford; 2JU on Long Island; NSF (the Naval Aircraft Radio Laboratory at the Naval Air

1EK Robert D. Huston, 19 Nevens St., Portland, Maine.
1FB Lawrence C. Cumming, Prout's Neck, Maine.
1HAA Irving Vermilya, Marion, Mass.
1NAQ J. C. Randall, 23 Harrison St., Hartford, Conn.
1SN Wm. B. A. Dodge, Beverly, Mass.
1TS Donald H. Mix, 40 Stearns St., Bristol, Conn.
1YB F. L. Southworth, Sec., Dartmouth College Radio Assn., Hanover, N. H.
2BG A. J. Lorimer, 243 Mackay St., Montreal, Quebec.

A. R. R. L. FADING REPORT

Receiving station call______Location________________Date_________

Time observations begin_________General reception this date_________

____

______________________________General character of strays

("static") this date______________________________

_____________ Transmitting station call_______ Wave length _____m.

Weather, wind direction, and strength, indicated by check mark below.

Weather:	Wind Direction:	Wind Strength:
Clear	N	Calm
Cloudy	NE	Light
Rain	E	Medium
Snow	SE	Strong
Sleet	S	Storm
Fog	SW	
Lightning	W	
	NW	

SIGNAL STRENGTH RECORD. Indicate average strength for each letter by a check mark (✓) in the proper square below.

	A	B	C	D	E	F	G	H	I	J	K	L	M	N	O	P	Q	R	S	T	U	V	W	X	Y	Z	
Very strong 9																											9
Strong 8																											8
Good 7																											7
Fair 6																											6
Rather faint 5																											5
Faint 4																											4
Just readable 3																											3
Very faint, unreadable 2																											2
Just audible 1																											1
Nothing 0																											0
	A	B	C	D	E	F	G	H	I	J	K	L	M	N	O	P	Q	R	S	T	U	V	W	X	Y	Z	

Fig. 9

____
Receiving Operator

A propagation reporting form used during the Bureau of Standards fading tests.

Station in Anacostia, DC); 8XK in Pittsburgh; 9ZN in Chicago; and 8ER in Ohio. There were 14 receiving stations, and additionally the transmitting stations listened when not transmitting. Standard reporting forms were utilized for ease of analyzing data as shown in the accompanying figure.

The figure below illustrates a typical plot of the resulting data (2 of a total of 1260 plots — quite a bit of data was generated!). The top plot is from 2OE (a coastal station in Freeport, New York) listening to 1AW on July 8, 1920. The bottom plot is 9ZJ (an inland station in Indianapolis much farther away) listening to 1AW at the same time on the same day. The horizontal axis consists of the time slots when 1AW was transmitting, and the vertical axis is the relative signal strength.

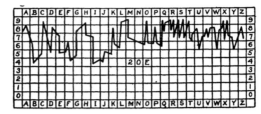

Transmission by 1AW July 8, 1920.

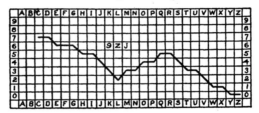

Received signal strength at 2OE (Freeport, New York) and 9ZJ (Indianapolis, Indiana) from 1AW transmissions from West Hartford, Connecticut.

Preliminary Conclusions

Fading in New England appeared to be the worst, with less severe fading as one went south or southwest. At points in Pennsylvania, Ohio, Indiana, Illinois and Michigan, fading was not even approximately as bad as in New England.

Three types of fading were identified — very rapid and very abrupt (period of ½ to 5 seconds), moderately rapid and more gradual (period of 10 seconds to 5 minutes), and a very gradual slow drift (period of 5 minutes to several hours).

Fading was not solely a land phenomenon. Data from the USS Ohio (150 miles east of Cape May, New Jersey) explicitly showed this.

It was stressed that these conclusions, because of the transmitting station and receiving station locations, favored the northeast quarter of the US. Reasons for this included a lack of stations in the southeast and southwest portions of the country. Also cited was a limit on the number of plots that could be analyzed. Remember, everything was done manually back then — there were no computers available to crunch data.

Regardless of the limitations of these fading tests, lots of good information was collected showing that amateurs could contribute to the science of radio. And more importantly, theories were put forward based on the data to explain the results (these theories needed much more work based on subsequent data and a better understanding of the ionosphere).

The Bureau of Standards---A.R.R.L. Tests of Short Wave Radio Signal Fading

By S. Kruse
Assistant Electrical Engineer, Bureau of Standards

Presented at meeting of the Radio Club of America, Columbia University, September 24, 1920

PART I.

THE Bureau of Standards—A.R.R.L. tests of short wave radio signal fading were run co-operatively by the Radio Laboratory, Bureau of Standards, and the American Radio Relay League for the purpose of gaining information useful in determining the cause of the swinging or fading of radio signals. The work was divided between the two organizations, the selection of stations and actual performance of the tests falling to the A.R.R.L.; while the work of general supervision, preparing the recording forms, correspondence, and the analysis of the results were done by the Bureau of Standards.

Test signals were transmitted by six stations each Tuesday, Thursday and Saturday night, from June 1 to July 17, 1920, inclusive. Five of the transmitting stations were A.R.R.L. stations. The sixth was the station at the Radio Laboratory of the Naval Air Station, Anacostia, D. C.

It is perhaps best to begin a discussion of this kind by defining the term "swinging" or "fading" of signals. This can best be done by example. Supposing that we are listening, at the Radio Laboratory in Washington to station 1HAA at Marion, Mass. 1HAA will call and be received with normal intensity, will begin the preamble of his message still at normal intensity, and then, as he starts to send the text, the signals rapidly become very much louder until within a few seconds they can be heard all over an ordinary room. Then as he proceeds the signals become fainter and may become so weak as to be unreadable or even inaudible for a number of words, and then again begin to become louder, so that by the time the station signs off, the signals are again very loud. It can readily be seen that this kind of thing makes communication very difficult, and on many occasions requires repetition time after time of a message which could otherwise be copied "solid" the first time. In short-wave work swinging is so prevalent that a standard abbreviation has been devised to inform the sending station that his signals are swinging, and at present, in amateur communication this abbreviation, "QSS", is heard quite as often as QRM and QRN, which mean respectively "interference" and "atmospherics," the other two worst difficulties encountered in short wave communication. It is then of interest to attempt to find some explanation as to the cause of swinging, with the possibility in mind that if we know the cause, there may be a remote chance of avoiding the difficulty. Swinging has not been much investigated in the past, for several reasons. It is primarily a long-distance phenomenon, that is to say, long-distance compared to the range of the station which is sending. Most commercial communication is done well within the range of the transmitting station where not much swinging is encountered. In addition to this, commercial communication is done on long wave lengths on which swinging is not very severe nor very rapid. At present, however, the use of short-wave sets is very much on the increase, not only in amateur practice but also by airplanes, in military work, and in low-power ship communication. It seems worth while to attempt to investigate fading at short waves particularly. Naturally, since our ideas as to the cause of fading are rather vague, an investigation depending on a network of stations (rather than one sending and one receiving station) would be the most instructive. The thought that data on the fading of radio signals can be secured by co-operation with a network of amateur radio stations follows at once, as it is here only that one can find a large number of well equipped short-wave stations whose operators are thoroughly familiar with the apparatus and also able to give time and effort to the performance of an investigation. Last spring, therefore, I suggested to Mr. L. E. Whittemore of the Radio Laboratory of the Bureau of Standards that we place before the American Radio Relay League a plan for a system of fading tests in which the A.R.R.L. stations would do the transmitting and receiving, while the supervisory and clerical work and the analysis of data fell to our laboratory. During the following week such a plan was worked out tentatively by Mr. L. E. Whittemore, Miss H. H. Smith and myself.

Laboratory tests of the method of recording the variations in signal intensity having shown that satisfactory results could be secured without the use of any instruments other than the regular receiving equipment, the Bureau of Standards then officially proposed the plan to the A.R.R.L. The plans were received favorably, especially as they offered an opportunity of finding out with some definiteness what could be done in the way of summer transmission with amateur stations. It has developed since that Mr. H. P. Maxim, and Mr. K. B. Warner, respectively President and Secretary of the A.R.R.L., had discussed a similar plan and were about to write to the Bureau when our letter was received.

The plans for the tests were completed at a conference in the Bureau of Standards Radio Laboratory on April 7 at which there were present: for the American Radio Relay League, Mr. H. P. Maxim, and Mr. K. B. Warner; and for the Bureau of Standards, Dr. J. H. Dellinger, Mr. L. E. Whittemore, and the writer. Commander A. H. Taylor, USNRF, in charge of the Radio Laboratory, Naval Air Station, Anacostia, D. C., as well as Dr. S. J. Mauchley and Mr. A. Sterling of the Department of Terrestrial Magnetism, Carnegie Institution, Washington, were present and offered valuable suggestions. The tentative plans were brought into working shape, and the sending stations agreed upon. Mr. Maxim and Mr. Warner offered the use of their station 1AW at Hartford, Conn., and Commander Taylor the use of station NSF at Anacostia, subject to the approval of the Navy Department. Commander Taylor's offer of NSF was opportune as there was no Washington station capable of good 250-meter transmission which was available for the tests. Both 1AW and NSF did excellent work in the test series, the transmission of the latter station being at times little short of phenomenal.

During the following weeks, Mr. K. B. Warner and the officers of the Traffic Department of the A.R.R.L. did much hard

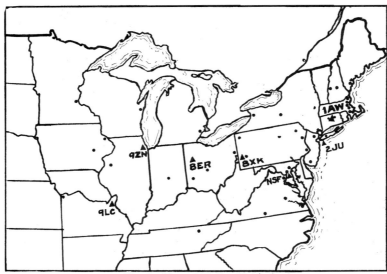

Fig. 1—Map of Station Network.

work in selecting recorders properly located, and known to be well enough equipped as to apparatus and experience, who could also find time to take part in the tests.

The Station Network

The station network finally developed is shown in Fig. 1 where the sending stations are indicated by triangles with the call of the station alongside, while the recorders are indicated by circular dots. There were seven sending stations and fifty-one recorders.

Considerable criticism of the lay-out of the fading system was occasioned by the fact that only the northeast quarter of the United States was covered. There were reasons for this. There were almost no stations in the southeast part of the country and not a great many in the southwest. Also such stations as there are, report comparatively little fading. It seemed, then, that not a great deal of information would be obtained from the southern stations. In addition, there is a limit to the number of curves which can be analysed. The amount of work involved in handling the 1260 curves which were received can hardly be appreciated by anyone who has not attempted a job of this kind. The decision to confine the tests to the northeast was a unanimous one in the conference, and the results have shown it to be sufficiently correct. Experimentally the A.R.R.L. has run some nation-wide tests, largely to see what transmission conditions were. The reason for the wider spacing of stations west of Pittsburgh is a double one. To begin with, there are fewer stations west of Pittsburgh, and although it might have been possible to secure as many west of Pittsburgh as we did to the east, we did not think this was necessary. The winter range of stations in the Mississippi and Ohio Valleys is enormous compared to that of eastern stations. It did not occur to us that the Mississippi Valley summer conditions are enormously different from the winter conditions, while on the eastern coast ranges do not change particularly with the season. The station arrangement, therefore, which would have been satisfactory for a winter test was not so for the summer test. The western stations, 9ZN at Chicago and 9LC at St. Louis, were working under a considerable handicap, and it became necessary later to add station 8ER at St. Marys, Ohio, in an effort to secure more complete records.

Station Description—Senders.

1AW—Station 1AW at Hartford, Conn., is operated by Mr. H. P. Maxim, President of the A.R.R.L., and Mr. K. B. Warner, Secretary of the same organization. 1AW does not need much advertising. The station location is directly to the east of a large hill toward which the antenna is directive. There are no hills to the north or south and the country is level to the east for about two miles, after which it drops sharply to the Connecticut River. The soil is a heavy clay which is usually very wet in the winter. The station is surrounded by houses at a distance of about 75 feet, and there are trees in all directions except east. The antenna (Fig. 2)[1] is a bent fan of 17 wires spaced three feet apart at the high end and which is elevated 80 feet. All wires are continued through the spreader at the low end (elevation 50 feet) to the anchor gap at the transmitting apparatus which is located in the basement. The ground system consists of a network of buried wires as well as wires to ground rods and to all the metal pipes in the building. The radiating system has a resistance of 5 ohms and a capacity of 0.0011 microfarad. The sending set (Fig. 3)[1] is of the 60-cycle non-synchronous rotary gap type. Either an Acme or Thordarson transformer is used. In either case the input is about 780 watts. A Dubilier mica condenser of 0.01 microfarad capacity is used. The rotary gap is unusual, consisting of a shaft mounted in bronze bearings and carrying 4 metal arms revolving between two fixed electrodes. The rotor diameter is 15 inches and the speed 7000 RPM. It will be seen that while the spark rate is low the peripheral speed of this gap is very much higher than usual. Because of the high speed, or perhaps because of the compressed air traveling before the rotating electrodes, unusually good quenching is obtained so that close coupling with consequent high efficiency may be used. The normal antenna current is 5½ amperes and the decrement quite low.

The second station, **2JU**, operated by Mr. C. J. Goette, is located in Woodhaven, L. I., near Jamaica Bay. There are no large buildings or trees in the neighborhood and the land is very level and slightly marshy.

The antenna is a four-wire L, 50 feet high, 85 feet long, and 10 feet wide. The ground system consists of a lead to the water pipe and an eight-wire fan buried directly under the antenna which is directive eastward.

The sending set (Fig. 4)[2] employs a United Wireless 1-k.w. open-core transformer with a 30,000 volt secondary. This transformer is well known among amateurs under the nickname of "the coffin," which its box resembles. The condenser consists of two Dubilier mica units in series. Each unit has a capacity of 0.014 microfarad. The oscillation transformer is the familiar "pancake". The rotary gap is of

---
1. Omitted. See July 1920 QST, page 35.
2. Omitted. See August 1920 QST, page 35.

the gear type, having eight teeth, and is driven by a synchronous motor. A tone differing noticeably from that of a non-synchronous rotary is obtained.

NSF is the Naval Aircraft Radio Laboratory at the Naval Air Station, Anacostia, D. C. This station is under the direction of Commander A. Hoyt Taylor, USNRF. The transmitting set at NSF employs two electron tubes of the General Electric type P. (Navy type CG916) operating in parallel. The filament and plate circuits are fed by the same motor generator set, and the total input to the tubes is about one kilowatt. The plate circuit supply is at 2000 volts direct current, the tone being produced by a motor driven chopper disc, which is placed in series with the key as a shunt to the grid condenser so that the tubes block and cease oscillating whenever either the key or the chopper opens the circuit. The circuit is the familiar one sometimes referred to as the Meissner circuit, both grid and plate circuits being untuned and coupled to the common antenna coil. The antenna is a multiple tuned one 75 feet high and 235 feet long with three down-leads, to the center one of which the sending set is coupled. At 250 meters the current in each down-lead is 2.3 amperes, thus giving a total of 6.9 amperes in the antenna.

For transmitting speech the above described set is used as a power amplifier, the grid being adjusted so that the set does not oscillate. To the grid is coupled the output circuit of a small aircraft radio telephone set. The antenna currents are nearly the same for telephone as when using the set in the ordinary manner.

8XK, the fourth testing station, operated by Mr. F. Conrad of the Westinghouse Electric and Mfg. Co., Pittsburgh, Pa , has become very well known during the past winter as one of the very few short-wave, high-power, ICW stations. The antenna system at 8XK consists of a 6-wire L antenna 120 feet long, suspended 50 feet from the ground over a similar counterpoise elevated 12 feet. A third network buried beneath the counterpoise is used as a ground.

The sending set (Fig. 5)[3] employs two transmitting tubes of a type similar to the General Electric Company's "U" type in the familiar circuit using one coil as a common antenna, plate and grid coil. The plate power is obtained from a ½-kilowatt 110-volt, 900-cycle generator from an airplane transmitter of the type employed on the NC planes. This generator is driven by a direct current motor at such a speed that the frequency is 700 cycles. A transformer steps the 110-volt supply up to 3000 volts which is applied to the plates of the tubes through a high-frequency choke coil. No chopper is necessary to secure an audible tone with this type of transmitter. The antenna current is normally about 5½ amperes. This is measured in the antenna lead.

9ZN—Station 9ZN at Chicago, operated by Mr. R. H. G. Mathews is perhaps the best known station in the network, 9ZN having operated under the present call since several years before the war and during the time doing excellent long-distance work. 9ZN is located in a vacant block on Sheridan Road within 30 feet of the sea wall of Lake Michigan. The aerial (Fig. 6)[4] hung between two steel towers is a vertical fan of 10 wires spaced 15 feet apart at the top and brought together near the station roof; all wires continue through to the antenna switch. The height of the fan is 95 feet. The grounding system consists of 28 wires 30 and 150 feet long buried inshore from the station. In addition, two 100-foot wires in the lake and a considerable number of ground rods near the station are used. The fundamental wave length of the antenna is 300 meters. For miles around 9ZN the country is some of the most level in the United States. The soil is very thin and is underlaid by many feet of sand, which is moist at all times. Two transmitting sets are used at 9ZN, one of which is a 500-cycle Telefunken set, (Fig. 7)[4] no detailed description of which is available. In the 60-cycle non-synchronous rotary gap set the transformer is a United Wireless open-core "coffin" similar to the one used at 2JU. The condenser is of plate glass in oil with about 0.008 microfarad capacity, the rotary gap a seven-point gear type driven at 3600 r.p.m. The antenna current at 9ZN is unusually high, about 8.7 amperes at 250 meters, and somewhat over 9 amperes at 425 meters. This is probably an indication of very low antenna resistance.

8ER—Station 8ER at St. Mary's, Ohio, is operated by Mr. and Mrs. Charles Candler. 8ER under its pre-war call of 8NH established a record, unequalled, I believe, by any other amateur station, of being heard in every state of the Union. The location of 8ER is unusually favorable. The country about St. Mary's is absolutely level. There are no hills for many miles in all directions. Even along the streams the land is very flat. There are no tall buildings near 8ER and only a few large trees to the east. All stations in this portion of Ohio are able to do unusually good work. The antenna is a six-wire L, 55 feet high and 65 feet long. The grounding system consists of a number of 7-foot ground rods also connected to the water

---

3. Omitted. See September 1920 QST, page 32.

4. Omitted. See January 1920 QST.

pipes and to a cistern. No information is available as to the antenna characteristics. The sending set is of the non-synchronous type with 60-cycle supply, Thordarson transformer, gear type rotary, and glass plate condenser in oil.

9LC—9LC at St. Louis is the only one-half kilowatt station in the system. It is operated by Mr. W. E. Woods, who has become well known in connection with his work at the Otter Cliffs receiving station of the Navy Department and his pre-war work with station 9HS at St. Louis. There are no tall buildings or trees near 9LC. There is a street car line about 200 feet from, and parallel to, the antenna but no interference has been experienced. Not much is known about the topography near 9LC. In general the country about St. Louis is flat. The antenna is a five-wire

a shunt condenser but by means of a variable inductor in series with the secondary. A great increase in sensitiveness is secured, as the ratio of inductance to capacity in the circuit is much improved over that obtained when using a shunt condenser. The plate circuit of the tube contains another variable inductor by means of which the degree of regeneration can be controlled. For spark or ICW reception the set is usually operated with the largest degree of regeneration which will not distort the spark tone. Far more regeneration can be used with low spark tones than with high. It is possible that this is the reason why a low spark rate has been found far more effective in amateur practice than the high pitches favored in commercial work. Almost without exception the recorders used a "soft" or gas

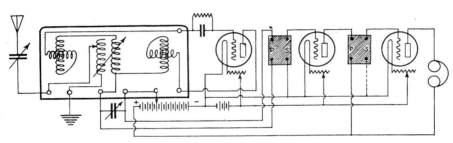

Fig. 8—Paragon receiving set circuit.

L, 55 feet high, 65 feet long, and 12 feet wide. The sending set consists of an Acme ½-kilowatt transformer, six Murdock condenser sections, of 0.0017 capacity each, connected in parallel and oil immersed to prevent brushing between leads. Either a quenched gap or a Benwood enclosed rotary is used. The Benwood rotary is a gear type gap enclosed in an air-tight aluminum case which serves not only to muffle the crash of the discharge but also provides a more favorable atmosphere for good quenching. The radiation is 4½ amperes at a decrement of 0.03. 9LC had, during the past winter, a range attained by very few one-kilowatt stations. During these tests, however, the unusually severe summer conditions of the Mississippi Valley did not give this station the opportunity to perform as well as some of the others in the system.

Station Description—Recorders.

With a single exception every recording station used a short wave receiving set of the type originally put on the market under the name of the Paragon receiver by the Adams-Morgan Co. The circuit of this set is shown in Fig. 8. The tuning of the primary circuit is accomplished by means of a switch on the inductance and a series condenser in the antenna lead. The secondary circuit is not tuned by means of

tube as the detector and "hard" or high vacuum tubes for the amplifier. Minor variations of the circuit occurred, such as the provision of taps on the B battery as a means of varying the plate voltage of the detector tube.

The recorders, with few exceptions, used four or six wire L antennas about 60 feet high and 60 feet long. These were suspended by means of electrose insulators and, in most cases, copper wire, No. 12 or thereabouts, or 7 strand phosphor bronze, was used. The ground connections in most cases were to water pipes; in some cases to buried networks. A few recorders used harp antennas.

All of the transmitting operators except the one actually sending at the time acted as recorders. The stations which served as recorders only are listed below:

Additional Recorders.

1AE S. B. Young, 294 Ashmont St., Dorchester, Mass.
1AK H. C. Bowen, 168 Belmont St., Fall River, Mass.
1BG G. Faxon Shorey, Melrose, Mass.
1CK P. F. Robinson, 149 Hollis Ave., Braintree, Mass.
1CM H. B. McLane, 342 Union Ave., Laconia, N. H.
1DG Stuart Briggs, 94 Walnut Place, Brookline, Mass.

1EK Robert D. Huston, 19 Nevens St., Portland, Maine.
1FB Lawrence C. Cumming, Prout's Neck, Maine.
1HAA Irving Vermilya, Marion, Mass.
1NAQ J. C. Randall, 23 Harrison St., Hartford, Conn.
1SN Wm. E. A. Dodge, Beverly, Mass.
1TS Donald H. Mix, 40 Stearns St., Bristol, Conn.
1YB F. L. Southworth, Sec., Dartmouth College Radio Assn., Hanover, N. H.
2BG A. J. Lorimer, 243 Mackay St., Montreal, Quebec.

A. R. R. L. FADING REPORT

Receiving station call_____ Location_____ Date_____
Time observations begin_____ General reception this date_____
_____
_____General character of strays
("static") this date_____
_____Transmitting station call_____ Wave length_____m.

Weather, wind direction, and strength, indicated by check mark below.
Weather: Clear   Wind Direction: N   Wind Strength: Calm
          Cloudy   NE   Light
          Rain   E   Medium
          Snow   SE   Strong
          Sleet   S   Storm
          Fog   SW
          Lightning   W
                                       NW

SIGNAL STRENGTH RECORD. Indicate average strength for each letter by a check mark (✓) in the proper square below.

		A	B	C	D	E	F	G	H	I	J	K	L	M	N	O	P	Q	R	S	T	U	V	W	X	Y	Z	
Very strong	9																											9
Strong	8																											8
Good	7																											7
Fair	6																											6
Rather faint	5																											5
Faint	4																											4
Just readable	3																											3
Very faint, unreadable	2																											2
Just audible	1																											1
Nothing	0																											0
		A	B	C	D	E	F	G	H	I	J	K	L	M	N	O	P	Q	R	S	T	U	V	W	X	Y	Z	

Fig. 9

_____
Receiving Operator

2BK C. E. Trube, 6 Livingston Ave., Yonkers, N. Y.
2FG F. H. Myers, 45 Albany Trust Bldg., Albany, N. Y.
2JE J. L. Eddy, Jr., 19 Washington St., New Rochelle, N. Y.
2OE S. L. Raynor, College Court, Freeport, N. Y.
2TT A. Rechert, 181 Waverly Place, New York City.
2YM YMCA Radio Club, 153 E. 86th St., New York City.
2ZM L. M. Spangenberg, 25 South Fourth Lake View, N. J.
3BZ W. T. Gravely, Danville, Va.
3EN T. C. White, Jr., 303 Riverview Ave., Norfolk, Va.
3JR H. A. Snow, 1656 Newton St., NW., Washington, D. C.
3NB Marcus Frye, Jr., Box 187, Vineland, N. J.
3SU A. B. Chism, 3729 M St., N.W., Washington, D. C.
3UA E. B. Duvall, 4004 Park Heights Ave, Baltimore, Md.
3ZA C. A. Service, Jr., Bala, Pa.
3ZS C. H. Stewart, St. Davids, Pa.
4AT O. A. Gulledge, Ft. Pierce, Fla.
5DA W. C. Hutcheson, Wind Rock, Tenn.
8AAN A. H. Benzee, Jr., 207 Sumner Pl., Buffalo, N. Y.
8ABI Harrison Daniels, 424 W. First St., Dayton, Ohio.
8BQ H. M. Walleze, 234 Vine St., Milton, Pa.
8CE R. C. Ehrhardt, 117 South Blakely, Dunmore, Pa.
8DA A. J. Manning, 252 McKinley Ave., Salem, Ohio.
8ER Mr. and Mrs. Charles Candler, St. Marys, Ohio.
8IB R. C. Higgy, 50 E. 18th Ave., Columbus, Ohio.
8WY Lord Bros., 531 Beach Ave., Cambridge Springs, Pa.
8XU Sibley College, Cornell University, Ithaca, N. Y.
8ZW J. C. Stroebel, Jr., Wheeling, W. Va.
9DT C. W. Patch, Villa St., Dubuque, Iowa.
9ET W. L. Tomson, 1163 North Broad St, Galesburg, Ill.
9NQ J. H. Burke, Galesburg, Ill.
9ZC J. A. Gjelhaug, P. O. Box 154, Baudette, Minn.
9ZJ F. F. Hamilton, North Alabama St., Indianapolis, Ind.
9ZL H. J. Burhop, Naval Radio Station, Manitowoc, Wisc.
WWV S. Kruse, Radio Laboratory, Bureau of Standards, Washington.
NSF L. C. Young, Radio Laboratory, Naval Air Station, Anacostia, D. C.

Operation

The network performed excellently throughout. After the first two days in which the usual delays occurred, no sending station failed to transmit its test schedule excepting on a very few occasions when the cause of the failure was beyond the control of the operator. The average distance of transmission was 400 miles. When it is considered that no station in the system used an input of over one kilowatt, that communication was at 250 meters where static is usually at its worst, and that the season was the most unfavorable for radio work, it would seem that only very meager results could be expected. Actually, however, an average of 26 recorders stood watch every evening and on no occasion were less than 20 on duty. This performance did not decrease during the period of the tests, the operators having the necessary interest to spend night after night at their instruments struggling with the uproar due to atmospherics. More than half of the schedules listened for were copied in the form of 1260 curves sufficiently good to be used in the final analysis.

The tests were all made at a wave length of 250 meters, under permits issued by the Radio Inspection Service, Department of Commerce. These permits were not necessary for the special amateur stations 9ZN and 8XK nor for the Naval Station NSF. The method of recording the variations of signal intensity is shown in Fig. 9. The test schedule consisted of the alphabet, each letter sent five times at a speed equal to eighteen words per minute, so that the alphabet required about three minutes for transmission. As each letter was received the operator indicated on this chart the intensity at which it was heard, so that when the schedule was complete a curve had been secured showing the swinging during the three-minute period. The intensity scale used may not seem especially satisfactory but its use was unavoidable since an audibility meter cannot be used satisfactorily with a regenerative receiving set, and as a matter of fact; the performance of the method is very good under severe tests. A laboratory test of the method can be seen in Fig. 10. Buzzer transmission of the actual schedule was sent through the primary of an ordinary coupler to the secondary of which two headsets were connected in series. The operators independently recorded the intensity of signals which was varied during transmission by altering the coupling. It will be seen that the curves are alike excepting as to the judgment of the average strength of the signals, so that one curve lies higher on the chart than the other. Many such tests were made, and in no case were the results less satisfactory than those shown on this chart. A test of the method under actual operating conditions is shown in Fig. 11, where Mr. K. B. Warner and H. P. Maxim, at 1AW, Hartford, Conn., recorded the signals from 2JU at Woodhaven, Long Island, simultaneously. The curves do not represent variations in received power since a receiving set operating near the critical point at which it begins to regenerate has something of the characteristics of a generating set and amplifies weak signals more than strong ones.

Method of Testing

The method of running an actual test was as follows: At 10 p.m., eastern standard time, all the sending stations listened for time from Arlington. At 10:10 the first station, 1AW, at Hartford, Conn., (Fig. 1) made a long QST call, saying repeatedly "Bureau of Standards—A.R.R.L. Fading Test." Both the call and the notice were repeated, then the station started to send the test schedule, repeating each letter five times as has been mentioned. All recorders able to hear 1AW tuned in during the QST, and thereafter left all adjustments alone and recorded signal intensity. After the schedule 1AW signed off.

Three tests were made each week, on Tuesday, Thursday and Saturday evenings, the transmission by 1AW coming at 10:10 p.m. eastern standard time, 2JU at 10:20, NSF at 10:30, 8XK at 10:40, 9ZN at 10:50, 9LC at 11:00. After being added to the list of senders, 8ER also transmitted at 11:00. The ranges are sufficiently small in the Mississippi Valley during the sum-

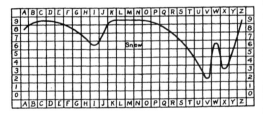

Laboratory Test of Recording Method

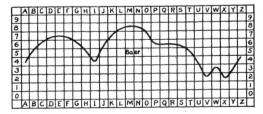

Fig. 10

mer time so that no interference occurred between 8ER and 9LC.

On every test night each recorder who was on watch filled out one curve sheet (Fig. 9) for each sender that he could hear. At the close of the week he sent in all the sheets made during that week. The original intention to record atmospherics, by means of the various symbols shown, was abandoned as no recorder was able to note signal and static strength simultaneously. Weather conditions are shown roughly by checking the proper words at the lower left corner of the sheet. Recorders were asked to indicate on the lines above the chart, the swinging at various waves,

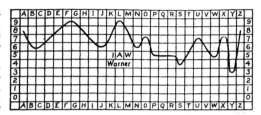

Transmission by 2JU – July 1, 1920

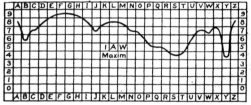

Fig. 11—Two operators receiving at same station.

general reception conditions on various waves, and any special conditions. Most of them did this very well and also used this space for indicating general static conditions during the evening. The exact method of recording varied, as it was modified during the tests by reason of improvements suggested by the observers. At first our impression was that the swinging would be very slow, hence the intention was to use a check mark for each group of five letters. This was not adequate as the swinging was often more rapid than could be so shown. Several observers suggested a different observation form in which one column was allowed for each letter, that is to say, five times as many columns as in the present form. This would have been good but clumsy; even the present form is exceedingly unhandy when large numbers must be analyzed. Another suggestion was that a continuous curve be drawn by moving the pencil slowly as the signals come in. This sounds well, but in practice is subject to violent errors when long slow fading takes place, as the temptation to keep the pencil moving in the same direction is irresistible when the curve has continued in the same direction for, say, 20 seconds. The result of this tendency, which appeared both in the field and in laboratory tests, is that slow

(Continued on page 37)

**BUREAU OF STANDARDS—A.R.R.L.
TESTS OF SHORT WAVE
RADIO SIGNAL FADING**
(Concluded from page 12)

swings are exaggerated, turns in the curve appear too late, and small variations are omitted. Mr. L. C. Young of NSF suggested the method which proved best in practice, that of using dots for each letter and drawing in the curve later. In this way, attention is paid to each letter, and the tendency for the pencil to acquire a "drift" is checked.

(Part II, to be presented in the December QST, will describe the results of these tests, illustrated with curves of various classes of fading.)

The Bureau of Standards---A.R.R.L. Tests of Short Wave Radio Signal Fading

By S. Kruse

Assistant Electrical Engineer, Bureau of Standards

Presented at meeting of the Radio Club of America, Columbia University, September 24, 1920

PART II.

Results of Tests.

The test system began operations June 1, 1920. The results here given are, with few exceptions, those obtained on the test sheets of the last four weeks of the run, that is to say, from June 15 to July 17. The first three weeks of the test were run while winter conditions were gradually changing to summer ones and before the system had gotten properly under way. As three other tests are to be run during the other seasons it was thought best to consider the last part of this test which was run in summer weather. The additional information which could have been obtained from analysis of the first three weeks of the test would not at all have compensated for the additional men and labor involved. The results of transmission by station 9LC at St. Louis, Mo., were also eliminated as only a few records of any value were obtained. As has been explained, station 8ER at St.

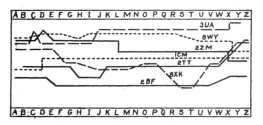

Transmission by 9ZN July 8, 1920

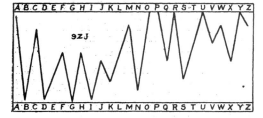

Fig. 12—Normal 9ZN curves.

Marys, Ohio, was added to the transmission system and the records on this station are considered instead of those on 9LC.

During the entire first week, the curves that were received seemed to mean nothing. In Fig. 12 are shown representative curves for station 9ZN. Those in the upper half of the sheet which were secured

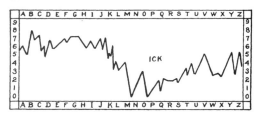

Transmission by 8XK - July 6, 1920.

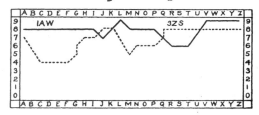

Fig. 13—Normal 8XK curves.

by 3UA at Baltimore; 8WY at Cambridge Springs, Pa.; 2ZM at Clifton, N. J.; 1CM at Laconia, N. H.; 2TT at Yonkers, N. Y.; 8XK at Pittsburgh, Pa.; and 2BF at Montreal, Canada, are entirely representative curves for this station, which has the distinction of fading less than any other station in the system, its peculiarity being that it is, in general, heard steadily or else not at all. The curve below, which was secured at 9ZJ at Indianapolis, is a very unusual one for transmission from 9ZN and would lead to the suspicion that the receiving apparatus at 9ZJ was at fault, except for the fact that on this and other evenings normal curves were secured on all other stations at 9ZJ and almost without fail 9ZN swung violently. In Fig. 13 are shown some curves secured from transmission of 8XK at Pittsburgh, Pa. 8XK swung more rapidly than any other station in the test, often going from extremely

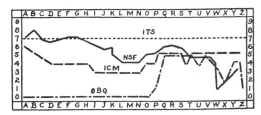

Fig. 14—Normal curves on 2JU.

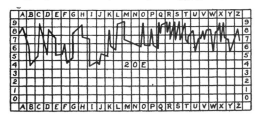

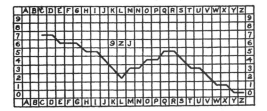

Fig. 15—1AW as copied on coast and inland.

seldom being as steady as 9ZN nor varying as violently as 8XK. Typical curves for 2JU are shown in Fig. 14 and for 1AW as copied on the coast and inland in Fig. 15.

Check Curves

The tests had not been in progress very long, however, before the first evidence began to appear that we were securing some sort of information. This evidence first appeared in the shape of similar curves from various receiving stations. At Washington there were four recording stations. Two of these, (3JR and WWV) are about one mile apart. The curves obtained at 3JR were generally checked with fair accuracy by WWV when that station was on watch, which unfortunately was not often. The curves at 3SU, about four miles southwest,

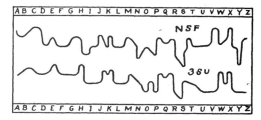

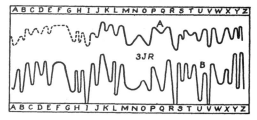

Fig. 16—Check by three stations.

could be depended upon to check the curves of 3JR and WWV with fair exactness about half the time. At other times only partial checks were secured or else the curves were of totally different shape. NSF, Naval Air Station, Anacostia, 5 miles south, was several times checked by 3SU and 3JR but not by WWV. We do not believe that this failure to check throughout the group was the fault of any of the observers, as at the same time that NSF failed to check with any other Washington observer it checked with 3NB at Vineland, N. J., while at the same time 3SU and 3JR checked each other. In several instances 3JR was checked by 3UA in Baltimore, 40 miles northeast. An excellent example of the group check is shown in Fig. 16. The first two curves, obtained by 3SU and NSF, are sufficiently alike, so that there is no doubt of their checking. The curve turned in by 3JR, labeled $3JR_b$, at first

loud to absolute silence in less time than is taken to sound one letter of the Continental alphabet. The sensation when receiving 8XK is exactly as if someone opened the antenna switch and instantly reclosed it. The intensity of signals does not vary slowly—letters simply drop out. The curve shown in the figure which was secured at 1CK, Braintree, Mass., is not a typical 8XK curve, as in this case the variations, while rapid, were gradual enough to form some sort of a curve. The curves shown below, which were secured at 3ZS in St. Davids, Pa., and at 1AW in Hartford, Conn., are not at all typical of 8XK, and, in fact, for this station amount to freaks. 2JU, 1AW, NSF, 8ER and 9LC lay between these limits, fading rapidly at times, slowly at others, and

sight has no resemblance to the other two; however, when it was redrawn with an amplitude the same as that of the other two curves, the resemblance at once appeared. This is the curve labeled 3JR₁.

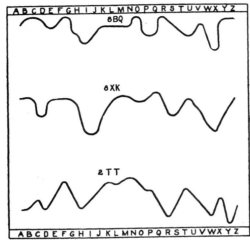

Fig. 17—Checks by distant stations.

It is believed that by this time there will be little doubt that the method is capable of securing results which indicate definitely in what manner the signals are varying at a given receiving station, so long as the signals do not vary with extreme rapidity, in which case audibility meters or any other device known at present for measuring signal intensity variation would be perfectly hopeless.

An example of check curves from stations some distance apart is shown in Fig. 17 on the transmission of NSF July 8. The recorders are 2TT in Yonkers, 8XK at Pittsburgh, and 8BQ at Milton, Pa.

Regional Characteristics.

In New England violent and rapid swinging seems to be the rule. This grows less severe as one goes south or southwest and at points in Pennsylvania, Ohio, Indiana, Illinois, and Michigan it is not even approximately as bad.

There seemed to be, roughly, three types of swing:
(a) a very rapid and very abrupt kind which sound as if the sender had simply omitted a letter or two. The length of the swinging cycle in this case is from ½ to 5 seconds.
(b) a moderately rapid and more gradual type which gives curved lines almost entirely, the period being from ten seconds to five minutes. This is the commonest type of swinging.
(c) a very gradual slow "drift" of all stations in one direction from the recorder, a cycle taking anywhere from five minutes to several hours.

The first two types are both shown in the upper graph of Fig. 13, obtained at 1CK, Braintree, Mass., on the sending of 8XK, July 6.

The first type of swing is, as far as I have observed, purely a one-station phenomena. The second type also is not followed by other sending stations nearby, but when one sender is swinging in this manner, others near him seldom fail to swing at a similar rate though not in synchronism. This is the most aggravating type of fading as one station swings in while another is going out, so the station being copied is blanketed before it goes out of audibility.

In the long slow third type of swinging all sending stations near each other swing slowly together. Where the swing is unusually slow it is noticed that during the early part of the evening stations in one direction will be heard best while those in another are inaudible, the condition perhaps reversing later in the evening. This sort of swinging cannot be shown by short tests and usually does not cause much

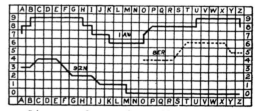

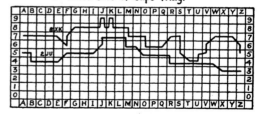

Fig. 18—Fading over water.

difficulty in handling traffic, since stations remain "swung out" long enough so that they do not have to work, or else "swung in" long enough to clear traffic. This type of swinging is especially characteristic of the Mississippi Valley.

Fading is not solely a land phenomenon. The curves obtained at 4AT, Ft. Pierce, Fla., on the transmission of 1AW and 2JU are normal although transmission is almost entirely over water. Fig. 18 shows curves obtained on July 6 on board the U. S. S. Ohio, at that time 150 miles east of Cape May, N. J., by Mr. L. C. Young of NSF. These are similar to those turned in by Mr. Young from NSF, at Anacostia.

Traveling Curves.

Similar curves are not always simultan-

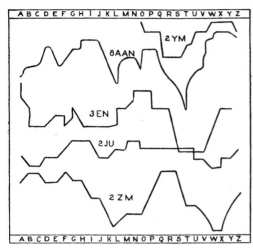

Fig. 19—Traveling curves.

eous. There is such a thing as a traveling curve. By the traveling curve is meant one which appears successively at different recording stations. Thus in Fig. 19 the same "dip" in the curve which appeared at 2YM in New York City on the letter R reached 8AAN at Buffalo, N. Y., at the letter S, 3EN at Norfolk at U, 2JU at Woodhaven, L. I. and 2ZM at Clifton, N. J. at W. This phenomenon occurred many different times, and in almost every instance where there was a clearly defined direction of travel of the curve it was away from the sending station. I cannot think of any reason for this rule, and believe it to be accidental and due to limited data. For this reason, it was thought best to ignore curves that appeared at only two stations, although some thirty-two such were found in which the curves were beyond question the same. Of the type which passed through three or more stations, sixteen were found.

No definite relation between the weather and either transmission or fading has been found nor has any relation between the weather and the direction of best transmission been found in a way that is at all convincing.

Explanation of Cause of Swinging.

Variations in the intensity and direction of received waves have been explained by a number of people as due to reflection and refraction of the waves before arriving at the receiving station. (See Scientific Paper of the Bureau of Standards, No. 353, "Variation in Direction of Propagation of Long Electromagnetic Waves," by A. H. Taylor, USNRF). The variations observed in these tests were actual changes in received power. A satisfactory explanation, based on reflection and refraction effects, involving the existence of interference bands such as are obtained with light, was suggested and discussed by various members of the conference of April 7. The results of the tests seem to bear out this explanation very well.

In Fig. 20 we have at S a source of monochromatic light (say red) from which rays of light travel to the receiving screen by two different paths, first along the straight line SA joining the source and the screen, and second along the line SA'A. Supposing the length of the path SA differs from that of the path SA'A by one wave length of red light, then the rays arriving at A by the two paths will be in phase and will add their amplitudes so that the result is more intense red light at A than would be obtained without the reflector. At another point B, however, the light arriving by the the path SB will not be in phase with that arriving by the path SB'B and hence they will not reinforce each other in the same manner. If the length of SB differs from that of SB'B by one-half a wave length of red light the two waves will differ 180 degrees in phase and hence will tend to cancel each other. If the amplitudes are the same they will cancel so that complete darkness re-

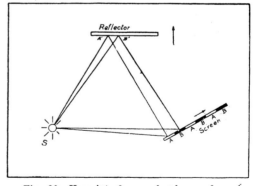

Fig. 20—How interference bands are formed.

sults. Thus there will be along the screen regions AAA, where the light is more intense than without the reflector, and between these, other regions BBB where there is almost complete darkness. If the reflector is tilted or moved in any direction except its own plane, these interference bands will move along the screen. Supposing the motion is in the direction of the arrow, the bands will move as shown by the arrow at the screen. Suppose now that we have at C an eye which is observing the light arriving at this point. This eye will see alternately red light and darkness.

If we consider the case of radio transmission, the source S becomes a sending station, the eye at B becomes a receiving station, and the waves electromagnetic waves. The whole phenomenon takes place on a much enlarged scale, consequently the reflector must also be of considerable size. It seems that a large cloud, fog bank, mass of fumes from an industrial plant, or perhaps the Heavyside layer may operate in this capacity. It is entirely probable that interference bands may also result from waves arriving over two paths, neither of which is direct. In this case movement of a reflecting or refracting member in either path may change the signal intensity. Where the waves have been repeatedly reflected before arriving the chances for violent and rapid swinging are much increased. If we accept the theory that fumes from smelters or steel mills may collect in sufficient masses to act as reflectors, this seems a plausible reason for the phenomenally rapid and erratic swinging of station 8XK which is located in a region of many such plants. It is just as well, however, to admit at once that other prominent stations in the same region, namely 8DA at Salem, Ohio, and 8ZW at Wheeling, W. Va., do not at all duplicate these rapid swings. The rapid swings of 8XK are, however, not due to the sending apparatus, as at the same time that one recorder will hear anywhere from 15 to 28 swings for 8XK, others will hear three or four. We have no record of 8XK being received without fading except by stations very close by. Reflecting need not necessarily be involved in the production of interference bands. Refraction will answer just as well to change the direction of the waves if we can find a mass of vapor whose dielectric constant differs from that of the normal atmosphere through which the waves are traveling. Neither the reflecting nor the refracting body need be at high altitudes. They may be at the elevation of the sending and recording stations and to one side of the line joining them.

Inverse Curves

Another type of curve may be designated as the inverse curve. The curve appearing at one station is found inverted at another. The upper part of Fig. 21 shows inverse curves received at 1TS, Bristol, Conn., and 8ER, Saint Marys, Ohio, from 2JU at Woodhaven, L. I. Singularly enough the cases of inverse curves are, without exception, simultaneous; that is to say, the positive peak of the curve appears at one station on the same letter for which the negative curve appears at the other; again, without exception, each case in which the curves are undoubtedly inverses is that of a very slow swing which lasted from 1 to 8 minutes. It is this simultaneous appearance of the curves which makes them difficult to explain, and leads to the suspicion that they are coincidences. A special case of inverse curves was that in which the positive curve was obtained at both station 3JR, Washington, and 3UA, Baltimore, while the negative curve was obtained at both 3BZ, Danville, Va., and 3BN, Norfolk, Va., giving complete check on the observations. The transmitting station was 2JU. It will be noted that the stations of a pair which obtained the same curves are at about the same distance from the sender, suggesting at once the thought that we have traveling curves, and the case is the special one in which the fading was sufficiently regular so that the fading curve which appeared at a particular station would be repeated

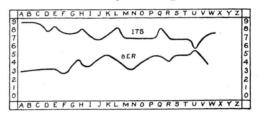

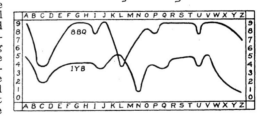

Fig. 21—Inverse check curves.

by others near it and the fading bands were spaced so regularly that it was possible to find further along the line of their travel other stations at which a dark band was appearing while a light one was crossing the first stations. With enough recorders it might be possible to trace in this manner with a fair degree of accuracy, the system of light and dark bands.

Clearly defined inverses are not frequent. Six inverses were found during the last four weeks which were fairly definite. One of these is shown in Fig. 21 for the transmission of 2JU on July 1 as received at 1TS, Bristol, Conn., and 8ER, St. Marys, Ohio. There does not seem to be any reason why stations so situated should obtain curves having any definite relation to each other. Perhaps inverse curves are purely accidental. Certainly they would be more convincing if more numerous.

The other inverse curves obtained were as follows:

Date	Sender	Recorders	
7/3/20	8XK	8ER	1TS
7/6/20	8ER	9ZJ	3NB
7/8/20	1AW	1CM	8AAN
7/8/20	2JU	3BZ	8AAN
7/8/20	8ER	3BZ	3UA

A possible inverse curve system is shown in Fig. 22, for the sending of 2JU on June 1. 8IB is at Columbus, Ohio, 8DR at

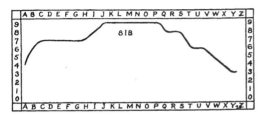

Transmission by 1AW — June 1, 1920

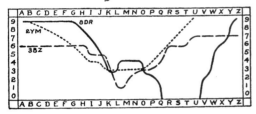

Fig. 22—Checks and inverses; also a doubtful traveling curve.

Detroit, 2YM in New York City. The curve at 3BZ (Danville, Va.) is possibly a traveling curve related to the one at 2YM.

Distance Effect

Fading is a long distance phenomenon. Repeated attempts were made at 1TS in Bristol, Conn., 12 miles removed from 1AW, to secure fading on 1AW by detuning the receiver or by dimming the tube filaments so as to decrease the signal intensity. The intensity remained perfectly uniform, however, and showed not the faintest tendency to fade. The same observations were made by 2YM and 2JE in New York, on the transmission of 2JU, Woodhaven, L. I., also by 3SU, 3JR and WWV in Washington on the transmission from NSF at Anacostia. This does not mean that there is a fixed distance below which fading does not occur. What it does mean is that fading does not occur until the distance is a considerable proportion of the normal transmission range of the station. In cases where transmission conditions are very bad, fading will occur at distances which are short. For instance, the distance from Washington to Baltimore is only 40 miles. It is almost impossible for stations in these two cities to work together on any wave length below 500 meters, as signals swing violently at all times. Similarly, the distance from Lawrence, Kansas, to St. Louis, Mo., is about 120 miles, a very short distance as radio transmission goes in this region. Yet, so far as I know, successful communication was never accomplished before the war by a St. Louis station with any station in Lawrence, Topeka, Leavenworth, Kansas City, or any of the surrounding towns. That the statement regarding ranges in the region is correct may be seen from the fact that any of the stations in the cities just mentioned could work over St. Louis to stations in Tennessee and Kentucky with perfect ease, while at the same time St. Louis stations could work over the state of Kansas, say, to Danver, without any difficulty at all. I am of the opinion also that fading does not occur in general within the daylight range of a station. This statement will not bear very close inspection, as in one of the cases just mentioned, that of transmission from Washington to Baltimore, the cities are within daylight range of each other. Signals do not fade in the daytime; on the contrary, in this particular case, they are stronger than at night. But, as stated, signals fade very badly at night.

Determination of Transmission Conditions.

In an attempt to connect fading with weather conditions and with normal transmission, it was desirable to establish some sort of a criterion as to the excellence of transmission on a particular date. No really good way of doing this was found. The method adopted can be best explained by example. In order to establish the normal intensity at which station 8XK at Pittsburgh was heard at 1CM, Laconia, N. H., the mean intensity of the signals of 8XK at 1CM for each day was first established by inspection of the curves obtained at 1CM on that date. The question then arose whether in averaging the intensities for the test period, those evenings should be considered on which 1CM had listened but failed to hear 8XK. If the failure was due to a defect in the apparatus, the results for the evening should, of course, be thrown out. It was decided however, that the operation of the stations was constant enough so it could safely be assumed that apparatus failures had not occurred. The mean intensity was accordingly obtained by averaging the intensities on all the evenings in which 1CM listended for 8XK, regardless of whether the station was heard or not. The mean intensity so obtained was then used in determining whether on a particular schedule, the reception of 8XK at 1CM was good, normal, or poor. No definite relation between weather and transmission was found.

Almost without exception the recorders stated that they believed fading was not a variation in signal strength but a shift of wave lengths, as they could recover a station which had swung out by retuning the receiving set. We requested them not to attempt this since it would be impossible to tell whether the variations in received signal strength were due to a change in incoming power or due to mistuning. A laboratory check of this scheme showed conclusively that two observers could not get results that were even approximately alike if the receiving apparatus was retuned during the test. For this reason the QST call preceding transmission was made very long so that tuning might be finished before the test started. Subsequently it was found that when ICW signals were being received they could not be recovered by retuning when they had faded out. This observation was checked by several of our recorders at Pittsburgh, Chicago, and Hartford.

A possible explanation of this difference between spark signals and ICW signals, which also explains the apparent shift in wave length, may be given, following the ideas used by A. H. Taylor in explaining the difference between the variations of direction observed with damped and continuous waves. (Bureau of Standards Scientific Paper 353, already mentioned). Return to Fig. 20 and the formation of interference bands. Our source was monochromatic and a single set of interference bands, alternately red and black, resulted. An eye which could see only red light would then see alternate red light and darkness as the bands passed across it. Supposing the source of red light were replaced by one of white light. Interference bands of red light would still be produced and the red-seeing eye would still see alternate red light and darkness. If, however, another eye, a blue-seeing eye, were placed alongside of the red-seeing eye, it would see alternate blue light and darkness, and since the wave length of the two is not the same the interference bands would not be at the same places. Hence while one eye had darkness the other one would be out of phase with it and would have some light. Thus, by using the proper eye it would be possible at all times to see some light. The radio reception case is similar to the rather fanciful light system. The spark transmitting set emits not one wave but a band of wave lengths; the receiving set, however, can detect only one of these waves. Regenerative sets are notoriously very sharply tuned. If then the condition is such that a dark band for the particular wave length at which it is tuned is crossing the receiving station, it will detect no signals, although at the same time power is arriving on a slightly different wave length still within the band of wave lengths emitted by the sending apparatus. While there is some disagreement about this band, most of the recorders consulted agree that the wave length variation detected lies within the band of wave lengths normally emitted by the sending station.

With an ICW station we have the case of the monochromatic source. Only one wave length is being emitted. Hence when a dark band for that wave length crosses the receiver no signals can be found. At close range this does not hold true, since an ICW transmitter emits other wave lengths too weak to be detected at a distance which give the effect of a particular wave at close range.

An excellent example of this is NSF, which at first had great difficulty in initially "raising" distant stations although after they had tuned NSF in, the signals were reported as very loud. This is sufficient proof that NSF, at a distance, is very sharp. In Washington more difficulty by far is experienced in tuning out NSF than in tuning out 3KM, 3XF or 3JR, all of which are 1 K.W. spark transmitters nearer by.

The side frequencies of the ICW transmitter are those which differ from the main frequency by the tone frequency. Mr. Conrad of 8XK has suggested a possible means of avoiding QSS based on the double system of inverse bands presented above. His suggestion is the use of an ICW or CW transmitter emitting two waves some ten meters apart, and two independent receivers tuned to these two waves. It would be necessary to have these two receivers working into a common amplifier or perhaps into the two halves of a split head set. Mr. Conrad has attempted to operate an ICW transmitter in this manner but we do not know at present with what degree of success. It will be seen that an ICW transmitter is not the answer to the fading problem.

The statement made regarding the general opinion as to the rate of fading in various parts of the country was confirmed by the tests. Fading in the Mississippi Valley is of the type designated as "C". In the region around Pittsburgh all three types of fading are found, mainly "B" and "C", while in New England the "A" type of fading seems to be chronic, regardless of the location of the sending station. This seems remarkable since many of the New England records were those for 1AW, 2JU and NSF, all close to this region.

Summary

Test signals were transmitted three nights each week during June and July,
(Concluded on page 22)

A.R.R.L.—B. S. FADING TESTS
(Concluded from page 19)

1920, by six sending stations operating at 250 meters wave length and observations of the intensity of the signals were made by fifty recording stations. An average of twenty-eight recorders listened for the test schedules on each of twenty-one evenings, obtaining 1260 curves of signal intensity variation.

Frequent checks between curves at adjacent and sometimes distant receiving stations were found. Traveling curves, appearing successively at various recording stations, were found. No definite connection between weather and transmission was found. Inverse curves were found but infrequently and are not considered as other than chance variations. Three types of fading were observed, a rapid and very abrupt type, appearing mainly in New England, a less rapid and less abrupt type found in all parts of the test territory, and a very slow type covering large territories and affecting all sending stations in the region alike.

There is no marked difference in the manner of fading for various types of sending sets. However, a damped wave that has faded out can often be recovered by retuning, which cannot be done for continuous waves.

The tests furnish good evidence in support of the belief that radio signal variations such as fading and swinging are caused by varying reflection and refraction of the waves.

"MacMillan Expedition Nears Arctic Daybreak" by K. B. Warner, 1BHW

By Carl Luetzelschwab, K9LA and Ward Silver, NØAX

In June 1923, another first was recorded for Amateur Radio. Donald H. Mix, 1TS, accompanied Donald R. MacMillan, renowned Arctic explorer, as the ARRL operator on the schooner *Bowdoin* when she sailed from Maine to "the top of the world" on a 14-month trip in the interests of science. The following figure shows the major Amateur Radio players in this endeavor.

On board the *Bowdoin*, after unpacking the expedition's crates of equipment. Left to right are F.H. Schnell, ARRL Traffic Manager; D.H. Mix, WNP's operator; K.B. Warner, Editor of *QST*; M.B. West, the Zenith engineer who designed the station; and Dr. MacMillan the *Bowdoin*'s captain.

The MacMillan expedition was likely the first Amateur Radio DXpedition ever undertaken with two-way capability — sending Godley to Europe during the Transatlantic Tests was for one-way communications only and two-way communications across the Atlantic Ocean would not occur until November later that year. (To find the articles on the MacMillan expedition in the *QST* online archives on the ARRL website, use the keywords "macmillan" and "wnp", selecting the years 1923 and 1924.)

Numerous expeditions followed suit as word got around of the amateur's flexibility, wireless know-how and dedication to the job. Radio operators with amateur experience were often chosen as part of the crew. Even if an amateur was not operating the expedition's equipment, it was common in those early days of a blurry boundary between amateur and professional for amateurs to serve a part of the "home team" to handle communications with the expedition.

In addition, amateurs were encouraged to listen for transmissions from expeditions. Far more numerous than commercial stations, amateurs listened from many more locations and were sometimes in a better receiving location and able to copy messages unintelligible elsewhere. One of the better-known of these expeditions was the Byrd Expedition of 1926 for which "…press messages…will be an important part of the traffic. Amateurs receiving any such messages are requested to forward them by collect telegraph… immediately upon receipt." The pages of *QST* are filled with news of upcoming and ongoing expeditions well into the 1950s. ARRL members can find the articles in the *QST* online archives by searching for the keyword "expedition." Clicking on the highest-numbered Results page will take you to the earliest articles.

One of the last and best-known expeditions with an Amateur Radio station set sail for neither the Arctic nor the Antarctic. The *Kon-Tiki*, a 45-foot balsa raft launched from Peru, carried the 15-watt CW and AM station LI2B on its 4000-mile journey to Polynesia in 1947. Equipped for 40, 20, 10 and 6 meters with tube radios operated from dry cells and hand-cranked generators, the station kept the expedition in contact with the Norwegian embassy and weather services through amateur relay stations in Southern California and elsewhere. (A summary of the *Kon-Tiki* expedition can be found in the December 1947 issue of *QST*.)

While the days of expeditions using dog sleds and balsa rafts are (mostly) over, Amateur Radio still plays a part in connecting us with human beings at the far edges of our frontier. Only this time, instead of the frontier being over the horizon, it is above it! Every day, the orbits of the International Space Station take it over every person on the planet. Equipped with several types of ham radio equipment, it is not unusual to hear the astronauts making a contact with a school or just person to person to hear a voice from Earth. Wherever humankind goes, Amateur Radio will be there, too!

MacMillan Expedition Nears Arctic Daybreak

IT was rather a hard job to keep the MacMillan Arctic Expedition schooner "Bowdoin," WNP, in communication with the U.S.A. during January. In spite of the fact that this month is accounted one of the best radio periods of the year, WNP's signals have been very faint and fading violently; so that, altho more reports have been received than usual, actual communication has been carried on with difficulty. It is quite perplexing to us why this should be so. Nor, indeed, have we any idea why it should be that, ever since c9BP and u7DC first broke thru the barrier and linked their

The 88-ft. schooner "Bowdoin", frozen in the Arctic ice off a barren shore. Is radio a comfort in such a location? Write your own answer. (From a photograph made by MacMillan on a previous expedition.)

respective countries with WNP, the northwestern states should hear the "Bowdoin" with more or less regularity while it is seldom that the signals are heard east of the Mississippi. One reason of course is that Operator Mix does most of his work with c9BP at a time favorable to the latter, midnight to 3 A.M. Pacific time, or 3 a.m. to 6 a.m. Eastern time when but few eastern operators are listening, but at that it seems the signals simply are not getting thru to eastern points except on rare occasions.

Again we record c9BP, Prince Rupert, B.C., as the best contact point, working Mix seven reported times in January and handling almost a hundred messages. Again u9DKB, Minot, N. D., has been second only to c9BP, working WNP four times and handling about 25 messages. u7CO and u6XAD worked him twice each, 7CO handling 3 messages; and u7OM and c4HH once each, the latter handling a dozen messages.

WNP was heard by W. L. Shiel at Dunedin, New Zealand, while working u9ZT on the night of Nov. 25th, N.Z. time. That is splendid DX. Mix also has succeeded in copying numerous European amateurs during the Transatlantic Tests, reporting the following: French 8BM, 8ARA, 8BF, 8AZ; Dutch PCII, NAB2, PA9; British 5AT, 2ON, 6XX, 2OD, 2NO, 5KO, 6NI, 6YA, 2NM, 2KW, 2NI, 2IN, 2SZ, 2ZU. As far as we know he doesn't know anything yet about the new short-wave work, as his tuner only goes down to about 145 meters.

That Coolidge Message

As we described in our last issue, the A.R.R.L. handled President Coolidge's message of holiday greetings to the Expedition. The unknown "5" station which participated turns out to be c5GO in Vancouver, B.C., so the routing of the message was u1HX-u8ZZ-c5GO-c9BP-WNP. Barnsley handled the reply too, but as time was short he wired direct to A.R.R.L. headquarters, where it was turned over to the Radiocorp for delivery to the President, the original message having been filed with the R.C.A. Permission has been received from the White House to publish the text:

MEMBERS OF MACMILLAN EXPEDITION IN NORTH GREENLAND DEEPLY APPRECIATIVE OF YOUR HOLIDAY GREETINGS AND WISHES FOR NEW YEAR ALL'S WELL ON THE BOWDOIN IN THE MIDDLE OF LONG ARTIC NIGHT.
MACMILLAN

Some Pretty Relaying

Station WOAW, operated in Omaha by the Woodmen of the World in co-operation with the Omaha "World-Herald" has been one of the best-heard broadcasting stations at WNP. It occured to the station management to put on a special Christmas program for MacMillan and his men, and so the "World-Herald" asked 9DXY, Quinby, Omaha City Manager to forward a message to WNP asking for their selections. Then enused a pretty bit of relaying. Unable to raise a 7 on the night in question, 9DXY gave the message to 9BOF in Salem, S.D., who forwarded it to 9CAA in Denver. Thence it went to 7ZU in Polytechnic, Mont., to 7ABB in Everett, Wash. 7ABB was unable to hear WNP during this particular week, so broadcast the message under a QST. It was received OK by WNP and a program immediately selected by the members of the crew and transmitted by WNP as a message to 9DKB, Minot. As 9DKB has difficulty in working into Omaha, he mailed the message to the "World-Herald." And thus a special Christmas program of their own selection was broadcast to the MacMillan party by WOAW.

The "Bowdoin" is now approaching the end of the long Arctic night. Already they have a little daylight every noon. Soon their days will be as long as their nights, and in a few months more they will be having almost all daylight and the chief difficulty will be to get the traffic off during darkness. Then when the ice breaks up in midsummer the little "Bowdoin" will turn her nose towards home, expecting to return to Main in September. That means that you fellows who want the fun of working WNP had better try hard right now.

January reports on WNP follow; unless otherwise shown, calls listed report hearing WNP.

Jan. 1, 9CDO-6BUH; Jan. 2, 1ER, c9BP sent 18 msgs., 9ASC, 9AFM; Jan. 4, c9BP sent 11 msgs., 6ALO, 9DKB; Jan. 6, c9BP sent 7 and recd. 6 msgs., 9DKB; Jan. 7, c9BP sent 13 msgs., 7MN; Jan. 8, c9BP sent 4 and recd. 14 msgs., 6CBL, 6XAD and 9DKB both worked WNP and sent press and one message; Jan. 9, c9BP recd. 9 msgs., 7MN, 5ML, 6CBL, 9CNS, 9CCK; Jan. 10, 9EFH, 6CBL, 9DKB; Jan. 11, c9BP sent 8 and recd. 2 msgs., 9DKB sent 3 msgs., 7MN. 9EFH; Jan. 12, 7CO recd. 1 msg., 6CBL, 9DKB, 6XAD sent 300 wds. press; Jan. 13, 6CBL; Jan. 14, c4HH worked WNP, 9DKB; Jan. 15, 7CO recd. 2 msgs., 1CMP, 9DKB; Jan. 16, c4HH; Jan. 17, 9DKB sent 2 and recd. 11 msgs., 6CBL; Jan. 19, 7RD, c4FV, 9BSM, 9DGC; Jan. 20, 9DKB sent 1 and recd. 4 msgs., 6CDV; Jan. 21, 1AJF, 6CJQ; Jan. 24, 9EFO.

—*K.B.W.*

"Radio Astronomy"
by Byron Goodman, W1DX

By Carl Leutzelschwab, K9LA and Ward Silver, NØAX

Karl Jansky, working for Bell Telephone Labs, was tasked to determine sources of interference in transcontinental cable systems. In completing this work, Jansky discovered a radio signal in 1932 that was associated with the Milky Way galaxy. Its origin was strongest in the Sagittarius constellation — the center of the Milky Way galaxy. This source was too weak to affect cable communications, so no further work was done by Bell Telephone Labs.

But there was no need to worry — Amateur Radio came to the rescue to continue the investigation of extraterrestrial noise. Grote Reber, W9GFZ, upon hearing of Jansky's work, built his own radio telescope in his backyard in Wheaton, Illinois. It was a 31-foot diameter dish, and he began his observing program at 160 MHz in 1939.

From his data, Reber put together sky maps that confirmed that parts of the sky were "bright" at radio frequencies. Reber published his sky contour maps in the April 1949 issue of *Sky and Telescope* (also in the *Astrophysical Journal*). A sample of Reber's sky maps is supplied in the following figure. It's interesting to realize that an Amateur Radio operator was the only one looking at the sky at radio wavelengths from 1939 to 1949. His homebrew telescope was moved to the national observatory at Green Bank, West Virginia, in the 1960s.

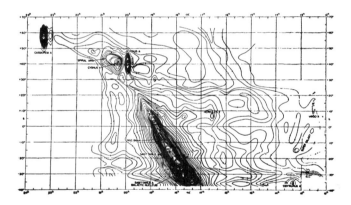

Grote Reber, W9GFZ, created this radio map of the summer sky at 250 MHz. Reber's antenna was an array of 96 helix antennas. The lines on the map represent contours of equal noise strength in the sky.

Reber, characterized as "The first radio astronomer who knew what he was building" by Dr. Philip Morrison (ex-W8FIS), eventually moved to Tasmania in 1954. There, he could pursue his interest in the 0.5 to 3 MHz medium frequency (MF) range. Tasmania proved to be a good selection, as the local noise level was extremely low and allowed him to receive MF signals from outside the ionosphere. Even then, low-band operators were moving to quiet locations in pursuit of DX!

Today, amateurs are still involved in radio astronomy. For example, NASA's Radio Jove project (**radiojove.gsfc.nasa.gov**) encourages amateurs and interested students of radio astronomy to construct and aim simple antennas at the planet Jupiter. Large bursts of radio static are emitted by the giant planet in the mid-to-upper HF range, centered on 20 MHz. The improvement of low-noise receivers and the availability of high-gain antennas enable amateurs to observe in the upper-UHF and microwave ranges, too.

Radio Astronomy

A New Tool for Studying the Universe

BY BYRON GOODMAN, W1DX

AMATEURS have been conditioned to think of radio as basically a medium for two-way communication, although the broad-minded ones will admit that radio can also be used for broadcasting, TV, telemetering, radar, navigational aids, remote control and a few other things far removed from amateur radio. There is still another use of radio, one that isn't too widely known, that should certainly stir the imagination of any amateur who has been thrilled by DX on any ham band. It's called "radio astronomy."

Most people think of astronomy as the study of the universe by optical means, with equipment ranging from unaided keen eyes to telescopes and cameras of the magnitude used at Palomar. Radio astronomy began with some observations by Karl G. Jansky of the Bell Telephone Laboratories back in 1931, when he built a rotating directive antenna system for studying the direction of arrival of static on the short waves. In the absence of all static Jansky found some residual noise coming from the direction of the center of our galaxy. In the late 30s, Grote Reber, W9GFZ, of Wheaton, Ill., built a parabolic reflector in his backyard for the systematic study of what he called "cosmic static."

Radio astronomy came into its own directly after World War II. Developments in microwave receiving equipment and antennas had moved ahead in great strides during the war, and it had been observed (but kept secret) that at least two types of radio noise come from the sun. One is an intense and variable component associated with sunspots and occurring at meter wavelengths, and the other is a steady emission at centimeter wavelengths. Since our sun is a star, it was reasonable to expect that radio signals from other stars might be received, and radio astronomy gained new impetus.

Before describing what is currently being done in radio astronomy, it might be well to mention two things. Some readers may wonder why anyone should bother to try to detect weak radio noise from extraterrestrial sources when we have big telescopes available for visual observation. The answer to that is simply that radio is another tool, one that can be used during the day and night without regard to optical "seeing" conditions. Further, it has the ability to "see" through dust clouds in space. And, as we will mention later, additional information on the universe has already been obtained that is impossible to collect by optical means. The second point is that two "local" types of radio astronomy that will just be mentioned in passing are (1) using radar to observe and study meteors regardless of light conditions, and (2) moon radar experiments.[1]

[1] Kauffman, "A DX Record: To the Moon and Back," *QST*, May, 1946.
"Lunar DX on 144 Mc.!", *QST*, March, 1953.

This bank of 96 (4 by 24) helical beam antennas is the largest radio telescope antenna at Ohio State University at the present time. The helices are backed up by a steel-mesh ground plane measuring 22 by 160 feet, and the coaxial line feed is arranged so that the antenna can be operated with all helices in phase (for the sharpest beam) or with the two halves of the array in phase opposition (split-lobe pattern). (*Photograph courtesy Department of Photography, Ohio State University.*)

May 1956

Real DX

Two discoveries in radio astronomy spurred the present high interest in the subject. The first was the discovery in 1946 of discrete noise sources, or "radio stars," that couldn't be associated with any visual object. The first in this category was a noise source in the constellation of Cygnus, and it wasn't until 1953 that this was identified as two distant galaxies in collision. The identification of this strong source, approaching the intensity of the undisturbed sun, carried with it an astonishing implication. Since the distance from the earth of this source is 200 million light years (5), it can be shown that similar sources, if they exist, could be detected by radio at a distance beyond the reach of the largest optical telescope. To an astronomer, demonstrating a tool that will reach beyond the largest optical telescope is like leaving a kilowatt rig on the doorstep of a brand-new General Class licensee — the event will be noticed!

The second discovery was that the atomic hydrogen spectral line at 21 cm. (1420.405 Mc.), predicted by theory and confirmed in the laboratory, could be observed by radio means. Consequently, it is possible by radio astronomy to detect concentrations of hydrogen gas and determine their directions from us. A clue to the speed of movement can be obtained by the shift in frequency, or Doppler effect, and a map of our galaxy is being made from these observations.

Radio Astronomy in the U. S.

Work in radio astronomy is being carried on in many parts of the world. In England a 250-foot diameter parabolic reflector is being completed that will be used for the observation of radio sources. The Netherlands, Australia, France, and Canada have already contributed to the knowledge of radio astronomy, and research is in progress in other countries such as Russia, India, Japan and Sweden. In the United States, most of the work is being carried on at universities, although the Naval Research Laboratory in Washington, D. C., has a 50-foot parabolic reflector of cast aluminum, the National Bureau of Standards has a 25-foot dish at Boulder, Colo., and the Carnegie Institution of Washington, D. C., a large fixed dipole array called a "Mills Cross."

The antennas used for radio astronomy run all the way from stacks of Yagis through rhombics and parabolas to the bank of 96 helical antennas used at Ohio State University. The radio astronomy projects at O.S.U. are headed by Dr. John Kraus, Professor of Electrical Engineering, whom pre-war amateurs will remember as W8JK of the "close-spaced beam" and other antenna fame. Dr. Kraus was kind enough to furnish the writer with the illustrations and information contained in this article, and to arrange for a guided tour of the telescope site several miles from the campus in Columbus, Ohio. From a few remarks dropped at the conclusion of the interview, we wouldn't be too surprised to hear W8JK back on the air some day, but restricting his operations to terrestrial limits after exploring the universe will undoubtedly seem rather confining. (Yes, the word "mundane" fits, but we resisted the temptation.)

The radio astronomy work at O.S.U. began in the fall of 1951 with a small array of helical antennas that grew to the present beam by the fall of 1952. With this antenna system, and with the 250-Mc. receiving system built under the supervision of Donn Van Stoutenburg, a radio map of the sky was obtained. This is the way the sky would appear to our eyes if our eyes were sensitive only to a "radio color" of 250 Mc. The detailed mapping of the sky was carried out and is continuing under Dr. H. C. Ko.

Although the 96-element helical antenna is a beautiful sight to behold, with its beam width of 1° by 8°, plans are going ahead for a still more ambitious antenna with higher gain and narrower bandwidth. As shown in the sketch, this antenna will use a tiltable plane reflector working into a fixed paraboloid that will in turn reflect the signals into a horn antenna at the focus of the paraboloid. Present plans call for a 70-foot high paraboloid 700 feet long, although the ultimate objective is a paraboloid 2000 feet long. At 1 meter this latter system would have a half-power beam-width of 0.1° by 1°! The object of these huge systems is, of course, to increase the gain and the resolution (ability to separate sources). The design principles have already been confirmed by a 12-foot model working at a wave-

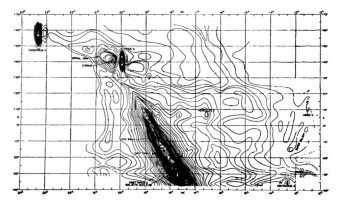

Radio map of the summer sky, made at 250 Mc. with the 96-helix antenna. The lines represent equal "brightness" contours of radio radiation.

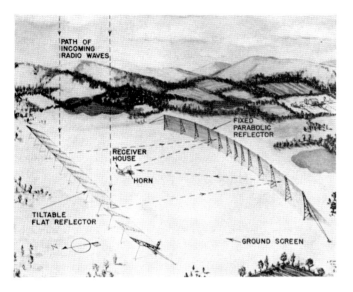

This super radio telescope, designed by Dr. Kraus, is soon to be built at O.S.U. When completed, the parabolic reflector will measure 700 feet in length by 70 feet in height.

length of about 1 centimeter and used for celestial observations.

Receivers used for radio-astronomy observations must, of course, be built with the lowest practical noise figure, since the sensitivity of the system depends upon the gain of the antenna and the noise figure of the receiver. The bandwidth of the receiver may be a few kc., as when studying the 21-cm. hydrogen signals, or up to several Mc. when observing radio stars. The receiver must be very "gain-stable" if the measurements over a period of time are to be compared, and a common practice is to provide for periodic comparison with a standard noise source.

Amateur Radio Astronomy

Somewhat overwhelmed by the large antennas we learned about, we assumed that Dr. Kraus wouldn't hold out much hope for amateur radio astronomy. To the contrary, he explained that amateurs could make observations with relatively simple equipment and might be able to contribute something, in the same way that amateur astronomers have done useful work in the field of optical astronomy. As examples, he pointed out that radio noise from the sun can be observed at meter wavelengths, and that many of the better-equipped 10-, 6- and 2-meter stations should be able to observe the solar signals. He also pointed out that recently at O.S.U. they have been getting signals from the *planet* Jupiter. We did a double take on this one, because we had assumed that the only extraterrestrial sources were hot stars and not cold planets. Dr. Kraus explained that with a "radio telescope" consisting of 12 half-wave dipoles pointed at Jupiter they occasionally receive relatively strong signals on 11 meters that sound more like static than the usual hiss-type noise received from thermal sources. It is also observed that these signals are obtained when the "white spot" of Jupiter is facing the earth, although they aren't observed every time the white spot comes around to our side of Jupiter. One of the theories that has been advanced, and probably the most acceptable one to date, is that the signals they hear are generated by violent lightning storms on Jupiter. The Jupiter signals were first detected last year, by Drs. B. F. Burke and K. L. Franklin of the Carnegie Institution.

And that's the very brief story of radio astronomy, just enough to whet the appetite of the readers who have come this far with us. If you want to read more about it, a bibliography is included at the end of this article. If you want a crack at a science that is not yet too cut-and-dried, here is your opportunity. It isn't ham radio as it is generally known, and we can't promise your SWL cards to the sun and Jupiter will be acknowledged for some time, but you will have to admit that it's *real* DX!

Bibliography

Books: Lovell and Clegg, *Radio Astronomy*, published by John Wiley and Sons, N. Y. C., 1952.

A good general book on the subject, with some elementary treatment of both radio and astronomy. Considerable space is devoted to meteor observations, but the entire field is covered.

Pawsey and Bracewell, *Radio Astronomy*, published by Oxford Univ. Press, London, 1955.

Somewhat more technical than Lovell and Clegg.

Articles: Hagen, McClain and Hepburn, "Discrete Radio Sources at 21 Cm.," *Proc. IRE*, 42, 1811, 1954.

Kraus, "Radio Telescopes," *Scientific American*, March, 1955.

Wild, "Radio Waves from the Sun," *Scientific American*, June, 1955.

Many articles have appeared in other issues of *Proc. IRE* and *Scientific American*, as well as in *Nature* and *Sky and Telescope*.

May 1956

"ARRL-IGY Propagation Research Project" by Mason Southworth, W1VLH

By Carl Leutzelschwab, K9LA and Ward Silver, N0AX

After the Bureau of Standards requested help from radio amateurs in the shortwave fading tests of 1920 as described earlier in this chapter, it was just a matter of time before amateurs would again be called upon to help gather information on the science of propagation. The IGY (International Geophysical Year) provided this opportunity.

The IGY ran from July 1957 through December 1958. In addition to measurements in many areas of science, the IGY performed worldwide ionosonde measurements of the ionosphere that eventually led to a model of the E and F regions.

The radio amateur's contribution in the IGY was tied to our earlier discovery of transequatorial propagation (discussed in the Propagation chapter). To gather more information on this interesting VHF mode, the ARRL set up the Propagation Research Project during the IGY to collect reports of possible 50 MHz and 144 MHz ionospheric propagation, evaluate them and transcribe the data onto punched cards.

The 50 MHz reports were then analyzed by the Radio Propagation Laboratory at Stanford University by Southworth, W1VLH; Villard, W6QYT; and others. A summary of the results was reported in the *Journal of Geophysical Research* in 1960 (see the References table at the end of this book). An abstract of the paper states that three different types of previously undiscovered equatorial propagation occurring at night were observed by hams.

The Propagation Research Project generated nearly 300,000 individual reports from nearly 600 observers on the 50, 144 and 220 MHz bands. The quality and scope of the data received from hams led to continued amateur participation in the International Geophysical Cooperation effort of 1959 in which additional 50 MHz observations were collected. As Southworth stated at the end of his June 1959 *QST* article, "If all this makes you feel that amateur propagation studies are important and mean business, you're right!"

Hams who participated in the Propagation Research Project received this four-color certificate to acknowledge their support of International Geophysical Year scientific programs.

The ARRL—IGY Propagation Research Project

V.h.f. Contact Data to Be Collected on a Worldwide Scale

BY MASON P. SOUTHWORTH,* W1VLH

> • Since the accompanying article introduces a new ARRL program, perhaps a few words of introduction for its author are also in order. Although W1VLH is officially a newcomer to the Headquarters staff, many of you already know him for his *QST* articles on "things v.h.f." during recent years. These have been turned out while spending his college vacations working in the ARRL laboratories.
>
> Mason graduated from Trinity College, Hartford, in 1955 and from Rensselaer Polytechnic Institute in 1956. He is a member of Phi Beta Kappa, Sigma XI, Tau Beta Pi, Eta Kappa Nu, and Sigma Pi Sigma honorary societies as well as the IRE and their Professional Group on Antennas and Propagation. With this background plus several years of v.h.f. hamming experience it was only natural that W1VLH should go to work on the project announced in this article. He will be in charge of a special ARRL office which will collect and analyze the reports to be sent in by v.h.f. amateurs.

THE WORTH of amateur observations is recognized in many scientific fields, and amateur workers of many kinds will participate in the coming International Geophysical Year. Therefore it was only natural that a place be made for hams in the course of planning the radio-propagation aspects of IGY.

The IGY itself and the reasons for its being were discussed by Dr. Berkner in the July issue of *QST*, and anyone who has not read this background article by now should certainly do so. The possibilities for amateur participation in connection with tracking the satellite of Project Vanguard, and setting up communications networks to furnish moral support to the Antarctic groups and help give notice of special events were mentioned in the same issue. Another amateur project, whose purpose is to gather radio propagation data is, perhaps, to be the most important and worthwhile of all. This involves the reporting of v.h.f. DX contacts made by several means of propagation which, although fairly common to a good many hams in practical communication, are still incompletely explained theoretically.

When there is a job to be done, one tries to pick the best means for doing it. Just so in this case. When it comes to gathering data about propagation phenomena, it's hard to beat a large number of reporting stations operating at all hours of the day and night. If a series of observing stations had to be set up especially for the IGY, the cost of this phase of the program would be enormous, and results would still not be as complete as could be furnished by existing amateur stations with their wide distribution. Therefore, when information on propagation was desired for IGY, hams were a natural for the job.

ARRL and IGY officials got together as early as the fall of 1955 to see what could be done about setting up a program of amateur observations to supplement the more exact — but of necessity limited — information obtained from scatter soundings and the like. The program which evolved from these talks has now taken on a definite form. The work will be done by ARRL under an Air Force contract. Dr. Wolfgang Pfister of the Air Force Cambridge Research Center will be the consulting scientist on the program. The writer will be in charge of collecting and analyzing the data for ARRL.

The program will be concerned with v.h.f. propagation in three main categories: transequatorial scatter on 50 Mc., auroral communication on any amateur frequency above 50 Mc., and sporadic-E skip. In order that no interesting phenomena may be missed, details of any amateur v.h.f. work over unusual distances will be solicited. It will then be up to the special ARRL IGY Staff to sort them out, if the reporting amateur is unable to do so himself.[1]

The first work in the three fields mentioned above was done by amateurs using the v.h.f. bands. Transequatorial scatter was turned up when amateurs in Mexico began working South American stations on 50 Mc., at times when communication should not have been possible, according to any means of propagation then known. Later 50-Mc. operators in many parts of this country and Canada made similar contacts at "wrong" times, and the medium by which these came about is still far from completely understood. It was for the purpose of gathering more data on this phenomenon that scientists working out the scope of the IGY program first conceived the idea of enlisting the aid of radio amateurs.

(Continued on page 118)

---

* ARRL-IGY Project Coordinator

[1] — Basic details of v.h.f. propagation may be found in any recent edition of the ARRL *Handbook*. 50-Mc. DX was described in May, 1955, *QST*, Page 22. V.h.f. dx phenomena were discussed in detail in *QST* for February, 1951, p. 46.

ARRL — IGY

(Continued from page 15)

Long-distance propagation of v.h.f. waves by means of reflection from the auroral curtain, and from sporadically-ionized patches of the *E*-region of the ionosphere was discovered by amaturs two decades ago, and their observations have been used effectively in studying these phenomena on many occasions. Notable examples are the Cornell University Auroral Project organized with ARRL assistance, and the RASO program conducted by O. P. Ferrell under Air Force contract. Because use of amateur v.h.f. bands is currently at an all-time high, and because the IGY is a worldwide and concentrated scientific effort on many fronts, timed to coincide with the expected peak of a solar activity cycle, the ARRL-IGY program is an unparalleled opportunity for amateurs to contribute to man's knowledge of radio wave propagation.

To make the most of this project, reports from amateurs in all parts of the country will be needed. If you live in one of the less populous sections and make relatively few contacts, don't feel that you can't contribute much. Your reports will be, if anything, more valuable than those from fellows whose areas are well represented. In fact, it isn't necessary to have a v.h.f. transmitter or even an amateur license to help out. Accurate heard reports will be useful supplements to lists of two-way contacts. It goes without saying that this program is made-to-order for the Technician licensee. Many of these fellows have already found out what fun 50-Mc. operation can be, but for those who haven't here's a chance to really make that "ticket" count for something. Not to be overlooked in this project are our brother amateurs from south of the equator. Their cooperation will be essential, of course, in the equatorial-scatter phase of this program. Their help will be solicited through member societies of the International Amateur Radio Union, as well as the pages of *QST*.

The reporting involved in the program will go something like this: All contacts and heard reports which are suspected to have resulted from one of the propagation types outlined above will be listed on the special forms to be available. These forms will be made up so that the desired information can be taken from the regular station log, insofar as possible. Regular operation will, of course, be encouraged. At bimonthly intervals these report forms will be returned to the ARRL office handling the program.

Then the project staff takes over. First the data will be sorted as to propagation type and time of occurence. Contacts will be selected which are representative of conditions at any given time. From the information furnished about these contacts, calculations of such things as distances and mid-point locations will be made. The resulting data will then be arranged in a form suitable for analysis. At this point the really important job of study and correlation begins. This will go on during the IGY period, and probably afterwards when the data from other projects is available. If all this sounds rather involved, remember that all the reporting stations have to do is to operate faithfully and send in suitable data on their contacts.

The International Geophysical Year itself will run from July 1, 1957 until December 31, 1958. In almost any new project, certain "bugs" develop. To circumvent this, it has been decided to start collecting data on January 1, 1957, six months early. Thus, we should be in full swing by the actual beginning of the IGY. Do not think that the data collected during this trial period will be wasted — far from it. We can use all the information that we can get. In fact, there has been some talk of the possibility of continuing an investigation of this sort even after the IGY is over. This will depend on the cooperation received from you, the radio amateur.

If you are equipped to operate or listen on any band from 50 Mc. up, and want to take part in what may become one of the major accomplishments of amateur radio, write in and let us know. Send your letter to the writer, in care of ARRL Headquarters. Bear in mind that the program is in a formative state. Aims and procedures may be modified as the need arises or as new ideas come along. In fact, we hope that the program will remain flexible all during its existence, since it can contribute the most only by being adaptable to new concepts. If you have any suggestions as how this work can be made more worthwhile, let us know that too. Further and more detailed information will be coming up shortly through the pages of *QST*. In addition, there will probably be a monthly bulletin which will be sent to contributing stations. It will contain program news, reports sent in which are of special interest, and reports of the project results as information comes in.

Amateur Radio's Contributions to Antenna Design

By Jim Breakall, WA3FET

Amateurs were responsible for all types of antennas in the beginnings of radio. In 1886, Heinrich Hertz forced an electrical spark to occur in the gap of a dipole antenna in his system. He used a loop antenna as a receiver and observed a similar disturbance. By 1901, Marconi was sending information across the Atlantic Ocean on a regular basis. For the transmit antenna, he used several vertical wires in the form of a fan monopole attached to the ground. In Europe, the receive antenna was a 200-meter wire held up by a kite. In 1906, Columbia University had an Experimental Wireless Station at which they used a transmitting aerial cage made up of wires suspended in the air. In 1908, they formed what is thought to be the first Amateur Radio club and later got the call 2XM. Beginning in 1919, Harold Beverage, 2BML, experimented with long wire receiving antennas into the 1920s, resulting in the Beverage antennas still used today for low-band reception, particularly DXing.

Other than the dipole and vertical, the most famous antenna used by radio amateurs is the Yagi. The Yagi antenna was invented in Japan and the first paper describing it was published in 1926. The original idea for this antenna design was reportedly developed by Shintaro Uda and refined with Hidetsugu Yagi, both at Tohoku Imperial University, Sendai, Japan. The original work was also published in Japanese. Yagi then went to America and gave the first English-language presentations on the antenna in 1928, which led to its widespread use. Hence, even though the antenna is often called a Yagi antenna, Uda probably invented it and a more proper name would be the Yagi-Uda antenna.

Other types of antennas used by radio amateurs in the 1930s and 1940s were phased arrays of wires, parabolic dishes, and horn antennas. Radio astronomy is a direct descendant of Amateur Radio, mainly resulting from the work of Grote Reber, W9GFZ. He spent his summer holidays in 1937 building a parabolic dish antenna 10 meters in diameter made of wood and iron to receive signals on what he called the "ultra high" frequency of 160 Mc (MHz).

Another ham who made significant advances in antenna design was John Kraus, W8JK, a professor at Ohio State for many years after World War II. He invented a number of antennas during his career, many of which benefitted Amateur Radio. These include the 8JK phased-array beam, the corner reflector and the helical beam. He also made many contributions to radio astronomy, designing and building "The Big Ear" radiotelescope at Ohio State University (**www.bigear.org**).

Antennas have always and *will* always be a key element of Amateur Radio. The cover of February 1922 *QST* shows the antenna of 1BCG, participant in the Transatlantic Tests.

With the advent of computers and techniques for modeling and simulating antennas in the 1960s to the 1980s, it became possible to accurately predict antenna performance on a computer as opposed to having to actually build and measure antennas. Software packages such as the *Numerical Electromagnetics Code* (*NEC*) and *MININEC* appeared on mainframes and PCs. These programs could accurately determine antenna patterns, input impedance, gain, and other parameters in the actual environment of ground and other objects. The author and others such as Brian Beezley, K6STI; Roy Lewallen, W7EL; Jim Lawson, W2PV; Dean Straw, N6BV; Dave Leeson, W6NL; John Devoldere, ON4UN; and L.B. Cebik, W4RNL, worked to produce software packages and algorithms, enabling the radio amateur to model antennas and surroundings. Furthermore, the author and others introduced sophisticated optimization techniques that allowed Optimized Wideband Antenna (OWA) Yagis to be constructed with superior characteristics of gain, front-to-back ratio and bandwidth compared to trial-and-error designs of the past.

In this section, we present some of the monumental *QST* articles on antennas by such names as Beverage, Kraus, Lawson, Maxwell, Sevick, Beezley, and others covering all types of innovations and inventions in the field of antennas and transmission lines, developed by amateurs for use in Amateur Radio.

Beaming to the Future

What will the future bring? Innovations such as metamaterials may allow new miniature antennas to be made or antennas to be placed right up against a metal ground plane. New techniques in antenna matching (called *non-Foster*) may allow small antennas to be used over a wide bandwidth with excellent gain and VSWR characteristics. It is clear that radio amateurs will take part in all of these new developments and make strong contributions as has been the case over the last century of technology.

"The Wave Antenna for 200-Meter Reception" by Harold H. Beverage, 2BML

By Jim Breakall, WA3FET

Most Amateur Radio operators are familiar with horizontal dipole and long-wire antennas well above ground. The unterminated long-wire antenna with the feed point near one end has a bidirectional radiation pattern in-line with the wire that gets more directive as the wire gets longer.

A Beverage (or wave antenna), named after its inventor, Harold H. Beverage, 2BML, is essentially a long-wire antenna that is terminated at the opposite end from the feed point and mounted at a low height in wavelengths above the ground. Because of its low efficiency due to proximity to the lossy ground, the Beverage antenna is mainly used for receiving. At high frequencies (HF) and lower, the background noise from man-made, atmospheric and extra-terrestrial sources is quite high. As long as this noise picked up by an antenna is higher than the receiver front-end amplifier noise, efficiency is not the important criterion; signal-to-noise (SNR) is the desired goal in receiving. The higher the amount of signal received compared to the background noise (higher signal-to-noise ratio or SNR), the better the reception.

In 1919, Harold Beverage experimented with receiving antennas similar to the Beverage antenna described above at the Otter Cliffs Radio Station south of Bar Harbor, Maine. In 1921, antennas we now call Beverages (up to nine miles long!) were installed at RCA's Riverhead, New York, Belfast, Maine, Belmar, New Jersey, and Chatham, Massachusetts receiver stations for receiving low-frequency, long waves. Harold Beverage received a patent for this antenna in 1921 and it has since taken his name as the type of antenna.

In 1927, an array of four phased Beverage antennas three miles long and two miles wide was built by AT&T in Houlton, Maine. This was used for the very first transatlantic telephone system and is perhaps the largest Beverage antenna ever constructed commercially. These commercial Beverage antennas clearly provided excellent directivity for reception, but a huge amount of space was required. They were also physically far too large to be practically rotated and therefore installations had to use multiple Beverages beaming in different directions to provide a choice of azimuthal coverage.

The following article by Harold Beverage, published in 1922, had a special note that radio amateurs were given the privilege to experiment and use this wave antenna as set forth by RCA, owner of the license. This clearly has been put to use over the years in Amateur Radio with much experimentation and implementation by scores of low-band enthusiasts and contesters.

One of the reasons for its high popularity on the low bands is that it is fairly simple to construct a highly directive receive antenna as long as one has the space required. It consists simply of a long wire (at least one or more wavelengths) suspended above and close to the ground, oriented in the direction of the required reception. The far end in the direction of the station to be received is terminated in a non-inductive resistor (300 to 600 Ω) that has a value close to the characteristic impedance of the system against ground. The feed end away from the direction of reception is fed with a matching transformer to transform the higher impedance (300 to 600 Ω) to the normal coaxial cable impedance of 50 or 75 Ω. Other configurations exist with wires sloping down from the center to the ground at each end and also two-wire designs that allow switching of reception in two directions. Some excellent references for the design and theory of Beverage antennas are the *Beverage Antenna Handbook* by Victor Misek, W1WCR; editions of *Low-Band DXing* by John Devoldere, ON4UN; and the website of Tom Rauch, W8JI (**www.w8ji.com**).

In the following *QST* article from 1922, the abstract says, "It is absolutely a classic in the literature of Amateur Radio, and we are proud of it." After a century of technology in Amateur Radio, there is no more truer statement than this about this remarkable and everlasting antenna known as the Beverage. It is clear that radio amateurs will keep it alive and well clear into the this next century of technology with the contributions and usage by hams.

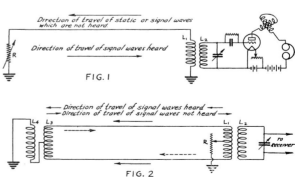

The Beverage termination was important to give it directivity. Several schemes were devised for one- and two-wire antennas, eventually combined in a two-wire, switchable antenna.

A Magazine Devoted Exclusively to the Radio Amateur

The Wave Antenna for 200-Meter Reception

By H. H. Beverage
Engineer, Radio Corporation of America

> *For a year now QST has been endeavoring to secure reliable information on the so-called Beverage Wire or wave antenna, which for special purposes is the best arrangement known today. With the approach of our Transatlantic Tests the matter became of even greater moment and we appealed to the Engineering Department of the Radio Corporation of America. They had never done any practical work with it on amateur wave-lengths but very courteously arranged for a series of special tests at their Belmar station, where engineers were sent and numerous lengthy tests conducted on this special subject. The following article, written especially for the A.R.R.L. and QST, is the result. It is absolutely a classic in the literature of amateur radio, and we are very proud of it. We acknowledge our gratitude to the Radio Corporation and its engineers for their very kind co-operation.*
>
> *No license rights are to be inferred from the publication of this article, but attention is called to the fact that amateurs are given the privilege of using the wave antenna as set forth and to the extent indicated in the current catalogue of the R.C.A., the owner of the license rights.—Editor.*

THE Wave Antenna is a new type of unidirectional antenna which has been developed by the author and Messrs. Chester Rice and E. W. Kellogg of the General Electric Co., and is covered by patents and applications. This antenna has been in existance for some time, but was first brought to the attention of the amateurs by Mr. Paul F. Godley, who described it in his report on the reception of American amateurs at Ardrossan, Scotland. The full theory of this antenna is scheduled to appear in an A.I.E.E. paper for the Pittsburgh convention in November, so this paper will be confined to very elementary theory and practical considerations.

Theory

If a wire is suspended in space, it has a certain capacity and inductance per unit length which bear a definite relation to each other. This relation may be expressed as $1/\sqrt{LC}=V$, where V is a constant. This constant is the velocity of light. For example, if L and C are expressed as the capacity and inductance per meter, then $V = 3 \times 10^8$ meters, which is the velocity of light in meters per second. If a larger wire is used, or if two or more wires are used instead of one, in the ideal case the inductance decreases in the same ratio as the capacity increases, so that $L \times C$ is always a constant. This means that, for the ideal wire, the currents induced in that wire will always travel along it at the velocity of light, independent of the size or number of wires.

A practically-constructed wire must be supported at several points and must run

One of the "Beverage Wires" erected at Belmar for these tests.

horizontally within a few feet of the earth. The effect of the supporting insulators and the proximity of the earth is to increase the capacity in a greater ratio than the inductance decreases, so the velocity of the currents on a practical wire is always somewhat less than the velocity of light On short wave-lengths, however, the velocity approaches very close to the velocity of light, generally between the limits of 85% and 98% of the velocity of light for 200 meters, depending upon the size and number of wires.

In order to make the antenna unidirectional, it is necessary to stop the reflections at the end farthest from the receiver end. This is accomplished very simply by placing a non-inductive resistance between the antenna and ground at the far end. If this resistance is made equal to the "Surge Impedance" of the wire, it absorbs all of the energy and prevents any of it from being reflected back to

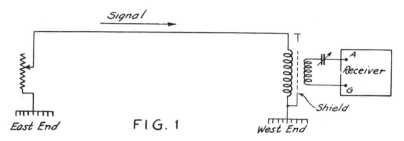

FIG. 1

In Figure 1 is shown the simplest form of Wave Antenna. It consists simply of a wire, at least one wave-length long, stretched in the direction of the transmitting station. For explanation purposes, it may be assumed that the transmitting station is east of the receiving station, and that the receiver is placed at the west end of the antenna, as shown. The travelling wave from the transmitting station moves from east towards the west at the velocity of light. As the wave moves along the antenna, it induces currents in the wire which travel in both directions. The current which travels east moves against the motion of the wave and builds down to practically zero if the antenna is one wave-length long. The currents which travel west, however, travel along the wire with practically the velocity of light, and, therefore, move along with the wave in space. The current increments all add up in phase at the west end, producing a strong signal, as shown by curve A in Figure 2. In like manner, static or interference originating in the west will build up to a maximum at the east end of the antenna, as shown by curve B in Figure 2.

If the east end of the antenna were open or grounded through zero resistance, all of the energy represented by curve B would be reflected and would travel back over the antenna to the west end, where part of the energy would pass to earth through the receiver and part would be reflected again, depending upon the impedance of the receiver winding. The horizontal plane intensity diagram would be bi-directional, as shown in Figure 3. The reception from the west is not as good as from the east because some of the energy is lost due to attenuation in the wire as the reflected wave travels back from east to west.

the receiver. The intensity characteristic becomes unidirectional, as shown in Figure 4.

The value of the surge impedance depends upon the size, number, and height of the wires above ground, but is independent of the length of the wire. For practical construction with one or two No. 12 copper wires, the surge impedance lies between the values of 200 and 400 ohms. The surge impedance is theoretically equal to $R = \sqrt{L/C}$, where L and C are the inductance and capacity per unit length.

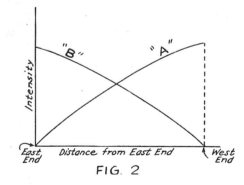

FIG. 2

Godley used the simple form of wave antenna, as shown in Figure 1. However, this is not the most practical form as it is necessary to go to the far end to make adjustments of the damping resistance.

Feed-Back Antennae

If two parallel wires are used, the wave antenna becomes very flexible and the receiver may be placed at either end with local control of the damping. In Figure 5, for reception from the east, the receiver at the west end is replaced by the primary P of a transformer T_2. The primary is coupled to the secondary S as closely as possible, and feeds the energy over the two wires as a transmission line. A second transformer T_1 at the east end feeds the energy from the transmission line into the receiving set. The energy fed over the transmission line circulates around the line

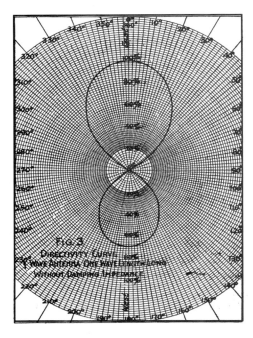

as in an ordinary metallic-circuit telephone line, and, therefore, the currents pass through both halves of the primary of T_1 in the same direction, inducing voltages in the secondary which feeds into the receiving set. On the other hand, currents coming over the wires as an antenna, that is, from the west, are equal and in phase on both wires, and upon passing to ground through the two halves of the primary of the output transformer T_1, they pass through the winding in opposite directions and neutralize. With this circuit, the energy reaching the receiver is the same as it would be if the receiver were placed at the west end, excepting for the transmission line losses, which ordinarily are 20 to 25% with proper design. With this feed-back system, the operator can make adjustments of the surge resistance without leaving the station, and can listen to the signals while he is making the adjustments.

Figure 6 is equivalent electrically to Figure 5, but in this case the transformer T_2 has been replaced by a simpler circuit. By grounding one wire and leaving the other wire open, the energy is reflected on each wire, but the reflected currents on the transmission line are 180 degrees out of phase on the two wires, and, therefore, a difference of potential exists across the terminals of the primary of transformer T_1 exactly the same as when the reflection transformer T_2 of Figure 5 was used. If the ground resistance at the reflecting end is zero, the reflection of energy with the connections of Figure 6 would be 100% efficient, and the only loss would be the transmission line losses. The open-ground reflection connection is preferable to a transformer, on short wave-lengths particularly.

It is possible to damp a two-wire antenna from either end. In the case of Figure 6, the signal from the east built up to a maximum at the west end, and was then reflected up to the east end, where the receiver and damping circuit were placed. In the case shown in Figure 7, the receiver is placed at the west end as in the case of the simple antenna of Figure 1. Instead of placing the damping circuit at the east end, however, it is placed across the transmission line at the west end where the receiver is. This damping circuit is practical-

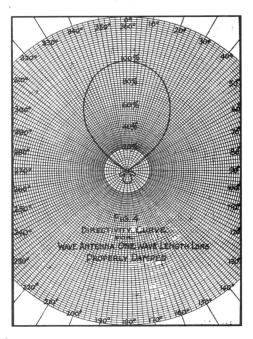

ly just as effective as it would be if actually placed at the far end. This circuit also has the advantage that the desired signals do not pass over the transmission line, and the transmission line losses are avoided.

In order for the damping circuit to be effective, it is necessary that the two wires of the antenna be joined through an inductance which is of high impedance compared with the impedance of the damping circuit. The best way to acomplish this result is to use a coil with a mid-point tap, as shown at N in Figure 7. With respect to the transmission line, the two halves of this coil are adding, so the inductance across the line is high. With respect to the receiver, however, the two halves of the coil are oposing, so that the impedance in series with the output transformer amounts only to the leakage reactance of the coil N, which can be made very small. A satis-

eliminate. This is made possible by making the damping-circuit reactance, either slightly capacitive or slightly inductive, instead of purely resistive. In some cases it may be desirable to reflect a small amount of energy to neutralize undesirable signals from the back end. This is readily accomplished by adjusting the resistance and capacity of the damping circuit. The capacity and inductance in this damping circuit are usually found to practically neutralize each other for the best adjustment; that is, they should tune approxi-

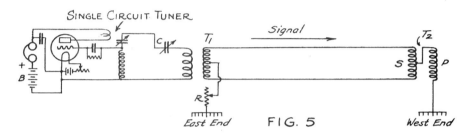

FIG. 5

factory coil for N for 200 meters was a 24-turn coil seven inches in diameter, with a tap at 12 turns for feeding the output transformer T. This coil was about 0.3 millihenries across the line, or 1900 ohms at 300 meters, and nearly 3000 ohms at 200 meters, which was high enough to have no appreciable influence on the damping circuit, and yet had low enough leakage reactance to allow the signals to pass to the receiver without noticeable weakening.

mately throughout the band of wavelengths it is desired to receive. If the wave-length being received is varied over wide limits, it is necessary to readjust the damping circuit condenser for best results, although the adjustment is usually quite broad. The resistance does not need readjustment except in special cases.

For a range of 180 to 360 meters, the damping circuit consists of an inductance of about 0.08 millihenries, a variable con-

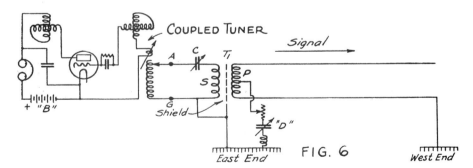

FIG. 6

Damping Circuits

In Figures 6 and 7, damping circuits "D" are shown which consist of resistance, inductance, and capacity, in series. Due to distortion on the antenna, to back-wave effects, to interfering signals or static coming from such a direction as to be received on one of the little "ears" on the back of the antenna, as shown in Figure 4, etc., it often happens that there are appreciable residuals which it is desirable to

denser of 0.0015 mfd. maximum capacity, and a non-inductive resistance variable in steps of one ohm from 0 to 500 ohms. A General Radio decade box is ideal for this purpose. However, ordinary resistance wire potentiometers, inductively wound, have been used with entire success in damping circuits. It is necessary to select a potentiometer with sufficiently low inductance to tune well below the shortest wave it is desired to receive; then the inductance of the potentiometer is taken into account when calculating the value of inductance to be used in series with the resistance and capacity. In this manner the inductance of the potentiometer used for the variable resistance may be tuned out, and the damping circuit may be made pure resistance for any one particular wave-length.

Other wire lines may be crossed at right angles without undesirable effects. In cases where it is not feasible to run the wave antenna in line with the desired signals, it is possible to get good reception with the antenna somewhat off line by sacrificing signal intensity. By referring to Figure 4 it is seen that for the average antenna one wave length long it is possible

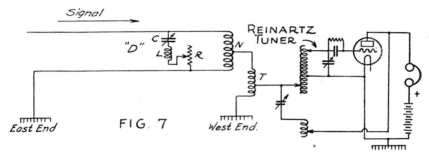

FIG. 7

When the damping circuit is placed across the transmission line as shown in Figure 7, the value of the damping resistance may vary considerably with wavelength, becoming lower for short wavelengths, due to the increase in attenuation at short wave-lengths partially damping the antenna. In other words, the transmission line acts as a resistance in series with the damping circuit, and the transmission line resistance becomes appreciable at short wave-lengths.

Antenna Design

It is obvious from the theory of the wave antenna just given that it must either point towards the desired signals or that it must point directly away from the desired signals. In case the antenna is pointed away from the signal, then the maximum signal occurs at the far end and must be brought up over the transmission line to the receiver, as shown in Figure 6. In case the antenna is pointed towards the signal, it is necessary to put the damping circuit on the transmission line, as shown in Figure 7. It is possible to use a single antenna for reception from either direction by switching arrangements to change to either the connection of Figure 6 or that of Figure 7 at will. It is preferable on short wave-lengths to point the antenna towards the signal, using the connections of Figure 7, but the feed-back of Figure 6 gives practically the same results, excepting that the signals are not quite as loud due to the transmission line losses.

It is necessary to run the wave antenna in as straight a line as possible and not nearer than 200 feet to other parallel wires, such as telephone and power wires, as the influence of these wires is liable to distort the directive characteristic of the antenna.

to be 45 degrees off line before the signal drops to half intensity. Beyond 45 degrees the signal falls off very rapidly. Twenty degrees off line, the signal intensity has fallen off only 10%, so very good reception may be obtained. If the antenna is two

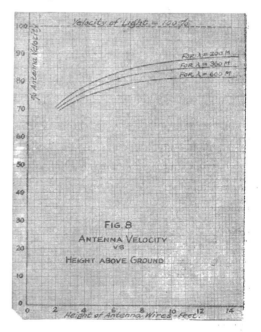

wave-lengths long, it is more directive, and it is not possible to receive well if it is more than 25 or 30 degrees off line.

The antennae are constructed of copper or other non-magnetic material, although

Mr. Cutler of 7IY reported in the October *QST* that he has obtained good results on a galvanized iron wire. The size of the wire is usually between No. 10 and No. 14 B.&S., although it is possible to get fair results even with No. 18 bell wire. The usual construction is to put up two wires

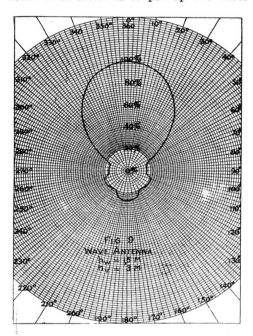

on a cross arm about two to three feet long. The wires are suspended by porcelain cleats, or in more permanent construction standard telephone pins and high grade insulators are used.

The height of the wires above ground has a marked influence on the velocity of the currents along the wires when the wires are close to the ground, but if the wires are ten feet above the ground there is very little to be gained in velocity by making them higher, as shown in the curves of Figure 8. These data were taken on an antenna at Belmar, N. J., by Mr. H. O. Peterson. This antenna extended over fairly conducting soil. The character of the soil underneath the antenna influences the velocity to some extent, but the data of Figure 8 are about the average velocity. These curves show that the velocity becomes lower at longer wavelengths.

If the velocity is too slow, then the currents in the wire lag in phase behind the wave in space, and a point is soon reached when the current in the wire from the far end is so far behind in phase that it not only does not add to the increments from points close to the receiver, but may actually subtract. The maximum length that it is feasible to use is that length at which the current in the wire lags 90 degrees behind the wave in space. This length is given by the formula:

$$L = \frac{\lambda}{4\left(\frac{100}{C} - 1\right)}$$

where
λ = wave-length in meters.
C = signal velocity on antenna expressed in per-cent velocity of light.

For example, from Figure 8 we find that the velocity of the currents in the two wires suspended at a height of 10 feet is about 88% of the velocity of light for 200 meters, so the maximum usable length is:

$$L = \frac{200}{4\left(\frac{100}{88} - 1\right)} = \frac{200}{.544} = 367 \text{ meters.}$$

Therefore it is not feasible to use a two-wire antenna suspended at a height of 10 feet more than two wave-lengths long for 200 meters. By increasing the height, the velocity will increase, and longer wires may be used. Figure 8 shows that the velocity increases slowly with height above 10 feet, so the wires must be much higher to be of material advantage. Making the wires too high introduces a difficulty on short waves which does not occur on long waves, and that is the "end" or vertical-antenna effect. The effective height of a 200 meter wave antenna is about 5% to 10% of its horizontal length, depending upon the nature of the earth beneath the antenna, etc. If an antenna is 200 meters long, therefore, its effective height will be between 10 and 20 meters. If the antenna

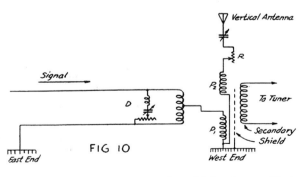

is on supports 10 feet high, the vertical or end effect may be equivalent to an effective height of nearly 3 meters, distorting the directive curve. In Figure 9 is shown the directive curve of a wave antenna of 15 meters effective height with a vertical or end effect of 3 meters superimposed upon it. It will be noted that the end effect may mount up to very serious proportions if the antenna is made too high. It is, however, possible to balance this end effect by means of a separate vertical antenna, as shown in Figure 10. P_1 is the standard primary, while P_2 is a second primary coil of about the same number of turns, which is wound over P_1 but in the opposite direction. How-

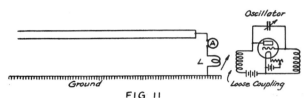

FIG 11

ever, in practice, the end effects seem to be very much smaller than predicted theoretically, so as a general rule if the antenna is not over 10 feet high the end effects are so small that it is not worth the trouble to balance them. From the above considerations, it is evident that 10 feet is a good average height for short wave antennae.

Design of Transformers

With the feed-back circuit of Figure 6 only one transformer is necessary. The output transformer T_1 was made up on a 7-inch cardboard tube. The primary P was 20 turns of No. 24 B.&S. D.C.C. copper wire, with a tap at ten turns or the exact center. Over the primary was placed a shield consisting of a piece of tinfoil insulated from both windings by paper. This shield was grounded to cut out capacity currents between primary and secondary. It is important that the tinfoil be not quite a complete turn around the primary; the ends must not touch or it will act as a short-circuited turn and introduces high losses. The secondary consisted of five turns of No. 18 bell wire wound over the tinfoil shield. The center of the secondary winding was lined up carefully over the center of the primary winding; otherwise the transformer would not be balanced. With the circuit of Figure 6, the transformer balance was tested by opening both wires at the west or reflection end. When the transformer T_1 was properly balanced, the receiver was quiet, indicating that the two halves of the primary were perfectly symmetrical with respect to the secondary.

Transformer T_1 of Figure 6 was designed to work with a coupled receiver. The secondary of the output transformer was connected in series with the primary of the receiver and was tuned by the series condenser C. This same transformer can also be used with a single-circuit tuner like the Westinghouse RC or the General Electric AR-1300 tuner. For 200 meters, it is usually better to use a separate condenser C outside of the tuner condenser, as shown in Figure 5, but for longer wave-lengths this series condenser may be omitted.

When the circuit of Figure 7 was used, the transformer described above was used with success but better results were obtained by cutting the primary turns down to 15 turns instead of 20 turns. This transformer is shown in Figure 1, but may be used with the connections of Figure 7. A tinfoil shield is used between primary and secondary, and is grounded as shown. In all of these transformers the coupling between primary and secondary should be as close as possible.

In Figure 7 an auto-transformer T is shown. The total turns are 15, and the receiver is tapped off at 5 turns. The diameter of the turns is 7 inches, but smaller diameters have been used by increasing the number of turns to make the same inductance. This auto transformer connection has been adapted to a Reinartz tuner with excellent results by Mr. Bourne at 2BML.

Determination of Surge Resistance and Velocity

The velocity and surge resistance were easily determined by oscillator tests. An oscillator was coupled to the antenna, as

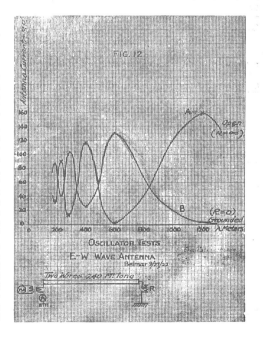

shown in Figure 11. In the antenna circuit was included a coupling coil L consisting of only two turns. The far end of the antenna was left open for the first test, and a resonance curve of the antenna was taken. The curve is plotted as Curve A in Figure 12. Then both wires of the antenna were grounded at the far end and the resonance curve taken again. This curve is plotted as Curve B in Figure 12. In order to find the velocity, it is necessary to calculate what the resonance points would be if the velocity of the currents on the wires was equal to the velocity of light.

The length of the antenna was carefully measured. In the case of this particular antenna at Belmar, the length was 240 meters. Assuming that the velocity of the currents on the antenna is equal to the velocity of light, the first resonance point with the far end of the antenna open will be the quarter-wave oscillation as in an ordinary antenna. The wave-length will be 4 x 240 = 960 meters. The next resonance point will be the three-quarter wave oscillation, or 4/3 x 240 = 320 meters. The next will be the 5/4 oscillation, or 4/5 x 240 = 192 meters, etc., for all odd multiples of the quarter wave oscillation. In like manner, with the far end of the antenna grounded the antenna will oscillate at all even multiples of the quarter wave oscillation. These calculated values are recorded in the table below. In the next column, the observed values taken from Figure 12 are recorded. By dividing the calculated value by the observed value, we get the actual velocity at that particular wave-length in terms of per-cent of velocity of light.

Calculation of Velocity of Currents on Antenna

Length = 240 meters, 2 No. 10 wires, 3 meters high.

Mode of Oscillation	Wave-length Calculated	Wave-length Observed	Velocity on Wires Velocity of Light
1/4	960	1200	80%
2/4	480	590	81%
3/4	320	390	82%
4/4	240	280	85%
5/4	192	220	87%
6/4	160	180	89%

To determine the surge resistance, a non-inductive resistance was placed between antenna and ground at the far end, and the resonance curve taken again. Figure 13 shows the results of this test on the Belmar antenna. Curve A, with 500 ohms at the far end, shows broad but unmistakable resonance points at open oscillation wave-lengths. On the other hand Curve B, with 200 ohms at the far end, shows grounded resonance points. Curve C, with 300 ohms at the far end, shows no resonance points, indicating that the antenna is quite aperiodic. Therefore the surge resistance for this particular antenna is approximately 300 ohms. The downward bend of Curve C below 200 meters is not due to the antenna but is due to the oscillator output falling off when the coupling condenser approached zero.

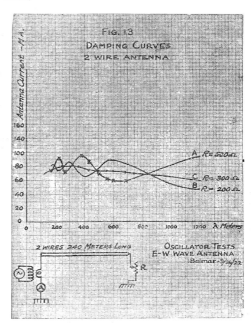

When one of the wires was grounded at the far end and the other wire was left open, and the damping resistance was placed across the wires at the station end, as shown in Figure 7, a smooth curve, similar to Curve C of Figure 13, was obtained when the non-inductive resistance was 500 ohms. In this case, however, there were slight irregularities in the curve which do not appear in Curve C of Figure 13.

Figure 14 shows the resonance and damping curves taken on a single-wire antenna by Mr. R. B. Bourne at 2BML-2EH. This wire was 195 meters long, and was suspended from trees at a height varying from 15 to 20 feet. It is interesting to note that Mr. Bourne's antenna has a velocity of approximately 93% of the velocity of light at 200 meters and, therefore, shows that a single wire may be used up to a length of over three wave-lengths or approximately 2000 feet. Such an antenna should show very directional properties, but lacks the flexibility and ease of adjustment of the two-wire antenna.

Performance

Two 200-meter wave antennae were erected at Belmar, one running west from the station, and the other running south.

These antennae were arranged with switching such that the connections of Figure 6 or Figure 7 could be selected at will on either antenna. That is, the west antenna could be used for reception from either the east or the west, and the south antenna could be used for reception from either north or south. For comparative purposes a flat-topped single-wire antenna 40 feet high was erected. The effective height of this vertical antenna was estimated as approximately 8 meters. The signals on the wave antennae were about 50% stronger than on the vertical, giving an effective height for the wave antennae of 12 meters. This figure corresponds to about 5½% of the horizontal length of the wave antennae.

Listening tests on these antennae showed marked directive properties, as expected. Listening south, most of the stations heard were in the 3rd and 4th districts, but careful adjustments were necessary to eliminate 2nd district stations to the north. With the antenna directive towards the

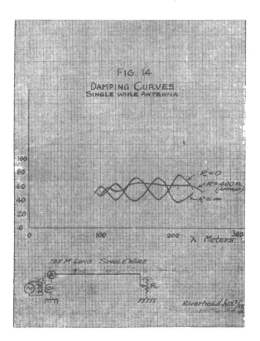

north, the best reception was from the 1st and 2nd districts, although several 8th district stations were heard. The east-west antenna worked better than the north-south antenna, probably because the ground resistance at both ends was less than an ohm, whereas the ground resistance at the far end of the north-south antenna was very high, nearly 300 ohms, making it difficult to operate the damping circuit effectively. The reception from the west was excellent, great numbers of 3rd, 8th, 5th, and 9th district C.W. stations being heard without interference from 1st and 2nd district stations. With the antenna directed east, only local 2's, Long Island 2's, and a few 1's were heard. There was considerable static reduction at times on the eastward reception, as the static was often heavy in the south or west.

On the 360-meter broadcast station wavelength, very good results were experienced in eliminating interference, particularly when using the antenna for west reception, and cutting out New York and Schenectady interference. Station WOC at Davenport, Iowa, was received particularly well on the wave antenna at times when reception was impossible on the vertical antenna due to local interference.

Even on 600 meters, these wave antennae showed very good directivity, particularly for reception from ships at sea.

Mr. Bourne's antenna at Riverhead, L. I., runs in a direction about ten degrees north of west. He reports his results as follows: "Signals from the south and southwest come in with about 25% to 50% increase in signal strength over a vertical antenna 60 feet high. Signals from New England are, in general, very weak, and in some cases cannot be heard at all when using the wave antenna. No interference from ships or shore stations using commercial wave-lengths has been noticed. WSA, at Easthampton, about 20 miles away, at times has a very strong harmonic on about 225 meters, which interferes seriously with 200 meter reception when the ordinary antenna is used, but due to the fact that this station is southeast, no interference is experienced when using the wave antenna. Radiophones on 360 meters come in with about the same intensity as with the vertical antenna, but often the signal-static ratio is much improved with the wave antenna, and, as with 200 meter reception, interference from WSA and WBC (East Moriches, 10 miles away) is entirely done away with."

The amount of static reduction experienced with the 200-meter wave antenna at Belmar depended entirely upon the distribution of the static at different times. On several occasions very marked improvement was noted in the signal-static ratio when receiving from the east and north, and sometimes when receiving from the west, but it was rarely observed to make any marked improvement when receiving from the south.

The author wishes to acknowledge the valuable assistance received from Messrs. H. O. Peterson, R. B. Bourne, and A. B. Moulton, in the collection of these data on the 200-meter wave antennae.

"A 14-Mc. Rotary Beam Antenna for Transmitting and Receiving" by John Shanklin, W3CIJ

By Jim Breakall, WA3FET, and Ward Silver, N0AX

Aside from the dipole, probably no antenna design has had as much impact on Amateur Radio as the Yagi — more accurately, the Yagi-Uda array — first described in IRE papers published in 1926 by Professor Uda and 1927 by Professor Yagi, both of Tohoku Imperial University in Japan. Their antenna was one of the first, if not the first, utilizing parasitic elements that re-radiate signals from energy supplied by a nearby driven element.

Initially, the antenna was intended for use with wireless power transfer, which is an active area of experimentation even today, nearly a century later. While those experiments were not sufficiently successful, the antenna did focus radio frequency signals through constructive and destructive interference created by the direct and re-radiated signals.

The Yagi utilizes a combination of wave transit time, reactance of the parasitic elements, and a 180-degree phase shift in re-radiated signals to form the radiation pattern of the antenna. Thus, the final radiation pattern of the antenna (and other parameters) depend primarily on element length and spacing to set up the proper phase relationships for the desired enhancement in the forward direction and cancellation in the reverse direction.

The first extended description of an amateur Yagi antenna came in a January 1929 *QST* article by Ross Hull describing propagation experiments on the new 28,000 kc band. (The article is featured in the Propagation section of this book. A short Stray in the 1928 October issue of *QST* is reproduced here.) Amateurs and professionals were just discovering radio at these high frequencies. It was still somewhat of a mystery as to the characteristics of the Kennelly-Heaviside Layer, as the ionosphere was then named, especially at these high frequencies. Antennas that could be varied in both vertical and horizontal directivity were needed to investigate propagation. The wavelength of the 10 meter band being relatively short, a Yagi's elements were short enough for construction on a wooden frame, and so the beam era of Amateur Radio got its start.

As more experience was gained with the Yagi, more of them were built and soon it was time to describe the antenna in detail for wider application. The following article by John Shanklin, W3CIJ, is the first detailed construction article for an amateur Yagi antenna. Unlike the more common horizontally-polarized Yagis that came into wider use after inexpensive and lightweight aluminum tubing became available, this antenna used wire elements held vertically between two wooden booms. The booms are held aloft on a 50 foot wooden pole and a girder made of "pine flooring and plaster lath." The antenna, weighing a svelte 300 pounds, was turned manually by ropes.

The vertically-polarized antenna also accomplished another first — stacking of Yagis. The antenna looks very

> **Strays**
>
> The erection of the 28,000 kc. (10-meter) beam antenna at 1CCZ has given the natives of Wianno, Mass. (where the station is located) one of the biggest thrills they have had for years. One village rumor has it that the affair is a private Ferris Wheel but this is flatly contradicated by some inhabitants, who insist that it is to be the new Dirigible for a trans-atlantic flight. "Dear me, that is a wonderful ship," one lady remarked on catching a glimpse of it through the trees, "but how will you ever get it down to the water when it's finished?"

The first note in the amateur literature of the Yagi antenna being used. Note that "village rumors" have plagued the ham with a beam since the beginning!

Possibly the first amateur Yagi ever constructed at the station of W1CCZ in 1929.

similar to what is commonly done on 2 meters today with a pair of Yagis side-by-side. Vertical polarization was probably the only practical option for amateurs building the array as a hobby, but placing two in an array allows considerable sharpening of the azimuthal beamwidth. The resulting gain was estimated and measured to be approximately 6 dB over a dipole.

The author mentions that the antenna works well for both transmit and receive with the stations reduced off the side, clearly indicating high directivity. This also confirms *reciprocity*, which is the property of receiving and transmitting with the same directivity, one of the primary antenna theorems. A front-to-back and front-to-side ratio of 3 to 5 R (receiving) units is noted and "the results in reception are a balm to interference-harassed ears."

Other practical notes abound. The antenna was fed with open-wire line and "Zepp feeders," a necessity since flexible coax was not yet a feature of the amateur station and this particular antenna was located "650 feet from the shack"! The antenna was fed from one side with the feeders between the beams transposed to account for line length. An impedance-matching section is then used to produce the right impedance for the feed line down the hill. A close look also shows that the extra vertical guying cables were broken up with insulators so they were electrically short enough not to interfere with the relationships of the driven and parasitic elements.

It would be interesting to build this antenna today using modern materials. Such a project is well within the capabilities of an experienced antenna and tower rigger! The same feeder technique could be used to match the antenna to 50-Ω coax, as well. It would be interesting to be able to say, "Antenna here is a 1934 W3CIJ stack!"

A 14-Mc. Rotary Beam Antenna for Transmitting and Receiving

An Effective Way of Increasing Transmitted and Received Signal Strength

By John P. Shanklin, W3CIJ*

ALTHOUGH the general idea of directional antennas for both transmitting and receiving has attracted the interest of most of us at one time or another, the very nature of a fixed type directional system, concentrating its

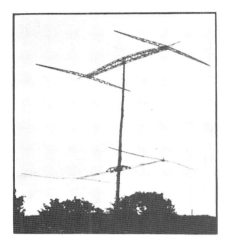

W3CIJ'S ROTARY 14-MC. BEAM ANTENNA MAKES A STRIKING APPEARANCE ON ITS PRIVATE HILL 650 FEET FROM HIS SHACK

energy along one path toward a limited group of possible receivers, runs contrary to the amateur's natural desire to communicate with anybody in almost any direction. The fixed type of directional antenna system is, therefore, of limited use in amateur work. While it may be of great advantage for communication in the particular direction toward which it points, it is a decided handicap to communication in every other direction.

What we want, then, for our work is a directive system that can be pointed in any direction. The only alternative to this would be a number of separate systems, one for each direction in which we might have occasion to work—which, of course, is completely "out" for most of us. But the antenna system of adjustable directivity is not. In fact, the rotary 14-mc. directional antenna system that has been in use at W3CIJ for some time has shown the idea to be entirely

* Marion, Va.

practicable and, by the excellent results it has given with a 50-watt 'phone-c.w. rig, has demonstrated that such a system is more than worth the expense and work required to construct it and get it into operation.

For instance, on three typical nights when, with a good non-directional antenna, only occasional VK's were heard and these were mostly unreadable, using the beam for both transmitting and receiving seven out of eight VK's heard were worked. Five reported the 'phone readable and one QSO was entirely on 'phone. With the beam swung around to point on Europe, several good 'phone QSO's have been had with stations there, and the ease with which they have been worked has given me the idea of going after a 'phone W.A.C. as soon as time permits.

The many requests for descriptions of the system that have been received from fellows contacted while using it show that it has widespread interest among hams.

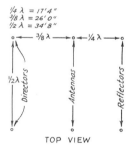

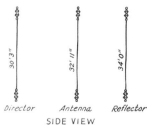

FIG. 1—SPACING AND LENGTH OF THE ELEMENTS OF THE BEAM
Note that the reflector wires are slightly longer than the antennas while the directors are slightly shorter. The percentage values are given in the text.

DESIGN AND CONSTRUCTION

As shown by the accompanying diagrams, there are six essential elements. First there is a pair of half-wave radiators, separated a half-wave and excited in phase. These are backed up by a pair of reflectors spaced a quarter-wave behind the antennas and a half-wave from each other. Finally, there is a pair of directors in front, the latter being spaced three-eighths-wave from the radiators and one-half-wave from each other.[1] The direction of transmission is, of course, along a line at right angles to the plane of the radiators and from the reflectors toward the directors. The dimensional arrangement of these elements is shown in the upper part of Fig. 1. The spacings between the elements are shown in wavelength fractions and in actual dimensions for a frequency of 14,200 kc. (wave-length, 21.13 meters), the center of the 14-mc. amateur band.

The lower portion of Fig. 1, the side view, shows the lengths of the respective elements for this frequency. These were calculated on the following basis: Antenna (radiator), 95 per cent of a half-wave in length; reflectors, 98 per cent of a half-wave in length; and directors, 87 per cent of a half-wave in length. The "tuning" was done entirely with a yard-stick when the beam was put up. The experimental check with instruments, made after the power was turned on, showed that nothing needed to be changed.

Fig. 2 shows the method of feeding the antennas, the feeders being connected to the lower ends of the radiators in Zepp fashion. Transposition of the feed line half way between the two radiators, as shown, is necessary to excite the

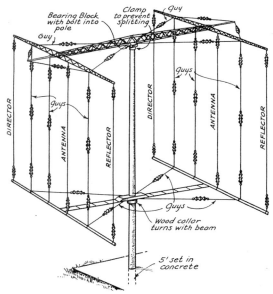

FIG. 3—A PERSPECTIVE DRAWING OF THE COMPLETE ASSEMBLY
The wood pole carrying the beam is 50 feet in height.

two antennas in phase. As is also shown in this figure, the feeders are extended a quarter-wave from one of the antennas, this quarter-wave section being shorted at its outer end. This extension is used as a folded half-wave antenna serving as a linear-impedance matching transformer to which the transmission line is coupled, as illustrated. It acts very much the same as a doublet-type antenna using the "Y" feed method—except that the quarter-wave section does not radiate. The transmission line used has a characteristic impedance of 520 ohms (No. 12 wire spaced 3 inches or No. 10 wire spaced 4 inches). When tapped on 3 feet 7 inches from the jumper, the whole system puts the same load on the transmitter as a 520-ohm resistance dummy load. With a 600-ohm line (No. 12 wire spaced 6 inches or No. 10 wire spaced 10 inches) the transmission line would be tapped on 4 feet 2 inches from the jumper. The 520-ohm line used here is 650 feet long.

Fig. 3 and the photograph show the complete assembly of the beam, while Fig. 4 illustrates the construction of the main girder and the end supports which carry the elements. The transmission line connections, although not shown in Fig. 3, are as previously described in connection with Fig. 1.

A good husky wooden pole of about 50-foot height carries the whole load. This is set in concrete, to insure its remaining rigidly vertical. Pine flooring and plaster lath are the materials

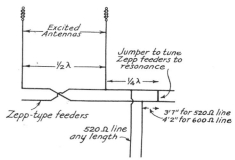

FIG. 2—HOW IMPEDANCE MATCHING IS PROVIDED AT THE ANTENNA TERMINAL OF THE TRANSMISSION LINE
The coupling idea is the same as that used in the familiar Y-fed doublet-type system.

[1] For a discussion of the action of wave reflectors and directors in this type of antenna system, see, "Beam Transmission of Ultra-Short Waves," by H. Yagi, *Proc. I.R.E.*, June, 1928. A similar combination was used in the 28-mc. tests at W1CCZ, described in *QST*, October, 1928, and January, 1929.—EDITOR.

from which the main girder and end supports are made, the cost of the wood being about $15 and the whole works weighing only about 300 pounds. The tongue and groove were removed from the 1-inch by 3-inch pieces of flooring to make the 3-inch pieces, and those serving as the 1-inch by 2-inch pieces were cut down further to the latter dimension. This type of construction has been

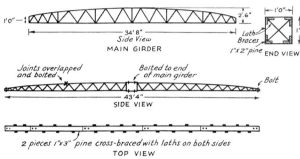

FIG. 4—DETAILS OF THE MAIN GIRDER AND END SUPPORTS THAT CARRY THE BEAM ELEMENTS

3-inch pine flooring and ordinary plaster lath are the materials used.

found satisfactory, although undoubtedly variations from it would serve as well. With the woodwork painted black, using roof and bridge paint, the structure has a striking appearance perched on its 60-foot hill.

With the bearing block on top and the collar at the bottom properly fitted, the beam is readily turned in any direction in a few minutes by means of a couple of rope stays. Once set at the desired position, pointed to dump the signals into the part of the world of interest at the moment, the ropes are pegged down to keep the beam from turning with the wind. To keep the feeders from becoming tangled up when the beam is turned, the line from the shack is anchored to

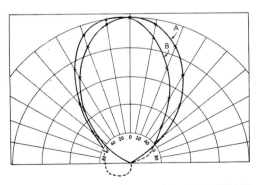

FIG. 5—THE THEORETICAL AND EXPERIMENTAL FIELD PATTERNS ARE IN GOOD AGREEMENT

The theoretical power gain as compared to a non-directional half-wave antenna is approximately 6 db, representing a power gain ratio of 4. Which is one way of making 50 watts behave like several hundred.

the pole below the lower bearing point and flexible jumpers of sufficient length are connected between the line terminals and the quarter-wave coupling section of the beam. A pulley and weight arrangement keeps the line running to the shack taut under varying conditions of weather and temperature. Although rotating the antenna through 180° puts some kinks in the jumpers, operation does not seem to be affected to any noticeable extent.

The other end of the transmission line is coupled either to the transmitter or receiver. The coupling to the transmitter is as conventionally used for any two-wire line (See the *Handbook*). For coupling to the FBXA receiver, a one-to-one transformer is used with 8 turns on each winding, both on the same 1-inch diameter form. The turns are spaced slightly, but the two coils are coupled together closely for best results, small-size wire being used to minimize capacity coupling to the line. Since the antenna is directional for receiving along the same line that it is directive for transmission, the system works both ways on the same QSO with equal effectiveness. The results in reception are balm to interference-harassed ears, both QRM and QRN being considerably minimized by the directivity. Off-beam signals leak through, but are weakened 3 to 5 points on the R scale. The beam action seems to be equally good over the whole 14-mc. band.

PERFORMANCE, MEASURED AND PRACTICAL

Fig. 5 shows the calculated horizontal field pattern (A) and the measured field pattern (B) of the beam. The intensity meter used in getting the experimental curve consisted of a Type 33 tube used as a diode rectifier, with both grids and the plate tied together, a 0-1 milliammeter connected in the output circuit giving the indications. Before taking the measurements it was calibrated on 60-cycle a.c. In taking the measurements the intensity meter was set up 10 wave lengths from the beam and the beam was then revolved through 180°, measurements being taken at a sufficient number of settings. The dotted portion of curve "B" is approximate, the reading being too small in this region to be determined accurately.

Theoretically the beam should boost the signal approximately 6 *db* over a non-directional antenna or, in other words, should give a power increase of 4 times—which means that the 50 watts here is effectively made equal to some several hundred watts with a nondirectional antenna. My calculations give the maximum concentration of radiation in the vertical plane to be between 20° and 40° above the horizontal, with

(Continued on page 68)

A Rotary Beam Antenna

(*Continued from page 34*)

considerable radiation as low as 10°. However, since the antenna is on a sharp 60-foot knoll the concentration of radiation at low angles is probably somewhat greater.

As an illustration of direct comparison of the beam and an ordinary non-directional antenna in actual communication, one evening W5AOT was contacted while the beam was aimed at Europe, nearly in the opposite direction. Switching over to a non-directional antenna he reported the signals *R8* while they were only *R3* to *R4* from the back of the beam. Several days later, in a subsequent QSO, with the beam pointed west, he gave reports of *R9*-plus on the beam and only *R3* to *R4* on the same non-directional antenna as had been used in the previous test. The later QSO was made under poor 14-mc. conditions, providing a striking example of the gain of the beam over the ordinary type antenna under such conditions as are commonly experienced on this band.

All that now remains is to make the rotation of the beam more convenient. Some day I'm going to install ropes and pulleys down the hill at the shack—and turn the beam with a crank, right from the operating position.

"Directional Antennas with Closely-Spaced Elements" and "The T-matched Antenna" by John D. Kraus, W8JK

By Jim Breakall, WA3FET

John D. Kraus, W8JK, was born June 28, 1910 in Ann Arbor, Michigan and died July 18, 2004 at the age of 94 in Delaware, Ohio. He received a Bachelor of Science, a Master of Science, and a Ph.D. in physics at the age of 23, all from the University of Michigan in Ann Arbor. During World War II, Dr. Kraus was a civilian scientist with the US Navy and was responsible for "degaussing," a technique for neutralizing the electromagnetic fields of steel ships to make them safe from magnetic mines. He also worked at Harvard University's Radio Research Laboratory where he contributed to developing radar countermeasures. After World War II, he took a faculty position at Ohio State University where he spent the rest of his entire career and became the McDougal Professor of Electrical Engineering and Radio Astronomy. The Antenna and Propagation Society of IEEE twice awarded him its Distinguished Achievement Award. The last award was in 2003 with the inscription "for a career of outstanding innovation and invention in the field of antennas, and for the many students he has taught and inspired to excel in electromagnetics."

In 1950, Kraus published the first edition of his classic and monumental book *Antennas* (McGraw-Hill). This book set standards and was referred to by many as the "Antenna Bible," especially for its detailed description of the helical antenna that Kraus invented. The helical beam has been used extensively in Amateur Radio and commercially for satellites and other applications for circular polarization. Kraus also developed other innovative antenna ideas such as the "W8JK flat-top beam," the "corner reflector," the "T-match antenna," and the "W8JK 5-band rotary beam antenna," all described in *QST*. He also had numerous published articles in professional journals on all of his ideas throughout his career. The following two *QST* articles, "Directional Antennas with Closely-Spaced Elements," and "The T-matched Antenna," are clearly amateur antenna classics and hallmark contributions to this *Century of Technology* book.

Being an avid Amateur Radio operator and a friend of famous radio astronomer and radio amateur Grote Reber, W9GFZ, Kraus was fascinated by the recent discoveries of radio noise from space and the potential to use radio waves rather than visible light to "see" the universe. At Ohio State, one of his major accomplishments was that he designed and directed construction of the "Big Ear" radio telescope (**www.bigear.org**). This large antenna was able to detect and discover some of the most distant known objects at the edge of the universe and conducted sky surveys mapping the radio stars. Kraus was also closely identified with efforts and activity related to the Search for Extraterrestrial Intelligence, or SETI. He even edited and published the first magazine about SETI, *Cosmic Search*.

The "Big Ear" was one of the largest radio telescopes ever built. [Permission to use photo given by Dr. Jerry R. Ehman, retired professor and radio astronomer, Ohio State University Radio Observatory; AC8IV.]

The first *QST* article, "Directional Antennas with Closely-Spaced Elements," was really something new for the time in 1938. Most radio amateurs were using some configuration of simple dipoles and were not that familiar with the concept of gain. The W8JK flat-top beam as reported in this article allowed a compact arrangement of two closely-spaced (in wavelengths, only 9 feet at 14 MHz) horizontal dipoles fed 180 degrees out of phase. This created a bidirectional pattern with a gain of about 4 dB over a single dipole. It could be fed with various feed arrangements usually with 600 Ω open-wire line and even could work at any frequency from 14 to 28 MHz, with a gain of 6 dB over a dipole at 28 MHz. This was really a true "beam antenna" and was used by countless radio amateurs for many years, some even making the W8JK rotatable.

Consisting of two or more closely-spaced dipoles fed out-of-phase, the "8JK" was one of Amateur Radio's first beam antennas. [Permission to use photo given by Dr. Jerry R. Ehman, retired professor and radio astronomer, Ohio State University Radio Observatory; AC8IV.]

The second *QST* article, "The T-matched Antenna," was actually written by Kraus and Stocker S. Sturgeon, W8MPH, also from Ann Arbor, Michigan. In 1940, when this article was published, a widely used method was the delta or "Y-matched" system to feed a half-wave dipole antenna from a high impedance open-wire transmission line. The concept was to feed the dipole at points separated from the center so the impedance would be much higher than the center-fed 73 Ω. This would then match whatever impedance transmission line was available, normally 600 Ω at the time. Another advantage was that the dipole did not have to be broken (insulated) in the center which would give extra strength, for example, if the antenna was made out of tubing. What this article showed is that a simpler and more convenient arrangement could be used as proposed by Kraus and Sturgeon, and they called it the T-match. It later became very popular for feeding Yagi antennas with a simple half-wave 4-to-1 balun to transform 200 Ω to 50 Ω. It also led to the gamma match which became a very popular method to feed a Yagi.

If ever there is an antenna hall of fame, a radio astronomer's hall of fame, or a radio amateur's hall of fame, clearly one of the first inductees in each would be Ohio State University professor emeritus Dr. John Kraus, the father of the W8JK beam, the helical antenna, the T-match, the corner reflector, and "Big Ear."

Directional Antennas with Closely-Spaced Elements

By John D. Kraus,* W8JK

ONE of the simplest and most efficient radiators used on short waves is the horizontal half-wave antenna.[1] Offhand it might not appear that two such antennas would make a good radiating system, if placed parallel to each other a small fraction of a wavelength apart and fed with currents 180 degrees out of phase. It is true, however, that this arrangement forms a simple and very compact directional antenna.

Fig. 1 is a sketch of two half-wave radiators oriented in the horizontal plane as described and placed high above the ground. The spacing may be a small fraction of a wavelength. If the wires

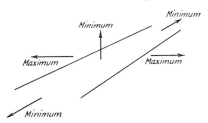

FIG. 1—TWO HALF-WAVE ANTENNAS CLOSELY SPACED AND WITH CURRENTS 180 DEGREES OUT OF PHASE
The arrows indicate the directions in which radiation is a maximum and a minimum.

are not placed too close together, the pair will radiate the same power as would a single half-wave antenna with the same input. But, because of the close-spacing and out-of-phase currents, the direction in which the radiation takes place is profoundly altered. G. H. Brown[2] was the first to point out the advantages of using such close spacing.

As indicated by the arrows in Fig. 1, the radiation from the pair is very small—theoretically zero—off the ends and also vertically. The radiation horizontally broadside is a maximum and is considerably greater than from a single half-wave antenna fed with the same power.

Fig. 2 shows the close spacing idea applied to a number of practical directive antenna systems. The type of Fig. 2-A is 32 feet long. It has two half-wave radiators spaced one-eighth wavelength and fed at the center. The cross-over feeds the two radiators 180 degrees out of phase. The feeders connect on at the middle of the cross-over. The radiation from the antenna is maximum in both directions broadside and minimum off the ends. The gain in both directions broadside is as much as or more than in the one preferred direction when a half-wave radiator is used with a reflector one-quarter wavelength behind. Dimensions are given for fundamental operation in the 14-Mc. band. The antenna is actually a multi-band affair, giving approximately the same horizontal bi-directional pattern on 28 Mc. as on 14 Mc., or on any frequency between these two bands. When used on 56 Mc. the horizontal pattern has four lobes. For fundamental operation on 28 Mc. the dimensions of Fig. 2-A should be halved. This smaller array would have about the same bi-directional pattern on both 28 and 56 Mc.

An antenna of about the same size as the one of Fig. 2-A is shown in Fig. 2-B. This antenna is end-, instead of center-fed. An array having two sections, which uses four half-wave elements, is shown in Fig. 2-C. It is 62 feet long. The array of Fig. 2-D has 4 sections or 8 half-wave elements and is 112 feet long. The antennas of Fig. 2-B, C, and D have the bi-directional pattern only on their fundamental frequency—14 Mc. in this case. When operated on 28 Mc. their horizontal patterns will have four main lobes. For fundamental operation on 28 Mc. the dimensions should, of course, be halved.

CONSTRUCTION

To make one of these antennas as a unit so that it may be supported between two poles it is convenient to use spreaders, which, for a 14-Mc. antenna, are about 9 feet long. These may be either of bamboo or 1- by 1-inch strips of wood. A suggested arrangement for a two-section antenna is given in Fig. 3. Since the antenna bears a striking resemblance to one of the "T" or flat-top types popular a decade or two ago, it is called a "flat-top beam."[3]

The cross-over at the middle of the flat-top is made by using two 6-inch feeder-spreader insulators, one placed horizontally at the center and the other vertically half-way between the center and one end of the wooden spreader. The two-wire feed line comes up from below and con-

---

*Arlington Blvd., Ann Arbor, Mich.
[1] An excellent treatment of the characteristics of horizontal antennas has been given by George Grammer, *QST*, Nov., 1936, and March, 1937.
[2] G. H. Brown, "Directional Antennas," *Proc. I.R.E.*, Jan., 1937.
[3] J. D. Kraus, "Small But Effective Flat-top Beam," *Radio*, March and June, 1937.

January, 1938

nects on to the cross-over at the horizontal center insulator. In order to get greater separation at the cross-over, the insulators may be made longer by fastening two 6-inch feeder spreaders end-to-end. The wire length at the cross-over is of necessity a few inches more than the spacing. Thus, the wire length at the cross-over of a 14-Mc. antenna (8 feet 8 inches spacing) may be about 8 feet 11 inches.

The line used to support the long wooden spreaders at each end of the flat-top should preferably be of rope. In case a 4-section flat-top is used, a method of accomplishing the additional cross-overs is indicated by dotted lines in Fig. 3. One vertical feeder-spreader insulator is used at the middle of the long wooden spreader. The recommended spacing lengthwise between the sections of the flat-top is about 2 feet.

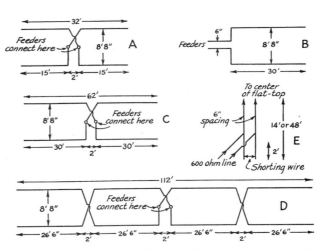

FIG. 2—FOUR TYPES FOR USE IN THE 14-MC. BAND

A and B are single-section types, C a 2-section, and D a 4-section. For fundamental operation on 28 Mc. the dimensions should be halved. Approximate dimensions for a matching stub to feed the 2-section antenna of C are given in E.

FEEDING

The main characteristics of a flat-top directional antenna are the closely-spaced elements, about one-eighth wavelength apart, and currents 180 degrees out of phase. All the elements are driven. The spacing is not critical but one-eighth wavelength seems to be about optimum when 180-degree phasing is used, and is recommended. The mutual coupling between closely spaced out-of-phase wires is such that the impedance at the center of the half-wave elements becomes quite small and, inversely, quite large at the ends. Accordingly, the current flowing at voltage nodes is very high.

The dimensions are not critical and the values of Fig. 2 are recommended for use on any frequency in the 14-Mc. band. Compensation is made for any small variations when the antenna is tuned up.

Either Zepp feeders or a matching stub and 600-ohm line can be used to feed the antennas. The Zepp feeders or the stub connect at the center of the cross-over in the flat-top as shown in Fig. 3. The approximate dimensions for a stub to feed the antenna of Fig. 2-C is indicated in Fig. 2-E. With more sections the 600-ohm line will connect farther from, and with fewer sections closer to, the shorting wire on the stub.

Where the line is not over a wavelength or two long, the Zepp type of feed is very practical. It is also convenient if one expects to use the same flat-top beam on a number of bands. For example, the antenna of Fig. 2-A may be series fed at the transmitter on 14 Mc. and parallel fed on 28 Mc. The feeders in this case would be either one-half or one wavelength long, approximately, since this antenna is fed at a current loop (voltage node) on 14 Mc. A matching stub for this antenna would also be either one-half or one wavelength long on 14 Mc. and about 8 feet either longer or shorter on 28 Mc. The other antennas, Figs. 2-B, C, and D, are all fed close to current nodes as used on 14 Mc. so that matching stubs to feed them should be either one-quarter or three-quarter wavelengths long. It is often convenient to use a three-quarter wavelength stub as one may be able to adjust it from the ground after the antenna has been pulled up into place. It is advisable to use good 6-inch spreader-insulators throughout the stub and 600-ohm line.

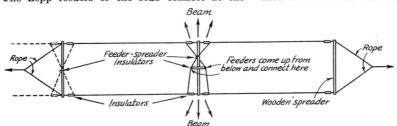

FIG. 3—TOP VIEW SHOWING CONSTRUCTION OF A 2-SECTION ANTENNA WHICH IS POPULARLY TERMED A "FLAT-TOP" BEAM

Method of making cross-over if extra sections are added is shown by dotted lines at left.

In adjusting the stub the antenna is shock-excited from another antenna or from an r.f. line coupled loosely to it. The shorting wire on the stub is then adjusted for a maximum of current through the short. The transmission line is next connected on the stub a foot or two above the short and adjusted up or down the stub until the

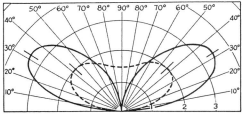

FIG. 4—COMPUTED RADIATION CHARACTERISTICS IN THE VERTICAL PLANE FOR A SINGLE HALF-WAVE ANTENNA (DASHED) AND A 2-SECTION FLAT-TOP (SOLID) BOTH AT A HEIGHT OF THREE-EIGHTHS WAVELENGTH ABOVE GROUND

standing waves along the transmission line are a minimum. A sensitive r.f. current meter (0-200 ma.) equipped with a single turn loop and an insulated hook can be used to slide along one side of the transmission line, so that readings may be made quickly at four or five points along the line spaced about an eighth wavelength apart. Insulation of the antenna and feeders from the transmitter plate supply voltages is, of course, important in any installation.

PERFORMANCE

Because of the out-of-phase currents, the vertical radiation from the flat-top antenna approaches zero. As a result, the maximum radiation in the vertical plane is lowered to a smaller vertical angle. In Fig. 4 the vertical radiation characteristics of a single half-wave antenna (dashed curve) and a 2-section or 4-element flat-top antenna (solid curve) are compared for a height in both cases of three-eighths wavelength above ground. The plane in which the radiation is shown is at right angles to the antennas. The relative field strength is plotted in arbitrary units, and the curves are calculated on the basis of the same power to both antennas. Perfectly conducting ground is assumed, but with horizontal antennas and the height being considered the patterns for ordinary ground would probably be quite similar.

It is apparent from Fig. 4 that the radiation maximum is lowered from about 43 degrees in the case of the half-wave antenna to about 32 degrees for the flat-top. The maximum gain of the flat-top over the half-wave does not occur at these angles, however, but rather at lower ones—15 degrees and less. It is these low angles which are frequently the most effective in long distance communication. The effect of lowering the vertical angle of maximum radiation from a flat-top beam is most pronounced at heights up to a half wavelength or so above ground. At greater heights the angle of the lowest lobe becomes nearly the same as that for a single half-wave antenna. For 14-Mc. DX a height of three-quarters to one wavelength above ground seems worth while.

Although much of the gain comes through vertical directivity, the horizontal gain is also important. This depends mainly on the number of sections used. Fig. 5 shows the measured horizontal radiation pattern for a single-section antenna (see Fig. 2-A). The maximum radiation is broadside and the minimum is off the ends of the antenna. The radiation is 3 db down at an angle of about 35 degrees off the center line of the beam (broadside). At 70 degrees the signal is over 20 db down, representing a front-to-side signal power ratio of well over 100 to 1. The relative field strength is plotted in decibels, the minimum signal observed being taken as 0 db.

The power gain of a single-section flat-top compared to a single half-wave antenna is over 4 db. When used on its second harmonic the gain

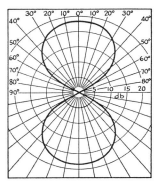

FIG. 5—MEASURED HORIZONTAL RADIATION PATTERN OF SINGLE-SECTION FLAT-TOP ANTENNA
The relative field strength is plotted in decibels.

is about 6 db. The horizontal radiation as measured from a 2-section flat-top (Fig. 2-C) is only slightly narrower, the signal being 3 db down at about 30 degrees off the center. Thus, a 2-section flat-top puts out a very satisfactory signal over an angle of about 60 degrees in each direction broadside, and a usable signal over an even wider angle. The null off the ends, however, is very pronounced. Three 2-section antennas arranged at angles of 120 degrees with respect to each other should give good coverage over 360 degrees. The gain of a 2-section flat-top is over 6 db. A 4-section array would have over 8 db gain and a still narrower pattern than the 2-section type.

A pair of double-Zepp antennas, one stacked one-half wavelength above the other, is a familiar

(*Continued on page 37*)

Directional Antennas

(Continued from page 13)

bi-directional array of 4 elements. In many cases, especially where the lower double-Zepp is not very high off the ground, a 2-section flat-top should give somewhat improved performance, that is, if the flat-top is placed at the same height as the upper double-Zepp of the pair. A 2-section flat-top should also give more gain over a much wider horizontal angle than 4 co-linear half-wave antennas in phase and at the same height above ground.

The small dimensions of the flat-top antenna make it suitable for use in many locations. Through the use of close-spacing the gain is exceptionally good for an array of its size.

The T-Matched Antenna

Feeding the Radiator With An Untuned Line

BY JOHN D. KRAUS,* W8JK, AND STOCKER S. STURGEON,** W8MPH

The delta or "Y-matched" system is widely used to connect an open-wire untuned transmission line to a half-wave antenna. This familiar arrangement is shown in Fig. 1.

The use of the "Y" or fanned-out section between the transmission line and the antenna is convenient in some cases. However, there are many installations where it would be more convenient to extend the transmission line at uniform spacing to within a very short distance of the antenna. An arrangement of this type is provided by the "T match" shown in Fig. 2-A. The transmission line divides at a point close to the antenna, and each wire extends parallel to the antenna for a short distance before making a right angle bend and connecting to the antenna.

Referring to Fig. 2-A, L is the length of the antenna, D the distance along the antenna between the points where the line connects to it, A the distance from each end of the antenna to the nearest tap, and S the spacing between the antenna and the parallel wire of the "T match". In constructing an antenna it is only necessary that either A or D be specified. For convenience, however, both are given. Open-wire lines of any convenient characteristic impedance can be used for feeding a half-wave antenna by means of the "T match". For a 600-ohm line, the recommended dimensions are as follows, where f is the operating frequency in megacycles:

$$L = \frac{475}{f} \text{ feet,}$$

$$D = \frac{114}{f} \text{ feet,}$$

$$A = \frac{180.5}{f} \text{ feet,}$$

$$S = \frac{114}{f} \text{ inches.}$$

As an example, an antenna cut for the center of the 14-Mc. band (14.2 Mc.) would have the following dimensions: $L = 33$ feet 5 inches,[1] $D = 8$ feet, $A = 12$ feet 8 inches, and $S = 8$ inches. These dimensions are suitable for matching an

* Arlington Blvd., Ann Arbor, Mich.
** 1032 Vaughn St., Ann Arbor, Mich.
[1] Note that this formula for the antenna length gives a slightly longer length than the usual formula. — ED.

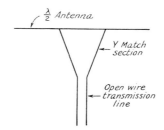

Fig. 1 — Delta or Y-matched half-wave antenna.

open wire line having a characteristic impedance of about 600 ohms. A line of this impedance can be constructed of No. 12 wire, spaced about 6 inches.

The performance of the "T" match is excellent and is entirely comparable with the delta or Y match. Tests involving changes of several variables have been made with T-matched horizontal half-wave antennas at W8JK. These variables included antenna dimensions, frequency and height above ground. A variation of only about 10 per cent in the standing-wave ratio on the transmission line was observed over the frequency range of the 14-Mc. band.

It appears that the dimension D is not critical. Although the length L is not particularly critical, it is important that it be fairly close to the resonant value. For a simple half-wave antenna made of No. 12 wire, the dimensions given above are close to optimum. If tubing is used for the radiator, it may be desirable to shorten L by about one per cent. When using a T-matched half-wave as the driven element of a beam antenna, some change in D may also be desirable.

An arrangement for supporting the center of the "T match" is shown in Fig. 2-B. Two insulating strips, of paraffined wood or ceramic material, are used to maintain the spacing at the

---

Although aware of its advantages, many amateurs hesitate to use an untuned transmission line to their antenna because the usual delta match is often awkward and sometimes hard to adjust. Here is a modification of the system that takes up less room and should be much easier to get going.

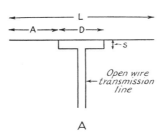
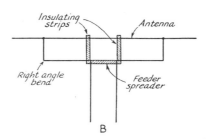

Fig. 2 — The T-matched half-wave antenna (A) and a method of supporting the matching section (B). Dimensions are given in the text.

center and to carry the weight of the transmission line. An approximate right-angle bend is made at each end of the "T," adjacent to where the wires connect to the antenna. By using sufficiently heavy wire (No. 12 or heavier) this bend can be made self-supporting.

Two-Wire Antennas

The T-matched half-wave can be regarded as an intermediate step toward the 2-wire half-wave antenna.[2] An antenna of this type is shown in Fig. 3-A. With the antenna in free space, the resistance at the antenna terminals is about 300 ohms.

Another type of 2-wire radiator is the extended antenna shown in Fig. 3-B. This is a 2-wire three-quarter wave antenna. Both wires are opened at the center, the transmission line connecting across one of them. The feed point resistance is about 450 ohms.

The dimensions given in Fig. 3 are suitable for operation in the 14-Mc. band. For 28 Mc. these dimensions, both length and spacing, should be halved. Thus, for example, a 2-wire half-wave antenna for operation in the 28-Mc. band is made 17 feet long, with 6-inch spacing. The arrows on the wires indicate the current distribution on the antennas at a given instant. The radiation characteristics of the 2-wire half-wave antenna are similar to those of a simple single-conductor half-wave. The principal change is the increase in the feed point radiation resistance from about 70 to 300 ohms. The radiation characteristics of the 2-wire three-quarter wave antenna are similar to those of a single-conductor extended half-wave type. Either of the 2-wire antennas may be fed satisfactorily with open-wire transmission lines of 400 to 600 ohms characteristic impedance. Although the feed point resistance of the 2-wire types may appear on paper to be somewhat low for the direct connection to a 600-ohm line, excellent results can be obtained with such an arrangement. The 2-wire antennas also have the advantage of a very flat response over a wide frequency range.

The 2-wire three-quarter wave antenna is slightly more directional than a half-wave antenna, concentrating more radiation at right-angles to the antenna. However, all of the antennas described in this article, both T-matched and 2-wire types, are much similar to a simple half-wave antenna in radiation characteristics and are not beam antennas in any sense. The antennas described can be regarded as simple types in which the matching arrangement is included as an integral part of the radiating system.

We appreciate the assistance of Henry Newburgh, W8MDA, in certain of the tests on the T-matched half-wave antenna.

---
[2] J. D. Kraus, "Multi-Wire Doublet Antennas," *Radio*, May, 1939, and June, 1939; and "Multi-Wire Dipole Antennas," *Electronics*, Jan., 1940.

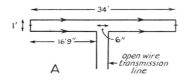

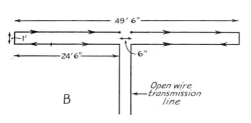

Fig. 3 — The 2-wire half-wave antenna (A) and the 2-wire three-quarter wave antenna (B). Dimensions are given for the 14- to 14.4-Mc. band.

"The 'Quad' Antenna" by George Grammer, W1DF

By John Stanley, K4ERO, HCJB engineer (retired)

When I arrived at HCJB in 1973 I found that the large technical staff there included a number of largely self-taught folks along with some highly qualified graduate engineers. In the earliest days, much of the work was done by the "hams." Clarence Moore, W9LZX, had limited technical qualifications, as he was well aware, but his contagious enthusiasm for radio and tireless experimentation was a major factor in making the cubical quad a widely used and praised antenna. Though Clarence worked much of his life in the technical arena, he also serves as a good example of a radio amateur in the best sense of the word. He was simply someone whose love for radio advanced the state of the art.

In May of 1947, Clarence applied for a patent on an antenna he called a quad. In that application he states, "The theory underlying the present invention is not too well understood but extensive tests have demonstrated that an antenna is provided having substantially no high voltage points." A reading of the patent in light of modern antenna theory demonstrates that in 1947 the quad was, indeed, not well understood, even by its inventor. A quad does, of course, have voltage peaks on the wires at the points ¼-wavelength from the feed point. The antenna was successful in the high altitude of Quito more because of its two-turn elements, which spread out the strong E fields, than for the quad shape. The two turns also stepped up the feed point impedance, similar to a folded dipole, important for feeding with open lines.

The original HCJB quad consisted of two turns of wire that had a lower E field strength — reducing corona at high power and high altitude — and a higher feed point impedance for open-wire feed line. [Photograph provided by John Stanley, K4ERO]

The single-element, two-turn loop antenna that Clarence first tested at Radio Station HCJB, in Quito, Ecuador, was not exactly the "cubical quad" of later ham radio fame, but certainly in its direct ancestry. The patent, finally granted in 1951, included a unidirectional version with a reflector loop, also with two turns. The patent also mentioned use on 28 MHz, and Clarence's good results with a 10 meter quad led many others to try the design as it was introduced in the following article by George Grammer, W1DF, in January 1949 *QST*.

With lower sunspots, 10 meter propagation faded and the quad excitement had waned somewhat when in January 1955, S.B. Leslie, W5DQV, presented a 20 meter version in *QST*. By then it was called a cubical quad due to the shape of the two-element version. Later, others added additional elements and additional bands and the quad, as we know it today, was off and running.

Quads have continued to be used for broadcasting. A 24-element array on 4 booms with 6 quad elements each, was used from Pifo, Ecuador on 21 MHz while beaming to Europe. Clarence donated this antenna to HCJB after founding Crown International, Inc. in Elkhart, Indiana, where he also had a similar antenna on the factory roof. HCJB used a 5-element quad for 26 MHz with a rotator to beam to Japan, North America and Europe during the Cycle 21 sunspot peak. HCJB Australia used a 2-element quad rated at 50 kW for South Pacific broadcasting. Other stations, such as ELWA in Liberia, have used horizontal "lazy quad" antennas for NVIS coverage on the tropical broadcast bands.

Today the quad is used with director and reflector elements. HCJB uses this 24-element quad on 4 booms with 6 elements each while beaming programs to Europe on 21 MHz. [John Stanley, K4ERO, photo]

While some claims for the quad have not stood up under *NEC* analysis, one thing cannot be denied. If you are on an island with lots of bamboo and no aluminum tubing, the quad will certainly be the beam antenna of choice. Since many prime DX locations are in places like that, the quad has possibly done more to add to the country totals of DXers than any other antenna design.

• *Technical Topics* —

The "Quad" Antenna

THE current fashion in antennas on the ten-meter band appears to be the "quad"[1] — so named, perhaps, because it is built in the shape of a square or quadrangle, or perhaps because the total length of wire in an element is four half-wavelengths. The most-used version consists of a two-turn loop, ¼ wavelength on a side, backed up by a similarly-constructed reflector, as shown in Fig. 1. Provision is made in the reflector for inserting reactance to obtain optimum phasing.

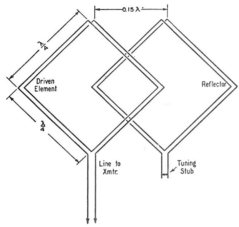

Fig. 1 — The "quad" antenna, using driven element and reflector, each consisting of a two-turn square loop ¼ wavelength on a side.

Since the only purpose served by using two turns instead of one is to obtain an impedance step-up (as in the folded dipole), it is convenient to look on the driven element as a single-turn square loop having a total length of one wavelength. This is shown in Fig. 2-A. The only possible current distribution, if the transmission-line currents are to be equal and opposite, is that shown by the arrows. There is a current loop at the input terminals, B, and at the opposite corner, A. Current nodes occur at corners C and D. With the loop mounted vertically in the position shown, the currents in the various sides can be divided into horizontal and vertical components as shown in Fig. 2-B. It can be seen that the vertical components tend to cancel each other, while the horizontal components are all in the same direction. The result is that a square loop in this position is horizontally-polarized. If corner B is closed and the input terminals are moved to C or D, the polarization becomes vertical.

It has been pointed out by W. van B. Roberts[2] that loops of this type can be considered as instances of a general case that includes the folded dipole as one limit and a short-circuited half-wave transmission line as the other. If the folded dipole of Fig. 3-A is stretched out into a square as in Fig. 3-B, we have the loop of Fig. 2. Further stretching forms a shorted half-wave line, as shown at C. The input impedance of the folded dipole is known to be approximately 300 ohms, and that of the shorted half-wave line is zero. Consequently, we might reasonably expect that the impedance of any loop formed by the stretching process would have an intermediate value of input impedance. So far as we know, no analysis of this particular conformation has been published.

As a radiator, the loop of Fig. 2 can be looked upon as being equivalent to two horizontal dipoles stacked vertically, with each having a length equal to the diagonal of the square. The two are separated by the distance between what might be called the "effective centers" of current in each bent dipole. In dipole CAD the highest current is at A, but current also is distributed along CA and AD. The "effective center" is therefore below A, but it is nearer to A than it is to the center of the loop. Similarly, the highest current in dipole CBD is at B, and the "effective center" is nearer to B than to the center of the loop. Since the diagonal of the square is approximately 0.35 wavelength, the separation of the

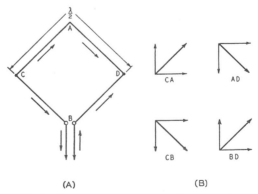

Fig. 2 — Instantaneous current flow in a square loop and resolution into horizontal and vertical components.

---

[1] This antenna system is believed to have originated at HCJB, Ecuador.
[2] W. van B. Roberts, "Input Impedance of a Folded Dipole," *RCA Review*, June, 1947.

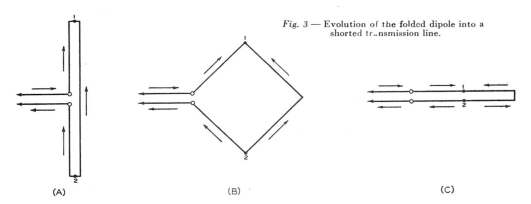

Fig. 3 — Evolution of the folded dipole into a shorted transmission line.

two equivalent dipoles is less than 0.35. It is known that the gain with broadside half-wave dipoles at 0.35 spacing is about 2 db. and drops to 1 db. with ¼-wavelength spacing. We might expect, therefore, that the gain from the equivalent dipoles would be between 1 and 2 db. On the other hand, the equivalent dipoles are shorter than ½ wavelength and the reduction in length can be expected to result in some loss. It would appear questionable, therefore, whether such a loop would have any significant gain over a half-wave dipole.

This reasoning was confirmed by measurements using model antennas at 144 Mc. Field-strength measurements comparing the square loop with a dipole showed that the loop had a gain of about 0.5 db. at a height (center of loop) of one wavelength above the flat roof on which the measurements were made. At a height of about ¾ wavelength the two antennas gave the same field, but below this height the simple dipole showed a gain over the loop, the dipole being 1.5 db. better at a height of about 0.6 wavelength, the lowest height used. This behavior with respect to height may be the result of the fact that at a given center height the corner of one dipole in the loop is almost 0.2 wavelength below center. If so, it shows the importance of height in a stacked system.

Using a Reflector

There appears to be no more reason for using the folded or two-wire reflector shown in Fig. 1 than there is for using folded parasitic elements in the ordinary type of beam antenna. Folding an antenna element (folded-dipole fashion) does not change its characteristics when viewed externally; it is simply an expedient for making the input impedance as seen by the transmission line assume a desired value. The reflector used in our measurements was a single-turn loop having a closed phasing stub at the bottom corner. The stub supplies the inductive reactance required to make the parasitic loop act as a reflector.

Measurements showed that when the stub was adjusted to optimum length the gain over the simple loop was approximately 7 db. — considerably more than is usually obtained from a reflector. This is no doubt the result of the configuration of the system, which does not have a very close physical resemblance to the customary straight-line elements. The gain over a half-wave dipole at the height at which this measurement was made — just under one wavelength — was between 7 and 8 db.

For comparison, a simple reflector of the ordinary type was tried at the same spacing (0.15 wavelength) with a half-wave dipole. The measured gain of this set-up was a little over 4 db., which is in line with previous measurements [3] although possibly not the maximum that could be secured by careful adjustment of spacing and reflector tuning. Wire elements, rather than tubing, were used in this case. Nevertheless, there is no doubt in our minds that the two-loop quad system shows a worth-while gain over the simple

[3] R. G. Rowe, "Gain vs. Element Spacing in Parasitic Arrays," *QST*, April, 1947.

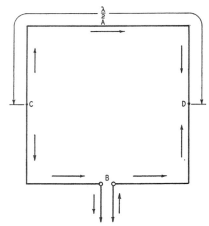

Fig. 4 — Square loop fed at center of one side.

form of two-element beam using a driven element and reflector. The quad gain over a dipole is comparable with that obtained from three-element beams [3] provided the antenna is installed at a height of at least one wavelength.

Since there appears to be little difference in gain, the choice between a two-loop quad and a 3-element beam can be made on the basis of other features. From the adjustment standpoint the quad appears to be simpler; it is only necessary to adjust the stub on the reflector as against adjusting both reflector and director in the 3-element beam — adjustments that usually interlock. Although folding the driven element does raise the impedance as seen by the transmission line, it was obvious in our tests that the terminal impedance does not match a 300-ohm line very closely. No facilities were available at the time for making a reasonably accurate measurement of either impedance or s.w.r. at 144 Mc. Constructionally, it appears to be a matter of choice. The quad is about 8 feet on a side at 29 Mc. (the wire length is figured from $468/f$ for a half-wavelength) and thus requires cross members a little over 11 feet in length. The spacing between the two loops is just under 5 feet at this frequency ($492/f$ for a half-wavelength in space).

An alternative method of mounting and feeding a square loop is shown in Fig. 4. The current distribution is similar, except that the current loops occur at the centers of the top and bottom wires and the current nodes at the centers of the vertical members. The cancellation of the vertically-polarized radiation is more obvious in this case (a similar principle is used in the well-known Bruce curtain), and it is equally obvious that the horizontally-polarized components are in phase. In Fig. 4, the high-current portions of the antenna are actually horizontal and are separated by $\frac{1}{4}$ wavelength; their length is also $\frac{1}{4}$ wavelength. A loop of this type, without a reflector, showed a consistent gain of about 0.8 db. over a half-wave dipole at all heights except the lowest (0.6 wavelength), where the two were equal. Its behavior with a loop reflector has not yet been investigated. — *G.G.*

"The Multimatch Antenna System" by Chester Buchanan, W3DZZ

By Jim Breakall, WA3FET, and Ward Silver, N0AX

In the time before this article appeared in *QST*, a "multiband" antenna meant an antenna that could be "loaded up" on multiple bands through tuned feeders, an antenna coupler, an impedance matching network or other means. The end-fed Zepp and center-fed doublets were the order of the day. Then came Buchanan's article.

While he had published an article in *Radio & Television News* (December 1950) about a dual-band antenna, the *QST* article that follows extends the idea to more bands and presents not only what we now called a trap (or trapped) dipole, but the first multiband rotary beam antenna, too, the now-ubiquitous "tribander." The W3DZZ trap dipole design covers all five (at the time) HF ham bands from 3.5 through 28 Mc (MHz). The triband Yagi design works on 14, 21 and 28 Mc (MHz).

The use of tuned circuits in antennas was uncommon prior to Buchanan, although there were many designs that used tuned feeders or stubs. Some of the designs used stub or feeder placement to achieve a suitable impedance on more than one band. For example, a Hints & Kinks item by S.L. Seaton, VK6MO, from November 1941 *QST* uses multiple tuned feeders on a single Zepp antenna, although only one feeder is selected at a time. So the W3DZZ design rather burst onto the scene and as later articles on its various implementations would note, it generated a lot of interest in the *QST* readership!

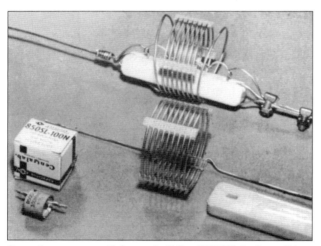

One of numerous articles on building W3DZZ designs, this photo from October 1956 *QST* illustrates how to construct traps for wire antennas.

The article itself covers a lot of fundamentals along with presenting construction information. Buchanan shows how a parallel resonant circuit, one of the most important in RF circuit design, behaves at resonance (very high impedance), below resonance (as an inductor), and above resonance (as a capacitor). Every electrical engineer and General class exam student learns the extreme cases — at dc the capacitor is an open circuit and the inductor is a short, while at infinite frequency, the situation is reversed. In between those extremes, by choosing the right combination of values for each and the correct lengths of the wire sections, the result is an antenna that presents a resonant impedance on more than one band. This is the first time that had been presented in the amateur literature. Based on those principles, Buchanan then extends the concept to create antennas that will resonate on odd multiples of half-wavelengths to get an antenna that works on 80 through 10 meters.

The triband beam also has some interesting features from today's perspective. On 10 meters, there are two reflectors which makes it a 4-element beam although the extra reflector has been shown to be unneeded. The T-match is used to allow the antenna to be fed with 75-Ω twin lead, based on the work of John Kraus, W8JK, a few years earlier. While the familiar gamma match had been introduced by H.H. Washburn, W3MTE, in *QST* in 1949, coaxial feed lines were still new and this particular antenna used the balanced feed system. Another innovation here is the use of the telescopic tapered aluminum elements for strength and concentric aluminum tubing in the traps. Compare this design to the 1934 article introducing the Yagi made of wood and wire with a weight of 300 pounds!

There were no real measurements of performance except to say that people were happy with it. An understatement, to be sure! If one had time, it would be interesting to model the W3DZZ with today's sophisticated software to just see what the modeled performance would be. One would have to figure out the inductance and capacitance of the traps, and that is not easy in modeling.

How did Buchanan come upon and develop his design? We don't know and there is little that describes the process. Nevertheless, it is clear from the details provided and the well-thought-out method of trap construction that a significant number of hours were consumed in the design and trial-and-error phases. In this era of modeling software, we tend to forget just how much work was involved in antenna design before computers came along!

Buchanan's creation spread quickly around the world and is still being produced commercially in simple three-element tribanders that have been on the market with little change except in the production materials since the mid-1950s. The many following articles on every aspect of the antenna — traps, tubing, tuning — led to many thousands of home-built antennas, as well. The authors have had many, many contacts and received boxes of QSLs over the years in which the other station reports "the antenna is a W3DZZ" or "ANT HR DZZ." That a design nearly 60 years old is still vital and useful to the amateur community says a lot about how the importance of its invention and the vision of its creator.

The W3DZZ beam designs were introduced as commercial products beginning in 1955-1956 such as this version from the Frederick Tool and Engineering Corp. Traps for wire antennas were also available from numerous companies.

The Multimatch Antenna System

Unique Design Providing Essentially Constant Impedance Over Several Bands

BY CHESTER L. BUCHANAN,* W3DZZ

> • For a long time, hams have been searching for a single antenna that could be fed efficiently with a low-impedance transmission line on several bands. At last a simple but ingenious design by W3DZZ provides a solution. He has applied some well-known but neglected principles to both wire and parasitic-beam antennas.

RADIO transmitters and receivers have enjoyed rapid development in flexibility to the point where changing bands is a matter of only spinning a dial or two and flipping a couple of switches. In contrast, the operation of a single antenna on several bands is usually done only at the expense of high standing waves on the feed line, because of the wide variation in antenna feed-point impedance from band to band.

Some work done by the author several years ago in connection with a dual-band parasitic array[1] has led to the development of a simple wire antenna covering five bands, from 80 to 10 meters. This antenna can be fed with a low-impedance transmission line without incurring excessive s.w.r. on any of these bands.

Basic Design

The fundamental principle of the system can be explained with the aid of Fig. 1. In Fig. 1A,

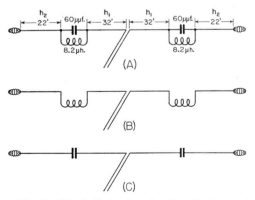

Fig. 1 — Sketch illustrating the three fundamental modes of the multimatch antenna.

---

* 4671 Lacy Ave., Washington 23, D. C.
[1] Buchanan, "Duo-Band Ham Antenna," *Radio & Television News*, December, 1950.
[2] Morgan, "A Multifrequency Tuned Antenna System," *Electronics*, August, 1940.

sections h_1 constitute a half-wave dipole for some frequency f_1. This dipole is terminated in lumped-constant trap circuits resonant at f_1. Additional wire sections, h_2, extend beyond the traps. If the system is excited at frequency f_1, the traps serve to isolate the dipole much as though insulators were inserted at these points.[2]

At frequencies much lower than f_1, the traps no longer isolate the dipole, but act simply

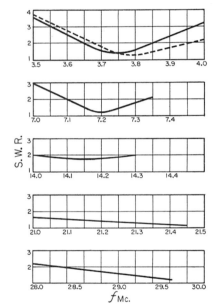

Fig. 2 — S.w.r. measurements made on the antenna of Fig. 1A. The dashed lines show measurements made on a 122-foot dipole in the same location for comparison.

as loading inductances in a second dipole whose electrical length is made up of h_1, h_2 and the inductive reactance of the traps, as in Fig. 1B.

At frequencies much higher than f_1, the traps again cease to isolate the sections, the traps now acting as series capacitances, as in Fig. 1C.

Another important consideration in this multiband system is that low impedance at the center feed point of the antenna occurs not only at its fundamental resonance but also at any odd harmonic of the fundamental.

By applying these principles, and by proper selection of the values of L and C in the traps, and choice of lengths for h_1 and h_2, it has been possible to arrive at a design where the system operates as follows:

1) Sections h_1 form a half-wave dipole resonant

in the 40-meter band. The traps, resonant at the same frequency, isolate this dipole from the outer sections.

2) The inductive reactance of the traps is such that the entire system, including sections h_2, resonates as a loaded half-wave dipole for the 80-meter band.

3) The capacitive reactance of the traps at higher frequencies is such that the entire system resonates as a 3/2 wavelength antenna on 20, 5/2 wavelength on 15, and 7/2 wavelength on 10 meters.

The antenna is fed with 75-ohm Twin-Lead, and Fig. 2 shows the results of s.w.r. measure-

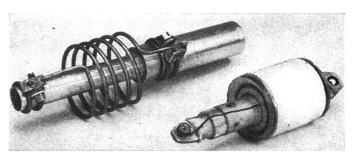

Lightweight weatherproof traps made by the author. To the left is the type inserted in beam elements, while the other one is suitable for wire antennas.

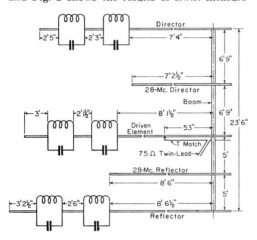

Fig. 3 — Dimensions of the 3-band parasitic beam found optimum at W3DZZ. Dimensions are, of course, duplicated on the opposite side of the boom.

ments made across each band. Proper dimensions are given in Fig. 1A.

Trap Construction

The values of C and L used in the traps are quite critical. The capacitance should first be adjusted accurately to 60 $\mu\mu f.$, then the inductance should be trimmed until the trap resonates at 7200 kc. This should be done before the traps are inserted in the antenna. The inductance will be approximately 8.2 μh. The traps made by the author are 6 inches long and weigh only 6 ounces and the Q is well over 100. They will withstand the voltage developed by a 1-kw. transmitter. Samples are shown in the photograph. The wire-antenna capacitor is made up of concentric lengths of 1-inch and ¾-inch aluminum tubing separated by polystyrene tubing with ⅛-inch walls, molded around the inner conductor. The polystyrene is also flowed into a series of holes in one end of the outer conductor so that the strain of the antenna will not pull the assembly apart. The inductor is wound with No. 14 wire and is concentric with the capacitor. The inductor is weatherproofed by molding it in insulating material. Other construction might be used, of course. As an example, a conventional inductor and capacitor could be enclosed in a plastic box, suspended across an insulator. This would, however, add to the weight.

A Three-Band Parasitic Beam

The principle of isolating sections of an antenna with resonant traps has been applied to a parasitic beam antenna that operates on 10, 15 and 20 meters. This array with dimensions is sketched in Fig. 3. The array is a five-element job on 10 meters, with two reflectors spaced approximately 0.15 wavelength, and two directors spaced approximately 0.2 wavelength. On the other two bands, three elements are active. On 15 meters, spacings are approximately 0.22 wavelength for the reflector and 0.29 for the director. On 20 meters, the approximate spacings are 0.14 and 0.2, respectively.

Fig. 4 shows a breakdown of a suggested method of construction of the three main elements. Each element starts out with a 12-foot center section to which various sections are added at each end. Provision is made for adjusting the length from the center of the element to the first (28-Mc.) trap, the length between traps, and the section on the outside of the second (21-Mc.) trap. The photograph shows an example of the array traps used by the author. Here,

(Continued on page 130)

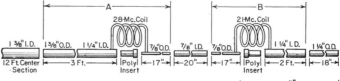

Fig. 4 — Breakdown of the element assembly. Sections *A* and *B* are assembled permanently. Other sections may be telescoping for adjustment. Detail of the polystyrene inserts is at the right. The ⅞-inch o.d. sections should be inserted to a depth of 2¾ inches.

March 1955

Multimatch Antenna System

(Continued from page 23)

again, the capacitor is made up of concentric aluminum or dural tubing separated with polystyrene, and the coil is concentric. In each capacitor, the polystyrene insert (Fig. 4) should provide a tight fit to both sections of tubing, and the insert should be driven into the outer conductor to the shoulder. The inner conductor should be driven into the insert for a distance of 2¾ inches (thus protruding 2 inches inside the outer conductor). This gives a capacitance of approximately 25 $\mu\mu$f. The trap inductors are wound with No. 8 wire. The 10-meter inductors have 5 turns 2½ inches in diameter, with the turns spaced approximately ½ inch. The 21-Mc. inductors are similar, but have 7 turns. As with the wire-antenna traps, the inductors should be adjusted for resonance near the center of each band before they are installed. The ends of the inductors are wound around the element sections and fastened with clamps. The array is fed with a T match to 75-ohm Twin Lead.

Fig. 3 shows the element dimensions used by the author. Antennas of this type, in both wire and beam forms, have been installed by many amateurs, using traps constructed by the author. Without exception, all have been enthusiastic about the performance.

"Yagi Antenna Design" by Jim Lawson, W2PV

By Jim Breakall, WA3FET

To learn about the passion, intensity, and just how meticulous was Dr. James L. Lawson, W2PV, read "To Win the World From Schenectady: The 25th Anniversary of the Last W2PV Contest Operation" in the *National Contest Journal* for November 2006. He was truly a legend in contesting, but one could equally argue that he was even more of a legend in antennas from the volumes of articles on the Yagi antenna and his book *Yagi Antenna Design*. Lawson contributed three *QST* articles on broadband inverted-V design and vertical arrays but really made his lasting impact with a nine-part article series on Yagi antennas in *Ham Radio*. These groundbreaking and remarkable articles on the Yagi antenna clearly formed the basis of his book.

Now long out of print, Lawson's book covered a wide range of topics and was the definitive amateur reference on Yagis for many years.

It could be said that the Yagi has been the most popular gain antenna in Amateur Radio, especially among the DXCC Honor Roll members and contesters. The Yagi was invented in Japan and has been used in amateur community since the late 1930s. Many simply designed these antennas with the reflector 5% longer and the directors 5% shorter than the resonant driven element! There was little if any research into optimized designs and what happens if the element lengths and spacing were changed. This was because it is extremely tedious, if not impossible, to change these parameters experimentally by trial and error and obtain any really optimum results. It is just too difficult a task without the help of computers and modern optimization techniques.

Lawson reported his work on scaling and especially on element tapering in a series of articles in *Ham Radio* from August 1979 thru December 1980. These articles showed, for example, that 20 meter elements may have to be lengthened as much as 12 inches or more to equal the free-space length of an equivalent constant-diameter element. Without taking these things into account, Yagi performance could be very poor — especially when trying to achieve high front-to-rear sidelobe levels. These articles are clearly the best collection of references on Yagi design to date at that time in history.

W2PV had a very clear style of writing and meticulously explored all details. He produced charts and patterns from computer modeling, somewhat primitive at the time compared to modern methods and computer power, showing what could be done and how to do it. It is remarkable and necessary reading for anyone wanting to know the complete history and understanding of the important antenna known as the Yagi.

The ARRL extended those articles in the classic 1986 book, *Yagi Antenna Design*, now out of print but sought after by antenna designers. W2PV showed in the book how to use computer-aided optimization, a technique that is now commonly used by many amateurs on their home PCs. At the time of his research, it took powerful mainframe computers to do this optimization properly. He was the first to introduce this design technique for Yagis and showed its principle advantage in the ability to optimize gain, front-to-back ratio or sidelobe minimization.

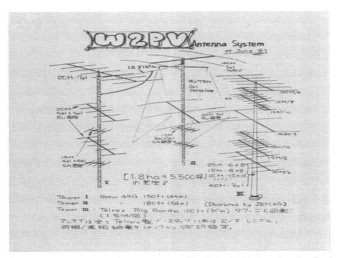

The Lawson antenna farm, captured in this 1981 drawing by Tack Kumagi, JE1CKA, was the precursor for super-stations around the world today.

One big problem at the time with Yagi performance characteristics was the achievable operating bandwidth, typically 200 kHz or less at 20 meters. His writings clearly showed that all of these things could be greatly improved over antiquated cut-and-try methods and led the way to modern Optimized Wideband Antenna (OWA) design via sophisticated global optimization software and advanced antenna simulation software.

The following chapter from *Yagi Antenna Design* describes W2PV's extensive work with stacking Yagis. It is a typical example of W2PV showing the way forward through solid engineering and practical technique.

CHAPTER 6
STACKING

This chapter addresses the use of multiple Yagi antennas arranged into a coherent antenna system. The number of potential arrangements is unlimited, but certain basic configurations deserve detailed analysis because they have attractive properties. To start, I shall limit the discussion to systems where the individual Yagi antennas are all physically identical and aligned for maximum radiation in the same direction. Moreover, to ensure that each Yagi contributes to the overall main radiated wave front in a coherent manner, I shall limit the configurations to those in which the Yagi positions (say, for example, the reflector end of the boom) lie in a plane perpendicular to boom direction. Usually all of the Yagis are coherently excited by the same driver current (magnitude and phase). Using identical Yagis positioned in such a plane helps maintain a uniform radiated pattern over a desired frequency band. The overall system beam pattern can be pointed in azimuth only by mechanically rotating the entire system. The radiated beam from a mechanically fixed (system) array of laterally spaced Yagi antennas can, in principle, be steered by changing the excitation phase to each Yagi antenna. However, the beam quality generally deteriorates. Such mechanically fixed, electrically steered phased arrays are not considered here.

The overall system array can be viewed as a large-area aperture illuminated in a quasi-uniform way by the individual Yagi antennas. So long as the individual Yagi antennas are not too far apart (so that illumination is relatively uniform), the system gain should be proportional to the total effective aperture area. The system beam pattern should also show an angular width inversely proportional to the aperture dimension. Thus, in concept, a horizontal array of Yagi antennas (horizontally polarized) should produce a narrow horizontal system beam pattern; similarly, a vertical array of Yagi antennas (horizontally polarized) should produce a narrow vertical system beam pattern.

We must consider the system array over ground; in this case all of the effects mentioned previously (Chapter 5) will occur. Recall that ionospheric paths over the earth primarily favor low radiation angles (up to, say, 20 degrees); moreover, this whole range of antenna radiation angles should be covered to accommodate a continuous range of great circle distances, as well as different multi-mode ionospheric paths. We shall see that, by vertically stacking two or more horizontally polarized Yagis over ground, it is possible to improve significantly low-angle performance (over that of a single Yagi antenna over ground) without reducing the azimuthal coverage. This improved result comes about through a suppression of otherwise useless radiation at the higher angles.

Vertical Stacking Arrangements

For Amateur Radio communications, relatively wide horizontal or azimuthal coverage is generally desirable, not only to make a given contact less sensitive to critical beam heading but to accommodate the many occasions in which the communication path is somewhat skewed due to ionospheric conditions. Wide azimuthal coverage is especially desirable under contest conditions, where it is advantageous to have the beam simultaneously illuminate the largest desired Amateur population. So, a horizontal array of Yagi antennas doesn't appear as desirable as a vertical stack; therefore I shall not attempt analyses of such horizontal arrays.

Vertically stacked Yagi arrays are now in reasonably wide use; these require a supporting mast. If the stacking separation is large (which we shall find desirable), the large mast must be entirely rotatable and, of course, very rugged mechanically. Such a mast, including its foundation, is a major undertaking.

Two interesting variations of this system are not as formidable. The first variation is a stacked Yagi antenna array offset from a fixed tower. The offset allows simultaneous rotation of the Yagi antennas over a range in azimuth of about 300 degrees; at either end of this range, the antennas are designed to nest around the mast. I use this construction for a 28 MHz stacked six-element Yagi antenna system on a Rohn 45 guyed mast. It works very well and is cost effective.

The second variation is to use a fixed mast with the top Yagi antenna fully rotatable and a second, lower, Yagi antenna fixed in a preferred direction. This is a particularly interesting variation for contest operation, especially on the lower frequencies where the mast must be very high. My 7 MHz system is a good example. A full-sized, three-element beam is fully rotatable on top of a 180 foot Rohn 45 guyed mast. A second full-sized, three-element beam is fixed at 90 feet, which is aimed at Europe. Thus, in the European direction, full stacking is available; in all other directions the top beam can be used alone. Moreover, it is easy to excite both beams and activate two azimuthal directions simultaneously, or it is also possible to switch instantly from one direction to another without losing the normal time to turn the large Yagi antenna. I have found the flexibility of this system to be very helpful in many situations.

Excitation

For all types of stacked arrays, I have found it useful to provide a switching system that allows operation of each Yagi independently or both together. When only high-angle radiation is desired, the lower antenna is usually best. For lower angles of radiation, the combined stack is better. It is easy to arrange such a switch using conventional relays and quarter-wave coaxial transformers; a practical system is shown in Fig. 6.1 for two stacked Yagi antennas.

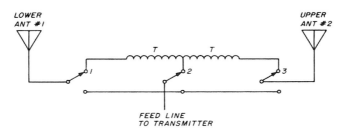

Fig. 6.1 — Both, lower, or upper (BLU) switching system. *T* is a quarter-wave transformer of 70 ohm coaxial cable.

The relays may have to be compensated by small shunt capacitors if their series inductance is too large. The relay box should be mounted on the mast about half way between the Yagi antennas. Extension to more than two stacked Yagi antennas is equivalently easy. However, the particular scheme will depend on the way in which power is to be split between all Yagi antennas.

Because of these various excitation techniques, it is desirable to compute not only the properties of a vertically stacked Yagi system, but the properties of the individually excited Yagi antennas. Two complicating problems arise. First, not only is a single Yagi antenna over ideal ground not the same antenna as in free space, but it is further changed by all other Yagi antennas as well as their ground images. This is true even if all other Yagi antennas are not driven. To some extent their elements will be parasitically excited by the single driven Yagi antenna. This means that the computation for a single Yagi must be carefully made to account fully for all the parasites and images in its local field.

Second, if only the top Yagi is rotatable, the performance of the single lower antenna alone will depend on the relative azimuthal orientation of the two antennas. In this case it is instructive to compute three cases: parallel, orthogonal, and antiparallel orientations.

Two-Array Stack

Let us now choose some representative horizontally polarized stacking arrangements over flat, ideal, ground and compute their theoretical performance. I shall present computed *H*-plane patterns over the range of elevation angles of interest. The *E*-plane pattern over ideal ground is, of course,

Table 6.1 — Performance of a two-array stack of three-element Yagis for different combinations of heights.

Fig. 6.2	height lower (λ)	height upper (λ)	both gain (dBi)	both angle (deg)	both F/B (dB)	lower gain (dBi)	lower angle (deg)	lower F/B (dB)
A	0.30	0.75	14.30	21	21.4	11.41	41	19.0
B	0.375	0.75	14.38	21	20.0	11.69	36	27.4
C	0.45	0.75	14.41	21	18.8	12.01	31	23.4
D	0.60	1.50	15.55	11	18.2	13.80	24	21.0
E	0.75	1.50	16.27	11	13.9	13.80	20	22.6
F	0.90	1.50	16.58	11	19.4	13.72	16	25.4
G	0.90	2.25	15.41	8	23.8	13.83	15	37.5
H	1.125	2.25	16.06	8	28.7	14.10	13	25.3
I	1.35	2.25	16.74	7	19.8	14.02	11	25.8
J	1.00	3.00	14.97	6	30.7	14.09	14	23.3
K	1.50	3.00	16.11	6	22.9	14.18	9	25.8
L	2.00	3.00	16.86	5	32.9	14.19	7	36.0

Fig. 6.2	height lower (λ)	height upper (λ)	upper gain (dBi)	upper angle (deg)	upper F/B (dB)	lower alone gain (dBi)	lower alone angle (deg)	lower alone F/B (dB)
A	0.30	0.75	13.54	18	29.0	11.54	37	22.9
B	0.375	0.75	13.39	18	23.7	12.20	32	47.8
C	0.45	0.75	13.32	18	20.1	12.82	29	28.4
D	0.60	1.50	13.96	9	23.9	13.67	23	19.5
E	0.75	1.50	13.71	9	16.0	13.84	19	25.3
F	0.90	1.50	13.83	9	18.9	13.94	16	31.2
G	0.90	2.25	14.31	6	30.8	13.94	16	31.2
H	1.125	2.25	14.19	6	29.9	14.08	13	24.2
I	1.35	2.25	14.00	6	21.3	14.13	11	37.2
J	1.00	3.00	14.22	5	30.8	14.04	14	25.5
K	1.50	3.00	14.31	5	24.6	14.17	9	26.5
L	2.00	3.00	14.20	5	34.1	14.24	7	27.3

zero everywhere. The plots show not only how well the overall system performs at the important low angles, but also what may be sacrificed at the higher angles, which are occasionally useful. Two basic Yagi designs are used. They are the same three-element beam (boom = 0.3 wavelengths) and the same six-element beam (boom = 0.75 wavelengths) shown in Table 5.1.

I shall start with two stacked, identical beams over ground. In practice, the height of the upper beam will be fixed at the overall mast height. The placement of the lower antenna will be made at some lower position. It is interesting to understand the tradeoffs involved in the height of the lower antenna. I shall choose, for illustrative purposes, four different heights for the upper beam, and for each of these cases, three different heights for the lower beam. All heights are expressed in wavelengths at the central design frequency. Tables 6.1 and 6.2 show computed results for all these cases. These tables also refer to Figs. 6.2 and 6.3, which display detailed *H*-plane patterns for all cases.

Stacking 6-5

Table 6.2 — Performance of a two-array stack of six-element Yagis for different combinations of heights.

Fig. 6.3	height lower (λ)	height upper (λ)	both gain (dBi)	both angle (deg)	both F/B (dB)	lower gain (dBi)	lower angle (deg)	lower F/B (dB)
A	0.30	0.75	15.52	20	23.2	12.78	33	15.8
B	0.375	0.75	15.60	20	20.2	13.06	27	26.1
C	0.45	0.75	15.61	19	18.2	13.22	24	26.2
D	0.60	1.50	17.47	11	22.5	15.11	21	21.6
E	0.75	1.50	17.28	11	14.0	15.10	19	16.7
F	0.90	1.50	18.10	11	23.3	15.73	16	38.8
G	0.90	2.25	18.00	8	31.2	16.06	15	24.7
H	1.125	2.25	18.42	8	29.2	16.31	12	49.0
I	1.35	2.25	18.60	7	19.9	16.22	11	22.6
J	1.00	3.00	17.34	6	39.7	16.38	14	35.5
K	1.50	3.00	18.71	6	32.9	16.61	9	39.1
L	2.00	3.00	19.24	5	25.5	16.59	7	27.1

Fig. 6.3	height lower (λ)	height upper (λ)	upper gain (dBi)	upper angle (deg)	upper F/B (dB)	lower alone gain (dBi)	lower alone angle (deg)	lower alone F/B (dB)
A	0.30	0.75	15.56	17	21.7	13.39	30	17.3
B	0.375	0.75	15.22	17	17.6	13.96	27	24.0
C	0.45	0.75	14.75	17	14.6	14.51	25	30.0
D	0.60	1.50	16.40	9	30.3	15.18	21	23.7
E	0.75	1.50	16.06	9	17.8	15.60	18	21.5
F	0.90	1.50	16.08	9	24.6	16.16	15	29.1
G	0.90	2.25	15.16	6	57.5	16.16	15	29.1
H	1.125	2.25	16.55	6	31.3	16.32	12	33.5
I	1.35	2.25	16.24	6	21.7	16.38	10	32.3
J	1.00	3.00	16.68	5	41.2	16.36	14	37.7
K	1.50	3.00	16.76	5	36.5	16.59	9	41.7
L	2.00	3.00	16.58	5	26.2	16.68	7	45.2

Note that each figure has several curves: one for the combined stacked performance (solid line); one for the lower antenna alone (dotted line); one for the upper antenna alone (dashed line); and, where applicable, what the lower antenna only would show if no upper antenna were physically present (broken solid line). In the second and third cases, both antennas are physically present, but only one is driven (all nondriven elements act as parasites).

An examination of Tables 6.1 and 6.2, and especially the *H*-plane patterns of Figs. 6.2 and 6.3, reveals a number of interesting and important characteristics of these simple, vertically stacked systems. Table 6.1 shows the maximum gain and corresponding elevation angle for each case of a stacked pair of three-element beams. Also shown is the F/B ratio, which we know varies with the exact element complex currents, which in turn are influenced by the mutual impedances to all other elements. Table 6.2 shows the equivalent quantitites for the stacked pair of six-element beams.

Note from these tables that the smaller values of overall antenna mast

6-6 Chapter 6

combination	curve
both	solid
lower	dots
upper	dashes
lower alone	chain-dots

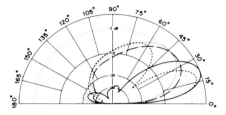

Fig. 6.2A — *H*-plane radiation pattern for two three-element Yagis at 0.3 and 0.75 wavelengths above ground.

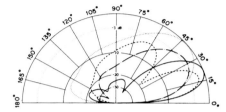

Fig. 6.2B — *H*-plane radiation pattern for two three-element Yagis at 0.375 and 0.75 wavelengths above ground.

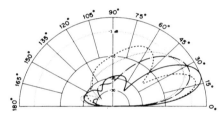

Fig. 6.2C — *H*-plane radiation pattern for two three-element Yagis at 0.45 and 0.75 wavelengths above ground.

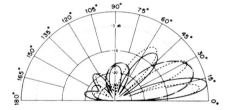

Fig. 6.2D — *H*-plane radiation pattern for two three-element Yagis at 0.6 and 1.5 wavelengths above ground.

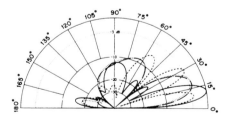

Fig. 6.2E — *H*-plane radiation pattern for two three-element Yagis at 0.75 and 1.5 wavelengths above ground.

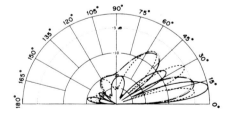

Fig. 6.2F — *H*-plane radiation pattern for two three-element Yagis at 0.9 and 1.5 wavelengths above ground.

Stacking 6-7

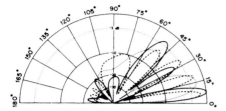

Fig. 6.2G — H-plane radiation pattern for two three-element Yagis at 0.9 and 2.25 wavelengths above ground.

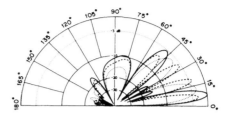

Fig. 6.2H — H-plane radiation pattern for two three-element Yagis at 1.125 and 2.25 wavelengths above ground.

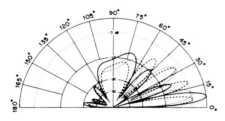

Fig. 6.2I — H-plane radiation pattern for two three-element Yagis at 1.35 and 2.25 wavelengths above ground.

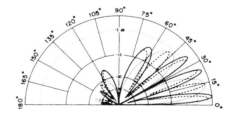

Fig. 6.2J — H-plane radiation pattern for two three-element Yagis at 1.0 and 3.0 wavelengths above ground.

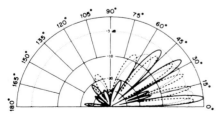

Fig. 6.2K — H-plane radiation pattern for two three-element Yagis at 1.5 and 3.0 wavelengths above ground.

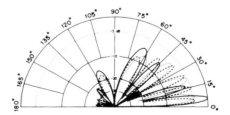

Fig. 6.2L — H-plane radiation pattern for two three-element Yagis at 2.0 and 3.0 wavelengths above ground.

6-8 Chapter 6

combination	curve
both	solid
lower	dots
upper	dashes
lower alone	chain-dots

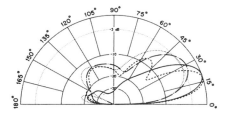

Fig. 6.3A — *H*-plane radiation pattern for two six-element Yagis at 0.3 and 0.75 wavelengths above ground.

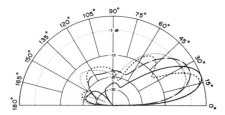

Fig. 6.3B — *H*-plane radiation pattern for two six-element Yagis at 0.375 and 0.75 wavelengths above ground.

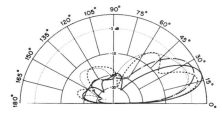

Fig. 6.3C — *H*-plane radiation pattern for two six-element Yagis at 0.45 and 0.75 wavelengths above ground.

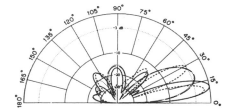

Fig. 6.3D — *H*-plane radiation pattern for two six-element Yagis at 0.6 and 1.5 wavelengths above ground.

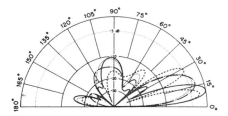

Fig. 6.3E — *H*-plane radiation pattern for two six-element Yagis at 0.75 and 1.5 wavelengths above ground.

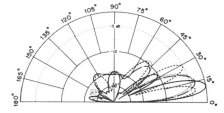

Fig. 6.3F — *H*-plane radiation pattern for two six-element Yagis at 0.9 and 1.5 wavelengths above ground.

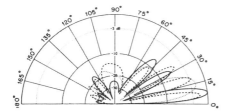

Fig. 6.3G — *H*-plane radiation pattern for two six-element Yagis at 0.9 and 2.25 wavelengths above ground.

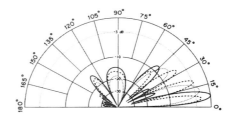

Fig. 6.3H — *H*-plane radiation pattern for two six-element Yagis at 1.125 and 2.25 wavelengths above ground.

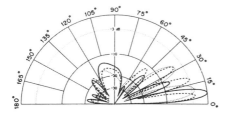

Fig. 6.3I — *H*-plane radiation pattern for two six-element Yagis at 1.35 and 2.25 wavelengths above ground.

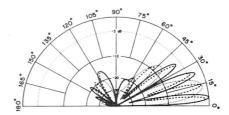

Fig. 6.3J — *H*-plane radiation pattern for two six-element Yagis at 1.0 and 3.0 wavelengths above ground.

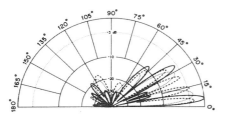

Fig. 6.3K — *H*-plane radiation pattern for two six-element Yagis at 1.5 and 3.0 wavelengths above ground.

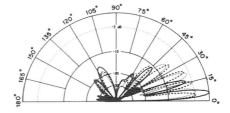

Fig. 6.3L — *H*-plane radiation pattern for two six-element Yagis at 2.0 and 3.0 wavelengths above ground.

6-10 Chapter 6

height do not give as much overall maximum gain as the higher antennas; this gain deficit is more severe for the six-element beams than for the three-element beams. This is the same general result previously obtained for single antennas over ground (Chapter 5); it results from the same phenomenon; that is, the natural increased free space directivity of the larger Yagi antennas reduces the gain potential at the higher elevation angles required for the lower antennas.

Note also from these tables that the exact placement of the lower Yagi antenna does not markedly influence the stacked maximum gain of the system but usually does significantly affect the angle of the lower antenna radiation. Note also that the excellent free space *F/B* ratio can be significantly affected by stacking; it is most strongly affected when the stack spacing is small and where the number of (adjacent) parasites is large, for example, especially the first three cases in Table 6.2.

To properly assess all of these stacked Yagi antenna systems, it is necessary to look at the *H*-plane (elevation angle) patterns shown in Figs. 6.2 and 6.3. It is instantly clear that excellent stacked coverage (solid line) of the crucially important zero to 20 degree elevation angles requires a reasonably high system (more than one wavelength) but not too high (less than 2.5 wavelengths). Above the first main lobe of radiation the patterns are quite varied; it is helpful to understand the basic reasons for these variations. Fig. 6.4 shows a simplified sketch of the two Yagi antennas above ground, each one represented on this diagram by a point. The lower antenna is at height h_L and the upper one is at height h_U; also shown are the image antennas below ground at heights of $-h_L$ and $-h_U$, respectively. Note that at an elevation angle, ϕ, the radiation from the lower antenna lags that from the upper antenna by a distance $(h_U - h_L)\sin\phi$. This phase lag causes the pair of antennas to interfere both constructively and destructively. At certain values of ϕ, which I shall designate ϕ_P, destructive interference will be complete and produce a radiation pattern null. Since the phase lag between the two antennas above ground is identical to that between the two images below ground, the overall radiation will also show these nulls where

$$\phi_P = \sin^{-1}[(n + \tfrac{1}{2})/(h_U - h_L)] \qquad (6.1)$$

where *n* can take on integer values starting with zero (0, 1, 2, …).

Now, from Fig. 6.4, note that the radiation from the image pair (which is excited out of phase with the real antenna pair) further lags by a distance $(h_U + h_L)\sin\phi$. Thus nulls will also occur in the overall pattern due to ground reflections at values of ϕ which I shall designate as ϕ_G where:

$$\phi_G = \sin^{-1}[m/(h_U + h_L)] \qquad (6.2)$$

where *m* can assume integer values (0, 1, 2, …). As an example, consider Fig. 6.3L where h_U is three wavelengths and h_L is two wavelengths. Equa-

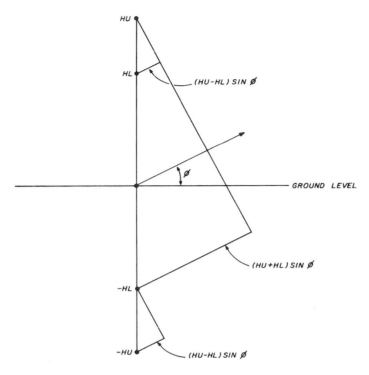

Fig. 6.4 — Diagram of two-array stack over ground, showing phase lags for each antenna and its image.

tions (6.1) and (6.2) predict that nulls should occur (within the range 0 to 60 degrees as follows:

ϕ_P = 30 degrees

ϕ_G = 0, 11.5, 23.6, 36.9, 53.1 degrees

Fig. 6.3L clearly shows these minima. Moreover, note from Fig. 6.3L that the upper envelope of gain falls off substantially with increasing elevation angle; this general result is caused by the natural free space directivity of the individual Yagi antennas. Note that this effect is much more pronounced for the larger six-element Yagi antennas (Fig. 6.3L) than for the smaller three-element equivalent stack (Fig. 6.2L).

Thus, the overall *H*-plane pattern is the result of three effects: first, the natural free space directivity of the individual Yagi antennas; second, the interference effect of the two real antennas; and third, the interference effect of the above ground system with its image counterpart. All three effects have different angular dependencies; it is therefore not surprising that the overall resultant can be quite varied and complex.

For those readers interested in constructing a vertically stacked Yagi antenna array, a careful scrutiny of Tables 6.1 and 6.2 and especially all of the relevant figures is quite enlightening. It is apparent that there is no single ideal design; nevertheless, there are a number of salient points that are worth noting.

1) A mast height (upper antenna height) of 0.75 wavelengths is really not high enough to get very much additional gain from stacking, especially with large Yagi antennas.

2) The higher systems provide better low-angle performance than the lower systems but sacrifice (sometimes needed) high-angle performance. They also provide less gain sacrifice due to ground images for big antennas and through increased antenna spacing provide less spoiling of the inherently good individual Yagi free space characteristics.

3) The important (lowest) first lobe gain is only weakly dependent on the placement of the lower antenna. The gain alone would favor h_L somewhat above $h_U/2$ (see for example Figs. 6.3G, 6.3H, and 6.3I); nevertheless, a lower placement (wider element spacing) will result in smaller beam interactions.

4) Mutual coupling or interaction between Yagi antennas tends to spoil the otherwise excellent properties of a single Yagi. This spoiling is most pronounced for low systems where spacings are small, not only to ground but between Yagi antennas (see for example Figs. 6.2A, 6.2B, and 6.2C). This spoiling can be easily seen in the altered patterns of the lower beam when the upper beam is physically present (dotted line) and when the upper beam is absent (broken solid line). You can also see the effect that stacking has on the F/B ratios (Tables 6.1 and 6.2) and also (not shown) the effects on the calculated driving-point impedances of both upper and lower Yagi antennas.

5) Interactive effects are also more serious when large Yagi antennas are used. This general result is anticipated and is due to the larger number of adjacent parasites; it is illustrated by comparing the dotted and broken-solid curves of Figs. 6.2B and 6.2C with those of Figs. 6.3B and 6.3C.

6) Any good stacked array (for example, Fig. 6.3G) will benefit by the Both, Lower, Upper (*BLU*) switch arrangement where at high angles a fill in the performance can be made (usually) using the lower antenna only. Best higher angle fill occurs when the placement of the lower antenna is at or preferably below $h_U/2$. A good practical height is $h_U/3 < h_L < h_U/2$. Note that a good fill obtained in this way slightly compromises maximum gain; however, this compromise is really not very serious.

7) With the *BLU* switch available it is interesting to compare perfor-

mances. In all cases, at the very lowest angles, Both and Upper give essentially identical results, that is, the stack is just as good as the upper antenna alone. However, the stack always accepts a broader range of vertical angles in its first lobe (due to its lower average height) and at its peak has more gain than either upper or lower alone. This gain advantage is one to three dB depending on the particular stack. Although this may not seem very impressive, experience demonstrates that the stack can indeed provide a commanding performance advantage over a single Yagi antenna and, coupled with the broader vertical coverage of the first lobe, will be more consistent.

8) A number of excellent stacked arrays can be chosen from these figures. As a good example note Fig. 6.3D. I have operated a stack very much like this on 14 MHz for several years; experience shows this to be a superb performer even without a *BLU* switch arrangement. Figures 6.3E and 6.3F also look very attractive, but the closer beam spacing results in increased variations in *F/B* properties and probably would require a *BLU* switch for best high-angle fill. For a higher stack note the excellent gain performances of Figs. 6.3G through 6.3I. However, for any of these cases, a fill seems desirable by the use of a *BLU* switch; note that for best fill at some higher angles the *upper* antenna should be used. For a very high stack Fig. 6.3J provides exceptional stacked gain, and by the additional use of the lower antenna for fill, it accommodates radiation angles up to nearly 30 degrees. However, at the 30 degree angles the system performance is abysmal, giving essentially zero response for any setting of the *BLU* switch.

"Transmission Line Transformers" by Jerry Sevick, W2FMI

By Jim Breakall, WA3FET

Jerry Sevick, W2FMI, was a renowned authority on antennas and transmission line transformers and was best known among radio amateurs as the author of the following books: *Transmission Line Transformers, Building and Understanding Baluns and Ununs*, and *The Short Vertical Antenna Handbook*. He is also known for the following *QST* articles "The Ground-Image Vertical Antenna" (1971), "The 20-Meter Vertical Beam" (1972), "A High Performance 20-, 40- and 80-Meter Vertical System" (1973), "The W2FMI Ground-Mounted Short Vertical" (1973), "Constant-Impedance Trap Vertical" (1974), "A Resistive Antenna Bridge...Simplified" (1975), "Simple RF Bridges" (1975), "Simple Broadband Matching Networks" (1976), "Short Ground-Radial Systems for Short Verticals" (1978), and "Measuring Soil Conductivity" (1981). That is almost one article every year in *QST* — he was a very prolific and knowledgeable author. The ground-mounted short vertical article and the antenna itself created quite a remarkable interest in that such an small antenna (6 foot high on 40 meters) could produce such a loud signal mainly because of the very excellent ground system (115 radials) and low-loss matching (transmission line transformer) techniques.

W2FMI with his famous short vertical: 6 feet tall on 40 meters.

Many people may not know that Dr. Sevick attended Wayne State University on an athletic scholarship and was drafted by two professional football teams. He also became a US Army Air Corps pilot in World War II where he was introduced to radio and electronics while serving for the military. He is quoted as saying that the discovery of ham radio changed his life and his career goals. After returning from World War II, he decided to go to Harvard University and earned a Ph.D. in Applied Physics. He went on to teach at Wayne State University and even worked at WXYZ-TV in Detroit as a local weather forecaster. Jerry finally got a position at the prestigious Murray Hill research center of Bell Laboratories in New Jersey. When he retired, he was the Director of Technical Relations at Bell Labs.

The book *Transmission Line Transformers* describes the main network design solution to match coaxial cable to his short ground-mounted vertical antennas. In the book he extensively studied the characterization and design of these transformers for low impedance applications. Later, he also presented a series on baluns in *Communications Quarterly* and a series on ununs (unbalanced to unbalanced transformers) in *CQ* magazine. Several commercial companies now sell baluns and ununs that are derived from Dr. Sevick's designs.

The fourth edition of this book includes new chapters on transmission line transformer efficiency, power combiners, mixer transformers, and equal-delay transformers. Dr. Sevick clearly describes the fundamentals underlying the balun designs of Guanella and Ruthroff. In addition, he constructed and measured hundreds of real transformers to establish practical levels of bandwidth and loss performance. He also provides many results that show his designs have higher performance than conventional magnetic flux-coupled transformers.

In closing, I remember that while a student at Penn State, I met Dr. Sevick who was the head of an outside technical advisory industry group for our Electrical Engineering Department tasked to give advice on how to improve our department. I will never forget just how soft-spoken and how interested he was to discuss antenna theory with me. He was so knowledgeable and so friendly and really was interested to motivate me to keep studying and learning as much as I could about antennas and radio. He was really a very unique and amazing individual and a "Ham's Ham."

A W2FMI-designed bifilar-wound impedance transformer with taps to provide 1.5:1, 2:1, 3:1 and 4:1 impedance ratios.

Chapter 1

Analysis

Sec 1.1 Introduction

There are two basic methods for constructing broadband, impedance-matching transformers. One system employs the conventional transformer that transmits the energy to the output circuit by flux linkages; the other uses the transmission line transformer to transmit the energy by a transverse transmission line mode. With techniques exploiting high magnetic efficiency, conventional transformers have been constructed to perform over very wide bandwidths. Losses on the order of one decibel can exist over a range of a few kilohertz to over 200 MHz. Throughout a considerable portion of this band, losses of only 0.2 dB are possible. On the other hand, transmission line transformers exhibit far wider bandwidths and even higher efficiency. The stray inductance and interwinding capacitances are generally absorbed into the characteristic impedance of the transmission line. As such, they form no resonances that could seriously limit the high-frequency response. Here the response is limited by the length of the transmission line and the deviation of the characteristic impedance from the optimum value. With transmission lines, the flux is effectively canceled in the core and extremely high efficiencies are possible over large portions of the pass band—losses of only 0.02 to 0.04 dB with certain ferrite core materials. Therefore, rather small structures can easily handle hundreds of watts of power.

In a general comparison, it can be said that the transmission line transformer enjoys the advantage of higher efficiency, greater bandwidth and simpler construction. The conventional transformer, however, remains capable of dc isolation.

All of the analyses on transmission line transformers to date have involved the use of bifilar windings (two windings interleaved). This is because conventional transmission line theory can be readily used to explain the concept of a two-winding device. As will be shown in later chapters, higher order windings such as trifilar and quadrifilar can also operate in a true transmission line mode, exhibiting high efficiencies and wide bandwidths with a variety of impedance ratios previously unreported.

The earliest presentation on transmission line transformers was by Guanella (ref 1) in 1944.[1] He suggested the concept of coiling parallel wires to form a choke that would reduce the undesired mode in a balanced-to-unbalanced matching application. Before this time, this type of device, known as a balun (balanced to unbalanced), was constructed from quarter- or half-wavelength transmission lines and had very narrow bandwidths. Other writers followed with further analyses and applications of the balun transformer introduced by Guanella (refs 2-8). In 1959 Ruthroff published his work on this subject (ref 9). It was considered to be the cornerstone for the popularity and more general use of this highly efficient and very wide bandwidth transformer. Many extensions and applications of his work were published and are included in the reference list (refs 10-27). This book should serve in the same manner as a contribution to the further development and elaboration of transmission line transformer knowledge.

The purpose of this chapter is twofold: (1) to review Ruthroff's approach to the analysis and understanding of these new wide-band transformers, and (2) to present additional material to form a basis for the chapters that follow.

Sec 1.2 The Basic Building Block

The single bifilar winding shown in Fig 1-1 is the basic building block for the understanding and design of all transmission line transformers. I have discovered that higher orders of windings (trifilar, quadrifilar, and so on), also perform in a similar transmission-line fashion. They will be discussed in Chapters 6 and 7.

An inductive reactance can be formed by coiling the transmission line. The purpose of the reactance is to isolate the output from the input circuit while still allowing energy to be transmitted to the output circuit by the normal transmission line mode. Low-frequency

---

[1]Each reference in this chapter can be found in Chapter 12, References.

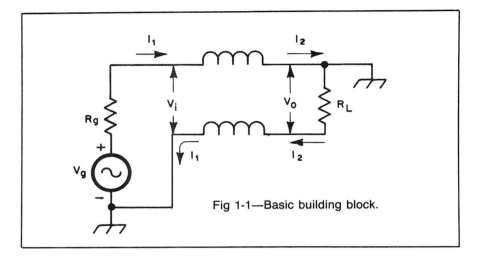

Fig 1-1—Basic building block.

capabilities can be improved by winding the transmission line on a core with properties to enhance the longitudinal choking action. Similarly, a straight transmission line can also be combined with a suitable medium (usually ferrite), to enhance the longitudinal reactance.

Transmission properties are inherently broadband if the characteristic impedance of the line is equal to the terminating impedance. If not, standing waves will exist and a dip in the frequency response will occur when the transmission line is a quarter-wavelength long. The depth of the dip depends on the ratio of terminating impedance to characteristic impedance of the transmission line.

In most applications, the transmission lines cannot be terminated in their characteristic impedances and standing waves will occur. The objective, then, is to minimize the standing waves by choosing the optimum value of characteristic impedance and to keep the transmission line as short as possible as governed by the required low-frequency response. By keeping the lines short, the output voltage V_o, more closely approximates the input voltage V_i, thus allowing for better high-frequency response.

The circuit, as connected in Fig 1-1, performs as a phase-reversing transformer. Since both ends of the load resistor, R_L, are isolated from the input circuit by the coil reactance, either end of the resistor can be grounded depending on the desired output polarity. If a balanced output is desired, the center of the resistor can be grounded

Analysis 1-3

instead. This isolation principle forms the foundation for the popular 1:1 and 4:1 balanced-to-unbalanced transformers.

Sec 1.3 Analyses of 4:1 Impedance Transformer

The analyses presented here are for a 4:1 unbalanced-to-unbalanced transformer, but a similar approach can be used for the 4:1 balanced-to-unbalanced transformer. A simple extension of these analyses can be equally applied to windings of a higher order (ie, trifilar, quadrifilar, etc). Fig 1-2 shows the circuit model for the 4:1 unbalanced-to-unbalanced transformer used in the analyses.

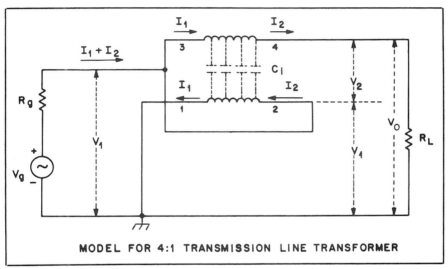

Fig 1-2—Circuit model for 4:1 unbalanced-to-unbalanced transformer.

Sec 1.3.1 A Simple Analysis

If the transmission line is very short compared to a quarter-wavelength, and the inductance (because of coiling), is sufficient to isolate the output from the input such that only transmission line currents flow, then

$$I_1 = I_2 \qquad \text{(Eq 1-1)}$$
and
$$V_2 = V_1 \qquad \text{(Eq 1-2)}$$

Since terminal 2 is connected to terminal 3, it presents a gradient to the ground of V_1 along both windings (they are tightly coupled), and the output voltage V_o, becomes

$$V_o = V_1 + V_2 \quad \text{(Eq 1-3)}$$

Using Eq 1-2, the output voltage can be written as

$$V_o = 2 V_1 \quad \text{(Eq 1-4)}$$

From Eq 1-1, the output current I_2 becomes equal to one-half of the input current and the transformation ratio ρ, becomes

$$\rho = \left(\frac{V_o}{V_1}\right)^2 = 4 \quad \text{(Eq 1-5)}$$

and maximum transfer of power occurs when

$$R_L = 4 R_g \quad \text{(Eq 1-6)}$$

It will be shown later that for optimum performance, the transmission line is seldom terminated in its characteristic impedance. Thus, the high-frequency performance is limited by the effect of standing waves. Even though the currents in the line are always equal and opposite, thereby canceling any flux in the core, the major change is that the transformation ratio becomes a complex quantity and deviates from 4:1. The loss at the high end is therefore generally caused by a mismatch and not by a real loss in the transformer.

At the low frequency end, insufficient capacity coupling comes into play between the conductors. Autotransformer action also occurs, thereby lowering the efficiency. Even the autotransformer action fails at the very low end because of insufficient magnetizing inductance.

The following section contains a rigorous analysis of the transmission line transformer. The reader who may not be interested in the theory of the device may proceed with Chapter 2.

Sec 1.3.2 The Ruthroff Analysis

As with conventional transformers, Ruthroff divided his analysis into two parts. One part deals with the high-frequency end. Here, sufficient reactance of the coiled lines occurs, so the input and output circuits are effectively isolated, leaving only transmission-line currents and voltages. The other part examines the low-frequency end.

Here, the series impedance, Z, of each half of the bifilar winding is compared to the load impedance, R_L.

The High Frequency Response

From Fig 1-2, Ruthroff derived the following equations:

$$V_g = (I_1 + I_2)R_g + V_1 \qquad \text{(Eq 1-7)}$$

$$V_g = (I_1 + I_2)R_g - V_2 + I_2 R_L \qquad \text{(Eq 1-8)}$$

$$V_1 = V_2 \cos\beta\ell + jI_2 Z_o \sin\beta\ell \qquad \text{(Eq 1-9)}$$

$$I_1 = I_2 \cos\beta\ell + j\frac{V_2}{Z_o}\sin\beta\ell \qquad \text{(Eq 1-10)}$$

where
  $\beta = 2\pi/\lambda$
  ℓ = the length of the transmission line
  Z_o = the characteristic impedance.

Eqs 1-7 and 1-8 are the input and output voltage loop equations. Eqs 1-9 and 1-10 are the conventional transmission line equations for current and voltage along length ℓ.

This set of equations is solved for the output power P_o, where

$$P_o = |I_2|^2 R_L \qquad \text{(Eq 1-11)}$$

The result is

$$P_o = \frac{V_g^2(1 + \cos\beta\ell)^2 R_L}{[2R_g(1 + \cos\beta\ell) + R_L\cos\beta\ell]^2 + \left[\frac{R_g R_L + Z_o^2}{Z_o}\right]^2 \sin^2\beta\ell} \qquad \text{(Eq 1-12)}$$

From Eq 1-12, the conditions for maximum power transfer are obtained by letting $\ell = 0$ and setting the first derivative of P_o with respect to R_L equal to zero at $\ell = 0$

$$\left.\frac{d P_o}{d R_L}\right|_{\ell=0} = 0$$

The transformer is found to be matched when $R_L = 4R_g$. By minimizing the coefficient of $\sin^2\beta\ell$ in Eq 1-12, we find the optimum characteristic impedance value to be $Z_o = 2R_g$. By setting $Z_o = 2R_g$ and $R_L = 4R_g$, Eq 1-12 reduces to

$$P_o = \frac{V_g^2(1 + \cos\beta\ell)^2}{R_g[(1 + 3\cos\beta\ell)^2 + 4\sin^2\beta\ell]} \quad \text{(Eq 1-13)}$$

Dividing the equation for available power

$$P_{available} = \frac{V_g^2}{4R_g} \quad \text{(Eq 1-14)}$$

by Eq 1-13, the normalized function is calculated as

$$\frac{P_{available}}{P_{output}} = \frac{(1 + 3\cos\beta\ell)^2 + 4\sin^2\beta\ell}{4(1 + \cos\beta\ell)^2} \quad \text{(Eq 1-15)}$$

As is shown in Eq 1-13, the output is zero when the transmission line is an electrical half-wavelength.

For the more general case where Z_o is not at the optimum value of $2R_g$, divide Eq 1-14 by Eq 1-12 to get the set of curves shown in Fig 1-3. Fig 1-3 shows that the loss, because of mismatching, is a very sensitive function of the characteristic impedance, Z_o.

Ruthroff also derived equations for the input impedances seen at either end of the transformer with the opposite end terminated in Z_L. They are:

$$Z_{in}(\text{low impedance end}) = Z_o\left[\frac{Z_L\cos\beta\ell + jZ_o\sin\beta\ell}{2Z_o(1 + \cos\beta\ell) + (jZ_L\sin\beta\ell)}\right] \quad \text{(Eq 1-16)}$$

and

$$Z_{in}(\text{high impedance end}) = Z_o\left[\frac{2Z_L(1 + \cos\beta\ell) + jZ_o\sin\beta\ell}{Z_o\cos\beta\ell + jZ_L\sin\beta\ell}\right] \quad \text{(Eq 1-17)}$$

Pitzalis, et al, plotted these impedances as a function of various values of Z_o as compared to the optimum value $Z_o = 2R_g$ (refs 12, 13). They found that the input impedances were also sensitive

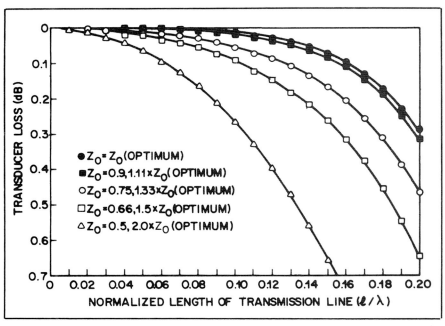

Fig 1-3—Transducer loss as a function of normalized transmission line length in a 4:1 unbalanced-to-unbalanced transformer for various values of characteristic impedance, Z_o.

to the value of the characteristic impedance. Looking into the low impedance side of the transformer, the following concepts could be generalized:

1) For a Z_o greater than the optimum value:
   a) The real part of Z_{in} increases only slightly with increasing frequency and values of Z_o.
   b) The imaginary part of Z_{in} becomes positive and increases with frequency and values of Z_o.
2) For a Z_o less than the optimum value:
   a) The real part of Z_{in} decreases greatly with increasing frequency and decreasing values of Z_o.
   b) The imaginary part of Z_{in} becomes negative and increases in magnitude with frequency and values of Z_o.

The Low Frequency Response

Transmission line transformers have a low-frequency cutoff that is determined by the falloff of primary reactance as the frequency is decreased. The series inductance of the coiled transmission line determines this reactance. Therefore, the longer the length of the line (more turns), the greater the series inductance and the lower the cutoff frequency. This is in conflict, however, with the high-frequency performance as noted before. A high permeability material placed close to the transmission-line conductors acts on the external fringe field present. It can greatly increase the inductance and thus provide a low cutoff frequency with fewer turns. For his low frequency analysis, Ruthroff used the 4:1 unbalanced-to-balanced transformer shown in Fig 1-4.

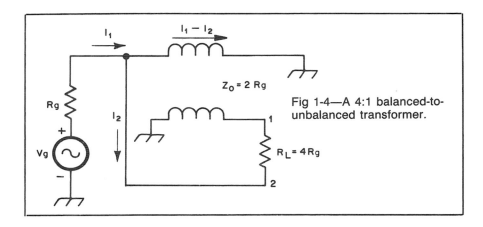

Fig 1-4—A 4:1 balanced-to-unbalanced transformer.

By denoting the series impedance of each half of the bifilar winding as Z, he arrived at the following loop equations:

$$V_g = (R_g + Z)I_1 - (Z + kZ)I_2 \quad \text{(Eq 1-18)}$$

and

$$V_g = (R_g - kZ)I_1 + (R_L + Z + kZ)I_2 \quad \text{(Eq 1-19)}$$

where k = the coefficient of coupling between the two windings.

Analysis 1-9

Solving for the ratio of input and output currents I_1/I_2, and assuming the series impedance of the winding to be much greater than the output load R_L, he arrived at

$$\frac{I_1}{I_2} = \frac{R_L + 2Z(1 + k)}{Z(1 + k)} \approx 2 \qquad \text{(Eq 1-20)}$$

which is necessary in a 4:1 transformation ratio.

To test for the balanced nature of the load voltage, Ruthroff then calculated the voltages from points 1 and 2 to ground. The voltage from point 2 to ground is

$$V_{20} = V_g - I_1 R_g \qquad \text{(Eq 1-21)}$$

When the transformer is matched,

$$V_g = 2I_1 R_g \qquad \text{(Eq 1-22)}$$

resulting in

$$V_{20} = I_1 R_g \qquad \text{(Eq 1-23)}$$

Similarly

$$V_{10} = I_2 Z - kZ(I_1 - I_2) \qquad \text{(Eq 1-24)}$$

Using Eq 1-20, Eq 1-24 becomes

$$V_{10} = ZI_1 \left[\frac{Z(1 + k)^2 - kR_L - 2kZ(1 + k)}{R_L + 2Z(1 + k)} \right] \qquad \text{(Eq 1-25)}$$

Assuming $k = 1$ and $Z \gg R_L$, Eq 1-25 becomes

$$V_{10} = I_1 Z \left[\frac{-kR_L}{R_L + 2Z(1 + k)} \right] \approx -\frac{I_1 R_L}{4} \qquad \text{(Eq 1-26)}$$

When the transformer is matched, ie, when $R_L = 4R_g$, Eq 1-26 then becomes

$$V_{10} = -I_1 R_g = -V_{20} \qquad \text{(Eq 1-27)}$$

1-10   Chapter 1

Therefore, the center point of R_L is at ground potential and the load is balanced to ground.

Further analytical and experimental information on the series inductance, Z, will be presented in Chapter 2. There, the low-frequency characterization of the 4:1 unbalanced-to-unbalanced transformer will be discussed.

"*MININEC*: The Other Edge of the Sword" by Roy Lewallen, W7EL

By Jim Breakall, WA3FET

Roy Lewallen, W7EL, is best known for his antenna modeling software, *ELNEC* and *EZNEC*, which have both been used by countless numbers of radio amateurs. *EZNEC Pro* is also used by many professional antenna experts and companies. *ELNEC* was his first antenna modeling software, written for *MS-DOS* and based on *MININEC*. *MININEC* was developed originally for the Apple II computer in 1982 by Jim Logan and Jay Rockway of the US Navy, as a smaller version of the much larger and sophisticated *Numerical Electromagnetics Code* (*NEC*) developed at Lawrence Livermore National Laboratory (LLNL) in Livermore, California.

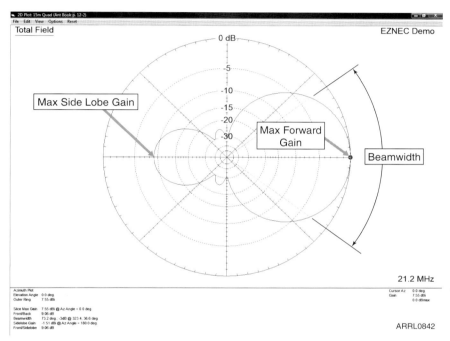

EZNEC provides antenna modelers with convenient and intuitive visual descriptions of antenna performance, such as the radiation pattern of this 2-element quad antenna.

MININEC and *NEC* both kept improving in the 1980s and 1990s, and computer power kept getting more memory and more speed as well. Numerous versions added features such as corrections for telescopic tubing in *NEC*-2 and *NEC*-4 and frequency shifts from wire diameter changes in *MININEC*.

Roy saw the important usefulness of bringing antenna modeling software to the ham community and wrote the first versions of his software, *ELNEC*, based on *MININEC*. Roy added something extremely valuable called a Graphical User Interface (GUI) to the *MININEC* engine that allowed the user to see the antenna model and display antenna patterns, currents and so on. He also created a very simple geometric input method to construct the wire antenna structure, connect feed line, add loads, and make other changes. It was really a breakthrough in making computer-based antenna modeling within reach of every amateur with simplicity and clarity.

With the computer power that exists today, corrections to the software problems of the past, and even more user-friendly features, it is possible to model just about the most sophisticated amateur antenna installation in existence. Roy is a very knowledgeable person about antennas and other subjects and has been very successful from his friendly personality and willingness to always listen and help his customers.

W7EL also has written many excellent articles and technical correspondence for *QST* over many years, including: "Notes on Phased Verticals" (1979), "An Optimized QRP Transceiver" (1980), "Try The "FD Special" Antenna" (1984), "The Impact of Current Distribution on Array Patterns" (1990), "A Simple and Accurate QRP Directional Wattmeter" (1990). He has had many articles in other publications such as the *ARRL Antenna Compendium*, and *QEX*.

W7EL's many talents are on display in the Optimized QRP Transceiver (August 1980 *QST*) that remains a QRP classic more than thirty years after the original article.

Two articles from the *ARRL Antenna Compendium* are most noteworthy. One is "The Simplest Phased Array Feed System — That Works" in the *ARRL Compendium, Vol. 2* and recent editions of the *ARRL Antenna Book*. Showing how to calculate "phasing line" lengths that actually create the intended phase shift, this became known as the Lewallen Method for proper phasing of vertical arrays and was written about extensively by John Devoldere, ON4UN, in his excellent many editions of the book *Low Band DXing*. Another important article was "Baluns: What they Do and How They Do It," in the *ARRL Antenna Compendium, Vol. 1*. It is an excellent explanation on the theory of and how to measure the performance of baluns.

In the following article "*MININEC*: The Other Edge of the Sword," Roy carefully explains the background and theory of *MININEC* and how it can be used to model amateur antennas. He covers many important aspects involving how to pick the number of segments for antennas, how to model wires at a junction and sharp angles, how to model closely spaced wires, how to place sources, and how to model antennas over ground, and errors if guidelines are not followed. He also talks about some of the important limitations of *MININEC* at the time that have been modified to work properly in the more modern editions.

In closing, two other important radio amateurs have to be mentioned in antenna modeling, Brian Beezley, K6STI, and Professor L. B. Cebik, W4RNL (Silent Key), who both were good friends and collaborators with Roy. Both are also very monumental and legendary contributors to the field of antenna modeling for radio amateurs.

MININEC:
The Other Edge of The Sword

MININEC antenna-modeling software is powerful and popular. But you need to know about its limitations to use it effectively. Here's the lowdown.

By Roy Lewallen, W7EL
5470 SW 152 Ave
Beaverton, OR 97007

Since the dawn of Amateur Radio, *predicting* antenna performance has been justifiably regarded as nearly impossible. No wonder: The only available tools for doing so have been analyses of textbook antennas (that bear a resemblance to our backyard creations to the same extent that a horse resembles a camel), testimonials, folklore and an awesomely lavish dose of "horse puckey."

Now, however, we have been armed with a sharp and powerful sword against decades of antenna-design darkness. But that sword is double-edged and some of us are getting pretty bloody from self-inflicted wounds as we blaze new trails in antenna design.

Our sword is, of course, the powerful antenna-modeling program *MININEC*. One of its edges is its ability to help us answer questions about antennas; its other edge is its limitations which, should we fail to recognize and carefully avoid them, can lead us to conclusions that are embarrassingly and profoundly wrong. For example, from a letter I recently received: "My personal favorite is the 45 dB gain I get [with a dipole] at 0.110 feet [high, over poor ground]. Boy, am I gonna be a big shot on 75 meters now!"

The only error the writer made was not being aware of one of *MININEC*'s basic limitations (discussed later). Tongue firmly in cheek, he had recognized that the answer was ridiculous, but sometimes we're not so lucky and the errors are tougher to spot.

Your ability to avoid the sword's other edge will greatly improve if you take time to gain a basic understanding of what *MININEC* is and how it works.

MININEC was written in BASIC for IBM®-compatible personal computers by J. C. Logan, N6BRF, and J. W. Rockway of the Naval Ocean Systems Center in San Diego. Both the source code and compiled program are available as public-domain software.[1,2] In addition, several commercial programs that use *MININEC* calculation code and additional features have appeared.[3-5] The limitations I'll describe

[1]Notes appear on page 22.

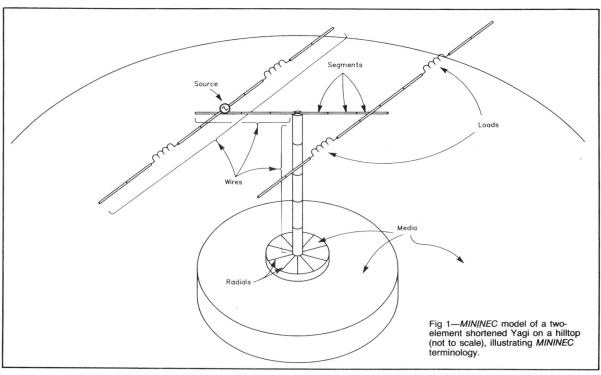

Fig 1—*MININEC* model of a two-element shortened Yagi on a hilltop (not to scale), illustrating *MININEC* terminology.

are, in general, shared by these and other derivative programs. Some variants work around some of the program's limitations, but some also add constraints of their own. Before you use any modeling program, thoroughly *read the documentation* and carefully observe the program's limits.[6] The most important thing you can do is to ask yourself: Does the result *make sense*?

How *MININEC* Works

MININEC is an extremely versatile and powerful program that permits you to "build" an antenna of straight conductors (called *wires*—you choose the diameter), put voltage *sources* and lumped impedances (*loads*) wherever you choose, place the structure over a realistic ground (if desired), and observe the input impedance, current distribution, and near and far fields at any azimuth or elevation angle. (See Fig 1.) Active (driven) and passive (parasitic) structures can be modeled. With some skill and understanding, you can accurately model anything from rhombics to rain gutters and towers to tribanders.

Let's take a closer look at *MININEC*'s operation. You enter the antenna description by specifying the diameters and end points of the wires and the number of *segments* into which they're to be divided for calculation (more about this later). End points are defined in an XYZ coordinate system. A free-space or ground-plane environment can be specified. If you choose a ground plane, it can be perfect or made of one or more sections (*media*) having finite depth, conductivity and permittivity and, if desired, radial wires. Sources and loads can be placed in series with any of the wires. (See Fig 1 for an example.) After entering the antenna description, you select one of several analysis options.

MININEC uses a procedure known as the *method of moments*.[7] In *MININEC*, each wire is divided into a group of equal-length segments for calculation. A uniform current is assumed to flow in a region extending to both sides of each segment junction (see Fig 2). These regions of uniform current, centered about the segment junctions, are called *pulses*. In any analysis, the program first calculates the self-impedance at each pulse and the mutual impedance between each pulse and all the others. If a ground plane has been specified, the impedances to and from the "image" antenna created by the ground plane are also calculated. This operation consumes the majority of the total computation time, reported by the program as *fill matrix*. The result is an internally stored matrix of impedance values. The program then solves an Ohm's Law equation using the values in the impedance matrix, a source-voltages matrix, and a matrix of the unknown pulse currents, reporting *factor matrix*. After this step, the impedances seen by the sources, as well as the currents at each pulse, are available. If near- or far-field analysis is requested, the contribution

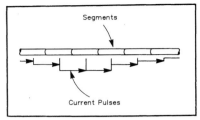

Fig 2—Illustration of the relationship between segments and pulses.

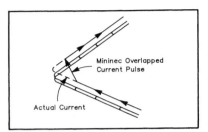

Fig 3—Pulse overlap at wire junctions can cause problems if it's not accounted for.

of each current pulse to the total field is calculated. If a ground plane has been specified, direct and reflected rays are summed to obtain the total field strength at each point of the near or far field.

The Limitations

MININEC's authors did an amazing and commendable job of reducing some very complex mathematical operations to a level that a PC can handle in a reasonable amount of time. But to do so, they had to make some compromises. Most of the program's limitations are due to these consciously chosen compromises.

Wires

In *MININEC*, every antenna must be described using only *straight wires* as the basic model building block. With some ingenuity, though, a wide variety of structures, including towers, top hats, rotators, rain gutters and even garages, can be adequately modeled. But overlapping wires *aren't* automatically connected by the program. For example, four wires are required to model an **X**-shaped structure if the conductors are connected at the center of the **X**. No limit is imposed on the minimum wire radius, and the program will produce accurate results with wire radii as large as 0.01 λ.

Number of Segments

It's up to you to decide how many segments to break each wire into for analysis purposes. To make an appropriate choice you have to have some knowledge of the trade-offs involved. Because the results become more accurate as the number of segments is increased, *MININEC* users naturally tend to use a large number of segments. Two factors suggest caution here. First, the size of the complex-impedance matrix calculated by the program goes up as the *square* of the number of pulses. (The number of pulses is approximately equal to the number of segments.) Therefore, *MININEC* and all its derivatives have some limit on the allowable number of pulses. Second, analysis time increases approximately as the square of the number of segments.

So, just how many segments are required to "do it right"? There's no exact answer, because the analysis accuracy nearly always improves with more segments. A straightforward (but time-consuming) way to determine if you've used enough segments is to increase the number of segments, rerun the analysis and see how much the results change. Some rules of thumb work well and can be used as a starting point if particularly good accuracy is required. As I'll describe, you need to take special care at wire junctions, especially where wires are connected at an acute angle.

Straight Wires

If you want to look at the pattern of an antenna with straight elements (like a Yagi), eight to ten segments per half wavelength are adequate. The pattern won't change much as you increase the number, although the program may give more accurate null depths with more segments. If you require *really* accurate feed-point impedances, use more segments.

Connected Wires—General

It's easiest to understand some of the problems of connecting wires if you have an understanding of what *MININEC* does at wire junctions. An unconnected wire is left with a zero-amplitude half-pulse at its end. However, the end pulses of later-defined connecting wires have nonzero current amplitudes. The half-pulse that extends beyond one of these wires is overlapped onto the lowest-numbered connecting wire (Fig 3). *This half-pulse of current takes on the segment length and wire diameter of the lower-numbered wire.*

When the program does its calculations, it considers only the pulse center or end points. When the straight-line path between the pulse ends becomes substantially different from the actual current path, errors result. This occurs wherever wires are connected at a nonzero angle. Accuracy also suffers when wires having greatly different segment lengths are connected. John Belrose, VE2CV, has observed[8] that the best results are obtained with square loops when the segment lengths are the same on all legs. He also observes that, as a rule, segment lengths on connected wires should differ by no more than a factor of two. Both rules are reasonable considering the way *MININEC* handles connections, and both rules have experimentally been proven sound.

February 1991   19

Table 1
Feed-Point Impedances Reported by MININEC†

Straight Dipole

Segments	Impedance (ohms)
10	74.073 +j 20.292
20	75.870 +j 21.877
30	76.573 +j 23.218
40	76.972 +j 24.053
50	77.222 +j 24.517

Bent Dipole

Segments	Impedance (ohms)
10	11.509 −j 76.933
20	11.751 −j 53.812
30	11.819 −j 46.934
40	11.848 −j 43.783
50	11.861 −j 41.988
14††	11.312 −j 43.119

†Impedances for a straight 0.5-λ dipole and dipole bent horizontally at its center at a 45° included angle, with various numbers of segments. Both antennas have a wire radius of 0.001 λ and are placed 0.5 λ above perfectly conducting ground.
††Tapered segment length. See text.

Wires Connected at Right Angles

Wires connected at a nonzero angle require more segments than unconnected wires or those connected at a 0° angle. Eight to ten segments per half wavelength are required for reasonable results if the connection angle is 90° or less and the segment lengths of both wires are equal. Far-field accuracy of a one-wavelength-circumference square loop is reasonably good with four segments per leg, although once again the impedance accuracy improves with more segments.

Wires Connected at Acute Angles

This is where *MININEC* becomes tricky. Accuracy can rapidly degrade as wire-connection angles decrease, although here again the impedance loses more accuracy than the far-field pattern. An example is shown in Table 1. The *MININEC*-calculated impedance of a dipole is reasonably accurate when the antenna is divided into only ten segments. When the same dipole is bent at a 45° included angle, more than 30 segments are required for similar accuracy. In both cases, however, ten segments produce far-field patterns that are virtually indistinguishable from those produced using more segments. The only way I know of to evaluate these cases is to change the number of segments and see what happens. Described next, however, is a technique that you can use to reduce the number of segments required for wires connected at sharp angles.

A Technique for Improving Accuracy

MININEC's accuracy can be markedly improved at wire junctions with only a slight increase in the total number of segments. This is done by tapering the segment length, making it short in the vicinity of the wire junction and increasing it at greater distances. Typically, only a few extra wires are required. This technique is illustrated in Fig 4 for the bent dipole of Table 1. Wires 1, 2 and 3 and their counterparts on the other half of the dipole have only one segment each. The remainder of the half-dipole is one four-segment wire. These segments are just slightly longer than when the dipole was made up of 10 segments total. The net result, shown in the last row of Table 1, is that the impedance for this 14-segment model is similar to the 40-uniform-segment model.

Close-Spaced Wires

MININEC documentation includes analysis of parallel wires at various spacings and finds the program to be well-behaved even when wires are very close together. Nonetheless, it cautions, "Whenever a model has close spacing, however, it is advisable to examine the results very closely to ensure proper behavior." Some time ago I analyzed a typical open-wire transmission line and found it necessary to make the segments no longer than three times the wire spacing. With longer segments, dramatic impedance errors resulted. More recent experiments have indicated that the problem is caused not by the close spacing, but by the connection at the ends of the two wires. The wire connecting the end has a maximum possible segment length equal to the wire spacing. The rule of having no more than a 2:1 segment-length ratio (see *Connected Wires—General*) on connected wires is violated unless the main wire-segment lengths are no more than twice the wire spacing. The tapered-segment-length approach outlined above can be successfully applied in this situation.

Additional factors limit your choice of the number of segments to use. Because *MININEC* assumes that current is uniform along a pulse, segment lengths should be short enough that the current in the real antenna doesn't change much in this distance. Therefore, the maximum segment length shouldn't exceed about 0.1 λ. *MININEC* documentation also states that segment length should always be greater than 10^{-4} λ, and greater than 2.5 times the wire radius.

Sources and Loads at Multiwire Junctions

This one can be a real surprise. When you place a source or load at a junction of more than two wires, you have to be very careful, or the source or load won't end up where you thought! Sources and loads can be placed only at pulses (segment junctions), so to understand the problem you need to know how *MININEC* assigns pulse numbers. Here are the rules it uses:

See Fig 5. Pulse numbering begins at end number 1 of wire number 1. A pulse number is assigned to each segment junction on the wire, and at a wire end if the end is connected to ground or an already-defined wire. No pulse numbers are assigned to open wire ends. After pulse numbers are assigned to the first wire, pulses are assigned to wire number 2, again beginning at end 1, and so forth.

Wire 1, shown by itself in Fig 5A, has four segments to which three pulses are assigned. Pulse numbers 1-3 belong to wire 1. In Fig 5B, wire 2 is added. Note the assignment of pulse number 4, which belongs to wire 2 since it didn't exist until wire 2 was defined. When wire 3 is added in Fig 5C, pulse number 8 is assigned *to the same physical junction as pulse number 4*, in accordance with the above rule. Pulse 8 belongs to wire 3. Now suppose the antenna in Fig 5 is a groundplane with two drooping radials, and we want to place a source at the base of wire 1, the main radiating portion. If we specify pulse 4 for the source position, *the source ends up on wire 2*, as shown in Fig 6. If the source is producing I amperes, I amperes flows in wire 2, and the return current of I amperes splits between wires 1 and 3—not the desired result. The same thing happens if pulse 8 (Fig 5C) is specified, except that wire 3 gets the full current and the return current splits between wires 1 and 2. Putting the source at pulse number 1 gets it on wire 1 all right, but 25% of the way up from the junction. *There is no way to place the source on wire 1 at the wire junction as this antenna has been defined.* This is because there's no pulse belonging to wire 1 at the bottom (end 1) of wire 1. *The only way to achieve the desired result is to avoid placing the source in the lowest-*

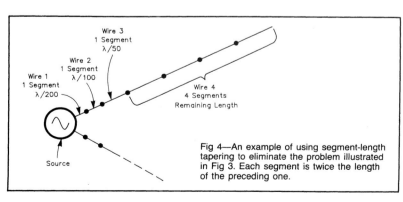

Fig 4—An example of using segment-length tapering to eliminate the problem illustrated in Fig 3. Each segment is twice the length of the preceding one.

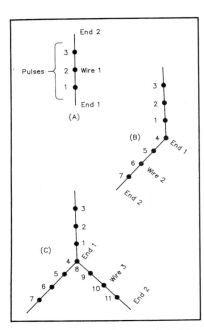

Fig 5—Pulse assignments are made in the order that wires are defined. See text for explanation.

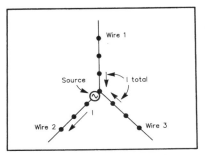

Fig 6—Result of placing a source at pulse 4 on the antenna shown in Fig 5C.

numbered wire (the one defined first) in the group sharing a common junction. To make sure you've put the source where you think you have, always look at the currents and *make sure they make sense*. Load placement behaves the same way, but mistakes can be harder to spot, so be extra careful when placing loads at multiwire junctions.

When only two wires are connected, there's no problem. Regardless of which wire the common pulse belongs to, the entire source or load current flows in both wires.

Ground—General

Probably the most misunderstood limitation of *MININEC* is its ground-modeling capability. Even though the program permits you to define a real ground in considerable detail, this definition is used *only for calculating far-field patterns*. *MININEC* uses *perfectly conducting ground* when calculating impedances and currents if either a perfect or real ground is specified. Ground has several effects on antennas.[9] Let's look at them one at a time and see how this simplification affects the accuracy of results.

Impedance and Gain

The feed-point impedance of an antenna changes with antenna height. The magnitude of this effect depends on antenna length, diameter, and orientation, and the ground characteristics. The impedance change of a half-wave dipole above ground is well documented.[10] When a dipole is at least 0.2 λ above ground, its impedance is nearly the same whether the ground is real or perfect, so *MININEC* results are adequate. If the antenna is lower, however, *MININEC* results can deviate greatly from the true impedance of an antenna over real ground. Specifically, the resistance reported by *MININEC* will be lower than it really is. This in turn leads to excessively high reported gain, as noted by the correspondent quoted earlier. I don't have any information on longer dipoles (such as the extended double Zepp), but I suspect that these antennas must be somewhat higher than 0.2 λ before *MININEC* gives accurate impedance results. Vertical dipoles have about the same impedance over real ground as over perfect ground, so *MININEC* results are satisfactory for these antennas at any height.

Ground System Losses and Efficiency

Efficiency of ground-mounted low-impedance vertical antennas is frequently the most severe limitation on such an antenna's performance. In such antennas, power is lost due to feed-point return current flowing through lossy ground in the vicinity of the antenna base. Placing radial wires around the base of the antenna raises efficiency by reducing this loss. A common way to determine the loss in such an antenna is to measure the feed-point resistance and compare it with the resistance of a similar element over lossless ground. The loss is simply the difference in the resistances, and usually this is nearly all ground loss.

Because *MININEC* uses a perfect ground for impedance calculations, it always reports the impedance seen over a perfect ground. Therefore, *MININEC* can't be used to determine the impedance or efficiency of antennas fed against ground; you can't use the program to evaluate the effectiveness of radial systems, for instance.

Low-Angle-Radiation Attenuation

Vertically polarized waves, in particular, are attenuated when reflected from lossy ground, leading to the well-known phenomenon of low-angle radiation attenuation.[11] *MININEC* models this correctly as part of the far-field calculation. If radials are specified, they modify the conductivity of the ground on which they are placed. *MININEC* documentation cautions that the radial calculations are accurate only for large numbers of radials.

One additional caution is necessary when specifying ground constants. It's frequently convenient to model antennas at 299.8 MHz, where a wavelength is one meter. If you do this, *you must scale ground conductivity in proportion to the frequency.*[12] For example, an antenna operating at 7 MHz over ground having a conductivity of 0.002 S/m will behave like a size-scaled antenna operating at 299.8 MHz over ground with $0.002 \times (299.8 \div 7) = 0.086$ S/m conductivity. However, even with a ratio this large, neglecting to scale ground conductivity usually won't be apparent in the far-field patterns, except at very low angles.

Multiple Media

Other limitations appear when the ground is broken up into several pieces (*media*). Once again, it's helpful to understand how *MININEC* functions in this regard.

Height of Ground Under the Antenna

It's important to realize that *MININEC* always assumes a ground-plane height of 0 (Z = 0 in *MININEC*'s XYZ coordinate system) when calculating impedances and currents. Also, it regards a wire-end Z coordinate of zero as meaning that the wire is connected to ground (except when the antenna is being modeled in free space). For these reasons, the region of the ground plane immediately under the antenna must have a height (Z coordinate) of zero. If you're modeling an antenna on top of a hill, the top of the hill must have a Z coordinate of zero, with the rest of the hill having negative Z coordinates.

Other Concerns

At each elevation angle, *MININEC* looks for reflection from ground. It begins at the most distant medium and looks for the intersection of the direct and reflected rays. This process is repeated for all other media. *MININEC* uses the innermost reflection point it finds; it makes no attempt to evaluate multiple reflections or those from corners. *MININEC* doesn't look between the antenna and the reflecting point or beyond the reflecting point. Therefore, the program assumes that RF passes through hills and cliff walls with no shielding or reflections. A puzzling simplification is that the program assumes a height of zero for all media during the process of determining the wave-reflection point to be used for far-field calculations, although media height is taken into account during summation of the incident and reflected rays. This can lead to pattern errors with media of differing heights. If you have access to a compiler, you can easily patch *MININEC*'s source code to overcome this deficiency. See the appendix for details.

These ground approximations were pur-

February 1991 21

posely made to keep the program length and speed compatible with PCs. We can hope that improved ground-modeling code will become available in the future as PCs continue to increase in speed and power.

Loss

MININEC doesn't automatically account for loss. Therefore, be wary of antennas with low feed-point resistances. The answers might be entirely legitimate, but only if there is no loss in the antenna structure. In the lossy real world, these antennas just won't work. Whenever you see a surprisingly high gain, look at the feed-point resistance and you're likely to find it's very low. Imitate reality by adding loads having a few ohms of resistance at each source (and anywhere else the current is high) and watch what happens to the gain!

Frequency-Related Errors

At least two writers have reported apparent frequency-dependent errors in *MININEC*.[13,14] This was determined by comparing *MININEC* results to those of *NEC*, a much more sophisticated mainframe program. Their observations were that, for certain frequencies and element diameters, the two programs seem to give similar results at slightly different frequencies. The only specific example of this I've seen was provided by Peter Beyer, PA3AEF.[15] It shows *NEC* and *MININEC* analyses of a 10-element 144-MHz Yagi. The *NEC* analysis was done at 144.5 MHz. *MININEC* analysis is closer to the *NEC* results when done at 145 MHz than at 144.5 MHz. I ran some brief experiments to see if there is, indeed, a frequency-sensitive error *within MININEC*. I scaled the same antenna for different frequencies and analyzed them with *MININEC*. No frequency-dependent effects (resonance shift, etc) were found, but the tests were far from exhaustive, and the program's *absolute* accuracy is what's in question. My feeling is that the differences arise because of the much more sophisticated way in which *NEC* deals with currents. I hope we'll see more about this phenomenon in amateur publications. In the meantime, be careful when trying to get high accuracy from *MININEC* analysis of highly directional structures, especially at VHF and UHF.

Bugs

I know of only two actual bugs in *MININEC*. They both deal with Laplace ("S-parameter") loads. One causes an overflow and the other is very obscure and highly unlikely to affect you. If you'd like some further description and fixes for the bugs, contact me.

Summary

All modeling tools, no matter how elaborate, powerful and expensive, have limitations. Absolutely none of these can be used sensibly unless you're constantly conscious of their limitations. *MININEC* is no exception. You must always be alert for answers that don't seem quite right. Are the impedance and gain values *reasonable*? If the antenna is symmetrical, is the pattern symmetrical about the axis you intended to specify? Do the currents change abruptly from one segment to another?[16] Do the results seem too good to be true? *If so, they probably are!*

We owe *MININEC*'s authors a great debt of gratitude for the pioneering work they have done. They've put fast, accurate antenna analysis within the reach of thousands of amateurs. The program they have created is very useful for analyzing a variety of antenna designs. Wielded properly, *MININEC* can be a powerful tool—a weapon against a decades-long void in knowledge about antenna design. This article should help you avoid the other edge of the sword.

APPENDIX

If you have access to BASIC compiler software (eg, Microsoft® *QuickBasic*, Borland *Turbo Basic*), you can patch the *MININEC* source code to improve *MININEC*'s handling of multiple media of different heights, then recompile the program.† Of course, the source code could be run directly with a GWBASIC interpreter, but the speed will be so slow as to render the program virtually useless. In the following code segments, the added lines have no line numbers since such are not required by the compilers.

702 T3 = −SIN(U4)
IF ABS(R3) < 0.00001 THEN ATU4 = 100000 ELSE ATU4 = ABS(T3/R3)
703 T1 = R3 * V2

756 FOR J = 1 TO NM STEP −1
IF B9 > U(J1) * (1 + ATU4) THEN 759
758 J2 = J1
Note: Delete line 757
[IF B9 > U(J1) THEN 759].

If the program is to be compiled with Microsoft *QuickBasic*, one other change must be made. In *MININEC*, "IS" is used as a variable. Because "IS" is a reserved word in *QuickBasic*, it must be changed. (If you're using a different compiler, check its documentation to see if this change is required.) Change "IS" to "ISX" in the following lines: 1592, 1593, 1596, 1605-1609, and 1612.

†Patched *MININEC* in compiled form is available from the author on an MS-DOS 5¼- or 3½-inch disk for $3 postpaid to the US, Canada, and Mexico. Add $3 airmail postage to other countries.

Notes

[1]*MININEC* is available from National Technical Information Service (NTIS), US Department of Commerce, 5285 Port Royal Rd, Springfield, VA 22161, tel 703-487-4650. Order no. ADA181681 (software and documentation).
[2]A technical reference describing the program is J. C. Logan and J. W. Rockway, *The New MININEC (Version 3): A Mini-Numerical Electromagnetic Code*, NOSC TD 938, Naval Ocean Systems Center, San Diego, CA, 1986. It is available as document number ADA181682 from NTIS (see note 1). This is a highly technical manual.
[3]J. Rockway, J. Logan, D. Tam and S. Li, *The MININEC System: Microcomputer Analysis of Wire Antennas*, available from Artech House, 685 Canton Street, Norwood, MA 02062. Includes several programs with source code and a comprehensive manual.
[4]*MN* and *MNjr*, by Brian Beezley, K6STI. Available from Brian Beezley, 507½ Taylor St, Vista, CA 92084.
[5]*ELNEC*, by Roy Lewallen, W7EL. Available from Roy Lewallen, PO Box 6658, Beaverton, OR 97007.
[6]Documentation files for *MN* and *ELNEC* are available on 5.25-inch diskettes from their authors for $5 and $3, respectively. Add $3 for postage to locations outside North America. See notes 4 and 5 for addresses.
[7]A good description of the method of moments is included in J. D. Kraus, *Antennas*, 2nd edition (New York: McGraw-Hill, 1988), pp 359-408.
[8]J. S. Belrose, VE2CV, ARRL Technical Advisor, private correspondence.
[9]An excellent description of these effects appears in G. L. Hall, ed., *The ARRL Antenna Book*, 15th edition (Newington: ARRL, 1988), Chapter 3.
[10]See note 9, p 3-11, Fig 16.
[11]See note 9, pp 3-1 through 3-6 and 3-10.
[12]G. Sinclair, "Theory of Models of Electromagnetic Systems," *Proceedings of the IRE*, Nov 1948, pp 1364-1370.
[13]P. Beyer, "Antenna Simulation Software," *Proceedings of the Third International EME Conference*, Thorn, Netherlands, Sep 9-11, 1988. Thanks to Warren Butler, W2WD, for bringing this to my attention.
[14]R. Cox, "An Update on Computer-Aided Antenna Design," *1990 Central States VHF Conference Proceedings*, published by ARRL. Thanks to *QST* Assistant Technical Editor Rus Healy, NJ2L, for bringing this to my attention.
[15]Peter Beyer, PA3AEF, private correspondence.
[16]Positive current flow is defined as being from end 1 to end 2. Current reversals at wire junctions are normal if wires are connected "head to head," ie, end 1 to end 1 or end 2 to end 2.

New Products

The ARRL and QST in no way warrant products described under the New Products banner.

SIMPLEX REPEATER

☐ Brainstorm Engineering has introduced its model SR3 Simplex Repeater. Based on digital voice recording and delayed playback, the SR3 is primarily intended for multistation communications on a single frequency where the stations don't have solid simplex communications capability, or as a voice mailbox. With the optional DTMF decoder, the SR3 can be used as a repeater identifier. Maximum message length is 64 seconds (with four memory ICs installed), and the SR3 comes with 16-second recording capability. Specifications: power requirement, 11.6-15 V dc at 200 mA; audio input, 0.1-2 V rms; audio output, 5-500 mV; 1.75 × 10.5 × 6 inches (HWD). Price class: $230-$330, depending on configuration. For more information, contact Brainstorm Engineering, PO Box 415, Montrose, CA 91021-0415, tel 818-249-4383, fax 818-846-2298.

"A Receiving Antenna that Rejects Local Noise" by Brian Beezley, K6STI

By Jim Breakall, WA3FET

Brian Beezley, K6STI, has written numerous programs for modeling antennas, optimizing Yagis, and determining the effects of terrain on antennas: *YO* — Yagi Optimizer, *AO* — Antenna Optimizer, and *TA* — Terrain Analyzer. All of these programs ran in MS-DOS, were highly interactive, and utilized extensive computer graphics to display results and objects being modeled. Unfortunately, Brian decided to retire from amateur radio software in response to the reported pirating of his software — disappointing because Brian's software was always very ingenious, extremely fast, and very user-friendly and accurate.

Released in the early 1990s, *YO* was remarkable for several reasons; its speed, visualization during calculation, and optimization. He achieved such fast computation results by programming the main computing algorithms in machine language (rare in today's programming environment), producing a fantastic increase in speed. This and other unique computing methods he employed were able to produce the visual effects of changing length and spacing of Yagi elements on the screen while at the same time seeing the effects on patterns, gain, VSWR, and current. This was really something different from traditional modeling of antennas which entailed waiting for the results in several seconds to minutes at that time. Brian's calculations were like seeing changes in Yagi antennas in real-time.

YO was also one of the first times that computer optimization was also seen generally by radio amateurs. Computer optimization is an area of mathematics and computer science that can find designs with the best antenna performance for maximum gain, minimum sidelobes (best front-to-back ratio), minimum VSWR, and so on. K6STI applied it to Yagis in *YO* and was able to produce antenna designs that could be optimized in ways that were not possible before his program. He also was able to do it over frequency ranges, as well, and display the results graphically.

He later went on to develop a more general antenna modeling software package, *AO*, based on the *MININEC* algorithm with corrections to agree with *NEC*. (See the introduction for the previous article by Roy Lewallen, W7EL, for more information about antenna modeling software.) *AO* could model any antenna but had the important unique addition of an optimizer to achieve any desired goal of gain, sidelobe reduction, VSWR minimization, or other parameters not only for Yagis but for *any* type of antenna. At the time, this was clearly a breakthrough in antenna modeling for radio amateurs.

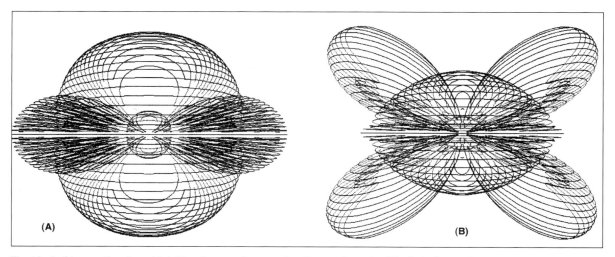

The kind of innovation for which Beezley was known, the diamond stack of Yagis in figure B produces significantly better main lobe performance (the central region) over the customary H-frame array in (A). The figure also illustrates the output of his antenna modeling software.

TA was another very interactive and graphics intensive program written by K6STI for analyzing the effects of irregular terrain in the vicinity of an antenna on radiation skywave elevation patterns. It is based on a specialized technique called the Geometrical Theory of Diffraction (GTD) to predict simulated radiation patterns in irregular terrain. *TA* was and still is a great program. Later, Dean Straw, N6BV, produced very impressive software such as *YTAD* (*YT*) and presently *HFTA* (HF Terrain Analysis). These techniques now have been used by many hams to predict what effects the surrounding terrain has on their antenna systems sometimes, allowing them to enhance antenna system performance greatly.

Brian is truly someone who likes to take something that looks really challenging and then apply himself and his genius to make it happen in a way that nobody else can seem to do. The following paper is one such antenna design and technique that allowed the minimization of local noise with a special receive antenna. The K6STI Loop set off a long sequence of innovative designs using small loops with carefully phased geometries to greatly improve receive performance on the lower bands where communication is often limited by atmospheric and man-made noise.

Brian has also written several other articles and technical correspondences over the years from 1991 to 2001. There are many including myself who would like Brian to come out of retirement and see what other magical software he could produce to help Amateur Radio.

A Receiving Antenna that Rejects Local Noise

Simplicity and performance combine to give birth to a compact antenna you'll want to have!

By Brian Beezley, K6STI
3532 Linda Vista Dr
San Marcos, CA 92069

Noise can make a ham's life miserable on any amateur band. As we approach the minimum of the sunspot cycle, many hams are discovering that noise can be particularly frustrating on the low bands. In summer, static crashes caused by thunderstorm lightning can totally mask weak signals on the 160, 80, and 40-meter bands. During other seasons, power-line noise, noise from household appliances, and incidental radiation from home electronic products often limits reception.

A recent *QST* article by Floyd Koontz, WA2WVL,[1] describes a small receiving antenna for the low bands that provides a cardioid directional pattern. This pattern can reduce noise and QRM from the rear. As I marveled at the elegance and simplicity of Floyd's design, I realized that the antenna did have one shortcoming: Because it is vertically polarized, the antenna responds strongly to local noise propagated by ground waves. I wondered whether it was possible to devise a receiving antenna to better reject local noise.

The Ground Wave

Most hams who operate HF are familiar with the sky wave (or space wave) that's responsible for long-distance ionospheric propagation. See Figure 1A. The space wave has two components: The *direct wave* propagates along a straight line from the transmit antenna toward the ionosphere. The *ground-reflected wave* bounces off the earth's surface and heads in the same direction.

The space wave also exists for local propagation, as shown in Figure 1B. The direct wave travels in a straight line between the transmit and receive antennas, while the ground-reflected wave takes a midpoint bounce. But when the antennas are close to ground, the direct and reflected waves nearly cancel, leaving a very small residual space wave. When the antennas are right at the earth's surface, the waves cancel completely. So what makes local com-

Notes appear on page 36.

munication possible? Answer: A third wave, called the *surface wave,* that exists for antennas close to ground. This wave diminishes in intensity as you increase antenna height. The surface wave exists *only near the surface of the earth*. The combination of the direct wave, the ground-reflected wave, and the surface wave is called the *ground wave*.[2]

Surface-wave intensity varies with frequency and ground conductivity. It's stronger at low frequencies and for highly conductive ground. But the most important property of the surface wave is its polarization sensitivity. The surface wave is much weaker for horizontal fields. For example, on 80 meters the broadside ground-wave response of a short piece of wire is about 34 dB lower when oriented horizontally. The difference is about 42 dB at 160 meters.[3]

The surface wave makes local AM radio broadcasting possible. Because of the poor propagation of horizontally polarized ground-wave signals, AM broadcasters universally use vertical polarization. The same phenomenon causes vertical anten-

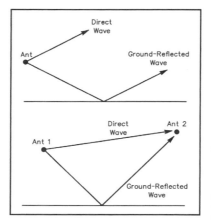

Figure 1—At A, the direct and ground-reflected components of the space wave for ionospheric propagation. At B, the space-wave components for local propagation.

nas to pick up much more local noise than horizontal antennas do. Even if a noise source has a stronger horizontal component, by the time the field reaches the receive antenna, the vertical component almost always dominates.

These facts suggest that the first requirement of a receiving antenna with low response to local noise is insensitivity to vertically polarized radiation, the dominant component of the ground wave. Surprisingly, simply avoiding the use of vertical wires isn't enough. An antenna composed only of horizontal wires can still respond to vertical fields.

A Low Dipole

Figure 2 shows the ground-wave response of an 80-meter dipole 10 feet high. An easy-to-install, inconspicuous dipole like this is sometimes used for receiving when the transmit antenna is vertically polarized. The pattern shows the electric-field strength 10 meters above ground at a distance of 1000 meters for an input power of 1 kW (the dipole exhibits the same pattern on receive). This geometry might be representative of that for a noisy power pole. Although the pattern may look similar to that of a free-space dipole, I think you'll be surprised to know that the wire is oriented broadside to the pattern null. A low dipole actually responds to ground-wave fields best off its ends!

Here's an explanation for this peculiar behavior: The dipole has no response to the vertical component of a broadside ground wave because the electric field is perpendicular to the wire. The antenna responds only to the weak horizontal component. The vertical component also is perpendicular to the mirror image of the antenna formed by the ground-reflected wave. But away from broadside, the dipole, its image, or both, have a nonvanishing projection in the vertical plane. This enables the dipole to respond to the vertical component of a ground wave. In addition, lossy earth causes the surface wave to develop a radial component in the direction of propagation. Away from broadside, the radial compo-

September 1995 33

Figure 2—Azimuthal plot of the ground-wave response of a 10-foot-high 80-meter dipole. The input power to the antenna is 1 kW. The peak electric field is shown.

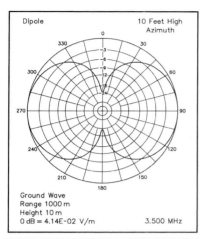

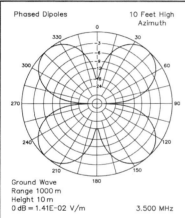

Figure 3—Azimuthal plot of the ground-wave response of two parallel dipoles 10 feet apart, 10 feet high and fed out of phase. The input power to the antenna is 1 kW. The peak electric field is shown.

nent also projects onto the wire and induces current. The vertical and radial components induce maximum current when the surface wave arrives in line with the wire.

When compared to a quarter-wave vertical with four radials elevated 10 feet above ground, the low dipole has a 12.5 dB lower ground-wave response in its most sensitive direction in line with the wire. For sky-wave signals arriving at 20° elevation from their weakest direction (also off the ends), the dipole has 10 dB lower response than the vertical. Therefore, the low dipole has a signal-to-noise ratio advantage of 2.5 dB for signals and noise arriving from their worst-possible directions. In the most favorable directions broadside to the wire, the S/N advantage peaks sharply at 26.1 dB.

Raising the dipole broadens the broadside S/N peak and improves S/N off the ends. For example, for signals arriving at 20° elevation, a dipole at 50 feet has an S/N advantage over the reference vertical of 6.3 dB in line with the wire and 25.6 dB broadside. If you have just a single noise source and you can rotate a high dipole, you should be able to come within a few decibels of the latter figure most of the time. But when multiple noise sources in different directions arise (typical for power-line noise in times of low humidity), rotating the antenna won't help much. The S/N advantage of the high dipole then is likely to be near the worst-case figure.

These numbers illustrate the advantage of horizontal receiving antennas and substantiate the notion long held by amateurs that "verticals are noisy." But you can reduce ground-wave noise much more effectively if you don't rely on a simple horizontal wire.

Canceling Ground-Wave Components

Although a horizontal wire responds only weakly to a broadside ground wave, its response is substantial off the ends. If you could somehow eliminate the end response, you'd be left with the low broadside response and whatever residual response developed at intermediate angles.

Figure 3 shows the ground-wave response of two parallel dipoles 10 feet apart and 10 feet high fed out of phase. The phasing cancels everything arriving off the ends of the wires. The end nulls combine with the low broadside response to create a residual cloverleaf ground-wave pattern. The peak of the cloverleaf is 9.3 dB down from the peak end-response of a single dipole.[4] (Wire losses are ignored here to illustrate the cancellation principle.)

This antenna is just a very-close-spaced W8JK endfire array. Although it makes a good receiving antenna for the low bands, it's pretty large. And there's still considerable ground-wave pickup in the cloverleaf peaks. If the wires somehow could remain parallel for all directions, it might be possible to achieve complete cancellation of the vertical and radial components of the ground wave.

In some sense, the sides of a circular loop are parallel everywhere. Current amplitude and phase vary little in small loops of regular shape. Therefore, the currents in opposite sides of such loops are nearly equal and out of phase. Unlike a W8JK array, a small horizontal loop does not have a null anywhere along the ground. But its ground-wave response is uniformly low in all directions because the antenna responds only to the weak horizontal component. Everything else cancels out (or nearly so).

A small loop usually is defined as one with a total conductor length of less than 0.1 λ. But unless you use large-diameter conductors to minimize RF resistance, loops this small are inefficient. A pream-

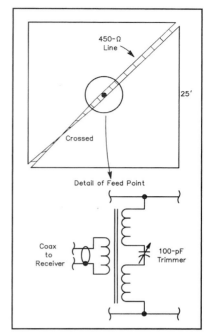

Figure 4—Basic diagram of the 80-meter low-noise loop antenna showing detail of the feedpoint arrangement. The antenna measures 25 feet on a side, is 10 feet high, and made of #14 wire. It's fed at opposite corners with phasing lines made of #14 wire spaced 1.5 inches. A small ferrite transformer at the junction of the phasing lines matches the antenna to 50 Ω coaxial feed line and also functions as a balun. The trimmer capacitor (a capacitance of about 40 pF is required) in series with the antenna-side winding resonates the loop at 3.5 MHz.

plifier may be needed to overcome receiver noise. You can increase the output of a loop by increasing its size, but the larger you make it, the less constant the current becomes. This reduces ground-wave cancellation.

The antenna of Figure 4 overcomes this difficulty by using two feedpoints, each on opposite sides of the loop to force current balance. One of the phasing lines is twisted to maintain proper phase.[5] This loop can be made quite large and still exhibit very low response to ground-wave noise.

A Practical Design

The 80-meter loop of Figure 4 has a perimeter of 0.36 λ. It's 25 feet on a side, 10 feet high, and made of #14 wire. It's fed at opposite corners with phasing lines made of #14 wire spaced 1.5 inches. A small ferrite transformer at the junction of the phasing lines matches the antenna to 50 Ω and also functions as a balun. A trimmer capacitor (about 40 pF is needed) in series with the antenna-side winding resonates the loop at 3.5 MHz.

34 QST

The ground-wave response of this particular loop is shown in Figure 5 and its sky-wave response in Figure 6. For signals arriving at 20° elevation, the worst-case sky-wave response is 20.5 dB below that of the reference vertical. This signal level is quite usable on 80 meters without a preamp. Because the loop reduces ground-wave noise at least 45.1 dB, S/N improvement is 24.6 dB for the worst-case combination of signal and noise directions. If you use a preamp and adjust for equal signal levels, ground-wave noise will be four S units lower on the loop *no matter what direction it comes from!* For signals arriving at higher angles, S/N enhancement approaches 30 dB.

Both the ground-wave noise pattern and sky-wave signal pattern are very uniform in azimuth. The antenna is essentially omnidirectional with an overhead null, just like a vertical. An overhead null is useful for reducing near-vertical-incidence sky-wave signals from nearby stations. (The loop rejects their ground-wave signals along with local noise.)

Although the S/N performance of this loop is not particularly sensitive to height, you can increase output level substantially by raising the antenna well above ground. For example, if you raise the loop to 50 feet, the output increases 15.2 dB for signals arriving at 20° elevation. At this height, the output level is only 5.3 dB below that of the reference vertical. You'll never need a preamp with a loop this high. The S/N advantage drops 0.1 dB. At a height of 20 feet, output increases 7.2 dB and S/N drops 0.6 dB.

You can shrink the loop to 10 feet on a side. The S/N advantage increases 0.5 dB, but the signal level drops 6.5 dB. You can raise the signal level 3.4 dB by doubling the loop side lengths to 50 feet, but the S/N advantage then drops 7.9 dB. You can thus trade-off loop size, S/N enhancement, and signal level. If you use smaller wire, output drops. For example, it's 1.7 dB lower for #22 wire.

Although this loop is a narrowband device and must be carefully resonated, the resonance is much broader than that of a typical small loop. You can get away with a single capacitor setting for both 3.5 and 3.8 MHz if you're willing to accept somewhat lower signal levels. The capacitor setting does not affect the patterns or sky-wave-to-ground-wave ratio—it simply alters output level.

The input resistance at the junction of the phasing lines varies over a wide range with loop size, height, and phasing-line characteristic impedance. The input resistance is about 40 Ω for the loop of Figure 4 at a height of 10 feet. A transformer using a type-77 ferrite core (such as an FT-82-77, FT-114-77 or FB-77-1024) with 9 turns of any size enameled wire on the coax side and 8 wire turns on the antenna side provides a good match to 50-Ω coax.[6] The

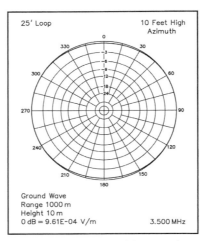

Figure 5—Azimuthal plot of the ground-wave component of a 25-foot-square, 80-meter loop at a height of 10 feet. The input power to the antenna is 1 kW. The peak electric field is shown.

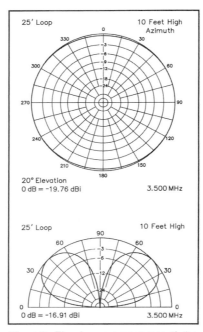

Figure 6—The sky-wave responses of the 10-foot-high, 25-foot-square, 80-meter loop. At A, the azimuthal plot; at B, the elevation plot.

input resistance drops to about 20 Ω when the loop is raised to 20 feet and to about 15 Ω at 50 feet. Use 13 turns of wire on the coax side for 20 feet and 15 for 50 feet.

Although the optimum transformer turns ratio varies with antenna height, little output is sacrificed if you use a fixed ratio. For example, output is only 1 dB less than optimal when a loop designed for 10 feet is used at 50 feet. If you're determined to obtain the best possible match, use 16 turns of wire on the coax side and tap the winding for lowest SWR (alternatively, a switch can be used to select any of two or more taps). Use the lowest possible power when measuring SWR. It's easy to puncture the dielectric of a small trimmer capacitor with a momentary blast.

The antenna's resonant frequency shifts when the phasing lines get wet. If you use true open-wire line with plastic spacers, the frequency shift will be less than 100 kHz. But if you use 450-Ω line with segmented polyethylene dielectric, the resonant frequency decreases more than 200 kHz when the line becomes thoroughly damp. Although this won't affect signal-to-noise ratio, output drops in the desired frequency range. You may be tempted to try phasing lines of 300-Ω twinlead routed inside PVC tubing to avoid moisture effects, but line impedances this low work only for smaller loops.

This antenna should be constructed as symmetrically as possible to maximize cancellation of the vertical and radial components of the ground wave. Make the loop perfectly square and accurately align it in the horizontal plane. Cut the phasing lines to the same length. Although these loops perform well near houses, fences, and towers, try to install the antenna as far from other conductors as possible to maximize current balance. Use the shortest possible leads to interconnect the matching components. Although it's probably unnecessary, I like to split the antenna-side transformer winding and put the tuning capacitor in the center to promote equal currents in the phasing-line conductors.

To minimize the number of supports, a loop about 17 feet on a side can be constructed using a 20-meter quad spreader. You can mount the spreader well up on a tower to increase output. Alternatively, you may be able to eliminate supports altogether by stringing a loop in your attic or garage. However, the current balance of indoor loops may be degraded by electrical wiring, plumbing, heating ducts, or other nearby conductors.

On-the-Air Performance

Ed Andress, W6KUT, located in the San Diego surburb of Poway, constructed a loop 21 feet on a side and 10 feet high. Ed describes his antenna in an article starting on page 37. Ed's location is subjected to strong, chronic power-line noise. On 80 meters, Ed uses a pair of phased quarter-wave verticals for transmitting. We used the verticals as a reference when evaluating the loop. A 20-dB preamp was available. With the preamp, signals near loop resonance were about equal to those from the verticals.

The loop performed as expected. It dramatically enhanced the signal-to-noise ratio of most sky-wave signals. Sometimes the verticals did better during a momentary change in propagation; occasionally a particular noise arose that the loop didn't attenuate much. But overall, the loop was far superior. It made little difference on strong signals. It made listening to moderately strong signals much more pleasant. It let us copy weak signals that were buried in the noise and unreadable on the verticals.

During times of no detectable power-line noise, we often noticed a curious effect: The loop still enhanced signal-to-noise ratio by one or two S units, making copy of moderately weak signals more pleasant. On these occasions, we were unable to hear the telltale, raspy buzz of power-line noise (or any other noise signature) when we listened with the transceiver's AM detector. Unless noise happens to arrive at low angles and signals at high, there's no reason for the loop to enhance sky-wave S/N. We believe that the unidentified noise is local and propagates by the ground wave. We speculate that it may be the sum of hundreds of weak man-made noise sources in the densely populated suburb. (The superposition of a large number of noise sources tends to be characterless even when the individual sources aren't.)

Total Ground-Wave Cancellation

If you stack two of these loops vertically and bring both feed lines into the shack, you can form a deep null on the horizon for all azimuth angles by combining the signals with a fixed amplitude and phase offset. Except for azimuth-response irregularities caused by nearby conductors and small elevation-angle differences due to range, this system will cancel all ground-wave components. This noise canceler was to have been the original subject of this article. However, a single component loop worked so well in practice that I decided total ground-wave cancellation was overkill.

Comparison with Other Antennas

A conventional, single-feedpoint, small loop about two feet on a side—oriented horizontally—yields roughly the same S/N enhancement as the loop of Figure 4. However, output will be down about 46 dB from the reference vertical. You'll need a low-noise preamp with a loop this small unless your receiver has a very low noise figure. Still, even with a preamp, a conventional small loop makes an attractive, low-profile alternative. You must construct a low-output antenna like this carefully to avoid stray pickup. A single capacitor setting won't provide good output levels on both phone and CW.

The WA2WVL cardioid antenna attenuates thunderstorm static and ground-wave noise to the rear. If you're seldom troubled by omnidirectional local noise, it should make a more effective receiving antenna than the loop described in this article. The cardioid also requires fewer supports and less space. As a bonus, it's inherently broadband.

If you have room for a two-wavelength Beverage, it will outperform the WA2WVL cardioid on sky-wave noise and should reduce ground-wave noise arriving more than 45° off boresight by at least 15 dB. If local noise near boresight isn't a problem, a long Beverage can tremendously improve your receiving capability.

The easiest way to improve reception on 80 or 160 meters is to use the most sensitive horizontal antenna available at your antenna switch. Many hams with 80-meter verticals find that switching to a 40-meter dipole or beam improves copy of weak signals even though the antenna is nowhere near resonant on 80 meters. When just a single noise source is active, you should be able to null it by broadsiding a 40-meter rotary.

Scaling the Antenna to Other Frequencies

While I've used the 80-meter band for illustration in this article, it's easy to scale the design to other frequencies. Simply multiply lengths, heights, transformer turns and capacitor values by the number you get when you divide 3.5 by the target frequency in MHz.

That said, I don't recommend this antenna for use above 40 meters. If you're using a vertical antenna on the upper HF bands, do yourself a favor and replace it with the highest horizontally polarized antenna you can manage. Not only will your receive noise decrease, your transmit signal almost certainly will improve due to higher ground-reflection gain.[7] (Exception: If your vertical radiates over saltwater, keep it!) If you're already using a horizontal wire on upper HF, I think your next antenna project should be a rotary beam rather than a receiving loop.

Notes
[1] Floyd Koontz, WA2WVL, "Is this Ewe for You?" *QST*, Feb 1995, pp 31-33.
[2] Frederick Terman, *Radio Engineers' Handbook*, 1st ed (New York: McGraw-Hill, 1943), pp 674-709.
[3] *MININEC*-based antenna-analysis programs do not compute the surface wave, nor can they accurately model antennas close to ground. I used *NEC/Wires 2.0* with its surface-wave and Sommerfeld-Norton ground options for all antenna models in this article. All models assumed average ground characteristics (dielectric constant 13, conductivity 5 mS/m).
[4] A small cloverleaf peak requires very close wire spacing. For example, the peak is down only 5.4 dB for a spacing of 50 feet.
[5] The feed arrangement is like that of an Alford Loop. In fact, the low-noise receiving antenna really is just a variant of the VHF/UHF loop devised by Andrew Alford for a different purpose in 1940. See Terman, pp 814-815.
[6] Don't be tempted to eliminate the transformer and connect 50-Ω coax directly to a loop. The transformer functions as a current balun. It keeps noise current induced on the coax shield from entering the receiver. Just a little pickup by the shield can pollute the low-noise output of a loop.
[7] For example, on 20 meters, a horizontal dipole only 35 feet high has 3 to 6 dB broadside gain over a vertical dipole at low angles over average ground.

New Products

HAMTRONICS WWV RECEIVER

◊ Ever wish you had a shortwave set for receiving time signals and geophysical propagation data from WWV? Today, many hams operate only on the VHF/UHF bands, and spending a lot of money for a shortwave receiver is out of the question. Enter the Hamtronics model RWWV, a low-cost, crystal-controlled, 10-MHz AM superhet for receiving WWV.

The RWWV comes on one printed circuit board; it's easy to build and align, and it's powered by one 9-V battery (or a 9-12 V dc power supply). The little receiver needs only a small whip antenna (or a short piece of wire) for good reception. It even has a squelch circuit to mute the speaker when reception fades into the noise.

In addition to showing you how to set up the RWWV, the instruction manual explains the informational broadcasts you'll hear on WWV.

Price: $59 kit; $99 wired and tested; shipping $5 US surface mail, $8 airmail.

For details, or to request a catalog detailing Hamtronics' many offerings, contact Hamtronics Inc, 65-F Moul Rd, Hilton, NY; tel 716-392-9430, fax 716-392-9420.

VHF-DX, AN AFFORDABLE PC-BASED LOGGER FOR VHF/UHF CONTESTING

◊ *VHF-DX*, from VHF Products, is a logger designed for high-performance VHF/UHF contesting, general logging and awards-chasing from 50 MHz to 10 GHz. It supports all ARRL VHF/UHF contests, tracks grid squares and easily logs rover contacts—satellites, too. *VHF-DX* even outputs your contest logs in ARRL Standard File Format for easy contest-entry submission.

The program automatically tracks grid squares worked by band for the League's VUCC award program, and handles satellite QSOs with ease, adding the satellite name and transponder mode to your log.

The package includes a program disk and a printed instruction manual. Price: $10.95 plus $1 shipping (specify disk size, PC compatibles only, 512k RAM minimum). VHF Products, PO Box 22391, Chagrin Falls, OH 44023-0391; tel 216-543-2748.

Amateur Radio and Radio Circuit Design

By Ward Silver, N0AX

Beginning with designs originally published in the experimenter and "electrical" magazines of the day, amateurs rapidly ignited a steady fire of innovation that continues today. As described by articles in the chapter "Spark and Early Radio," amateur spark stations evolved rapidly, often challenging commercial and military stations for access to the ether. In the tsunami of radio development that followed, amateurs faced two primary challenges — to hear and to be heard. The first proved to be the more daunting, at least initially, but the first century has been an alternating sequence of first pushing the receiving envelope then the transmitting. There is always a station to be logged that is just a little further away or weaker in strength!

When development of receivers was in its infancy, the designs were evaluated on the basis of "can signals be heard at all" or *sensitivity*. Early detectors such as the Branly coherer were quite insensitive by modern standards, for example. The introduction of vacuum tubes solved most of the sensitivity problems. That led to the next accomplishment — reducing the number of tuning controls required to move the receiver from signal to signal by adopting Armstrong's superheterodyne architecture in the 1920s.

Once stations were easily heard and the tuning process was streamlined, the problem then became *selectivity* — how to separate the many signals present so that only one at a time was heard. The "single-signal" receiver introduced by Lamb in the early 1930s was a major advance. This was accompanied by increasingly sophisticated transmitter designs, such as those described by Millen during the same period. Transmitters rapidly progressed from basic crystal-controlled, single-band MOPA (master oscillator power amplifier) designs to operate on multiple bands, variable-frequency oscillators (VFOs) became practical, power levels continually increased, and new demands were placed on stability and signal purity.

Taking advantage of advances made during World War II, a series of further refinements in receiver architecture led to both single- and multiple-conversion designs with differing strengths and weaknesses that were introduced to Amateur Radio through the 1950s and 1960s. During this period, improvements to filter, mixer and amplifier circuit design came quickly.

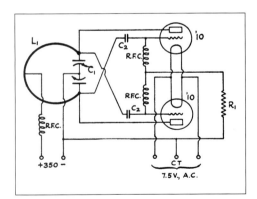

In the 1930s, 56 MHz (Mc then) was an extremely high frequency and even then the wiring layout became part of the circuit as shown by the way L1 is drawn in this oscillator created by James Lamb, W1CEI.

Sensitivity remained an issue on the VHF and higher bands, however, as low-noise amplifying devices with gain at those frequencies were simply not available to amateurs (or most professionals, for that matter). In the mid 1950s, however, semiconductor theory and performance was advancing rapidly, leading to new types of devices and transistors that could be applied to the problem. Low-noise parametric amplifiers using the new varactor diode were one such advance pioneered by amateurs alongside professionals, making possible early amateur "moonbounce" contacts through the 1960s and beyond.

During the post-war period, single-sideband and frequency modulation became part of Amateur Radio. This required new methods of modulation and filtering, driving innovation in circuits and circuit design techniques. The change from open-wire parallel conductor feed line to the newly available and inexpensive coaxial cable required wholesale changes in transmitter output and impedance matching circuitry. Amateurs also had to adapt their construction techniques to the rapid adoption of television (and the high-gain TV-set IF amplifiers operating at 21 MHz), meaning an end to breadboard haywired transmitters and the beginning of all-metal enclosures and extensive harmonic filtering.

Amateur gear then began to change from being based on tubes to transistors and then integrated circuits. The performance level of electronics available to amateurs rose dramatically, but that created new problems such as receiver linearity and oscillator noise performance. Articles in *QST* and *Ham Radio* by Rohde and Hayward, just to name two well-known authors, addressed how to get the most out of the new circuit topologies and devices. For an illustration of just how much performance changed, listen to a band during a major contest on mainstream amateur receivers from the 1960s and from today!

Circuit Design Going Forward

With so much of analog and discrete electronics being subsumed by programmable and application-specific devices or implemented as software, is the era of advances in circuit design past? After all, the most recent article selected for this section is from 1975! To be sure, as far as wireless communications is concerned, the days are long-gone when tinkering with an op-amp and bins of resistors and capacitors was state of the art. The same theme — analog is dead — has been echoed in the professional literature for years but it simply isn't so.

Going forward, circuit design will still require innovation at the interfaces where analog meets digital. Hybrid applications in which wireless meets some other technology will demand new techniques. For example, as I-Q modulation schemes took the stage, the Tayloe mixer by Dan Tayloe, N7VE, was invented. New devices, such as the memristor, and new materials, such as graphene, will open the door to entirely new functions for circuits, new power levels, new frequencies and more.

Power amplifier design is a new challenge for amateurs. We have receivers with outstanding linearity and the ability to pick out a tiny signal in the midst of thundering pileups. Yet our transmitters generate excessive spurious products from intermodulation and noise. Clearly, there is work to be done on spectrum cleanliness! The reign of the tube as the amplifying device of choice above a few hundred watts is also challenged. New high-power solid-state devices and modules are becoming available at prices amateurs can afford — does this remind anyone of the introduction of tubes themselves to Amateur Radio or the explosion of innovation fueled by cheap surplus equipment after World War II?

Digital circuit design — once the domain of discrete logic gates — is hardly standing still. It is now possible to "compile to silicon" as mathematics are translated directly into logic structures that are then programmed into arrays of digital circuitry in ICs. An amateur can dream up the math in the morning and have a working prototype device after lunch!

Finally, as amateurs learned years ago, above microwave frequencies the wiring, the component and the function all begin to blur into one physical structure. With the upper limit of Amateur Radio climbing rapidly toward 1 THz (imagine a megamegahertz!) there will be plenty of new frontiers to explore that will change even the definition of "circuit."

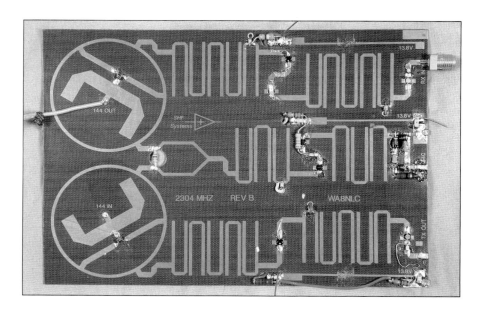

A no-tune, microwave-to-VHF transverter designed by Jim Davey, WA8NLC, for the 2.3 GHz band. By integrating components with the circuit board layout, amateurs can create functional circuits at very short wavelengths.

"The One-Control Superheterodyne" by James McLaughlin

By Ward Silver, NØAX

Long accustomed to the front panels of our radios being of the "one big knob" design, modern amateurs may be excused if they find it hard to imagine that in the early 1920s tuning a good-quality receiver once required the adjustment of three or more controls! Imaging trying to tune through a band or find a specific station if every change in frequency required tuning or neutralizing every RF stage and optimizing the filament voltage and grid bias of each tube in the receiver — an exercise requiring a steady hand and lots of patience.

A home-built 1930s TRF-Autodyne receiver from the collection of Al Klase, N3FRQ. The center tuning knob, below the lighted dial, is the "bandspread" control. It actuates two small capacitors that tune the RF amp and detector simultaneously. The knobs at the upper right and upper left are the "band-set" controls. The detector band-set is used to select the desired portion of a coil set's tuning range, and then the RF band set is tweaked for maximum signal.

Usually built on breadboards or in wooden cabinets, controls for these *tuned radio frequency* (TRF) receivers were also affected by the proximity of the operator's hand and, because of coupling between circuits inside the receiver, the adjustments often affected each other. Along with drift and poor selectivity (by today's standards), keeping a station tuned in required almost constant attention to tuning. Thus, it is no surprise that the lead-in to the article states, "We consider it the outstanding development in recent "superhet" progress, as it provides the simplest imaginable control for what is admittedly the best reception arrangement known today." Note that transmitters were crystal-controlled — a significant advance in and of itself — and VFOs were still in the future.

The superheterodyne concept having just been recently introduced to Amateur Radio, the article is obliged to point out that tuning now requires that the oscillator and amplifier stages (referred to as the "first detector" stage in the article) be tuned to have a constant *difference* in frequency (the intermediate frequency). This is more complicated problem than tuning a series of stages to the same frequency and at a similar rate.

The solution is three-fold and includes an alignment procedure. First, the primary tuning capacitors are "gang-tuned" by means of coupled gears turned by the single front-panel control. Setting the physical position of the variable capacitor plates is critical so that the capacitance tracks properly across the band of interest — the broadcast band in this article — maintaining proper alignment. (Note also the special proprietary "Super-Multiformer" transformer used with the multi-tube IF amplifier stages.)

Second, the inductors are carefully designed with mechanical drawings for each so that when the coils are reproduced, their inductances are very close to the desired value. This particular design could be made a multiband design through the use of plug-in inductors, but the author constructed a single-band design with the coils soldered in for stability.

Finally, mechanical construction quality is stressed throughout the article. By building the receiver on a sturdy metal chassis with a consistent layout, variations in tuning and other behaviors could be minimized. Tuning dials required careful layout if the calibration was to correspond closely to the designer's intended tuning curve. This allowed the receive frequency to be calibrated in exact frequency — even listing specific stations — and not "logging" scales that were calibrated by the user after setting up the radio.

The article concludes, "As to results — at Rochester, New York we have been able to bring in Pacific Coast stations on a loud-speaker on an average of three nights a week in the middle of August, which is not the best time of year to obtain good reception…"

Clues About Today's Future

The single-knob design remained dominant in communications receivers — amateurs, commercial and military alike — for more than 80 years. This is a reflection of the way we model the radio spectrum mentally: low frequencies are "over here" and high frequencies are "over there." The spectrum has but one dimension, frequency, and the stations are as beads on a string.

Only recently has the software-defined radio (SDR) with its screen-style display and use of a pointing device such as a mouse started to make inroads. The new visual representation of the spectrum (compared to the traditional receiver) adds more information in the form of time and other information about the calling station. Whatever user interface can be imagined can be implemented through software and maybe some interesting hardware. Nevertheless, many hams feel uncomfortable without that knob, leading to "soft knobs" on the screen and external knobs read by the software!

Hams who grow up with new types of receivers and the new user interfaces for them will have a very different way of imagining the radio spectrum, so their equipment designs and operating methods are likely to be different, too. What will they imagine and what kind of operating will they do without a knob?

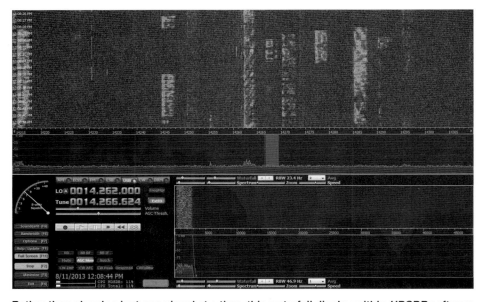

Rather than showing just one signal at a time, this waterfall display within *HDSDR* software shows a number of signals from 14.215 to 14.305 MHz.

The One-Control Superheterodyne

By James L. McLaughlin

Research Engineer, Precise Manufacturing Corporation

> Following closely on his recent article in *QST* describing the One-Control Neutrodyne, Mr. McLaughlin has produced a superheterodyne operated by but one control which we take great pleasure in presenting to our readers in this article. We consider it the outstanding development in recent "superhet" progress, as it provides the simplest imaginable control for what is admittedly the best reception arrangement known today. Although this article describes a set for the broadcast wavelengths, Mr. McLaughlin's control idea of course is applicable to superheterodynes designed for any other bands.—Editor.

WHEN the public first became interested in radio broadcasting several years ago it was introduced to receiving apparatus having numerous controls. It was taken for granted that such apparatus had to have several controls to be of any consequence, and if a person had a set with more knobs than his next-door neighbor's it was generally considered that his was the superior set. In fact it gave the impression that he had mastered a great deal of radio engineering to be able to operate such a tuner. This novelty has now worn off and the tendency is towards sets with the minimum number of controls. This is a very healthy state of affairs because it shows that radio has passed from the novelty stage to a status similar to that of the automobile—it has become a modern convenience. And therefore it is necessary that receiving devices be designed with such simplicity that the layman may operate them with little knowledge of the principles involved.

Besides being simple in operation a receiving set must be sensitive and selective or it will be useless. The two most sensitive and selective types of receivers at the present time are the Superheterodyne and

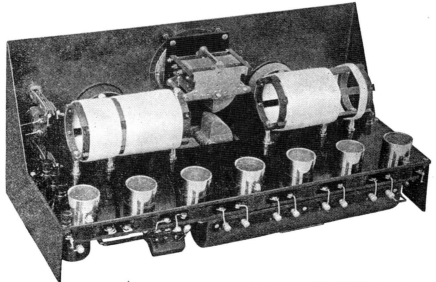

FIG. 1—A REAR VIEW OF THE SET THAT DOES THE TRICK, showing particularly the location of the two geared condensers and the inductances for the oscillator and tuner. Incidentally, note how the front panel and the sides are formed from one piece of sheet metal, the sides supporting the horizontal panel which carries the sockets.

those sets employing "neutralized" radio-frequency amplification. The measure of sensitivity and selectivity depends entirely upon how well made the sets are and not upon how many tubes they use. I have seen some of both type that tuned as broadly as a single-circuit receiver and were about as sensitive as a one-tube set.

In the Neutrodyne type of receiver we can simplify the filament control to one rheostat but beyond that we can do nothing electrically that will simplify its operation. We still have three or more tuning controls, depending on how many stages of tuned radio-frequency amplification are used. But by means of gears or some other mechanical device we can connect these several controls in such a manner that all the circuits are tuned simultaneously to the same wavelength. The set being electrically all right, the success of such an arrangement depends upon how well the mechanical work is done. Such a receiver

FIG. 2—THE BOTTOM OF THE SET, showing location of the transformers, fixed condensers, etc. The long black case in the left foreground is a "Super-Multiformer", a multiple transformer serving all the intermediate-frequency stages.

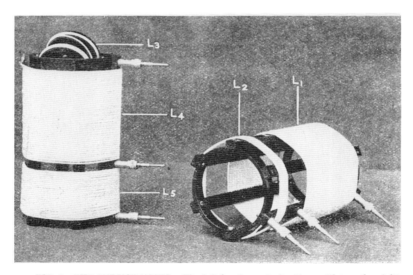

FIG. 3—THE INDUCTANCES. The left-hand one is for the oscillator, the right-hand for the tuner. Note the very efficient low-loss construction, the windings being carried by a light frame of narrow hard-rubber strips. The plug-in connectors make it possible to substitute other inductances for different wavelength bands. The success of one-control superheterodynes built from this article will depend largely upon the fidelity with which these inductances are duplicated electrically, so they should be carefully studied. See also the dimensional drawing, and consult the hook-up for the winding data.

was described by the present author in the August (1924) issue of *QST*.*

Examining the Superheterodyne

Let us now look into the possibilities of simplifying the control of the superhetero-

*Aavailable from *QST's* Circulation Department.

dyne. We can control the filaments of the tubes as in the Neutrodyne. This leaves us with one tuning control and one oscillator control. We may also have a stabilizing control for the intermediate-frequency amplifier but this may be eliminated by neutralizing the amplifier as described by this author in the June issue of *QST*.* Even if the tube capacity is not neutralized, this control may be made very stable by careful and proper design of the transformers used in the intermediate-frequency amplifier, so that it may be ignored here.

The first thought that occurs is to couple the two remaining controls as was done in the One-Control Neutrodyne, but this will not work because these two circuits are not to be tuned to the same frequency but to a constant *difference* in frequency which must equal the frequency of the intermediate-wave amplifier. It is quite a different problem and much more complex. Let us imagine the tuner of our superheterodyne has a range from 200 to 600 meters, and that the intermediate-frequency amplifier is tuned to 40 kilocycles. If the tuner is set, say, at 200 meters or 1500 kilocycles, the oscillator must be tuned to 205 meters (1460 k. c.) or else to 195 meters (1540 k. c.), either of which will produce a beat frequency of 40 k. c. We will not go into the reason for this or into the theory of superheterodyne operation, as this has been very fully covered in recent issues of *QST*.[1] Now let us change our tuner to 600 meters or 500 k. c., which we will call the maximum wavelength. To give the same beat frequency of 40 k. c. our oscillator now will have to be set at 650 meters (460 k. c.) or at 550 meters (540 k. c.)

From this we see that the wavelength ratio between tuner and oscillator does not remain constant but varies more or less directly with the dial setting; that is, as we go from minimum wavelength towards the maximum wavelength we have to change the wavelength of the oscillator more rapidly than we do that of the tuner. If only we had straight-line-frequency variable condensers the problem would be simple, for then if we had identical inductances in the first detector and in the oscillator we could gear the condensers of these two circuits together at a frequency difference of 40 kilocycles and the beat frequency would be the same over the whole range; but such condensers cannot be obtained on the market and we will have to look for some other solution.

---

[1] See particularly "Building Superheterodynes That Work," a series edited by S. Kruse, appearing in *QST* for June, July and August, 1924.

A Way Out

Looking at Figure 5 we see how the tuning curves of the first-detector circuit and oscillator circuit must look when plotted to produce a constant difference of 40 kilocycles over the whole tuning range, if the tuning condensers of the two circuits are identical. A study of these curves suggests that we design the inductances of both these circuits so that such tuning curves may be produced. Right there is our solution. When the proper ratio of inductance, capacity and distributed capacity in both of these circuits is found it becomes a simple matter to make a one-control superheterodyne. In the following description all

FIG. 4—THE SUB-PANEL carrying the two 23-plate Cardwell condensers and their gears. The control knob goes on the extension shaft of the bottom gear. Data on the gears are given in one of the drawings.

the specifications of the inductances are given so that the reader of average skill may duplicate the results.

The Construction

Two .0005-μfd. (500 μμfd.) Cardwell condensers are used to tune the two circuits and are geared together so as to be operated by one control. Figure 4 shows the gear construction, and dimensions and details are given in one of the drawings.

The cover of this number of *QST* illustrates the front of the receiver and shows the indicating arrangement that is used. The control knob, in the center of the panel, was taken from an Accuratune dial and is connected to the lower condenser

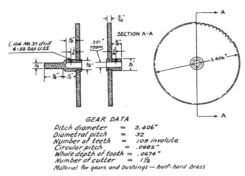

and gear. The two glass windows above this dial show the indicator, the left-hand one being used for calibration and the listing of important stations while the right-hand one indicates condenser settings so that stations that are not listed may be logged. (See also Fig. 6.) The small left-hand knob is the rheostat which controls all the tube filaments. This could be replaced if desired by a fixed resistance, as the filament temperature is not critical in any of the tubes. The small right-hand knob is a potentiometer and controls the grids of the amplifying tubes. This was found not at all critical, due to the design of the amplifying unit, and once set one could tune over the whole range and have the amplifier remain stable and still work at maximum amplification. Two jacks are shown on the right-hand side of the panel for the head-phones and loud-speaker, while between them is the filament control switch. The panel itself is 1-16" brass, with a baked crystal finish; working dimensions and layout are shown in one of the drawings.

The Inductances

Figure 3 shows the construction of the oscillator and tuning inductances. Their physical dimensions are given in a separate drawing, and the number of turns in each winding is shown under the wiring diagram. They were made so they could be removed readily from the circuit and others placed in to cover another wavelength range. In the photograph the left-hand coil is the oscillator inductance. The lower winding is the plate coil; the upper one is the grid coil; and the small coil inside at the top is in series with the grid coil, forming a small variometer, and is used to balance the circuit. The right-hand inductance is the first-detector tuner. The smaller winding is the antenna coil, the larger one the grid coil.

Figure 1 is a rear view of the receiver and gives a good idea of the position of these inductances in the completed set. The coils are kept over 2" away from everything except at their extreme ends. The seven sockets are arranged at the rear edge of the set. Beneath the sockets is a sub-panel which supports the intermediate-frequency amplifying unit, which is a Precise "Super-Multiformer", the audio-frequency transformer, bypass condensers, etc. This view clearly shows the short grid and plate leads required to make connections between transformers and sockets.

Figure 2 shows the underside of the layout and gives a clear idea of the "Super-Multiformer",[2] which really is the heart of the outfit and is chiefly responsible for the sensitivity and stability of this set. Alongside of this, to the right, is the Precise audio transformer. At the right-hand lower side is shown a 200-M.H. choke coil, which is required in the oscillator plate feed. Above this is the ½-μfd. by-pass condenser which shunts the

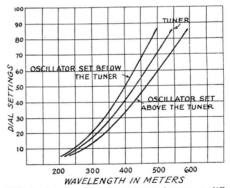

FIG. 5, showing how a constant frequency difference between tuner and oscillator involves an increasing difference in wavelength as the tuning wavelength is increased.

batteries, while above the audio transformer the C-battery of the audio stage may be seen. The layout of sockets is such that the first tube looking from the antenna end of the set (left-hand end in Fig.

---

[2] The "Super-Multiformer" is a multiple transformer for superheterodynes developed by the Precise Mfg. Corp., of Rochester, and takes the place of the four separate intermediate-frequency transformers that otherwise would be used. Although the basis of the set described in this article, Mr. McLaughlin's one-control idea is applicable to sets using other good makes of intermediate-frequency transformers. —Ed.

2, right hand end in Fig. 1) is the first detector; the next three are for the r.f. amplifier, the next is the second detector, then the audio amplifier, while the last one is the oscillator. This arrangement keeps the length of leads between oscillator circuit and oscillator socket approximately the same as between tuner circuit and tuner socket. The only coupling between these circuits is through

results were obtained using no plate voltage other than that supplied from the filament battery when the plate return was connected to the positive side of the A-battery as was done with the first detector, but 45 volts was found to be sufficient to bring in the loud signals to the best advantage as well as the weak.

In the second detector no grid condenser or leak is used, as generally the voltage

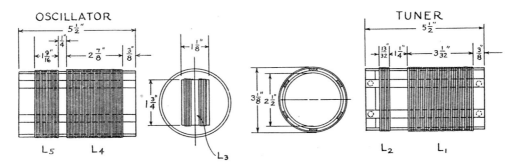

DIMENSIONS OF THE INDUCTANCES—Care should be taken to duplicate these as nearly exactly as possible. See Fig. 3 also. The end rings are sawn from bakelite tubing of 2½" inside diameter and having a 3/32" wall. The longitudinal hard-rubber strips are 3/8" x 3/16". The wire is No. 18 D.C.C. throughout.

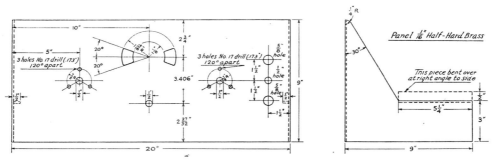

LAYOUT DIMENSIONS FOR THE METAL PANEL

the battery leads and stray coupling between the coils themselves (the separation is 6"). This was found much superior to the customary arrangement of choking the first detector with energy from the oscillator.

The Circuit

No plate voltage was used on the first detector other than that supplied by the A-battery. (See wiring diagram.) This improved reception greatly and was of big help on weak signals. The oscillator was supplied by a 45-volt B-battery, instead of the customary 90 volts. In fact excellent

applied to the grid of this tube is sufficient to shift the operating point to the bend in the characteristic curve and thus obtain detection.

Adjusting the Set

After all the parts are mounted and wired up and both condensers set to exactly the same capacity, the small coil in the grid circuit of the oscillator is adjusted until the oscillator and tuner circuits are correctly balanced. This adjustment can be found readily. Connect antenna and ground to the set, and set the potentiometer over to the negative side so that the long-wave amplifier is in a state of oscillation. Set the condensers at, say, minimum or five or ten degrees, and move the potentiometer back until the amplifier is just barely oscillating. Then adjust the small coil in the oscillator grid inductance until the "rushing" sound that is heard is at its loudest. This will indicate that both

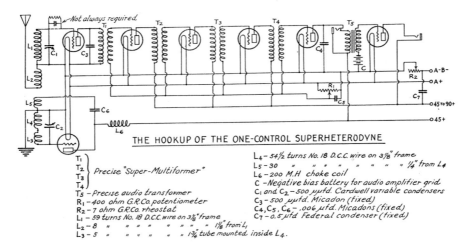

THE HOOKUP OF THE ONE-CONTROL SUPERHETERODYNE

T₁, T₂, T₃, T₄ — Precise "Super-Multiformer"
T₅ — Precise audio transformer
R₁ — 400 ohm G.R.Co. potentiometer
R₂ — 7 ohm G.R.Co. rheostat
L₁ — 59 turns No. 18 D.C.C. wire on 3⅛" frame
L₂ — 8 " " " " " " 1⅛" from L₁
L₃ — 5 " " " " " " 1¾" tube mounted inside L₄.
L₄ — 54½ turns No. 18 D.C.C. wire on 3⅛" frame
L₅ — 30 " " " " " " ¼" from L₄
L₆ — 200 M.H choke coil
C — Negative bias battery for audio amplifier grid.
C₁ and C₂ — 500 μμfd. Cardwell variable condensers
C₃ — 500 μμfd. Micadon (fixed)
C₄, C₅, C₆ — .006 μfd. Micadons (fixed)
C₇ — 0.5 μfd. Federal condenser (fixed)

the "rushing" sound should be of approximately the same intensity. If it is not, readjust the small coil and note how much variation is required to compensate for this change in tune. Then set the condensers at maximum or nearly so. If the coils have been made correctly the noise will still be heard. If it is necessary to change the small coil again, it is clear evidence that the condensers and coils are out of balance and that sufficient care has not been taken in building and adjusting them, because when both condensers are set at exactly the same capacity and coils built as specified it is only necessary to set this small coil once, at any condenser setting, and the circuit will be balanced for all settings in its range.

When the proper setting of this coil is found it is advisable to lock it in some manner. In our case we soldered it securely, so there would be no chance of its becoming loose and throwing the circuits out of balance.

Results Obtained

It is certainly a strange sensation to turn one knob and hear station after station come in without any further adjustment. With the calibrated scale on this set it is a very simple matter to find the desired station.

As to results—at Rochester, New York, we have been able to bring in Pacific Coast stations on a loud-speaker on an average of three nights a week in the middle of August, which is not the best time of the year to obtain good reception, so you can imagine what it will do in the good radio season.

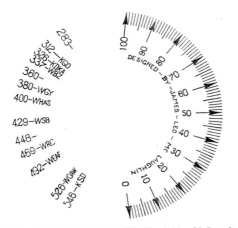

FIG. 6—THE TUNING CHART of Mr. McLaughlin's set illustrated in this article. These are the scales that show through the two little windows that may be seen in the photograph on our cover. The set has a wavelength range from 180 to 580 meters, although only a little more than 90 degrees of the condensers are actually used for the interesting waves between 300 and 550 meters.

circuits are set at the proper frequency to produce the beat-frequency required for the amplifier. Then move the knob which controls the condensers to, say, fifty degrees;

"Short-Wave Receiver Selectivity to Match Present Conditions" by James Lamb, W1CEI (later W1AL)

By Ward Silver, NØAX

"For the present it is satisfaction enough that a way has been found to make a sizeable dent in the particularly acute QRM afflicting us in these piping days of amateur radio, what with some 30,000 of us at it now and more joining up every day, *and more than double the effective width of our bands at the same time*." With those words in 1932, Lamb introduced an enormous improvement in CW reception, the dominant mode of the day.

Italicized for emphasis here, he also noted the importance of spectrum efficiency, echoing the transition from spark to CW and presaging a long sequence of improvements: AM to SSB, ever-narrowing bandwidths of FM phone transmission, PSK31, WSPR, and more to come. All of those improvements, however, are a consequence of changes in the transmitted signal. Lamb's improvement was contained entirely within his new "single-signal superheterodyne" receiver, although it depended on improvements elsewhere to be useful.

In a series of *QST* articles throughout 1932, Lamb made the case for better selectivity while examining the requirements for oscillator stability in both the transmitter and the receiver. The first explained the need and the second laid out the performance requirements for stations at both ends of the contact.

Aside from the band simply being more crowded, the primary problem on the receiving end of the circuit for "straight superhets" was that each incoming RF signal generated an audible beat note at *two* frequencies of the adjustable local oscillator (LO), above and below zero-beat. Modern-day hams who have operated a direct-conversion receiver have experienced the effective doubling of signals on the band, and the extra signals create a great deal of QRM. If those "other" signals could be eliminated, a lot of QRM would simply disappear.

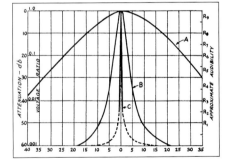

The responses of two typical receivers of the day and a "single-signal" receiver. (A) is for a receiver using one stage of tuned RF and a regenerative detector. (B) is for three stages of tuned RF and a regenerative detector. (C) is the "single-signal" receiver. The dB scale at the left shows the attenuation away from the frequency to which the receiver is tuned. The scale at right shows approximately the corresponding signal audibility in the "R" system.

The primary innovation introduced by Lamb was in placing a quartz crystal in series with the IF amplifier's signal path and offsetting the oscillators so that the image signal on the undesired side of zero beat was suppressed by the response of the IF amplifier's tuned circuits. An alignment sequence then optimized the overall circuit response to minimize receiver bandwidth and thus reject both mixer output products from nearby signals and the unwanted image on the "wrong" side of zero beat. The dramatic reduction in bandwidth also reduced received noise, improving signal-to-noise ratio and the effective sensitivity of the receiver without adding any additional amplification — a strategy still being pursued today. (The use of quartz crystals as filters had been suggested a decade earlier as the article notes, but had not been applied to amateur receivers previously.)

Yet a good filter was not quite enough to completely solve the problem. As the article clearly states, "...the ability of this receiver to make practical use of its high selectivity depends entirely on the stability of the received signal and the high-frequency oscillator."

It would not do much good, for example, to build highly selective receivers if the transmitted signal drifted, chirped, or was a "weeper" (signals that "climb or dive throughout every dash and dot"), too unstable to remain within the receiver passband during reception. Similarly, hum and ripple from power supplies — even raw ac modulation — were still quite commonly heard on signals with the effect of spreading the signal across the passband. The oscillators and circuits of the receiver had to be highly stable as well so that the receiver would remain centered on a signal without requiring constant readjustment.

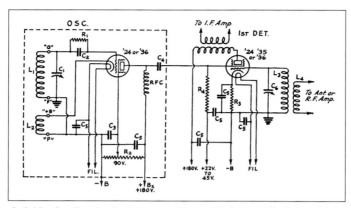

A tickler feedback, electron-coupled oscillator and first-detector combination designed by Lamb that was more stable than previous designs and could be adapted to existing receivers and converters.

The improvement in *system* performance from end-to-end required changes across the system and had a profound effect on amateur operating and construction practices. One consequence of improved selectivity, for example, meant that the tuning controls required much finer adjustment. Tuning a receiver with "1 k.c. selectivity" was much different than before! Enter fine-tuning or "bandspread" in the form of small variable capacitors in parallel with the main tuning capacitor.

Mechanical construction became much more important since rigidity and solid construction were needed if tuned circuits were to stay on frequency. Shielding between stages became an absolute necessity so that the hard-won selectivity was not spoiled by signals radiating from one stage to another. Electrical isolation was important for the same reasons. Changes and improvements cascaded forth from the sketch-pads of equipment designers as they met the challenges of modernization. The result was a receiver that could be used to make CW or AM QSOs today.

From this story we gain a valuable and timeless insight about wireless communication: Certainly, improving one aspect of a key piece of equipment is a significant achievement, but that performance improvement ripples across the entire communications system. It may enable or even demand changes in circuitry and components. New capabilities lead to new applications, and they may even change the way we think about the entire system and radio itself.

Short-Wave Receiver Selectivity to Match Present Conditions

Constructional and Operating Features of the Single-Signal Superhet

By James J. Lamb, Technical Editor

PERHAPS those of *QST*'s readers who had the perseverance to wade through the previous article on things wrong with our high-frequency receivers, and on receiver selectivity generally,[1] will begin this, its sequel, with justifiable foreboding. They may be apprehensive, just a bit suspicious that such a more or less involved discussion must needs beget a fearfully monstrous machine to put those abstractions to work. Chuck that illusion right at the start. The rig that does the business is nowhere near as entangling as the principles on which it is based. The burden of this piece is a practical "how-to-do-it," with some "why" and a little "how-not-to-do-it" thrown in for insurance. The aim here is to show how one job of receiver construction has succeeded in overcoming the basic defects of the receivers we have been using, to give the essentials of its building and adjustment, and to suggest such diversifications and modifications for future development as experience with this example have shown to be possible or advisable. The fact that, as far as we know, this receiver is the first model of its type, containing a first-time combination of several unusual features, makes inevitable a process of evolution. Undoubtably it will have successors little resembling (and perhaps disowning) their parent. Let that be so. For the present it is satisfaction enough that a way has been found to make a sizeable dent in the particularly acute QRM afflicting us in these piping days of amateur radio, what with some 30,000 of us at it now and more joining up every day, and more than double the effective width of our bands at the same time.

Many of these thousands are putting clean, steady signals on the air. Transmitter development has not been dormant. But the receivers aren't able to do them justice. Actually, most of the receivers in use to-day are essentially of the same breed as the autodynes of fifteen years ago, differing basically from the original "detector and one-step" only in the stage of r.f. that has been added to the front end and, sometimes, the audio filter that has been tacked on behind. Except for their occasional post-detector audio selectivity for c.w., such ability as they have for discriminating between signals could be duplicated by any well-constructed and carefully operated job of the low-loss era, the "two-circuit" (modern "pre-selection") tuners of that earlier day just about breaking even in point of selectivity with the 1932 tuned r.f. jobs. (They had to be that good. Ever get tangled in a little spark QRM?) Two sets of audio beat notes for every carrier, unstable oscillating detectors that block on strong signals, the rotten signal getting through with undeserved preferment to steady d.c., background racket, QRN — all as of yore.

> *The method of reception disclosed in this article establishes a new standard in amateur receiver performance, bringing it to par with crystal-controlled transmission. The receiver described is capable of thoroughly useful selectivity that not only greatly increases the effective width of our bands but also places the deserved high premium on the good steady signal, and watt for watt, puts the unsteady signal in the background where it belongs. Adoption of this kind of receiver by the advanced amateurs for whom it has been designed will do much to discourage the rotten note.*
> *— EDITOR.*

The root of these faults in performance, as was pointed out in the June article, is shortage of effective r.f. selectivity in combination with lack of stability, oscillator stability in particular. The gross result of these deficiencies is that our bands sound as if there were at least twice as many c.w. signals as there really are. When the receiver is tuned across the bedlam, each signal pops up on either side of zero beat. And when we tune in a signal on the "north" side of its zero beat, likely as not we find ourselves afflicted with an interfering beat-note from the "south" side of another (complex to visualize but easy to recognize). Hence, the first step toward multiplying ham-band utility by two and toward single-signal c.w. selectivity: Make each signal give but one set of audio beat notes, all on the one side of zero beat; get rid of the audio-frequency image. Then the next step: Narrow down the response on that one side until it becomes but a few-cycle slice out of any c.w. band. The first step can be realized to a considerable degree

[1] Lamb, "What's Wrong With Our C. W. Receivers?", *QST*, June, 1932.

with no more selectivity than that possessed by superhets of standard design *in combination with the off-set tuning scheme suggested in the previous article.* The second is realized by augmenting this selectivity with a sharp filter. Of course there must also be stability, flexibility in control and kindred features not common to other receivers of our acquaintance.

THE ESSENTIAL ELEMENTS

It has been intimated that the receiver must be a superhet and, unless the future brings forth developments to change the situation, that is so. This is not really undesirable, however. Despite prevalent impressions to the contrary, for ordinary service a high-frequency receiver of the superheterodyne type, when given the consideration that it deserves, can be made less noisy, more sensitive and far more selective than any tuned radio-frequency receiver of equivalent cost. When extraordinary service is demanded, as it must be for r.f. selectivity measurable in hundreds of cycles, superhet reception becomes the only recourse. Imagine the number of tuned circuits, tubes and plug-in coils that would be necessary for just one band in a t.r.f. set that would give the selectivity obtainable with a two-stage i.f. superhet — to say nothing of the ganging nightmare, inevitable instability and cost. Where high selectivity is the quest, then, *it must be obtained in an r.f. amplifier whose tuning can be peaked and remain fixed.* That's the i.f. amplifier of a superhet. To make such a fixed-tune amplifier useful over a wide signal-frequency range, there has to be a frequency conversion. Every signal must be changed to the intermediate frequency. That's taken care of by the high-frequency oscillator and first detector of the superhet. In the first detector the incoming signal is beat against (heterodyned by) the output of the oscillator so that the difference between their two frequencies is the frequency to which our fixed intermediate amplifier is tuned and into which amplifier the detector output is fed. The frequency of the local oscillator may be either intermediate-frequency higher or i.f. lower than the signal frequency. It is in this that the superhet differs from other kinds of receivers.

HIGH-FREQUENCY CIRCUITS AND THE I.F. FILTER ARE CONTAINED IN ONE UNIT, SHOWN HERE COUPLED TO A TUNED R.F. BROADCAST RECEIVER (LEFT) DOING DUTY AS THE I.F. AMPLIFIER

The aluminum cabinet is 17¾ inches wide by 9¾ inches deep by 7 inches high, inside dimensions. The closed compartment at the right contains the high-frequency oscillator.

The complete chain of events is more vividly shown in the picture of Fig. 1, an attempt to portray graphically the treatment a c.w. signal would receive between antenna and output of an ideally ultra-selective superhet. Of course all the links are not absolutely essential to every receiver. The stars mark the ones that constitute the bare minimum. The picture is largely self-explanatory, with the possible exception of the pre-selection and high-frequency image elimination of "B." Because many high-frequency superhet designs seem to ignore this feature — and suffer image trouble as a consequence — it merits explanation.

Since the intermediate-frequency is the difference between the oscillator and signal frequencies, and since the oscillator may be either i.f. higher or i.f. lower than the signal frequency, *it is possible to get the same intermediate frequency from two different signal frequencies at the same time.* An illustration: The i.f. amplifier's resonance frequency is 525 kc. The ham signal being received is on 7100 kc. The oscillator is tuned 525 kc. *higher* or to 7625 kc., beating with the signal to give the intermediate frequency. The antenna is coupled right into the first detector, with but one tuned circuit between it and outdoors. Parked on 8150 kc. and banging away at his A, B, C's is a high-power commercial — and his signals rattle the 'phones "R9 plus." How come? The oscillator frequency is exactly 525 kc. *lower* than his frequency *and there isn't enough selectivity ahead of the first detector to keep his signal from getting in along with the ham signal to which the receiver is supposed to be tuned.* That's radio-frequency image interference.[2] The cure? Put enough selectivity ahead of the first detector to keep the r.f. image response down below the danger line. Add a pre-selector. For convenience in coupling and to give a little additional gain, this pre-selector can be simply a tuned r.f. stage. This element makes other improvements, too. It improves the signal-noise ratio by keeping out background and

---
[2] Not to be confused with this is the pseudo-image interference caused by two incoming signals that heterodyne each other to produce intermediate frequency, even with the oscillator switched off. It also is eliminated by pre-selection.

static of the lower r.f. kind that might be passed readily to the i.f. amplifier if it once got to the detector; it prevents radiation of the high-frequency oscillator output via the antenna; with c.w. reception it keeps stray output of the i.f. beating oscillator from getting into the i.f. amplifier through the first detector; and, of course, it adds its bit to receiver sensitivity and all-around selectivity. Which brings us to the block diagram of Fig. 2 and the line-up of the actual receiver.

As shown by the division of the diagram into two sections, the receiver is built in two units. The one at the right, whose constructional details are given in this article, contains the high-frequency circuits and the i.f. filter. The intermediate-frequency and audio unit at the left may use a b.c. receiver chassis as a foundation, as noted, or may be a specially built unit such as will be described in a subsequent article. These two units mount one above the other in the same relay rack that holds the Class B audio amplifier-modulator described in December, 1931 *QST*, and other permanent laboratory equipment. Both superhet units go behind one common panel and for that reason the illustrations of this article show the controls temporarily mounted. The circled letters tie in with the links of Fig. 1, correlating the receiver elements with the processing described in that figure. The operating controls of the receiver are shown connected by the dash-lines to the elements with which they are associated. A mental picture of the complete receiver in this form will aid considerably in following the detailed description of the elements that go to make it up and will clarify the operating procedure.

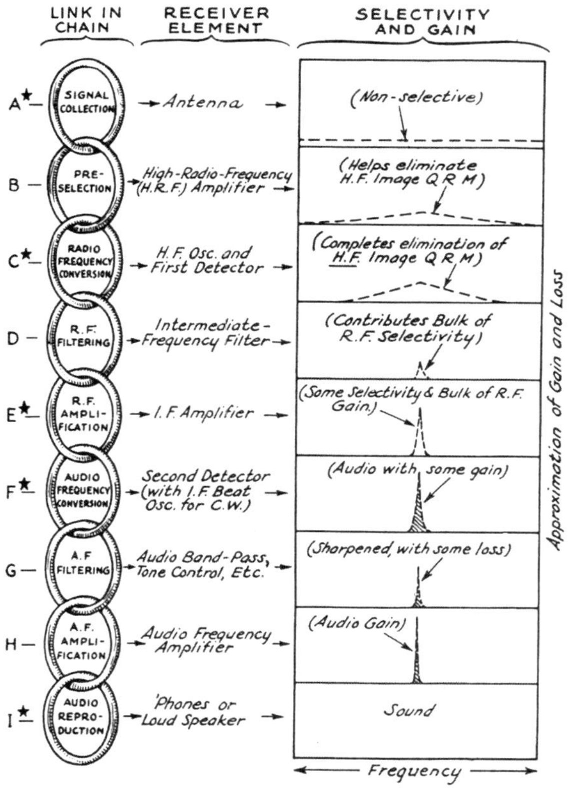

FIG. 1 — THE PROCESSING CHAIN OF SUPER-HETERO-DYNE RECEPTION

THE HIGH-FREQUENCY CIRCUITS

The three receiver elements that have to deal with high frequency (as contrasted to intermediate and audio frequencies) are the r.f. pre-selector stage, the first detector and the h.f. oscillator. The r.f. stage and first detector input circuits are tuned to the incoming signal frequency and the oscillator to a frequency that is higher or lower than the signal by an amount equal to the intermediate frequency. Designing the tuned circuits for the r.f. and first detector stages is therefore identically the same as for the r.f. and detector of an ordinary receiver. In fact the coils and tuning condensers can be borrowed intact, as they have been in this case. Referring to the circuit diagram of Fig. 3, and the notated top and bottom views, the arrangement of the pre-r.f. and first detector stages is recognizable as little different from that of the r.f. and regenerative-detector stages of the National SW3 chassis[3] which serves as their foundation. Tube sockets, coils, tuning condensers, are in their original positions. A few circuit changes, provision for r.f. gain control, resistor-capacitance circuit isolation, substitution of six-prong sockets and tube shields for the 58's,[4] the addition of some helpful shielding, constitute the differences.

The 3/32-inch thick panel fronting the whole of the unit is 17¾ inches wide by 7 inches high. Machine screws fasten the 9½-inch by 9-inch r.f.-detector base-plate to it 2 inches from the bottom and ⅝-inch in from its left edge. The base-plate has a ½-inch turned-down edge all

---

[3] Millen, "A Combination A.C. and D.C. Amateur-Band Receiver," *QST*, Sept., 1931.
[4] Characteristics on page 35, June *QST*, and socket connections on page 30, July *QST*.

August, 1932

around which serves for its fastening to the panel and to the left side of the oscillator compartment, against which it butts. Inter-stage shielding is provided by the semi-baffles which measure 6 inches back from the panel, 4½ high and 3¼ inches wide. These are also of 3/32-inch thick aluminum and are fastened to the base-plate and panel but not at the top or sides. This may seem like a half-way measure, but it was deemed advisable to use this semi-baffle type of shielding rather than to risk common couplings through the imperfectly grounded top and probably noisy contacts at the sides. The effectiveness of the shielding, freedom from contact noise and lack of instability have proven the idea to be justifiable. The rear end of the tuning condenser alley is blocked off by the 3½-inch high by 4-inch wide aluminum baffle-plate which is fastened at the bottom only. It should be noted that ¼-inch square brass pieces, drilled and tapped for 6-32 screws, are used for fastening these above-deck shields and are used generally in the assembly of the unit. This type of construction is not only more sturdy than that resulting when screws and nuts are used but is also a time-saver where frequent assembly and dis-assembly are inevitable in the fitting process.

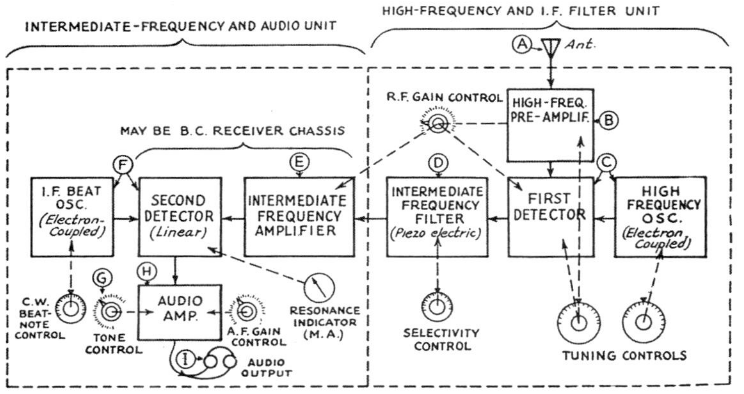

Not to be overlooked is the 8¾- by 2-inch baffle running front to back on the underside, isolating the pre-r.f. and first detector circuits down there. It is also fastened by the tapped brass-rod method. This shielding, together with the r.f. filtering in the grid and plate circuits, is unquestionably responsible in considerable measure for the notably noise-free performance of the receiver. It demonstrates as erroneous the belief that r.f. amplification ahead of the first detector in a high-frequency superhet must make the thing noisy.

FIG. 2 — BLOCK DIAGRAM OF THE ESSENTIAL ELEMENTS OF THE SINGLE-SIGNAL SUPERHET SHOWING HOW THEY ARE RELATED AND CONTROLLED

The circled letters tie in with the chain of Fig. 1.

Since band-spread coils of the type used require seven terminals (the tuning condenser is connected across only part of the secondary), each has its individual grid lead with a clip for connection to the tube. To accommodate coils of the non-band-spread type, the grid leads indicated by the dotted lines in Fig. 3, and shown fastened to the dummy plugs in the photograph, are brought out from the coil-socket terminals that connect to the condenser stators. When not in use they are kept out of mischief by the small pieces of bakelite rod conveniently mounted on the inner sides of the compartment shields. The special six-terminal coil sockets are mounted on 1⅞-inch square platforms, each elevated ⅞-inch above the baseplate on four U-shaped strips of brass. Leads from these sockets are taken to their terminations by the most direct routes. The antenna connections are made to a pair of G.R. jacks mounted on a small strip of bakelite at the left-front on the upper deck, in preference to bringing them in beneath and from the back. Neither terminal grounds on the shielding, permitting doublet antenna connection. The idea is that the antenna is supposed to have coupling to the grid of the pre-r.f. stage only — and precautions that prevent other couplings are in order.

Coil specifications for the amateur bands are given in Table I, the coils for both r.f. and first detector being identical. If coils for a National SW3, SW5 or SW58 happen to be available they can be used, although it is recommended that the grid leak and condenser of the detector coils be either shorted or removed and a jumper substituted. Plate detection, not grid detection, is wanted in this stage. The small adjustable compression type condensers (CT), integral with the detector coils, are handy for spotting the bands in the middle range of the dial scale.

In order to reduce unwanted coupling through grid-return circuits and, at the same time, to adapt the circuit to automatic gain control (as used for 'phone in the complete receiver), the blocking condensers C_5 and C_9 are connected between the lower ends of the grid coils and the grounded rotors of the tuning condensers. Isolating resistors R_1 and R_4 provide the desired filtering, their common connection being brought out to the terminal marked "$-C$." For manual gain control, this terminal is grounded, as indicated, and connected to the moving contact of the variable resistor R_1. The other terminal of this resistor connects to the cathodes through the resistors R_2 and R_5, which cathode resistors provide optimum bias for maximum sensitivity with the gain control in the full-on position.

The value of 5000 ohms specified for the first-detector cathode resistor has been found more satisfactory than other values tried. This size resistor, in combination with the low screen-grid voltage (22 volts or a little less) seems to provide greatest first-detector sensitivity.[5] The resistor R_{10} in the gain-control circuit is simply a bleeder to give complete cut-off of sensitivity by maintaining a minimum flow of current through the gain-control circuit. Connections to this circuit are shown in dotted lines because it is external to the high-frequency unit, being actually contained in the i.f. unit (or b.c. receiver chassis used as such). Screen-grid resistors R_3 and R_6 serve both for filtering and for providing good screen-grid voltage regulation, compensating for the tendency for the screen-to-cathode voltage to change when the control-grid bias is varied by gain-control resistor R_{11}. Although these resistors and those in the grid return circuits might be omitted, their presence contributes worthy improvements in

[5] Cf. Chinn, "A High-Frequency Converter," QST, June, 1931.

receiver operation. The same applies to the high-frequency chokes RFC_1.

In mounting these resistors and chokes, especially the terminals that connect to supply leads, small scraps of 1/16-inch bakelite or fiber with soldering lugs riveted to them are placed as may be convenient and fastened by machine screws with thick washers to space them from the base-plate. The same gadgets are used for heater supply and other external connections that are usually awkward to make. A batch of them can be made up in a few minutes with no more than bakelite or fiber scrap and some brass or copper rivets for materials.

In contrast to usual practice in high-frequency superhets, inductive coupling between the oscillator output and grid circuit of the first detector is utilized successfully in this receiver. This is made completely satisfactory by the

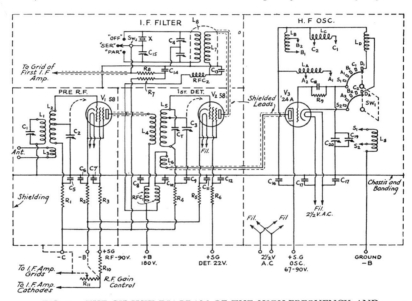

FIG. 3 — THE CIRCUIT DIAGRAM OF THE HIGH-FREQUENCY AND I. F. FILTER UNIT

L_1, L_2, L_3 — Normal primary, secondary and antenna windings of National band-spread coils for r.f. stage. See Table I.
L_4, L_5, L_6 — Same as above for detector stage. See Table I.
L_7, L_8 — I. f. filter input transformer. See text for details.
L_A, L_B, L_C, L_D, L_S — Oscillator coils. See Table II.
C_1 — Antenna trimmer condenser, 50-μμfd. midget.
C_2, C_3 — Ganged 100-μμfd. variable condensers. (Two National Type ST-100 with insulating coupling, or two-gang National Type 2 SE-100 or Hammarlund MCD-140 M).
C_T — 2 to 35-μμfd. adjustable condenser, one in each detector coil form. (Hammarlund EC-35).
C_4 — Double-section filter tuning condenser (selectivity control), 140-μμfd. per section. (Hammarlund MCD-140 M).
C_5 to C_{17}, inclusive — 0.01-μfd. mica bypass condensers.
C_{18} — 250-μμfd. mica grid condenser.
C_{19} — Oscillator padding condenser, 200-μμfd. midget. (Hammarlund MC-200 M).
C_{20} — Oscillator tuning condenser, 3-μμfd. min., 20-μμfd. max. Midget type with fitted front and rear bearings. (Hammarlund MC-20 M Special).

R_1, R_4, R_7 — Grid circuit isolating resistors, 250,000-ohm 1-watt.
R_2 — Pre-r.f. cathode resistor, 300-ohm 1-watt.
R_3 — Pre-r.f. screen-grid resistor, 5000-ohm 1-watt.
R_5 — Detector cathode resistor, 5000-ohm 1-watt.
R_6 — Detector screen-grid resistor, 50,000-ohm 1-watt.
R_8 — Grid coupling resistor for first i.f. stage, 1-megohm.
R_9 — Oscillator grid leak, 100,000-ohm 1-watt metallized type.
R_{10} — Bleeder resistor for gain control circuit, 100,000-ohm 1-watt.
R_{11} — Variable gain-control resistor, 2000-ohm tapered type.
SW_1 — Oscillator coil switch, two-circuit five-position. Mounted on National coil-switching panel.
SW_2 — Filter switch, single-pole double-throw miniature knife type or single-circuit three-position rotary type.
RFC_1 — High-frequency r.f. chokes (National Type 100).
RFC_2 — Intermediate-frequency choke (Hammarlund shielded Type SPC).
All circuit "grounds" to chassis are bonded by No. 18 copper wire soldered to each terminal.

August, 1932

peculiar stability of the electron-coupled oscillator — its relative imperviousness to frequency change with variations in its load circuit tuning. The whys and wherefores of this have been covered in a previous article [6] and need not be repeated here. The coupling is provided by L_6, the normal tickler winding of the plug-in detector coil, connected for series plate feed to the oscillator. The shielded lead between the oscillator plate and coupling coil is very short, as shown in the top view, running through the side of the oscillator compartment directly from oscillator plate to coil-socket terminal. This lead (and other shielded leads throughout the receiver) is a piece of Belden shielded cable such as that used for ignition systems, etc. It should have low capacity between conductor and shield, and the shield should make positive connection with the chassis.

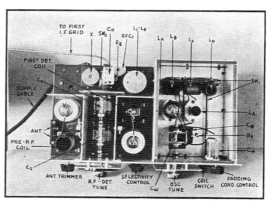

THE TOP PLAN, SHOWING THE ABOVE-DECK ARRANGEMENT IN DETAIL
Adequate shielding contributes to stability and freedom from noise.

THE HIGH-FREQUENCY OSCILLATOR

As we have said before, and it will bear repeating, the ability of this receiver to make practical use of its high selectivity is completely dependent on the stability of the received signal and of the high-frequency oscillator. Selectivity and stability, stability and selectivity — they are as closely identified with each other as ham and eggs. Therefore every reasonable means to the end of making the oscillator stability duplicate that of the best ham signals is worth pursuing. The circuit, rugged parts, sturdy mechanical construction, all are to be sought out and applied as rigorously as we know how. No claim is made that the ultimate has been attained in this particular job. But its performance marks it as a considerable advance in the right direction.

The circuit is the electron-coupled type adapted for indirectly heated tubes as described in April *QST*. The first trial of this circuit in a hamband superhet immediately demonstrated that it was head and shoulders above every other that had been used in our experiments *insofar as electrical stability was concerned*. The frequency would stay put remarkably with usual voltage variations and with tuning of the coupled load circuit. But its own tuning had to be precisely adjustable and had to be unaffected by mechanical instability. Therefore, coil mounting, condenser bearings, mechanical coupling between dial and condenser, and even the dial itself — all these mechanical things became responsible for stability rather than the purely electrical properties of the circuit. Even temperature effects that could be tolerantly ignored in most receivers began to assume importance. Hence the leaning to mechanical considerations in this oscillator. The schematic diagram and specifications for parts used are given in Fig. 3, while the mechanical construction is illustrated in the plan view.

The oscillator compartment is completely enclosed and is built of 3/32-inch aluminum sheet. Its inside dimensions are 5¾ inches high by 7 inches wide by 9¼ inches deep. The overall height of the sheet forming the sides is 6¾ inches so that there is a sub-base space of 1-inch depth. The two sides and back are formed by bending a single piece, although three separate pieces could be used just as well. The panel serves as the front. The convenient ¼-inch square brass rod, drilled and tapped for 6-32 machine screws, is used for fastening at the corners and for supporting the base-plate and

TABLE I
PRE-R.F. AND DETECTOR COILS

	Band			
	1750-kc.	3500-kc.	7000-kc.	14-mc.
L_1 and L_4* Turns	40	22	16	8
Size wire	34 d.s.c.	30 d.s.c.	34 d.s.c.	34 d.s.c
L_2 and L_5 Turns	64	35	21	10
Length	1 9/16″	1 7/16″	1 9/16″	1½″
Size wire	30 enam.	22 enam.	22 enam.	22 enam.
Tap, turns from ground end.	No tap‡	16¾	5¾	2¼
L_3 and L_6† Turns	6	4	4	3
Size wire	34 d.s.c.	34 d.s.c.	34 d.s.c.	34 d.s.c.

* Wound between turns of L_2 and L_5, starting from bottom.
† Wound in slot at bottom of form.
‡ Tuning condenser across whole coil.
Six-prong coil forms, 1½-inch diameter. For further details, see pages 13 and 14, *QST*, Sept., 1931.

[6] Lamb, "Stabilizing Superheterodyne Performance," *QST*, April, 1932.

the cover which measures 7⅜ by 9⅛ inches. The lower edge of the sub-base compartment is cut away sufficiently along its right and rear sides to leave a small gap between it and the bottom of the outer case, but the left edge is fastened to the bottom, having a piece of drilled and tapped ¼-inch square brass rod for fastening. The bottom view of the chassis shows this.

Within the compartment, the tuning condenser C_{20} is mounted on a small bakelite platform supported from the floor by four legs made of the quarter-inch brass rod, fastened to the platform and bottom by 6–32 machine screws threaded into the drilled and tapped ends of the legs. A flexible coupling is used between the condenser shaft and dial drive. The grid leak and condenser are carried on this same mounting by a small brass angle. The UY-type tube socket and UX-type coil socket are supported from the bottom by the spacing bushings that come with the Hammarlund Isolantite sockets, through which run the fastening screws. The National coil and switch panel is held in place rigidly by screws through the bottom and left side, into the 6–32 inserts provided in the R39 panel. The front-panel bearing for the quarter-inch round switch shaft was obtained from a midget condenser that had served its time. Alternatively, the removable threaded sleeve from a telephone jack that is made that way can be used. The hole just fits a quarter-inch shaft. The shaft itself is 8 inches long. The 200-$\mu\mu$fd. variable padding condenser C_{19} is mounted on the panel to the right of the tuning condenser, its occasional adjustment permitting less rigorous mechanical treatment than that required by its smaller partner. The oscillator tuning dial should be carefully considered for its mechanical properties. It should have a knob-to-shaft ratio of at least 20 to 1; be independent of the condenser shaft for mechanical support; be free of back-lash; and, preferably, have a flexible driving member between the knob and condenser shaft. It need not have a precisely calibrated scale. The precision Type N National dial, for instance, is not as well suited to this job as the older Type B that was finally adopted. So much for mechanical details — now for those of the circuit.

OSCILLATOR SWITCHING AND BAND SPREADING

Although coil switching was rejected as impracticable for the pre-r.f. and first detector circuits, because of the large number of terminals involved and the limited flexibility it would impose, coil switching has been adopted wholeheartedly for the oscillator. Whereas some three or four coil terminals would have to be switched simultaneously in each of the r.f. and detector stages, only two are involved in the electron-coupled oscillator — the grid and cathode; and whereas only one frequency range could be covered with each pair of coils in the other stages, at least four and even six or more ranges can be obtained from each oscillator coil. By using oscillator output either higher or lower than the incoming frequency and by using oscillator harmonics in addition to the fundamental, the four ham-band coils specified (one band-spreading two ranges) serve for at least 20 frequency ranges. With some duplication, these ranges include commercial point-to-point, the short-wave broadcasting channels, expedition frequencies, etc., *even though the circuit is designed primarily to give complete band-spread on each of the amateur bands 1750-, 3500-, 7000- and 14,000-kc.* In fact it goes even further. To make the spread of the 500-kc. wide 3500-kc. band conform to the "kilocycle" spread of the rest, the exclusively c.w. portion, 3500 to 3900 kc., has been given a whole range for itself — and the 3900- to 4000-kc. 'phone band has been given another! What's more, we have used the umpteenth harmonics in operating this receiver on 56 mc.

One method of band-spread tuning has been shown for the r.f. and first-detector circuits, in which the tuning condenser is connected to an extra tap, across part of the inductance. This high-L is advisable in circuits where selectivity and amplification of weak signals are at stake, because there is a voltage step-up to the grid of the tube. But in the case of the oscillator, where convenience is desirable, efficiency is secondary and stability is all-important, another type of band-spread tuning is in order. One that we like has been adopted for this job. A tuning condenser of small capacity range, in parallel with a larger adjustable padding condenser and in coöperation with the right inductance, spreads each band over all but a small margin at either end of the scale. This works out especially well because the tuned circuit becomes increasingly high C as the frequency becomes greater, thereby improving the proportionate stability. The tuning condenser has a minimum capacity of 3 $\mu\mu$fd. and a maximum of 20 $\mu\mu$fd., a range of 17 $\mu\mu$fd., while the padding condenser in parallel has a maximum capacity of 200 $\mu\mu$fd. In attempting to reduce the oscillator band-switching to a single operation, the scheme of equipping each coil with its own adjustable mica-type padding condenser was first tried. This was satisfactory for frequencies up to about 7000 kc., but on the higher ranges the creeping caused by the normally inconsequential temperature coëfficient of these condensers condemned them to rejection in favor of the air-dielectric type. The bulk and greater cost of the air type (midgets) dictated that a single condenser would have to do for all ranges, adding an operation to the band-switching but improving the stability and flexibility more than enough to make up for the inconvenience.

The coil design hangs on the frequency of the intermediate amplifier, because the oscillator

August, 1932

output must be intermediate frequency higher or lower than the incoming signal frequency. While the choice of intermediate frequency may be sometimes a matter of individual preference, where the amateur bands are the primary consideration there are factors that narrow it down to a limited range. The i.f. must be low enough to permit reception at the lowest ham-band frequency, 1715 kc., and still not so low as to make it difficult for the pre-selector to prevent image interference at the higher amateur frequencies where the tuned input circuit becomes less effective. Experience suggests that something between 1600 and 450 kc. would meet these requirements. But the gain of the i.f. amplifier would be greater at the lower frequency. Therefore the lower frequency is to be favored. To keep out of the broadcast band and to avoid inter-

150 kc. for the 7000-kc. band and 200 kc. for the 14,000-kc. band. The specifications for the coils, including the ranges covered by the oscillation generation circuits, are given in Table II. It should be noted that the 3500-kc. band coils are designed so that the oscillator output is 525 kc. *lower* than the signal-frequency (referred to as "low-beat") and that the oscillator output is 525 kc. *higher* than the signal frequency ("high-beat") for the other bands. This was done to make the "B" and "C" coils more useful for covering other ranges.

As a diversion from our usual ham procedure, these coils were not designed by the cut-and-try method but the complete specifications were worked out in advance, using a "Lightning Calculator."[7] Every one hit its range right on the nose the first trial — greatly relieving the

TABLE II

Coil	Signal Band, kc.	Osc. Range, kc.	Osc. Output used	Induct-ance, µh	No. Turns	Length of Coil	Size Wire (B. & S.)	Cathode tap, turns from Ground End	Approx. Padding Capacity (C_{19})
L_A	1715–2000	2240–2525	Fund. (High-beat)	65	64	1⅛"	28 d.s.c.	20	62 µµfd.
L_B	3500–3900	2975–3375	Fund. (Low-beat)	45	48	15/16"	28 d.s.c.	15	49 µµfd.
L_C	3900–4000	3375–3475	Fund. (Low-beat)	12	27	1"	20 d.s.c.	9	173 µµfd.
	7000–7300	3763–3913	2nd Harm. (High-beat)	12	27	1"	20 d.s.c.	9	136 µµfd.
L_D	14,000–14,300	7263–7463	2nd Harm. (High-beat)	2½	12*	1"	18 enam.	4	181 µµfd.
L_S	Available For Any Special Range That May Be Desired								

* Spaced diameter of wire. All other coils close-wound.
All forms 1-inch diameter. These coil specifications are suitable for any i.f. between 500 and 550 kc. with oscillator tuning capacity range of 17 µµfd. or more. Other oscillator ranges between 20,000 and 1400 kc. are available by suitable adjustment of C_{19}, and harmonics may be used for still higher ranges.

ference from possible amateur-frequency harmonics of the i.f. heterodyne oscillator that is to be used for c.w., an intermediate frequency between 500 and 550 kc. was finally decided upon for this receiver. The oscillator coils were designed accordingly.

The LC combinations are worked out so that the oscillator fundamental output frequency is used for the 1750- and 3500-kc. bands, and so that second-harmonic output is used for the 7000- and 14,000-kc. bands. This use of the second harmonic for the higher-frequency ranges was found necessary to eliminate the last vestige of reaction of first detector tuning on oscillator frequency. The second harmonic gives completely satisfactory heterodyning and the fundamental component does not cause harmful detector overloading. When designing for second-harmonic output, the frequency range covered by the LC circuit is half that of the output range,

tedium of the "how-many-turns" business. If they are made up exactly as specified and if the two variable condensers have the capacity ranges given, no juggling of windings should be necessary. To make the cathode taps without interrupting the winding process, a small tab of varnished cambric is slipped under the proper turn, with ends up in the form of a loop, as that turn is put on. When the coil is completed, the insulation is scraped off and the tap soldered without danger of injury to the insulation of adjacent turns. Finally, each coil is given a coating of clear Duco or airplane dope. Coils A, B, C and D are mounted with machine screws in the "cradles" molded for them on the panel (which, by the way, is the same as that used in the National NC5 converter), while coil S takes the plug-in position. The grid taps are soldered to the switch points on the front and the cathode taps to the cor-

[7] See page 76, June QST.

responding points on the back. The extra grounding switch arm on the front is removed to allow use of all five switch positions, shorting of one coil to prevent interlocking being unnecessary in this tuning system.

When the oscillator construction is completed, it can be tested by connecting temporary supply leads, with a small milliammeter in the positive screen circuit. At each switch position, the screen current should kick upward sharply when the control grid of the tube is touched. With the cover of the oscillator compartment off, the signal picked up on a regenerative receiver should be clean and steady. If there is a main carrier with a family of chirps on either side it indicates what the Britishers call "squegging" — too much feedback or too much grid-leak resistance. If the leak is not more than 100,000 ohms, the screen voltage is too high and should be reduced.

This completes the high-frequency circuits and brings us to the filter.

THE I.F. FILTER

Before deciding on the type of high-selectivity intermediate-frequency filter circuit for the receiver, several possible forms were investigated. The first was the straight multi-section type, consisting of a flock of coils and tuning condensers. This was immediately rejected because of its complexity in construction and adjustment, and because of the high losses that would necessitate additional amplification. The next was a single circuit with regeneration. Trial of this brought discouragement in the form of instability. It would give noticeable selectivity as between weak or moderate signals but immediately broadened out and became ineffectual on strong signals, where it was most needed. It was also tricky in adjustment and spilled over into oscillation on the slightest provocation. The next form to suggest itself was the electro-mechanical filter, the quartz crystal. Its "stiffness," its equivalence to a very large inductance in series with a very small capacity and a resistance, makes its L/CR very large — pointing to extremely sharp resonance and high efficiency. Its stability is so well known as to need no comment.

Dr. Cady first suggested the use of the quartz resonator as a sharp electric wave filter [8] over ten years ago and recently its use as such has been greatly accelerated. We recall that the series resonator as a filter in a receiving circuit was tried

---

[8] Cady, "The Piezo-Electric Resonator," *Proc. I. R. E.*, April, 1922.

several years ago by Paul Zottu in Dr. Cady's laboratory at Wesleyan University. A wide variety of applications has been made by the Bell Telephone Laboratories, Radio Corporation of America and others. A quartz filter is also used

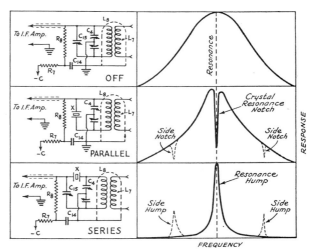

FIG. 4 — THE SELECTIVITY CHARACTERISTIC OBTAINED WITH FILTER SWITCHING

In the "Off" position the circuit performs as a transformer with tuned secondary, making the receiver a "straight" superhet. In the parallel position the crystal has the same characteristic that it would have in the usual oscillator circuit, putting a sharp peak on the curve at a frequency slightly off its main resonance frequency and acting as a rejector for a signal right on its resonance frequency. This connection is useful for both 'phone and c.w., taking out heterodyne interference when the interfering carrier is shifted into the notch. In the "Series" position maximum selectivity for c.w. reception is obtained, the circuit performing as a very sharp acceptor for one frequency and a rejector for other frequencies. The side notches with the parallel connection and the side humps with the series connection are caused by the secondary resonance peaks characteristic of the quartz crystal. Their slight effect can be nullified for c.w. reception by a low-pass audio filter cutting off at about 1000 cycles.

in the Stenode broadcast receiver, recently given considerable publicity in England and this country, its use therein being to secure high r.f. selectivity for modulated signals (particularly broadcasting), prior to linear detection and subsequent restoration of the audio component relationship by a compensating circuit of progressive high-frequency response — to make up for the progressive side-band attenuation or high-note loss inevitable with high r.f. selectivity. Whether or not this method of reception for modulated signals is sufficiently effective under amateur 'phone conditions has not been definitely determined. Using the crystal as a parallel resonator, to be described immediately, has given more satisfactory results up to the present.

For c.w. reception of steady signals, the sharp r.f. filtering provided by the quartz crystal as a series resonator is completely practicable. That audio-frequency amplitude modulation is ironed out makes things all the better. Our c.w. signals are supposed to be pure r.f. carriers of a single

August, 1932

frequency and they may remain so until the second detector is reached. There should be no audio-frequency modulation and there are no side bands involved until the carrier has been heterodyned in the process of detection. For reception of the less steady signals, awaiting the day when all get into the top bracket, provision is made to broaden the response with a tuning adjustment which may well be called the selectivity control. When a still less steady signal is encountered, one that is too unstable for the series-resonator type filter at its broadest, or when 'phone reception is desired, a flip of the filter switch either puts the crystal in as a *parallel* resonator or cuts it out altogether. Therefore there are three distinct ranges of selectivity available, sufficient to meet any requirement, with a selectivity control to regulate the degree of each. The circuit and specifications of the filter circuit are included in Fig. 3 while the analysis of the filter operation is given in Fig. 4. The receiver may be built without the quartz crystal, of course, providing its owner with a top-notch straight superhet. But ultimate inclusion of the crystal should be contemplated.

Contrary to expectations, the carrier sensitivity of the receiver is in no wise reduced by the series quartz filter. In fact, for steady c.w. carriers the signal at the second detector is actually greater with the "Series" connection than with the "Off" connection (as shown by the increment in second detector plate current), probably because the low-decrement quartz filter tends to encourage regeneration and gain in the first i.f. stage. Moreover, the apparent sensitivity for steady c.w. signals is much greater with the series filter because of the large improvement it makes in the signal/background ratio. Unsteady signals are treated much less cordially, as would be expected, and are relegated to the background in direct proportion to their instability. For instance: "Xtal d.c." that is ordinarily QSA3 becomes QSA5; wobbly "r.a.c." that is ordinarily QSA5 can be made QSA3 or so — and the crystal signal can be copied right through it.

The filter input circuit is simply a conventional r.f. transformer with its secondary tunable by the double-section midget condenser C_4, maximum capacity of each section 140 $\mu\mu$fd., 70 $\mu\mu$fd. for the two sections in series. This is the selectivity control. The transformer is contained in the shield can behind the first detector compartment. The tuning condenser is directly underneath, with its Isolantite base bolted to the side of the oscillator compartment and its shaft coupled by a flexible unit to the ¼-inch brass rod running out to the selectivity control knob on the panel. The plug-in crystal holder and filter switch are mounted on the small bakelite panel to the left of the transformer. The adjustable phasing condenser C_{15} is fastened to a bakelite extension at the top. The shielded choke, RFC_2, is between the transformer and small panel, at the rear edge. The insulated terminals of this choke extend through the base. For greater convenience in operation, it is suggested that a single-circuit three-position rotary type switch with panel control be substituted for the s.p.d.t. miniature knife switch shown.

The transformer shown has primary and secondary windings of the "Diamond Weave" type (made by the F. W. Sickles Co.)[9] with close coupling between the two coils. A home-made transformer of the straight solenoid type, used in the preliminary development model that preceded this receiver, is somewhat more bulky but works satisfactorily. For the benefit of those who may wish to roll their own, the latter transformer has the following specifications:

Primary:
  Diameter of form, 1 inch (bakelite tube).
  Length of coil, 2 inches.
  Size wire, No. 34 d.s.c.
  No. of turns, 195.
  Approximate inductance, 400 microhenries.
Secondary:
  Diameter of form, 2 inches (bakelite tube).
  Length of coil, 2 inches.

RESISTORS AND BY-PASS CONDENSERS PREDOMINATE IN THE SUB-BASE REGION, DOING THEIR PART TO MAKE THE RECEIVER STABLE AND "QUIET"

---

[9] 300 Main St., Springfield, Mass. Alternatively, the 465-kc. i.f. transformers made for s.w. superhets (Hammarlund, Silver-Marshall, etc.) could be used with the adjusting condensers removed.

Size of wire, No. 34 d.s.c.
No. of turns, 195.
Approximate inductance, 1.3 millihenries.

For No. 32 d.s.c. wire, the primary and secondary each should be wound with 220 turns (length of coil 2⅝ inches), other specifications remaining the same. The primary is mounted inside the secondary and concentric with it. The diameter of the primary could be larger (say 1½ inches, inductance 800 microhenries), other specifications remaining the same. With the circuit as shown, this transformer will tune from 500 to 800 kc. approximately. Since it would require an individual coil shield of about 4-inch diameter, shielding the whole filter circuit in a box would be preferable.

Experience with a number of quartz crystals (both X- and Y-cut) ground for use as oscillators at broadcast-band frequencies has shown that the crystal filter presents no special problem. Both X- and Y-cuts seem to have a pair of secondary humps, one either side of the major peak, as suggested in Fig. 4. The amplitude of these side humps is considerably less than the main peak, however, and their importance is reduced still further by the selectivity of the succeeding stages. It should be noted that these humps are not in harmonic relationship to the crystal's major frequency but are the result of other modes of vibration determined by the dimensions and shape of the plates. Even crystals that work at only one frequency in the conventional oscillator show these humps when they are used as resonators. The response of the crystal, and hence the efficiency of the filter, is considerably better with an air-gap between the quartz plate and top electrode. Therefore an air-gap mounting should be used. The size of the gap is not critical. A spacing washer (bakelite with a hole in it to accommodate the crystal), slightly thicker than the crystal and placed between the top and bottom electrodes, will do nicely. The gap need not be adjustable. The mounting shown in the photograph is one of several of the G.R. air-gap type that were picked up, broadcast-band crystals included, in a second-hand store.

The phasing condenser C_{15} is used with the series resonator to balance out the residual audio-frequency image for c.w. reception, as will be explained in the following paragraphs.

TUNING UP

It is not necessary, nor would it be advisable, to kick off operating tests with this high-frequency unit coupled into an i.f. unit whose acquaintance was yet to be cultivated. The better plan is first to line up the high-frequency and filter unit with a good t.r.f. broadcast-receiver of known performance doing i.f. duty, thus isolating preliminary adjustments to the new piece of apparatus. The shielded output lead (length not more than 2 feet) from the filter unit is connected directly to the control grid of the first stage in the b.c. receiver, having a grid clip for that purpose, and the ground post of the h.f. unit is connected to the ground terminal of the b.c. set. The unit's

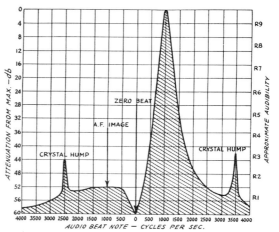

FIG. 5 — THE PICTURE OF SINGLE-SIGNAL C.W. SELECTIVITY

Actual audio response curve of the receiver for a 1000-cycle beat note. This represents the cumulative selectivity of all the tuned circuits, including the i.f. filter in the "Series" connection and two tuned-primary tuned-secondary i.f. transformers. No audio-frequency filtering was used in running the curve. The crystal (and i.f. amplifier) resonance frequency is 528 kc. Even with this order of selectivity high-speed keying is reproduced cleanly. Still higher selectivity can be obtained but puts tails on the signals.

power supply can be a 2½-volt filament transformer and either a "B" eliminator tapped to give the usual voltages or a 180-volt block of "B" batteries. The usual antenna and ground are connected to the unit's antenna terminals. After the oscillator has been given its preliminary test, as outlined previously, the routine procedure is as follows:

1. Tune the b.c. receiver to about 550 kc., being careful not to land on the carrier of a local station. Set its volume control at maximum.

2. Set the filter tuning condenser (selectivity control) at about two-thirds capacity. With a small screwdriver (one made of quarter-inch wood dowel or bakelite rod preferred), adjust the phasing condenser (C_{15}) to near minimum capacity — about 8 turns of the screw from maximum. The filter switch should be in the "off" position, shorting the crystal terminals. The crystal is not necessary for these tests or for straight super-het operation afterwards, incidentally.

3. Insert the 3500-kc. band coils in the pre-r.f. and detector stages and set the ganged tuning at about mid-scale.

August, 1932

4. Set the oscillator tuning condenser C_{20}, at midscale and the coil switch at position "C." Starting at maximum capacity, carefully turn the padding condenser C_{19} towards minimum, listening for ham 'phones When the band is located, leave this condenser set and go back to the r.f.-detector tuning, adjusting the ganged condensers, antenna trimmer and detector-coil trimmer for maximum response. There are two settings of the oscillator padding condenser at which the 'phones should be heard, one near maximum and one at about mid-scale. The near-maximum position should be used to give the low-beat for the 3900- to 4000-kc. 'phone band. More precise calibration of the oscillator settings and adjustment of the r.f.-detector tuning can be made with a heterodyne frequency meter or other calibrated oscillator, a milliammeter connected in the plate-feed circuit of the second detector serving as a resonance indicator. Things are simplified if the b.c. set has a.v.c. and a tuning meter. If the receiver happens to be a superhet and a series of "burps" is experienced with tuning of the high-frequency oscillator, suspect harmonics from the b.c. set. Modern broadcast jobs are supposed to be free from such but some models still have them.

Failure to get results with this procedure must mean that there is a defective part or that a mistake has occurred in the construction. As with any new piece of equipment, maximum performance follows continued playing with the adjustments, each detail contributing to the whole.

C.W. RECEPTION — OFF-SET ADJUSTMENT

The i.f. beating oscillator arrangement shown on page 16 of June *QST* should be rigged up to modulate the second detector for beat-note reception. It should be completely shielded as shown in the diagram on that page and it should be tunable to the low-frequency end of the broadcast band, assuming that a t.r.f. set is to be used as the i.f. unit. A milliammeter should be connected in the "plus B" lead to the second detector. With the i.f. beating oscillator shut off, fire up the heterodyne frequency meter or other low-powered local oscillator that is to serve as the signal generator and tune it in on the receiver. Adjust the tuning and the selectivity control for maximum deflection of the plate milliammeter, adjusting the antenna trimmer and r.f. gain control so that the second detector is not overloaded. Several peaks of maximum current would mean that the i.f. circuits are out of gang, necessitating adjustment of the b.c. receiver's r.f. trimmers. This is easily done, using the detector plate meter as a resonance indicator. After setting the high-frequency tuning for peak signal at the second detector we are ready for the off-set adjustment that is the first step towards single-signal reception. Results are certain if the following instructions are followed closely.

1. Tune the first oscillator so that the detector plate current just begins to fall off. Tune towards *minimum* capacity (higher frequency) if a low-beat oscillator range is being used; towards *maximum* capacity (lower frequency) if a high-beat range is being used The idea is to put the frequency of the signal going through the i.f. amplifier on the *low* side of i.f. resonance.

2. Turn on the i.f. beat oscillator and tune it into audio beat with the i.f. signal, approaching from the low-frequency (maximum condenser capacity side). Adjust for a note of 1000 cycles or so.

3. Tune the high-frequency oscillator back and forth "through zero beat," simultaneously adjusting the selectivity control for maximum difference between "signal" and "image" response.

4. Repeat the procedure several times to get the swing of it and for most satisfactory adjustment. If the i.f. amplifier has any sort of steep-sided resonance curve, a very effective signal to audio-frequency image ratio can be realized. The i.f. amplifier to be described in next month's article has such selectivity.

ADDING THE QUARTZ FILTER

If the frequency of the crystal is known, set the b.c. receiver to it. If not, rig up a temporary oscillator with the crystal and use it as a signal generator to tune up. Then put the crystal in the filter circuit with the switch set on "Series." Repeat the previously described adjustment for maximum signal at the second detector, but omit the off-set tuning. Everything is "on the nose" with the sharp filter. Be particularly precise in adjusting the h.f. oscillator and selectivity control because the peak of resonance will be very sharp. Again turn on the i.f. beat oscillator and adjust it for a suitable beat note, as before. Then tune the high-frequency oscillator "through zero beat," so that the weaker note on the other side is about the same pitch as that on the peak. Then adjust the phasing condenser, C_{15}, using a wood or bakelite screwdriver, *to the point where there is a sharp minimum response to the image signal*. Go through this procedure several times to get the "feel" of it. This gives real single-signal selectivity for c.w. The final result should sound like the curve of Fig. 5 looks. Picking the right peak of the crystal may be confusing at first, but landing on the best one is not difficult after a little experience.

Experience with the system also will reveal what can be done using the parallel resonator connection for both 'phone and c.w. reception. The wide range of selectivity obtainable by adjustment of the selectivity control, with the switch in any of its three positions, is a revelation in receiver operation. This feature is to ham-band traffic conditions what free-wheeling, automatic clutch and all the trimmings are to modern

(Continued on page 90)

Short-Wave Receiver Selectivity to Match Conditions

(Continued from page 20)

motoring. One can pull the really steady signal through otherwise impossible mazes of a.c. hash, separate good signals of equal strength when they are as close together as 500 cycles, drag 14-mc. c.w. out of automobile QRM that puts any other receiver out of the running — and even go in and get a d.c. signal that is between the carrier and a 1000-cycle side band of a 500-cycle supply crystal rig. All these things, and more, have been done with this receiver, both with a selective t.r.f. broadcast receiver as the intermediate unit and with the completely modern companion unit that will be described next month.

"2, 6, and 10 with Crystal Control" by James Millen, W1HRX

By Ward Silver, NØAX

In the 1930s, amateurs who wanted to try out the bands above 20 meters (15 meters was not opened to hams until 1952) faced significant challenges: tubes with good performance at those frequencies were not available at reasonable cost, standard circuit construction techniques were not at all suitable for those high frequencies, and available circuit designs — especially oscillators — were not reliable above 20 Mc (MHz).

This all changed during World War II when terrific advances in radio technology were made under great duress. New components, new circuits, and new methods of building reliable equipment all burst onto the amateur scene with the conclusion of hostilities. The wireless world had changed dramatically while Amateur Radio was off the air — if Rip Van Winkle had been an amateur, his experience on awakening would approximate that of amateur operators who were eager to make use of the great advances that had been made while they were off the air!

The first challenge for the home-building amateurs was to generate a stable, low-power signal to work with. As the article notes, pre-war overtone crystals were quite touchy — even fracturing if not used just right. The key to building a proper oscillator was a better crystal and tight control of oscillator construction. So key, in fact, that a commercial unit from Bliley Electric was specified for consistent performance at these high frequencies. (Founded in 1930, Bliley's history is maintained online at **www.bliley.net/xtal**.)

Bliley was a familiar name to amateurs from the 1930s as long as crystal-controlled equipment was in wide use. Now Bliley Technologies (www.bliley.com), the company produces specialized oscillator and signal generator products.

BLILEY CRYSTALS / Quartz and Tourmaline
Powerful — Accurate — Uniform Quartz Crystals supplied at your dealer close to specified frequency, 0.05% calibration: 1750, 3500Kc bands, $5.50. 7000Kcs, $9. Quartz mounting, $2.50. Tourmaline Discs: 7Mc band, $12. 14Mc band, $14. Tourmaline mounting, $2.50. 525Kc Lamb-super mounted crystal, $9.50. 100Kc. Std. Freq. mounted bar, $12.00.
BLILEY PIEZO-ELECTRIC COMPANY
Masonic Temple Bldg., Erie, Pa.

As a small digression, the "tri-tet" oscillator mentioned in the article was introduced to amateurs by James Lamb, W1CEI, in 1933. The name is an abbreviation of "triode-tetrode" and the circuit is based on an oscillator formed by the cathode, control grid and screen grid of a tetrode or pentode (such as the 6AG7 in this design). Some of the current also circulates in the plate circuit and forms the output of the oscillator. This design was quite reliable and offered good isolation of the input and output circuits.

The 829B and 2E26 tubes used in the transmitter were also available as surplus at very affordable prices — "a few dollars" — after the war. The 2E26 tube was still in wide use by popular "tube strip" VHF FM transmitters and as a final amplifier tube in amateur designs throughout the 1960s. If the builder was careful with layout and neutralizing (note that the neutralizing "capacitors" were just short pieces of wire, arranged carefully at the tube inputs and outputs), plenty of power could be obtained from these seemingly-simple transmitters, opening up the lower VHF bands for regular operation. The increase in amateur activity then lead to discoveries in propagation — just as the amateur's "exile" to the "useless" shortwave bands in the 1920s opened communication on those bands.

Accumulating experience with short leads, low RF impedance connections, careful attention to component placement, and the use of components suitable for use at high frequencies served amateurs well as they pushed above 144 MHz to 220, 432, and even 1296 MHz. Because state-of-the-art components were too expensive, amateurs became skilled at using lower-frequency devices beyond the usual design frequency limits. As better components became available, they were then able to quickly adapt them to amateur service as well.

Homebrew equipment at 50 MHz (left) and 144 MHz (right) required careful attention to lead length, component selection, and circuit layout as shown in these construction detail photographs of October 1954 *QST* projects by Ed Tilton, W1HDQ, and Mason Southworth, W1VLH.

While this particular article by a well-known and skilled amateur-professional presented a solid and buildable project that helped open up these bands for amateurs excited to be back on the air after the wartime hiatus, it was by no means the only such circuit design appearing in *QST* and in other amateur publications. Amateur Radio was busy expanding its frontiers to catch up with design advances made during the war, fueled by a flood of surplus equipment and components, along with wide availability of new materials, particularly plastics.

Note also the "Stray" item at the bottom of page 70 that refers to a War Department manual, *Suppression of Radio Noises — TM11-483*. The spread of electronic apparatus into more and more fields, coupled with Amateur Radio growing by leaps and bounds, also meant that new forms of interference were beginning to be troublesome in the post-war period. Immersed in today's seeming sea of "unintentional emitters," the 21st century's hams yearn for those relatively RFI-free days before television which was still a few years in the future.

2, 6, and 10 with Crystal Control

A Three-Band Transmitter with 829B Final

BY JAMES MILLEN,* W1HRX

Recent developments in crystals, crystal-oscillator circuits and ultrahigh-frequency components make it possible to construct a high-performance compact 10–11-meter transmitter, of 100 watts or so input, that is also capable of quick shift with relatively little decrease in power output to the 2- and 6-meter bands. Also, the availability of 829Bs in the surplus-tube market at this time helps materially in holding down the cost of the tubes needed in the construction of such a transmitter. The transmitter to be described takes advantage of both factors.

Crystals & Oscillators

The transmitter was designed around the new Bliley Type CCO-2A crystal-oscillator combination, which uses the Type AX2 crystal for 10–11-meter operation and the new Type AX3 crystal, operating on the third "overtone" frequency, for 48- to 54-Mc. output.

The "overtone" type crystals are not nearly so tolerant of circuits and operating conditions as their low-frequency counterparts, and satisfactory performance with respect to efficiency, output and stability depends critically on the use of the right oscillator tube, coil sizes, circuit components and layout. Using the CCO-2A unit and AX3, which are designed to work as a team, assured us optimum performance without the headaches that go with the cut-and-try that is usually necessary to get high-frequency crystals working to complete satisfaction. The oscillator is used either to drive an 829B power amplifier directly, for 6- or 10-meter output, or with additional multiplication through a 2E26 tripler for

* % The Millen Mfg. Co., Malden, Mass.

• Here's a neat little job incorporating a new unit designed for h.f. crystals and having an output stage using the popular 829B. On 10 and 6 there are only two stages altogether; a tripler is added for 2 meters.

output on the 2-meter band.

The basic circuit of the oscillator unit is the familiar Tri-tet, with sufficient revamping and modification so that the usual problems of self-oscillation and other difficulties are eliminated. In addition, the features needed to obtain the best performance with crystals operating on the third "overtone" frequency are included. One of the difficulties with crystals of this type in the past has been their tendency to fracture when not used in just the proper circuit and under just the right conditions.

The Bliley unit is semienclosed in a small metal case, as shown in the accompanying photograph of the transmitter. A tuning control and a crystal socket are located on the front face. The oscillator tube, a 6AG7, plugs into a recessed socket, mounted below the top surface of the unit. Band-switching is provided by means of a double-pole single-throw switch located on the top of the case; this permits a choice of oscillator output (with the appropriate crystal) on either 10–11 or 6. For final output on 2 meters it is necessary to use frequency tripling from the 6-meter output of the oscillator. The power and output terminals are located on the back of the crystal unit so that short direct leads into the transmitter chassis are possible.

The transmitter can be used as shown or can be fitted with a panel for relay-rack mounting. There are only three tubes — 6AG7, 2E26, and 829B — and the 2E26 is used only when 144-Mc. output is required. This view shows the amplifier 2-meter coils in place.

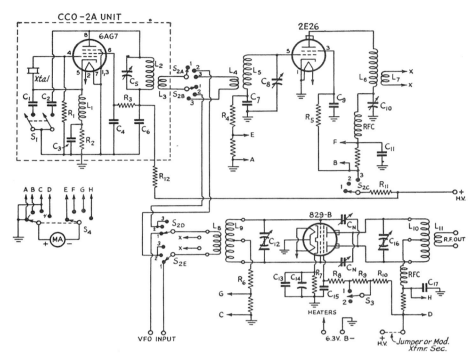

Fig. 1 — Circuit diagram of the 2- to 11-meter transmitter.

C_1 — 50-$\mu\mu$fd. Erie Ceramicon.
C_2 — 40-$\mu\mu$fd. Erie Ceramicon.
C_3, C_4, C_6, C_7 — 0.0022-μfd. mica, 500 volts.
C_5 — 25-$\mu\mu$fd. midget variable (Millen 26025-5).
C_8 — 35-$\mu\mu$fd. midget variable (Millen 20035).
C_9, C_{11}, C_{13}, C_{15}, C_{17} — 470-$\mu\mu$fd. mica, 500 volts.
C_{10} — 15-$\mu\mu$fd. midget variable (Millen 20015).
C_{12}, C_{16} — 10-$\mu\mu$fd.-per-section split-stator, double-spaced (Millen 23912A).
C_{14} — 25-μfd. electrolytic, 250 volts d.c.
C_N — Neutralizing condenser; see text.
R_1 — 22,000 ohms, ½ watt, carbon.
R_2 — 220 ohms, 1 watt, carbon.
R_3 — 6000 ohms, 2 watts, carbon.
R_4 — 0.1 megohm, 2 watts, carbon.
R_5 — 50,000 ohms, 1 watt, carbon.
R_6 — 3900 ohms, 1 watt, carbon.
R_7 — 50 ohms, 10 watts, wire-wound.
R_8 — 5000 ohms, 10 watts, wire-wound.
R_9 — 0.1 megohm, 2 watts, carbon.
R_{10} — 10,000 ohms, 10 watts, wire-wound.
R_{11} — 5000 ohms, 10 watts, wire-wound.
R_{12} — 7500 ohms, 10 watts, wire-wound.
L_1 — 9 turns No. 14 enam., close-wound, ½-inch i.d., air core.
L_2 — 8¾ turns No. 14 enam., double-spaced, ½-inch i.d., air core.
L_3 — 2 turns No. 22 double-spaced, ½-inch i.d., air core.
L_4 — 2 turns No. 18 ins. wire, ⅝-inch diam.
L_5 — 8 turns No. 10 bare, ⅝-inch diam., double-spaced.
L_6 — 6 turns copper tubing, ½-inch diam., double-spaced.
L_7 — 2 turns No. 18 insulated, ½-inch diam., wound between bottom turns of L_6.
L_8 — 27–30 Mc.: 3 turns 7–22 insulated, ⅝-inch diam., wound between middle turns of L_9.
  50 Mc.: 3 turns No. 20 tinned, ⅝-inch diam., interwound with middle turn of L_9.
  144 Mc.: 1 turn No. 18 enam., ⅜-inch diam.
L_9 — 27–30 Mc.: 12 turns No. 16 tinned, ⅝-inch diam., center-tapped.
  50 Mc.: 6 turns No. 14 tinned, ⅝-inch diam., center-tapped.
  144 Mc.: 2 turns ⅛-inch tubing, ⅜-inch diam., spaced 3/16 inch between turns, center-tapped.
L_{10} — 27–30 Mc.: 2 coils 12 turns each No. 16 tinned, center-tapped, spaced ⅝-inch between coils.
  50 Mc.: 2 coils, 5 turns per coil, ⅛-inch tubing, ⅞-inch diam., spaced ½ inch between coils, center-tapped.
  144 Mc.: 2 turns ⅛-inch tubing, ⅞-inch diam., spaced ⅝-inch between turns, center-tapped.
L_{11} — 27–30 Mc.: 6 turns No. 14 tinned, ⅝-inch diam., 1½-inch leads.
  50 Mc.: 6 turns No. 14 tinned, ⅝-inch diam., ½-inch leads.
  144 Mc.: 2 turns ⅛-inch tubing, ⅞-inch diam., spaced 1/16-inch between turns.
(NOTE: Grid coils, L_8 and L_9, mounted on Millen 40407 jack-bar; plate coils, L_{10} and L_{11}, mounted on 40403 jack-bar except 27–30-Mc. coil, which is on 40203 jack-bar. Complete coils are] the 48,000 series.)
RFC — 75 turns No. 30 enam., ¼-inch diam., close-wound on large-value resistor.
S_1 — D.p.s.t. toggle.
S_2 — 3-pole 3-position ceramic wafer, 2 gang.
S_3 — S.p.d.t. toggle.
S_4 — 2-pole 4-position ceramic wafer.
NOTE: The milliammeter *MA* used in the unit has a range of 0–50 ma. This range is used for grid-current readings and the range is extended to 0–500 ma. for plate readings. Shunts AE and CG should have negligible effect on the meter readings; values of 120 ohms are used in the unit. Shunts BF and DH must be adjusted for the meter used; they are each 1.5 ohms in the unit.

September 1947

The 829B tube — readily available now for only a few dollars in the surplus market — is capable of an input of about 100 watts and an output of approximately 70 watts, without forced ventilation. If a blower or other means for air-cooling is available, these excellent high-frequency push-pull p.a. tubes can be forced to even higher outputs. In addition, the 829B is an easy tube to drive, requiring only about 2 grid watts with 100 watts plate input.

The tripler is cut in and out of the circuit by means of a three-pole three-position wafer-type switch that connects the oscillator output link to either the 2E26 or 829B and disconnects the plate and screen voltages from the 2E26 when that tube is not needed. The grid and plate coils of the 829B stage are plug-in, and it will be observed in Fig. 1 that the proper link connections to the grid coil for the different bands are made by using an extra set of contacts on the coil forms and sockets.

Provision is made for driving the 829B on 10–11 meters from a VFO; in the transmitter shown in the illustrations, this was done by running a pair of leads to binding posts on the rear of the chassis, leaving the leads permanently connected to the 829B grid link. An alternative arrangement that permits disconnecting the VFO by using extra switch wafers ganged with S_2 is suggested in the diagram. The simpler arrangement shown in the photographs has no bad effects electrically, but makes it necessary to disconnect the leads from the VFO when crystal control is used.

The milliammeter is switched by means of a two-pole four-position wafer switch and is so shunted as to give readings for tripler grid current, tripler plate current, power-amplifier grid current and power-amplifier plate current. In addition, a toggle switch is provided, as indicated at S_3 in the circuit diagram, for reducing power input during the tuning-up procedure.

Construction Details

The transmitter was constructed for table-top operation without a panel, and is built on a 3 × 3 × 17-inch chassis. Starting with the crystal unit at the left-hand end of the chassis, the components are mechanically laid out in a straight line, directly in sequence according to the circuit. Immediately following the crystal unit is the 2E26 tripler, with its associated tuned grid-input circuit below the chassis and with its plate circuit above. The grid and plate inductors for the tripler are not changed in band-shifting and consequently can be wound to be self-supporting, using heavy bare or enameled wire or copper tubing.

The tripler plate inductor is supported at one end by a polystyrene stand-off to provide an extremely short, flexible lead from the coil to the tube plate connector, and at the same time provide a rigid mounting for that end of the plate inductor. The other end is supported directly on one of the stator terminals of the plate tuning condenser. Plate voltage is fed in at this same point through a v.h.f. r.f. choke that is mounted in a novel manner by passing it through a rubber grommet in the chassis in such a way that the low-potential end of the choke is insulated from the chassis and supported by the grommet while the high-potential end is in the clear. A silver-mica by-pass capacitor is placed between the ground terminal on the 2E26 tube socket, the adjacent tie-point on the chassis itself and the low-frequency end of this choke coil.

As shown in the top view, the output of the tripler is link-coupled to two of the prongs on the socket for the 829B grid coil. This is a new polystyrene socket (Millen 41407) having a dual set of link contacts, an arrangement that eliminates the necessity for complicated switching when, as in this case, a multiplier stage must be cut in or out when changing bands. The particular coil plugged in at any time has its link make contact with the directly-associated link socket contacts.

The 829B amplifier occupies the right half of the chassis. The tube is mounted horizontally, with its input and output circuits shielded from each other by means of the socket mounting plate. Even though this "shelf" has side brackets, the aluminum shield furnished for the socket (Millen 33999) should also be used. The top view of the chassis does not show this shield, as it is hidden from view by the mounting shelf. This same socket mounting plate also carries the 829B neutralizing condensers, which are readily constructed from feed-through bushings and adjustable pieces of bus bar, whose position, relative to the tube plates, can be readily adjusted to secure the extremely low neutralizing capacity required for this particular tube. The pieces of bus bar should be bent as shown in the photo-

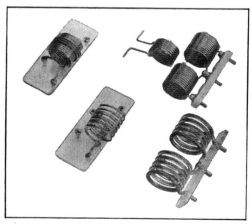

The two coils at the top are the amplifier grid and plate coils for 10–11 meters; the 6-meter coils are at the bottom.

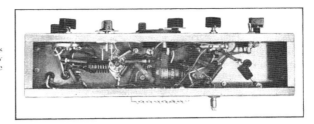

In this bottom view the 2E26 grid coil is just to the left of the tube socket and below the tuning condenser. Relatively little of the r.f. wiring is below the chassis.

graph so that the free ends can be swung toward or away from the plates of the two sections of the 829B. The over-all length should be such that the straight portions at the ends are opposite the bottoms of the plates, and the length of these portions should be about one-half inch.

The grid tuning condenser for the 829B is mounted so close to the socket that lead lengths of only approximately one-half inch between the two socket grid terminals and the condenser are required. The polystyrene coil socket is mounted directly on the variable condenser by means of small right-angle brackets, thus permitting the socket contact-lug to be soldered directly to the condenser terminals at the exact point at which the leads from the grids are also attached.

On the output side of the 829B, a similarly symmetrical and compact circuit arrangement requires plate leads only one inch in length from the plate connectors to the stator terminals of the dual output condenser. The coil socket is mounted and connections to the condenser made in the same way as in the grid circuit. The center connection of the plate coil is brought directly down to the plate r.f. choke, which is supported by a grommet in the chassis in the same way as the previously-mentioned choke in the tripler circuit. The output plug-in coil socket differs from that used in the 829B grid circuit in that provision has been made for an adjustable link which, when swung to the desired coupling, can be locked into place by means of the knurled locking supports.

On the rear of the chassis is mounted the terminal strip to which connections are made for filament and plate power, and also a pair of binding posts to which VFO input may be fed when it is desired to use the transmitter with an existing 10–11-meter band VFO.

In general, the wiring and mechanical assembly are straightforward and not at all tricky. There are a few points, however, worth special comment. These concern the ground leads, especially around the tripler. One-quarter inch braid is used for essentially all grounding circuits, in order to reduce high-frequency impedance of the ground connections at these points to a minimum. On the tripler socket, Contacts 4, 7, 8 and 1 are tied directly together with a piece of ¼-inch braid, which in turn continues on to an adjacent contact on the chassis. It is to this particular strap that one of the socket contacts in the silver-mica by-pass condenser from the plate choke is gounded, as well as the ground or rotor terminals from the 2E26 grid tuning condenser. The grid connection to this input tuned circuit is less than ¾ inch long and there is another piece of braid directly from the No. 5 or grid contact on the socket, down to the stator spindle of the grid tuning condenser.

It is also important in mounting the two high-frequency plate-circuit chokes to see that the cold end is supported by the grommet and *only* the cold end.

The arrangement of the controls is such that should the builder desire to mount the transmitter chassis in a cabinet or on a relay-rack panel, a neat-appearing symmetrical panel arrangement will result. If this is done, a small rectangular hole should be cut in the panel to expose the crystal socket, rather than attempting to remount the crystal socket from the crystal-oscillator unit on the panel itself.

In the initial tests on the transmitter illustrated, an interesting experience was had in connection with link circuits. Stranded wire was used between the 2E26 plate link and its termination on the 829B grid-coil socket. It was found that although the 2E26 was operating normally with adequate power in the plate circuit, yet insufficient grid drive was being obtained on the 829B. The difficulty was discovered to be caused by a single broken strand in the flexible lead wire connecting the two stages! Of course, another piece of wire, with no broken strands, cured the trouble; but perhaps it might be just as well in applications of this kind to use a solid lead covered with varnished cambric. Certainly then there could be no question of a hidden broken strand dissipating the missing power.

The actual connection of the transmitter to the power supply is simplified by the inclusion of divider resistors in the transmitter itself. The negative high-voltage ground and the ground side of the heater are connected to Post 1 on the terminal strip. The other side of the heater is connected to Post 2 and the high voltage is connected to Post 3. For c.w. operation, Posts 4 and 5 are connected by a jumper; on 'phone a Class B modulator is connected between the same two posts.

Operating Notes

The adjustment and operation of the transmitter are straightforward. Those who have used 829s before do not need to be reminded of the necessity for neutralizing them or told how to do it, but those who have not will find the process very simple. The neutralizing preferably should be done with the amplifier operating on 2 meters, and the transmitter should be tuned as described later but without plate voltage on the 829B (the plate voltage may be disconnected by leaving the modulation-transformer terminals open). The positions of the neutralizing "condensers" — the short lengths of wire mounted on the stand-off insulators as shown in the photograph — are then varied, keeping them symmetrical with respect to the tube, until the 829B grid current remains constant when the plate tank condenser, C_{16}, is swung through resonance. The adjustment is not too critical.

For 10–11-meter operation the bandswitch is set to Position 2, the crystal oscillator switched to the 10–11 position and the toggle switch, S_3, to the "tune" position. The meter switch should be set in Position 3, so as to read the 829B grid current. A crystal for the correct frequency (between 13.6 and 13.7 or 14 to 14.85 Mc.) is then plugged into the CCO-2A crystal unit. Final-amplifier grid and plate coils for 10–11-meter operation should be plugged into their respective sockets.

After allowing the heaters to reach operating temperature, the plate voltage is applied and the oscillator tuned for maximum 829B grid current. After that, the 829B grid tank condenser is adjusted for maximum grid current. The meter switch is then set in Position 4 so as to read the 829B plate current. This should be adjusted to minimum by means of C_{16}. After this has been done, the "tune-transmit" switch should be set in the "transmit" position. The antenna coupling link is then adjusted for maximum output. The 829B grid- and plate-tank adjustments are then corrected to give optimum performance.

The power amplifier can be operated from a VFO by connecting its output to the binding posts on the back of the chassis, switching the band-change switch to Position 1 and following the procedure just outlined, except insofar as the crystal oscillator is concerned.

The procedure on 6 meters is very similar except that a 25- to 27-Mc. crystal is used, S_1 is set for 6-meter output, and the 50–54-Mc. grid and plate coils are plugged in the 829B circuit.

Adjustment on 2 meters is very much the same, and is tabulated below:

1) Turn bandswitch to Position 3. Set S_1 in the CCO-2A to the 2-6-meter position.
2) Turn toggle-switch S_3 to "tune" position.
3) Turn meter switch to Position 1 (reads 2E26 grid current).
4) Plug in 24–24.22-Mc. crystal.
5) Plug in 144–148-Mc. final-amplifier grid and plate coils.
6) Turn on filament voltage.
7) Turn on plate voltage after heaters are up to temperature.
8) Tune C_5 for maximum grid current.
9) Tune 2E26 grid tank condenser, C_8, for maximum grid current.
10) Turn meter switch to Position 2 (reads 2E26 plate current).
11) Tune 2E26 plate tank condenser, C_{10}, for minimum grid current.
12) Turn meter switch to Position 3 (reads 829B grid current).
13) Tune 829B grid tank condenser, C_{12}, for maximum current.
14) Turn meter switch to Position 4 (reads 829B plate current).
15) Tune 829B plate, C_{16}, for minimum plate current.
16) Turn S_3 to "transmit" position.
17) Adjust antenna coupling to final amplifier for maximum output.
18) Recheck 9, 11, 13 and 15.

The transmitter can be operated from a single 600-volt supply that is capable of delivering 250 ma., or the 600-volt supply may be used for the 829B alone and a separate supply delivering about 300 volts at 100 ma. used for the 6AG7 and 2E26. Under normal operating conditions the 6AG7 plate current is 35 ma. and the 2E26 plate current 75 ma. The plate potential on the 829B can be increased to 750 volts for c.w. operation, with a total plate-and-screen current of 160 ma. On 'phone, the plate-and-screen current should not exceed 150 ma. at 600 volts. However, if forced air-cooling is used the plate current can be increased to 200 ma., at 750 volts for c.w. and 600 volts for 'phone.

Strays

W6JQV provides his DX contacts with a QSL service de luxe. Recently, while working XU6GRL, "Doc" Stuart requested QSL by mail. "Oh, that won't be necessary," responded Hal, "I'll bring it over." And so he did, W6JQV's ocean-hopping work with the airlines making it an easy matter to deliver the card in person!

— · · · —

We are indebted to W3CPT for bringing to our attention a War Department technical manual entitled "Suppression of Radio Noises — TM11-483," which may be obtained (supply limited) from the Superintendent of Documents, G.P.O., Washington, D. C. The cost is 20¢ in cash, certified check or money order — no stamps. This publication makes an excellent supplement to Harold G. Price's article in May *QST*, "Eliminating Car Noise in 28-Mc. Mobile Reception."

"Experimental Parametric Amplifiers" by Frank Jones, W6AJF

By Ward Silver, NØAX

New types or variations of components are always of interest to amateurs who put them to use as soon as they are available. With so many advanced amateurs employed in labs of all sorts, the distinction between amateur and professional tends to blur as applications are developed for these devices. A particularly good example of this sort of amateur innovation is the *varactor diode*.

In the early 1950s, the only amplifying game in town for amateurs was the vacuum tube. Vacuum tubes gave reasonably good performance at VHF and UHF, but due to thermal noise and other characteristics of tube circuits, they were limited in their ability to provide low noise figures. Professionals were working with masers (which stood for microwave amplification by the stimulated emission of radiation), the predecessor of the laser, but masers were not amateur devices. Transistors with useable gain at VHF and UHF were still years away.

Bell Labs researchers Uhlir and Bakanowski were able to devise a structure and method for producing a reverse-biased junction diode to use as a voltage-controlled capacitor. A couple of years later, Microwave Associates and other manufacturers produced the first practical varactor diode components with performance and packaging suitable for use in VHF, UHF and even microwave applications. The professional literature was full of papers about the theory and use of varactor diodes.

By using a process similar to modulation or passive mixing, the voltage-controlled capacitance of the varactor diode could be employed to transfer energy from a pump signal to the desired signal, creating amplification. But the theory behind the process could be fierce as illustrated by this classic W1CJD cartoon.

Amateurs working professionally in the field were quick to relay the information to their peers. The four-part series of *QST* articles by Ross Bateman, W4AO, and Walter Bain, W4LTU, beginning in December 1958 makes excellent reading for information about the diode itself and how it could be used for frequency conversion and amplification. (See the references that are provided in the Appendix.)

The basic idea behind the parametric amplifier is very similar to modulation or mixing in which a fixed-frequency local oscillator (LO) is used to create signals (sidebands or mixing products) at the sum and difference frequencies of the input signal and the LO. The parameter that does the amplifying in the parametric amplifier is the varactor's reactance, which is varied by the LO or "pump" oscillator signal as if a variable capacitor's plates were being varied at an RF rate. The "idler" frequency of the parametric amplifier corresponds to an unwanted product from a mixer.

How to put the new varactors to work in amateur stations was still an open question until the featured article by Frank Jones, W6AJF, appeared in the August 1959 issue. Working to develop parametric amplifiers for 144 and 220 MHz, Jones had very little practical information to support his efforts. Long before the Internet, technical journals and manufacturer data sheets were about all anyone had to work with. Nevertheless, Jones — a VHF/UHF DXer — stuck with it and came up with the amplifier you can read about here.

As the article indicates, there were "vague notions of how to put the new devices to practical use." There were equations describing the device functions and some news of experimental equipment, but reducing these to practice was a time-consuming process. The article describes how the multi-resonant coaxial line was developed to provide the tuned circuits for the pump, signal and idler frequencies, all in a single structure.

Jones alludes to many hours spent trying different approaches, ruining fragile tuning capacitors, and even destroying one of the precious new diodes. One look at the coaxial line's resonance structure in the article's Figure 2 and the tuning procedure at the end of the article illustrates how much effort it must have taken to get the first unit up and running with satisfactory results! This is Amateur Radio's experimental nature at its finest. What amateurs may lack in laboratory resources, they make up in persistence and steady learning, pursuing many false leads on their way to practical, working designs.

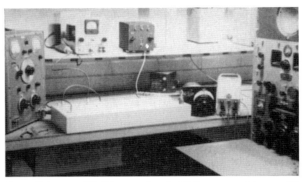

Ross Bateman, W4AO, constructed this parametric amplifier for use at 144 Mc (MHz) using a 900 Mc pump oscillator and a Microwave Associates diode.

Today's amateurs also have new components, such as the memristor and advanced transistors that work at millimeter wavelengths. As operating frequencies tunnel upward toward the previously unimaginable terahertz region, even the choice of materials used to construct electronic components and structures is changing. Graphene's electronic properties are just being explored, organic dyes and polymers are being employed as one-molecule switches, and nanostructures such as carbon tubes and fibers are creating wires, contacts and even antennas! Surely amateurs will put these to work just as they have every other new component since the coherer.

> The projects W6AJF describes here were undertaken at a time when little or no practical information was available that would enable an amateur to build working models of these new devices. The reader, on the other hand, has the benefit of the work of Bateman and Bain, detailed in a four-part series in December, 1958, through March, 1959, QST, to help him understand what early-bird W6AJF had to find out for himself. A careful reading of the articles by W4AO and W4LTU is recommended as preparation for this one, particularly to the newcomer to the parametric-amplifier field.

Working Toward Lower Noise Figures in Reception at 144, 220 and 420 Mc.

BY FRANK C. JONES,* W6AJF

Experimental Parametric Amplifiers

LIKE many other amateurs who have made a specialty of long-distance v.h.f. and u.h.f. work, the writer was extremely interested when news of the parametric, mavar or reactance amplifiers began to appear in print. But like other amateurs (and most of the professionals, too) we had only vague notions of how to put the new devices to practical use. After many hours of experimental work with a varactor diode from Microwave Associates, practical ideas began to emerge.

Many days were wasted in some of the early tests, as almost no experimental information was available. Learning about these new techniques had to be done the hard way, at the expense of much sheet metal, broken plunger-type trimmers, coax fittings and even one varactor diode. This cost of being early in a new field was well worth the effort, however, for at this writing we have one good amplifier on 144 Mc., a better one on 220 Mc., and a couple of good 432-Mc. units. Further work on 432 Mc. and a 1296-Mc. project are planned.

Some Preliminary Findings

Lowest noise figures and best amplification were obtained with a varactor diode in an amplifier, rather than an up-converter. Tests were made at 144 Mc. with up-conversion to 432 and 1296 Mc. The 432- and 1296-Mc. receivers had noise figures of 4 to 5 and 8 to 10 db., respectively. This deteriorated the over-all noise figure with the up-converter, so the final result at 144 Mc. was never below 2 db. Since a noise figure of 2½ to 3 db. was already available with several good 2-meter converters using tube amplifiers, the up-converter didn't offer much improvement. The up-converter arrangement had the added disadvantage of requiring a highly stable pump power source.

On the other hand, a straight-through parametric amplifier apparently gets down under 1 db. at 144 and 220 Mc., and the pump stability requirement is not nearly so severe as with the up-converter. The up-converter is not as regenerative as the amplifier, and it seems to depend for its over-all signal gain on the extent to which the signal frequency is up-converted. A 1296-Mc. receiver gives more gain from a 144-Mc. up-converter than does a 432-Mc. receiver and, despite the higher noise figure of the 1296-Mc. receiver, the over-all noise figure is about the same.

The over-all noise figure of an up-converter system is given by

$$F = F_1 + \frac{F_2 - 1}{G_1}$$

*850 Donner Ave., Sonoma, Calif.

The 220-Mc. parametric amplifier ready for use at W6AJF. Regulated power supply, left, is for the pump oscillator, in the small box at the rear.

August 1959

Interior of the 220-Mc. amplifier, with the varactor and short pump line at the far left. Signal input and output coupling loops are the center of the line. Note that the half-wave line, used in the 220- and 432-Mc. amplifiers, is mounted on insulating standoffs.

where F_1 is the numerical value of up-converter noise figure, F_2 is that of the receiver used as the i.f. system, and G_1 is the gain of the up-converter or amplifier, as the case may be.

One down-converter was built, with a varactor diode and pump oscillator, but it showed a loss in gain and a poor noise figure, when compared to the up-converter system. Further up-converter tests are planned here in the near future.

One That Didn't Work — And Why

The first parametric amplifier for 144 Mc. built here used a silver-plated coaxial line, with a 3/8-inch inner conductor and a 1 3/4-inch outer conductor, about 12 inches long, shorted at one end. A small tuning capacitor and the varactor diode were connected from the open end of the inner conductor to the grounded shell, with a blocking capacitor in series with the diode. A variable oscillator covering 250 to 350 Mc. was used as the pump, with a regulated plate supply, variable from 0 to 90 volts. The best pump frequency within the above range was around 285 Mc. Pump energy was fed in through a tap on the line about one inch from the grounded end. Coupling loops for the 144-Mc. input and output were about 3 inches long, mounted close to the inner conductor and series tuned with small trimmers. Moderately good noise figure was indicated, but the unit was unstable and very difficult to maintain in operation. Because one idler frequency was close to the signal frequency the amplifier was very ineffective in the presence of auto ignition, line noise or other external interference, and the system responded to signals on the idler frequency nearly as well as to the desired ones.

These limitations seemed to eliminate as undesirable the only type of circuit that had been mentioned in amateur literature up to that time. At 432 and 1296 Mc. this image effect might not be troublesome, as external noise is far lower there, and amateur QRM is not much of a problem.[1] On 144 or 220 Mc., however, on-the-air results were very disappointing, and the design was of little use, other than to gain experience.

Practical Working Models

Then followed a long period of paper and sheet-metal work on parametric amplifiers for 144 and 220 Mc. The idea of a cylindrical coaxial tank was abandoned, as a line built into a long box of square cross section would serve equally well and, if made with a removable side, would be much more readily worked on. The line impedance should be known for working out practical dimensions. The impedance of a cylindrical coaxial line is found from the formula

$$Z = 138 \log_{10} \frac{D}{d}$$

The impedance of a line built in a long box with sides equal to the diameter of a cylindrical line has an impedance 10 to 15 per cent higher. Use of a 1/4-inch inner conductor in a box 2 1/4 inches square results in a line impedance of about 140 ohms. Boxes 12 inches long and 2 1/4 inches square were used in the 144- and 220-Mc. amplifiers described herewith.

---

[1] Bateman and Bain pointed out in March *QST* that use of a pump frequency of twice the signal frequency fundamentally limits the over-all noise figure to no lower than 3 db., though noise figure measurements may make it appear that much lower noise figure is being achieved.—*Ed.*

The 144-Mc. amplifier uses a quarter-wave line, with the inner conductor grounded at the right end. Pump line and varactor are at the left, with signal input and output coupling at the right end.

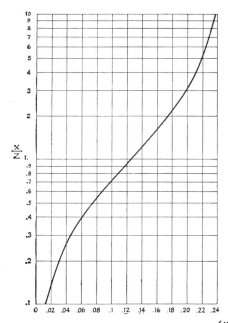

Fig. 1—Curve showing normalized input reactance $\left(\dfrac{X}{Z}\right)$ versus length in wavelengths of short-circuited coaxial or parallel-line circuits. X is the inductive reactance of the line and Z is the characteristic impedance.

for 220 Mc. These reflect smaller capacitances across the open ends of the line, so only a guess can be made of the net capacitance at the end.

The Microwave Associates MA-460A varactor diode had a "zero" capacitance marking of 6.6 $\mu\mu$f. This plus 1 to 2 $\mu\mu$f. from the small tuning capacitor gives about 8 $\mu\mu$f. at the varactor end of the line.

The inductive reactance of the short pump-frequency line, in series with the diode capacitance to ground, cancels a small portion of the diode capacitive reactance. For this reason, the pump line should be short; perhaps an inch or so for 144- or 220-Mc. amplifiers. The receiver with which the amplifier is used must have enough selectivity at 220 Mc. to keep any 280- or 720-Mc. signals or noise from getting into the first mixer. A few slug-tuned circuits at 220 Mc. should accomplish this.

In Fig. 1 is shown a curve which gives the capacitive reactance, normalized to the characteristic impedance, required for resonance at the input terminals of a short-circuited transmission line, for lengths up to about one-quarter wavelength. If an open-circuited line with equal capacitance at each end is used, the length obtained from the curve of Fig. 1 must be multiplied by a factor of 2. The wavelength in inches for any frequency can be calculated from the expression, $\dfrac{11{,}800}{f_{\text{mc}}}$, which gives figures of 53.5 inches for 220 Mc., 42 inches for 280 Mc., 23.6 inches for 500 Mc., and 16.4

Four frequencies are involved in the operation of the parametric amplifier: the signal frequency, the pump frequency and two idler frequencies. The idler frequencies are equal to the sum and difference of the first two. The proper value of impedance for each frequency must be present for parametric amplification with a varactor diode.[2]

A typical amateur design for 220 Mc. will be described, since the procedure outlined gave reasonably good results when applied to actual construction. A line impedance of 140 ohms was chosen, as this could be made easily with available components, as mentioned above. As a starting point a pump oscillator frequency of 500 Mc. was used. The upper idler frequency was then 500 plus 220, or 720 Mc. The lower is 500 minus 220, or 280 Mc. By a process of elimination, the coaxial line circuit shown in Fig. 2 was arrived at.

A half-wave line was chosen for 220 Mc. as the two idler frequencies could be tuned more readily with this design. One or more tuning capacitors for the idler frequencies are placed across the line circuit at the grounded or zero-voltage point

---

[2] The author appears to have used a more complex approach than is necessary here. Theory and practice indicate that only the lower of the two idler frequencies need be considered in the design of a parametric amplifier. The relatively low pump frequencies used by W6AJF may account for the need for taking the upper idler frequency into account in his experience. — Ed.

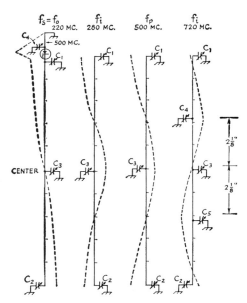

Fig. 2—Voltage distribution and tuning points on a 220-Mc. line 10 inches long, with a characteristic impedance of 140 ohms. Idler frequencies of 280 and 720 Mc. result from the use of a pump frequency of 500 Mc. and a signal frequency of 220 Mc.

inches for 720 Mc. For a capacitance of 8 $\mu\mu f.$ at each end of the line, the value of X at 220 Mc. is 84 ohms, at 280 Mc. 70 ohms, at 500 Mc. 40 ohms, and at 720 Mc. 28 ohms. Each of these divided by 140 gives the $\frac{X}{Z}$ on the vertical scale of Fig. 1. Reading the values of line length from the curve gives the length to a zero-voltage point from each end of the capacity-loaded circuit.

The actual values plotted in inches in Fig. 2 are obtained by multiplying the wavelength in inches for each frequency by the decimal values of Fig. 1. These were 5, 3.15, 1.0, and 0.82 inches, respectively, from each end, neglecting end effects. For resonance in the 220-Mc. band, this line would be approximately 10 inches long. To make Fig. 2, several vertical lines were drawn 10 inches long, or scaled into 10 equal parts. The relative voltage or impedance at 220 Mc. is shown as the dotted line with a null at the center. Tuning the line to 220 Mc. is done with a 3-$\mu\mu f.$ variable capacitor, C_1, in parallel with the diode capacitance and, at the other end, by a 10-$\mu\mu f.$ capacitor, C_2. The null can be set at the exact line center by running C_1 and C_2 in opposite directions when the coax line is being tested without a pump oscillator in preliminary alignment.

Next, consider 280 Mc., a proposed idler frequency. The null will be about 3 inches from each end of the 10-inch line, as shown in the second line of Fig. 2. To make the 4-inch middle section of the line become a shortened half-wave circuit at 280 Mc., capacitor C_3 can be added at the exact center without affecting the 220-Mc. circuit, if it is balanced properly. This value of C_3 can be calculated by the reverse process, using Fig. 1. The two 2-inch sections each side of the center are short-circuited lines at 280 Mc., having a length of $\frac{2}{42} = 0.048\lambda$. From Fig. 1, 0.048$\lambda$ corresponds to an $\frac{X}{Z}$ value of 0.33, and since $Z = 140$, $X = 140 \times .33 = 46$ ohms, or 12 $\mu\mu f.$ at 280 Mc. Actually, the reactance of C_3 is one-half this value since it is tuning two line sections in parallel so $C_3 = 24$ $\mu\mu f.$

The same method can be used to calculate C_3 in the third line at 500 Mc. Obviously, the same value of C_3 cannot be used for both 500 and 280 Mc., so the 500-Mc. function is moved up to the shorter line on the other side of the varactor, as shown at the top of the left-hand drawing in Fig. 2. A short line with a large tuning capacitance will offer enough impedance at the pump frequency to function by varying the pump oscillator power into this circuit. Either the lower idler frequency or the pump frequency can be moved to this short line, but in general it is better to put the oscillator into the short line. If this line is about 1 inch long, $\frac{1}{23.6} = .045\lambda$. From Fig. 1, $\frac{X}{Z} = 0.3$ and $X = 140 \times 0.3 = 42$ ohms. C_4 is thus equal to 7.5 $\mu\mu f.$, including some capacitance through the varactor and the long circuit.

Consider the 720-Mc. idler frequency. The first null occurs about 0.8 inch in from each end of the 10-inch line. If it weren't for C_3, which is needed for the other idler frequency, the line would be nearly resonant since there is approximately a half wavelength (8.2 inches at 720 Mc.) between these nulls on the 10-inch line. But the presence of C_3 makes it necessary to have a null at the center of the line so C_3 will have no effect at 720 Mc. Adding equal capacitances, C_4 and C_5, at the correct points will tune the 10-inch line to 720 Mc. by multiple resonance. The distance from the end null to the center is $5 - 0.8 = 4.2$ inches, and half of this is $\frac{4.2}{2} = 2.1$ inches. This length represents $\frac{2.1}{16.4} = 0.128\lambda$ and from Fig. 1, $\frac{X}{Z} = 1.0$. Thus, $X = 140$ and $C = 1.6$ $\mu\mu f.$ at 720 Mc. Doubling this value for C for tuning the two sections in parallel gives $C_4 = C_5 = 3.2$ $\mu\mu f.$

The effects of C_4 and C_5 on C_1 and C_2, and then on C_3, can be calculated, and amount to a slight increase in the effective capacitance at C_1 and C_2. Thus in tuning C_1 and C_2 their values would be set at about ½ $\mu\mu f.$ less than originally calculated. C_4 and C_5 are physically so near the null points at 280 Mc. that C_3 would be only a tiny bit less than calculated.

All this looks fine but several factors have been neglected or their effects guessed at for simplification. All tuning capacitors and even the varactor have inductance in the leads or plungers. Fortunately, this effect is small enough so careful adjustment of all capacitors and variation of the

The 432-Mc. amplifier has the pump energy inserted near the center of the half-wave line. Idler tank and varactor are at the right of this photograph.

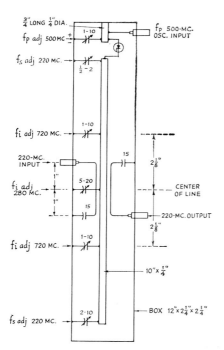

Fig. 3—Dimensions of the 220-Mc. parametric amplifier. The 220-Mc tuned circuit is a half-wave line. Pump energy is fed into the short line at the top of the amplifier.

pump oscillator frequency will usually result in hitting the magic spot of proper amplification at low noise levels. If a high pump frequency such as 1000 to 1400 Mc. is used, the two idler frequencies also will be very high and the capacitor lead inductance will completely upset calculations. That is probably the reason why the 432-Mc. amplifier is still not completely satisfactory.

The dimensions of Fig. 3, based on the foregoing calculations, have been found to make a very good 220-Mc. amplifier. If the varactor "zero" capacitance is something more or less than 6 $\mu\mu f.$ the dimensions may have to be changed, since too much capacitance at C_1 which — in effect, is across the varactor — may prevent proper "pumping." More data and more varactor diodes of different capacitances will have to be tested to study this effect. It would seem desirable for the varactor capacitance to be around 4 to 6 or 7 $\mu\mu f.$ for v.h.f. operation and 2 or 3 $\mu\mu f.$ for u.h.f. bands. The 432-Mc. band is a little high in frequency for a 6-$\mu\mu f.$ varactor and perhaps it would be easier to get a lower-capacitance unit into operation on this band.

The sketch in Fig. 3 gives the essential dimension and locations of capacitors for the 220-Mc. amplifier. Aluminum about $\frac{1}{16}$-inch thick is suitable for the box if copper (heavy flashing sheet) is used for the end pieces. These should have bent-over lips on all four sides. The ends can be fastened into the aluminum sides with a couple of sheet-metal screws on each side. The $\frac{1}{4}$-inch diameter center conductor should be soldered into the sheet copper end pieces for the 144-Mc. unit. In the 220- and 432-Mc. units only one end needs to be copper since the half-wave line is floating free of ground on a pair of small poly or ceramic insulators.

Fig. 4 gives the dimensions found suitable for 144 Mc. with a 6-$\mu\mu f.$ varactor. The dimensions in Fig. 5 for the 432-Mc. unit are for the same varactor diode. Miniature plate-type capacitors were used at first for tuning, but caused the circuit Q to drop too much. Later, copper solder lugs were made up to fit over the shafts to clamp against the box side, and then bent around for soldering to the ground lugs on the capacitors. The Q went back up and, since several of the glass piston-type trimmers which had been substituted had been broken due to carelessness, the little plate-type capacitors were put back into the 220- and 144-Mc. amplifiers.

Variable capacitors for the input and output links at 432 Mc. (near the center of the long line) were so large and space-wasting that very small 5-$\mu\mu f.$ NP0 fixed capacitors were used to tune out most of the link reactance at 432 Mc. Moving the 1-inch long insulated links (BNC coax fitting to 5-$\mu\mu f.$ capacitor) closer to or farther away from the center line is necessary in getting the amplifier to fire up properly. Similarly at 220 Mc., fixed 15-$\mu\mu f.$ ceramic capacitors (with minimum possible lead lengths) were finally used in series with the 2-inch links. At 144 Mc., two 30-$\mu\mu f.$ capacitors were substituted for the 5- to 40-$\mu\mu f.$ capacitors shown in the photograph of this amplifier. The links in this case were 3 inches long (including the capacitor). The 144-Mc. unit was modified as shown in Fig. 4 after the photographs were made.

Alignment Suggestions and Miscellaneous Notes

Alignment isn't easy unless one is lucky. Every tuning control reacts on the others, so a lot of patience and a diode noise generator are needed. The first step is to get a reference reading with the receiver connected directly to the noise generator. Then connect the parametric amplifier into the coax line between the noise generator and the receiver. Leave the pump oscillator turned off but have the varactor diode in place. (Handle it carefully!) Tune the end capacitors for best noise figure. If this is more than 20 per cent above the noise figure without the amplifier, adjust the input and output links also. Once you get the noise figure down near the original value, the signal circuit end tuning should be touched up slightly, because it is possible to get amplification off resonance and lose about 1 db. of noise figure. If the unit has a half-wave line, try to get it balanced up so a short circuit with a small screw driver to the box at the line center has no effect on the noise figure.

The next step is to turn on the pump oscillator and slowly increase its output. For safety, keep the oscillator input to less than one-half watt. The pump-circuit tuning and the idler-frequency

August 1959

adjustments have to be worked back and forth until the parametric amplifier begins to show some gain in the output reading with the noise generator on. When the right combination of all tuning adjustments and correct pump frequency are found, the pump power into the amplifier should be reduced to a point which gives from 5 to 15 db. gain, with the amplifier well below the oscillating point. Connecting to an antenna may upset the amplifier unless the antenna system has a flat line of the same impedance as the noise generator. Again, a slight adjustment of the controls will make the amplifier operate normally with an antenna.

In the three units described here, two 6AF4 parallel-line oscillators are used. One has parallel ¼-inch rods spaced less than ¼ inch edge to edge, with a small butterfly tuning capacitor at the end opposite the tube. Plate current is fed into the plate side through a 2000-ohm resistor at the center of the line, and a 10,000-ohm grid leak to ground connects to the other rod near its center. The tuning range is from about 700 to 830 Mc. The 425- to 550-Mc. oscillator has similar construction with 4-inch lines. These are not ideal, and a more mechanically and electrically stable oscillator for these ranges could be built with a heavy flat-plate line of lower impedance and greater physical length.

The 432-Mc. amplifier shown here uses approximately 800 Mc. as the pump frequency.[1,4] By careful adjustment it has been possible to get an improvement of about 3 db. in noise figure over a 416B amplifier normally used at W6AJF on this band.

The 220-Mc. amplifier shows nearly 3 db. improvement over a 417A tube amplifier normally used on this band. The 144-Mc. unit shows from 1 to 2 db. improvement over a 417A tube amplifier. These improvements indicate that the parametric amplifiers are not far from a noise figure of 1 db. The 220-Mc. unit tuned up most readily with a pump frequency of 520 Mc. and the 144-Mc. unit with the pump at about 475 Mc. The pump frequencies may be changed a few megacycles without ill effects if the idler adjustments are varied. These frequencies apply only to these particular units with the one varactor used in all three.

Spurious Radiation

In some recent tests on the 144-Mc. amplifier for spurious output the pump frequency was set at 482 Mc. and the adjustments made for

(*Continued on page 138*)

---

[4] Better results could be obtained with a higher pump frequency. Something of the order of 1500 Mc. or higher is recommended for use with 432 Mc. amplifiers.

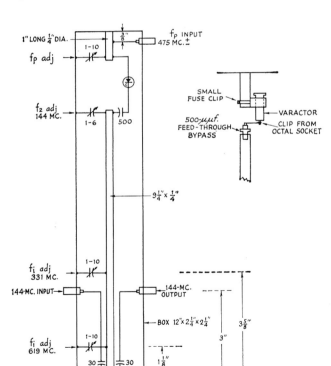

Fig. 4—Dimensions of the 144-Mc. amplifier using a quarter-wave line. Method of mounting the varactor is similar to that employed in the 220-Mc. amplifier, except for the blocking capacitor needed because of the grounded inner conductor.

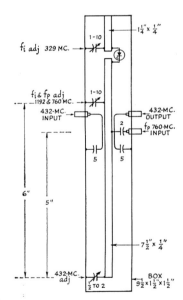

Fig. 5—Dimensions of the 432-Mc. amplifier, using half-wave tank circuit. Varactor mounting is similar to that used in the 220-Mc. amplifier.

Parametric Amplifiers

(Continued from page 16)

best average reception over 144 to 144.2 Mc. The signal generator was connected into one jack at 144.1 Mc. with outputs up to 100,000 microvolts available. The usual 2-meter receiver was disconnected and an APR-1 receiver tuning 300 to 1000 Mc. was substituted. By using another signal generator in the 450-Mc. range, the input to the APR-1 receiver could be found by the substitution method. At the pump frequency of 482 Mc. the output across 50 ohms measured 80,000 microvolts or 80 millivolts. A high-Q 144-Mc. circuit between the antenna and the parametric amplifier is indicated for reducing radiation from this source.

The unwanted output at the two idler frequencies, 626 and 338 Mc., was in direct proportion to the signal input at 144 Mc. It measured 5000 microvolts for a 10,000-microvolt input, 500 for 1000, and 50 for 100, at the lower idler frequency of 338 Mc. At the upper frequency of 626 Mc. the outputs were 2000, 200 and 20 microvolts, respectively. Since the parametric amplifier would probably only be used on signals of 1 microvolt or less, the outputs at 338 and 626 would be less than 1 microvolt — not enough radiation to worry about. However, the pump oscillator output would still be up near 80 millivolts, or about 125 microwatts into a 50-ohm dipole. A carefully designed high-Q coaxial tank circuit tuned to 144 Mc. would reduce this oscillator radiation by a factor of about 100 without sacrificing more than 1 db. in gain and noise figure. A small neon bulb across the top of this extra tank circuit would probably fire when a high-powered transmitter in the station is keyed, thus protecting the varactor diode against overload when the antenna relay isn't self-shielding for the receiver input side. **QST**

"Defining and Measuring Receiver Dynamic Range" by Wes Hayward, W7ZOI

By Ward Silver, NØAX

By the early 1970s, the transistor began to replace vacuum tubes, particularly in receiver front-end RF amplifiers, preamplifiers and mixers. With tube receivers, sensitivity was a primary concern (particularly above 20 MHz), but transistors had plenty of gain in those frequency ranges and even more at lower frequencies. Soon, amateurs discovered a new problem — *non-linearity* and *intermodulation*. The author of this introduction vividly remembers his first experience with a highly-sensitive transistorized receiver encountering the strong signal environment of the ARRL DX CW contest!

By the mid-1970s, new terms had entered the amateur lexicon: *blocking, gain compression, intermodulation products, intercept points, odd- and even-order*, and so forth. The challenge was now to create solid-state receivers that could handle the strong signals on the bands. To evaluate different designs, however, new tests and a thorough understanding of the phenomena was required.

Enter Wes Hayward, W7ZOI. A widely-respected receiver designer, in the following article, Wes summarized the issues at hand, defined the metrics and tests by which performance was to be evaluated, and even provided simple circuits for test equipment that could be built by amateurs. While there are other articles discussing receiver linearity, this particular example is noteworthy for capturing the discussion and placing everyone on a relatively even footing.

Today, receiver linearity is considered *the* most important overall aspect of receiver performance. The measured performance of new models in *QST* Product Reviews and by third-party labs such as Sherwood Engineering (**www.sherweng.com/table.html**) are eagerly awaited by amateurs around the world.

Receiver design, however, is undergoing rapid change. Digital signal processing (DSP) functions and applications gained wide acceptance over the past decade. Software-defined radio (SDR) architectures are displacing the traditional superheterodyne designs that have dominated the field for 80 years. These raise new questions, such as how does clock jitter during the digitizing process manifest itself in the received signals? What is the effect of signal quantization and special algorithms on weak signals at the receiver's noise floor? What are the appropriate performance metrics, test protocols, and equipment? There will also be new mysteries to unravel as the analog and digital portions of a receiver interact.

Amateurs use receivers differently than commercial, military and academic operators. Signals on the amateur bands are closely spaced and of widely differing strengths. Signals using different and incompatible modes are crowded into the amateur band segments, adjacent to and even on top of each other, making reception a challenge. Even as more and more digital signals fill the bands, amateurs will still be copying signals "by ear" for the foreseeable future. All of these constraints and requirements will present significant new challenges to receiver designers.

Each of these new technologies brings with it new performance issues requiring new metrics and new measurements. Along with the new issues will come the need for each to be explained to amateurs — the cause of the behavior and its effect on operating, the metrics by which it is characterized and measured, and the means of comparing different products and designs. Thus, we hope for more articles such as the one that follows to guide us through the stormy seas of innovation throughout radio's second century.

Main operating screen of the popular *PowerSDR* transceiver control program for SDR radios, illustrating the power of digital signal processing.

A top-performing amateur receiver as of mid-2013, the SDR-architecture Elecraft KX3. Featuring an IMD dynamic range of up to 103 dB and a reciprocal-mixing dynamic range (RMDR) of 114 dB at 2 kHz signal spacing, the low power transceiver is the size of a large paperback book.

DEFINING AND MEASURING
Receiver Dynamic Range

BY WES HAYWARD,* W7ZOI

PRIOR TO THE late 1950s, the excellence of a communications receiver was thought to be commensurate with the number of signal conversions employed. A triple-conversion, 20-tube "super blooper" was the rage of the day. Then Goodman enlightened us with his paper, "What's Wrong with our Present Receivers?" His outlook contributed to the current popularity of single-conversion designs.[1]

The present trends in receiver design reflect an even more careful approach. Not only do we strive for suitable sensitivity, selectivity, stability, and frequency accuracy, but we also try to realize these ends without compromising receiver performance in the presence of a band filled with very strong signals. A number of superlatives are used to describe such a modern receiver, both by the amateur constructor and by the manufacturer. Phrases like "wide dynamic range," or "excellent immunity to cross modulation," are common. One manufacturer even claims in his receiver advertisement, "Adjacent-signal overload is nonexistent!"

What do these terms mean? How wide is the dynamic range of a receiver? How immune is it to cross modulation, to blocking, to intermodulation-distortion effects? All of these parameters *can* be measured and specified. The purpose of this presentation is to review some of the basic measurement concepts which are used to define the performance of a receiver. Having an understanding of these measurements, we will be in a position to make a better selection in the purchase of a receiver, or to do a better job in the construction of our own homemade "machine."

The initial impression of some amateurs is that these measurements can be done *only* with expensive and sophisticated test equipment. This is partially true, for highly accurate measurements can be realized only with high-quality test gear. However, surprisingly accurate and meaningful measuring can be done with simple equipment which can be built easily and calibrated by the amateur experimenter in his basement workshop. Suitable circuits will be presented later in this article.

* 7700 S.W. Danielle Ave., Beaverton, OR 97005.

Fundamental Considerations

Before we discuss the measurements for receiver evaluation some of the basic phenomena which limit the performance of an amplifier or mixer will be considered. These include intermodulation distortion, blocking (gain compression) and cross modulation. A typical test setup is shown in Fig. 1. The equipment includes a pair of signal generators, a hybrid combiner, the amplifier under test, and a spectrum analyzer. The reader should not be terrified by this collection because much less will be required for the more limited task of receiver evaluation. The function of each of these items will be outlined.

While most signal generators are calibrated in terms of output voltage, the real concern is not with the voltage from the generator but with the *power* available. The fundamental unit of power is the watt. However, the unit which is used for most low-level rf work is the milliwatt, and power is often specified in dB with respect to one milliwatt, or in dBm. Hence, 0 dBm would be one milliwatt. The output of a typical QRP transmitter might be +33 dBm, or 2 watts. A signal arriving from a 50-ohm antenna at the input terminal of a receiver might be 1 μV, or −107 dBm.

The convenience of a logarithmic power unit like the dBm becomes apparent when signals are amplified or attenuated. For example, a −107-dBm signal which is applied to an amplifier with a gain of 20 dB will result in an output of −107 dBm +20 dB, or −87 dBm.

The signal generators used in the test setup are, ideally, calibrated accurately in dBm. For receiver work they should be capable of producing output power from 0 dBm down to −140 dBm or even lower. The generators should have extremely low leakage. That is, when the output of the generator is disconnected, we should not be able to detect any signal in the most sensitive receiver tuned to the generator output frequency. Ideally, at least one of the signal generators should be capable of amplitude modulation. A suitable lab-quality piece would be the HP-8640B.

A hybrid combiner is essentially a unit with three ports (i.e., three spigots or coax connectors). The device is used to combine the signals from a

July 1975

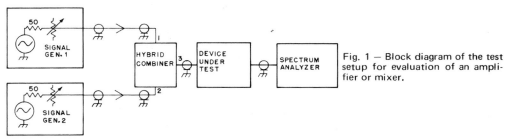

Fig. 1 — Block diagram of the test setup for evaluation of an amplifier or mixer.

pair of signal generators. Note the labeling on the hybrid combiner shown in Fig. 1; this box has the characteristic that signals applied at ports 1 or 2 appear at port 3, and are attenuated 6 dB. However, a signal from port 1 is attenuated 30 or 40 dB when sampled at port 2. Similarly, signals applied at port 2 are isolated from port 1 some 30 to 40 dB. The isolating properties of the box are needed in order to prevent one signal generator from being frequency- or phase-modulated by the other. A second feature of a hybrid coupler is that a 50-ohm impedance level is maintained throughout the system. A commercial example of a hybrid coupler of this kind is the HP-8721A.

The final piece of gear in our experimental arrangement is the spectrum analyzer. This box is essentially a receiver. However, it has a few features not usually found in an amateur receiver. First, the output information is not audio energy in a pair of headphones, but is a "blip" on the face of a CRT. Second, a spectrum analyzer is an electronically swept instrument, with the span of frequencies displayed being selectable by the operator. Finally, the spectrum analyzer is a calibrated instrument. That is, by examining the signals which are displayed on the screen, the operator can read directly the power amounts of the signals in dBm. Typical analyzers on the market also have selectable bandwidth or resolution. High quality examples for the lab are the Tektronix 7L13 or the HP-8553.

This equipment can now be used to study a simple test amplifier, or for that matter, any two-port device. This setup could also include a mixer if we assume the associated local oscillator to be included in the box labeled "device under test." For our example we will use a simple one-stage amplifier.

For the first experiment assume that one of the generators is turned off. Set the other generator to the frequency of interest, and adjust the output to a power of, say, −44 dBm. Remembering that the hybrid has an attenuation of 6 dB, the power available at the input to the amplifier is −50 dBm. We now tune the spectrum analyzer to the same frequency, and observe the output of the amplifier. With a signal of −30 dBm, the gain of the amplifier is determined to be 20 dB. Now we increase the generator output by 10 dB and notice an output of −20 dBm. The gain is still 20 dB. As this is continued, however, the gain decreases. For our hypothetical example, when the power available at the amplifier input is −10 dBm, we would expect an output 20 dB higher, or +10 dBm. Instead, only +9 dBm is observed. This is the point of 1 dB of gain compression and is the phenomenon which usually leads to desensitization, and ultimately, to blocking in a receiver.

It is interesting also to decrease the signal-generator output. For a time the output signal is observed in the analyzer at a level 20 dB above that of the generator. However, a point occurs eventually where the output energy is buried in the noise. This level will be determined by the noise figures of the amplifier and the spectrum analyzer and by the bandwidth of the system.[2]

Further Testing

The next experiment in the evaluation of the amplifier uses both signal generators to perform two-tone intermodulation tests. Two signals of equal level are injected into the input of the amplifier at slightly different frequencies, F_1 and F_2, and the output is studied. The so-called third-order, intermodulation-distortion products will appear at frequencies of $(2F_1 - F_2)$ and $(2F_2 - F_1)$.[3] Assume that the two input frequencies

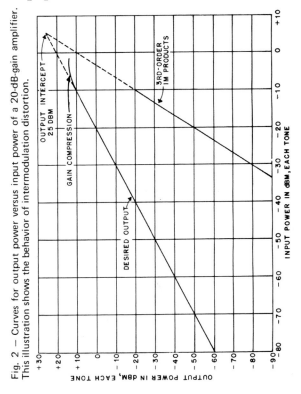

Fig. 2 — Curves for output power versus input power of a 20-dB-gain amplifier. This illustration shows the behavior of intermodulation distortion.

are 14,040 and 14,060 kHz. The third-order IM products will then appear at 14,020 and 14,080 kHz.

Assume that the input power to the amplifier is −20 dBm for each of the input "tones." If the spectrum analyzer is set to sweep from 14 to 14.1 MHz, the desired outputs of 0 dBm each are seen, indicating again that the amplifier has 20 dB of gain. The hypothetical amplifier also produces signals at '020 and '080 at a level of −50 dBm. In this case, the IM products are 50 dB down from each of the two tones. Since the peak envelope power (PEP) of the output is 6 dB above each of two equal tones in a two-tone test, the IM would be 56 dB below the PEP output. Although the latter definition is often used by manufacturers of amateur gear, the more conventional designation will be used in this article.

The really interesting property of inter-modulation distortion is the way the distortion levels change as the drive power changes. If 10 dB of input power is subtracted from each signal-generator output, the two major outputs will decrease by 10 dB. However, the distortion products will decrease by 30 dB to −80 dBm each.[4] The IM is now 70 dB down from each of the desired output tones.

The output power may be plotted as a function of the input power of the tones in a graph of the kind shown in Fig. 2. In this curve, the abscissa shows the input power for each tone. The ordinate (vertical axis) represents output power. Two curves are shown. The upper one is merely the level of each of the desired outputs, while the steeper curve represents the power output of each of the distortion products. From the first experiment we found that our output ceased to be linear at an output of +9 dBm (1 dB gain-compression) point). Hence, it is not meaningful to extend the measurements to higher power levels. However, we can extrapolate each of the two curves beyond the powers where we actually do measurements. These portions of the curve are shown dotted in Fig. 2. The result of this extension of the curves is that the two plots eventually cross each other. The output power associated with this intersection is called the third-order, IM-output intercept, or the IM intercept. This number is a very useful figure of merit for the designer, for it defines essentially the IM performance of the amplifier for all power levels. In the example the intercept point is +25 dBm. Knowing the intercept, output power "X" dB below the intercept will lead to IM products which are 2"X" dB down from each of two equal tones.[5]

In the first experiment gain compression was measured using only one signal generator. The same experiment can be performed with two tones. One generator is set for a medium-level output, such as −50 dBm. The other generator is moved 10 or 20 kHz away from the first, and its amplitude is increased until the first signal, as observed in the spectrum analyzer, decreases by 1 dB.

Cross Modulation

Cross modulation can be measured in a similar fashion. The first generator is set to deliver a cw output of −50 dBm. The second generator is set up for amplitude modulation at a 30% level. The output power of the second generator is increased until a 1% modulation appears on the first signal. The difficulty encountered with cross-modulation measurements arises from the fact that many signal generators create (unwanted) additional modulation sidebands. These can confuse the results seen on the spectrum analyzer. The best cure is to run the output of the second generator (the one with modulation) through a crystal filter which will pass the carrier and the desired modulation sidebands, but not the higher order sidebands.

The foregoing phenomena will limit the ability of the amplifier to handle strong signals. If this amplifier were, for example, the rf amplifier in a communications receiver, we would hear the IM-distortion products in the receiver during such an experiment. However, we have said nothing about dynamic range. This will depend not only upon the amplifier ability to handle strong signals, but also upon its capacity to work simultaneously with small signals, which have not been specified. This will depend, in this experiment, upon the noise figures of the amplifier and spectrum analyzer, and upon the system bandwidth. Blanket statements sometimes found in the "ham" literature claim that a given amplifier has, for example, a "140-dB dynamic range." Such comments are meaningless.

Receiver Measurements

The experiments presented in the foregoing discussion can be extended easily to the study of a receiver. The appropriate test setup is shown in Fig. 3, where the amplifier under test and the spectrum analyzer of Fig. 1 have been replaced by the receiver and an audio voltmeter.

The fundamental discussion used a hypothetical amplifier which was "designed" to yield numbers which were typical but consistent with simple arithmetic for ease of explanation. The example used to illustrate the receiver measurements, on the other hand, is quite real, being the writer's home-built, solid-state cw receiver.[6] The apparatus used

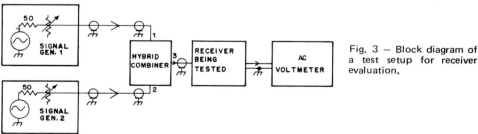

Fig. 3 — Block diagram of a test setup for receiver evaluation.

for evaluation was the collection of lab-quality gear mentioned earlier.

The first experiment is to measure the receiver equivalent noise floor. This is done by means of a single generator which is tuned to the same frequency as the receiver. Output from the generator is increased until the ac voltmeter at the audio-output jack of the receiver shows a 3-dB increase. In the writer's receiver, the input level available at the antenna terminal was -142 dBm. This measurement indicates the minimum signal which could be detected with the receiver. This level is defined as that which will produce the same audio-output power as the internally generated receiver noise. Hence the term noise "floor."

This measurement was cross-checked by using lab-quality equipment to determine the noise figure of the receiver. The two measurements corresponded within 1 dB. The noise figure was about 6 dB.

The noise floor of -142 dBm measured for the writer's receiver is typical of many of the receivers on the market with cw filters being used. With a "tangential sensitivity" of -142 dBm, these receivers will show a 10-dB signal-to-noise ratio with an input signal of approximately .06 microvolt. Rarely are commercial receivers specified so closely, even though they may be capable of this sensitivity. Much better sensitivity is possible. However, it is generally pointless in receivers for the hf bands. Noise figures as high as 20 dB are often suitable up to the 7-MHz band for use in locations plagued with high antenna-noise levels. Even on the ten-meter band, noise figures under 8 or 10 dB are rarely usable.

The next measurement concerns blocking. Both signal generators are used. One is set for a weak signal of roughly -110 dBm (S5 or so), and the receiver is tuned to this signal. The other generator is set about 20 kHz away from the desired frequency, and is increased in amplitude until the receiver output drops by 1 dB. This occurred at a level of -21 dBm, or 121 dB above the noise floor in the author's receiver. This measurement is somewhat suspect with the writer's receiver, since the stop-band attenuation of the first crystal filter is not this good. A blocking measurement is indicative of the signal level which may be tolerated at the antenna terminal without rendering the receiver totally useless.

Two-Tone IM Tests

The more enlightening measurement is to evaluate the two-tone IM performance of the receiver. For this measurement it is often useful to place a step attenuator between the hybrid coupler and the receiver. This allows two equal tones to be varied at the same time. The two signal generators were adjusted for an output of -10 dBm each at 14,040 and 14,060 kHz. The receiver was tuned to 14,080. An IM product was noted immediately. The step attenuator was adjusted until the IM product produced an output which was 3 dB above the noise level. This is similar to the measurement of the noise floor, where the signal is tangential

with the noise. This occurred for input signals of -57 dBm., or 85 dB above the noise floor. Hence, the two-tone *dynamic range* of the receiver is 85 dB. This figure is one of the most significant parameters which can be specified for a receiver: it is a measure of the range of signals that can be tolerated while producing essentially *no undesired spurious responses*. It is generally a conservative evaluation, for other effects such as "crossmod" or blocking will occur only for signals well outside the dynamic range of the receiver. Also, when a receiver is optimized for dynamic range, it is generally close to optimum for immunity from these other stronger and undesired responses.

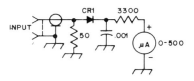

Fig. 4 — Circuit of a simple rf power meter. Full-scale sensitivity is approximately +17 dBm. See text for calibration details.

If the bandwidth of the receiver is changed, the dynamic range will change. For example, if the bandwidth of the receiver is increased by a factor of 10, the equivalent noise floor will increase by 10 dB. However, it will not be necessary to increase the two primary input tones by 10 dB in order to bring the IM response back up to a level tangential with the noise floor. (Note the curve in Fig. 2, where IM products climb three times as steeply as do the inputs.)[7] On the other hand, an attenuator ahead of the receiver will not change the dynamic range. Rather, it will shift it toward higher power.

Another useful measurement is the noise-modulation performance of the receiver.[8,9] This is done with a signal generator set 10 or 20 kHz away from the receiver frequency. The output level of the generator is brought up until a slight increase in

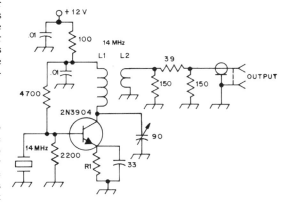

Fig. 5 — Diagram of a test oscillator which is suitable for making IMD measurements. L1 has 24 turns of No. 22 enam. wire on an Amidon T50-6 toroid core. L2 is 3 turns of No. 22 enam. wire over L1. R1 is selected to provide the desired output amount (220 ohms is a typical value).

the audio-noise output of the receiver is noted. This output is the result of noise from the receiver local oscillator, *or* from the signal-generator output mixing in the front-end mixer. In order to remove noise from the generator, the ideal measurement approach is to run the generator output through a very narrow crystal filter prior to application to the receiver.

Since a good crystal filter was not available at 14 MHz, only a qualitative noise-modulation experiment was done. A generator was set 100 dB above the receiver noise floor, and a slight increase in receiver output was noted 10 kHz away. The receiver was then tuned toward the generator frequency. When the two were within about 2 kHz of each other the noise output started to increase dramatically. At 1-kHz spacing, a beat note was first heard. While this measurement is not completely meaningful, because of the lack of a suitable crystal filter, it did show that the dynamic range of the receiver was not being compromised by local-oscillator noise. Noise-modulation effects are quite often the ultimate limitation in receivers, especially where very steep-skirted crystal filters are used in the i-f.

Home-Constructed Measurement Gear

The tests outlined earlier are performed easily if high quality lab test gear is at hand. However, meaningful tests can also be done in the home lab when using relatively simple equipment which an amateur can build. While the accuracy of such measurements will be compromised over the results obtainable with the higher quality apparatus, the results will be useful in receiver optimization. If care is used in the design, construction, and calibration of the equipment, the results may even be surprisingly accurate.

The intent of this section is to outline the kinds of measurement techniques which may be applied in the home lab. It is the purpose here to demonstrate feasability rather than to present projects for duplication. Hence, in the interest of brevity, many of the details will not be presented.

The basic requirement for performing a receiver evaluation is to provide stable signals to the receiver which have *well known power-output amounts*. Hence, the essential underlying problem is one of rf power measurements. Shown in Fig. 4 is a simple rf power meter which has a full-scale sensitivity of approximately 50 mW, or +17 dBm. This unit is the ultimate in simplicity, consisting of nothing more than a 50-ohm termination, a hot-carrier diode, one resistor, one capacitor, and a meter. Weiss[10] pointed out that power meters of this kind may be calibrated with dc. This is based upon the observation that the circuit is essentially a peak-reading voltmeter. For example, a power of 50 mW into a 50-ohm resistor would result from a peak voltage of 2.24 volts across the resistor. Hence, a dc voltage of 2.24 across the 50-ohm resistor would yield an equivalent meter reading. A dc calibration of the writer's power meter agreed within 0.5 dB of a more careful calibration with lab-quality equipment. Clearly, a gadget of this kind is a real workhorse in the amateur lab.

Shown in Fig. 5 is a simple crystal-controlled oscillator which is suitable for IM measurements. This circuit is virtually identical with that used in many QRP transmitters. The output is obtained through a 6-dB, 50-ohm attenuator. This serves the purpose of providing a little buffering, and ensuring that the output impedance is close to 50 ohms. A pair of these oscillators will be required for IM and blocking measurements.

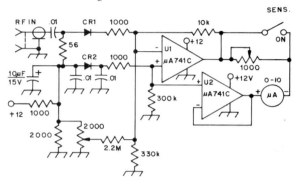

Fig. 6 — Circuit for a square-law detector. The sensitivity is below −26 dBm. See text for information on CR1 and CR2.

Once one of these oscillators is built, the emitter resistor may be adjusted for an output power of +7 to +10 dBm. Lower power levels are then obtained easily with a step attenuator. Such a device is constructed easily from inexpensive slide switches, half-watt 5% tolerance carbon resistors, and an enclosure fabricated from scrap pc board. Suitable units are described by Daughters and Alexander.[11] Although simple, these attenuators are surprisingly accurate, and are flat well into the vhf range. The unit used in the author's shack has eight sections with cumulative amounts of 1, 2, 3, 6, 10, 10, and 10 dB, yielding a maximum attenuation of 42 dB.

It is useful to measure much lower rf power directly. Shown in Fig. 6 is a relatively simple rf detector which is capable of detecting signals as low as −26 dBm. The basis of this "microwatt meter" is a diode, CR1, which is biased with a standing current of about 20 microamperes.[12] The key to achieving good sensitivity is to bias the diode from a low-impedance dc source. This is achieved by means of an operational amplifier, U1, with feedback. A second similar diode, CR2, is used for temperature compensation, although it has no rf applied to it. The other op amp, U2, merely provides a low-impedance reference for the meter. This instrument is calibrated easily while using one of the oscillators shown in Fig. 5 (and with the step attenuator). Although hot-carrier diodes were used ultimately, 1N914s gave similar sensitivity.

Note that a bootstrapping process is now being used for calibration. Initially a dc measurement was employed to calibrate a high-level power meter. This meter was then used to calibrate a high-level rf source. This source is then attenuated and used to calibrate a more sensitive detector. The

July 1975

process may be continued an arbitrary number of times, although the errors in the measurements will accumulate.

The low-level power meter of Fig. 6 can be extended to lower levels with suitable amplifiers of either broadband or narrow-band design. A broadband amplifier using three 2N5179s is included with the author's detector. It provides a sensitivity of under −60 dBm with a 3-dB ripple, and a bandwidth of 50 MHz. This combination has turned out to be an extremely useful general-purpose measurement tool. When used with a signal generator and a step attenuator, for example, filters may be evaluated over a 50-dB range. A small loop of wire at the end of a piece of coax will serve as a super-sensitive "rf sniffer." A suitable bank of filters could make the machine function as a rudimentary spectrum analyzer.

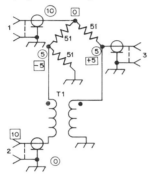

Fig. 7 — Illustration of a hybrid coupler. The isolation properties result from bridge action and the balun behavior of T1. The latter consists of 10 bifilar turns of light-gauge enamel wire on a 0.37-inch OD ferrite toroid core.

A workable hybrid combiner is shown in Fig. 7. This box is nothing more than a simple rf bridge. The three ports are labeled the same as was the hybrid unit used in Figs. 1 and 3. Shown in circles are the rf voltages at various points in the circuit, resulting from a 10-volt excitation at port 1. Similarly, in square boxes are the signals resulting from 10 volts of rf at port 2. The isolation transformer is wound on a ferrite toroid (Amidon FT-37-12-125) with a permeability of 125. A lower permeability powdered-iron core should not be used.

As might be expected, the hybrid device can be used also as an rf bridge. In this "return-loss bridge" mode, rf excitation is applied to port 1, the load to be adjusted to 50 ohms is connected to port 3, and the detector is tied to port 2. The virtue of such a bridge is that measurements can be made at very low power levels.

The most difficult and critical item to build and calibrate is an rf source which can be used to measure the noise floor of the receiver under test. A circuit suitable for this purpose is shown in Fig. 8. Again, a simple crystal-controlled oscillator is used as the rf source. However, in this case the oscillator must be extremely well shielded and decoupled from the battery. The latter should always be used for a power supply. Significant attenuation is provided by the enclosure which houses the oscillator. The unit is built in a box made from scraps of double-clad pc board. After the attenuator resistors are adjusted to provide something close to an S7 signal in a receiver, the box is soldered shut, crystal included. Several partitions are used in the attenuator portion of the circuit.

While this low-level source could, in principle, be calibrated with an extension of the bootstrap process used to calibrate the rest of the equipment, the errors would probably be excessive. A better method would be to borrow a calibrated signal generator from a local amateur. Many such units have appeared on the surplus market, or through the MARS program, and should not be hard to locate. Then, the low-level source of Fig. 8 can be compared with the signal generator in a receiver.

The crystal-controlled source, once calibrated, will be every bit as good as all but the best signal generators, for the leakage will be quite low. No output should be detectable in a fairly well-shielded receiver when the two units are grounded together. Attaching only the receiver antenna post to the homemade generator output terminal should yield a detectable signal. This source can then be used with the step attenuator for tangential-sensitivity measurements, or directly without attenuation as the "desired" signal in blocking measurements. Even if it is not possible to calibrate this source, it will be quite useful for comparative measurements.

The author's low-level source has an output of −112 dBm at 14 MHz. Used in conjunction with the home-constructed step attenuator, the measurement results agree with those obtained with lab-quality instrumentation, within one dB.

The final item needed for receiver evaluation is an ac voltmeter. A simple unit is shown in Fig. 9.

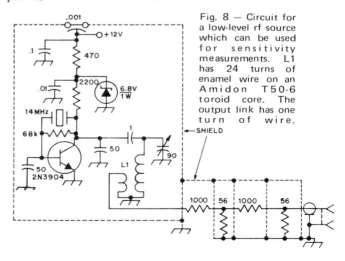

Fig. 8 — Circuit for a low-level rf source which can be used for sensitivity measurements. L1 has 24 turns of enamel wire on an Amidon T50-6 toroid core. The output link has one turn of wire.

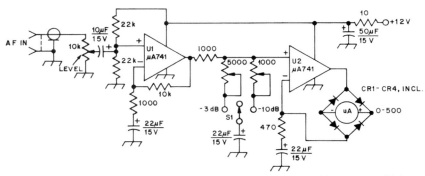

Fig. 9 — Simple audio voltmeter. CR1-CR4, incl., are 1N914s. M1 is a 500-μA meter. S1 is a spdt toggle switch (center off).

This equipment is not calibrated on an absolute basis. However, 3 dB and 10 dB of attenuation can be switched in for measurement purposes. The internal adjustments are made easily by temporarily tacking a 51-ohm resistor across the input terminal, then driving the input with the step attenuator. Audio power is applied to the step attenuator from an audio generator with a −10-dB 50-ohm pad in the output.

Conclusions

With the inexpensive modern semiconductors available to the radio amateur, high performance receivers can now be built. However, the "ultimate" receivers will come only from those builders who are willing to perform careful measurements during their design efforts. Ideally, these measurements are performed best with the high quality lab instruments presently available. However, a suitable job can also be done with rather simple homemade equipment if it is calibrated carefully.

Using readily available components, and care in measurement, it should be possible for the experimentally inclined amateur to build a receiver with a dynamic range of 100 dB or more. Using more exotic components, the current state of the art is probably somewhere around 140 dB. Receivers of this caliber, however, are not available on the amateur market.

Considering the fact that the measurements needed to specify blocking and dynamic range can be performed by the amateur who uses simple equipment he has built, it does not seem unreasonable that we, as consumers, demand more realistic and complete specifications from the receiver manufacturers. In a similar vein, it is this writer's opinion that similar data should be included in ARRL evaluations of Recent Equipment. This would not only be useful to the potential customer, but also to the builder who needs a goal for his own work.

References

[1] Goodman, *QST* for Jan., 1957.

[2] The noise figure of an amplifier, a mixer, or a receiver, is the input signal-to-noise ratio divided by the output signal-to-noise ratio. The input noise is usually assumed as originating in a resistor at a temperature of 290 degrees Kelvin. The reader unfamiliar with the definition and the subtleties of the noise-figure concept should review Nelson's, "A Little Bit About Noise," *73 Magazine* for January, 1967.

[3] The transfer characteristics of most real amplifiers can be expressed as a power series:

$$V_{out} = K_0 + K_1 V_{in} + K_2 V_{in}^2 + K_3 V_{in}^3 + \ldots$$

The term of normal interest is the linear term $K_1 V_{in}$. The other terms describe the distortions in the amplifier. If two input signals of equal amplitude, A at frequencies f_1 and f_2 are considered, the input signal is

$$V_{in} = A[\cos \omega_1 t + \cos \omega_2 t]$$

where $\omega_N = 2\pi f_n$

If this input signal is substituted into the cubic term of the power series, $K_3 V_{in}^3$, a number of terms result, including some of the form

$$V_{out} \propto A^3 \quad \cos(2f_1 - f_2) 2\pi t + \cos(2f_2 - f_1) 2\pi t$$

These are the so-called third-order intermodulation distortion products. A more complete outline of this analysis is found in *Electronic and Radio Engineering*, Chapter 10, McGraw-Hill, 1955.

[4] It follows directly from the analysis of footnote 3 that

$P_{IM} = K P_{out}^3$. Taking the log of this expression,

P_{IM} (in dBm.) = $3 P_{out}$(dBm) + $10 \log K$.

P_{IM} is the power of the IM product and P_{out} is the desired amplifier output power.

[5] Measuring the output intercept allows the constant of footnote 4 to be evaluated. The numbers presented in the example used in the text are typical of a quality bipolar transistor amplifier biased for a collector current of 20 mA, with a collector load resistance of 50 ohms.

[6] Hayward, "A Competition-Grade CW Receiver," *QST* for March and April, 1974.

(Continued on page 43)

Dynamic Range *(Continued from page 21)*

[7] It may be shown that if the bandwidth is changed from B to B' the dynamic range, D will go to D' where:

$$(D'/D) = (B/B')^{2\ 3}$$

Here, the dynamic ranges are expressed as algebraic ratios rather than in dB.

[8] A good discussion of noise in oscillators is given by Priestley, "Oscillator Noise and Its Effect on Receiver Performance," *Radio Communication* for July, 1970.

[9] The on-the-air effects of noise modulation are outlined in Part I of footnote 6.

[10] Weiss, *Ham Radio Magazine* for Oct., 1973.

[11] Daughters and Alexander, *73 Magazine* for January, 1967.

[12] This detector works essentially in the square-law region. If the series of footnote 3 is considered with a sine-wave input at a single frequency, it may be shown that a dc term results in the output from the quadradic term, $K_2 V_{in}^2$.

+[EDITOR'S NOTE: Concerning the intercept-point method, agreement between experiment and theory will be satisfactory with the devices normally encountered in receiver applications. Diode balanced mixers and Class A amplifiers would be typical examples. However, the method should not be considered a suitable one for *all* circuits where nonlinearities exist. For example, class AB or B linear power amplifiers often exhibit IMD products (with a two-tone test signal) that may increase with additional input-signal level, then drop, then increase again. From a mathematical outlook, this means that the amplitude of the third-order distortion products are not directly proportional to the cube of the signal voltage, but behave in a more complex manner. Therefore, it should not be assumed that the third-order products will *always* increase by 30 dB for every 10 dB of signal-power increase.]

Amateur Radio, Modes and Networks

By Ward Silver, NØAX

Modes in the Second Century

Let's start with modes. The story of Amateur Radio is a long and fascinating tale of modes — new ones constantly appearing and evolving, old ones falling into disfavor or staying active on the bands. When the regulations have allowed them to do so, amateurs have been eager to adopt, adapt and invent modes. Just tune through the "digital segments" of today's bands and you'll get an earful of amateur ingenuity.

But what is a "mode," really? The FCC's method of defining emission designators is the standard for establishing whether hams are permitted to transmit a particular type of signal (see **wireless.fcc.gov/services/index.htm?job=licensing_2&id=industrial_business** or just do an Internet search for "FCC emission designators"). There is a simpler, if less precise, approach that enables a broader discussion.

Hams can think of a mode as a package of three elements that make up a communication "pipe." The first element is the air link (what is actually transmitted) describing the signal you would observe at the terminals of an antenna. The second element is the information carried by the signal that a receiver would extract, such as characters or speech. The final element is the protocol or procedural rules that govern the exchange of data through the pipe — anything from CW prosigns and Q signals to the packet structure and error-correction rules of the latest version of PACTOR.

Hams are nothing if not inventive, and so there are a multitude of "pipes" on the bands. Some are adaptations or adoptions of commercial or military technology, such as RTTY, which combined mechanical teleprinters with FSK and AFSK modulation of amateur transmitters. CW and AM date from the time when there was little distinction between "amateur" and "professional" so we all pitched in to push the state of the art along. Packet radio's AX.25 is an amateur adaption of the commercial X.25 protocol, extended to allow data transmission over audio channels. SSTV and CLOVER and PSK31 (and numerous other digital modes) were purely amateur inventions. D-STAR was developed under a program sponsored by the Japan Amateur Radio League (JARL) specifically for amateur digital voice and data. The list is long: the modes and their variations supported in the digital communications software package *fldigi* by David Freese, W1HKJ, (**www.w1hkj.com/fldigi.html**) number approximately 100!

A review of the literature reveals a rapid increase in the number and type of digital modes, including digital voice, that began in the

Amateur Radio teletype pioneer John Evans Williams, W2BFD, is shown testing a high-speed paper tape sending unit for his 2 meter teletype system in 1948. The first amateur two-way RTTY contacts took place in 1946.

1980s and continues through the present day with no sign of slowing down. What happened? Two things — loosening of restrictions on data encoding and the application of network technology to create novel and useful digital systems.

A New Kind of "Net" Operation

Prior to 1978, US and Canadian amateurs were restricted to using the archaic (by that time) 5-bit Baudot code and radioteletype. After receiving approval to use ASCII codes from their telecommunication regulators, Canadian amateurs began developing packet radio and terminal node controllers. The initial Montreal Protocol eventually led to AX.25, so-named because it was the amateur version of the wired-network protocol X.25.

The FCC relaxed the restrictions on US amateurs in 1980 and the race was on! Packet radio spread like wildfire throughout the decade, developing into an international network with bulletin boards, digipeaters and messaging systems all operating over Amateur Radio. Although it was overtaken by the development of the Internet, packet radio and several of the systems built around it were adopted commercially, first for low-bandwidth data and then at higher rates, such as in the Mobitex and GPRS systems.

There was no reason that other packet protocols couldn't be used. Bell 202 AFSK encoding over FM voice links was well-suited for 1200-baud data, but the AX.25 packet structure could encapsulate other protocols. Examples include Phil Karn, KA9Q's adaptation of TCP/IP (the main Internet transport protocols) in his *NOS* software, and *ROSE*, which was based on aspects of the X.25 protocol. (More information about the history of packet radio is available at **www.tapr.org/pr_intro.html**.)

This is the original TNC that started the Amateur Radio packet system. Designed by the Vancouver (British Columbia) Amateur Digital Communications Group, the bare board and parts could be purchased as a kit.

During this period and all through the 1980s, there was a very strong synergy between amateur packet radio and the larger field of computer networking. Many of the principal developers of early amateur packet radio also worked professionally in some networking-related field and ideas originally proposed for ham radio often found a home in the non-ham world, as well. For example, Karn's TCP/IP software was developed primarily for ham use, but it developed quite a following in the non-ham world for Internet access over dialup modems. Both worlds contributed a lot of operational experience, with hams focusing on making it work over low quality channels, mobile/portable operation, and the like. As a result, it's very hard to separate the ham from non-ham worlds of computer networking because they were so tightly interwoven during their early development. Amateur Radio deserves a great deal of credit for its role in contributing to the now-ubiquitous, planet-wide communication system.

As the Internet spread, the amateur packet network shrank but packet radio's robust characteristics and inexpensive equipment requirements enabled the development of two other groundbreaking systems: *APRS* (by Bob Bruninga, WB4APR, **www.aprs.org**) and *PacketCluster* (by Dick Newell, AK1A). The former

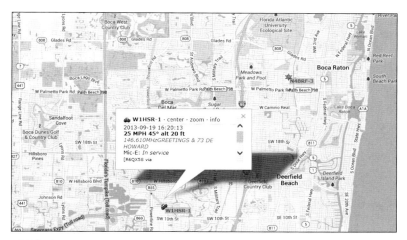

APRS, the Automatic Packet Reporting System, allows the collection and display of data from individual stations who transmit position and other data periodically via packet radio. Here, a map from the website aprs.fi shows the track of Howard, W1HSR, driving near his home in Florida. (Map courtesy of Google Maps)

combined position data from a navigation system with the packet radio system of relay stations known as digipeaters to create a tracking system in which the transmitting station information could be viewed using a web browser. *PacketCluster* was a specialization of the bulletin board systems that were popular before the World Wide Web became ubiquitous. Users connected to a cluster system and received "spots" — information about DX and contest station activity that helped them compete. The cluster functionality has been carried over into Internet-based systems, such as DX Summit (**www.dxsummit.fi**). Both APRS and *PacketCluster* have been the basis for widely used commercial products.

By the early 1990s, it was obvious that computing and networking technology was developing so fast that trying to manage each new combination of modulation, encoding and protocol was completely impractical. As a result, in October 1995 the FCC released §97.309(a)(4) which specifies that amateur stations transmitting RTTY or data signals "…may use any digital code that has its technical characteristics publicly documented." In other words, as long as bandwidth, symbol rate and emission type rules were satisfied, a ham could invent new digital technology, publish its specification online, and start using it on the air. (A list of such publications is available on the ARRL website at **www.arrl.org/technical-characteristics**.)

Taking advantage of low-cost consumer wireless data equipment, hams are today building high-speed networks using channels on the 2.4 GHz and 5.8 GHz amateur bands that are shared with unlicensed services. Wireless routers and similar gear are used to construct systems such as Broadband-Hamnet and HSMM-Mesh (**hsmm-mesh.org**). Amateur networks taking advantage of amplifiers and high-gain antennas span entire regions with high-speed data links.

Connections to the Future

While the introduction of new modes and systems continues at a rapid pace, there continue to be regulatory and technical obstacles in the path of digital Amateur Radio. As these are addressed, hams will proceed in accordance with the rules, whatever they may be.

The regulatory challenges of the near future will be first-and-foremost those of retaining amateur access to the sought-after VHF/UHF/microwave bands. Above 1 GHz, amateur use of these bands has been light due to the cost of equipment and limited communication opportunities. Just as consumer demand is making low-cost components and equipment available, the same interests want and need more spectrum. It will be a struggle to retain enough of our allocations to support meaningful utilization and innovation.

Other administrative obstacles regard bandwidth and symbol rate limits. There is an ongoing discussion between the FCC, the ARRL, and other interested parties to determine how to proceed in the US. While other countries have fewer restrictions on digital modes, US amateurs are still limited to 300 baud (symbols

A wireless router and "barbeque grill" antenna (not shown) for the 2.4 GHz band's amateur channels, supported by a 12 V battery-powered UPS, signal mirror and compass, are all that is needed to set up a high-speed network link over a 9 mile path. [Lynn Jelinski, AG4UI, photo]

per second) on the HF bands and other limits apply on the VHF/UHF bands. (For example, PACTOR-4 and ROS — weak signal radio chat — are illegal in the US due to limits on symbol rate and spread-spectrum transmissions, but legal elsewhere.) It is likely that some relaxation will occur in the next few years, but the exact form of new rules is yet to be determined.

There are also questions about the type of data that can be transmitted and about messaging versus speech for digital voice systems such as D-STAR, amateur versions of the Digital Radio Mondiale (DRM) system, and the new *CODEC 2* for HF digital voice by David Rowe, VK5DGR. Proprietary techniques including codecs, protocols and data compression cause the open amateur systems to collide with copyright and patent restrictions. That these questions are being asked is a sign that innovation is alive and well in the digital age of Amateur Radio.

Technical challenges abound, as well. HF channel characteristics are notorious for the distortions and noise they inflict on digital signals. Noise and fading make error-detection and error-correction crucial to developing a useful communications system. Long-distance communication must often take place at very low signal-to-noise ratios, requiring sophisticated encoding and correlation schemes to extract data. Codes designed for moonbounce (JT65) at VHF and above are being applied to digital operation on the lower HF bands (JT9) where atmospheric noise and not path loss is the primary concern. Users of wideband modes such as spread spectrum, which are limited to the upper UHF bands and microwaves, face difficulties from primary-secondary allocation issues, limits in band size, available transmitter power and other problems.

Finally, there are open questions of hybridization with the Internet and other non-amateur technologies. Should ham radio systems embrace or avoid "back-channel" connections that use commercial networks? If a hybrid system is created, is it "real" ham radio? What about transmitting non-amateur data over amateur links? With each step we have to examine our principles, our history, and the need to experiment and push boundaries. Looking back, we find that with every major advance in communication technologies, concerns were raised about how to integrate them with Amateur Radio as it was then practiced: spark-to-CW, AM-to-SSB, packet radio, email systems. And with each advance, hams figured out how to maintain that special ham radio "flavor" to preserve our unique combination of experimentation, enjoyment and utility. I have confidence that we will continue to meet the myriad challenges and persevere in "advancing the radio and communications arts" as we have for 100 years.

"What Is Single-Sideband Telephony?" by Byron Goodman, W1DX

By Ward Silver, NØAX

Along with numerous other advances made during the years of the Second World War, amateurs were also waking up to a brand-new mode of phone operation: single-sideband or SSB. Better known as those "Donald Duck" signals that couldn't be translated into recognizable speech by AM detectors, SSB — then called SSSC for single-sideband, suppressed-carrier — was a whole new world for amateur voice operation. So new, in fact, that most of the January 1948 issue of *QST* was devoted to explaining it technically and operationally.

Though SSB had been described in *QST* in 1935 by James Lamb, W1CEI, and the first amateur SSB stations were on the air in 1933-1934, the mode remained on the sidelines, so to speak, until wartime technology improvements made it practical for amateur use. SSB was relatively new in the commercial and military worlds, too. Using complex (for the time) crystal filters for removing the unwanted sideband and carrier was within the capabilities of commercial and military users but were still rare in amateur equipment. The Hartley method of creating the SSB signal with 90-degree phase shifts had been invented in 1924 but, as analog designers well know, was hard to realize in a product. The Weaver method of using low-pass filters and quadrature mixers was not described in the literature until 1956. In that same year General Curtis Lemay, W6EZV, coordinated tests comparing AM to SSB for aircraft use in which SSB performed far better, giving momentum to the military's use of SSB.

Eldico introduced an SSB transmitter in 1950 and numerous manufacturers such as Central Electronics, Hallicrafters, RME and others were advertising SSB equipment throughout the 1950s. The introduction of the Collins KWM-1 SSB transceiver in 1957 signaled the high point of early SSB equipment manufactured for the amateur market. The change was on and by the mid-1960s, most amateurs had converted to (or could at least use) SSB. Byron Goodman's April 1958 *QST* Product Review of the KWM-1 was correct in predicting "the end of one era and the beginning of another."

The changes ushered in by SSB were system-wide, just as the "single-signal receiver" simultaneously raised the standard level of performance and the technological level of amateur equipment. At a minimum, receivers now needed a BFO to

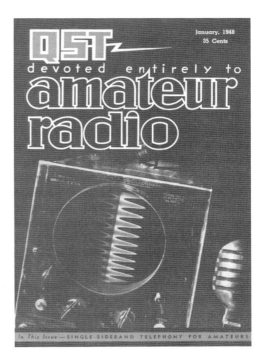

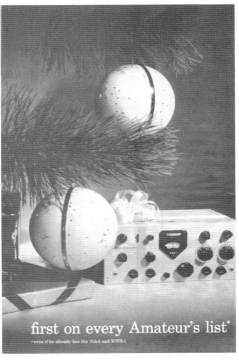

The Collins KWM-1 was a compact CW and SSB transceiver suitable for home or mobile use. It offered state-of-the-art performance in a single piece of equipment, spelling the end of the era of the separate transmitter and receiver.

replace the missing carrier that was filtered (or phased) away in the transmitter. Higher receiver precision and stability were required, too, better than 10 to 20 cycles while listening. This was state-of-the-art at the time.

There were myriad other changes required, as well. First and foremost, a convention for which of the sidebands (upper or lower) to use had to be established. Numerous suggestions about mixing schemes and sideband inversion have been put forth, but the standard for using LSB below 10 MHz and USB above seems to have come from the international commercial environment, captured in CCIR Recommendation 249 (1959).

Amateurs also had to change their transmitting amplifier chains as well, doing away with Class C designs and multipliers in favor of "linear" amplifiers operating in Class A or B and frequency mixing designs that shifted the sideband frequency but did not alter the relationship of frequencies within the sideband. The need for sideband generation also had a major hand in pushing the adoption of crystal lattice filters in both receiving and transmitting equipment.

Operating also changed as the forest of carrier heterodynes gave way to a "nonspeech rumpus which the brain can readily ignore or reject," as Goodman suggests here. True, signals were definitely narrower, but the requirement for linear amplification gave QRM an opening, leading to terms like "splatter" and "buckshot." And with the carrier no longer being required, voice-break-in became possible and voice-operated-transmit (VOX) control circuits filled the pages of magazines and handbooks.

What Is Single-Sideband Telephony?

A Few Facts About the New 'Phone Technique

BY BYRON GOODMAN,* W1DX

THE history-making single-sideband suppressed-carrier transmissions of W6YX and WØTQK have aroused considerable interest in the transmission and reception of these signals, and well they might, since it is not at all unlikely that most of us will be using the system within a few years. The name describes the thing of course, but it doesn't tell all. Neither does this article, but it should give you a start toward understanding the stuff.

Everyone knows that a regular a.m. 'phone

• The year 1947 will go down in amateur radio history as one of the big ones, since it was in October of that year that the first amateur 14-Mc. single-sideband suppressed-carrier transmissions were made. But most hams would rather make history than read about it, so this article is intended to give you a nodding acquaintance with the principles involved in s.s.s.c. transmission and reception.

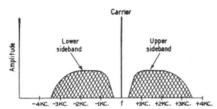

Fig. 1 — The normal a.m. signal consists of a carrier and a pair of sidebands. The crosshatched areas represent the frequency range of the sidebands.

signal takes up space frequency-wise that can be represented by the sketch in Fig. 1. The carrier frequency, designated by f, is a single frequency. The "sidebands" take up room on either side of this frequency, depending upon the audio frequencies present in the modulation. The crosshatched areas in Fig. 1 represent the frequencies occupied by the sidebands.

At the receiver, the usual practice is to center the carrier in the passband of the receiver, and to use a receiver with a response curve capable of passing both sidebands. This is shown in Fig. 2, where the sketch of Fig. 1 has been superimposed on a typical selectivity curve of a receiver. However, it is not at all necessary to receive *both* sidebands, and this fact has been used by McLaughlin [1] to reduce heterodyne interference. A response curve of a receiver capable of receiving only one sideband is shown in Fig. 2 as a dotted line. Under such conditions, nothing is omitted from the original signal, since one sideband is all that is required. As W1DBM aptly puts it, "both sidebands are saying the same thing." [2]

* Assistant Technical Editor, *QST*.
[1] McLaughlin, "Exit Heterodyne QRM," *QST*, Oct., 1947.
[2] Rand, "The Q5-er," *QST*, December, 1947.
[3] Crosby, "Exalted-Carrier Amplitude- and Phase-Modulation Reception," *Proc. I.R.E.*, Sept., 1945.

However, while one sideband can be eliminated without impairing the quality one iota, the *carrier* cannot be eliminated, or even reduced appreciably, if the modulation percentage is high. If, for example, the single-sideband receiver curve of Fig. 2 (the dotted line) were such that it cut into the carrier, the carrier would be reduced in the receiver. This in turn would give a signal that, so far as the detector was concerned, would look like an *overmodulated* signal, since the proper carrier-to-sideband proportions would not have been preserved. On the other hand, the sideband (or sidebands) can be reduced, leaving the carrier the same, with no ill effects other than to reduce the effective modulation percentage that the detector sees. This is the principle of "exalted-carrier" reception. [3]

The point that the carrier must be present in

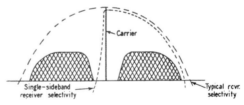

Fig. 2 — In normal reception, the a.m. signal is centered on the selectivity characteristic of the receiver. However, if the receiver has considerable selectivity, as shown by the dotted line, equally good reception is obtained by passing only one sideband through the receiver.

the receiver along with the sideband (or sidebands) before proper detection can take place is an important one to remember in this discussion.

Carrier Suppression

There is really no need to transmit the carrier of a 'phone signal, provided the carrier is put back

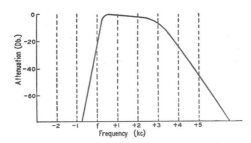

Fig. 3 — The filter required for sideband elimination requires very rapid attenuation in a range of about 1000 cycles. The characteristic shown above would be suitable for such work — the normal carrier frequency would be placed at *f*.

on the signal before audio detection takes place. Methods have been known for years for "suppressing" the carrier, and their effectiveness has been proven by a good record of commercial use. The two common types of modulators that suppress the carrier during modulation are the "balanced" modulator (using tubes) and the "ring" modulator (using diode rectifiers in a bridge or lattice arrangement). Both of these take the modulation frequencies and the carrier frequency and give an output that consists only of the sidebands (along with a few combinations of carrier *harmonics* that have to be filtered out). Of course the carrier suppression isn't perfect, but suppressions on the order of 40 to 60 db. are not difficult to obtain, and careful balancing has brought the figure up to 100 db.

But neither Johnny Q. Ham nor anyone else is going to get very far with a system that only suppresses the carrier. While it is easy to transmit, it is practically impossible to receive. The mathematics of the thing shows that the carrier has to be reinserted with the same *phase* relation to the sidebands that the original carrier had. This means, therefore, that it would have to have exactly the same *frequency and phase* relationship as the original carrier, and no frequency drift could be tolerated, since any at all would cause a phase change. So that's out the window.

However, the same mathematics shows that if *one* sideband is received, the carrier can be reinserted in *any* phase, and in practice the frequency can be off by 10 or 20 cycles without impairing the quality too much. That's more like it. While 10 or 20 cycles seems like incredible stability for a receiver, it isn't outside the realm of possibility at all and, in fact, receiver stability has been sneaking up on us over the years without our realizing it. But more of that later.

Sideband Suppression

There are two classical methods of eliminating one sideband. One is a brute-force method that

[4] Honnell, "Single-Sideband Generator," *Electronics*, Nov., 1945.

consists simply of lopping off one sideband by using a very selective filter. This is the method used by the commercials. Another more delicate and subtle system requires an elaborate arrangement incorporating 90-degree phase shifts of carrier and audio signals. It has been used,[4] but it isn't easy.

You can't just dismiss that filter with a sentence or two. In the first place, it has to have a characteristic similar to that shown in Fig. 3, and filters like that aren't easy to come by. The frequency *f* represents the carrier frequency at which the filter is used, and the important thing about the filter is the slope of the curve between "+0.5 kc." and "-0.5 kc." Notice that within this 1-kc. range the attenuation goes from 0 to about 50 db. The slope on the other side of the filter is unimportant, just so long as it permits the sideband to pass without excess attenuation. Filters with a characteristic like that of Fig. 3 are not easy to obtain, and the filter is usually designed for a low frequency, since the selectivity in cycles decreases as the frequency *f* is increased. The filter characteristic shown in the McLaughlin article[1] would be satisfactory, and this was obtained at 50 kc. Fifty or 75 kc. probably represents the upper frequency limit for effective sideband filters, unless one resorts to crystal lattice-type filters, infinite-rejection circuits and other complex dodges.

Frequency Changing

Our s.s.s.c. transmitter now begins to take shape. It will start off with a modulator that suppresses the carrier, and then we'll go through a filter that will lop off one sideband, after which we'll have to get the signal to the operating frequency and out on the air. Fig. 4 shows the signal as far as we've gone.

As mentioned earlier, this filtering of the sideband would be done at some low frequency, and we have the problem of getting to the operating frequency. We can't do it by frequency multiplication, any more than we can in conventional a.m. *after* modulation. So the next big point we run across is that you *heterodyne* the signal when you change frequency in s.s.s.c. work. This is old

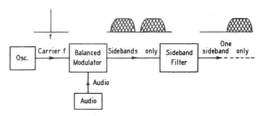

Fig. 4 — The basic system for obtaining an s.s.s.c. signal. The carrier and audio frequencies are fed into a balanced modulator, where the sidebands are generated minus the carrier. The signal is then passed through a filter that removes one sideband.

stuff, of course — we do it all the time in receivers and converters. So, if our output from the sideband filter is on 50 kc. and we are headed for 14,250 kc., we would feed the single sideband into a mixer with an oscillator running at, say, 600 kc. This would give beats of 550 and 650 kc. To use only one, we would run the output of the mixer through a 550-kc. filter (a stage of i.f. amplification). Then to get to 14,250, we would beat this signal against a 13,700-kc. oscillator and run the output through enough selective stages to wipe out the undesired 13,150-kc. signal. All this is shown in Fig. 5. To make the job of the filters a little easier, balanced modulators can be used for the mixers, so that the local-oscillator signal is eliminated in the output. In Fig. 5, the local-oscillator signal is shown in the output of each mixer, as would be the case in conventional mixer circuits.

It is also apparent from Fig. 5 that it is only necessary to change the frequency of the last local oscillator in order to change the output frequency. Thus a basic s.s.s.c. exciter and modulator would consist of the stages shown in Figs. 4 and 5. The frequencies wouldn't be the same, necessarily, but the principles involved would be. The entire unit would use receiving tubes and, for the most part, receiver components.

Amplification

It has been pointed out that frequency changing involves the use of heterodyning instead of multiplication in s.s.s.c. technique. We also have to forget about our cherished Class C amplifiers, because the s.s.s.c. must be amplified in a Class A or Class B stage; i.e., an amplifier that reproduces the input signal without distortion. But our receiver techniques are generally Class A, and Class B amplifiers are no strangers to the 'phone man who has been using one for a modulator for the past 14 years. We don't even have to worry about too-careful adjustment of these Class B amplifiers. They are more tolerant with no carrier, unlike the critical "linear" amplifiers everyone shies away from. And, unlike audio Class B amplifiers, they don't have to be push-pull.

So there you have the fundamentals at the transmitter end: carrier suppression in a balanced modulator, sideband rejection in a sharp filter, frequency changing by heterodyning, and amplification in Class A or Class B amplifiers.

Reception

The receiver end is a lead-pipe cinch. All you have to do is tune in the signal and put back the carrier in the right place! Fortunately, any communications receiver is set up to do this, although the technique seems a little strange at first. The first thing you do is turn off the a.v.c., although you can leave it on while you tune in the sideband if you want. You tune in the sideband, as indicated by maximum strength in the 'speaker (or maximum *swing* of the S-meter, if the a.v.c. is on). With a.v.c. off, switch on the b.f.o. and adjust its control, *not* the main tuning control, until the signal clears up and begins to sound like something human. As you vary the b.f.o., you will get various types of inverted speech and deep and falsetto voices, but when you hit it right the speech will sound as natural as any other signal. It may be necessary to back off the manual gain quite a bit, particularly if you have a weak b.f.o. in the receiver. In any event, it's a good idea to run with reduced i.f. gain, because you have no a.v.c. to hold the gain down in the receiver, and you can't afford to have any stage in the receiver overloaded, since the linearity will be destroyed.

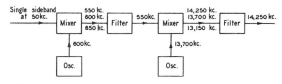

Fig. 5 — Frequency changing in an s.s.s.c. system is done by heterodyning the sideband to a new frequency and filtering out the undesired beat products. The diagram above shows how a single sideband might be taken from 50 kc. to an operating frequency of 14,250 kc.

The Advantages of S.S.S.C.

What does all this get you? Some of the benefits won't show up until a number of stations are using the system, but here are a few of the obvious advantages: Transmitting only one sideband, the receiver bandwidth has to be only half as great, for the same fidelity, as it does for double-sideband reception. This gives an immediate 3-db. improvement in signal-to-noise, since reducing the bandwidth by a factor of 2 decreases the noise by the same amount. The power required at the transmitter end for equivalent double- and single-sideband signals at the receiver is considerably less in the case of s.s.s.c. transmission. There is no carrier power to be supplied, and all of the power goes into the one signal-generating sideband. For example, a kilowatt 'phone using double sidebands and the usual carrier requires that a kilowatt of power be supplied to the r.f. amplifier plus the power consumed by the 500-watt modulator. The same signal is obtained at the receiver in the s.s.s.c. system by furnishing power to the final amplifier equal to what would be drawn by a Class B modulator capable of delivering 250 watts of audio. The saving in transmitter input is plenty! When you aren't talking you have no output signal, so there is no good reason why you can't carry on excellent duplex work right on your own frequency! With

(Continued on page 126)

Single-Sideband 'Phone

(Continued from page 15)

no heterodynes between carriers, there is no heterodyne interference, the big bugaboo of 'phone as practised today. This fact, coupled with the obvious one that your signal occupies only half the spectrum space it does with conventional a.m., will make room for many more 'phone signals in the same number of kilocycles. With selective receivers that pass only one sideband, the number of clear channels is exactly doubled, but there is still another advantage. Suppose the interfering station is only 500 cycles removed; i.e., the two carriers, if they were transmitted, would be separated by that amount. And suppose that the same relative sideband (upper and lower) had been suppressed in each case. The unwanted signal would ride through the receiver along with the desired one, but it would be completely unintelligible. It would only manifest itself as monkey chatter in the background, there would be no interfering heterodyne, and one signal could probably be copied through the other. You know what two equal-strength signals 500 cycles apart can do with conventional a.m. — now you can see why we're so enthusiastic about the possibilities of s.s.s.c.

With only a single sideband transmitted, you can expect less trouble with selective fading, the kind caused by the sidebands coming in with the wrong relative phase to each other and the carrier.

We promised to mention receiver stability. You will recall that the carrier has to be reinserted with an error of less than about 20 cycles for full naturalness, but the requirement is only about 50 cycles for intelligibility. For many years this seemed like an insurmountable obstacle in the way of amateur s.s.s.c., but it is no longer so. Our present receivers, after they are warmed up, are capable of such stability over the period of a transmission, as has been demonstrated by the satisfactory reception of W6YX and WØTQK by many stations. By using crystal-controlled high-frequency oscillators, we should have no trouble with s.s.s.c., even on 29 Mc. This improved stability of receivers has been sneaking up on us over the years, and it only took the transmissions of W6YX and WØTQK to show that amateur s.s.s.c. is here and practical!

"A New Narrow-Band Image Transmission System" by Copthorne MacDonald, W4ZII/2 (WA2BCW, VY2CM)

By Ward Silver, NØAX

With so many professional resources at work in the communications industry, truly new amateur inventions tend to be rare, but they *do* occur in a variety of fields. One such invention was slow-scan television, introduced in the August and September 1958 issues of *QST* by Copthorne MacDonald, then W4ZII, a student at the University of Kentucky. MacDonald had studied facsimile systems along with the experimental "Picture Phone" system from Bell Labs and a competing system from Dage Electronics. He decided that what those systems accomplished over wired networks, amateurs could do over a communications-quality voice channel and set to work in 1957.

A few months later, he had the prototype of a slow-scan television (SSTV) system assembled and working. The image was taken from a photographic negative by a cathode-ray tube (CRT) flying-spot scanner. The video output of the scanner amplitude modulated a 2000 Hz carrier (which then became a sub-carrier in the transmitted signal) with sidebands extending from 1000 to 3000 Hz that was the input signal to a regular amateur 'phone transmitter. A 120-line image could be transmitted every 6 seconds with a bandwidth sufficient for about 120 pixels in each line of the image. At the receiver, the output audio modulated the intensity of an electron beam sweeping across the face of a long-persistence P7 phosphor CRT. In an interesting twist, the initial testing of the system was done on the 11 meter band which was lost to amateurs shortly thereafter and became Citizen's Band in September of 1958.

Testing continued, and by 1961 it had become apparent that the AM-based system was too susceptible to noise and fading. The encoding of the image information was then changed to a constant-amplitude FM-based system in which the video intensity was represented by the audio frequency. A tone range of 1500 to 2300 Hz represented black to white, respectively. Sync pulses were sent as 1200 Hz tones with a short pulse (5 ms) acting as the horizontal sync (line-to-line synchronization) and a long pulse (30 ms) as the vertical or frame sync. This greatly improved image quality and remains the standard for analog monochrome SSTV to this day.

Not content to simply define a workable system, MacDonald then went on to develop buildable designs for a SSTV monitor (March 1964 *QST*) and a SSTV vidicon-based camera system (June, July and August 1964 *QST*). These designs laid the foundation of amateur analog SSTV that would anchor the mode for nearly four decades. It is safe to say that these four 1964 articles, preceded by the initial introduction in 1958 and the improved modulation system in 1961, were groundbreaking. SSTV also found its way into spacecraft systems used by NASA and other agencies, although in a different format than used by hams.

The self-contained, compact slow-scan monitor introduced by MacDonald in the March 1964 issue of *QST*. The monitor included the complete sync/video and display system for either received signals or the output of cameras or flying-spot scanners.

There are numerous current modes that comprise today's SSTV. The most popular analog modes are named "Martin" (European) and "Scottie" (North American) and both can transmit color images. A current list of variations (**www.sstv-handbook.com/download/sstv_05.pdf**) covers nearly three pages! In addition,

Color SSTV images are transmitted from the International Space Station (ISS) as part of the Amateur Radio program for astronauts. The downlink frequency is 145.800 MHz and operational news is available at ariss-sstv.blogspot.com.

amateurs have adapted Digital Radio Mondiale (DRM) — a digital data transfer protocol suitable for use on HF bands — to transfer image files, although this is more of a file-transfer mode than a video or image mode.

SSTV continues to evolve and find new applications, nearly 60 years after its appearance on the 11 meter band in 1957. An amateur SSTV station is installed and active on the International Space Station, transmitting images from orbit on the downlink frequency of 145.800 MHz. Amateur public service communications teams use SSTV to capture images of disaster sites for emergency response and rescue teams. Wherever there is a need to squeeze an image through an audio-bandwidth channel, SSTV will be there.

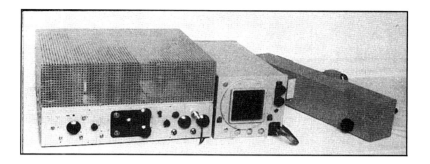

A New Narrow-Band Image Transmission System

In Two Parts

Part I—Principles of Slow Scan Picture Reproduction

BY COPTHORNE MACDONALD,* W4ZII/2

FOR THE past twenty years or so the conventional wide-band TV system and various mechanical-scanning fascimile systems have been the only common methods of transmitting images by electrical means. Recently, however, another method has been used to transmit images over wire lines. This method involves using television type pick-up and reproduction devices with slow scanning rates to produce narrow bandwidth video signals.

The Bell Telephone Laboratories' "Picture-Phone" system uses a live pick-up camera to

*49 St. Mary's Place, Nutley, N. J.

Above: These three units contain all the specialized picture transmitting and receiving equipment, ready to be connected to an ordinary phone transmitter and communications receiver. The shielded chassis at the left contains the sync, sweep, power supply, and receiver amplifier circuits. The detector, low-pass filter and 5-inch cathode-ray tube for receiving are in the center unit. At the far right is the light-tight box containing the flying-spot scanner. The modulator chassis is mounted on the rear of the scanner unit.

In this cathode-ray picture transmission system, facsimile communication becomes possible without moving parts. By thus eliminating the precision mechanical scanners and reproducers used in ordinary facsimile, picture transmission and reception by amateur stations is made immediately practicable. The final record picture is easily made by photographing the receiving cathode-ray tube display, or the composite video and sync signal can be recorded on magnetic tape with any home-type recorder, for playback at any subsequent time.

The system takes no greater band width than voice communication, and the signal can be transmitted and received with any equipment suitable for phone work.

generate the video signal, a magnetic storage drum to freeze the action, and special "Iatron" image-storing cathode-ray tubes to reproduce the image. A 60-line picture, 40 lines wide, is scanned once every 2 seconds and can be sent over ordinary phone lines.

Dage Electronics developed a system for use with "high-fidelity" phone lines which are flat from 60 c.p.s. to 5000 c.p.s. or higher. Both these systems employ expensive components and, consequently, have not been widely used.

Upon reading about these "wired" systems the writer became intrigued with the possibility of utilizing the slow-scan principle for image transmission by radio. In September, 1957, he started the design and construction of a low-cost slow-scan system which is especially adapted to the transmission characteristics of amateur phone equipment. This work was undertaken as a personal project in an independent problem course at the University of Kentucky.

Briefly, the system uses a cathode-ray tube flying-spot scanner to develop a 120-line picture, scanned once every 6 seconds, from a slide em-

August 1958

bodying an inexpensive photographic negative. The video output of the scanner amplitude-modulates a 2000-c.p.s. carrier, resulting in an audio-frequency signal consisting of the 2000-c.p.s. carrier and video side bands extending both ways in frequency to 1000 and 3000 c.p.s. This signal is then fed to the radio transmitter's modulator. At the receiving end, the audio-frequency output of the communications receiver is processed and the picture is presented on the screen of a low-cost electrostatically-deflected cathode-ray tube with a long-persistence P_7 phosphor.

The system can be used with almost any amateur phone transmitter and receiver with no changes necessary in the regular station equipment. The slow-scan unit merely plugs into the transmitter mike jack and receiver headphone jack. Air tests on the 11-meter band indicate that conditions and equipment which give good phone transmission, with a reasonably good signal-to-noise ratio, will also transmit satisfactory pictures. The actual type of modulation used in the transmitter seems to be relatively unimportant so long as the audio output of the receiver is a reasonably good replica of the input to the transmitter modulator. Plate modulated a.m. was used in all the tests made so far with good results, as the pictures show. Eleven-meter s.s.b. was non-existent in the Lexington area during the testing period, but this mode of transmission should be quite satisfactory, and the required frequency accuracy of the reinserted carrier should actually be less than for phone reception. N.f.m., with limiter stages in the receiver, could be used to reduce the effects of fading on picture transmission.

While the system presents a less detailed image than conventional facsimile it is adequate for many purposes, and the system is superior to existing facsimile in certain other respects. For one thing, the transmission time is a few seconds instead of minutes. This increases flexibility of operation by permitting rather rapid alternation of voice and picture transmission over the same circuit. This would, of course, be of vital importance in emergency work where all transmissions must be kept short. Also, by presenting ten scans every minute instead of one every few minutes, it should be possible to dodge the intermittent interference so prevalent on the ham bands. Also, the slow-scan system uses inexpensive and readily-available components, and if cost is not a factor a live-pickup Vidicon camera could easily be added to the system. The slow scanning rate, of course, requires that all images be still, but this should not be too great a disadvantage with the type of material which the ham is likely to transmit.

The System

The important system characteristics are listed below:

Number of lines: 120
Aspect ratio: 1:1 (square picture shape)
Vertical repetition rate: 6 seconds
Horizontal frequency: 20 c.p.s.
Modulation: Amplitude-modulated 2000-c.p.s. subcarrier. (White level, 0-20 per cent of maximum amplitude; black level, 50 per cent to 75 per cent of maximum; sync level, maximum amplitude.)
Pass band required: 1000–3000 c.p.s.
Synchronization: Maximum-amplitude carrier bursts coinciding with retrace periods. (Approximately 0.015 second for vertical pulse and 0.0015 second for horizontal.)

Many possible combinations of sweep times, aspect ratios, and audio carrier frequencies were studied in an attempt to find the most suitable combination. The maximum possible vertical sweep time is limited to about 6 seconds because the brightness of the P7 phosphor on the receiver cathode-ray tube face decays too rapidly to

This picture shows the kind of resolution that can be obtained with the 120-line scanning system described here. Taken off the monitor during transmission.

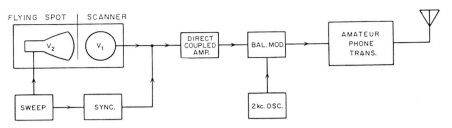

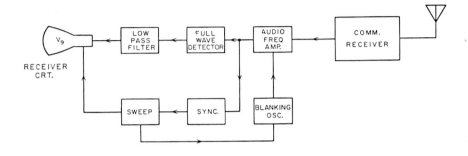

Fig. 1—The separate transmitting and receiving setups are shown in this block diagram.

retain bright picture detail much longer than this. The 1:1 aspect ratio is a picture shape which makes efficient use of a round cathode-ray tube screen, and does not favor the viewing of horizontal objects as the usual 4:3 aspect ratio does. The band-width requirements of the flying-spot scanner video output are d.c. to approximately 1000 c.p.s. The 2000-c.p.s. subcarrier frequency was chosen because it permits the upper video side band to fall within the 300–3000-c.p.s. pass band considered representative of current amateur practice, and provides at least two cycles of carrier for each cycle of modulating frequency.

Modulation polarity was selected to make low level represent white and high level represent black, for two reasons. First, the synchronizing pulses, being at the infrablack level, will blank the cathode-ray tube retrace if the receiver retrace and sync trigger time is less than the duration of the sync pulse. Second, strong noise pulses appear black rather than bright white as they would if high amplitude represented white.

Simple rectangular pulses lasting the duration of the retrace period permit synchronization of the receiver sweep oscillators. Since the vertical pulse is only about one-third the length of a scanning line, it is completed well before the next horizontal sync pulse starts. This avoids the need for serrating the vertical sync pulse to prevent upsetting the horizontal sweep, as is necessary when the pulse is over one line in length.

The picture transmitting and receiving circuits were combined in a single unit with common power supply and sweep circuits, in order to keep the cost as low as possible. As shown in the block diagram of Fig. 2, send-receive switches make the appropriate sync connections and, on "transmit," also feed the output signal into the video receiver to permit the outgoing picture to be monitored on the receiver cathode-ray tube (V_9). The simplified block diagrams in Fig. 1 represent the circuit connections on "transmit" and on "receive." These diagrams, along with the details of the Fig. 2 block diagram, will be explained in the discussion to follow. Actual circuitry and mechanical details will be described in Part II of this article.

Picture Transmission

The flying-spot scanner consists of a light-tight aluminum box with a 908-A cathode-ray tube (V_2) mounted at one end. The tube faces the other end where a 931-A photomultiplier tube (V_1) is mounted so that light from the cathode-ray tube will strike it. A slit in the side of the box directly in front of the cathode-ray tube allows insertion of a slide, which consists of a size 120 or 620 photographic negative mounted on a 3×5-inch cardboard frame. The slide is held in position in the scanner by its cardboard edges in such a way that the transparent portion of the slide is in intimate contact with the glass face of the 908-A cathode-ray tube. Thus any light which appears on the surface of the 908-A passes through the photographic negative before it strikes the photocathode of the photo-multiplier tube, some 8 inches away.

In operation, a small bright spot on the cathode-ray tube face is caused to sweep across the tube in raster fashion by the horizontal and vertical sweep voltages. The 908-A is a 3-inch electrostatically deflected tube with a P5 very-

August 1958

short-persistence screen, whose brightness decays to 1 per cent of its orginal value in 35 microseconds. The spot, therefore, remains a spot at the sweep frequencies used and does not leave a "tail" of undecayed brightness behind it as it sweeps across the tube. The spot faintly illuminates the cathode of the 931-A photomultiplier, and the intensity of the illumination is inversely proportional to the photographic density of the negative at a point directly in front of the spot. The small photocathode current is amplified approximately 40,000 times by the secondary-emission action of the dynodes. The voltage across the multiplier anode load resistor is, then, a video signal whose instantaneous amplitude follows the variations in picture brightness as the negative is scanned.

Plate-coupled 6SN7 multivibrators are the heart of the sweep and sync generation circuits. The 20-c.p.s. horizontal multivibrator (V_{17}) is synchronized with the 60-cycle power line, not only as a convenience in keeping its frequency constant, but to insure that any hum in the video will result only in variations in picture shading, not diagonal hum patterns. The vertical multivibrator (V_{14}), with a period of about 6 seconds, is triggered by the horizontal oscillator during a horizontal retrace period. This insures that the vertical retrace will always occur at the beginning of a line, which is necessary for proper positioning of the vertical sync pulse.

Sweep capacitors, charged through resistors from B+, are discharged during retrace periods by current from the multivibrators, channeled through isolating diodes (V_{15}). The saw-toothed voltage developed across each capacitor is coupled directly to the grid of its associated sweep amplifier, half a 6SN7 (V_{16}). One of the horizontal and one of the vertical deflection electrodes of the 908-A are internally tied to the tube's anode which is returned to a positive centering potential. The other deflection electrodes are connected to the V_{16} plates, putting the varying saw-toothed plate potential directly on the deflection electrodes.

The rectangular pulses developed by the multivibrators during the retrace periods are combined in a dual-diode tube (V_{12}) to form a composite sync signal. This signal is coupled to the photomultiplier load resistor where it is added to the video signal. The grid of a d.c. amplifier (V_{3A} — triode half of a 6U8) is also connected to this point. Since the sync pulses drive the triode beyond cutoff, the output voltage

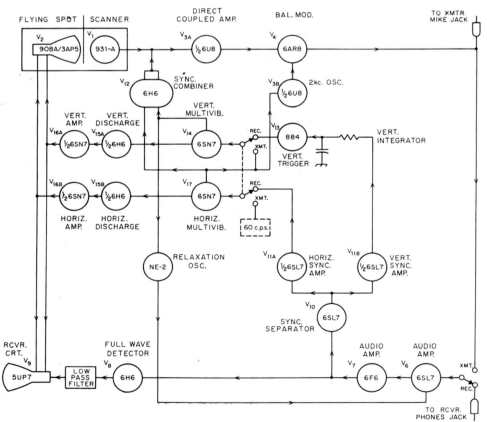

Fig. 2—Complete block diagram, showing transmit receive switching and stage functions.

consists of video during the sweep period and of sync pulses, clipped to constant amplitude, during the retrace periods. The ratio of sync level to video level is controlled by the cathode-ray tube's brightness control, increased brightness raising the video level and reducing the ratio.

Since the video signal at this point has important components from d.c. to 1000 c.p.s., it is evident that it cannot be applied directly to the ordinary transmitter modulator which attenuates frequencies below about 300 c.p.s. To surmount this difficulty, the video is directly coupled to the control grid of a 6AR8 sheet-beam tube used as a balanced modulator (V_4). This tube can be thought of as a miniature beam tetrode with two plates and two deflection electrodes. In operation, the 2000-c.p.s. output of a synchronized electron-coupled Hartley oscillator (V_{3B} —pentode half of the 6U8) is applied in push-pull to the deflection electrodes in the 6AR8. This causes the electron beam to be deflected back and forth from one plate to the other at the 2000-c.p.s. rate. The beam current is controlled by the grid voltage and is therefore proportional to the level of the video signal. The output is taken from the plates through a push-pull transformer. The balanced push-pull connection prevents the original 0- to 1000-c.p.s. video signal from appearing in the output, the only output being the 2000-c.p.s. carrier and its side bands. This output may be connected directly to the transmitter modulator. It should be noted here that, although the image source is a photographic negative, signal polarities have been handled so that the transmitted image is positive — that is, clear negative is black level, dense area is white.

Picture Reception

A three-stage audio-frequency amplifier, using a 6SL7 (V_6) and a 6F6 (V_7), amplifies the signal from the communications receiver (or directly from the video generator) to a peak level of about 100 volts. This signal is coupled through an isolation transformer to a full-wave diode detector (V_8). The output of the detector is fed to the grid of the 5UP7 cathode-ray tube through a low-pass filter which passes 0–1000 c.p.s. without attenuation or excessive nonlinear phase shift, but which effectively removes the ripple.

The 100-volt signal is also applied to an i.f. type full-wave triode sync separator (V_{10}) which separates the sync pulses from the composite sync and video signal. These pulses (actually a series of short pulses; one for each alternation of the 2000-c.p.s. carrier) are amplified by the two halves of a 6SL7 (V_{11}), one output going to synchronize the horizontal multivibrator, the other to an RC integrating circuit. The vertical pulse is approximately 10 times as long as the horizontal pulse, and the higher integrator output voltage, when driven by a vertical pulse, is sufficient to separate the vertical from the horizontal.

In conventional TV the vertical oscillator is brought into sync by changing the oscillator

Test picture transmitted by radio over a 7-mile path. The signal-to-noise ratio (peak sync pulse amplitude to peak noise, 12 db.) was in the range where "snow" is evident in the picture.

frequency slightly. This could be a lengthy process with an oscillator that makes only one sweep every six seconds. To solve this problem the integrated vertical sync pulse is used to fire an 884 gas triode (V_{13}). The 884 plate is directly connected to one of the vertical multivibrator plates, providing positive triggering action during almost any part of the vertical sweep period.

Since the retrace times on receive are the same as on transmit, and since an appreciable time is required for vertical sync pulse integration, blanking of the receiver cathode-ray tube is not assured. To insure blanking, a neon-bulb relaxation oscillator, fired by the vertical multivibrator plate voltage during retrace, is coupled to the receiver audio amplifier. The burst of tone signal from the oscillator is amplified, detected, and fed to the cathode-ray tube where the voltage extinguishes the beam for the entire retrace period.

Tests

Since the transmitting and receiving circuits use the same power supplies, sweep oscillators, and sweep amplifiers, it was impossible to have the actual picture transmitter located at one point and the picture receiver at another. In order to conduct tests, therefore, it was necessary to tape record the audio-frequency picture signal. While even the home-type recorders have adequate frequency response, some of the less expensive machines have appreciable "wow" or other forms of instantaneous speed variation which cause a slight skewing of lines in the picture. The effect is most noticeable when viewing an image containing vertical lines, and appears slight in an image of a face.

Incidentally, tape recordings could be a big help in getting started with this mode of trans-

(Continued on page 140)

Image Transmission
(Continued from page 15)

mission. For instance, a club could build a picture transmission unit as a club project, and this could be used to make recordings of the members' slides. Armed with recordings of the pictures he wished to transmit, the individual ham would then only have to build receiving equipment.

Local air tests were made over 1-mile and 7-mile distances on the 11-meter band, under a variety of transmission conditions. K4KYY played the video tape through his plate-modulated a.m. rig, and the signal was received on the NC-300 at W4JP, the University of Kentucky's station. These tests yielded information about the signal-to-noise ratio required for faithful picture reproduction. The figure of interest is the ratio of the sync pulse amplitude of the receiver output signal to the receiver peak noise output when receiving the unmodulated r.f. carrier. When this ratio was greater than about 26 db., the received picture quality was equivalent to that observed when monitoring transmissions with the picture received fed directly with the outgoing picture signal. With a 20-db. ratio the quality was still good, but with some snow present. When the ratio dropped to about 12 db. the picture contained considerable snow, but call letters could still be distinguished. In all these tests the black level was set at 50 per cent of the sync level.

K4KYY and PJ2AO tried valiantly to make a satisfactory long-distance test, but 11 meters had slipped a little too far into the summer slump for success. Phone signals were only slightly above the noise, and the signal received at W4JP from PJ2AO, who had recorded and played back the signal sent by K4KYY, was well down into the noise. While this test didn't produce conclusive results, the successful operation of conventional a.m. facsimile systems indicates that long distances can be covered if the signal-to-noise ratio is sufficiently high.

A New Narrow-Band Image Transmission System

*In Two Parts**

Part II — Circuit and Construction Details

BY
COPTHORNE MACDONALD,**
WA2BCW, EX-W4ZII

Inside view of the flying-spot scanner, with slide in place. The knob at the rear actuates a cam arrangement for moving the cathode-ray tube back and forth so the face of the tube can be placed in contact with the photographic negative containing the subject to be transmitted. The outboard chassis at the left contains the subcarrier oscillator and modulating circuits. Inside the box in the foreground, but not visible in this photo, is the photomultiplier tube.

PART I of this article described a low-cost method for transmitting images with conventional ham gear, a method which may be of interest to experimentally-inclined amateurs. The system, by combining television and facsimile techniques, permits a 120-line picture to be transmitted by almost any amateur phone transmitter and received on the station's communications receiver. The interested reader is referred to Part I for a discussion of the system's features and principles of operation. In this issue the actual circuitry will be described, with emphasis on the critical points, in order to help the reader who might like to build similar equipment make the most of his junk box.

> Here are the circuit details of the equipment described in outline in Part I of this article. The experimenter will find plenty of scope for trying out ideas of his own, since the basic system permits many variations. Discarded TV receivers and war-surplus c.r. indicator gear can be dug into for many of the components.

Transmission Circuitry

The schematic of the combined transmission-reception apparatus is shown in Fig. 3. The cathode-ray tubes (V_2 and V_9) and the photomultiplier tube (V_1) require a high negative voltage for operation. A scope-type transformer with an electrostatically-shielded 2.5-volt filament winding for the V_2 heater is used in conjunction with a half-wave rectifier to develop approximately 2000 volts d.c. If the transformer (T_1) suggested in the parts list is used the rectifier should be a 2X2; other transformers may require a different tube. R_{20} should be selected to provide 1300 to 1500 volts across filter capacitor C_1, and will have a value of 1 or 2 megohms. Old scopes provide a fertile field for conversion to slow-scan use, but the available voltage should be at least 1500 for sufficient receiver cathode-ray tube brightness. The photomultiplier tube is quite sensitive to voltage changes so NE-2 neon bulbs were wired across the voltage-dividing resistors to regulate the dynode voltage at about 65 volts per dynode stage. The 450 volts B+ can be obtained from any supply capable of delivering approximately 200 ma. The +105- and −105-volt supplies were regulated by OC3/VR105 regulator tubes.

---
* Part I of this article appeared in *QST* for August, 1958.
** 49 St. Mary's Place, Nutley, N. J.

The grid resistor (R_{24}) of V_{3A} is also the photo-multiplier anode load resistor; thus the grid of V_{3A} is at some negative potential whose actual value depends upon the setting of the V_2 brightness control (R_{18}) and the density of the picture being scanned. The large negative pulses coming from the sync-combiner diode (V_{12}) during retrace periods are attenuated by the R_{21}-through-R_{24} network but are still of sufficient amplitude to drive V_{3A} beyond cutoff. The voltage-dividing network in the V_{3A} plate circuit and V_4 grid circuit permits direct coupling of the video and sync signals to the balanced modulator.

The white-level control (R_{27}) should be adjusted so that the tone output of the balanced modulator [1] is close to zero during the scanning of white portions of the picture. A scope connected to the output jack (J_1) during transmis-

---

[1] This is not the conventional type of balanced modulator, the accepted definition of which is a modulator whose output contains side bands but no carrier. In the present case, a balanced circuit is used to produce an ordinary a.m. signal, but with the *modulating* signal balanced out in the output circuit. This is necessary because the modulating signal and carrier are so close in frequency. — *Ed.*

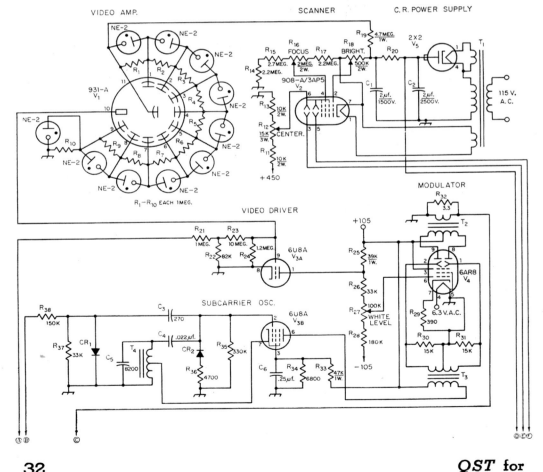

Fig. 3—Signal-generating and reproducing circuits for slow-scan picture transmission. Unless otherwise indicated, capacitances are in $\mu\mu f.$, resistances are in ohms, fixed resistors are ½ watt, variable resistors are composition potentiometers, ½ watt. Capacitors marked with polarity are electrolytic; others may be paper, ceramic, or mica as available or convenient. With the exceptions listed below, component designations are primarily for text reference.

C_5—See T_4.
C_{10}—See text.
CR_1, CR_2—1N34 or equivalent.
J_1, J_2—Microphone-type connectors.
L_1—12 henrys, 20 ma. (Thordarson 20C52).
R_{20}—1 to 2 megohms, 1 watt (see text).
R_{31}—Slider type resistor.
S_1—S.p.d.t. toggle or rotary.
S_2—2-pole 5-position rotary (Centralab PA-2019).
T_1—Scope transformer, to deliver approx. 2000 volts d.c.; see text (Thordarson 22R40; 1800 volts at 2 ma.; 2.5 volts at 2.2 amp. or 6.3 volts at 0.6 amp.).

T_2, T_5, T_6—Audio output transformer, push-pull plates to voice coil.
T_3—Audio interstage or small modulation transformer, single plate to push-pull grids, ratio not critical (Triad M-1X).
T_4—Autotransformer or tapped inductance; see text. C_5 may be varied to suit any available tapped coil to resonate at 2000 c.p.s.
T_7—6.3-to-6.3-volt isolation transformer, 1.2 amp. (Stancor P-8191).
V_5—2X2, or to suit filament voltage available on T_1.

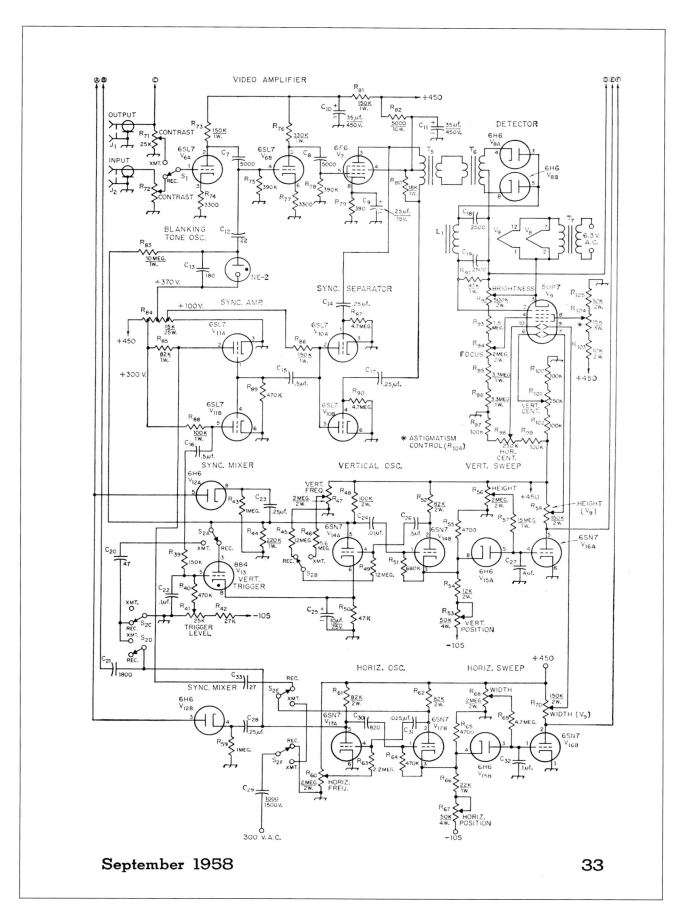

sion will permit this adjustment to be made, as well as setting the maximum black level at about 50-75 per cent of sync level with R_{18}. Fig. 4 illustrates the correct output wave form. No balancing control was provided in the balanced modulator, because the unwanted 0–1000 c.p.s. video was found to be 20 db. below sync level when checked on the scope with the 2000-c.p.s. carrier cut off.

The 2-kc. oscillator (V_{3B}) is an experimental circuit which permits the horizontal sync pulse to control the oscillations. It was felt that maintaining a constant time relationship between the sync pulses and individual cycles of tone might permit slightly more accurate synchronization than would be possible with a random relationship between the two. The results were inconclusive, however, with any advantage being a slight one. A standard oscillator circuit would probably serve just as well and would have a better output wave form. In the circuit used, T_4 is a high- to low-impedance headphone autotransformer. The CR_2-R_{36} combination improves the output wave form by limiting the negative grid-voltage swings so the tube is not driven to cutoff. This "gimmick" can also be applied to other types of oscillators. The oscillator output transformer (T_3) can be a small modulation transformer or single plate to push-pull grid interstage unit.

On "transmit" the horizontal multivibrator (V_{17}) is synchronized at a submultiple of the power line frequency by a voltage fed from the power transformer (external) through C_{29}. R_{60} controls the horizontal frequency and permits frequencies from 15 to 60 c.p.s. to be selected. The picture width is controlled by R_{68} which regulates the charging current of the sweep capacitor C_{32}. On retrace, V_{17B} is cut off and a heavy discharge current through V_{15B} pulls the grid voltage of V_{16B} to some negative value which depends on the setting of R_{67}. The charging rate during sweep is such that the grid never goes positive. A highly linear sawtooth wave, therefore, appears on the grid of V_{16B}; the tube amplifies this voltage, and it is fed directly to Pin 5 of V_2.

The vertical multivibrator has a sweep range of 1 c.p.s. to 1 cycle every 7 seconds, controlled by R_{47}. The oscillator receives a sync pulse from the horizontal oscillator through C_{20} during every horizontal retrace period. These pulses have no effect until the vertical oscillator approaches the triggering point, at which time one of the pulses triggers the oscillator. The rest of the vertical sweep circuit is similar to the horizontal, with R_{56} controlling flying spot scanner raster height, and R_{53} the vertical position. R_{12} is used to center the raster on V_2 and R_{16} focuses the flying spot.

The rectangular pulses developed during the multivibrator retrace periods are coupled to the cathodes of V_{12}, where they are combined to provide the video sync pulses fed to R_{21}. The sync pulse for the 2-kc. oscillator is coupled from V_{17A} through C_{21}.

Many substitutions can be made in the picture transmission circuits. While there is no inexpensive substitute for the 931-A, any cathode-ray tube with a P5 phosphor is suitable for V_2. The 5CP5 and 5JP5 are currently available on the surplus market. Miniature equivalents of the octal base tubes can be used, of course, and in some instances they cost less than the octal types used. Generally speaking, the R and C values in the sweep and sync circuits are noncritical; however, the time constants in the grid circuits of the multivibrators ($C_{24}R_{51}$, $C_{26}R_{49}$, etc.) should be adjusted for proper timing. Several balanced modulators were tried, but most failed to remain in balance over the wide range of control-grid voltage swing. The 6AR8 circuit was the most satisfactory in this respect, and it also provides plenty of output. If the output voltage from J_1 overdrives the first stage in the transmitter modulator, a pot or fixed pad may be installed to cut the gain.

Reception Circuitry

The audio from the communications receiver is fed into J_2 and is controlled in amplitude by con-

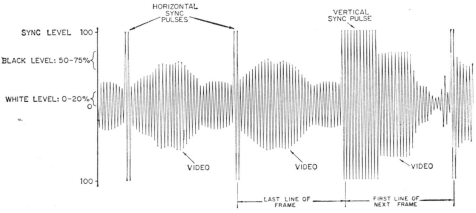

Fig. 4—Wave form of modulated 2000-c.p.s. tone. There are approximately 100 cycles of 2000-cycle carrier per line.

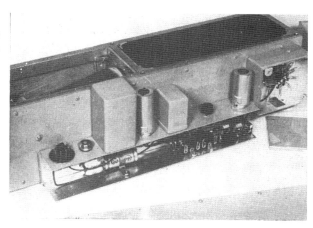

Side view of the scanner assembly with cover plates off the modulator chassis and 931-A socket shield. The 931-A socket, far right, has the dynode load resistors and neon-tube voltage regulators clustered about it. The tube immediately adjacent is V_3. Moving to the left, the components on top of the modulator chassis are the control knob for R_{27}, then T_3, V_4, T_2, the output connector for feeding the composite signal to the main chassis, and the power supply connector.

trast control R_{72}. During the monitoring of a transmitted image the contrast is controlled by R_{71}. These two controls can have a wide range of values from a few thousand ohms to half a megohm or more. The two small universal push-pull output transformers, T_5 and T_6, are connected to feed the amplified audio to V_8, the full-wave diode detector. The secondary of T_6 is at a potential of about -2000 volts d.c., but with the transformer mounted on small ceramic stand-off insulators there has been no trouble with insulation breakdown. Also at a high negative potential, and consequently mounted on stand-offs, is L_1. This choke is rated at 8 henrys at 40 ma. in its intended filter application, but it measures only 4.5 henrys at 2000 c.p.s. with no d.c. in the winding. Measuring the actual frequency response of the filter is the best check on performance. This filter should have no attenuation up to 1000 c.p.s., the point where a gentle roll-off starts.

In the cathode-ray tube circuit, R_{92} controls the brightness, R_{94} the focus, R_{98} the horizontal centering, R_{101} the vertical centering, R_{58} the vertical size, R_{70} the horizontal size, and R_{104} astigmatism. This last control is used to adjust the anode voltage to the point where optimum focus in the horizontal and in the vertical direction occurs at the same point on the focus control.

The sync pulses are separated from the composite video and sync signal in V_{10}. The pulses fed to the horizontal oscillator are amplified by V_{11A}. V_{11B} feeds the $R_{39}C_{22}$ integrating circuit which fires V_{13} when a vertical sync pulse charges C_{22} sufficiently. The firing level is controlled by R_{41}. Since the plate of V_{13} is directly connected to the plate of V_{14A}, the firing of the 884 will also trigger the vertical multivibrator. The $C_{25}R_{50}$ combination in the cathode circuit of V_{14A} is used to raise the bias on V_{13} after firing, until the bias on C_{22} has a chance to leak off. This is done so that noise or horizontal sync pulses soon after firing won't cause the tube to fire again. To operate properly, C_{25} should be in the neighborhood of 10 μf., not much larger.

The operation of the sweep circuits is the same during reception as during transmission. One additional event not previously mentioned is the triggering of the neon bulb blanking oscillator. During the sweep period, V_{14A} is cut off and the oscillator does not operate. However, during the conduction period the difference between the voltage at the plate of V_{14A} (about 50 volts) and the 370-volt return potential of the neon bulb is sufficient to allow the circuit to oscillate. The tone output is coupled to V_{6B} through C_{12}. The neon-bulb return voltage is a tap on R_{84}, which may be the bleeder resistor of the 450-volt power supply.

Several tubes may be substituted for the 5UP7: among them are the 3FP7, 5CP7, and 5ADP7, all of which are available on the surplus market. These tubes all have the post-deflection acceleration feature and can give a brighter picture than the 5UP7 if a high positive voltage is applied to the tube's third anode.

Mechanical Details

Physically, the equipment consists of three separate units. The largest of these is an old TV chassis upon which the power supply, sweep, sync, and receiver amplifier circuits are mounted. The important points here involve layout and insulation. In addition to the usual precautions in wiring the audio circuits, care must be exercised to reduce stray capacitive coupling between the two sweep oscillators. The steep wave forms in the horizontal oscillator are easily coupled to the vertical oscillator, where they may cause premature triggering. Several inches of separation between the two stages is recommended. The remainder of the layout is not critical. Adequate insulation should be used in the high-voltage

An old TV receiver chassis was used for the major portion of the circuitry. This assembly contains power supplies (built according to ordinary design methods) in addition to the circuits shown in Fig. 3.

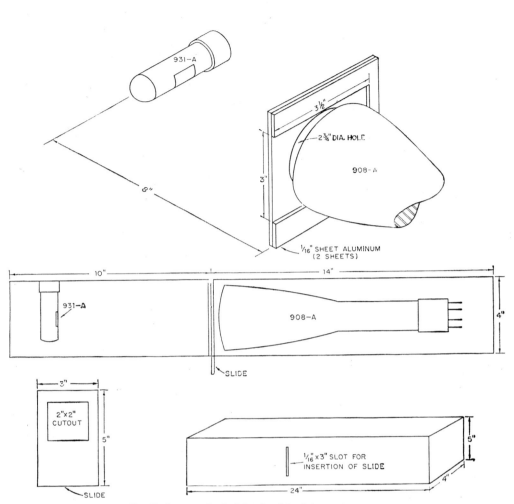

Fig. 5—Some mechanical details of the flying-spot scanner.

power supply, and the focus and brightness controls should be insulated from ground and connected to their knobs with insulated couplings.

The second unit contains the 5UP7 and the detector circuit. An ASB surplus radar indicator provided the chassis and mounting assembly for the 5UP7. Unfortunately, the magnetic shield which covered the 5BP1 originally used in the indicator was too narrow for the 5UP7 and had to be removed; the electron beam in the tube is therefore subject to deflection by stray magnetic fields. This may mean keeping the tube several feet away from power transformers.

The P7 phosphor is of the cascade type where the electron beam excites a short-persistence blue phosphor, which in turn excites a long-persistence yellow phosphor. The blue flash which accompanies the sweep is undesirable because of its extreme brightness and is therefore filtered out with a Wratten 15G gelatin filter which covers the face of the tube. Your photo dealer can obtain this filter for you.

The third unit, the flying-spot scanner, also has the 6U8, 6AR8, and voltage-regulating neon bulbs mounted on the back. The important constructional points are illustrated in Fig. 5 and in the photographs of the scanner. While this scanner has a framework of machined aluminum and sides of 1/16-inch thick aluminum sheet, equivalent results can be obtained with a much less elaborate arrangement. Actually, the first tests of the system were conducted with the scanner tube and photomultiplier in a cardboard box made light tight with masking tape, and with a negative taped to the face of the 908-A.

The aluminum scanner box was made as light tight as possible. A strip of felt covers the slot where the slide is inserted in order to reduce the amount of light entering here, and the interior is painted black to reduce reflection. Since it is desirable to have the negative directly against the face of the scanner tube during operation, the tube was mounted on a movable car-

(Continued on page 146)

line and with the loading coils in use, S_O would be 20 and D would be 1.1 db. The loading coils would be effective in reducing the reactance to negligible values only over a narrow band, probably about 100 kc., and for operation over a wider band the coils would have to be readjusted. This calculation has demonstrated that the use of such a "short" antenna without loading coils is undesirable, while with loading coils there are several undesirable features. Thus the use of such an antenna should be limited to situations where space is extremely restricted, as in mobile work.[3]

The antenna chosen for this second example is not entirely fictitious. One which we have used the past several years conforms approximately to this description except that ours is vertical, and the upper half is a war-surplus whip. On 14 Mc. it has been our old stand-by, mainly the one with which we hammered out a DXCC with powers not exceeding about 175 watts. On 21 Mc., in spite of its unorthodox nature, it loads very easily. It may not be the best antenna that can be built for this band (recently we have supplanted it with a miniature two-element beam which we hope to describe in a later article), but with it we have been WAC and have worked quite a bit of DX with little difficulty, some with only an 807 in the final. Since conditions became good on 28 Mc. most operation on that band has been with a beam, but when this antenna has been used it has got out quite well. And there was the time when for a joke we called a JA with 50 watts to an 807 — but the joke was on us because he came back on the first call and gave an S8 report!

---

[3] The author here has in mind the solid-dielectric type lines that have been the subject of discussion in the article. With open-wire line — i.e., parallel-conductor line using air or essentially all-air insulation — the line losses are not unduly high even with very high standing-wave ratios. Such a system requires tuned coupling at the transmitter, so the fact that the band width is narrow is not too great a handicap since the system can be easily reresonated when the operating frequency is changed. — *Ed.*

the negative directly against the phosphor in the 908-A, some parallax is present which could reduce the scanner resolution if precautions are not taken to minimize the effect. To help the situation, the 931-A was mounted about 8 inches from the face of the scanner tube, and the glass envelope of the 931-A was painted black, except for a $\frac{1}{2} \times \frac{1}{2}$-inch square section in front of the cathode which was left clear. The angle formed by imaginary lines drawn from the extremes of the exposed cathode area to the spot of light on the scanner is kept small in this way, thereby keeping down the parallax.

Conclusion

The equipment just described is certainly not the ultimate in design, but represents the first attempt to get a system of this type operating on the ham bands. Because of this, the experimenter has a wide-open field for originality in his circuitry, and all who are interested in constructing a system are urged to become familiar with the techniques employed in conventional TV, since many of them can be adapted for slow-scan use. An acquaintance with oscilloscopes, especially the direct-coupled variety, also would be valuable. While the amplitude-modulated audio-subcarrier method of modulation used in this system has the dual advantage of simplicity of circuitry and versatility of application, it is also technically possible to use the flying-spot scanner output to amplitude or frequency modulate an r.f. carrier directly. The experimenter may therefore want to make his equipment flexible enough to conduct these tests. Use that good old ham ingenuity, because this is an opportunity for amateur radio to make a real contribution to the art.

Acknowledgments

Thanks are extended to Dr. H. A. Romanowitz, Head of the Electrical Engineering Department at the University of Kentucky, whose cooperation and support made this project possible; and to K4KYY, K4HBG and PJ2AO for the help they gave with the air tests.

"The Making of an Amateur Packet-Radio Network" by David Borden, K8MMO, and Paul Rinaldo, W4RI

By Ward Silver, NØAX

As noted in the introduction to this section, packet radio was the first major data communications advance following the FCC's ruling that allowed hams to use ASCII data characters. Actually, the invention of packet radio *preceded* that ruling because Canadian hams in Montreal and Vancouver (primarily) had already established fundamental structures for packet radio in the preceding two years! Nevertheless, allowing hams on either side of the 49th parallel to use ASCII characters or codes in their transmissions had immediate and long-lasting benefits.

Packet radio and its underlying AX.25 protocol were much more than just a new mode or character set (see the list of references later in this book for the actual protocol, formally accepted by the ARRL in 1984). After all, the National Traffic System's human-powered Morse machines had for decades been linked in a coast-to-coast network of store-and-forward nodes that could organize according to predetermined routing tables or *ad hoc* — using today's terminology. Amateurs had also been using 5-bit Baudot and radioteletype to link stations since the late 1940s when teleprinters and terminal units became available at reasonable cost. Packet added a crucial element to the mix — computing power — in the form of the microprocessor and personal computer.

AX.25 was based on the X.25 protocol for computer-to-computer messaging over "wired" networks. Those networks often included microwave links along the way, but the protocol itself did not have to deal with the vagaries of RF propagation. That was taken care of by the equipment implementing the point-to-point link. Amateurs, on the other hand, do have to worry about the air link, which consists of transmitters, receivers, antennas and a modulated signal. They also have to comply with bandwidth and other restrictions on the transmitted signal that do not apply to commercial systems.

To exchange the AX.25 packets, amateurs had to replace the RF link equipment used by commercial systems with modems that could deal with the typical amateur VHF voice channel and commonly available equipment (an FM voice transceiver). The preferred solution was to use surplus Bell 102 (300 baud) and Bell 202 (1200 baud) FSK modems that would soon be available as integrated circuits. (RTTY FSK equipment could also be used at relatively low data rates.)

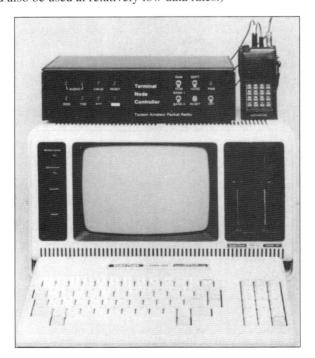

A typical packet station of the mid-1980s. A personal computer running terminal emulation software was connected to a standalone Terminal Node Controller (TNC) and a VHF FM transceiver.

Amateurs didn't have mainframes and mini-computers, so those had to be replaced with something affordable that had enough computing power to handle the modem interface, read and write the packetized data, display and accept ASCII characters, and interact with a user. The insight that made packet radio practical for a wide audience was to partition the system between data display equipment the amateur could afford (a simple ASCII terminal or PC running a terminal emulation program) and the Terminal Node Controller or TNC, which could deal with the data packets and the AX.25 timing constraints. Remember that this was a long time before sound cards, in the days when PC processor speed and memory were measured in megahertz and kilobytes!

That combination worked and worked well. TNCs were available first as kits from the Vancouver Amateur Digital Communication Group, then from the Tucson Amateur Packet Radio (TAPR, **www.tapr.org**), and finally as ready-to-go shack accessories from many vendors. The final piece of the puzzle was a pair of cables to connect the TNC to the microphone and speaker jacks of a VHF FM transceiver. (The cables, particularly the microphone jack cable, turned out to be surprisingly challenging due to the variety of connectors and pin assignments. Entire books were devoted to diagrams of cables for the different TNCs and radios.)

The AX.25 protocol's error-detection capabilities were brand new to Amateur Radio and created a "reliable transport" mechanism (data transferred correctly or not at all) suitable for transferring large blocks of data, such as the files amateurs were starting to generate on their new PCs. Amateurs were quick to adapt bulletin board system (BBS) software to packet connections, and many BBSs could be accessed via telephone modem or packet radio.

Reliable transport was a boon at VHF and higher frequencies where channel noise and fading were not too destructive. On the HF bands, however, the channel characteristics were very unkind to the long strings of FSK data required for efficient data transfer. In order to get any kind of throughput, the packets had to be kept short and so the effective data rate was quite low. This lead to the "TOR" (Teletype Over Radio") and other modes more tolerant of HF channel characteristics.

Nevertheless, packet radio enabled amateurs to create worldwide networks by using digipeaters, long-distance links, and a scheme of individual addresses similar to that of ARPAnet, which eventually became the Internet. Instead of "what's your email address?" the question was then "what's your home node?" Amateur Radio was connected and in a big way!

Packet radio is a key component of today's worldwide networks and for emergency communications. Software applications like *Airmail* or *Outpost* (shown here) wrap packet's reliable transport with an email-like client.

As we all know well, the Internet came along, then the World Wide Web, and the extensive network of packet digipeaters and nodes fell into disuse. That does not mean packet radio went away or that it won't continue to be a useful tool in the future! Packet at 1200 and 9600 baud forms critical links in local and regional networks that are used for the international Winlink system (see the Winlink 2000 article later in this section) and emergency communications teams. The APRS network (described in the next article) is built on packet digipeaters and VHF-to-Internet gateways to transfer position and other data from its users. Never fear, that "packet racket" will continue to be heard on the amateur bands for a long time to come!

The Making of an Amateur Packet-Radio Network

U.S. and Canadian Radio Amateurs are experimenting with packet radio. Plans are underway for an amateur packet-switched network to be built over the next few years.

By David W. Borden,* K8MMO, and Paul L. Rinaldo,** W4RI

October 16, 1981, is the date set for the ARRL conference on Amateur Radio Computer Networking at the National Bureau of Standards, Gaithersburg, Maryland.[1] This will be the setting for a get-together by North American radio amateurs who are eager to build a packet-switched network.

Store-and-forward packet-switching techniques date back to a 1964 study by the RAND Corporation. The term "packet" was coined in 1965 by D. W. Davies of the British National Physical Laboratory. In that year, the U.S. Advanced Research Projects Agency (DARPA) started working on time-sharing concepts that would lead to the activation of ARPANET in 1969. Since then, a whole new science of packet communications technology has matured, and numerous government and commercial packet-switched networks have emerged. This history and an excellent treatment of packet technology is covered in a recent book edited by Kuo.[2]

Amateur Radio packet experimentation got its start in Canada on September 15, 1978, when the Department of Communications (DOC) announced rules for the Amateur Digital Radio Operator's Certificate.[3] The DOC also established regulations for packet-radio transmissions and designated certain vhf and uhf subbands for packet emission. This kicked off packet activity in Ottawa, Montreal, Vancouver and elsewhere.

In 1975, the availability of microprocessors and inexpensive microcomputer kits gave personal computing a big send-off. Because ASCII was not at that time permitted in the ham bands, the choices for data communications were to convert to Baudot or to use the telephone lines. Couple this with the fact that many computerists do not have ham licenses, and you can see why telephone data communications became popular. In 1978, the Computerized Bulletin Board System (CBBS) was developed by Christensen and Suess.[4] There are now around 200 active CBBS systems in the U.S. and Canada. This picture was changed by FCC action, effective March 17, 1980, that legalized ASCII over the U.S. ham bands. This set in motion some experimentation with serial (start-stop) transmission of ASCII; i.e., just hook up the computer to your ham radio equipment through a modem, and let 'er rip! As only a short time passed, it became clear that packet transmission of ASCII offered some advantages. So, a handful of U.S. experimenters set out to catch up with the 18-month lead enjoyed by their Canadian counterparts.

Pardon Me, But . . .

What is a packet? A packet is a group of ASCII characters (information) surrounded by control signals and error-detection features. The control signals help recognize the presence of a packet and tell any intervening switching equipment where the packet should be sent. The error-detection feature works so well as virtually to guarantee that bad information will not be observed by the destination station. Table 1 illustrates a typical packet.

As may be seen, a packet is similar to a message format. In fact, it's a lot shorter than the average Amateur Radio or MARS message. Besides carrying smaller payload, the header and trailer components are designed to be read by computer, not by human operators. The computer, in this case, can be either a home computer programmed to perform this function or a packet controller — a single-purpose microcomputer board dedicated

---

Table 1

Format for a Typical Packet

Time ⟶

| SYNC | FLAG | ADR | CTL | DATA | FCS | FLAG |

⟵ *Direction of BIT Transmission*

SYNC — First packet in a group of packets contains 16 bits of alternating zeros and ones.
FLAG — 8 bits, always 01111110 (7E hex).
ADR — Address of the sending station, either assigned dynamically by the Station Node at sign-on or hard-coded into the Terminal Interface Program (8 bits).
CTL — 8 bits containing control information for handling the packet.
DATA — From 0 (supervisory packet) to 255 bytes of data in ASCII.
FCS — Frame Check Sequence — 16 bits, computed by the sending station and checked by the receiving station.
FLAG — 8 bits, always 01111110 (7E hex).

---

[1]Notes appear on page 30.
*Rte. 2, Box 233B, Sterling, VA 22170
**1524 Springvale Ave., McLean, VA 22101

to this task. There are advantages to the packet-controller board approach, such as (a) taking advantage of packet-controller chips on the market, (b) keeping the hardware costs low by not tying up the personal computer and (c) avoiding the necessity of generating new software for every type of computer as changes are made.

Following this philosophy, a typical vhf Amateur Radio packet station would look like that in Fig. 1. The terminal in this case could be either a cathode-ray tube (CRT) or printer and could operate in either ASCII or Baudot code. The Terminal Node Controller (TNC) of the type designed by Doug Lockhart, VE7APU, can be programmed by means of programmable read-only memories (PROMs) to handle serial or parallel communication with a wide variety of terminals, including computers. The other side of the TNC manages the line — sending and receiving packets in High-Level Data Link Control (HDLC) format.

Example Packet Transmissions

Assume that the source station wishes to send a two-page message to a destination station using packets. The transmission might be broken up into 48 packets, each containing the address of the source and destination, an information (data) field containing a part of the total message and a frame check sequence (FCS) for error detection. The source station would enter his message into a computer terminal attached to a Terminal Node Controller. The TNC would accept the message as input, break it up into packets, send the packets over the transmission medium (radio, in this case) and receive an acknowledgment of correct reception from the destination station for each packet sent. The destination station would also employ a TNC to receive the packets, acknowledge correctly received packets (ASCII ACK) or request retransmission of any bad packets (ASCII NAK or negative acknowledgment). Bad packets are detected using the FCS. An FCS is appended to each packet by the transmitting station. The receiving station computes what the FCS should be and compares that with the FCS supplied with the packet. If the two agree, the chances are very great that the packet is error free. If the two answers disagree, the destination station knows that the packet is bad and requests retransmission of that packet only.

We have yet to observe the benefits of packet radio. First, a channel can be utilized by a number of users through a time-sharing arrangement known as time-division multiplexing. These different conversations can take place on the same channel, apparently at the same time. In fact, each pair of users believes that the channel is theirs exclusively. Unless a station deliberately tells its TNC to monitor everything on the channel, the station will recognize only those transmissions meant for it.

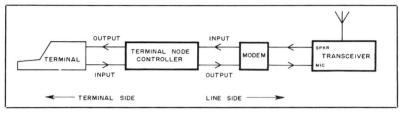

Fig. 1 — Block diagram showing a typical vhf packet-radio station. The arrows indicate the direction of data flow.

You might ask, "What happens when two users transmit at the same instant?" In ham radio, it's QRM. In packet terminology, it is called a "collision." There are all sorts of so-called contention schemes to avoid collisions, but they happen even in the best packet networks. In this case, the TNC performs a carrier-sense check (to see if anyone is using the channel). Just to reduce the possibility of two TNC boards hearing nothing and bursting packets at exactly the same time, a variable time delay is built in. Because the time delay at each TNC (user) is changing, repeated collisions between the same pair of users should not occur.

Local Repeaters

In packet terminology, Local Area Network (LAN) is used to designate a number of terminals within a small geographical area that are able to talk to one another through a common channel. That may be coaxial cable or radio. It is difficult for some people to feel comfortable with the term "packet repeater," because this type of repeater may be quite different from the usual ham 2-meter fm variety. Because local area network packet repeaters are still highly experimental, those now operating or in the construction stage in the U.S. and Canada represent different approaches. As examples of two implementations of local area networks using the same Vancouver TNC boards and HDLC protocol, let us look briefly at San Francisco and Washington, DC.

The KA6M/R local area network packet repeater was activated on December 10, 1980.[5] It is a single-frequency repeater that accepts packets, performs an error check on them and retransmits them when the packets contain no errors. The repeater itself uses a Z-80 microprocessor driving a custom-built board containing a Western Digital 1933 HDLC chip. Bell 202 1200-baud modems are used both at the repeater and by members of the net. Individual stations are using Vancouver TNC boards.

The WD4IWG/R repeater is a straightforward 2-meter fm voice repeater, which is also used by local AMRAD (Amateur Radio Research and Development Corp.) members for data communications. So, what comes in is repeated on the output frequency at the same time. This approach has the advantages of (1) using an existing repeater and (2) being able to sense the repeater output for presence of carrier before transmitting, avoiding collisions when the other station cannot be heard directly. Like those local networks in Vancouver, San Francisco and Hamilton, Ontario, the Washington, DC group is using the Vancouver TNC boards.

The local area network packet repeater scene is continuing to evolve with new compromises between doing it "right" and making do with what is available.

The Wider Network

The eventual goal is to tie these and many other local areas together to form a larger packet network. The focus, at the moment, is on interconnecting the various groups in Canada and the U.S. We are using the acronym AMNET to designate this wider network, which may go much beyond North America. Basic approaches, and possibly some tentative standards, for this network are the topic of the October 16 conference in Gaithersburg, Maryland.

There is general agreement that the bulk of the network traffic will be handled by the vhf or uhf packet repeaters deployed across North America. The spread of these repeaters could be as rapid as seen in past years with fm repeaters, but that depends upon enthusiasm and agreement of how to proceed. One view, perhaps the prevailing one, is that the intercity packet repeaters should be separate from the local area network packet repeaters. Also, it seems that the place for them is 220 MHz, and that they should operate at high signaling rates in the range of 1200 to 48,000 bits per second. The idea is to have the speed as high as practical in order to ensure that there is sufficient capacity to handle all intercity traffic. The higher speeds, however, require both wider bandwidths and greater power. So, the trade-offs are being studied. The lower speed (1200) would be necessary if, for some reason, we are unable to obtain an FCC rules change or waiver.

There is also a preference for the use of satellites for the long-haul circuits needed to "leapfrog" the vhf/uhf terrestrial network. Data communications channels are

October 1981   29

A Glossary of Packet-Radio Terms

Address — Element(s) of a packet frame that identify the source and/or destination stations by means of an agreed bit pattern.

CCITT — Consultative Committee for International Telegraph and Telephone, a part of the International Telecommunication Union (ITU).

CSMA — Carrier sense multiple access, a contention scheme in which stations listen for the presence of a carrier on the channel before sending a packet.

HDLC — High-Level Data Link Control, a packet transmission protocol developed by the International Standards Organization (ISO). It was derived from IBM's Synchronous Data Link Control (SDLC).

Flow control — The method used to regulate the rate of data exchange between the end users of the packet network in order to prevent system overloading. In general, the input is slowed down or stopped until the network handles the previous input.

Packet — (CCITT definition) A group of binary digits, including data and call control signals, that is switched as a composite whole. The data, call control signals and possibly error-control information are arranged in a specific format.

Packet switching — (CCITT definition) The transmission of data by means of addressed packets, whereby a transmission channel is occupied for the duration of transmission of the packet only. The channel is then available for use by packets being transferred between different data terminal equipment.

Protocol — A format and set of procedures for achieving communications.

Protocol layering — The International Standards Organization (ISO) has divided protocols into seven layers, from the lowest through the highest levels, as follows: Physical, Link, Network, Transport, Session, Presentation and Application. RS-232-C is an example of a Physical level protocol, HDLC a Link level.

Routing — A sequence of passing packets through various store-and-forward packet switches in a network to the desired destination.

Terminal Node — As used by the Vancouver Amateur Digital Communications Group, a user station in the packet network consisting of a Terminal Node Controller board, a data terminal (or computer), a modem and radio equipment.

---

assigned to AMSAT Phase III and later satellites in the planning stages. Hank Magnuski, KA6M, is the chairman for the AMSAT International Computer Network (AMICON) system architecture design group.

High-frequency (hf) packet circuits will be needed to fill in the gaps while the satellite capability is still not operational. Also, some hf capability should be maintained as a back-up system. An experimental hf packet circuit is being tested between AMRAD (WD4IWG) in Washington and ARRL (W1AW) in Newington to determine both equipment and software requirements for an operational circuit. Hf propagation restricts practical speeds to the general range of 75 to 600 baud, although 300 baud is the top speed presently permitted by FCC rules. The speeds of 300, 600 and 1200 baud are possible over ionospheric paths within the limitations of multipath distortion. Generally speaking, a radio signal that is operating on the maximum usable frequency (muf) has only one path, thus no multipath. However, lower frequencies (than the muf) can follow several paths within the same ionospheric layer, and suffer multipath distortion at higher speeds. This is a complex effect that varies by path distance and operating frequency, relative to the muf. The worst circuit distances for multipath are the shortest ones, e.g., under 300 miles — that between Newington and Washington. The best path distance is around 1000 to 1600 miles.

Getting Started

First, you need to do some reading. In addition to the references at the end of this article, you will find a number of books and magazine articles in many technical libraries. More to the point, you may wish to join one or all three of the following Amateur Radio groups that regularly publish newsletters with substantial packet information:

1) Amateur Radio Research and Development Corp. (AMRAD), monthly *AMRAD Newsletter* ($12). Gerald Adkins, N4GA, 1206 Livingston St. North, Arlington, VA 22205.

2) Vancouver Amateur Digital Communications Group (VADCG), *The Packet* ($10). Don Oliver, VE7AOG, 818 Rondeau St., Coquitlam, BC V3J 5Z3.

3) Hamilton and Area Packet Network (HAPN), *I-Frame de VE3PKT* ($10). Stu Beal, VE3MWM, 2391 Arnold Cres., Burlington, ON L7P 4J2.

If you decide to start with the Vancouver TNC board, you can order them from VE7AOG. The price is $30 for a bare board and all documentation. You will need to populate it with integrated circuits, resistors, capacitors and the switches required. You then plug in PROM chips containing the appropriate program and begin communicating. The total cost of the TNC is about $250 when you add up the costs of the board and parts.

Next, you will need a Bell 202 modem. These may be available as surplus at hamfests, but several manufacturers are now making them at affordable prices. If you contemplate only hf operation, your existing RTTY modem (AFSK keyer/demodulator) may be used at the slower speeds of 75 and 150 baud, possibly with some modification.

Some Cautious Conclusions

Amateur packet radio experimental activity is well under way. Local area networks have been set up in a number of places in Canada and the U.S. Network standards and protocols are beginning to take shape.

You can get involved by starting a local area network with just two (or more) hams within range of each other. One or more of the groups mentioned in this article can help you get started.

Notes

[1] "Call for Papers on Packet Radio and Computer Networking," *QST*, July 1981, p. 32.
[2] Kuo, *Protocol & Techniques for Data Communication Networks* (Englewood Cliffs, NJ: Prentice-Hall, 1981).
[3] R. Hesler, "Canadian Newsfronts: DOC Creates New Amateur License Class," *QST*, Dec. 1978, p. 61.
[4] Christensen and Suess, "Hobbyist Computerized Bulletin Board," *Byte*, Nov. 1978, p. 150.
[5] H. Magnuski and P. O'Dell, "First Packet Repeater Operational in U.S.," *QST*, April 1981, p. 27.

Bibliography of Packet Radio and Amateur Computer Networking

Abramson. "The ALOHA System," *Computer-Communication Networks*. Englewood Cliffs, NJ: Prentice Hall, Inc., 1973, pp. 501-518.
Borden. "Protocol". columns. *AMRAD Newsletter*, Feb. and later issues.
Bruninga. "A Multiuser Data Network — Communicating over VHF Radio." *Byte*, Nov. 1978, p. 120.
Caulkins. "PCNET 1979." *People's Computers*, Sept.-Oct. 1977.
Derfler. "Dial-up Directory." *73*, issues starting with Jan. 1980.
Felsenstein. "Community Memory — A 'Soft' Computer System." *Proceedings of the First West Coast Computer Faire*, April 1977.
Folts and Karp. *Compilation of Data Communications Standards*. New York: McGraw-Hill, 1978.
Fylstra. "Homebrewery vs. The Software Priesthood." *Byte*, Oct. 1976.
Halprin. "Hip Packet." *QST*, April 1981, p. 91.
Henry. "ASCII, Baudot and the Radio Amateur." *QST*, Sept. 1980, p. 11.
Hewlett-Packard. *Data Communications Testing*. Delcon Div., 690 E. Middlefield Rd., Drawer 7021, Mountain View, CA 94042, 1980, Manual Part No. 5952-4973.
Hodgson. "An Introduction to Packet Radio." *Ham Radio*, June 1970, p. 64.
Horton. "Distributed Network." *Byte*, Nov. 1978.
Isaak. "Standards for the Personal Computing Network." *IEEE Computer*, Oct. 1978, p. 60.
Kahn, et al. "Advances in Packet Radio Technology." *Proceedings of the IEEE*, Vol. 66, No. 11, Nov. 1978.
Kasser. "The Sky's the Limit: Ham Radio for Intercomputer Communication." *Byte*, Nov. 1978.
Kasser. "The Club Computer Network." *Byte*, May 1980.
Kleinrock and Tobagi. "Packet Switching in Radio Channels: Part 1 — Carrier Sense Multiple Access Modes and their Throughput-Delay Characteristics." *IEEE Trans. Commun.*, Vol. COMM-23, Dec. 1975, pp. 1400-1416 (and other papers in the same issue).
Levin. "Interpersonalized Media: What's News?" *Byte*, June 1980.
McCarthy. "DIALNET and Home Computers." *Proceedings of the First West Coast Computer Faire*, April 1977.
Newcomb. "Why not Just Use the Phone?" *Byte*, July 1978.
Palm. "Washington Mailbox: ASCII." *QST*, June 1980, p. 60.
Pank. "CB Computer Mail." *Proceedings of the First West Coast Computer Faire*, April 1977.
Pugh. "MCALL-C: A Communications Protocol for Personal Computer." *Dr. Dobb's Journal of Computer Calisthenics & Orthodontia*, 1980, No. 46, p. 16.
Riportella. "Satellite-Linked Computer Network, A Phase-III Hook-up for Your Keyboard." *Ham Radio Horizons*, March 1980, p. 48.
Rouleau. "The Packet Radio Revolution." *73*, Dec. 1978, p. 192.
Rouleau and Hodgson. *Packet Radio*. Blue Ridge Summit, PA: Tab Books, 1981.
Stoner. "Calling All Computers." *Byte*, Dec. 1978, p. 159.
Tesler. "Computer Networks." *People's Computers*, Sept.-Oct. 1977.
Wilber. "CIE Net." *Byte*, Feb. through April 1978 issues.
Williams. "ASCII at Last?" *QST*, Oct. 1978.

"Automatic Packet-Radio Location System (APLS) Proposal" by Bob Bruninga, WB4APR

By Ward Silver, NØAX

The packet radio network of nodes and digipeaters and gateways (stations that routed messages between the packet network and other networks such as the rapidly expanding Internet) enabled quite a number of interesting services. The best-known service was the bulletin board system or BBS that was essentially the same as the dial-up BBSs that were popular throughout the 1980s and early 1990s. (This was well before the World Wide Web was launched.) Another widely-used service was the *PacketCluster* variation of the BBS, broadcasting DX spotting and other information to logged-on stations. Once the Internet got rolling, though, those services changed over to online access to take advantage of the much higher data rates of the wired networks. But a third service was gaining popularity and is still in operation today — even expanding with new features — the Automatic Packet Reporting System (APRS, www.aprs.org).

APRS is thriving precisely because it was designed for use by roving, mobile stations disconnected from any wireless network, and there are plenty of those! As the following article from February 1991 *QEX* shows, the original proposal for an Automatic Packet-Radio Location System (APLS) grew out of public safety agency vehicle tracking systems that had just become practical at the time. While mobile telephones and data services now cover quite a bit of territory, it would still require a fair amount of accessory equipment to accomplish what APRS does. Since the APRS is an open standard and uses the stable, established communications infrastructure of packet radio nodes and digipeaters, it's much easier to extend and customize the system than commercial technology.

Reading through the list of field and data types, it is clear that Bruninga's vision for APLS/APRS was broad and prescient — a fully-formed information distribution system available to anyone with a TNC and a 2 meter transceiver. While some of the data definitions are no longer very useful (the comment "x" in a

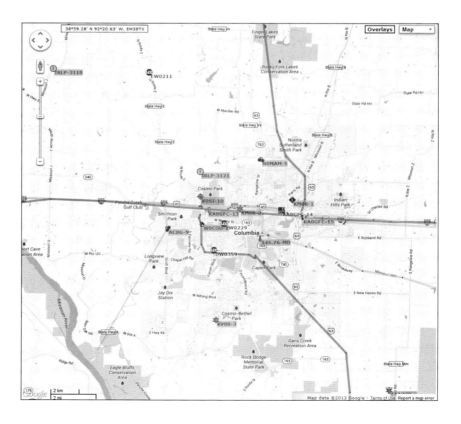

APRS station location and other information can be found via websites such as aprs.fi. The stations in and around Columbia, Missouri, can be seen here, including the position "trails" of stations passing through town. Other icons indicate weather or IRLP stations. (Map courtesy of Google Maps)

gateway field means "fax available"), the utility of the list is clear. Looking at the list of symbol definitions available for use today (**www.aprs.org/symbols.html**) gives an idea of the power of the system.

Another key element of the APRS messaging definitions that can be a lesson to all developers is that its controlling data elements and message contents are all in "plain text," meaning that a human can easily read them without special compression/decompression or translation software. This greatly aids in development and debugging, and enables new developers to support the system and add features. According to Bob Metcalfe, the creator of Ethernet, a network's value lies not in its speed but in its ability to form connections. Plain text, while not the fastest or more sophisticated choice, helped the APRS network to expand quickly.

The utility of APRS was immediately recognized by commercial developers who have adapted the basic principles to numerous messaging and location systems used by industry. This makes APRS and its underlying packet radio system an excellent example of amateur innovation flowing to the professional world.

With the mobile data networks expanding and accelerating, is there a future for APRS? Most assuredly. Its founder is still busily integrating features into the APRS specification, messaging (similar to mobile telephony's Short Messaging System or SMS) is taking off as an APRS feature, gateways to other amateur digital networks are being implemented such as the D-PRS system (**www.aprs-is.net/dprs.aspx**), and APRS is rapidly becoming a protocol of choice for scientific experiments that combine remote sensing with Amateur Radio in balloons, remote-controlled craft, water- and land-based monitoring systems and other applications.

An example of a self-contained APRS tracker, the R-Trak from RPC Electronics (http://rpc-electronics.com) includes a GPS receiver and 500 mW VHF transmitter. Power and antennas are all that is required to generate position messages to the APRS system.

AUTOMATIC PACKET-RADIO LOCATION SYSTEM (APLS) PROPOSAL

Most commercial mobile communications systems have evolved to include sophisticated data communication capabilities. The latest technology is automatic vehicle location systems (AVLS) that permits rapid dispatch and response since the location of every vehicle in the system is known instantaneously. By providing automatic station location information, the communication channel can be used for more critical information needs. On the amateur bands, the first and most critical period of any emergency net is the identification of net participants, their locations and capabilities. This initial period of operation uses up valuable time and energy. Amateur packet radio is ideally suited for automating net establishment and administration.

If we adopted a standard format for reporting location and capabilities over packet radio, simple computer programs could be used for collecting and displaying station locations. Color graphics could be used to display maps, station locations, and station capabilities. Simple programs could provide on-line real-time status displays that would be the envy of most public service agencies and officials.

APLS

The standard packet-radio format would be transmitted as a beacon about every ten minutes and would include up to three fields:

Location: Absolute - latitude, longitude
            Point - city or locally defined point
            Relative - range and bearing to a known point
            Offset - N, S, E, W offsets to a known point
Descriptors: Includes capabilities, affiliations, vehicle type, etc
Text: Remaining bytes left in one line packet that can contain free text, or amplifying remarks

Since tracking and display software must have precise definitions for extracting the information from monitored packets, the format for each field needs to be explicitly defined. The following formats are designed to be simple and also human readable. The field separators are the slash character followed by a one-character field identifier. The packet is identified as an APLS packet by the APLS characters in the TO: address of the standard packet format.

Field Type	Format	Comments
/L...	+dd:mm:ss	Latitude in degrees: minutes:seconds
	+dd.ddd	In decimal degrees (± 90 degrees)
/O...	+dd:mm:ss	Longitude in degrees: minutes:secs
	+dd.ddd	In decimal degrees (± 180 degrees)
/*...	Xxxx...x	City, airport or other defined point
/G...	XXnnxx	Grid square (defined by NW corner)
/B...	ddd	Bearing in degrees from /* location
/R...	mm.m	Range from /~ location in miles
/N...,/S..., /E...,/W...	mm.m	North-South and East-West offsets from /* location in decimal miles
/=	XxxXxX...x	Descriptors: Each letter represents a capability, affiliation, or location descriptor. The letters may be listed in any order, but alphabetically would help manual processing.

A	Ambulance	a	Aeronautical mobile
B	BBS	b	Briefcase portable
C	County	c	City
		d	Data/file storage and retrieval
E	Emergency org.	e	Emergency power
F	Federal	f	Fire station or vehicle
G	Government	g	Good location (for antennas, etc.)
H	Hospital	h	HF capability
M	Medical	m	MARS, Military Affiliate Radio
N	NET/ROM	n	National Traffic System station
P	Police	p	Printer for hard copy available
Q	CQ		
R	RACES	r	ARES station
S	State	s	Satellite capability

16 QEX

T	TCP/IP	t	ATV capability
		u	UHF 440-MHz capability
V	Voice frequency shown in text	v	VHF 220-MHz capability
W	Weather station		
X	Cross-country gateway	x	FAX available
4	Four-wheel drive	!	Command post or Headquarters
6	6-meter node	>	Enroute to location described in text
?	Press or Media	#	Telephone (optional number in text)
+	Red Cross	&	Multiple ops standing by
~	Marine/maritime	@	At location described in text

Usage

Although many descriptors can apply to most stations, only those items or fields necessary for the particular communication at hand should be used. For example, a beacon packet for a station with HF, satellite and ATV capability could contain more than 70 characters. For calling CQ on HF, only the location is typically of interest. Some examples for my station are shown below.

WB4APR>APLS:/L+38.59.27/0-76.29.25/
 =deghpstuv#/:301 267-4380

or

WB4APR>APLS:/*BWI/E5.2/S3.8/=deht (South and East of BWI airport)

or

WB4APR>APLS:/L+38.59.27/0-76.29.25/=Qh (CQ on HF)

or

WB4APR>APLS:/*Glen Burnie,MD/=Q (CQ on HF)

Map Display

The most interesting use of the APLS beacon information will be in the presentation of network size and location on map displays. Map scale and features would be user options. The minimum scale could be as small as 1 mile square for certain public service events, to worldwide for watching HF activity. Geographic features can be displayed or suppressed depending on screen congestion. For example, display categories may include Interstates, major highways, minor highways, water boundaries, marinas, airports, train tracks, city or county boundaries, city and town names, etc. Editing of map features is essential for tailoring local small scale displays.

Activity

Since the time of each packet is tagged by the receiving station, color can be used for displaying the latency of information. The location of new stations can be displayed on the color map in bright letters, maybe red. After a station has not been heard for more than 15 minutes, it decays to yellow letters. After 30 minutes, the station decays to green letters. After an hour, the station fades to gray, and after two hours it is dropped. The rate of decay is a user set parameter depending on the type of network being monitored.

Type of Location

Using the information contained in the capabilities field, monitoring programs can easily sort stations by type of vehicle or by type of location, such as medical care facilities or emergency communications points.

Implementation

No special hardware is required to implement APLS at the thousands of packet-radio terminals across the country. APLS information is transmitted in a beacon packet using the built-in beacon function of the standard TNC. Unfortunately, the use of beacons on packet radio developed a bad reputation back in the early days because of overall band congestion and misuse. If beacons are kept short and timed to occur infrequently, they can become a very valuable addition to our packet-radio system. If there are 30 stations in a net, beaconing for one second every 10 minutes uses less than 5% of the channel capacity. If the APLS format was not used, imagine how much channel capacity would be used if all 30 stations reported their location and capability in plain text!

Everyone can monitor APLS beacons simply by observing transmissions with the monitor mode turned on. If the channel is busy, all connected information packets can be filtered out by turning the MALL parameter off. With the MALL parameter OFF, only beacon packets and other packets not involved in a two-way connected QSO will be displayed. MCOM should also be off to reduce clutter on the screen. User-friendly software for display of APLS information can easily be written for any computer.

Standardization

Since standardization of format and descriptors is very important, it is essential that a single coordinating body be responsible for the assignment of descriptor characters and for addressing any needed changes to the format. The purpose of this article is to suggest a national standard for APLS and to eventually transfer the coordinating responsibility to the ARRL or other suitable national organization. In the meantime, please address all suggested modifications and changes to Bob Bruninga, WB4APR (at 115 Old Farm Ct, Glen Burnie, MD 21060). The format is extendible to other unforeseen applications by the additional definition of field identifiers. For the sake of programmers, however, it is hoped to keep additions and changes to a minimum.

—*from Bob Bruninga, WB4APR*

"PACTOR — Radioteletype with Memory ARQ and Data Compression" by Hans-Peter Helfert, DL6MAA, and Ulrich Strate, KF4KV

By Ward Silver, NØAX

The HF channel does horrible things to digital transmissions on their way to the receiver: noise, selective fading, multipath, interference, echoes, to name a few. The result is a very high error rate in received characters that makes high data rates all but impossible at the signal-to-noise ratios typical of amateur communications.

Beginning in the days of RTTY and electromechanical teleprinters, there was no choice. Character errors were just the price of exchanging FSK data on HF. As the price of digital logic components dropped, it became possible to add some firmware to the mix in the form of hard-wired communications circuits with a very limited amount of memory. A variety of improvements were achieved by the mode AMTOR (Amateur Teleprinting Over Radio), developed by Peter Martinez, G3PLX, which made its on-the-air debut in 1978. (Martinez also developed PSK-31 which is featured later in this section of the book.) AMTOR uses FSK with a 170 Hz shift and 100 baud symbol rate.

AMTOR adds two crucial improvements that made dramatic improvements over RTTY: error-detection/correction and automatic repeat request (ARQ). The 7-bit characters sent by AMTOR have a special structure with a 4:3 ratio of 1 and 0 bits. This can be verified by digital logic as a form of error detection. If errors are detected, a repeat is requested. In addition, a limited form of Forward Error Correction (FEC) is also supported that can correct single-bit errors. The result is a fairly robust, if slow, digital mode with an effective data rate of about 35 baud.

The slow speed of AMTOR and several variations (G-TOR is the best known) were a result of the limited processing power available. As personal computers and microprocessors increased in speed and memory prices dropped, more resources were available. Encoding and data compression technology were improving, as well.

While packet radio was performing fairly well at VHF and above, the mode exhibited poor performance in the presence of channel impairments typical of the HF shortwave bands. To achieve an acceptable error rate, the length of each packet had to be reduced to where data throughput became unacceptably slow.

PACTOR was developed with full awareness of the HF channel from extensive testing. This allowed optimization of certain protocol parameters and reduced protocol overhead dramatically. The first release of PACTOR could operate at either 100 or 200 baud depending on conditions, changing on-the-fly as required and without time-consuming resynchronization. Data packets similar to packet radio were used but with two important new features: memory ARQ and real-time data compression (Huffman encoding). The mode specification was released publicly in 1991 (**www.arrl.org/pactor**).

Memory ARQ does not throw away a packet received with errors. The packet is saved (both as received data bits and as a digitized analog signal) and subsequent packets are received and evaluated until a complete

Early multi-mode controllers like this PacTOR Controller from PacComm handled not only PACTOR-I but also AMTOR and RTTY. Other controllers, such as the classic PK-232 from AEA, offered PACTOR support, as well.

good packet can be assembled. This essentially prevents the "blocked" state of the packet radio protocol in which damaged packets are repeatedly discarded but no 100% correct packet can make it through, leading to eventual loss of the connection.

PACTOR immediately proved popular and began to displace the slower AMTOR mode, especially since PACTOR could transfer binary data. The automated "mailbox-style" operation enabled a robust worldwide system of data exchange to be developed, even extending to "PACSAT" satellites in low Earth orbit.

PACTOR-II, released in 1995, increased immunity to interference through software and hardware improvements, the ability to negotiate one of four different speeds depending on propagation and noise (up to 800 bits/s), differential phase-shift keying (DPSK) that reduces spectrum, and totally automatic operation (where allowed). The real-time data compression and encoding scheme of PACTOR-I was improved as well, although the protocol and the proprietary modem (**www.scs-ptc.com**) remain backward-compatible with PACTOR-I and a training sequence can be heard at the start of a contact as modems negotiate to see which protocol will be used.

PACTOR-III improved performance further. Released in 2002, its data rate averages more than three times higher than PACTOR-II with a top speed of 5200 bits/s. The bandwidth of a PACTOR-III signal can reach 2.4 kHz as the signal is spread across multiple tones to meet the requirement to limit the symbol rate to 300 baud. PACTOR-III is also backward-compatible with the two previous PACTOR modes.

Because modems for PACTOR-II and PACTOR-III are proprietary, amateurs felt the need to have a backup (or competing) mode to PACTOR that could operate on a wide variety of computers. While PACTOR-I software had been available for some time, implementing the more sophisticated PACTOR-II and -III were far more difficult. An initial attempt called SCAMP demonstrated the feasibility of supporting PACTOR-like communications on a sound card-based computer, but performance was not sufficient. Subsequently, the project was reattempted successfully, producing the WINMOR protocol. (Details are available at **www.winlink.org/winmor**; see the reference table later in this book for articles about WINMOR by Meuthing.)

Recently, SCS released a further upgrade, PACTOR-4, still backward compatible with its predecessor protocols, but with dramatically improved performance. Its maximum net speed is 10,500 bits per second, twice the maximum rate of PACTOR-III, but still occupies the same 2.4 kHz channel. The DSP software can operate at any of 10 signaling speeds, supports up to six notch filters automatically, and has an adaptive equalizer for channel conditions.

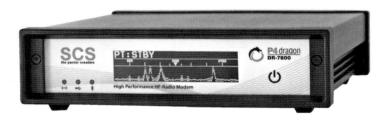

The P4dragon DR-7800 HF Radio Modem from SCS supports all levels of PACTOR though PACTOR-4. As of 2013, US hams may not use PACTOR-4 due to symbol rate limitations on the HF bands.

Yet PACTOR-4 cannot be used by US hams in the US ham bands. (MARS and foreign hams can use PACTOR-4 and the Winlink system also supports it.) Why? Because the PACTOR-4 symbol rate can be as high as 1800 baud, exceeding the current 300-baud limit by a factor of 6. This points out the need for modernizing the regulations for Amateur Radio as technology progresses. The current 300-baud limit on the HF bands has been in place for decades while the state of the art bypassed it long ago. A new regimen is needed if amateurs are going to continue to make meaningful advances and satisfy their Basis and Purpose in the second century of Amateur Radio.

PACTOR—Radioteletype with Memory ARQ and Data Compression

By Hans-Peter Helfert, DL6MAA
   Gustav-Müller-Strasse 8
   D-8948 Mindelheim
   Germany

and Ulrich Strate, KF4KV
   Lommerwiese 18
   D-5330 Köbigswinter 1
   Germany

Translated by Don Moe, KE6MN/DJØHC, from the November 1990 issue of cq-DL, *published by the German Amateur Radio Club.*

Introduction

In the past ten years, Amateur Radio teleprinting has increasingly evolved from an elite operating mode for specialists into a regular means of daily communications. Under closer scrutiny it is apparent however, that the largest extent of progress has mainly benefited the VHF/UHF operating mode packet radio. In the short wave segment, amateurs still have to make do with relatively modest technical standards and ease of operation.

The transition from "Steam RTTY" of the T37 era to AMTOR (SITOR) and packet radio (PR) undoubtedly represents a large qualitative improvement. However, the question may be asked whether mere adaptation of commercially used transmission protocols provides a favorable solution for Amateur Radio. In the case of PR above 30 MHz, this can certainly be answered with "yes," since here the transmission conditions of the original system (data lines via telephone) are virtually identical with those found on VHF/UHF. In contrast, a PR connection on the 80-meter band in the evening often results in a serious test of patience.

SITOR was especially developed for operation on short wave; but the system standard is still limited to the technical possibilities of the "TTL days" in the 1960s, even if the amateur designation "Microcomputer Teleprinter Over Radio" suggests something more.

All important AMTOR system parameters such as character set and maximum transmission rate are geared to the typical data terminal at that time, the mechanical teleprinter. Electronic intermediate storage devices, taken for granted today, were not feasible economically. Since new developments can scarcely be expected from the commercial side, such as for nonmilitary short wave radio at sea, radio amateurs are left to their own devices.

The authors of this article advocate the position that even in the era of satellite communications, efficient transmission protocols for short wave cannot be ignored. In accordance with aspects of information theory, this must also include the operating mode CW.

1. AMTOR—Strengths and Weaknesses

Before designing a new system from scratch, it is appropriate to look for possibilities of extending or improving existing technology.

The popularity of AMTOR (see Ref 1 for functional description) is well founded: the system is relatively uncomplicated and can be combined with available teleprinters.

Even at poor signal-to-noise levels usable connections can still be maintained. The rather high error rate under these conditions is tolerable in normal amateur conversations due to the high amount of redundancy in text.

This is a different story in the case of technical messages, such as modification instructions, programs or the like. In addition to the fact that every error can have disastrous effects, such texts are mostly in ASCII format. When transmitted in 5-bit Baudot code, ambiguity results which must either be tediously clarified or left to the intuition of the reader.

Recoding techniques, such as suggested in Ref 2, merely shift this problem to a different level. In addition to significant speed reductions, transmission errors can cause even more disagreeable side effects.

A further disadvantage of AMTOR, which is particularly significant for mailbox operation, is the low effective maximum speed of less than 35 bauds, resulting in insufficient usage of the available channel capacity during phases with good signal-to-noise ratios.

2. Basis for the Development of PACTOR

The authors began experimenting with derivatives of the AMTOR technology, such as longer blocks, doubling the speed, etc. Although these achieved significant improvements in performance, the principal weaknesses of AMTOR, inadequate error correction and ASCII incompatibility, could not be overcome. Thus the design of a completely new technique was begun at the end of 1987.

Since the new system combined important characteristics of packet radio and AMTOR, the name PACTOR was chosen (Latin: mediator). The synchronous, half-duplex basic structure of AMTOR was retained: Information blocks sent at fixed time intervals are acknowledged by the receiver with brief control signals (CS).

The length of the information blocks and thus the duration of the transmission cycle is an important factor in determining the flexibility of a system. On a noisy channel long packets scarcely have a chance of survival, resulting in the PR blocking effect, which is largely minimized by Memory ARQ in PT. On the other hand, during periods of strong interference, the probability of reception increases when shorter packet lengths are used. The price in this case is a lower maximum data rate on a noise-free transmission channel.

For example: AMTOR requires a cycle length of 45 bits in order to transmit the message content of 15 bits. Two thirds of the capacity are thus swallowed up by overhead.

To arrive at the most favorable PACTOR block lengths, long-term tests were performed with short wave FSK trans-

[1]References appear on page 6.

missions and the results were evaluated by computer. The result was an optimal cycle time of nearly two seconds, which was then reduced to 1.44 seconds in the final version of the system in order to achieve short break-in times. The overhead portion now takes up only one third of the transmission capacity.

In a synchronous transmission system, the stability of the clocks at both stations is very important. During the development of PT this problem was circumvented in a very simple way: the system clock at both ends was derived from the 50-Hz power grid, which provides a phase stable and reliable synchronization framework for nearly all of western Europe. Since relying on the power grid would have naturally restricted the system's usefulness, crystal control with phase correction is now the standard mode.

Due to the narrow bandwidth limitations imposed by regulations and the receiver filters, only FSK came into consideration as the modulation type. Under normal conditions, the typical short wave channel width using a 600-Hz filter permits 200 bauds at 200-Hz shift, which is achievable with customary filter converters without significant modifications.

During periods of phase distortion, such as multipath propagation, which can occur on winter evenings on 80 meters, the speed must be reduced to 100 bauds. In PT this is accomplished by optionally filling the blocks with 100- or 200-baud information. Since the main timing remains constant, the switch over can happen automatically without loss of synchronization as soon as requested by the receiving station.

As described in the previous section, the relatively high error probability with AMTOR is its central weakness. Therefore PT uses a longer acknowledgement signal (12 bits) as well as the cyclical error recognition code used in PR (16 bits), which practically eliminates the problem of unrecognized transmission errors. Only under these prerequisites can this new method for amateur RTTY be fully effective with the following features:

- Memory ARQ, summing method for reconstructing the original block
- On-line data compression (Huffman encoding).

Additional system characteristics:

- faster and more reliable change of transmission direction (break-in)
- 100% compatible to ASCII and transmission of binary data
- QRT confirmed at both stations
- independent of shift direction, no mark and space conventions
- optional attachment to frequency standards such as DCF-77
- unique call address using complete call signs
- comprehensive capability for other stations to read along
- simple hardware requirements
- comfortable operation

3. Important System Details

Since a complete specification of the protocol would exceed the limits of this article, the authors will provide a complete description in the PR mailbox network so that interested parties can obtain further information easily. Here only a few of the special aspects will be described as they differ from the corresponding AMTOR/PR procedures.

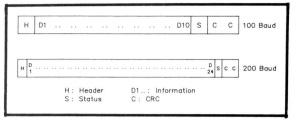

Fig 1—PACTOR packet format

3.1 Transmission Formats

a) Information Blocks

- All packets have the basic structure shown in Fig 1:
- Header: contains a fixed bit pattern for simplifying synchronization and reading along, also important for Memory ARQ
- Data: any binary information. 192 bits at 200 bauds, 80 bits at 100 bauds.
- Status: control byte containing 2-bit packet number, break or QRT request, transmission mode, etc.
- CRC: 16-bit block check code, effective on data, status and CRC.

b) Acknowledgment Signals

- PT uses four acknowledgment signals (CS1 to CS4), which correspond in their function to the AMTOR control signals except for CS4:
- CS1/CS2: normal acknowledgment function
- CS3: change of transmission direction (break-in), forms packet header
- CS4: requests a speed change at the sending station
- The acknowledgment signals have a length of 12 bits. The characters differ in pairs in 8 bits (Hamming offset) so that the chance of confusion is minimized. One of the most common causes of errors in AMTOR is the small CS Hamming offset of 4 bits.
- If the CS is not correctly received, the transmitting side reacts by repeating the last packet. The request status can be uniquely recognized by the 2-bit packet number so that wasteful transmissions of pure RQ blocks as in AMTOR are unnecessary.

c) Timing

- The receive pause between two blocks is 0.32 seconds. After deducting the CS lengths, 0.2 seconds remain (0.17 sec for AMTOR) for switching and propagation delays so that there is adequate reserve for DX operation.

3.2 Establishing Contact

The calling station (master) sends a special synchronization packet which only contains the call sign (address) of the called station (slave):

/Header/Address (8 bytes, 100 bauds)/Address (8 bytes, 200 bauds)/

Following synchronization, the slave responds with CS1, or CS4 if the 200-baud bit pattern was also recognized. Depending on channel quality the connection can be started at the optimal speed without delay. The number of significant synchronization bytes can be chosen by the slave. In practice, six characters should suffice. The unpleasant problem of ambiguous selcals in AMTOR is thus eliminated.

During the synchronization phase the relative shift direction is also determined. The converter or FSK setting of the two stations is irrelevant. Mark/space conventions can thus be dropped.

After receiving the first CS from the slave, the master begins sending normal information blocks. It has proven useful to send system specific data automatically at the beginning such as master call sign, software version number and other configuration parameter.

3.3 Changing Transmission Direction

Following each correctly received packet, the receiving station can transmit a CS3 (break-in). In contrast to AMTOR, an intermediate cycle containing no information is not required. The CS3 forms the header of the first information packet. In the ideal situation, the direction could be changed again in the next cycle, which would be advantageous for mailbox commands. Depending on whether only the CS3 header or the entire packet was received, the former master could reply with CS2 (repeat) or CS1/CS3.

Analogous to "+?" in AMTOR, the transmitting station can also request a break-in, which occurs by setting the BK status bit.

3.4 Changing Speed

Switching between the two speeds of 100 and 200 bauds is normally provided. Since an increase in speed is sensible only during good conditions and a reduction during bad conditions or a slow information flow such as manual text entry, each direction is handled differently in the protocol.

a) 200 -> 100 Bauds

Following receipt of a bad 200-baud packet, the receiving station can request a reduction in speed with CS4. While maintaining the time frame, the transmitting station will put the packets together with 100-baud information. The unacknowledged 200-baud information of the previous packet will then be repeated.

b) 100 -> 200 Bauds

A correctly received 100-baud packet could be acknowledged with CS4 which causes the transmitting station to double the speed. If the following 200-baud packet is not acknowledged after a predetermined number of attempts, the speed will automatically be set back to 100 bauds. The decision regarding a speed change is made at the receiving end. Normally this occurs by automatically evaluating the packet statistics such as error rate, number of retries, number of filler characters for manual text entry, etc.

3.5 Ending a Contact

In the normal ARQ protocol, the principle of mutual acknowledgment is violated at the end of a connection: One station sends the appropriate QRT signal and then switches the transmitter off. If the other station does not receive the QRT signal, it sends acknowledgment signals until the internal timer expires, which leads to undesirable interference, particularly in AMTOR mailbox operation.

PT solves this problem through a special mode: At the end of a connection special QRT synchronization packets are transmitted which contain the receiver address in the reversed order. If the slave station recognizes such a packet during the normal search phase, it responds with a single acknowledgment transmission in the established time frame. This process is repeated until the sending station has received the acknowledgment.

3.6 Data Compression

In amateur RTTY only constant length characters have been used to date. Frequently occurring letters such as E or N require the same transmission time as X or Q.

A frequency analysis of normal written texts shows that the average information content per character ("Entropy"[3]) only amounts to 4 bits, so that a normal ASCII transmission therefore contains nearly 50% ballast. Through clever encoding using variable character lengths, common in Morse telegraphy for the past 150 years, it should be possible to put this idle reserve to use.

The Huffman code (see Ref 3) used by PT approaches the optimal limit within a few percent so that nearly 100% increase compared to ASCII can be achieved in practice. This code can be automatically calculated as a tree structure based on the character frequency. The compression occurs by packet; the character lengths vary between 2 and 15 bits.

A prerequisite for using data compression methods is high data integrity. Techniques without block error recognition such as AMTOR are therefore not suitable.

3.7 Memory ARQ

Customary FSK RTTY converters route the demodulated received signal via a low-pass filter to a trigger stage where the binary data for the computer are extracted. Here a weakness becomes evident: The decision whether a signal is a "0" or a "1" is made outside the computer and is thus no longer accessible for "intelligent" analysis. The information whether a signal was only 1 millivolt or 1 volt above the threshold is lost forever. Additional distortions are caused by inaccurate calibration or drift of the trigger threshold.

In the past, error recognizing techniques for RTTY in Amateur Radio merely evaluated the information from complete blocks received error-free. It is obvious that this results in a significant waste of information particularly at poor signal-to-noise levels. In an ARQ system such as PACTOR, multiple repeats of an incorrectly received packet can be overlapped to recover the original information.

The ideal solution in the form of a direct computer evaluation of the audio receive signal is still constrained by the high price of the necessary signal processors. Practice with PACTOR has shown however, that important advances can be achieved using a low-cost 8-bit A/D converter instead of a trigger stage.

The incoming analog values are first converted to 0/1 decisions as before, but additionally are stored as a sequence of 8 bit values for later use. If the 0/1 evaluation does not yield a correct packet (CRC error), the analog values from subsequent repeats of the packet are combined into a "sum" packet which is then subjected to a 0/1 evaluation and CRC check.

There are two potential problems to be considered:

a) If the acknowledgement signal sent by the receiving station is not immediately heard, old RQ packets could be added to the sum for the new block.

b) Packets which were nearly completely destroyed, such as by an interfering carrier, should also be ignored.

To handle these cases, the information contained in the packet header is evaluated. This is inverted in phase

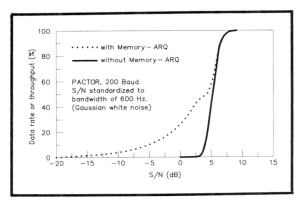

Fig 2—Increase in data rate when using Memory ARQ.

with the packet counter in order to guarantee a simple request recognition. Obviously unusable packets, such as those with a constant bit pattern or a destroyed header are not added to the summation.

Similar methods are used in professional transmission technology.[4] The term "Memory ARQ" comes from there.

Sample calculations confirmed in practice have shown that the data rate can be significantly improved at poor signal levels by using Memory ARQ. It is particularly apparent that the sharp PR limit at which the communication collapses has been eliminated. (See Fig 2.)

Memory ARQ can be limited to being used only if the error recognition technique has adequate reserve. In AMTOR a dramatic increase in the rate of incorrect characters would result.

3.8 Monitor Mode

The requirement that other stations be able to read the content of communications is specified in the Amateur Radio regulations. This is necessary when there are more than two active stations. PACTOR is similar here to the monitor mode in PR. The received bit stream is continuously evaluated and checked for valid packets according to CRC. Since several samples occur per bit and a separate CRC must be calculated for the two possible speeds, the capacity of the Z80 CPU is nearly at its limit in this mode. The result is an uncomplicated read-along operation, which works without operator intervention, in contrast to the L-mode in AMTOR.

Additionally an automatic CW identification occurs in 5-minute intervals.

3.9 Supervisor Mode

The definition of special control characters makes it possible to pass information from the receive buffer directly to the system level. Through this supervisor mode, various protocol versions could be automatically harmonized and thus future developments of the system could be taken into consideration.

4. Practical Operation

4.1 Hardware and Software

PT was designed from the start to be a self-contained system since a home computer solution (C64 or similar) nearly always has disadvantages such as space requirements, HF interference, etc.

The "PACTOR Controller" (PTC) was implemented as a single board computer based on the Z80 processor. Initially DL6MAA built a prototype with the new CMOS SMD chip TMPZ84C015 which contains all of the necessary Z80 peripheral modules. At the same time a compatible version was built by DF4KV using conventional Z80 components.

A battery-powered real-time clock is integrated along with two EIA-232 interfaces as terminal connections (XON/XOFF handshaking). The system status is displayed in a block of 12 LEDs, and an additional row of LEDs acts as a tuning indicator based on the incoming analog values. Important events such as connect or QRT are also signaled acoustically. The associated converter operates with filters. The output signal from the low-pass filter is fed via a level converter stage to the ADC input.

The software was developed primarily by DL6MAA and in addition to the pure PT system also contains a command interpreter with TNC compatible syntax. The free RAM memory is automatically configured as a private mailbox in which messages from callers can be deposited or read. The available program memory is large enough to accommodate additional software such as AMTOR or a CW keyer.

In the fall of 1989, DL2FAK installed a PTC on 80 meters with access to the message base of a 70-cm PR system. Using this PT link technique, ASCII compatibility and speed of the PT system were demonstrated very well.

In the meantime, further amateurs have become involved with PT tests: DK5FH, DF4WC, and DL3FCJ, who has developed a new PTC design with an integrated converter.

4.2 Operating Techniques

For users already familiar with packet radio, there is scarcely any adjustment needed. A series of commands allows checking and setting all important system parameters. Most commands can also be accessed by the remote station for reading directory contents, storing messages, etc.

5. Conclusion

PACTOR was developed as a purely amateur project in the context of the experimental radio service. Error robustness and short wave suitability were primary goals.

PTC kits based on the design of DL3FCJ should become available by the end of 1990. Interested parties can request circuit diagrams from the authors by sending an SASE. Programmed EPROMs and GALs are likewise available in limited quantity.

6. References

[1] L. Monz, DF8PD: Funkfernschreibverfahren. *cq-DL* 1/86. (Radio teleprinter techniques)

[2] A. Clemmetsen, G3VZJ: 10 Jahre AMTOR—Rückblick und Ausblick. *cq-DL* 2/89 (10 years AMTOR—review and prognosis)

[3] F. Topsoe: Informationstheorie. *Stuttgart* 1974. (Information theory)

[4] J. J. Metzner, D. Chang: Efficient Selective Repeat ARQ Strategies for Very Noisy and Fluctuating Channels. *IEEE Transactions on Communications*, vol. COM-33, May 1985.

"APLINK: The Delivery Systems"
by Jim Mortenson, N2HOS

By Ward Silver, N0AX

Most hams are aware of, if not familiar with Winlink, the worldwide system of email servers accessible via radio links. Most hams are not, however, familiar with how the system got started or that it had nothing to do with email at all! The original need addressed by *APLINK* software (the name is an abbreviation of AMTOR-Packet-Link) was to allow individuals using AMTOR on HF to contact bulletin board systems (BBS) that were then connected together with packet radio networks on VHF and UHF. Military Auxiliary Radio System (MARS) and National Traffic System (NTS) operations also adopted *APLINK*. The system achieved its broadest reach around the time of the 1990 Gulf War as it handled thousands of messages from military personnel.

APLINK is not a mode or protocol; it is a program that works with an AMTOR modem on one side and a BBS system on the other side. Nevertheless, it supplied a key interworking function that connected disparate modes and bands to enable worldwide communication. Note that in the following articles, hams using AMTOR on HF routinely connect to *APLINK* stations at BBSs thousands of miles away. Originally an MS-DOS program, *APLINK* migrated to the *Windows* environment and became what is now referred to as *Winlink Classic*. Both *APLINK* and *Winlink* were written by Vic Poor, W5SMM.

Table 1
Active APLINK Stations

Call	SELCAL	SysOp	Location	Frequency (kHz)
AH6D	AAHD	PAUL	HAWAII	14071.5*
DL0YB	DLYB	WERNER	GERMANY	14080.0
DU9BC	DUBC	FRED	PHILIPPINES	14072.0
G4SCA	GSCA	JOHN	ENGLAND	14070.0*
HL9TG	HLTG	GARY	KOREA	14073.5
K7BUC	KBUC	DEL	ARIZONA	14072.5*
KB1PJ/8	KBPJ	DAVID	OHIO	14070.5*
N0IA/7	NNIA	BUD	NEVADA	14070.5*
TG9VT	TGVT	JOHN	GUATEMALA	14074.0*
V51NH	VVNH	NICO	NAMIBIA	14070.0
VK2AGE	VAGE	GORDON	AUSTRALIA	14075.0*
VK2EHQ	VEHQ	PETER	AUSTRALIA	14070.5
VK6YM	VKYM	HERVE	AUSTRALIA	14081.0
WA1URA/9	WURA	FRANK	INDIANA	14071.5*
WA8DRZ/6	WDRZ	CRAIG	CALIFORNIA	14068.5*
WB7QWG/9	WQWG	BOB	INDIANA	14071.5*
ZF1GC	ZFGC	FRANK	CAYMAN IS	14070.5*
ZL1ACO	ZACO	NEILL	NEW ZEALAND	14072.5

*On multiple frequencies/bands.

In 1990 this was the entire worldwide network of AMTOR-accessible stations running the *APLINK* software!

In the 1980s, the wide-area packet network developed quickly and by developing some addressing conventions, amateurs were able to send messages worldwide. But the Internet was on the march and many BBS users migrated to the fast and easy email available online. The packet network and BBSs started falling out of favor, but the functionality of *Winlink* was still needed. Jim Jennings, W5EUT, translated the BBS side of *Winlink* to use Internet email instead, creating *Netlink*. This was the genesis of today's Winlink 2000 system that handles email via ham radio around the world. (A full accounting of the Winlink 2000 system's history is available at **www.winlink.org**.)

By themselves, AMTOR and packet radio were important amateur innovations. Adding the BBS component and linking them together was also important, but these remained separate until *APLINK* created the "pipe" that let information flow in completely new ways. A station with no network connection at all, just an HF radio with a simple AMTOR modem, could suddenly send and receive digital messages. Hams piloting a sailboat, a motor home, or just operating away from home now had digital connectivity — all they needed was a list of *APLINK* mailbox station frequencies and a bit of propagation!

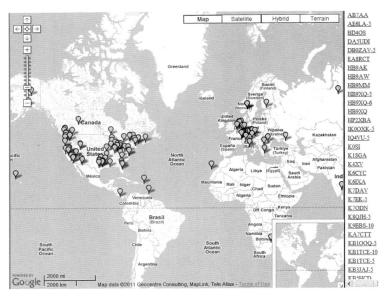

This map shows some of the Winlink 2000 Radio Mail Server (RMS) stations available on HF. Many more local stations can be accessed via VHF or UHF channels.

Of course, Winlink 2000 has grown far beyond the original BBS replacement system. With the addition of the email client software *Airmail*, the system looks and acts like Internet email. It is accessed by thousands of users every day from remote places all around the world. Winlink 2000 has become a key component of emergency communications teams worldwide. Will the growing spread of mobile data networks make Winlink 2000 obsolete in the same way Internet connectivity eroded the need for the BBS-packet radio networks? That's a question I'm sure the Winlink 2000 administrators think about all the time — maybe they're at work on the solution right now!

Public Service

Conducted By Steve Ewald, WA4CMS
Assistant Public Service Manager

APLINK: The Delivery Systems—Part 1

By Jim Mortensen, N2HOS
65 Holly Pl
Briarcliff Manor, NY 10510

APLINKing the World

While the AMTOR-to-packet traffic potential of *APLINK* isn't the fulfillment of Marshall McLuhan's "Global Village" (where everybody communicates instantaneously with everybody else), it comes close, even though a bunch of amateurs run the system. *APLINK* software runs on more than 50 stations scattered about six continents (even the Soviet Union joined the ranks in mid-1991, thanks to John Veale, G4SCA, of Plymouth, England).[1] The network offers any amateur with AMTOR capability the opportunity to participate in a service that operates around the clock and requires no more than 100 watts, yet transcends propagation and QRM problems by scanning multiple bands and frequencies. No other mode or service offers such interesting and flexible person-to-person, digital-communications capability.

Part 1 of this series covers the personal communications aspects of *APLINK* and the system's multiple-delivery systems. Part 2 will examine *APLINK* as a major new ingredient in Amateur Radio's public service capability. The columns assume that you're familiar with AMTOR and *APLINK* and have had experience with the mode and the mailbox service.

APLINK and AMTOR techniques were covered in my article in November 1990 *QST* ("A Beginner's Tour to and Through AMTOR," page 53). Software requirements have changed, however. When signing in for the first time, it's now only necessary to type (after the station's initial **GA+?**) your own call sign. Type **N2HOS<Return>**. The mailbox will ask you to confirm the call sign. Proceed as outlined in the article. There are also changes involving routing beyond the first *APLINK* station (see below).

To use screen-to-screen communications via *APLINK*, one step does it all. You deposit a message for me at "box" XYZ, I log in later and pick up the message and leave one for you. This basic delivery technique works without flaw. Timing depends solely on the addressee; if he doesn't log in, the message can't be delivered (the computer purges the message after 21 days).

If the bands collapse, you might try to leave the message in XYZ "AT" ABC (to be forwarded by the station that received your message). Error message! The *APLINK* stations will reject that address statement. Things have changed and that's where we go next—to the delivery systems beyond your initial *APLINK* contact.

Ya Gotta Know the Technique

The latest *APLINK* software requires hierarchical routing (H-Routing). Stations remind you in different ways, but there's no avoiding the new H-Routing protocol. The address hierarchy is straightforward. If the message is to go beyond the first station, start the address with the recipient's call sign, the destination call sign, then state or country, and finally the continent. A period (.) must be used to separate the tokens, which must be in order, from the most specific to the least specific (thus the hierarchy). For example, **SP N2HOS AT TG9VT.GTM.NA** or **AT GB7SCA.GBR.EU**.[2,3]

Delivery timing depends now on the actions of two operators. First, an *APLINK* system operator (SysOp) must manually trigger the forwarding action. The message will normally move within 24 hours (and often less). The message sits at the destination mailbox until the addressee fires up the rig, links with the right *APLINK* station and picks up his mail. Timing now slips a bit. Under the best circumstances, it might be 10-30 hours instead of 2-12. But *APLINK*-to-*APLINK* forwarding is efficient and predictable.

Growing Pains

Move to the next delivery method (from "A" for the AMTOR part of *APLINK* to the "P" for Packet mode) and we do a flip-flop. VHF packet offers insulation from solar activity, but suffers from a lack of predictability. Delivery is problematic—sometimes surprisingly fast, sometimes nonexistent. But if your message targets the computer of a non-*APLINK*-using ham, the HF-to-VHF switch is a necessary option. Address the message under the H-Routing rules and the *APLINK* SysOp will dump the message in the lap of a nearby full-service packet BBS (PBBS). If the addressee is in the immediate area, delivery availability is assured within hours or minutes. Otherwise, the journey begins and timing now relies not on 2-3, but on 4-14 pairs of hands. No wonder performance is unpredictable!

Packet handling of traffic from DX stations via *APLINK* is still in its formative period. The systems are there, but lack the organization to harness the power and make the transfer/forwarding process routine. It will come, but for now, PBBSs are swamped with traffic and SysOps have little time to give thought to this problem.

Keeping the Messages Moving

There are bright spots, however, and focused effort produces startling results. During the fall of 1990, at the peak of the Operation Desert Storm buildup, we glimpsed its potential. Bob Foster Jr, WB7QWG/9 (Indianapolis *APLINK*), passed hundreds of messages each week from the USS *Kennedy* (via John Troost, TG9VT, in Guatemala City) to families and friends in the US. Many of them had a common home-port destination, so Bob developed a packet route from Indianapolis to Norfolk, Virginia, that expedited the mail and had replies en route to the *Kennedy* within 24 hours. The operative word is *develop*. Apply patience, experimentation and cooperation in equal doses and you, too, might work out the kinks in your area.

Packet has the potential to be a primary cog in *APLINK*'s future. A few dedicated regional networks could interface with *APLINK* stations and serve the bulk of the US amateur population. This array could deliver an HF message to a VHF PBBS less than one or two hops—minutes to hours—from the final destination. Screen-to-screen, ham-to-ham traffic operators smile at the thought. Personal communications (still not quite the Global Village) nears perfection in this mailbox mode. Enjoy it when live QSOs aren't an option.

Don't Be Satisfied!

APLINK's value shrinks if it doesn't move high volumes of emergency or health-and-welfare traffic from HF to VHF packet to the local telephone call that's the final leg in third-party traffic handling. *APLINK* can do it, but it requires changes in routing, system and mode (digital to voice)—and in the ARRL National Traffic System (NTS).

The NTS, last but not least of the *APLINK* delivery systems, is proud of its tradition. The keepers of that heritage watch carefully as new technologies earn their place in the system. *APLINK* graduated with honors and is now the primary long-haul element in the NTS structure. Mail that enters the NTS is delivered, and the message is read over the telephone to the addressee.

Part 2 covers the details of using the *APLINK*-to-NTS message service and *APLINK*'s public service activity.

Notes

[1] Vic Poor, W5SMM, of San Antonio, Texas, developed software to solve the long-haul communication problems from his sailboat in distant waters. After trying and discarding HF packet, Vic switched to AMTOR and the new mode was born. The software is now in version 5.04 (at least) and is "freeware."

[2] The address **SP N2HOS AT WA1URA/9.IN.USA.NA** works in AMTOR, but fails to meet the needs of packet. Packet requires the @ in place of **AT**. New versions of *APLINK* software may handle this problem.

[3] The full listing of abbreviations is too large to include here. Complete tables can be downloaded from *APLINK* stations, or contact the *RTTY Journal*, 9085 La Casita Ave, Fountain Valley, CA 92708. A complete list of routing abbreviations and commands and the latest listing of *APLINK* stations is available.

Public Service

Conducted By Steve Ewald, WV1X
Assistant Public Service Manager

APLINK: The Delivery Systems—*Part 2*

By Jim Mortensen, N2HOS
65 Holly Pl
Briarcliff Manor, NY 10510

APLINK, an AMTOR-to-packet message gateway program, operated on an unprecedented scale during the Gulf War, but its role as a primary player in traffic handling began much earlier. John Veale, G4SCA, and David Speltz, KB1PJ, participated in the first display of *APLINK*'s public service power after the 1989 Armenian earthquake.[1] Veale and Speltz passed hundreds of health-and-welfare messages. The bulk of the traffic comprised American requests for survivor information, assembled in Cleveland via packet. The information was sent via AMTOR to Plymouth and relayed via SSB to the Soviet Union. They also teamed up with the International Red Cross and the United Nations Disaster Relief Organization (UNDRO) to pass urgent requests for drugs and medical gear needed at two hospitals involved in the tragedy.

Why was this traffic switched from SSB (as was used in the Mexico City earthquake) to AMTOR? Handling hundreds of names and addresses by phone can be done, but Veale found it so time consuming that he suggested AMTOR as the solution. Speltz set up the station and from then on, the digital mode took over the US-UK traffic. Throughout his experience, Veale says AMTOR proved itself as a reliable long-haul medium. "It reaches areas other modes can't reach."

APLINK has passed the test and performed admirably in public service third-party traffic handling. But it's only the beginning. With *Clover*, the capacity could increase dramatically.[2] Volume could grow six times or more, even though *APLINK* would continue to use the same amount (or less) of spectrum.

Kinks in the Chain

APLINK doesn't deliver third-party traffic; the system forwards messages for delivery by other hams. Somebody must pick the traffic out of the mailbox and aim it toward its destination. A packet, CW or SSB op must move a message to its destination, where someone must print out the message and telephone the addressee or read it to a VHF traffic net. In the latter case, the VHF operator must write it down, pick up the phone and deliver the message to the third party.[3]

It's this complicated, multilayered operation that's the last of the *APLINK* delivery systems. The NTS has been involved in delivering messages for 40 years. But how does it work now, with the new digital modes? Let's look at the structure of *APLINK*/NTS and the procedures for injecting a message into the system.

Ralph Duvall Jr, W3GL, of New Castle, Delaware, operated the first *APLINK* station dedicated to NTS traffic. There are now 11 full-service NTS-affiliated *APLINK* stations in the US, where the HF "chirp" meets the VHF "burrrrrrp" (see Table 1). Although there's a western/southwestern skew to the lineup, US and DX hams should address all NTS traffic to one of these stations.[4] All stations accept NTS traffic, but the traffic may not be picked up at unofficial stations. If it's not picked up, it gets handed off to the packet network for ultimate delivery or the other fates discussed last month.

During the selection process, the NTS required *APLINK* SysOps to have the ability to scan multiple frequencies, dedicate their systems to the NTS and drastically curtail their ham-to-ham and bulletin traffic. (There are those, myself among them, who feel that the second requirement has a negative influence on the NTS. *APLINK*'s foundation rests on such traffic: personal messages and DX bulletins for the worldwide RTTY community. It's unrealistic to cut any station out of that loop and maintain its viability with *APLINK* participants. The busiest stations, those that carry personal and DX traffic, were the stations that carried the bulk of the Gulf traffic. Activity generates activity. The reverse is also true and SysOp boredom poses a real threat. The NTS needs access, but redundancy might be a better answer than exclusivity).

Eleven stations await your traffic. Link with the station closest to the destination of your traffic. The closer the better. Select and move on to the addressing requirements.

Stop Before You Start

Don't send traffic unless you have the message already composed and safely tucked into a file, and you're ready to get it out of the file and into the transmit buffer. Practice that procedure if you aren't completely familiar with your software's file-handling routine. NTS traffic can't be typed on the fly.

You know how to "link" as the first step. Call the appropriate station and sign in as you normally would. Complete any other activity before you come to the NTS-traffic portion of your link. Proceed as outlined below.

Step 1 involves a special *APLINK* command. The SysOp sends **GA+?** and because your response is **ST 33519 at NTSFL <CR/LF>**, you're asked to confirm the details of the command. It says that this is an NTS message going to ZIP code 33519 in Southern Florida. Without that information, the message is bound for the scrap heap. The station then instructs you to go ahead with the message, which might look something like the following:

QTC 1 CLEARWATER FLORIDA 33519
NR 08 R HXG 41 N2HOS BRIARCLIFF NY
10510 0100Z NOV 11 1991
BARBARA METZGER, N4LIH
3005 SARAH DR
CLEARWATER, FL 33519
813-555-9999
I WAS GRIEVED TO HEAR OF THE LOSS OF YOUR VERTICAL IN YESTERDAY'S STORM X
I AM HAPPY TO OFFER YOU SOME USED ANTENNA WIRE FOR THE UPCOMING RTTY CONTEST X WILL SHIP EXPRESS COLLECT X REGARDS FROM YOUR FRIENDLY COMPETITOR
JIM MORTENSEN
NNNN

Line No. 1 is easy. **QTC 1** is your serial number for this message within the current transmission. The following message would be No. 2, etc. The rest of the line is composed of the city, state and ZIP code of the destination.

Line No. 2 grows in complexity. **NR 08** is the serial number for your own message count for the year or month. Suit yourself. **R** refers to the precedence of the message (R = routine, W = welfare, P = priority or EMERGENCY [always written out]). **HXG** is the handling instruction. Handling instructions are optional, but recommended. Seven (condensed) options are available (see the sidebar, "ARRL NTS *HX* Signals"). Then enter the originating station, followed by the number of words/groups in the body text. (Don't count headers or the address, but count the **X**, or stop character. Try to hold the word count to 25 or less). Finally, place of origin, time filed (in UTC) and date.

The NTS mandates a complete address, including ZIP code and telephone number with area code. Without it, the chances of delivery are slim. **NNNN** indicates to *APLINK* that your message is complete. Type **<CR/LF>** to conclude the message and turn the control over to the mailbox. Then, log off or continue with other traffic as desired. That's all there is to it! NTS wheels now grind fast or slow, but exceedingly well (we hope)!

Here's what happens: In theory, if every NTS *APLINK* hub surrounded itself with a cluster composed of 20-40 dedicated VHF

Table 1
NTS-Affiliated *APLINK* Stations

The following key stations are AMTOR-to-packet gateways running *APLINK* software that pass NTS traffic from HF to VHF packet for delivery (single 20-meter mark frequency shown):

Call Sign	AMTOR Selcal	State	Freq (kHz)
N6EQZ/7	NEQZ	WA	14,070.5
W7DCR	WDCR	OR	14,070.5
WA8DRZ/6	WDRZ	CA	14,068.5
N0IA/7	NNIA	NV	14,070.5
K7BUC	KBUC	AZ	14,071.5
KE5HE	KEHE	TX	14,070.5
KA0JRQ	KJRQ	IA	10,128 (30 meters only)
KK4CQ	KKCQ	FL	14,072.5
WA1URA/9	WURA	IN	14,068.0
W3GL	WWGL	DE	14,071.5
W1FYR	WFYR	NH	14,071.5

Pick up the complete list of stations and frequencies, outlined in Part 1 last month.

November 1991   81

ARRL NTS *HX* Signals

The following standard abbreviations are used in the preambles of all properly formatted NTS messages:

HXA	Collect call authorized by addressee.
HXB *X*	Cancel message if not delivered within *X* hours.
HXC	Report date/time of delivery to originating station.
HXD	Report identity of delivering/relaying station and time/method of delivery.
HXE	Get reply from addressee.
HXF *X*	Hold delivery until date *X*.
HXG	Delivery by mail or toll call not required.

packet stations, all the nodes would start an immediate push-pull movement of the traffic toward its destination. Within hours, Metzger's phone would ring. In practice, there are only two areas in the country where that might happen—California/Arizona and New England. The following examples show how it worked with two of my messages:

Florida. I linked with Jim Jennings, KE5HE, with a message for Barbara Metzger, N4LIH, in Clearwater, Florida. Jennings is in College Station, Texas. Somebody (per his/her assignment) linked, picked up the traffic and dropped it into the packet network in the Tampa area. Metzger received the call at 6 PM the next day, about 24 hours after I sent it. Good work.

California. I linked with N0IA/7 (Bud Thompson of Las Vegas) with a message for Geoff Preston, KB6WSQ, in Twentynine Palms, California. Thompson's station ported the message into the NTS packet network with no delay. The message was relayed by two or three packet stations until it arrived at the home of Jack Carter, K4WRM. He was in school at the time, but his TNC accepted the message and turned on its LED. Carter returned, saw the LED, fired up the computer, printed the message, called Preston, and went back to his studies. Elapsed time: About 15 hours. Excellent.

Making *APLINK* Work with the NTS

The majority of my test messages proceeded at a pace that deterred my interest in using the NTS (even allowing for my message-format errors and the unquestioned dedication of NTS members). Overall, however, the NTS may be a bit better than packet. Why? Reasons are plentiful.

APLINK/NTS works in California. Why? Let Thompson answer: "Our first rule is that we don't forward NTS traffic into the packet network until we've confirmed that the end-node PBBS for that ZIP code is NTS-active, and delivery/relay will occur. It's not enough that packet will relay NTS messages properly; they must be serviced in short order, rather than fester on the end-node PBBS."

The statement says so much about caring, recruiting, training, accountability, dedication and understanding, that I know my traffic will get there on time. Here *APLINK* is in an "active," not "passive," mode. Messages don't wait for messengers, but are pushed toward a known, live packet destination. The good thing about the NTS in this micro-environment is that it works and has a sense of mission. The group has shared values, the people at the keyboards and telephones have shared their interests, and the traffic reaches the destination on time. I like that, and sense that we can see the future of the NTS in that model.

But is that the mission of the NTS? Maybe, depending on your source. As an outsider, I look in and say that the NTS seems to operate with no agreed-upon sense of purpose, no definition of its ideals. There are old values, new values and old and new technologies. These divergent groups have convened, danced around the bonfire, laid out new boundaries and protocols, but have no shared convictions about the form or shape the new NTS should display. As an outside observer, I know that if the movers and shakers of the NTS can't agree on the ultimate destination, the organization will never get there.

If Ted Sharp, K6UYK, of North Hollywood, California, is right, "We can develop systems that allow hams to come on the air and find an accessible outlet for a message at almost any time of day, regardless of its destination."[5] If the California model is correct (and it does approach Sharp's ideal), the NTS should hasten to add more *APLINK* stations near major population centers (measure the distance in repeater hops from Miami, Minneapolis/St Paul, New York, Denver or Atlanta to the nearest *APLINK*/NTS outlet), and carefully recruit and develop the dedicated group of VHF packet ops who make the system go and keep the end of the line from "festering." Given that combination, it's possible to envision a system that rivals the DX PacketCluster in its effectiveness and shared passion; a system that would draw outsiders into the action.

This state-of-the-art system built around *APLINK* hubs could serve the bulk of the population centers and 80-90% of the population. The vastness of the Great Plains and deserts of the West would remain a challenge to the ingenuity of the best of the NTS traditions. The answer may be found in *PAMS* (Vic Poor's new *APLINK*-compatible Personal Amtor MBO). Maybe they would even decide to use WATS line telephones to solve the problem. (The Radio Amateur Emergency Network, RAYNET, sponsored by the Radio Society of Great Britain [RSGB] uses telephone and fax. Should we ignore these readily available options?)

If the *APLINK*/NTS future isn't tied to this kind of digital backbone, it's incumbent on them to define a more compelling future and let the amateur community know about it. Without such a platform, they won't be able to recruit, train and stimulate the keyboarders who, in Thompson's words "...are like vultures looking for action." Those vultures are the next generation, the people who'll keep the NTS alive, well and serving for the next 40 years.

Special People

I want to express my sincere appreciation to the hams who went out of their way to give me the benefit of their knowledge of the NTS (the opinions are all mine!). John Veale, G4SCA, was generous and assembled a tremendous amount of information. Ralph Duvall Jr, W3GL, the first (and for so long the only) *APLINK*/NTS station, is a treasure trove of historical knowledge. Dick Hoppe, ND5T, of Edgewood, New Mexico, was a tireless telephone companion. Nick Zorn, N4SS, of Milton, Florida, was another stimulating discovery. His commitment to the cause is exemplary. Ted Sharp, K6UYK, a CW traffic handler for countless years, sees the digital system with 20/20 vision. Thanks to Bud Thompson, N0IA/7, who has seen the future and knows how to run it. Thanks also to Frank Moore, WA1URA/9, of Grabill, Indiana, who led me into the digital world with his first NTS message to me three years ago; to Bob Foster Jr, WB7QWG/9, the past master of handling and forwarding tons of traffic, and to John Troost, TG9VT, of Guatemala City, who taught many of us what the spirit of *APLINK* is all about.

Notes

[1] John operates GB7SCA, Plymouth *APLINK*, the first such European station. It's also the RAYNET station for the UK, the official inlet/outlet for all European emergency traffic.
[2] *Clover* is a development of HAL Communications and Ray Petit, W7GHM, of Oak Harbor, Washington. *Clover* is based on phase-shift keying (FSK/AFSK). It achieves 600-baud throughput with a 500-Hz bandwidth under good band conditions. This could be the ultimate HF digital mode.
[3] In certain situations where there's a well-established regional cluster, the traffic is ported immediately to VHF packet.
[4] Ham-to-ham messages aren't generally considered illegal third-party traffic. See p 13-15 in the ARRL's *FCC Rule Book*. It states, "Where third-party traffic is normally prohibited between the US and other countries, where the third party is an amateur and eligible to be the control operator of the station, the third-party traffic is permitted."
[5] Read Sharp's Apr 1991 *QST* column (p 75). He's been in the NTS for years and is a thoroughly experienced traffic handler.

"Toward New Link-Layer Protocols" by Phil Karn, KA9Q

By Ward Silver, NØAX

The paper reprinted here is a single example of many that were published during what is surely one of the most intense periods of innovation in modern Amateur Radio. After the FCC's relaxation of rules restricting the types of characters that could be used (ASCII characters were first allowed for US amateurs in 1980), an explosion of digital creativity quickly followed. Not coincidentally, the telecommunication industry was also breaking out of its landline access model and starting to capitalize on research that had been accelerating throughout the 1970s. Readers of science history know that innovation usually comes in waves following some kind of breakthrough or new opportunity — such as an increase in available computing power.

Packet radio burst on the scene in 1978 from Canada as described elsewhere in this section. Based on the X.25 computer-to-computer protocol, packet radio networks began to be deployed and quickly began to attract users. As more users took advantage of ever-cheaper computers and self-contained TNC accessories, loading of the system started to affect performance and communications designers looked deeper at the fundamental structure of packet and other over-the-air protocols. Engineers working professionally on commercial data system and as amateurs on the growing digital data systems developed concepts that cross-fertilized each other frequently and widely.

One of these designers was Phil Karn, KA9Q. Most widely known for his *NOS* software that brought the TCP/IP protocol to packet radio, Phil was also taking a hard look at digital radio communications and suggesting ways to improve it. Building on the advancing power of computers available to the amateur, he introduces Forward Error Correction (FEC) to amateur protocols in this detailed and interesting paper that follows. Other topics include Sequential versus Viterbi Decoding and numerous details of what makes a protocol work (or not work) over a radio channel.

A regular presence at TAPR-ARRL Digital Communications Conferences, several of his contributed papers are listed in the reference table later in this book. Here you will find the genesis of TCP/IP applied to packet radio — with broader implications for the use of TCP/IP around the Internet, an open question at the time. The use of TCP/IP on Amateur Radio packet radio networks preceded the appearance of the public Internet. In fact, a block of 16.7 million IP addresses was set aside for Amateur Radio users worldwide in the 1970s through the efforts of Hank Magnuski, KA6M, when computer networking was in its infancy. Karn's packet radio TCP/IP software eventually made its way to dialup systems and then possibly into your mobile phone should it contain one of the common chip sets!

A paper on collisions in the packet radio network deals with the well-known "hidden transmitter" problem that plagues simplex radio channels where any station can transmit at any time. It also deals with the less well-known "exposed terminal" problem in which a station with wide-area receive coverage is unable to transmit when controlled by carrier sensing because it can hear the signals of too many other stations. Several alternatives are suggested with possible significant improvements in performance.

Another paper by KA9Q proposes a new channel access method (Multiple Access with Collision Avoidance, MACA) based on an older busy-tone model but implemented on a single radio channel. While MACA did not gain adoption in Amateur Radio, essential elements of it were incorporated into the IEEE 802.11 standard that you may know better as WiFi. Originally conceived specifically for amateur packet radio, MACA is an excellent example of ideas flowing bidirectionally between the ham and non-ham world because they had much the same problems. Even TCP/IP grew out of early research on non-amateur packet radio.

In the following paper's closing section, "Status and Open Questions," the final question is a good one: "Will the average amateur be willing to use this stuff?" The answer over the past two decades has been, "Yes, if the complexity is managed sufficiently." As it turns out, most hams, like members of the general public, are primarily interested in applying Amateur Radio to some end, even ragchewing. They may be aware of the complexities more than the lay person but too much of layers and configurations and protocols gets in the way of what they want to do with the technology.

Going forward, there is a core of hands-on technologists who revel in the complexity of communications technology. Advances are cyclic: Commercial technology is adapted to amateur uses where it is modified and enhanced, then re-circulated back to the commercial environment. As the ebb and flow of the currents wash more technology onto the shores of Amateur Radio, occasionally there is a lucky convergence and a new mode or application springs up to start the cycle over again so that amateurs can do whatever it is that they want to do with wireless — perhaps just talk about the weather as, yes, they "use this stuff."

Toward New Link-Layer Protocols

This paper from the Proceedings of the TAPR 1994 Annual Meeting *describes some exciting ways of improving packet radio.*

By Phil Karn, KA9Q

This paper describes an experimental new link-layer protocol for amateur packet radio use. It extends my earlier MACA scheme for dealing with hidden terminals by incorporating a powerful forward error correction (FEC) scheme: convolutional coding with sequential decoding. The resulting hybrid protocol combines the best of the FEC and retransmission (ARQ) techniques. It should perform very well in the presence of hidden terminals, noise and interference, particularly pulsed radar QRM like that often found on the 70-cm amateur band.

Introduction

AX.25 is now 12 years old.[1] Although it has become the universal standard link-level protocol for amateur packet radio, it is widely recognized as being far from optimal. The experience of the past decade plus significant advances in the computer technology now available to the radio amateur suggest that we look at much more sophisticated alternatives. These techniques have existed for many years, but only now have powerful modern PCs brought them within easy reach of the average radio amateur.[2]

This article gives a brief overview of forward error correction techniques and then describes the author's work in progress to develop a new general-purpose link-level protocol suitable for amateur packet radio use at speeds up to about 100 kb/s. This protocol combines the features of my earlier MACA (Multiple Access with Collision Avoidance) access scheme with forward error correction (convolutional encoding with sequential decoding performed in software) in what the literature calls a *Hybrid Type II ARQ/FEC protocol*.[3,4,5] This protocol should perform well over channels with error rates up to 10%, far beyond the capabilities of AX.25. It was originally motivated by, and should be especially well suited for, channels with radar interference. With the right modem, it should also perform very well over analog satellite transponders like those on AO-13.

Computer Technology—1994 Versus 1982

In the late 1970s and early 1980s, the best computer that most radio amateurs could hope to own included a 4- or 6-MHz Z-80 running CP/M, 240-kB 8-inch floppy drives, 64-kB RAM, and either a "dumb terminal" or a small memory-mapped video display. The introduction of the IBM PC in the early 1980s upped these capabilities considerably, particularly in address space, but these machines were quite expensive when first introduced.

Since the original PC was introduced, there have been several more generations of Intel microprocessors: the 80286, first used in the PC/AT; the i386; i486; and now the Pentium. The faster 486 CPUs are nearly 100 times faster than the 8088 used in the original IBM PC.

Other measures of personal computer system performance have increased even more dramatically. It is not at all uncommon to find amateur systems with 16 megabytes of RAM (256 times the 64-kB maximum with CP/M) and hundreds of megabytes, or even gigabytes, of hard disk (thousands of times the capacity, and hundreds of times the speed of the 8-inch floppies used with CP/M). These machines rival the high-end engineering work stations of just a few years ago.

Notes appear on page 9.

7431 Teasdale Ave
San Diego, CA 92122

And best of all, these machines have plummeted in price even as their capabilities have grown. The 8088 has long been obsolete; the 286 more recently so. Motherboards with the 386 chip are now selling for less than a hundred dollars, a sure sign that they, too, will soon be obsolete.

What Modern Computers Make Possible

When AX.25 was developed, it was reasonable to emphasize simplicity over functionality and performance. DARPA had already experimented with much more sophisticated and powerful packet radio protocols, error correction and signal processing techniques, but theirs was a government-funded research program with (by amateur standards) very deep pockets.[6,7,8] Amateurs needed a practical standard they could afford, even if it didn't work very well.[9]

But many of the sophisticated techniques used in the DARPA project are now within our easy reach. Thanks to their wide data paths and high-speed caches, chips like the 386 and 486 are especially well suited to CPU-intensive operations such as forward error correction. Yet amateurs have been slow to exploit these capabilities by updating their protocols.

Amateur packet radio urgently needs FEC. A common rule of thumb is that the packet loss rate should not exceed 1% for good performance with pure ARQ protocols like LAPB or TCP.[10,11,12] The typical amateur packet radio channel far exceeds this. Causes include nonoptimal modem designs and radio interfaces, poor signal-to-noise ratios and interference.

FEC is especially effective against radar. We share our 70-cm amateur band with military radar and, in the coastal cities, the periodic audio whine of a Navy radar is a familiar sound.[13]

Forward Error Correction— Background

Forward Error Correction (FEC) has been around for quite some time. It essentially began when Claude Shannon's revolutionary 1948 paper launched the field of information theory.[14]

Error correction is a very deep and often highly mathematical subject, about which dozens of textbooks and thousands of journal papers have been written. I could not possibly include a complete discussion in this paper. However, the basic principles are easy enough to understand.

Shannon proved that it is possible to send data over even a noisy channel with an arbitrarily low error rate, as long as the data rate is less than the channel capacity, defined by the famous formula.

$$C = B \log_2 \left(1 + \frac{S}{N} \right)$$

Unfortunately, Shannon did not show *how* one could achieve this capacity, only that it was theoretically possible. Practical systems have only begun to approach the Shannon limit, although some have come remarkably close (the *Voyager* spacecraft downlink operated at about 50% of the Shannon capacity of its channel).

With FEC, a receiver can use all *of the received signal energy.*

The basic idea behind FEC is to add redundancy to the data being sent so that some number of channel errors can be corrected, up to a limit. The encoded data are referred to as *symbols*, to distinguish them from the original user data bits.

Compare this with the more familiar ARQ scheme, where redundancy (eg, a CRC) is added to the data only to *detect* errors; if even one error occurs, the receiver discards the entire block of received data and waits for a retransmission. If this happens often, a significant amount of channel capacity and transmitter energy is wasted.

With FEC, a receiver can use *all* of the received signal energy; it doesn't have to throw any of it away. This actually allows one to reduce the transmitter power required for a given user data throughput. This reduction is called the *coding gain* of the code. Depending on the particular code, its implementation, the modem in use and the amount of redundant information added, coding gains can range from 1 to 8 dB or even more against additive white Gaussian noise (AWGN, eg, the thermal noise of a preamp and antenna system).

White noise is actually a worst case for FEC; certain codes can provide dramatically higher gains against nonwhite noise such as radar pulses, and against short deep fades. Coding gains of 40 to 50 dB or more against radar QRM are easily achievable, assuming that the receiver recovers quickly after each radar pulse.[15] The error rate in a radar-QRMed digital system depends primarily on the user data rate and the radar pulse duration and repetition rate. It is essentially independent of radar signal level over a wide range. For example, radar pulses 10-20 microseconds long are comparable to a bit time at 56 kb/s (17.8 microseconds). If the radar pulse power exceeds the desired signal power minus the required S/N demodulator margin, a data bit will be corrupted. However, if the receiver recovers rapidly after each pulse, the bits sent between the pulses will arrive unharmed no matter how much stronger the radar gets. At a repetition rate of 400 Hz, only every 140th data bit will be clobbered. This is an error rate of 0.7%, which is *easily* handled with just a modest amount of FEC. On the other hand, without coding communication would be almost impossible unless you could increase transmitter power to completely overcome the radar, and this is quite often impractical.

A similar situation exists with fading. If the fades are relatively short, coding can easily handle the situation no matter how deep the fades are.[16] The alternative is to increase transmitter power until there's enough margin even in the deepest fade, which may again be impractical. FEC essentially "smears" individual data bits over time on the channel so it is not necessary to receive an entire message, only enough of it to permit the decoder to fill in the missing spots from what it did get.

There is no free lunch, however; coding gains necessarily come at the expense of increased bandwidth. For example, the code I am currently using in my experiments provides a 4-dB coding gain against AWGN at the expense of doubling the required bandwidth by sending two encoded symbols for each user data bit. That is, if I have a 10-kHz channel capable of carrying 10 kb/s with 100 W of transmitter power, then my code enables me to send the same 10 kb/s with only about 40 W of power, but I need 20 kHz of bandwidth to do it. Or I could stay in my original 10-kHz channel, reduce my data rate to 5 kb/s, and reduce my transmitter power to only 20 W.[17]

Because all FEC schemes add some amount of redundancy to the user data being transmitted over the channel, it is important to distinguish between the user data rate and the encoded symbol rate as sent over the channel. Since it is the user data rate that ultimately counts, the literature uses the parameter E_b/N_0 rather than "signal to noise ratio" to define the performance of a coding system and modem. E_b is the received energy per user data bit; N_0 is the received noise spectral density.

Types of FEC

Block Codes

The earliest error-correcting codes inspired by Shannon's work were Hamming's "block" codes.[18] As the name implies, a block code operates on a fixed amount of data that depends on the particular code. Hamming's code has been used on several amateur spacecraft to correct radiation-induced memory errors; the memory word makes a natural code "block." This code can generally correct one error in each 8-bit byte of memory. Another popular block code, the Golay code, adds 11 redundant bits to 12 data bits to produce 23 bits for transmission. This is referred to as a (23,12) block code. This code can correct any combination of three or fewer errors in its transmitted block of 23 bits.[19]

Another important block code (out of many) are the Reed-Solomon codes, used in the compact disc and elsewhere.[20] Reed and Solomon actually defined a whole family of codes. Reed-Solomon codes can operate on multibit symbols (as opposed to binary symbols) and can be easily constructed with relatively large block sizes. These two characteristics together provide an excellent burst-error-correcting capability, which is especially useful when combined or *concatenated* with other error detecting and correcting codes. The Clover II HF modem, designed by Ray Petit, W7GHM, makes extensive use of Reed-Solomon coding.[21,22,23]

Convolutional Codes

Another class of error-correcting codes operates on an arbitrary stream of bits, rather than fixed-size blocks. These are the convolutional codes, sometimes called "tree" codes. In a more general form they are known as "trellis" codes and are found in modern dial-up telephone modems (eg, V.32 and V.32bis).

Convolutional codes are easily generated in hardware with a shift register, two or more exclusive-OR "parity trees" and a multiplexer. These operations are also easily implemented in software. The length of the shift register defines an important parameter called the "constraint length" K of the code. The larger K is, the better the code will perform (subject to the limitations of the decoding process as discussed below).

Because convolutional codes operate on continuous streams, they are specified by the ratio of the input data and output symbol rates. For example, an encoder that produces two encoded symbols for each user data bit is known as a "rate 1/2" code, often abbreviated to "r=1/2".

Convolutional codes have several interesting properties. They are especially easy to generate and provide excellent performance for a given amount of complexity. They are well suited to varying amounts of data, eg, variable length data packets. They are also readily adapted to *soft decision* decoding.[24] This uses symbol quality indications from the modem to aid the decoding process. For example, instead of slicing the demodulator output to binary 0 or 1 with a comparator, one uses an A/D converter to indicate the relative quality of each 0 and 1.[25]

When properly implemented, soft decision decoding yields a

$$\frac{2}{\pi} (2 \text{ dB})$$

performance improvement over 1-bit or *hard decision* decoding in the presence of AWGN. The code I'm using would therefore provide a 6-dB coding gain were I to use full-blown soft decision decoding, but this will have to wait for modems (most likely DSP-based) that provide soft decision samples.

My decoder currently accepts "unknown" as a received symbol value in addition to "one" and "zero." This 3-level *binary erasure channel* is a good model for a radar-QRMed channel where symbols are erased by radar pulses. Making this erasure information available to a decoder can dramatically improve its performance. For example, without erasure information the rate 1/2 code I'm using can, with considerable effort, barely correct a stream of symbols when the symbol error rate reaches 10%. However, if the modem can tell the decoder *which* symbols have been trashed by radar pulses (perhaps by running the receiver's noise blanker gate line to the decoder), then the decoder will continue to function even when nearly 50% of the received symbols have been erased—ie, when almost all of the redundant information added by the encoder has been removed by the channel.

A 3-level decoder is also useful for *puncturing*, another useful technique easily applied to convolutional codes. This involves simply not transmitting some fraction of the encoded symbols and substituting erasures in their place at the decoder.[26] Puncturing makes it easy to vary the coding rate (the amount of redundant information added to each user data bit) in accordance with changing channel conditions without having to change the encoder or decoder. This is important because the redundant information added by a coder is nearly useless overhead when the channel conditions are good enough to not require the code's full error correcting capability.

Sequential Versus Viterbi Decoding

There are two general classes of decoders for convolutional codes: sequential and minimum-likelihood (Viterbi). The sequential decoder is the older of the two, dating from the late 1950s.[27] The Fano algorithm for sequential decoding dates from the early 1960s and is still in use with few changes.[28]

> *The code would provide a 6-dB coding gain with soft decision encoding.*

Viterbi first proposed his algorithm in the late 1960s.[29] It has since become the most popular technique for decoding convolutional codes, primarily because of the availability of high speed VLSI hardware decoders.[30] The *Voyager* spacecraft down-link mentioned earlier uses convolutional encoding with Viterbi decoding, sometimes in conjunction with a Reed-Solomon block coder.

Both the sequential and maximum-likelihood decoders work by regenerating the data stream that, when passed through a local copy of the encoder, most closely matches the received encoded symbol sequence. Because the received symbols usually contain errors, the match is seldom exact; but as long as the error rate is not too high, the decoder will reproduce the original user data without any errors. This is possible because the effect of any particular user data bit is spread over many encoded channel symbols. For example, in the $K=32$ rate 1/2 code I use, each data bit affects 64 encoded symbols. Even when several symbols are lost, there is usually enough information left in the remaining symbols to reconstruct all of the original data bits. The coding gain of a convolutional code depends on the constraint length, K; the larger the better.

The main difference between the sequential and maximum-likelihood decoders is the way they regenerate the original data sequence that is fed through the decoder's local copy of the encoder for comparison with the received symbol stream. Both use what might be called "intelligent brute force," as each tests and discards many data sequences that don't work out. This requirement for "brute force" CPU crunching is why convolutional decoding is just now becoming practical for amateur use at reasonable speeds.

The Viterbi decoder explores every possible data sequence in parallel, discarding at each step those that can't possibly be correct. These parallel operations are well suited to hardware VLSI implementation. The number of data sequences that a Viterbi decoder explores in parallel is 2^K. Increasing K by 1 doubles the work that the decoder must do to recover each data bit. Viterbi decoders typically work with $K=7$ or $K=9$; larger values are very rare.

The sequential decoder, on the other hand, explores only one data sequence at a time, so its work factor is almost independent of K. As long as the sequence being tested produces symbols reasonably close to those being received, it keeps on going. When the decoder "gets into trouble," it backs up and methodically searches increasingly dissimilar data sequences until it eventually finds one that gets it back onto the right track. Much larger values of K are typically used with sequential decoders than with Viterbi decoders. My code uses $K=32$, a convenient value on modern microprocessors like the 386 and 486 with 32-bit registers.

Since larger values of K give better performance, this seems to tip the scales in favor of sequential decoding. However, the Viterbi decoder always operates at a constant rate, while the speed of the sequential decoder is a random function that depends strongly on the channel error rate; the higher the error rate, the greater and more unpredictable the decoding time becomes. At sufficiently high error rates, the decoding time of a sequential decoder becomes unbounded.[31] Any practical sequential decoder must therefore have a timer to keep it from running "forever" if it is inadvertently fed garbage or an extremely noisy packet. This makes the sequential decoder less attractive than the Viterbi decoder for real-time applications with strict delay limits such as full-duplex digital voice.

On the other hand, the *average* decoding time of a sequential decoder is often less than the fixed decoding time of a software Viterbi decoder running on the same CPU. This is important if (a) you've decided to implement your decoder in software to avoid the cost of a dedicated VLSI Viterbi decoder, and (b) you have a nonreal-time packet application such as file transfer, where it's the average decoding speed that counts.

An interesting property of sequential decoders with large values of K is that the probability of uncorrected errors becomes very small. It is much more likely that the decoder will time out first. This may make it unnecessary to include a CRC or other error-detecting code to ensure that the decoded data is correct; the decoder timer takes the place of a CRC check. We don't actually avoid the overhead of the CRC, though. A convolutional coder requires a tail of zeros at the end of every packet to return the coder to its starting state and to allow every user data bit to influence the full number of channel symbols. The tail length must be at least $K-1$ bits, or 31 for my code (I use 32 just to keep things in round numbers).

Whether the inherent error-detecting ability of my $K = 32$ sequential decoder provided by its time-out mechanism is comparable to that of a 32-bit CRC is an interesting question. I don't know yet.

So to recap, Viterbi decoding is usually preferable when the application requires a constant decoding delay and dedicated VLSI hardware decoders are available. Sequential decoding has the edge when a variable decoding delay is tolerable and a software implementation is required (eg, to minimize cost to the radio amateur who already has a PC). For these reasons I have chosen sequential decoding for my experimental protocol.[32]

Interleaving

Convolutional decoders work best when the symbol errors they correct are evenly distributed throughout the transmission. This is the case on channels limited by AWGN (thermal noise). However, errors caused by momentary interference and fading often occur in bursts. These can cause sequential decoders to get into trouble since the work factor goes up exponentially with the length of the burst.

Interleaving is the standard approach to this problem. The symbols from the encoder are rearranged in time before transmission and put back into their original order before decoding. Interleaving doesn't remove any errors, it simply scatters them in case they were adjacent on the channel.

Several classes of interleaving schemes exist. The particular interleaving scheme I've chosen for my protocol uses *address bit reversal*. Each symbol address is written in binary in the usual way with the high order bit on the left. Then the bits are reversed right-to-left, forming a new number. For example, the sequence

0 1 2 3 4 5 6 7

when bit-reversed becomes

0 4 2 6 1 5 3 7

Note that all even numbers are in the first half of the block, and all the odd numbers in the second half. Note also that when these numbers are again bit-reversed, the original sequence reappears.

Since address bit reversal only works when you have 2^N numbers, I need some way to extend this scheme to arbitrary length packets. To facilitate this, I first pad each data packet out to a multiple of 32 bits (64 symbols for my rate 1/2 code). Then I write the symbols as a 2-dimensional matrix with 64 rows, first going vertically down the columns and using as many columns as I need. Here is an example with 193 symbols, numbered 0 through 191:

```
 0    64   128
 1    65   129
 2    66   130
 .    .    .
 .    .    .
63   127   191
```

Then I interchange the rows by bit-reversing the row addresses:

```
 0    64   128
32    96   160
16    80   144
 .    .    .
 .    .    .
63   127   191
```

Now I actually transmit the symbols by transmitting horizontally across each row. The transmitted symbol sequence is therefore

0, 64, 128, 32, 96, 160, 16, 80, 144, ..., 63, 127, 191

At the receiver I reverse the process, restoring the symbols to their original order. Note how adjacent symbols from the encoder are always widely separated in time when they go over the channel; in particular, note how all of the even-numbered symbols appear in the first half of the transmission and the odd-numbered symbols in the second half.

Variable Rate Puncturing by Interleaving

I chose this particular interleaving scheme because it makes variable-rate code puncturing especially easy. Suppose I transmit only the first 32 of the 64 rows. This covers all of the even-numbered symbols in the stream; I've sent every other symbol. Since there are twice as many symbols as data bits, the effective code rate is 1/2 divided by 1/2, or 1 (ie, no redundant information, and no ability to correct errors). Now suppose we also send the 33rd row. This gives us 1/2 divided by 33/64, which is 32/33. This "high rate" code cannot correct as many errors as the original rate 1/2 code, but if this is good enough for the channel, we can avoid sending the other 30 rows. On the other hand, if the channel is poor, we simply send enough rows to lower the effective code rate until decoding is possible.[33] Adding the 34th row gives us a code rate of 16/17, and so on up to all 64 rows, which returns us to a rate 1/2 code.

Nothing says we have to send all of the rows in a single transmission. We could start by sending just the first 32 rows (no redundancy) and attempting to decode the packet with a tight timeout. Although we cannot actually correct any errors with only 32 rows, if any do occur the decoder will "get stuck" in the tail and time out, thus indicating that errors exist. If this happens, we can send additional rows until the receiver is finally able to decode the packet. In this way we send only as much redundancy as the channel currently requires. This is the idea behind the Type II Hybrid ARQ/FEC scheme mentioned earlier: use the power of FEC to deal with channel errors, but use the adaptability of ARQ to adjust the FEC overhead to that actually required by the channel.[34,35,36,37]

We send only as much redundancy as the channel requires.

What if the receiver cannot decode the packet even after we send all the rows? One possibility is to send the whole thing again and to use code combining at the receiver to add the two transmissions before decoding.[38] For example, if we send all of the symbols belonging to a rate 1/2 code twice, we have effectively switched to a rate 1/4 code. although this particular rate 1/4 code provides no additional coding gain over the original rate 1/2 code (since the retransmissions are identical), adding the two transmissions increases the total received energy (and E_b/N_0) by 3 dB.[39] Of course, this comes at the expense of halving the user data rate. We could take this scheme even further by adding more than two transmissions but we are eventually limited by the packet synchronization mechanism discussed in the next section.

This scheme can provide some of the benefits of soft decision decoding even when only hard decision samples are available from the modem. For example, the DARPA packet radio could combine two hard decision copies of a packet by erasing those symbols that disagreed between the two transmissions. (See Note 6.) Symbols that agreed were left unchanged. As we've already seen, a sequential decoder has a much easier time dealing with erasures than with errors.

Synchronization

Any packet protocol needs something to reliably flag the beginning of a packet. HDLC uses the 8-bit value 7E (hex) for this purpose, but since we want to operate reliably over very noisy channels this is not acceptable. As anyone who has ever operated a packet station with the squelch open and "PASSALL ON" knows, you don't have to wait very long for a 7E to appear by chance in random noise. And what if a packet is actually present, but one or more bits in the flag is in error? The entire packet would be missed. We *could* accept flags with, say, at most one bit in error but this would make the false alarm problem even worse.

The solution is to use a longer flag, or sync vector. The longer the sync vector, the easier it is to reliably detect real packets with errors while rejecting false alarms (triggering the sync detector on random noise). I have chosen a 64-bit sync vector for my protocol that consists of a 63-bit pseudo-random (PN) sequence (generated by a 5-stage shift register with feedback) augmented by an extra 0 to make 64 bits. The receiver correlates the incoming symbol stream against a local copy of the sync vector, and it declares synchronization whenever they match with 13 or fewer errors. This allows the detector to work reliably up to a channel error probability of about 20%, well above the error correcting capability of the rate 1/2 convolutional code (about 10%).[40] Yet the sync vector is so long that the probability of random noise triggering the detector is quite small.

Scrambling

Several higher-speed packet radio modems, eg, the K9NG/G3RUH 9600 bit/s FSK modems and the WA4DSY 56 kbit/s modem, use scrambling to ensure a sufficiently high bit transition density to allow the demodulator to recover clock regardless of the user's data sequence. However, the self-synchronizing descramblers they use have an unfortunate property: error propagation. Each channel error produces a characteristic pattern of several closely spaced data bit errors that depend on the particular polynomial being used. Without FEC this is of little consequence since even a single bit error is enough to ruin a packet, so extra errors can't make things worse. But with FEC, we don't want the modem to do anything to make the decoder's job harder. So we must disable the scrambling and descrambling functions.

This leaves us with the problem that scrambling was originally intended to solve: how can we ensure a good transition density on the channel no matter what the user sends? It turns out that the solution is relatively simple: we scramble the user's data ourselves, but we don't use a self-synchronizing descrambler. We use a fixed PN sequence that is started from a known point at the beginning of the packet and allowed to "free run" for the length of the packet. This type of scrambling doesn't propagate errors, but it does require independent synchronization—which we already have from the sync vector mechanism just described.

It may turn out that current modem clock recovery mechanisms are inadequate with FEC. FEC can operate with a E_s/N_0 far lower than that required to produce good data without coding, and it's entirely possible that existing modem clock recovery circuits won't work on these weak signals.[41] Other approaches may be necessary.

One possible approach is to perform the sync vector correlation function in a DSP modem on raw A/D input samples at some integer multiple of the incoming data rate. When the correlator output peaks, we can then start blindly counting off the appropriate number of A/D samples between each received symbol. If the transmitter and receiver clocks are closely matched in frequency and the packets aren't too long, this should provide reasonably accurate symbol timing for the entire packet without having to extract clock from those (noisy) symbols. If the clocks are too far apart for this to work, another possibility would be to buffer all of the raw A/D samples in the packet and post-process them looking for the sampling frequency that produces the best eye pattern for the packet as a whole.

Protocol Headers

The discussion of variable rate code puncturing assumed that we have had a reliable way to control it. But the control information can also be corrupted by channel errors. How can we deal with this? By always using full FEC coding for the packet header, regardless of the coding rate in use for the user data portion of the packet. Since the header is (hopefully) small compared to the user data, the overhead incurred by this is (hopefully) also small. To do this, though, we have to be very selective about what goes into the header.

The header in my protocol is currently 16 bytes (128 data bits or 256 encoded symbols) long. It contains the following information: source address, destination address, frame type, transmission length, previous frame error count and coder tail.

This decoder can easily keep up with a 56-ksymbols/s stream.

The coder tail is all zeros. As mentioned earlier, it is required by our use of a convolutional coder. Because we restart the coding process between the header and the data portion of the packet, each portion needs its own coder tail.

The source and destination addresses consist of the station call signs and SSIDs as in AX.25, but the call signs are more efficiently coded. Since there are only 36 legal characters in a call sign (the 26 letters in the English alphabet plus the ten decimal digits) there is no need to spend an entire 8-bit byte on each one. If we add "space" as a 37th character and use radix-37 encoding, we can encode into 32 bits any legal call sign up to 6 characters long.[42] Add 4 bits for an SSID and the complete address fits into 36 bits, as compared with 52 for AX.25.

The frame types are as follows:
- Request to Send (RTS)
- Clear to Send (CTS)
- User Data
- Negative Acknowledgment (NAK)
- Positive Acknowledgment (ACK)

The RTS tells the receiver of the sender's intention to send a certain amount of data. The receiver responds with a CTS that echoes this length. This tells the sender to go ahead with the actual data transmission, and it also has the important side effect of telling anyone else on the channel to remain quiet for the appropriate amount of time.

If the receiver is able to decode the transmission (the sequential decoder completes without timing out), it returns an ACK to the sender that it may proceed to the next block of data. Alternatively, if the timer expires before the sequential decoder finishes, the receiver returns a NAK. The NAK confirms to the sender that its transmission was received, but with too many errors. The sender then sends additional rows from the interleaver output, which the receiver combines with those symbols already received. If the receiver is still unable to decode the packet, the cycle repeats with additional NAKs and data packets containing additional rows of symbols until the receiver finally succeeds and returns an ACK. At this point the sender can continue to the next block of data.

Note that the NAK, like the CTS, also holds off other stations from transmitting so that they do not interfere. In fact, I may eventually merge the NAK and CTS messages into a single type, with the CTS simply being the special case of a NAK sent before any data symbols have been received.

It also goes without saying that should the sender receive neither an ACK nor a NAK in a reasonable time, it must retransmit its last frame. This can only occur if the channel was so poor that the heavily coded header could not be decoded, or perhaps even the sync vector was missed. If this is a temporary condition, then a retransmission will get things moving again.

The previous frame error count field is used in ACK packets to let the sender know how many errors were detected and corrected in the last packet. The sender can use this information to aid in deciding how many of the interleaver symbol rows to send up front in its next transmission, without having to wait for the receiver to ask for them with NAK messages. This helps minimize modem transmit-receive cycles when channel conditions are fairly constant. At the moment I actually have two previous frame error count fields: one for the last header received, and one (in ACK packets only) for the last data field received.

Status and Open Questions

Since sequential decoding is the heart of this protocol and by far the biggest consumer of CPU cycles, I have spent most of my time to date working on my implementation of the Fano algorithm in C. It now runs quite well on the 486-50. At the moment, this decoder can, on average, easily keep up with a 56-kilosymbol/s stream (eg, from a WA4DSY modem) as long as the symbol error rate is less than about 2%. More errors could be tolerated at lower channel speed, with a faster CPU, or with a better optimizing compiler, but this performance is already good enough to be quite useful.

The correlator that searches for the sync vector is another potentially CPU-intensive task. Although correlation is simpler than sequential decoding, the decoder runs only when a packet has actually been received, while the correlator may have to process a continuous symbol stream from the modem if it has no carrier-detect squelch.[43] So it is still desirable to make the correlator run as fast as possible in order to free up the maximum amount of CPU time for other tasks. I have implemented a correlator in assembler that runs at several hundred kilosymbols per second, with most of the time spent in the function that returns the next received symbol.

I have not yet finished the complete protocol, however. When I do, I will have plenty of work left. I need to answer the following questions:

1. Is a rate 1/2 code strong enough, particularly for the packet header? Should I consider using a rate 1/3 or even lower coding for maximum robustness?
2. Should I consider a block code (eg, Golay) for the packet header in order to eliminate the need for a coder tail?
3. What strategy should the sender use to decide how many rows (out of the 64 available) should be sent in any given transmission? How can I make best use of recent history (especially the receiver's observed error rate indication) to send just the required amount of redundancy for each packet in as few transmissions as possible?
4. Is 64 interleaving rows optimum?

Is the whole interleaving scheme optimum?
5. What is the optimum packet size for transmission? Should transmissions be large to decrease header and modem turnaround overhead, or should they be small to decrease the chances of a sequential decoding timeout and the resulting need to transmit additional redundancy?
6. Is relying on a decoder timeout sufficient to detect errors when a packet has been punctured back to rate 1 (no redundancy), or is a true CRC still required?
7. Does the MACA algorithm work well in the presence of stations too far away to reliably decode CTS messages, but close enough to cause harmful interference? Does FEC help this problem by improving the capture effect?
8. Can I make a sequential decoder that works well on soft decision samples such as those that might be produced by a PSK modem implemented in DSP, or is the sequential decoder's well-known sensitivity to incorrect soft-decision metrics a serious stumbling block? Can I compute the metrics on the fly according to observed noise levels to mitigate this problem?
9. Will the clock recovery circuits in existing amateur packet radio modems turn out to be the limiting factor instead of the error correcting capability of the code?

And last but not least,
10. Will the average amateur be willing to use this stuff?

Credits

I would like to thank several people for their advice and assistance: Franklin Antonio, N6NKF, and Klein Gilhousen, WT6G, for sharing their considerable expertise in the practical application of convolutional coding; Paul Williamson, KB5MU, and Bob McGwier, N4HY, for their insights and especially their patience in listening to my ravings; Andy Demartini, KC2FF, of Digital Radio Systems Inc, for his donation of two DRSI PCPA Type 1 interface cards; and Skip Hansen, WB6YMH, for his clever trick of turning a Zilog SCC into a simple and dumb serial/parallel converter.

Notes

[1] Fox, Terry, WB4JFI, ed, *AX.25 Amateur Packet-Radio Link-Layer Protocol*, Version 2.0, October 1984, ARRL. (Updates earlier versions dating from 1982.)
[2] Many of the fundamental references cited in this paper date from the 1970s or even earlier.

[3] Karn, Phil, "MACA—A New Channel Access Method for Packet Radio," *Proceedings of the 9th ARRL/CRRL Amateur Radio Computer Networking Conference*, London, Ontario, Canada, September 22, 1990, p 134.
[4] Kallel, Samir and Haccoun, David, "Generalized Type II Hybrid ARQ Scheme Using Punctured Convolutional Coding," *IEEE Transactions on Communications*, Vol 38, No. 11, November 1990, p 1938.
[5] Lin, Shu and Yu, Philip S., "A Hybrid ARQ Scheme with Parity Retransmission for Error Control of Satellite Channels," *IEEE Transactions on Communications*, Vol COM-30, No. 7, July 1982, p 1701.
[6] Kahn, R. E., Gronemeyer, S. A., Burchfiel, J., and Kunzelman, R. C., "Advances in Packet Radio Technology," *Proceedings of the IEEE*, November 1978, p 1468.
[7] Shacham, Nachum, "Performance of ARQ with Sequential Decoding Over One-Hop and Two-Hop Radio Links," *IEEE Transactions on Communications*, Vol COM-31, No. 10, October 1983, p 1172.
[8] Special issue on packet radio networks, *Proceedings of the IEEE*, January 1987.
[9] The military also discovered the same thing, with the ironic result that amateur packet radio technology found its way into several military applications.
[10] Automatic request-repeat: (re)send each packet until an acknowledgment is received.
[11] The connection-oriented part of AX.25, borrowed from X.25 Level 2.
[12] The Internet's connection-oriented transport level protocol.
[13] Much of the early work on FEC was prompted by the Navy's desire for reliable shipboard communication links that could tolerate local radar QRM. My present interest was initially prompted by the heavy radar QRM we often experience to our 70-cm 56-kb/s modems here in San Diego.
[14] Shannon, C. E., "A Mathematical Theory of Communication," *Bell System Technical Journal*, Vol 27, July/October 1948, pp 379-423.
[15] A pulse blanker is important to keep the radar energy out of the receiver AGC and IF filters. It can also directly aid the FEC process, as explained later.
[16] A radar QRMed channel with a pulse blanker at the receiver is really just a channel with infinitely deep fades during each pulse.
[17] The extra 3 dB of power reduction in the latter case is *not* part of the coding gain; it results directly from the 50% reduction in user data throughput.
[18] Hamming, Richard W., "Error Detecting and Error Correcting Codes," *Bell System Technical Journal*, April 1950.
[19] Lin, Shu and Costello, Daniel J., Jr., *Error Control Coding: Fundamentals and Applications*, Prentice Hall, 1983 (ISBN: 0-13-283796-X).
[20] Pohlmann, Ken C., *Principles of Digital Audio*, second edition, Sams, 1990 (ISBN: 0-672-22634-0).
[21] Petit, Raymond C., W7GHM, "The Cloverleaf Performance-Oriented HF Data Communications System," *QEX*, July 1990. Also, *Proceedings of the 9th ARRL/CRRL Amateur Radio Computer Networking Conference*, London, Ontario, Canada, September 22, 1990, p 191.

June 1994 9

[22] Petit, Raymond C., W7GHM, "Clover-II: A Technical Overview," *Proceedings of the 10th ARRL Amateur Radio Computer Networking Conference*, San Jose, CA, September 27-29, 1991, p 125.

[23] Henry, Bill, K9GWT, and Petit, Raymond C., W7GHM, "HF Radio Data Communications," *Communications Quarterly*, Vol 2, No. 2, Spring 1992, p 11.

[24] It is possible to "soften" the decoding of block codes, but with considerably more effort. Also see Chase, David, "A Class of Algorithms for Decoding Block Codes With Channel Measurement Information," *IEEE Transactions on Information Theory*, Vol IT-18, No. 1, January 1972.

[25] A simple comparator is really a 1-bit A/D converter, so we are just increasing the resolution of the A/D converter we already have.

[26] Obviously, the receiver has to know which symbols are not sent, otherwise it will get very confused.

[27] Wozencraft, J. M., "Sequential Decoding for Reliable Communications," Research Laboratory of Electronics, MIT, Cambridge, MA, *Technical Report 325*, 1957.

[28] Fano, Robert M., "A Heuristic Discussion of Probabilistic Decoding," *IEEE Transactions on Information Theory*, April 1963, pp 64-74.

[29] Viterbi, Andrew J., "Error Bounds for Convolutional Codes and an Asymptotically Optimum Decoding Algorithm," *IEEE Transactions on Information Theory*, Vol IT-13, No. 2, April 1967.

[30] Qualcomm, Inc, data sheets for Q1650, Q0256 and Q1401 Viterbi Decoder ICs.

[31] Jacobs, Irwin Mark, "Sequential Decoding for Efficient Communication from Deep Space," *IEEE Transactions on Communications Technology*, Vol COM-15, No. 4, August 1967, p 492.

[32] The DARPA packet radio project also chose convolutional coding with sequential decoding.

[33] Sending additional rows also increases the total transmitted energy. This increases the E_b/N_0 ratio, which also aids decoding.

[34] Kallel, Samir and Haccoun, David, "Sequential Decoding with ARQ and Code Combining: A Robust Hybrid FEC/ARQ System," *IEEE Transactions on Communications*, Vol 36, No. 7, July 1988, p 773.

[35] Mandelbaum, David M., "An Adaptive-Feedback Coding Scheme Using Incremental Redundancy," *IEEE Transactions on Information Theory*, May 1974, p 388.

[36] Metzner, John J., "Improvements in Block-Retransmission Schemes," *IEEE Transactions on Communications*, Vol COM-27, No. 2, February 1979, p 524.

[37] See Note 4.

[38] Chase, David, "Code Combining—A Maximum-Likelihood Decoding Approach for Combining an Arbitrary Number of Noisy Packets," *IEEE Transactions on Communications*, Vol COM-33, No. 5, May 1985, p 385.

[39] Pactor uses *Memory ARQ*, which is essentially a combining scheme on uncoded data. FEC and interleaving could improve Pactor's performance considerably without any increase in bandwidth.

[40] This provides some margin to allow successful code combining, which could allow us to operate above a 10% symbol error rate.

[41] Symbol energy-to-noise spectral density ratio, as opposed to E_b/N_0. For a rate 1/2 code, E_s/N_0 is 3 dB less than E_b/N_0.

[42] Some might like to see room for longer call signs. However, except for the rare special event station, all Amateur Radio call signs have been 6 characters or less and are likely to remain so for quite some time. In my opinion, the legal requirement for IDs with prefixes during reciprocal operation (eg, "W6/GB1AAA") is better met with a special ID frame every 10 minutes than by requiring everyone to make room for them in every packet header. I'm willing to be persuaded otherwise. Remember that this is still an experimental protocol.

[43] Good carrier detect circuits are already hard to build, and it will probably be almost impossible to make them operate quickly and reliably at the much lower E_s/N_0 ratios usable with FEC. And recall that one of the principles behind MACA is that carrier detect is essentially worthless in a hidden-terminal environment anyway.

"PSK31: A New Radio-Teletype Mode" by Peter Martinez, G3PLX

By Ward Silver, NØAX

Not content with having previously created the popular AMTOR mode, G3PLX continued innovating with PSK31. This has become one of the most popular digital modes, perhaps slightly less common than RTTY but rapidly gaining converts. PSK31 provides keyboard-to-keyboard communication with very little in the way of equipment needed — just a sound card and an audio connection to the radio microphone and speaker or headphone jacks. It also works quite well at low power levels, enabling very modest stations to communicate with excellent results. Surely there is some complex and intricate protocol at work?

You would be wrong to make that assumption. Martinez explains why as follows: "...with error-correcting modes, you only get good copy when you are linked to one other station. The copy is decidedly worse when stations are not linked, such as when calling CQ or listening to others. This makes it difficult to meet other people on the air, and there is a tendency to limit contacts to a few close friends or just mailboxes.

"These factors lead me to suggest that there is a case for a transmission system that is not based on the use of error-correcting codes, when the specific application is that of live contacts. The continued popularity of traditional RTTY using the start-stop system is proof of this hypothesis: There is minimal delay (150 ms), the flow of conversation is continuous, the error-rate is tolerable, and it is easy to listen-in and join-in."

Nevertheless, designing such a system, for that is what PSK31 is, can be quite a challenge. When the job was done, not only did amateurs have a new mode, but also a new method of encoding characters (Varicode) and a new display and tuning method (waterfall display). The latter has had an especially profound effect, changing the way the user views the spectrum and other signals.

PSK31 is also an excellent neighbor to other signals, taking up less than 100 Hz of band space to have a chat with another ham. On most days, in a single audio channel of 2.4 kHz or so, 10 or more signals can be visible at one time as the waterfall display creeps down the computer display. Some reception software can be configured to decode multiple PSK31 signals at the same time, allowing you to listen in on a number of ongoing QSOs.

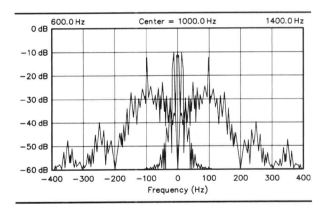

Comparison of the PSK31 spectrum with 100-baud, 200-Hz-shift FSK (AMTOR/PACTOR). The taller, three-peak signal at center is PSK31.

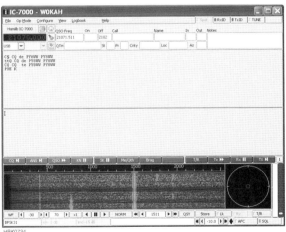

The waterfall display of digital mode software such as *fldigi* by David Freese, W1HKJ, shows several PSK31 signals in a slice of spectrum that is the same bandwidth required by a single voice signal.

PSK31: A New Radio-Teletype Mode

Many error-correcting data modes are well suited to file transfers, yet most hams still prefer error-prone Baudot for everyday chats. PSK31 should fix that. It requires very little spectrum and borrows some characteristics from Morse code. Equipment? Free software, an HF transceiver and a PC with Windows *and a sound card will get you on the air.*

By Peter Martinez, G3PLX

[Thanks to the Radio Society of Great Britain for permission to reprint this article. It originally appeared in the December '98 and January '99 issues of their journal, RadCom. This article includes February 1999 updates from Peter Martinez.—Ed.]

I've been active on RTTY since the 1960s, and was instrumental in introducing AMTOR to Amateur Radio at the end of the '70s. This improved the reliability of the HF radio link and paved the way to further developments that have taken this side of the hobby more into data transfer, message handling and computer linking, but further away from the rest of Amateur Radio, which is based on two-way contacts between operators.

There is now a gap opening between the data-transfer enthusiasts using the latest techniques and the two-way

High Blakeband Farm
Underbarrow, Kendal,
Cumbria, LA8 8HP
England

contact fans who are still using the traditional RTTY mode of the '60s, although of course using keyboard and screen rather than teleprinter. There is scope for applying the new techniques now available to bring RTTY into the 21st century.

This article discusses the specific needs of "live QSO" operating—as opposed to just transferring chunks of error-free data—and describes the PSK31 mode I have developed specifically for live contacts. PSK31 is now becoming popular using low-cost DSP kits. The mode could become even cheaper as the art of using PC sound cards is developed by Amateur Radio enthusiasts.

What is Needed?

I believe that it is the error-correcting process used in modern data modes make them unsuitable for live contacts. I have identified several factors; the first revolves around the fact that all error-correcting systems introduce a time-delay into the link. In the case of an ARQ link like AMTOR or PACTOR, there is a fixed transmission cycle of 450 ms or 1.25 s or more. This delays any key press by as much as one cycle period, and by more if there are errors. With forward-error-correction systems, there is also an inevitable delay, because the information is spread over time. In a live two-way contact, the delay is doubled at the point where the transmission is handed over. I believe that these delays make such systems unpleasant to use in a two-way conversation.

This is not so much a technical problem as a human one. Another factor in this category concerns the way that quality of information content varies as the quality of the radio link varies. In an analogue transmission system such as SSB or CW, there is a linear relationship between the two. The operators are aware of this all the time and take account of it subconsciously: They change the speed and tone of voice instinctively and even choose the conversation topic to suit the conditions. In a digital mode, the relationship between the signal-to-noise ratio (S/N) on the air and the error-rate on

July/Aug 1999 3

Table 1

The Varicode alphabet. The codes are transmitted left bit first, with "0" representing a phase reversal on BPSK and "1" representing a steady carrier. A minimum of two zeros is inserted between characters. Some implementations may not handle all the codes below 32.

ASCII*	Varicode	ASCII*	Varicode	ASCII*	Varicode
0 (NUL)	1010101011	+	111011111	V	110110101
1 (SOH)	1011011011	,	1110101	W	101011101
2 (STX)	1011101101	-	110101	X	101110101
3 (ETX)	1101110111	.	1010111	Y	101111011
4 (EOT)	1011101011	/	110101111	Z	1010101101
5 (ENQ)	1101011111	0	10110111	[	111110111
6 (ACK)	1011101111	1	10111101	\	111101111
7 (BEL)	1011111101	2	11101101	]	111111011
8 (BS)	1011111111	3	11111111	^	1010111111
9 (HT)	11101111	4	101110111	_	101101101
10 (LF)	11101	5	101011011	`	1011011111
11 (VT)	1101101111	6	101101011	a	1011
12 (FF)	1011011101	7	110101101	b	1011111
13 (CR)	11111	8	110101011	c	101111
14 (SO)	1101110101	9	110110111	d	101101
15 (SI)	1110101011	:	11110101	e	11
16 (DLE)	1011110111	;	110111101	f	111101
17 (DC1)	1011110101	<	111101101	g	1011011
18 (DC2)	1110101101	=	1010101	h	101011
19 (DC3)	1110101111	>	111010111	i	1101
20 (DC4)	1101011011	?	1010101111	j	111101011
21 (NAK)	1101101011	@	1010111101	k	10111111
22 (SYN)	1101101101	A	1111101	l	11011
23 (ETB)	1101010111	B	11101011	m	111011
24 (CAN)	1101111011	C	10101101	n	1111
25 (EM)	1101111101	D	10110101	o	111
26 (SUB)	1110110111	E	1110111	p	111111
27 (ESC)	1101010101	F	11011011	q	110111111
28 (FS)	1101011101	G	11111101	r	10101
29 (GS)	1110111011	H	101010101	s	10111
30 (RS)	1011111011	I	1111111	t	101
31 (US)	1101111111	J	111111101	u	110111
32 (SP)	1	K	101111101	v	1111011
!	111111111	L	11010111	w	1101011
"	101011111	M	10111011	x	11011111
#	111110101	N	11011101	y	1011101
$	111011011	O	10101011	z	111010101
%	1011010101	P	11010101	{	1010110111
&	1010111011	Q	111011101	|	110111011
'	101111111	R	10101111	}	1010110101
(	11111011	S	1101111	~	1011010111
)	11110111	T	1101101	127	1110110101
*	101101111	U	101010111		

*ASCII characters 0 through 31 are control codes. Their abbreviations are shown here in parentheses. For the meanings of the abbreviations, refer to any recent *ARRL Handbook*.

---

the screen is not so smooth. The modern error-correcting digital modes are particularly bad at this, with copy being almost perfect while the SNR is above a certain level and stopping completely when the SNR drops below this level. The effect is of no consequence in an automatic mailbox-forwarding link, but can badly inhibit the flow of a conversation.

A third factor is a social one: with error-correcting modes, you only get good copy when you are linked to one other station. The copy is decidedly worse when stations are not linked, such as when calling CQ or listening to others. This makes it difficult to meet other people on the air, and there is a tendency to limit contacts to a few close friends or just mailboxes.

These factors lead me to suggest that there is a case for a transmission system that is *not* based on the use of error-correcting codes, when the specific application is that of live contacts. The continued popularity of traditional RTTY using the start-stop system is proof of this hypothesis: There is minimal delay (150 mS), the flow of conversation is continuous, the error-rate is tolerable, and it is easy to listen-in and join-in.

Improving on RTTY

How, then, do we go about using modern techniques that were not available in the '60s, to improve on traditional RTTY? First, since we are talking about live contacts, there is no need to discuss any system that transmits text any faster than can be typed by hand. Second, modern transceivers are far more frequency stable than those of the '60s. We should be able to use much narrower bandwidths than in those days. Third, digital processors are much more powerful than the rotating cams and levers of mechanical teleprinters, so we could use better coding. The drift-tolerant technique of frequency-shift keying, and the fixed-length five-unit start-stop code still used today for RTTY are a legacy of 30-year-old technology limits. We can do better now.

PSK31 Alphabet

The method I have devised for using modern digital processing to improve on the start-stop code, without introducing extra delays due to the error-correcting or synchronization processes, is based firmly on another tradition, namely that of Morse code. Because Morse uses short codes for the more common letters, it is actually very efficient in terms of the average duration of a character. In addition, if we think of it in terms that we normally use for digital modes, Morse code is self-synchronizing: We don't need to use a separate process to tell us where one character ends and the next begins. This means that Morse code doesn't suffer from the "error-cascade" problem that results in the start-stop method getting badly out of step if a start or stop-bit is corrupt. This is because the pattern used to code a gap between two characters *never* occurs inside a character.

The code I have devised is therefore a logical extension of Morse code, using not just one-bit or three-bit code-elements (dots and dashes), but any length. The letter-gap can also be shortened to two bits. If we represent key-up by 0 and key-down by 1, then the shortest code is a single one by itself. The next is 11, then 101 and 111, then 1011, 1101, 1111, but not 1001 since we must not have two or more consecutive zeros inside a code. A few minutes with pencil and paper will generate more. We can do the 128-character ASCII set with 10 bits.

I analyzed lots of English-language text to find out how common was each of the ASCII characters, then allocated shorter codes to the more-common characters. The result is shown in Table 1, and I call it the *Varicode* alphabet. With English text, Varicode has an average code length—including the "00" letter gap—of 6.5 bits per character. By simulating random bit errors and counting the number of corrupted characters, I find that Varicode is 50% better than start-stop code, thus verifying that its self-synchronizing properties work well.

The shortest code in Morse is the most-common letter: "e", but in Varicode the shortest code is allocated to the word space. When idle, the transmitter sends a continuous string of zeros. Fig 1 compares the coding of the same word in ASCII, RTTY, Morse and Varicode.

PSK31 Modulation and Demodulation

To transmit Varicode at a reasonable typing speed of about 50 words per minute needs a bit-rate of about 32 per sec. I have chosen 31.25, because it can be easily derived from the 8-kHz sample-rate used in many DSP systems. In theory, we only need a bandwidth of 31.25 Hz to send this as binary data, and the frequency stability that this implies can be achieved with modern radio equipment on HF.

The method chosen was first used on the amateur bands, to my knowledge, by SP9VRC. Instead of frequency-shifting the carrier, which is wasteful of spectrum, or turning the carrier on and off, which is wasteful of transmitter power capability, the "dots" of the code are signaled by reversing the polarity of the carrier. You can think of this as equivalent to transposing the wires to your antenna feeder. This uses the transmitted signal more efficiently since we are comparing a positive signal before the reversal to a negative signal after it, rather than comparing the signal present in the dot to no-signal in the gap. But if we keyed the transmitter in this way at 31.25 baud, it would generate terrible key clicks, so we need to filter it.

If we take a string of dots in Morse code, and low-pass filter it to the theoretical minimum bandwidth, it will look the same as a carrier that is 100% amplitude-modulated by a sine wave at the dot rate. The spectrum is a central carrier and two sidebands at 6dB down on either side. A signal that is sending continuous reversals, filtered to the minimum bandwidth, is equivalent to a double-sideband suppressed-carrier emission, that is, to two tones either side of a suppressed carrier. The improvement in the performance of this polarity-reversal keying over on-off keying is thus equivalent to the textbook improvement in changing from amplitude-modulation telephony with full carrier to double-sideband with suppressed carrier. I have called

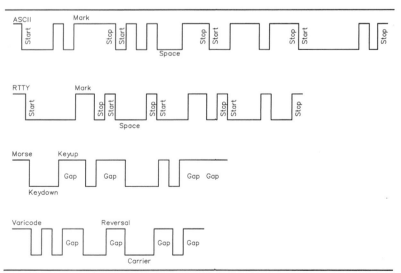

Fig 1—The word "ten" in ASCII, RTTY, Morse and Varicode.

July/Aug 1999 5

this technique "polarity-reversal keying" so far, but everybody else calls it "binary phase-shift keying," or BPSK. Fig 2 shows the envelope of BPSK modulation and the detail of the polarity reversal.

To generate BPSK in its simplest form, we could convert our data stream to levels of ±1 V, for example, take it through a low-pass filter and feed it into a balanced modulator.

The other input to the balanced modulator is the desired carrier frequency. When sending continuous reversals, this looks like a 1 V (P-P) sine wave going into a DSB modulator, so the output is a pure two-tone signal. In practice we use a standard SSB transceiver and perform the modulation at audio frequencies or carry out the equivalent process in a DSP chip. We could signal logic zero by continuous carrier and signal logic one by a reversal, but I do it the other way round for reasons that will become clear shortly.

There are many ways to demodulate BPSK, but they all start with a bandpass filter. For the speed chosen for PSK31, this filter can be as narrow as 31.25 Hz in theory. A brick-wall filter of precisely this width would be costly, however, not only in monetary terms but also in the delay time through the filter, and we want to avoid delays. A practical filter might be twice that width (62.5 Hz) at the 60-dB-down points with a delay-time of two bits (64 ms).

For the demodulation itself, since BPSK is equivalent to double sideband, the textbook method for demodulating DSB can be used. However, it can also be demodulated by delaying the signal by one bit period and comparing it to the signal with no delay in a phase comparator. The output is negative when the signal reverses polarity and positive when it doesn't.

We could extract the information from the demodulated signal by measuring the lengths of the "dots" and "dashes," as we do by ear with Morse code. It helps to pick the data out of the noise, however, if we know when to expect signal changes. We can easily transmit the data at an accurately timed rate, so it should be possible to predict when to sample the demodulator output. This process is known as synchronous reception, although the term "coherent" is sometimes wrongly used.

To synchronize the receiver to the transmitter, we can use the fact that a BPSK signal has an amplitude-modulation component. Although the modulation varies with the data pattern, it always contains a pure-tone component at the baud rate. This can be extracted using a narrow filter, a PLL or the DSP equivalent, and fed to the decoder to sample the demodulated data. Fig 3 shows block diagrams of a typical BPSK modulator and demodulator.

For the synchronization to work we need to make sure that there are no long gaps in the pattern of reversals. A completely steady carrier has no modulation, so we could never predict when the next reversal was due. Fortunately, Varicode is just what we need, provided we choose the logic levels so that zero corresponds to a reversal and one to a steady carrier. The idle signal of continuous zeros thus generates continuous reversals, giving us a strong 31.25-Hz modulation. Even with continuous keying, there will always be two reversals in the gaps between characters. The average number of reversals will therefore be more than two in every 6.5 bits, and there will never be more than 12 bits with no reversal at all. If we make sure that the transmission always starts with an idle period, then the timing will pull into sync quickly. By making the transmitter end a transmission with a "tail" of unmodulated carrier, it is then possible to use the presence or absence of reversals to squelch the decoder. Hence, the screen doesn't fill with noise when there is no signal.

Getting Going

So much for the philosophy and the theory, but how do you get on the air with this mode? In the first experiments on this mode in early 1996, the route to getting on PSK31 was to obtain one of several DSP starter kits. These are printed-circuit cards, usually with a serial interface to a PC, marketed by DSP processor manufacturers at low cost to help engineers and students become familiar with DSP programming. Some radio amateurs have started to write software for these, not just for RTTY but also for SSTV, packet, satellite and digital-voice experiments. They have audio input and output and some general-purpose digital input/output. The construction work needed is limited to wiring up cables, building a power supply and putting the card into a screened box. The DSP software is freely available, as is the software that runs in the PC to interface to the keyboard and screen, and can be obtained most easily via the Internet. It would certainly be possible to construct a PSK31 modem in hardware, although I know of no one who has done this yet.

However, it became clear late in 1998 that soundcards now common in personal computers are capable of performing the audio input/output function needed for PSK31, with the DSP software running in the PC. At Christmas 1998, I completed a basic *Windows*-based PSK31 program to use the soundcard. The availability of this program has dramatically increased the level of PSK31 activity worldwide. (It's available on the Web: **http://aintel.bi.ehu.es/psk31.html**—*Ed.*)

PSK31 Operating

Since PSK31 performance is the same when calling, listening or in contact, it's easy to progress from listen-

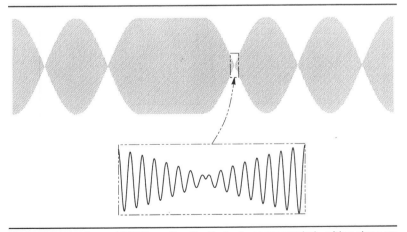

Fig 2—The waveform of BPSK sending the Varicode space symbol., with a close-up of the detail during a phase reversal.

ing to others, to calling CQ, two-way contacts and multi-station nets. The narrow bandwidth and good weak-signal performance do mean learning a few new tricks: First, set the radio dial on one spot. Then fine-tune the audio frequency, while listening through the narrow audio filter rather than the transceiver's loudspeaker, while using an on-screen phase-shift display to center the incoming signal within a few hertz. On transmit, since the envelope of the PSK31 signal is not constant (as is the case for FSK), it is important to keep the transmitter linear throughout. However, since the PSK31 idle is identical to a standard two-tone test signal, it is easy to set up. The worst distortion products will be at ±45 Hz at (typically) 36 dB below PEP.

So far, we've looked at requirements for a live-contact, keyboard/screen communication system, and proposed the narrow-band PSK31 mode as a candidate for a modern equivalent to traditional RTTY. This mode has now been in use on the HF bands by a small but growing band of enthusiasts for about two years. Now, let's look at two recent additions to PSK31.

A Second Look at Error Correction

After getting PSK31 going with BPSK modulation and the Varicode alphabet, several people urged me to add error correction to it in the belief that it would improve it still further. I resisted for the reasons that I gave earlier, namely that the delays in transmission, the discontinuous traffic flow and the inability to listen-in, all make error correction unattractive for live contacts. There is another reason. All error-correcting systems work by adding redundant data bits. Suppose I devise an error-correcting system that doubles the number of transmitted bits. If I wanted to maintain traffic throughput, I would need to double the bit rate. With BPSK that means doubling the bandwidth, so I lose 3dB of S/N and get more errors. The error correction system will have to work twice as hard just to break even! It is no longer obvious that error correction wins. It is interesting to note that with FSK, where the bandwidth is already much wider than the information content, you *can* double the bit-rate without doubling the bandwidth, and error correction *does* work. Computer simulation with BPSK in white noise shows that when the S/N is good, the error-correction system does win, reducing the low error rate to very low levels. At the S/N levels that are acceptable in live amateur contacts, it's better to transmit the raw data slowly in the narrowest bandwidth. It also takes up less spectrum space!

However, there was the suggestion that error correction could give useful results for bursts of noise, which cannot be simulated on the bench, so I decided to try it and do some comparison tests. The automatic repeat (ARQ) method of correcting errors was ruled out. Forward error correction (FEC) seemed to deserve a second look, provided the transmission delay was not too long.

I realized that comparing two systems with different bandwidths and speeds on the air would be difficult. Adjacent-channel interference would be different, as would the effects of multipath. There is, however, another way to double the information capacity of a BPSK channel without doubling its bandwidth and speed. By adding a second, 90° phase-shifted BPSK carrier at the transmitter and a second demodulator in the receiver, we can do the same trick that is used to transmit two color-difference signals in PAL and NTSC television. I call this quadrature polarity-reversal keying, but everybody else calls it quaternary phase-shift keying, QPSK.

There is a 3-dB S/N penalty with QPSK, because we must split the transmitter power equally between the two channels. This is the same penalty as doubling the bandwidth, so we are no worse off. QPSK is therefore ideal for my planned comparison experiment: The adjacent-channel interference, the S/N and the multipath performance would be the same for both.

In the next section, I will think of QPSK not as two channels of binary data, but as a single-channel that can be switched to any of four 90° phase-shift values. By the way, the clock-recovery idea used for BPSK works just as well for QPSK, because the envelope still has a modulation component at the bit-rate.

QPSK and the Convolutional Code

There is a vast amount of available knowledge about correcting errors in data that are organized in blocks of constant length (such as ASCII codes) by transmitting longer blocks. I know of nothing that covers error correction of variable-length blocks like Varicode. There are ways of reducing errors in continuous streams of data with no block structure. (This seems a natural choice for a radio link, since its errors don't have any block structure either.) These are called convolutional codes. One of the simplest forms does actually double the number of data bits; it is therefore a natural choice for a QPSK channel carrying a variable-length code.

The convolutional encoder generates one of the four phase shifts, not from each data bit to be sent, but from a sequence of them. This means that each bit is effectively spread out in time, intertwined with earlier and later bits in a precise way. The more we spread it out, the better will be the ability of the code to correct bursts of noise, but we must not go too far or we will introduce too much transmission delay. I chose a time spread of five bits. The table that determines the phase shift for each pattern of five successive bits is given in the sidebar "The Convolutional Code." The logic behind this table is beyond the scope of this article.

In the receiver, a device called a

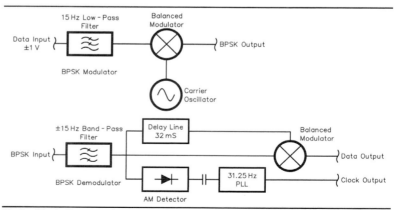

Fig 3—Block diagram of analog BPSK modem.

July/Aug 1999 7

Viterbi decoder is used. This is not so much a decoder as a whole family of encoders playing a guessing game. Each one makes a different "guess" at what the last five transmitted data bits might have been. There are 32 different patterns of five bits and thus 32 encoders. At each step the phase-shift value predicted by the bit-pattern-guess from each encoder is compared with the actual received phase-shift value, and the 32 encoders are given "marks out of ten" for accuracy. Just as in a knockout competition, the worst 16 are eliminated and the best 16 go on to the next round, taking their previous scores with them. Each surviving encoder then gives birth to two "children," one guessing that the next transmitted bit will be a zero and the other guessing that it will be a one. They all do their encoding to guess what the next phase shift will be and receive scores again, which are added on to their earlier scores. The worst 16 encoders are killed-off again and the cycle repeats.

It's a bit like Darwin's theory of evolution, and eventually all the descendants of the encoders that made the right guesses earlier will be among the survivors and will all carry the same "ancestral genes." If we record the family tree (the bit-guess sequence) of each survivor, we can trace it back to find the transmitted bit-stream. We must wait at least five generations (bit periods), however, before all survivors have the same great great grandmother (who guessed right five bits ago). The whole point is that the scoring system based on the running total ensures that the decoder always gives the most-accurate guess, *even if the received pattern is corrupted.* Although we may need to wait a bit longer than five bit periods for the best answer to become clear. In other words, the Viterbi decoder corrects errors.

The longer we wait, the more accurate it is. I chose a decoder delay of four times the time spread, or 20 bits. We now have a 25-bit delay from one end to the other (800 ms), giving a round-trip delay to a two-way contact of 1.6 seconds. I think this is about the limit before it becomes a nuisance. In any case, the decoder could change to trade performance for delay without incompatibility.

QPSK on the Air

PSK31 operators find QPSK can be very good, but it is sometimes disappointing. In bench tests with white noise, it is actually *worse* than BPSK, confirming the simulation work mentioned earlier, but in conditions of burst noise, improvements of up to five times the character error-rate have been recorded. This performance doesn't come free, however. Apart from the transmission delay, which can be a bit annoying, QPSK is twice as critical in tuning as BPSK. A QPSK signal will start to decode wrong when the phase shift is greater than 45°, and that will be the case when the tuning error is only 3.9 Hz. This could be a problem with some older radios. What tends to happen is that contacts start on BPSK and change to QPSK if it is worth doing and there is no drift. There is one aspect of QPSK that must be kept in mind—it is important for both stations to use the correct sideband—on BPSK it doesn't matter.

Extending the Alphabet

In English-speaking countries, virtually all the characters and symbols that are needed for day-to-day written communications are present in the 128-character ASCII set. However, many other languages have accents, umlauts, tildes and other signs and symbols that are not in the ASCII set,

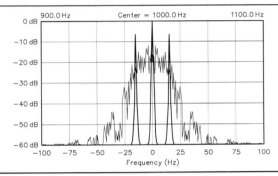

Fig 4—The spectrum of a BPSK signal, idling and sending data, compared with an unmodulated carrier at the same signal level. The carrier is the center pip; the smaller pips are the PSK31 reversals, and the large, ragged hump is noise shaped by the filter.

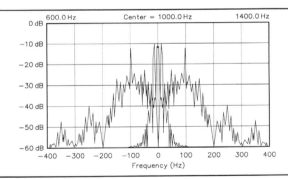

Fig 5—Comparison of the PSK31 spectrum with 100-baud, 200-Hz-shift FSK (AMTOR/PACTOR). The taller, three-hump signal at center is PSK31. The smaller, double-peak (±100 Hz) signal is FSK.

Fig 6—A screenshot of the *PSK31 Windows* program control panel, receiving a slightly noisy QPSK signal (notice the scope display at left). Fine-tuning controls for receive and transmit audio tones are near the bottom-center of the panel.

> **Is PSK31 Legal?**
>
> Some armchair lawyers have questioned the legality of PSK31 since its Varicode is not specifically mentioned as "legal" digital code in Part 97. Some confusion is understandable, give the wording of 97.309(a). However, the FCC clarified the meaning of the rules in an Order released October 11, 1995 (December 1995 *QST*, p 84). The Order (DA95-2106) reads in part: "This Order amends Section 97.304(a) of the Commission's Rules ...to clarify that amateur stations may use any digital code that has its technical characteristics publicly documented. This action was initiated by a letter from the American Radio Relay League, Inc. (ARRL)."
>
> The Order goes on to note that "The technical characteristics of CLOVER, G-TOR and PACTOR have been documented publicly for use by amateur operators, and commercial products are readily available that facilitate the transmission and reception of communications incorporating these codes. Including CLOVER, G-TOR and PACTOR in the rules will not conflict with our objective of preventing the use of codes or ciphers intended to obscure the meaning of the communication. We agree, therefore, that it would be helpful to the amateur service community for the rules to specifically authorize amateur stations to transmit messages and data using these and similar digital codes"
>
> Given that PSK31 is in the public domain for amateur use, that software is readily and freely available and that its emission characteristics clearly meet the standards of Section 97.307 for RTTY/data, there is little doubt that its use by FCC-licensed amateur stations is legal.
>
> However, just to complete the documentation, in a letter to the FCC dated January 27, 1999, ARRL General Counsel Christopher D. Imlay, W3KD, documented the technical characteristics of PSK31 in a manner similar to how CLOVER, G-TOR and PACTOR were previously documented. There is no need for PSK31 to be mentioned specifically in the rules, because CLOVER, G-TOR and PACTOR are simply given as examples.—*Dave Sumner, K1ZZ*

but are now used in everyday written text generated on computers. These extra symbols are now standardized worldwide in the ANSI alphabet, the first 128 characters of which are identical to ASCII, and the second 128 contain all the special symbols. Since the *WINDOWS* operating system uses ANSI, and most PC programs are now written for *WINDOWS*, I have recently extended the PSK31 alphabet in a *WINDOWS* version.

It is very easy to add extra characters to the Varicode alphabet without backwards-compatibility problems. In the early PSK31 decoders, if there was no "00" pattern received 10-bits after the last "00", it would simply be ignored as a corruption. In the extended alphabet, I let the transmitter legally send codes longer than 10 bits. The old decoders will just ignore them and the extended decoder can interpret them as extra characters. To get another 128 Varicodes means adding more 10-bit codes, all 11-bit and some 12-bit codes. There seemed little reason to be clever with shorter common characters so I chose to allocate them in numerical order, with code number 128 being 1110111101 and code number 255 being 101101011011. The vast majority of these will never be used, so it hardly slows the transmission rate at all, but it would not be a good idea to transmit binary files this way!

Summary

This article has identified some of the characteristics of modern HF data-transmission modes that have contributed to the decline in live QSO operation on these modes, while tradi-

> **The Convolutional Code**
>
> The left-most numbers in each column contain the 32 combinations of a run of five Varicode bits, transmitted left bit first. The right-most number is the corresponding phase shift to be applied to the carrier, with "0" meaning no shift, "1" meaning advance by 90°, "2" meaning polarity reversal and "3" meaning retard by 90°. A signal that is advancing in phase continuously is higher in radio frequency than the carrier.
>
> | | | | |
> |---|---|---|---|
> | 00000 2 | 01000 0 | 10000 1 | 11000 3 |
> | 00001 1 | 01001 3 | 10001 2 | 11001 0 |
> | 00010 3 | 01010 1 | 10010 0 | 11010 2 |
> | 00011 0 | 01011 2 | 10011 3 | 11011 1 |
> | 00100 3 | 01100 1 | 10100 0 | 11100 2 |
> | 00101 0 | 01101 2 | 1010 3 | 11101 1 |
> | 00110 2 | 01110 0 | 10110 1 | 11110 3 |
> | 00111 1 | 01111 3 | 10111 2 | 11111 0 |
>
> As an example, the "space" symbol, a single 1 preceded and followed by zeros, would be represented by successive run-of-five groups 00000, 00001, 00010, 00100, 01000, 10000, 00000, which results in the transmitter sending the QPSK pattern 2,1,3,3,0,1,2.
>
> Note that a continuous sequence of zeros (the Varicode idle sequence) gives continuous reversals, the same as BPSK.

tional RTTY is still widely used. By concentrating on the special nature of live-QSO operation, a new RTTY mode (I don't call it a "data" mode) has been devised, which uses modern DSP techniques and uses the frequency stability of today's HF radios. The bandwidth is much narrower than any other telegraphy mode. Fig 4 shows the spectrum occupied by PSK31 and Fig 5 compares this to the bandwidth of a PACTOR signal.

At the time of writing (February 1999) PSK31 is available for the Texas TMS320C50DSK with software written by G0TJZ, the Analog Devices ADSP21061 "SHARC" kit with software by DL6IAK and my own software for the Motorola DSP56002EVM. For the SoundBlaster card, DL9RDZ has written a *LINUX*-based program for the PC. Some commercially available DSP-based multimode controllers have already been upgraded to include PSK31 and more will follow. However, the most popular implementation of PSK31 so far is the *WINDOWS*-based soundcard program, which I have written for the soundcard. The DSP algorithms for PSK31 are being made available free-of-charge to bona-fide amateur programmers, so there should be a wide choice of PSK31 systems in the future.

News of the latest PSK31 developments and activity can be found at **http://aintel.bi.ehu.es/psk31.html** The site also contains a link to information for those who want to implement their own PSK31 modem.

"WSJT: New Software for VHF Meteor-Scatter Communication" by Joe Taylor, K1JT

By Ward Silver, NØAX

Rarely does a single technical advance turn an entire field of communication on its ear, so to speak, but Joe Taylor, K1JT managed to do just that by developing the *WSJT* software package. (**physics.princeton.edu/pulsar/K1JT/wsjt.html**) Most hams will correctly associate K1JT and his software with moonbounce or EME (Earth-Moon-Earth) communications, but his initial efforts were intended to improve on the high-speed CW (HSCW) techniques for working meteor scatter.

As Joe describes in the following article, in his early ham radio days he and his brother Hal, K2ITQ, operated a lot on the VHF bands, especially in the scatter modes. Education and professional academia then took priority, leading to his being awarded the 1993 Nobel Prize in Physics (along with Russell Hulse) for research on pulsars in binary star systems. Observing and measuring the pulsar itself was not the main achievement but, rather, establishing that the rate of change in orbital period of the pulsar confirmed the existence of gravitational radiation for the first time. Making the timing measurements required extremely precise techniques on a signal that was extremely weak, thus Joe became familiar with all sorts of signal processing to recover such a signal from the noise in which it was embedded. This turned out to have great benefits for Amateur Radio, as well!

As he approached retirement from Princeton, Joe's interest in Amateur Radio rekindled — a common story among hams — and he returned to scatter propagation, in particular meteor scatter. This is an interesting

The 1000-foot diameter Arecibo radio telescope where K1JT did the research on pulsars that led to a share of the 1993 Nobel Prize in Physics.

mode in which the "openings" are extremely short with a few seconds being considered long, leading to the characterization of the received signals as "pings" and meteor scatter operators as "ping jockeys." Manual meteor scatter communication on CW or SSB was not particularly robust, and the Europeans had refined the HSCW technique of sending bursts of Morse code at 8000 letters per minute, recording the received signals, and playing them back.

While HSCW was successful in working stations off of the ionized meteor trails, Joe set about devising a coding scheme and protocol that could take advantage of the computing resources of the typical ham shack equipment. The result was FSK441, a mode named for the type of modulation (FSK) and the symbol rate of 441 baud. As the article detailed, FSK441 worked so well that it has been adopted worldwide in pursuit of pings. During a meteor shower, listeners on the meteor scatter operating frequencies (50.250-50.270 MHz and 144.130-144.150 MHz) will hear the distinctive buzzing of FSK441 signals as they appear and disappear with each "burn" in the sky. In the following year, Joe optimized the mode for 6 meters and ionospheric scatter as JT6M.

If the story ended here, it would be a good story, but Joe was by no means finished. As he mentions in the article, the mode PUA43, developed for EME by Bob Larkin, W7PUA, was of great interest. The coding and modulation schemes in PUA43 had been quite successful although they were written for specific hardware. Taking the next step, the *WSJT* software suite was extended to support moonbounce communications with the mode JT65 in 2003 and JT4, optimized for use on the microwave bands.

It was if Joe had reached into the sky and brought the Moon close to Earth. No longer did moonbounce require large steerable arrays or dishes, kilowatt amplifiers, and ears trained to detect the faint echoes returning after a round trip of nearly one-half million miles. Stations equipped with 10 times less transmit power, a high-quality receiver and reasonably good preamplifier, and a few long-boom Yagi antennas were now "on the Moon." While this by no means diminishes the extraordinary skills, dedication, and technical contributions of the EME "analog" pioneers, JT65 was Promethean in making moonbounce more than a dream for many amateurs.

The rate of *WSJT* innovation is, if anything, accelerating. Now converted to open-source, numerous programmers are at work extending and refining the software. QRP and low-frequency HF operators adapted a version, JT65-HF, to communicate through atmospheric noise, and JT9 is in development just for those applications. WSPR was developed as an extremely low-power beacon mode to assess propagation. ISCAT supports ionospheric scatter. Variations on JT65 are in development to support moonbounce contest activity and speed up the QSO rate.

Just as CW leapt past spark, the adoption of digital coding and modulation is revolutionizing amateur communications. Contacts once considered impossible or only achievable under extreme conditions are now routine. The ability to make these contacts opens up possibilities for hams who can now imagine completely new methods and modes of operating, leading hams to think "I wonder if…" and that is the real driver of

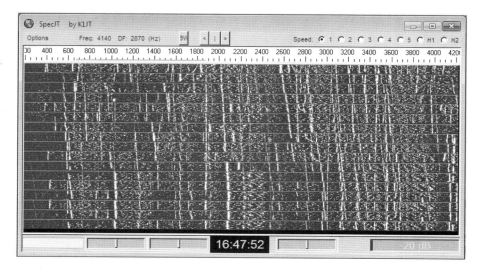

A waterfall display showing many dozens of JT65 signals audible at Arecibo in a 4 kHz passband after making the trip to the Moon and back. Note the Doppler shift on the signals.

By Joe Taylor, K1JT

WSJT: New Software for VHF Meteor-Scatter Communication

Interplanetary dust particles are plunging into Earth's atmosphere continuously. With this revolutionary software you can communicate over distances up to 1400 miles by bouncing signals off the ionized trails of these tiny meteors.

In February 2000 I started playing with meteor scatter on the 2- and 6-meter bands, using the relatively new computer-assisted high speed CW technique (HSCW). I had done some meteor and ionospheric scatter work in an earlier hamming life, more than 40 years ago.[1] My long-dormant interest in Amateur Radio having been warmly rekindled, I was anxious to see what advantages modern equipment and techniques might bring to this fascinating and always-available communication mode for VHF DX.

I quickly learned that the high-speed CW mode of carrying out meteor-scatter QSOs can be very effective. The mode was entertainingly described by Shelby Ennis, W8WN, in a recent *QST* article.[2] HSCW makes it possible to use the very brief "pings" of signals reflected from the ionized trails of meteors entering the Earth's atmosphere some 100 km above the surface. On the 50 and 144 MHz bands these pings can be received at almost any time from a moderately well equipped station at a distance of 500 to 1100 miles (800 to 1800 km). The pings typically last no more than a few tenths of a second at 144 MHz, so they are useless for voice communication or normal-speed CW. Indeed, single-sideband operators who get on during the peaks of major meteor showers call them "the abominable pings," and in order to make QSOs they wait patiently for the much less frequent "blue whizzers" whose stronger ionization can support two-meter SSB exchanges for a few seconds or longer. Outside the major showers, blue whizzers are so rare that they, too, are essentially useless for communication unless you are extremely lucky or willing to run in unattended "beacon" mode. As a result, SSB meteor-scatter contacts are virtually nonexistent on 2 meters except near the peaks of major showers.

On the other hand, pings from meteor trails with "underdense" ionization are nearly always available in usable numbers. Even 100-W, single-Yagi stations at suitable distances can usually hear several pings from each other in a 10 to 20 minute period. At typical HSCW speeds around 8000 letters per minute, a ping lasting 0.1 second contains about 13 characters—just about enough for your call, the other station's call, and perhaps a signal report. With coordinated timing, good frequency calibration, and some diligence, operators who take the time to learn the technique can easily complete QSOs this way. It's a fascinating way to work a bunch of new states, VUCC grid locators, or (if you live in Europe) DXCC entities. It can also work wonders for fattening your multiplier total in a VHF contest. You do not need an EME-class station, and best of all, you don't need to wait for a meteor shower or for one of those all-too-elusive band openings that usually happen when you had to be out of town.

Alas, all too few stations in North America have cared to put the effort into learning the HSCW technique for working meteor scatter. Our European friends have put us to shame in this respect; many hundreds of amateurs over there use the technique regularly. In our own hemisphere, HSCW meteor scatter has attracted surprisingly few converts. A North American High Speed Meteor Scatter Contest has been run for each of the past four years, and I've had great fun taking part in the 2000 and 2001 events. The total number of participants, however, has been under two dozen in any given year—and it seems that these include nearly all of the North American hams who have been active and HSCW-capable in those years.

Having learned International Morse as a youngster and never having lost my proficiency, I love CW as a mode of communication. But I also appreciate the progress that modern digital methods have brought to our hobby. Motivated in part by a desire to make VHF meteor-scatter communication accessible and attractive to a much larger number of fellow hams, and in part by a simple desire to show that it could be done, in April 2001 I set out to design a digital encoding scheme and software package to enable amateur QSOs using the brief pings from underdense meteor trails. The result has led to a computer program called *WSJT* (for "Weak Signal Communication, by K1JT") that implements a signal protocol called FSK441. The mode works so well that it has been rapidly embraced by the VHF fraternities in Europe and North America, and is now making inroads in Africa and the South Pacific, as well.

If your station is capable of weak signal SSB work on the 6 meter or 2 meter bands—say, if you have 100 W or more to a modest Yagi up at least 40 feet—then with the help of *WSJT* you should be able to work similarly equipped stations in the 500-1100 mile range at nearly any time

[1]Notes appear on page 41.

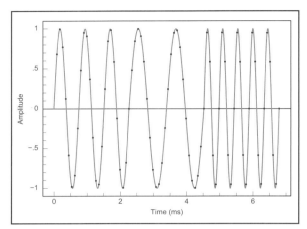

Figure 1—Audio waveform corresponding to the letter C in an FSK441 transmission. Each tone lasts for exactly 25 samples (filled circles) at the 11025 Hz sampling rate, or about 2.3 ms. Each character requires three tone intervals. The code for the letter C is 103, which means that the transmitted tones are at the frequencies 1323, 882 and 2205 Hz.

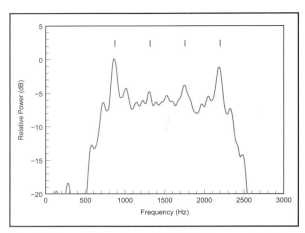

Figure 2—Computed spectrum of the FSK441 message "W8WN 27 K1JT 2727." The frequencies of the four basic tones are indicated by the tick marks above the spectrum. Note that nearly all of the transmitted power falls in the range 660–2425 Hz.

of the day or year. (On the minimum end of the scale, *WSJT* QSOs have been made with as little as 10 W, and I have worked N4KZ rather easily at 610 miles when he was using an 80-meter loop antenna on 6 meters.) With a higher antenna and more power, QSOs out to 1300 or 1400 miles become possible. A few QSOs have already been made with *WSJT* on 222 MHz, as well, and contacts on 432 MHz might be possible near the peak of a major meteor shower.

What Do I Need?

Like a number of other digital and quasi-digital communication modes that have recently become popular on the amateur bands, such as PSK31, MFSK16 and Hellschreiber, *WSJT* requires an SSB transceiver, a computer running the *Windows* operating system, and a soundcard interfaced to the radio's "microphone in" and "speaker out" ports. A 75 MHz Pentium-class computer is a minimum, and you will be happier with a faster CPU, especially if you want to use other programs (such as a Web browser) when running *WSJT*. Your computer should have at least 24 MB of RAM, 40 MB of free disk space, and a monitor with 800 × 600 or higher resolution. Microsoft *Windows* 95, 98, NT, 2000 and XP have all been used successfully. You will, of course, need a station capable of weak signal work on one or more VHF bands.

The *WSJT* program is available for download free of charge at the Web site **pulsar.princeton.edu/~joe/K1JT** and at the European mirror site **www.vhfdx.**

de/WSJT. Download the file *WSJT100.ZIP* for Version 1.00, or a similar file name with a higher version number, if one exists. Unzip the distribution file into a convenient directory such as C:\TEMP and then run SETUP.EXE in that directory to install *WSJT* to a permanent location of your choice. The default installation directory on most computers will be C:\Program Files\WSJT.

You will need a simple computer-to-radio interface like those required for such modes as PSK31, MFSK16, and Hellschreiber. The DTR or RTS line of one of the computer's serial communication (COM) ports is used to key your transmitter's push-to-talk (PTT) line. Connections are also required between the transceiver audio output and computer sound card input, and vice versa. Station accessories that accomplish these things are easy to build[3] and are available commercially from a number of sources advertising in *QST*. You will need a method of synchronizing your computer clock with UTC to an accuracy around one second or better. I heartily recommend a free software utility[4] called *Dimension 4*, which synchronizes your computer clock with atomic time standards at national timekeeping laboratories whenever you are connected to the Internet.

Sometime during the beta-test phase of developing *WSJT*, when I was getting swamped with requests for enhancements, Andy Flowers, KØSM, took pity on me and volunteered to help flesh out the online instructions I had written. With that collaborative effort as a start, further work at my end led to the presently available 13-page *User's Guide and*

Reference Manual. If you plan to give *WSJT* and VHF meteor scatter a try, I urge you to download the *User's Guide*, print it out, and read it carefully. Although many have shown that it is possible to install *WSJT* and learn to use it by trial and error, the manual should definitely be read by anyone serious about getting the most from *WSJT*.

How Does It Work?

The encoding scheme used in *WSJT* was designed to make the best use of signals just a few decibels above the receiver noise, exhibiting rapid fading and Doppler shifts up to 100 Hz, and typically lasting from 20 to a few hundred milliseconds. The Doppler shifts and effective path-length variations make any sort of phase-shift keying (for example, a system analogous to PSK31) a poor candidate for this kind of signal. Large and rapid signal strength variations make on-off keying difficult to decode reliably. In addition, such modulation is inefficient in spectral usage at high speeds, and is very prone to errors caused by atmospheric noise. After considering many possible encoding schemes and testing several of them under real meteor-scatter conditions (thanks to the patient and tireless early morning efforts of Shelby, W8WN, who has seldom refused my request for a schedule!) in early June I decided on a scheme that uses four-tone frequency shift keying at a rate of 441 baud. The adopted scheme has been given the technical name FSK441, although most people seem to be calling it simply "the *WSJT* mode."

In a normal FSK441 message, each character is encoded as three audio-frequency tones sent sequentially. Each tone can have one of four possible frequencies, so the maximum number of encodable characters is 4 × 4 × 4 = 64. For reasons described below, the four sequences that have the same tone sent three times in succession are reserved for a special purpose; in addition, the 15 remaining sequences that begin with the highest frequency tone are not used. This leaves 45 character codes available for general use. For the sake of consistency, and because I intended for *WSJT* also to implement the weak signal mode called PUA43, designed by Bob Larkin, W7PUA, I chose to use the same 43-character "alphabet" that is incorporated in that mode. This character set includes 26 letters, 10 digits, the space character, and the six special characters: . , ? / # $. Two available character codes remain undefined in FSK441.

Digital computers use binary arithmetic, and the basic unit of information is given the contracted name "bit" for "binary digit." When expressed in numerical terms, a bit can have the value 0 or 1. Since the FSK441 scheme uses four basic tones, base-four notation is the most convenient way of describing its code. For want of a better term, I call the digits of the base-four code "dits," rather than "bits." Each character in the FSK441 alphabet is described by a sequence of three dits, whose numerical values fall in the range 0 to 3. The full coding scheme of FSK441 is presented using this notation in Table 1. Three-digit numbers represent the three-tone sequences corresponding to each character. Tones 0 through 3 correspond to the audio frequencies 882, 1323, 1764 and 2205 Hz. Since the modulation rate is specified as 441 baud, or 441 dits per second, the character transmission rate is 441/3 = 147 characters per second. At this speed a ping lasting 0.1 seconds can convey a very respectable 15 characters of text.

The timing of FSK441 is such that each dit of each character consists of exactly two full cycles of the audio tone at 882 Hz, three cycles at 1323 Hz, four at 1764 Hz, or five at 2205 Hz. *WSJT* runs the computer sound card at a sampling rate of 11025 Hz and therefore each dit, 1/441 of a second long, requires exactly 25 samples for its representation in the digitized waveform. Each generated tone blends into the next one in a phase- and amplitude-continuous manner. An example of the generated signal is presented in Figure 1, which shows the audio waveform corresponding to the letter "C" (code 103; see Table 1). An FSK441 transmission contains no dead spaces between tones or between characters; the typical short messages exchanged in meteor scatter QSOs are sent repeatedly and continuously, usually for 30 seconds at a time. Different tones do not overlap in time, so there is little opportunity for even

Table 1
FSK441 Character Codes

Character	Tones	Character	Tones
1	001	H	120
2	002	I	121
3	003	J	122
4	010	K	123
5	011	L	130
6	012	M	131
7	013	N	132
8	020	O	133
9	021	P	200
.	022	Q	201
,	023	R	202
?	030	S	203
/	031	T	210
#	032	U	211
space	033	V	212
$	100	W	213
A	101	X	220
B	102	Y	221
C	103	0	223
D	110	E	230
F	112	Z	231
G	113		

a poorly adjusted transmitter to produce intermodulation products. For all of these reasons, the audio signal used to generate FSK441 signals is spectrally clean and largely confined to the range 660-2425 Hz, thereby making very effective use of the audio bandwidth of a modern SSB transceiver. In a well-designed and well-adjusted transmitter, the resulting RF spectrum will be similarly clean, and it will remain so even if Class C power amplifiers (or poorly designed solid state amplifiers driven into their limiting regions) are used. An example audio frequency spectrum is shown in Figure 2, computed for the message "W8WN 27 K1JT 2727." The four individual tones can be seen in the spectrum, as well as the sidebands produced by their keying pattern in this particular message. Tones 0 and 3 happen to be used more frequently than tones 1 and 2 in this message, so their spectral peaks are proportionally higher in the average spectrum.

WSJT has another highly effective ploy in its bag of tricks, based on the use of the reserved character codes 000, 111, 222 and 333. Originally I identified these four codes with the ASCII characters +, *, % and @, but I recognized that if a message were composed of any one of these characters sent repeatedly, with no intervening spaces, the transmitter would send a pure tone: an unmodulated carrier at the frequency of the suppressed SSB carrier plus that of the appropriate audio tone. I decided to define such transmissions as having the meaning of the most frequently used short messages in high-speed meteor scatter QSOs, namely R26, R27, RRR and 73. Because these shorthand messages are transmitted as single tones, they have very narrow bandwidths upon reception, even after allowing for the vagaries of propagation. They are therefore easy to recognize, both by ear and by the software. The narrow bandwidth means that a suitable DSP algorithm can dig the signals out of the noise very effectively, even if they are significantly weaker than the weakest decodable multi-tone messages. Single-tone messages have proven to be very effective and reliable, except where co-channel QRM is a severe problem. When pings are few and weak, they can speed up the average time to complete a QSO by a factor of two or more.

Decoding the Pings

The computer algorithm for decoding a received FSK441 message must be able to detect pings, carry out two stages of synchronization on the signals within the pings, and finally translate a sequence of measured frequencies back into a text message. The code that finds pings and determines their length starts by measuring the received power in the full receiver passband, smoothed and sampled at 20 ms intervals. When the signal exceeds the background level by more than a specified threshold, a ping is said to have started. When the power has dropped to at least 1 dB below the threshold, the ping is said to have ended. Pings with deep fading may be interpreted as several closely spaced pings.

The synchronization required for message decoding occurs in two stages. The program first identifies the starting points of the sequences of 25 consecutive waveform samples that convey each transmitted tone. This task is tractable because within properly phased 25-sample intervals, FSK441 signals always consist of a single tone. The decoding software therefore needs to align things so that a mixture of tones is not found in any such 25-sample sequence. The result of this process is a series of measurements of the received audio tone frequencies that reproduce the sequence generated at the transmitter. In practice, the software also needs to account for some frequency offset between transmitter and receiver, perhaps up to 200 Hz or so. Having made its best estimate of the frequency error, the program identifies each received tone with one of the four nominal FSK441 frequencies and labels it with a dit value in the range 0–3, as defined earlier.

The second necessary synchronizing step is to establish which dits in an arbitrary sequence are the *leading* members of the three-dit sequences defining characters in the message. For reasons of transmission efficiency, no special synchronizing information is embedded in an FSK441 message. Instead, the proper synchronization is established from the message content itself, making use of the facts that (a) three-dit sequences starting with "3" are never used, and (b) the "space" character is coded as 033, as shown in Table 1. Messages sent by *WSJT* always contain at least one trailing space—the software inserts one,

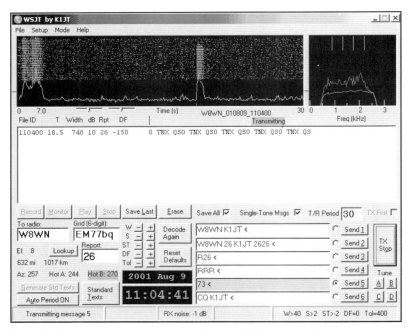

Figure 3—This screen-capture photo shows the main *WSJT* screen during a meteor scatter QSO with W8WN. Thunderstorms were present to the west of K1JT at the time, explaining the two static crashes near the beginning of the displayed 30-second recording as well as the noisier-than usual baseline of receiver background noise (the green line). The signal about 18 seconds into the record is a ping from an underdense meteor trail, and the message it conveyed is displayed in the central text box.

if you do not include it explicitly—and most messages will include additional spaces to improve readability. Other characters may have dits with value 3 in the second or third positions, but never in the first. Therefore, to properly synchronize a received signal the decoding algorithm examines the sequence of measured dit values, skipping through the time series in steps of three, and selects as the properly synchronized starting point a dit numbered N in the sequence such that none of the dits N, N+3, N+6, N+9, ... has the value 3. Under the conditions specified above, such a dit will necessarily be the leading one of an FSK441 character code.

After synchronization has been accomplished, message decoding is a snap. The sequences of dit values are converted from base-four notation into the computer's native binary arithmetic, and the numerical codes are converted to characters by means of a lookup table.

Two other subtleties of the decoding software are worth mentioning here. As you will quickly learn from listening to an FSK441 transmission, the audio waveform has a distinctive and easily recognizable "burbling" sound that is largely independent of the exact message content. This character can be described in terms of modulation of the signal power in each of the four tone frequencies, at the 441 Hz keying rate and its harmonics. The software readily detects this modulation; its absence implies that the signal being examined is *not* an FSK441 signal and that it may be safely rejected as interference or noise.

Single-tone messages are transmitted as pure carriers, and their effective bandwidths upon reception are essentially equal to the inverse of the duration of the ping. Even an extremely short ping of 20 ms duration will exhibit a bandwidth of only 50 Hz, far less than the modulated widths of the individual tones in a multi-tone message. Consequently, a different and much more sensitive detection method is appropriate. The spectrum of a ping suspected of carrying a single-tone message is examined with a spectral resolution of about 40 Hz, leading to very high sensitivity and an excellent ability to avoid spurious decodings.

Normal Operation

Figure 3 shows a screen-capture image of *WSJT* in operation at my station. At the top of the form are two graphical areas. The larger one displays a "waterfall" spectrogram in which time runs left to right and audio frequency increases upward. The signal displayed here is a 30 second recording from a QSO with W8WN; it includes two strong static crashes near the beginning, followed by a moderately strong ping about 18.5 seconds into the record. The green line at the bottom of this plot area represents the power in the full receiver passband, sampled every 0.1 second. The vertical displacement of each point on the green curve is proportional to the total power in all of the waterfall pixels directly above it, on a dB scale.

The smaller graphical window at the right displays two spectral plots, also on a dB scale. The purple line graphs the spectrum of audio-frequency noise, averaged over the full 30 seconds; in the absence of any strong signal, it effectively illustrates the receiver's passband shape. The red line displays the spectrum of the strongest detected ping. Yellow tick marks at the top of this plot area (and also at the left, center, and right of the larger area) indicate the nominal frequencies of the four FSK441 tones. The 441-baud modulation broadens out the pure tones so that their widths begin to approach their spacing, thereby creating an approximately flat transmitted spectrum for most messages. (Note, however, that local peaks may still exist in the spectrum, as illustrated in Figure 2.) In the red curve of Figure 3 you can just about recognize the peaks corresponding to the four basic tones. Each tone has been shifted slightly to the left, relative to the yellow tick marks, because of a small frequency offset between transmitter and receiver.

The large text box in the middle of the *WSJT* screen displays decoded text from any pings detected in the receiving interval. One line of text appears for each validated ping. Information in the text line in Figure 3 shows that the recording interval began at 11:04:00 UTC and that a ping was detected 18.5 seconds into the interval. The ping was 740 ms long, and peaked 10 dB above the noise. According to the somewhat arbitrary criteria coded into *WSJT* (which are made to be roughly equivalent to the operator-judged signal reports sent in high-speed CW meteor scatter work), such a signal rates a "26" signal report. The next number shows that the program estimates W8WN to have been transmitting at a frequency offset by –150 Hz relative to my receiver's frequency. Finally, the decoded message is shown, with Shelby thanking me for another fine 2-meter meteor-scatter ragchew over our 640-mile path.

You may have noticed that the two ping-like signals near the start of the 30-second receiving interval did not produce any decoded text. In the green-line plot and even in the waterfall spectrogram, these signals look very similar to the real ping later in the recording. However, they would not have sounded the same. As described earlier, the *WSJT* program has been taught how to recognize the "burbling" characteristic sound of an FSK441 signal. In the present instance the program would have examined the two early pulses, decided that they did not "smell quite right," and properly rejected them as noise.

A few additional comments on the decoded text in Figure 3 may be helpful. At 147 characters per second, a 740 ms ping should contain more than 100 characters. All displayed messages are truncated to 40 characters, however. Since the actual

December 2001 39

messages transmitted by *WSJT* are limited to a maximum of 28 characters, even the longest ones can be displayed to their full extent, perhaps with some repetition. Under some circumstances, *WSJT* gains additional sensitivity by detecting the repetition pattern of a message and averaging over all the cycles contained in the length of a received ping. This process is most useful for weak pings whose duration is 0.2 seconds or longer, and it can be especially effective on 6 meters where ping lengths are greater. When the program has taken advantage of message averaging, an asterisk is appended to the line of decoded text.

You can control the behavior of *WSJT* by selecting items from the four menus at the top of the screen and using the controls and text boxes in the lower part of the form. As one example, the "Options" item on the "Setup" menu causes the screen shown in Figure 4 to be displayed. This form permits the entry of various station parameters that typically do not change very often. I will not describe the functions of the on-screen controls any further here; you can readily guess the purpose of many of them from the labels visible in Figures 3 and 4, and they are described in full detail in the downloadable *User's Guide and Reference Manual*.

Standard Procedures

Meteor scatter is not a communication mode well suited to ragchewing! QSOs can be completed much more easily if you adhere to a set of standard procedures that have evolved from HSCW and other earlier techniques. A standard message format and message sequence helps the process considerably. *WSJT* generates standard messages automatically, as illustrated in the text boxes at the lower right of Figure 3. The formats of the messages are designed for efficient transfer of the most essential information: the exchange of both call signs, a signal report or other information, and acknowledgments of same. Timed message sequences are a must, and *WSJT* defaults to 30 second transmitting and receiving periods. Although other intervals can be selected, it helps to minimize QRM from nearby stations if everyone adheres to one standard. According to the procedures used by common consent in North America, the westernmost station transmits first in each minute.

At the start of a QSO you should send the other station's call and your own call alternately. Then, as the QSO proceeds...

1. If you have received less than both calls from the other station, send both calls.
2. If you have received both calls, send both calls and a signal report.
3. If you have received both calls and a report, send R plus signal report.
4. If you have received R plus signal report, send RRR.
5. If you have received RRR—that is, a definite acknowledgment of all of your

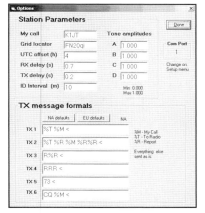

Figure 4—The "Options" screen of *WSJT*, called up from an item on the "Setup" menu. Use this screen to set a number of station parameters, typically ones that do not change frequently. Amplitudes of the four FSK441 tones can be set individually, if desired, to correct for certain transmitter idiosyncrasies. Programmable templates are available for establishing the format of standard messages, and default standards are provided for both North American and European conventions.

information—your QSO is officially complete. However, the other station may not know this, so it is conventional to send 73 (or some other conversational information) to signify that you are done.

Signal reports are conventionally sent as two-digit numbers chosen from non-overlapping ranges. The first digit characterizes the lengths of pings being received, on a 1-5 scale, and the second estimates their strength on a 6-9 scale. The most common signal reports are "26" for weak pings and "27" for stronger ones, but under good conditions reports such as "38" and higher are sometimes used. Whatever signal report you decide to send to your QSO partner, it is important that you do not change it, even if stronger pings should come along later in the contact. You never know when pings will successfully convey fragments of your message to the other end of your path, and you want your received information to be consistent.

Slightly different standard procedures have been adopted for high-speed meteor-scatter in Europe. You will undoubtedly find it useful to seek out and read additional information on current practices available on the Internet. Some good starting places are listed in the sidebar entitled "Meteor Scatter Resources."

The 6- and 2-meter calling frequencies in common use for *WSJT* in North America are 50.270 and 144.140 MHz. Typical practice for calling CQ is to send something like CQ U5 K1JT or CQ D9 K1JT, indicating that you will listen for replies up 5 kHz or down 9 kHz from your transmitting frequency, and will respond on that frequency. However, the easiest way to initiate a QSO is to post a one-line invitation on a Web page known as "Ping Jockey Central" (see sidebar). Someone at a suitable range from you will likely reply to such a posting, suggesting a specific frequency, and your QSO can begin. The ranges of frequencies now being used for *WSJT* in North America are 50.270-50.300 and 144.100-144.150.

Increasing Levels of Activity

Version 0.82 of *WSJT* was first made available to a group of about 20 volunteer beta-testers, nearly all of them HSCW veterans, on June 20, 2001. A majority of this group started making QSOs immediately, and they helped me to polish some of the program's rough edges and root out some bugs. An open beta release of Version 0.92 was announced on July 7, and within two more weeks the program was being widely used and discussed on VHF- and meteor-scatter Internet reflectors and DX clusters in both America and Europe. Release of a stable and more polished Version 1.0 of *WSJT* was announced on August 26. Since that time the installation package has been downloaded more than 1700 times from my own Web site, and more than 3000 times from the European mirror site.

Meteor Scatter Resources

For additional reading on the history and astrophysics of amateur meteor-scatter communications, as well as operating hints and details concerning practices in current use, the following references and Internet addresses are recommended.

1. The classic papers on amateur meteor-scatter communications are the two by Walter F. Bain, W4LTU: "VHF Meteor Scatter Propagation," Apr 1957 *QST*, p 20, and "VHF Propagation by Meteor-Trail Ionization," May 1974 *QST*, p 41. The second one is reprinted in the ARRL publication *Beyond Line of Sight*.
2. Many additional papers, unpublished hints, and extremely useful bits of information can be found on the Web pages **www.qsl.net/w8wn/hscw/hscw.html** and **www.meteorscatter.net/hsms.htm**, and links contained therein.
3. A number of highly useful explanatory files are bundled with a freely available program called *MS-Soft*, by OH5IY, available at **www.sci.fi/~oh5iy**.
4. At least two subscriber reflectors are devoted to meteor scatter communications. Their addresses are **hsms@qth.net** (primarily used in North America) and **meteor-scatter@qth.net** (primarily in Europe).
5. Meteor scatter schedules can be made in near real time by posting a message on the Web page known as Ping Jockey Central at **www.pingjockey.net/cgi-bin/pingtalk**.

I have made more than 150 contacts with *WSJT* myself, including 45 "initials" (first contacts with a new call sign). These QSOs include 19 states and 38 Maidenhead grid locators on 2 meters, and they do not include stations within 500 miles of me. Most of my contacts were made with a 160 W brick and an 11 element Yagi at 45 feet. Many other stations have been far more successful; for example, KØPW told me recently that in three months he had worked 73 initials and 30 states on 2 meters, using *WSJT*. I have counted more than 120 North American hams that are actively using the mode now, and additional calls are showing up every week. In Europe the activity levels appear to be substantially higher: I have heard estimates suggesting that at least 500 amateurs there are using *WSJT*, representing more than 50 DXCC entities. These numbers include extra activity centered around the Perseids meteor shower, which peaked on August 12, and it is likely that similar increases will occur near the peaks of the remaining members of the "big four" of the annual meteor showers: the Leonids around November 18, Geminids around December 13, and Quadrantids around January 3.

Another indicator of the growing interest in *WSJT* is its significant presence in the September 2001 VHF QSO Party, the first major North American VHF contest since the release of the program. I have no idea how many QSOs and multipliers were made using the mode during the contest, but I suspect the answer must be at least in the hundreds. I saw plenty of efforts to make *WSJT* schedules in advance of the contest period, and in the East, at least, the larger mountaintop "super stations" were involved. Without really trying very hard, I made 18 meteor scatter contacts during the contest, 17 of them being multipliers I would not otherwise have worked. These were not the quickest QSOs made during the contest, but they were not unreasonably long either. The median time to complete a QSO was 5 minutes on 6 meters and 13 minutes on 2 meters.

Looking Ahead

On a time-available basis, I hope to make further improvements in *WSJT*'s decoding algorithms and its convenience of use. Even more interesting, from a technical point of view, will be the incorporation of the extreme weak-signal mode known as PUA43. Unlike FSK441, PUA43 is designed for signals that are more or less constant in amplitude but buried deep below the level of the receiver noise. Even though quite inaudible, such signals can convey a slow but steady stream of information that is decodable by using DSP integration techniques. W7PUA and his collaborators have demonstrated the impressive capabilities of the PUA43 mode by making EME (moon-bounce) contacts with 150 W and single Yagis on 2 meters, and with 5 W and 10 foot dishes on 1296 MHz. To my knowledge, the PUA43 mode is presently available only in software written for the elegant home-brewed DSP-10 2-meter transceiver,[6] also designed by W7PUA. I hope to incorporate the mode into *WSJT*, as well, thereby making its capabilities available to amateurs using a much wider range of equipment.

As a sort of enticement for things to come, let me quote some numbers comparing the theoretical sensitivities and transmission rates of modes being discussed here, as well as the more familiar CW and SSB. In a typical transceiver's 2.5 kHz bandwidth, an SSB signal needs to be 4-6 dB above the noise to be copyable. Normal speech rates are two or three words per second; when one is sending call signs by voice as part of a minimal QSO, this means about three or four letters per second. In the same receiver bandpass, FSK441 signals can be copied at about 2 dB above the noise, and the special single-tone messages used in *WSJT* are copied down to 4 or 5 dB *below* the noise. The FSK441 transmission rate is a hefty 147 characters per second, but of course the useful throughput depends on the availability of meteors. Morse code at 20 WPM can be copied if it is about 6 dB below the noise in a 2.5 kHz bandwidth. (Note that such a signal would be about 1 dB *above* the noise in a 500 kHz bandwidth.) At 20 WPM, the throughput of CW is about 1.7 characters per second.

Amateurs customarily think of CW as being the most effective mode for weak signal communication, and the numbers just quoted seem to bear this out. However, please take note that a one-minute PUA43 transmission, containing 28 characters sent at 0.5 characters per second, can be copied all the way down to *some 27 dB below the receiver noise*. Post-detection averaging can yield nearly another 6 dB improvement in half an hour of alternating one-minute intervals of transmission and reception. The slower transmission rate, and even more importantly the coherent detection of the narrow band signal over 2-second intervals, accounts for the very substantial increase in signal to noise ratio.

PUA43 is a highly effective mode for VHF/UHF tropospheric propagation, in addition to EME. Because it works well with weak but steady signals, it nicely complements the short-ping capabilities of FSK441. With both PUA43 and FSK441 in its bag of tricks, the modest VHF station described earlier should be able to work out to 500 miles or so at any time with tropospheric propagation and the PUA43 mode, and from there out to 1100 miles and beyond by using FSK441 and meteor scatter. If you are within those distances of central New Jersey, I look forward to working you with one of these modes soon!

Joe Taylor was first licensed as KN2ITP in 1954, and has since held the Amateur Radio call signs K2ITP, WA1LXQ, W1HFV, VK2BJX and K1JT. Trained in the academic fields of physics and astronomy, he was Professor of Astronomy at the University of Massachusetts from 1969 to 1981 and since then has been Professor of Physics at Princeton University. His research specialty is radio astronomy, and he was awarded the Nobel Prize in Physics in 1993 for discovery of the first orbiting pulsar. He currently serves as Dean of the Faculty at Princeton and chases DX from 160 meters through the microwave bands. You can contact Joe at 272 Hartley Ave, Princeton, NJ 08540-5656; **k1jt@arrl.net**.

Notes
[1] Joe Taylor, K2ITP, "Working Ionospheric Scatter on 50 MHz," Dec 1958 *QST*, p 28.
[2] Shelby Ennis, W8WN, "Utilizing the Constant Bombardment of Cosmic Debris for Routine Communication," Nov 2000 *QST*, p 28.
[3] Steve Ford, WB8IMY, "PSK31 2000," May 2000 *QST*, p 42.
[4] Download the computer clock utility *Dimension 4* from **www.thinkman.com/dimension4**
[5] The *WSJT* home page is at **pulsar.princeton.edu/~joe/K1JT**
[6] Bob Larkin, W7PUA, "The DSP-10: An All-Mode 2-Meter Transceiver Using a DSP IF and PC-Controlled Front Panel," Sept 1999 *QST*, p 33, Oct 1999 *QST*, p 34, and Nov 1999 *QST*, p 42.

Amateur Radio in Orbit

By Jan King, W3GEY and Ward Silver, NØAX

On October 4, 1957, during the International Geophysical Year, the Soviet Union launched *Sputnik 1* which was the first artificial satellite of Earth. About 2 feet in diameter, it orbited the Earth every 96 minutes and was visible from the Earth's surface after dark. NØAX remembers being carried into the street by parents to look with the neighbors for the tiny and just barely visible dot of light moving through the stars. More to our interests, signals transmitted by the satellite on 20.005 and 40.002 MHz were monitored by Amateur Radio operators until the satellite's batteries became exhausted 22 days later. *Sputnik 1* eventually re-entered the Earth's atmosphere and burned up on January 4, 1958.

The launch electrified the world, setting off what became known as the "Space Race" with the enormous resources of the United States and Soviet Union competing for each advance and achievement. Who would have thought that a mere four years later, some "hobbyists" (professionally employed as scientists and engineers, to be sure) would build their own satellite, known as *OSCAR* (Orbiting Satellite Carrying Amateur Radio)? Ham radio's own "sputnik" (the word means "elementary satellite") lasted for the same 22 days.

Amateurs would go on to create dozens of satellites. Including the Cubesats built by teams from universities and other organizations, more than 100 amateur satellites have been launched. They have used frequencies ranging from 21 MHz through 47 GHz. (Allocations are also available on the 7, 14, and 18 MHz bands, as well as at 77.5, 134 and 248 GHz.) Twenty "birds" are currently shown as active and operational on the AMSAT website (Radio Amateur Satellite Corporation, **www.amsat.org**) either transmitting telemetry or retransmitting received signals back to Earth.

OSCAR 7, launched in 1974, is the oldest satellite of *any* type in orbit that is still functional. Built in W3GEY's basement, the satellite "went dark" in 1981 due to battery failure (a typical satellite lifetime) but came back to life 21 years later in 2002 after the fault cleared. Now it is running purely on power from its solar panels. These small satellites (by comparison to commercial and government satellites) have proven that very useful functions and scientific experiments can be performed on small platforms. AMSAT, *OSCAR*, and Amateur Radio more generally, have played a very important role in the evolution of small satellites that are beginning to take over the role of their larger brothers and displace much more expensive big satellite systems. The comparatively tiny CubeSats are beginning to be recognized by the science community as capable of doing "real science in orbit." None of this would have happened in the same way if it had not been for Project OSCAR followed by AMSAT.

AO-51, known as "Echo" (the octagonal satellite to the left is Unisat 3, another commercial "small satellite") ready for launch from the Baikonur Cosmodrome in Kazakhstan. (N4HY photo, courtesy AMSAT-NA.)

Hams not only hold the record for the oldest satellite in space, but we remain the only small satellite builders who have successfully carried out the accurate execution of a major burn maneuver of a bi-propellant motor with a total of four major bi-propellant burns in space on satellites AO-10, AO-13 and AO-40. No one else has yet attempted it, despite the huge surge in interest in small space systems around the world. Even so, very few amateurs know of these accomplishments and certainly no one outside Amateur Radio.

The need to control, manage and monitor satellites in orbit with the resources available to amateurs has also driven innovations in the communications link. Digital store-and-forward PACSATs were developed as a sort of orbiting bulletin board accessed via packet radio. Amateurs have developed robust communications protocols for uplinking control data, along with innovative antenna systems and sophisticated tracking software that control them.

The articles in this section touch on some of the amateur satellite success stories, but there are many, many more technical advances chronicled in numerous *QST* and *QEX* articles as well as related publications and proceedings of the amateur and professional communities. A number of these articles are listed in the reference table at the end of this book.

Satellites to Come

In recent years, university teams particularly have discovered the CubeSat form factor and the benefits of using Amateur Radio as the means of communications with the satellite. Amateur Radio provides a wide variety of frequencies and modes for the effort of passing an amateur licensing exam. This introduction to Amateur Radio has two major benefits. First, even if simply used as a means to an end, students embarking on a professional career are exposed to Amateur Radio and may continue to use and explore it. Second, continued use of Amateur Radio will lead to additional innovations from this growing new community. Clearly, this aspect of the Amateur Satellite Service will continue to expand.

Amateurs are also at a bit of a crossroads as to what kind of satellite programs they wish to pursue: small, single-purpose satellites or large multifunction platforms. Both have had their successes and failures. Opportunities exist to go forward with both, and so it is likely that hams will find their antenna systems tracking a wide range of birds. Even geosynchronous platforms are a possibility in partnership with commercial enterprises.

Manned spacecraft such as the International Space Station (ISS) and anticipated programs from a variety of nations will provide additional opportunities for Amateur Radio in space. Who will be the first to contact a lunar astronaut or maintain contact on a mission to Mars or an asteroid? Unmanned exploration probes may also have room for an amateur station tucked away somewhere, their faint whispers to be detected by a persistent and skilled ham. In short, as humankind's reach expands, so will Amateur Radio as it has been there all along.

Amateur Radio turned out to be "well-suited" to this experiment when a surplus space suit was fitted with an amateur transmitter and jettisoned from the ISS in February 2006. [Photo courtesy of NASA]

"The Oscar Satellite" by Harley Gabrielson, W6HEK

By Jan King, W3GEY and Ward Silver, N0AX

What do Ham, Yuri, Alan, Gus and Oscar have in common? All of them were launched into space in 1961. Ham refers to "Ham the Chimp," the first hominid animal in space, and his name was an acronym for the facility at which he was trained, the Holloman Aerospace Medical Center. The others are Yuri Gargarin (first human in space), Alan Shepherd (first American in space), Gus Grissom (second American in space), and finally, *OSCAR*, the first non-governmental satellite of any type and the first Amateur Radio satellite of many to come. (There was no number attached to that first flight. Numbering of *OSCAR* satellites began with *OSCAR II*.)

The very notion that in 1961, just as the space race was getting underway, ham radio operators could build a satellite capable of operating from Earth orbit was fairly preposterous. Not only did the satellite get built and work for 22 days, just as long as the *Sputnik 1* satellite, but it was also the first satellite of any type to be ejected as a secondary payload and enter a different orbit. Launched to the south onboard *Discoverer 36* from Vandenberg Air Force Base on the California coast, the satellite's 2 meter beacon signal, transmitting HI in Morse code, was first detected by KC4USA in the Antarctic and then by KL7EBM in Kodiak, Alaska.

Lance Ginner, K6GSJ, holding OSCAR 1 before launch. The satellite was plated in gold to reflect sunlight that would otherwise cause it to overheat. The stripes are black paint that would absorb just enough sunlight to maintain an even temperature in the spacecraft.

Built in its members garages and workshops by the Project OSCAR Radio Club (the oldest Amateur Radio club devoted to satellites and now incorporated as Project OSCAR, **www.projectoscar.net**), the satellite weighed only about 10 pounds. That made it one of the lightest amateur satellites until the CubeSat era some 30 years later. The cost has gone up, too. Most of that first satellite was built from donated materials and services, with a total cash outlay reported to be $68. There is more paperwork these days, although at the time, "Getting government approval proved to be pretty simple," reported original project member Chuck Townes, K6LFJ.[1]

---

[1] N. Corbett, "Ham-Built Radio Orbiting Earth," *Las Vegas Daily Optic,* 13 Dec 1961.

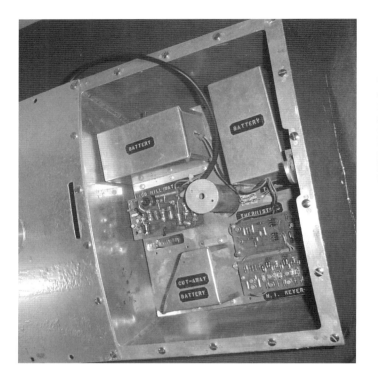

The internal circuitry of the OSCAR-1 backup that was restored and returned to the air in 2011 by ARRL Staff. Note that the printed circuit boards and transistors were new technology at the time. [S. Khrystyne Keane, K1SFA, photo]

Just as with the much larger instrumentation packages (typical payloads were 30 times heavier at about 300 pounds), *OSCAR* provided telemetry. Taking a cue from *Sputnik 1*, the rate at which the Morse code HI beacon was transmitted also encoded the internal temperature of the equipment. This would prove to be valuable in the design of subsequent satellites. You can listen to the signal of *OSCAR 1* on the AMSAT website at **www.amsat.org/amsat/features/sounds**.

What *OSCARs* Lie Ahead?

The specifications in the article being introduced here are mostly unimpressive by today's standards but were state-of-the-art in those early days of space flight. Other systems and equipment seen as groundbreaking today will surely be seen as primitive in future years but that is not the point, particularly in Amateur Radio which is charged with "advancing the art." Implicit in those advances is also "inspiration" as Jan King, W3GEY explains.

"Like every technically minded student of the 1960s I was totally fascinated by the manned space program (Mercury, Gemini and Apollo) and the activities of JPL [the Jet Propulsion Lab in Pasadena, California] were so exciting I stayed up all night to watch the touchdown of the first Surveyor spacecraft and the *Mariner 4* flyby of Mars. They were experiences for me that still have no bound. You must understand: the first photos of Mars were absolutely terrible but, the fact that you could see craters on Mars was totally mind expanding as it was not expected. By this time I was hooked on space and I graduated with my undergraduate degree in Physics and joined NASA's Goddard Space Flight Center…"

Manned and unmanned space flight may be considered common-place today, but humankind is just beginning to move beyond Earth orbit. Ham radio has been carried aboard the Space Shuttle and International Space Station for 30 years, but returning humans to the Moon is on the drawing boards along with discussions of missions to Mars and asteroids. Private enterprise has reached space on a regular basis. As the reach of humanity expands, so will the opportunities for amateurs to participate on levels ranging from observer to traveler, each one having the potential to inspire an inquisitive, adventurous mind to a career and discoveries that open eyes and minds all around the world.

There have been many amateur stations shown in QST which have been described by amateurs as being "out of this world." The Oscar beacon satellite, however, is the first one literally to make the grade! This paper is a review of the design and construction of this unit, touching briefly on the nature of some of the problems involved in building equipment that must operate in a space environment.

The Oscar Satellite

BY HARLEY GABRIELSON,* W6HEK

THE design objective of the Oscar program was to produce a package that would withstand the rigors of vehicle launch and that would work properly in the environment of space. The broad requirements called for equipment capable of radiating a 2-meter signal from orbit some 300 miles above the earth. This signal required a simple identifier, and it had to be capable of being heard and tracked by amateurs using relatively unsophisticated receiving equipment. A 140-milliwatt, crystal-controlled, c.w. transmitter, suitably keyed, and having an operating life of about three weeks, met these requirements.

Anticipating that the Discoverer vehicle was a likely source of launch into space, the packaging requirements for inclusion in this rocket were determined and were found to limit the equipment to a maximum weight of ten pounds contained within a rectangular-shaped configuration, curved to fit the outer circumference of the vehicle (Fig. 1).

The Reliability Problem

The most important consideration in building a suitable space-radio beacon was reliability. Construction of Oscar involved much more than simply whipping up a 140-milliwatt transmitter and keyer, and then providing a set of batteries ample to run it for a few weeks. Oscar must be physically rugged enough to withstand the rigors of a rocket launch, following which it must operate normally without the benefit of retuning or "knob tweaking." All this must be accomplished with the end in view that the equipment will be operating in a rather unusual environment — the utter cold and stillness of outer space!

It is not sufficient to use the best components and the most rugged and conservative design — although these are necessary and vital ingredients to ultimate success. In addition, it is necessary to prove the reliability of the design by subjecting the complete equipment package to punishment in the laboratory under conditions as strenuous as the worst to be expected in actual operation. It must be emphasized that the launch of any satellite is an "all or nothing" operation. There is no chance to call the rocket back to correct some defect observed after the launch has taken place! This sober thought remained uppermost in the minds of the Oscar crew responsible for the design and testing of the package. Failure of the equipment after launch meant that many thousands of man-hours of work, plus the hopes and dreams of the Oscar volunteers, would be to no avail. It also meant that valuable space in the launching vehicle would go to waste, and time and effort spent by others assisting this venture would

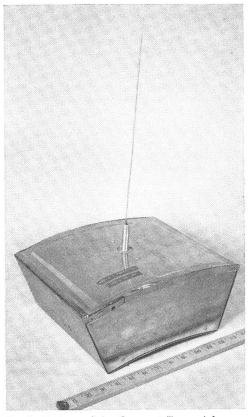

Fig. 1—Mock-up of the Oscar satellite used for preliminary design tests. The container is rectangular in shape and curved to fit the outer circumference of the launching vehicle. Final version of Oscar was gold-plated and had black strips across case to regulate internal temperature of package.

* Project Oscar Association, Box 183, Sunnyvale, Calif.

February 1962

Fig. 2—The Agena-B satellite, "mother ship" for Oscar. Used in the Discoverer program, the Agena-B tips the scales at more than 8500 pounds when it is boosted space-ward by the Thor IRBM vehicle. In orbit, Agena weighs about 1700 pounds after the liquid propellant has been exhausted. The Oscar satellite was placed in the aft equipment rack (extreme right in photograph). Once in orbit, the "piggy-back" Oscar beacon was ejected from the Agena, to go into its own orbit about the earth. Nose cone of Discoverer XXXVI was recovered in Pacific area after four days of orbiting about the earth, while Oscar continued on his journey alone!

have passed for naught. It was imperative, therefore, that every possible step be taken to make sure that Oscar would work once it had been blasted into the reaches of space. The Association, in addition, had to demonstrate to the launching agency that the equipment would meet the demands placed upon it, yet at the same time would not jeopardize the primary objectives of the launching vehicle. Further, it must be demonstrated that the Oscar equipment would have a high probability of performing correctly once it reached orbit.

The Oscar Package

The first design problem of any satellite package concerns the matter of the container in which the equipment is to travel. The housing must hold things together, and this is no mean task during the acceleration phase of the launch. In addition, the container must provide the proper temperature environment for the electronic components while they are whirling about in orbit. During the period the satellite is between the earth and the sun, the container is directly exposed to radiation from the sun without the benefit of protection from the atmosphere. On the other hand, for something less than half of the time the container will be hidden in the shadow of the earth and will be radiating its heat into the cold blackness of space. (The heat generated within the container by the equipment will have a negligible effect on the over-all heat balance.) The problem, therefore, is to cause the package to absorb the same amount of heat during the period it is exposed to sunlight as it loses by radiation during the time the satellite is hidden behind the earth. In this way, an average internal temperature can be maintained, well within the limits that the electronic components can withstand.

The heat balance of the Oscar package has been established by plating the surface of the container with gold to reflect most of the incident heat from the sun and then canceling part of the reflection by covering a portion of the gold surface with a pattern of absorptive paint which will absorb just the desired amount of heat to maintain the proper temperature balance.

This system of heat balance will establish an average temperature, but the day-to-night variations will be quite extreme unless a further precaution is taken. The electronic equipment in the Oscar package is protected by a thick coating of epoxy foam. The foam coating accomplishes two important functions: First, it helps strengthen the equipment by holding the components firmly in place. Second, the foam serves as a heat insulator which inhibits the transfer of heat into and out of the electronic gear. As a result, the internal temperature of Oscar will average out the extremes seen at the surface of the container. The final evaluation of this design feature will be obtained when the "HI" rate reports are reduced to equipment-temperature readings.

The Oscar container is made of a magnesium alloy to hold weight to a minimum and measures approximately 12 by 14 by 6 inches in size. It is curved to conform to the circumference of the Agena satellite. When the Agena achieves orbit, the "piggy-back" Oscar package is ejected upon command. An adapter fitting is rigidly attached to the Agena in the aft-equipment rack near the motor housing (Fig. 2). The Oscar satellite is fastened into this adapter and held in place with an explosive bolt holding an ejection spring under compression. Upon receipt of the ejection command the bolt is released by a pin-puller, permitting the spring to eject the ham satellite from the parent vehicle at a speed of about 5 feet per second (3 miles per hour). As there is no air resistance to slow it down, the Oscar satellite will continue to separate from the carrier satellite at this rate indefinitely. At the time of separation, a latch is released which al-

22

lows the antenna to spring upright into operating position. Dual snap-switches actuated by the release mechanism turn on the operating power to the 145-Mc. transmitter and Oscar is on the air!

The OSCAR Transmitter

In the interest of obtaining high primary-power efficiency, light weight and small volume, the Oscar transmitter is transistorized and is constructed upon a set of glass-epoxy printed wiring boards. This method of assembly provides the physical ruggedness and electrical stability required for the extreme environments which Oscar encounters. The r.f. and keyer assemblies are built as separate modules (Figs. 3 and 4). Modular construction makes it possible to use the functional units in later phases of the Oscar program, and also improves the flexibility of installation in the event that the container shape is changed at the last moment.

The R.F. Section

The r.f. unit, Fig. 5, consists of a 2N1493 crystal-controlled oscillator operating on the fifth overtone of the crystal to produce a 72.5-Mc. signal source. The signal is amplified by a 2N1506 buffer stage which is base-driven. The r.f. level of the buffer stage output is about 180 milliwatts. A Varicap diode doubler stage (VC_1) delivers approximately 140 milliwatts at 145 Mc. The output tank circuit is tapped at the proper point to provide a match to the 50-ohm coaxial line which feeds the antenna.

Curiously enough, one of the problems encountered during the development of the transmitter was that of too much power output! A fine balance had to be achieved between power output and primary battery life. Too much output meant that battery life would be unreasonably short. In the final unit, the over-all transmitter efficiency is better than 30 per cent at a power output level of 140 milliwatts. This balance permits good battery life, yet allows a good signal to be radiated.

The Keyer Section

A unique, recognizable identification was required for the Oscar satellite. A waiver was obtained from the FCC so that the Oscar call, W6EE, need not be transmitted. The symbols "HI" were chosen as the identifier as they are relatively easy to generate, because they have a low duty cycle, and because they are easily recognized on the air (even by phone men!). Last — but by no means least — the greeting "HI" is internationally recognized as a friendly salutation among amateurs. From the design standpoint, the important factor is that "HI" has a low duty cycle — that is, the time-off is large in comparison to the time-on, which helps minimize the average power drain of the transmitter r.f. section.

The transmitter keyer makes use of digital circuits which may not be familiar to many amateurs. Space does not permit a detailed description of the keyer in the present article, but the circuits in general are similar to those that have been used in electronic keyers. (For those readers who wish to pursue this fascinating subject further, the Navy publication, *A Handbook of Selected Semiconductor Circuits*,[1] should prove to be very interesting.)

The Antenna

A nondirectional antenna pattern is desired because the orbiting package will not be stabilized and quite likely will be tumbling as it revolves about the earth. But while it would be possible to generate a nondirectional radiation pattern, such a requirement would impose additional undesirable weight and complexity upon the Oscar package. For this reason, a simple ground-plane antenna is used. A quarter-wave monopole operates against the metal case of Oscar which (after a fashion) serves as the other half of the dipole. The resulting pattern, Fig. 6, is similar to that of a half-wave dipole in space. Here is one situation where the free-space pattern of an antenna is utilized in practice!

It would have been desirable if the deep nulls of the pattern could have been eliminated; however, they should have little detrimental effect upon signal reception. In fact, the roll rate of the package may be determined from the ampli-

[1] U.S. Government Printing Office, Washington, 25, D.C. BuShips NObsr 73231, NAVships 93484, price $2.25.

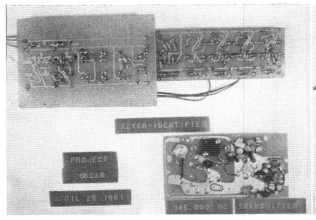

Fig. 3—Bottom view of Oscar printed-circuit boards. The electrical connections between circuit components are made by means of thin copper plated to the insulating board.

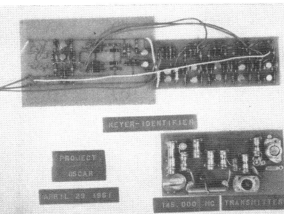

Fig. 4—The Oscar unit is built upon two printed-circuit boards. At top is the keyer and pulse-generator unit. The 145-Mc. transmitter is below. Sixteen transistors, a number of diodes and a "Varicap" semiconductor are used in these circuits.

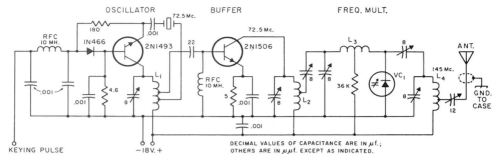

Fig. 5—The Oscar transmitter circuit. Tuning capacitors are 8-μμf. trimmers. R.f. coils are wound with No. 22 tinned wire on nylon forms, 0.2-inch diameter, threaded 20 turns per inch.

L₁—9 turns, tapped at 3 and 6½ turns.
L₂—9 turns center-tapped.
L₃—31 turns center-tapped.
L₄—7 turns, tapped at 2¾ turns.
VC₁—Variable-capacitance diode (Pacific semiconductors 115-10).

tude modulation of the signal produced by the rotation in space of the nulls. The antenna is held closely against the package during launch, but springs into a vertical position when Oscar is flung into separate orbit.

The Power Supply

During the preliminary study of the configuration, it was decided that small internal batteries would be sufficient to provide power for the beacon for three- to four-week operation at the 140-milliwatt power level. Characteristics demanded of batteries to be used in space application include the following: high power output per pound of weight, operation in any position, insensitive to temperature extremes, low electrical leakage, nonexplosive in event of failure, and capable of being used in a high-vacuum environment. Mercury cells similar to those used in the Vanguard satellite were selected to power the unit. Three 18-volt batteries were connected in parallel to meet the capacity requirement. Each battery is protected against reverse current by a series diode should one of the batteries fail in service. Two of the three batteries are sufficient to power the equipment for 30 days under normal operating conditions, giving a total transmitter life of about 45 days under ideal conditions. Debited against the total life must be the time consumed during pre-launch check-outs, leakage loss during the waiting period after assembly, and drop in efficiency of the cells at low temperatures. At the end of battery life, the voltage drops rapidly to the point where the equipment will cease operating. This serves as an automatic "turn-off" switch after the designed operating life of approximately 28 days has elapsed.

Testing the Oscar Beacon

Once the average amateur completes the construction of a piece of gear, he gives it a quick once-over to see that nothing looks amiss, then he turns on the power for the proverbial "smoke test." For a unit designed for operation in outer space, such a test is just a good beginning! For example, the operational tests must be much more thorough to insure that the unit is performing as intended, as once in the launching vehicle there is no means to realign *this*, or adjust *that!* Normal operational tests for the Oscar beacon include: D.c. power input level, r.f. power output, keying rate and proper code formation. These measurements are made during the environmental testing.

To insure that the unit will operate when it reaches orbit, the equipment is subjected to test conditions that are comparable to those expected in normal operation. These conditions include temperature extremes of 0 to +150 degrees F. (−35 degrees to +65 degrees C.), shock (50G, maximum), acceleration (15G, maximum), vibration (15G, maximum), and altitude (over 200,000 feet).

The detailed specifications required for the environmental testing of the Oscar payload were written by Nick Marshall, W6OLO. Suffice to say, these tests were passed with flying colors by the Oscar beacon. Laboratory equipment necessary to conduct these tests was utilized over week-end periods at some of the electronic laboratories located in the immediate area. Other items of test equipment were homemade, and their construction and use would be a story in itself.

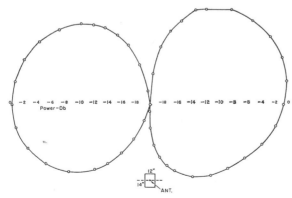

Fig. 6—Polar plot of Oscar radiation pattern with the container in vertical position, whip in horizontal plane. Plot in horizontal plane is a circle.

(Continued on page 132)

Oscar Satellite

(*Continued from page 24*)

Kudos

The work performed in the development, construction and testing of the Oscar beacon was the result of the cooperative efforts of a large number of radio amateurs and other interested persons working together on a voluntary basis. Nick Marshall, W6OLO, Project Oscar Technical Director, and Dick Esneault, W4IJC/6, Project Manager, made sure the project remained true to the original aim and supervised closely to a successful completion. Al Diem, W3LSZ/6, Project Engineer, designed the r.f. assembly and handled battery and encapsulation problems. Harry Hughes worked out the ideas and surmounted the problems of the code generator. Gail Gangwish and Doug Beck, WA6AAI, packaged the keyer assembly into launchable shape. The antenna work, including patterns, was done by C. A. Andrews, W6LHV, and Jim Daly. Wally Raven, WA6AID, and Jim Barnett were consultants on mounting and heating problems. Howard Linnenkohl, K6SSD, designed the container. Walt Read, W6ASH, got it built. Lance Ginner, K6FEJ, ran the injection tests. Jerre Crozier, W6IGE, handled the drafting and layout work. Chuck Smallhouse, WA6MGZ, Orv Dalton, K6UEY, and Herman Poole designed and built a second transmitter that served as a stand-by unit. Alf Modine, K6TWF, and Will Jensby wrote the test procedures.

There were gratis contributions of hard-to-obtain materials and services by local industries who had their spirit of adventure stirred by the project. Components, materials, laboratory and testing facilities were made available by Philco Corporation, Western Development Laboratories, Palo Alto, Calif., and by Lockheed Missiles and Space Co., El Monte, Calif. Transistors were contributed by Fairchild Transistor Co., Mountain View, Calif., Philco Corp., Radio Corporation of America, Diodes, Inc., and Pacific Semiconductors, Inc. Crystals were provided by X-tron, Inc., Oakland, Calif.; and Midland Crystals, Kansas City, Kansas; mercury batteries were supplied by Burgess Battery Co.

Countless other firms and individuals contributed suggestions and support to this unique project. To all of them, the Oscar Association extends its sincere thanks and points with pride to the results of this heartwarming amateur radio experiment: the "III" of Oscar as it circles the globe! [QST—]

"Making Use of the Oscar III Telemetry Signals" by Arthur Walters, W6DKH

By Jan King, W3GEY and Ward Silver, NØAX

Following the launch and 18-day life of *OSCAR II* in June of 1962, subsequent satellite operation generated intense interest in the amateur community. The successes of the first two satellites suggested that a more sophisticated satellite would supported by amateurs and that they were ready to try communicating *via* the satellite instead of just monitoring its beacons. Bear in mind that *Echo I*, the first passive communication satellite, and *Courier 1B*, the first active repeater in space had only been launched in 1960. In 1962, the first active relay satellite, *Telstar 1,* was launched as an experimental communications satellite to study telecommunications links through space. It seemed that there was a bit of commercial space race, as well, with amateurs in hot pursuit.

Thus the project to construct and launch *OSCAR III* was begun. Like *Telstar*, this satellite would not just reflect signals back to Earth but would receive, process, and retransmit them. This would be the first of many amateur satellites to carry a linear transponder. Signals transmitted in a 50 kHz wide band at 146 MHz would be retransmitted at 144 MHz with a power of 1 W. Because the transponder was linear, any amateur signal in the transponder's uplink band would appear in the downlink band.

Some of the *OSCAR III* project team celebrating three years of effort that ended in the successful operation of amateur radio's first spectrum translator. From left to right: Al Hurley, ex-9M2TC; Bill Orr, W6SAI; Bill Eitel, W6UF; and Lance Ginner, K6GSJ.

Other firsts achieved by the *Oscar III* team were the use of solar power to run the satellite with panels of the then-new photovoltaic cells, and the use of beacon transmitters separate from the main transponder was also new. As the article introduced here shows, telemetry from the satellite had also grown more sophisticated, using pulse-width modulation to encode two channels of temperature from the transmitter's output transistors and the satellite battery temperature, representing internal equipment temperature. The pulse bursts were sandwiched between transmissions of the now-familiar HI Morse messages.

All in all, readers are encouraged to browse through more than a dozen *QST* articles beginning in February of 1963 describing the operation of the satellite and how amateurs could receive its signals and, most importantly, transmit through it. State of the art? Amateurs were right up there with the commercial and military designers as *OSCAR III* beat the first commercial communications satellite, *Intelsat 1*, into space by less than a month! (All articles are available to ARRL members at **www.arrl.org**.)

Making Use of the Oscar III Telemetry Signals

BY ARTHUR M. WALTERS,* W6DKH

The Oscar III amateur radio space satellite incorporates three channels of vital telemetry data that will be transmitted to ground observers on 145.85 Mc. These channels will tell just how Oscar is behaving in his "out of this world" environment. This information is necessary to check the operation of the translator equipment, and also to provide data for future Oscar satellites. It is hoped that radio amateurs throughout the world will monitor the telemetry channels, in addition to using the translator. This article will illustrate how easy it is to "read" the telemetry signals and the proper way to interpret the readings. Calibration curves are included which translate the pulse information into the parameters measured.

A separate telemetry transmitter in Oscar III is driven by the telemetry equipment. It has an output power of about 25 milliwatts and is keyed on and off by several sources in a programmed manner. If all goes well, the keyed signals will tell the ground observer a number of things about conditions aboard the satellite.

The Telemetry Gear

A block diagram of the telemetry equipment is given in Fig. 1. The telemetry transmitter is actuated by a keyer which is driven from several sources, all of which are controlled by a rate multivibrator. The keying pattern is divided into two major parts, each of which lasts for four seconds. The first part of the sequence connects the telemetry transmitter to the diode matrix HI generator. The output from the matrix is a series of dots and spaces which make up the Morse Code greeting HI which is Oscar's signature. The word HI is sent twice at a rate of about 8 dots per second, taking four seconds to complete the sequence. The binary divider chain switches AND gates Nos. 1 and 2 so that the HI generator drives the keyer stage. Next, the transmitter and keyer are switched to the telemeter pulse generators. There are two of these, and they are selected one after the other; AND gates 1 and 2 control the switching, and AND gates 3 and 4 make the choice of generators. The first train of pulses from No. 1 generator represents T_1, the temperature of the transistors in the final amplifier of the translator. The pulse burst lasts two seconds.

AND gates 3 and 4 now switch the keyer to pulse generator No. 2, which represents T_2, the temperature of the main battery case within Oscar III. This reading indicates the average ambient temperature in the satellite. This 2-second pulse burst is followed by the HI signal, signifying a repetition of the telemetry cycle (Fig. 2).

The telemetry signals are a form of pulse-width modulation, and the pulse-width signals are triggered by the rate multivibrator. This multivibrator has a nominal frequency of 64 c.p.s. at 25° C. at a nominal battery voltage of −18 volts. Environmental tests have shown that changes in the multivibrator frequency for moderate temperature variations are quite minor and may be neglected unless the actual temperature of the package is greatly different than the design value.

The frequency of the rate multivibrator is arranged to vary as the potential of the −18 volt supply changes. Thus, as the main silver-zinc battery deteriorates over a period of 3 or 4 weeks, the rate of the pulses will decrease from about 69 c.p.s. at the beginning of orbit to around 37 c.p.s. after the main battery goes dead and the telemetry switches over to the solar-cell-charged auxiliary battery. The telemetry

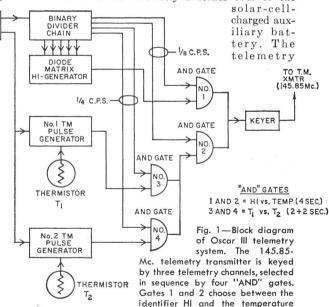

Fig. 1—Block diagram of Oscar III telemetry system. The 145.85-Mc. telemetry transmitter is keyed by three telemetry channels, selected in sequence by four "AND" gates. Gates 1 and 2 choose between the identifier HI and the temperature channels. Gates 3 and 4 choose between the two temperature channels. Calibration curves for the three channels are given in Figs. 3 and 4.

---

* Project Oscar, Inc., Foothill College, Los Altos Hills, Calif.

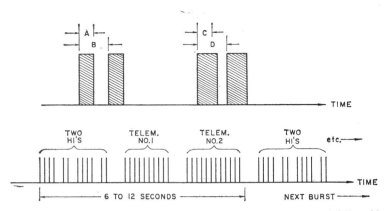

Fig. 2—A representation of the telemetry channels. Two HI's in Morse code are transmitted, followed by two bursts of telemetry. Each burst consists of a series of pulses, and each represents a temperature measurement made at a specific point in the satellite. The pulse rate of the complete sequence is related to the battery voltage and the duty cycle of the pulses in the two telemetry bursts conveys temperature information. The ratio of pulse width (A) to repetition rate (B) may be measured on the screen of an oscilloscope. One complete sequence (Channel 1, for example) should be expanded to fill ten divisions on the screen of the scope, and the duty cycle (A/B) may be read directly in percentage.

calibration curve for primary battery voltage versus pulse rate is shown in Fig. 3.

The telemetry pulse generators are Schmitt trigger circuits with a thermistor as one of the bias-control resistors. (A thermistor is a temperature-sensitive element whose resistance varies in accord with external temperature.) The circuits have been adjusted so that the pulse width is about 50 per cent (a square wave, as shown in Fig. 2) at normal operating temperature. The pulse width varies from about 20 percent at 0° C. to approximately 80 per cent at 60° C. Fig. 4 is a graph showing the relationship of battery voltage to pulse width, or duty factor.

Telemetry Measurements—Battery Voltage

Figs. 3 and 4 provide the necessary conversion data that will permit the ground observer to make the necessary measurements from the data telemetered from Oscar III. The only ground apparatus required is a sensitive v.h.f. receiver, an inexpensive oscilloscope, and a calibrated audio oscillator. Fig. 5 shows the equipment used to determine the pulse rate, which is the measure of primary battery voltage. The oscilloscope is connected to the output of the *detector* stage of the receiver and the receiver audio section is used only for monitoring purposes. During the telemetry bursts a "buzz" will be heard. The telemetry signal is tuned in and the audio oscillator adjusted to display a stationary pattern on the scope. There are many frequencies that will do this, but the proper one will be the same as the pulse rate, and will be between 35 and 75 cycles. During the early life of the satellite, the pulse rate is expected to be about 60 cycles, so this is a good starting point for initial oscillator setting. When the Lissajous pattern is stable, the audio frequency may be read from the dial of the oscillator. This is equal to the pulse rate (or pulse repetition frequency) of the keyer and represents battery voltage, as shown in Fig. 3.

Telemetry Measurements—Temperature

Fig. 6 shows the equipment adjusted to determine the pulse width and the two temperature measurements telemetered from Oscar III. An audio oscillator is not required. To accomplish the pulse-width reading, the oscilloscope sweep should be synchronized on the incoming signal (taken from the detector stage of the receiver). It is necessary to know whether the detector output of your receiver goes positive or negative with incoming signal, to prevent confusion of the "mark" and "space" portions of the telemetry signals.

In the presence of noise, there will be "jitter" in the synchronizing, so that an "educated average" will have to be taken. Sweep speed and horizontal-amplifier gain are adjusted so that one pulse cycle (one telemetry measurement) expands

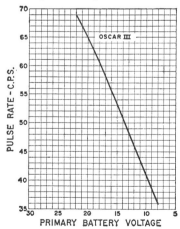

Fig. 3—Calibration curve for primary battery voltage as represented by pulse rate (cycles per second). The graph is linear, and may be reproduced by drawing a straight line through two reference points: At 22 volts, the pulse rate is 68.7 c.p.s., and at 8 volts the pulse rate is 36.0 c.p.s.

March 1965

to fill ten horizontal divisions on the screen. It is now possible to read directly the percentage of pulse "on" time to the time of full cycle (Fig. 2). A direct reading is possible if the pattern is adjusted to fill exactly ten horizontal divisions. Record pulse width of the first pulse train (T_1), followed by the pulse-width reading of the second train (T_2). The pulse width readings may be converted to temperature by means of Fig. 4.

The HI signal serves only the purpose of identification and as a timing signal to enable the ground observer to distinguish T_1 from T_2, and

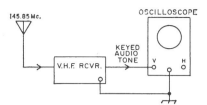

Fig. 6—Determining pulse width of Oscar III. The two temperature measurements shown in Figs. 2 and 4 may be made with this equipment setup. Oscilloscope sweep is synchronized internally.

does not enter into the readings as such. If desired, the pattern may be traced on the oscilloscope with a grease pencil for later measurement.

Be sure to make accurate records of your measurements. Log the date, time (GMT), and orbit number. The Oscar Association would appreciate receiving your data, which should be mailed to: Project Oscar Headquarters, Foothill College, Los Altos, California, U.S.A. Your participation and support in this activity will make future Oscars possible!

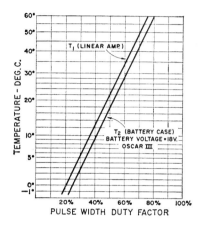

Fig. 4—Calibration curve for pulse width, representing temperature (degrees Centigrade) at two points in Oscar III. Curve T_1 is for the temperature of the linear amplifier, and Curve T_2 is for the temperature of the battery case. If, for example, the pulse width (ratio A/B, Fig. 2) is 60%, T_1 is 34° C. and T_2 is 28.5° C. This graph is plotted on Keuffel & Esser 359-51, Semi-Logarithmic, 1 cycle × 10 to the inch paper. The graph is linear, and may be reproduced by drawing straight lines through two reference points on each curve. These are: Curve T_1, 20% pulse width is at −0.5° C. and 70% pulse width is at 49.5° C.; Curve T_2, 20% pulse width is at −2.2° C. and 70% pulse width is at 42° C. It is recommended that these curves be redrawn on large graph paper for greater accuracy and that Figs. 3 and 4 be used merely for reference.

Strays

Those interested in Oscar satellite predictions are invited to write Thomas W. Petrie, 2459 Overlook Rd., #5, Cleveland Heights, Ohio 44106, for full details. Tom has access to a large, high-speed digital computer (UNIVAC 1107) and a computer program for calculating satellite predictions.

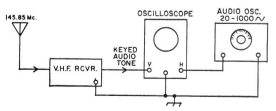

Fig. 5—Determining pulse rate of Oscar III. A stable v.h.f. receiver, plus an inexpensive oscilloscope and an audio oscillator are all the tools needed. The dial calibration of the audio oscillator should be checked against a standard (the power line, for example) for accuracy. A Lissajous pattern is created on the screen of the scope, and the audio frequency of the oscillator is adjusted to make the pattern stand still. The pulse rate of Oscar III is then equal to the audio frequency. Use Fig. 3 for conversion of pulse rate to primary battery voltage.

OSCAR III USERS: REMEMBER 3rd-PARTY RULES

V.h.f. men using Oscar III facilities for international communications may be faced with questions on international third-party communications for the first time since they left the "d.c. bands." A reminder then: messages and other communications — and then only if not important enough to justify use of the regular international communications facilities — may be handled by U.S. amateurs on behalf of third parties only with amateurs in the following countries: Bolivia, Canada, Chile, Colombia, Costa Rica, Cuba, Dominican Republic, Ecuador, El Salvador, Haiti, Honduras, Liberia, Mexico, Nicaragua, Panama, Paraguay, Peru, and Venezuela. Canadian amateurs may handle these relatively unimportant third-party messages with amateurs in Bolivia, Chile, Costa Rica, El Salvador, Honduras, Mexico, Peru, U.S. and Venezuela.

"OSCAR at 25: The Amateur Space Program Comes of Age" and "OSCAR at 25: Beginning of a New Era" by Jan King, W3GEY, Vern Riportella, WA2LQQ and Ralph Wallio, WØRPK

By Jan King, W3GEY and Ward Silver, NØAX

The *OSCAR III* satellite ushered in an active and successful period of satellite activity in which numerous advances, large and small, were achieved. Amateurs set their sights on lofty goals in orbit, hatching a stream of new "birds" year after year. By the late 1960s, as satellites of all sorts were launched, amateurs found they needed to replace the informal approach of fundraising and gaining access to launch vehicles. In response, AMSAT, the Radio Amateur Satellite Corporation (**www.amsat.org**), was created to manage projects, funds, and interaction with government and military agencies. Amateurs around the world had been contributing to the growing satellite program for some time. Soon AMSAT-UK and AMSAT-DL were formed along with satellite clubs and organizations in numerous other countries, such as JAMSAT in Japan and BRAMSAT in Brazil.

As satellite operations expanded, AMSAT groups took the lead in organizing and publishing information about the various programs. Nets and mailings lists and bulletins sprang up to disseminate information and get the word out to hams interested in space communications. Terms such as "earth station" and "spin fading" and the lingo of orbital mechanics became common in the amateur literature, eventually making their way onto the US amateur licensing exams. The ARRL added a Satellite DXCC award, encouraging pioneers who waited for orbits just right for brief contacts between stations at the very limits of satellite visibility. Hams learned about the Doppler shift, too!

The first generation (Phase I) of amateur satellites consisted of platforms that contained beacons, limited telemetry, and simple transponders and translators. Satellites of this type included *OSCAR 1* through *OSCAR 5* and a series of Russian *ISKRA* satellites that were deployed manually from the Salyut space station, similar to

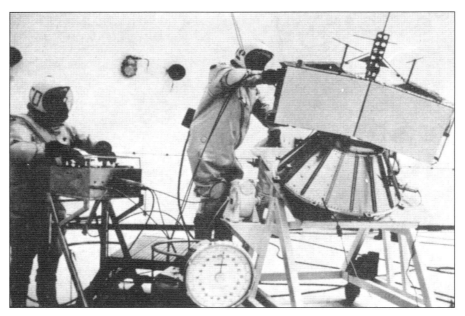

Prepping a satellite for launch is more than just topping off batteries and checking the antenna deployment mechanism. Shown here in protective suits, Dick Daniels, W4PUJ (right) helps Wolfgang Mueller from the rocket engine manufacturer MBB load the explosive, toxic propellant into the fuel tanks of *OSCAR 10* prior to launch in 1983.

the recent "SuitSat" launches. These didn't cost a lot of money to build or launch and their lifetime was fairly limited.

Phase II satellites added more features and longer lifetimes, launched into nearly circular low earth orbit (LEO) where signal strength was strong for the ground stations. This allowed amateurs with relatively simple equipment to make contacts with and through the satellites. (The recently reanimated *OSCAR 7* is a Phase II satellite.) Phase II satellites have been built by groups from many countries. Along with the US, UK, and Germany, satellites from Japan, Russia, India, Saudi Arabia, just to name a few are orbiting the planet right now. (More than 20 countries have launched an amateur satellite.)

The pinnacle of amateur satellite deployment was reached with the Phase III platforms such as *OSCAR 10, Phase 3D (OSCAR 40),* and *Echo (OSCAR 51)*. These were the most complex amateur satellites ever built, supporting extensive telemetry and multiple transponders or repeaters. The satellites could be reconfigured in different modes (uplink/downlink combinations) from ground control stations. The Phase III satellites were also launched into elliptical orbits so that they remained visible and useable over nearly half the planet's surface for hours at a time, quite different from the LEO satellites.

As of this writing (late 2013), active and operational amateur satellites are of the Phase II or CubeSat design (described in the following article), traveling in low Earth orbits and supporting one or two transponder or communication options. The International Space Station (ISS) is home to several amateur stations, including digipeaters and a station for direct contact between the astronauts and individual ground stations.

Calling Phase IV

With its emphasis on geosynchronous platforms and the associated need for resources, Phase IV has so far eluded the amateur satellite community although there have been some rumors of piggybacking on a commercial geosynchronous platform. Will we get to Phase IV in response to predictions of declining sunspots over the next few decades? In the first article of this pair written for the December 1986 issue of *QST*, King asks the prescient question of what must the satellites do if they are to grow beyond occasional use in Amateur Radio.

In the second article of the series, King goes on to discuss how Phase IV satellites would change the nature of satellite communications for the amateur. This was a watershed moment in amateur satellite history. At the time, packet radio had blossomed, hand-held FM transceiver capability was expanding as cost was declining, and the Internet was still years away from general use. Yet the "heavy lifting" required by Phase IV, along with the shorter-than-expected lifetimes of some of the more complex Phase III "birds" stalled the development of large and complex amateur satellites.

In the meantime, the most rapid growth in amateur satellites has been the CubeSat — a satellite built according to a standardized form factor and focused on a single function or experiment with some telemetry and a beacon transmitter. (See the next article in this section or visit the CubeSat website at **www.cubesat.org**.) This is bringing university-level students to Amateur Radio as they develop space-to-ground communication links to their satellites, which are often launched in large groups. This new avenue will provide opportunities for innovation in the Amateur Satellite Service perhaps based on new forms of modulation or networking between these minimal satellites to provide connections to hams down on Earth.

We still have the opportunity to pursue Phase IV goals. There are satellite service allocations at HF and EHF that have never been utilized. Improvements in radio technology continue to reduce the cost of space communication to the average ham. New digital modes and protocols optimized for the paths to, from, and even between satellites can raise the quality of communications significantly. The future is sitting on the launch pad.

OSCAR at 25: The Amateur Space Program Comes of Age

Twenty-five years ago this month, OSCAR I successfully achieved orbit around earth—and amateurs took their first steps into an exciting, new frontier, space communications.

By Jan King, W3GEY, AMSAT VP, Engineering
Vern Riportella, WA2LQQ, AMSAT President
Ralph Wallio, WØRPK, AMSAT VP, Operations
AMSAT, PO Box 27, Washington, DC 20044

In many fields, there are watershed events that mark transitions from one era to another. In aviation, Lindbergh's 1927 solo flight from New York to Paris was such an event. Suddenly, the continents were days closer. Similarly, the 1957 launch of Sputnik partitions history to the pre-Space Age and the Space Age.

In Amateur Radio, the watershed date is December 12, 1961. On that day, OSCAR I was launched. (OSCAR is an acronym for Orbiting Satellite Carrying Amateur Radio.) We predict that in the last decade of this millennium, the significance of that date will come more clearly into focus. It was then, historians of Amateur Radio will note, that the hobby took a sharp turn toward its future: space communications. It was then that ham radio got on track for its major theme in the 21st Century: proliferated networks of hams communicating via multiple media with satellites carrying the bulk of the mostly digital traffic (digitized voice, data and video as a minimum over the amateur equivalent of the Integrated Services Digital Network, ISDN).

On the eve of a quarter century of OSCARs, then, we thought it an appropriate juncture to step back and take the long view. How did we get here? Where are we? Where are we going? And how fast are we getting there?

One way to see where we are going is to chart trends. Mark a few points along a path and soon enough a trend can be discerned. For example, we can classify OSCAR mission complexity and operating environment into three, soon to be four, phases:

Phase 1—Short-lived beacon and/or transponder-equipped spacecraft, from OSCAR I through OSCAR 5, and the recent Russian ISKRA series, which were manually deployed from the Salyut space station.

Phase 2—Longer-lived, multitransponder or scientific spacecraft in low earth orbits, including OSCARs 6, 7 and 8, UoSAT-OSCARs 9 and 11, Fuji-OSCAR 12 and RS-1 through RS-8. (Many new satellites will be added in this class in the future since the low altitude often means strong signals.)

Phase 3—Longer-lived, multitransponder spacecraft in elliptical orbits, including OSCAR 10, Phase 3C (to be launched in 1987) and perhaps Phase 3D in 1990. Benefits of long duration of visibility are offset by complex tracking task.

Phase 4—Very-long-lived multitransponder, multimission geosynchronous spacecraft serving large regions of the earth. Currently undergoing serious study aimed at commencing general use in less than five years.

However, these coarse classifications don't speak to advancements in many engineering and operational areas that have gradually built on the past to produce the capabilities we enjoy today and will enjoy tomorrow. Improvements in power systems, function control, attitude control, telemetry systems and transponder operating frequencies and bandwidth all point toward an astonishing capacity in tomorrow's Phase 4 program. (Refer to Table 1.)

OSCARs I-IV were built by Project OSCAR of California. Australis-OSCAR 5 was built by students in Australia and was launched by NASA on a "ride" arranged

December 1986   15

Table 1
Capabilities Growth Comparison of OSCAR

OSCAR	Power	Function Control	Attitude Control	Telemetry	Beacon Transponder
I	Mercury battery	None	None	1-channel CW rate	2-m beacon
II	Mercury battery	None	None	1-channel CW rate	2-m beacon
III	Silver-zinc battery (transponder) solar cells 2.5 W & battery (beacon)	None	None	3-channel CW rate and pulse width	2-m/2-m transponder (50 kHz) 2-m beacon
IV	Solar cells 10 W & battery	None	Spin	None	2-m/70-cm transponder (10 kHz) 70-cm beacon
5	Manganese alkaline battery	1 ground command: beacon on-off	Spin & passive magnets	7-channels pulse width modulation	10-m, 2-m beacons
6	Solar cells 5.5-W NiCd battery	21 ground commands	Spin & passive magnets	24-channel CW	2-m/10-m transponder (100 kHz) 10-m beacon
7	Solar cells 15-W NiCd battery	70 ground commands	Spin & passive magnets	24-channel CW, 60-channel Baudot	2-m/10-m transponder 70-cm/2-m transponder (150 kHz) 10-m, 2-m, 70-cm, 13-cm beacons
8	Solar cells 15-W NiCd battery	5 ground commands	Spin & passive magnets	6-channel CW	2-m/10-m transponder 2-m/70-cm transponder (200 kHz) 10-m, 2-m beacons
9	Solar cells 17-W NiCd battery	Onboard computer & ground command	Gravity-gradient boom	105 channels ASCII Baudot synth-voice digital video CW	2-m, 70-cm, 13-cm, 10-GHz, 7, 14, 21, 28-MHz beacons
10	Solar cells 50-W dual NiCd batteries	Onboard computer & ground command	Spin & active magnets	64-channel ASCII Baudot	70-cm/2-m transponder 24 cm-70 cm (950 kHz) 2-m, 70-cm beacons
11	Solar cells 25-W NiCd battery	Onboard computer & ground command	Gravity-gradient boom & active magnets	156-channel ASCII Baudot synth-voice digital video CW	2-m, 70-cm, 13-cm beacons
12	Solar cells 8.5-W NiCd battery	Onboard computer & ground command	Spin & passive magnets	52-channel 66-channel CW PSK	2-m/70-cm transponders analog and digital (100 kHz) 70-m beacon
P3C	Solar cells 50-W dual NiCd batteries [Watts TBS]	Onboard computer & ground command	Spin & active magnets	64-channel ASCII Baudot	70-cm/2-m transponder 24-cm/70-cm transponder 2-m/70-cm transponder 70-cm/13-cm transponder digital transponder (500 kHz) 2-m, 70-cm, 13-cm beacons

by AMSAT. AMSAT built AMSAT-OSCARs 6, 7, 8 and 10 with its affiliated organizations and help from the ARRL (on OSCAR 8). UoSAT-OSCARs 9 and 11 are the products of the University of Surrey, England. Fuji-OSCAR 12 was a joint project of the Japan Amateur Radio Satellite Corporation (JAMSAT), the Japan Amateur Radio League (JARL), the Nippon Electric Company (NEC) and Japan's National Space Agency (NASDA). More on the history of the Amateur Satellite Program can be found in *The Satellite Experimenter's Handbook* (available from ARRL). Additional reading on FO-12 appears in the Oct and Nov 1986 installments of the Amateur Satellite Communications column and in the June, Aug and Oct 1986 issues of *QEX* (available from ARRL).

Power Systems

The application of solar-cell-driven battery recharging has been the single greatest improvement in OSCAR power-system design. Early projects predated usable solar-cell technology in terms of output, cost and reliability. While OSCAR III's solar cells and associated secondary battery powered the totally separate 2-m beacon for several months, the primary battery powering the transponder was depleted in 16 days. The first application of solar-cell technology that resulted in an extended working life was aboard OSCAR 6, whose Mode A transponder provided service to the Amateur Radio community for 4½ years, beginning October 1972.

The ultimate demise of every OSCAR project until AO-10 has been battery failure. Consequently, the baseline Phase 3 design includes an auxiliary battery, battery-charge regulator and a reliable means of switching between the two. This redundancy has not as yet been required aboard OSCAR 10, but continues as a vital insurance measure in Phase 3C, which is scheduled to fly in 1987.

Functional Control

The first application of ground-command capabilities for tuning the beacon transmitters on and off, flew aboard OSCAR 5. From this beginning, necessary to demonstrate remote-control capabilities to the FCC, hardwired functional control systems grew to accept as many as 70 different ground commands aboard OSCAR 7.

However, the big breakthrough was the successful application of software-driven onboard controllers, which have come to be known as Internal Housekeeping Units (IHU), beginning with OSCAR 9 and as flown on all OSCAR missions since. The IHU concept allows for at least two long-term benefits:

1) The ability to make decisions aboard the spacecraft, independent of ground control; and

2) The ability to upload new software representing better ideas designed after the bird is in orbit.

Attitude Control

The attitude of the spacecraft relative to the earth is important to ensure the best use of onboard antenna patterns and for thermal dynamics. Although spin stabilization was to be a feature of the ill-fated OSCAR IV mission, the OSCAR 5 project was the first to use both spin stabilization and passive magnets successfully. These attitude-control methods were entirely adequate for all transponder-equipped missions until the Phase 3 design. The scientific-studies payloads aboard OSCARs 9 and 11 require a completely different

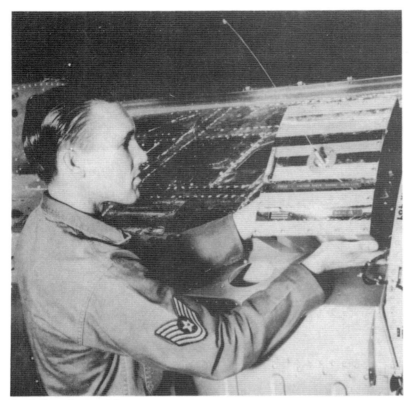

An Air Force Technical Sergeant admires the handiwork that went into designing and building the world's first nongovernmental communications satellite, OSCAR I. While circling earth, the 10-pound satellite transmitted the word "HI" in Morse code.

OSCAR I was the brainchild of Project OSCAR, a group of California hams. The members shown here are (l-r) Gail Gangwisch, Nick Marshall, W6OLO, Don Stoner, W6TNS, Chuck Towns, K6LFH, and Fred Hicks, W6EJU. Project OSCAR also was involved in later amateur satellites.

stabilization technique. A gravity-gradient boom is used for UoSATs.

The tri-star Phase 3 design requires active attitude control to respond to changing sun angles. This control is provided in the form of IHU-controlled electromagnets that are pulsed by navigational software as necessary to maneuver spacecraft attitude. Attitude is determined by sun and earth sensors and is processed by the IHU.

Telemetry

The encoding and transmitting of vital spacecraft operating parameters and conditions has evolved from methods undecipherable by anyone but the primary engineering team (as with OSCARs I, II and III) to transmission of telemetry units in CW, Baudot and ASCII codes with conversion tables available to anyone. In the future, we can look forward to transmission of actual engineering values in plain language, which will be especially useful for elementary and secondary educational purposes.

The quantities of parameters has evolved from just one, the internal temperature of OSCARs I and II, to as many as 156, as transmitted by OSCAR 11.

Beacons and Transponders

Amateur bands used for OSCAR missions have moved steadily higher in frequency as allowed by advances in technology and as the lower frequencies became more crowded with terrestrial operations. Through the years, both transponder efficiency and available bandwidth increased dramatically. OSCAR 10's 950 kHz of transponder bandwidth is more than equal to all preceding OSCAR missions combined.

Transition to the Next-Generation Satellites

Development and mastery of all of these areas has been necessary to bring us to the brink of the Phase 4 era. Without the successes achieved in power systems, functional control, attitude control, telemetry systems and transponders, we would not now be in the position to bring the advantages of satellite-borne transponder communications from the domain of the experimenter to the routine use by amateurs in many other facets of ham radio.

As is apparent, growth in OSCAR complexity and capability has been impressive since the humble beginnings in 1961. Despite the often-dramatic performance improvements between satellites within a generation, and even more so between satellite generations, working OSCAR has remained more or less an esoteric art; only about 3% of active US amateurs consider themselves "OSCAR-active."

A surprisingly high number of active US hams have tried OSCAR at least a couple of times. For one reason or another, they found it did not retain their interest; at least not in terms of the effort required to effect

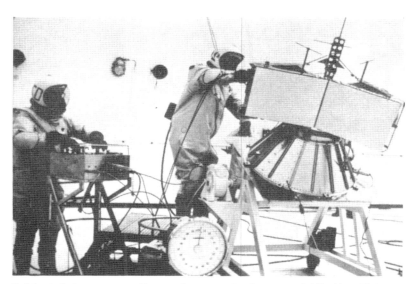

Building today's amateur satellites requires an outstanding range of skills. Here, Dick Daniels, W4PUJ (right), and Wolfgang Mueller (from the German rocket manufacturer, MBB) wear special suits while loading potentially explosive, highly toxic propellant into AMSAT-OSCAR 10 prior to its launch in 1983.

a QSO. And *that* seems to be a major theme with persons we've interviewed regarding their experiences with OSCARs. We've found that about 15% of all current hams have had at least one OSCAR QSO in their ham career. Why this group should outnumber the "regulars" by about 5 to 1 has been the source of protracted soul searching among our future-system architects. "Why," they justifiably ask, "is something so inherently interesting (space communication) such a disappointment in terms of obtaining and maintaining the interest of a large proportion of the amateur population?"

The question is significant in light of plans for our next generation of satellites, Phase 4. For, although the trend lines of past evolutionary growth in satellite capacity and functionality point to several potential growth areas, the consensus among AMSAT long-range planners is that it may be time for *revolutionary* growth instead of evolutionary growth in satellite-system architecture. It may be time for a change in the way we look at satellite systems and how they interact with the general Amateur Radio community.

Moreover, there is a special sense of urgency associated with this introspection. While technology advances have made more OSCAR capacity available to amateurs, it has also sharpened the appetite of commercial interests for the very heart of our hobby: our precious spectrum. The same technology that is making it possible to enhance present and future OSCARs ironically is placing our hold on the VHF/UHF spectrum at risk. Spectrum that was thought useless for commercial purposes years ago is now deeply coveted and eagerly sought by entrepreneurial interests.

The popularity of all prior OSCARs has been throttled by two main factors: access and functionality.

"Access" really means "ease of access" or, alternatively, "convenience." In order to be convenient, an OSCAR needs to appear regularly (at a given time of day), and it needs to be enduring (stick around for long enough for a few QSOs, at least). While AMSAT-OSCAR 10, in its high, elliptical orbit, has improved access in meaningful ways, the major drawback has been that it is not sun-synchronous. That is, its appearance tracked neither with the sun nor human activities (such as work/play schedules), which *are* synchronized with the sun. Nevertheless, AO-10 did provide endurance. It could be in view often for eight- or nine-hour periods, during which thousands of QSOs could transpire.

"Functionality" means, essentially, "What can I do with it?" The conventional wisdom holds that satellites will be truly popular when they can do more than 20 meters can do most of the time. If satellites could do what 20 meters does for less money, that would probably accelerate the popularization process. Well, AO-10 has done some of the things 20 meters does and some of the things it does not. Like 20 meters, AO-10 has provided international coverage. Unlike 20 meters, it has not been choked with QRM. Neither has AO-10 been tied to the sun in terms of when it's on and when it's off. Neither has AO-10 been notably affected by geomagnetic storms or sunspot cycles. But, whereas when 20 meters is very good, signals can be 40 dB over the noise, signals on AO-10 have rarely exceeded 12 dB above the noise. And, spin modulation (QSB) is an effect associated with satellites, not 20 meters.

The point is this: Given the traditional equipment and experience base of the active amateur community, there has been insufficient motivation to become satellite regulars. "What can I do with satellites that I can't do on HF?"

Given this reasonable question, then, let's look at revolutionary ways to provide communications which *can't* be accomplished using available HF techniques. For example, let's provide a way for linking the minimum Amateur Radio station, say a 2-meter hand-held radio, with another hand-held 10,000 miles away through a gateway or teleport in the vicinity of the hand-helds. Let's look at ways of trunking terrestrial packet networks into a global network. Let's consider how we might address emergency voice bulletins to a large portion of the Amateur community through thousands of repeaters across the country using an alert broadcast code and selective addressing from the next-generation OSCARs. Let's see what we can achieve with the latest in digital TV and compression techniques in a new amateur context. Most important, however, let's look at ways of making the next generation of OSCARs truly justify not only themselves in terms of intrinsic merit, but rather in terms of service they can provide to the public. *That* spells revolution, not evolution!

Next month, we'll take a look at the transponders and communications possibilities of the next-generation satellite, Phase 4.

OSCAR at 25: Beginning of a New Era

Easy-to-use space communications may at last be on the way. After 25 years as a technical novelty, AMSAT introduces a new generation of satellites. Public service and accessibility are the watchwords.

By Jan King, W3GEY,
  AMSAT VP, Engineering
  Vern Riportella, WA2LQQ, AMSAT President
  Ralph Wallio, W0RPK, AMSAT VP, Operations
  AMSAT, PO Box 27, Washington, DC 20044

Last month, we looked at the beginnings and the development of the Amateur Satellite Program from OSCAR 1 through Phase 3. This month, we'll look at the next-generation satellite, Phase 4, and its various transponders and communications possibilities.

In September 1986, Jan King completed a Phase 4 Engineering Study Plan. In it was depicted a preliminary architecture for a two-satellite geosynchronous system that AMSAT believes could be in operation by 1991-1992. The Plan suggested a one year course of study for Phase 4, during which specialists in various technical fields will look at each facet of the design. The design team will then advance the initial concept to a workable preliminary design. If, after the year, the team feels they have a design that meets the objectives, the AMSAT Board of Directors will be asked to authorize initial construction activities.

Working in parallel with the Phase 4 Engineering Study Team, comprising about two dozen experts, will be two other teams: the Ways and Means Team and the Operations and Applications Team. The Ways and Means Team will be looking into ways of developing resources to enable construction of Phase 4. Besides traditional scouting for donations, gifts and grants, these folks will be looking for donations of key resources (like rare skills), donations in kind (of specific hardware needed), and so forth. They will ferret out the $1-million-plus resources necessary to make this program turn real.

The Operations and Applications Team will be looking at two aspects:

1) How to optimize the strawman satellite architecture to the projected needs and capabilities of terrestrial users of the 1990-2000 time frame.

2) How to prepare the user community for the advent of truly easy-to-use satellite communications.

What will Phase 4 be like? How will it be to use? According to the preliminary (strawman) concept, initially there will be two satellites placed in geosynchronous orbits. The coverage areas (footprints) of each are shown in Figs 1 and 2. AMSTAR East would be positioned over the equator at 46.6° west. (AMSTAR is a preliminary designation for AMSAT's Phase 4 satellites.) From there, it would cover everything east to Helsinki and Durban and west to Seattle. AMSTAR West would cover everything from Boston west to Tokyo and central Australia. Although technically difficult, it might be possible to link the two birds (crosslink) in such a way as to enable a two-satellite QSO from, say, Athens to Melbourne.

What's especially attractive about the geosynchronous orbit is that the old bugaboo about tracking is gone completely! You just set your antenna at a given spot in the sky and, essentially, weld it in place. You never have to move it: no computers, no locators, no nothing; just AMSTAR in the sky 24 hours a day, 365 days a year providing the kind of facility

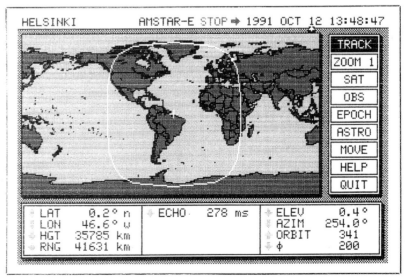

Fig 1—Footprint of AMSTAR East (see text).

January 1987 41

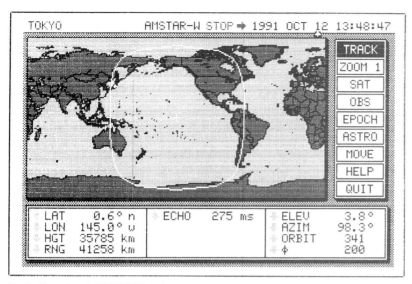

Fig 2—Footprint of AMSTAR West (see text).

a project sponsored by ARRL. Mode J has recently been reborn with its employment on the new Fuji-OSCAR 12 from Japan. As may be seen in Table 2, Mode J involves a 2-meter uplink and a 70-cm downlink. Mode J is especially popular in Japan because intense 2-meter QRM makes reception of the relatively weak 2-meter downlink of, for example, Mode B (70 cm up, 2 m down) very difficult. On the other hand, the 70-cm downlink is not subject to comparable QRM levels in Japan.

Mode L is a relatively new mode, having flown on AMSAT-OSCAR 10 in 1983 for the first time. With 24-cm uplink and 70-cm downlink and fully 800 kHz of bandwidth, it was designed as a safety valve to absorb anticipated user growth on AO-10's Mode B. That growth eventually did reach a stage where it would have likely spurred Mode L use, except that the Mode L transponder developed sensitivity problems. It was infrequently used for communications and occasionally for experimental purposes.

The combined Mode JL will have its first space test next autumn when the latest Phase 3 satellite, Phase 3C, is launched. With Mode JL, 2-meter and 24-cm uplinks each result in 70-cm downlinks. Given the user equipment shown for Mode J in Table 3, the SSB user can expect an average downlink signal-to-noise ratio (S/N) of 10.5 dB (see Table 4). Mode L users do a little better on average with about 11.3 dB

emergency communicators and ordinary would-be satellite users have been seeking for years.

What kind of communications services might be enabled by Phase 4? Let's look at the various transponders and examine briefly their capabilities (see Fig 3).

Mode JL

Mode JL is a combination of two modes (J and L) that have been used previously for OSCARs. Mode J (named for JAMSAT, our Japanese colleagues) first flew aboard AMSAT-OSCAR 8 in 1978 in

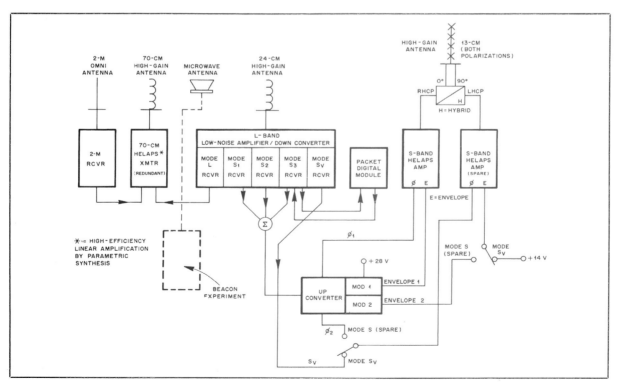

Fig 3—Block diagram of Phase 4's transponders and their capabilities (see text).

Table 2
General AMSTAR System Description, Space Segment

JL Transponder

- High-power linear transponder
- 120-W PEP output
- Mode JL: 2 meters and 24 cm up; 70 cm down
- 500-kHz-bandwidth downlink (approx 175 kHz at 2 m; 325 kHz at 24 cm)
- Global beam coverage, all bands
- Spacecraft antenna gain:
  2 m: 2.1 dBi
  70 cm: 12.5 dBi
  24 cm: 16.0 dBi

S Transponder

- Medium-power linear transponder
- 50-W PEP output
- Mode S: 24 cm (1260 MHz) up; 13 cm (2401 MHz) down

Subtransponders:
S_1: 100-kHz passband for "normal" mode (FDMA) global communications
S_2: 100-kHz passband for 20 voice repeater gateway interconnects (TDMA)
S_3: Packet gateway interconnect; nominally 19.3 kbits/s
S_4: The S_2 transponder used in broadcast mode
S_v: Integrated Services Digital Network (ISDN) transponder; 500 kbits/s

- Global beam coverage, uplink and downlink bands
- Spacecraft antenna gain:
  24 cm: 16 dBi
  13 cm: 16 dBi

Microwave Experiment

- Possible 10-GHz stable source for link tests and equipment alignment

Table 3
Preliminary User Equipment Requirements

Mode J

Receive antenna: 15.0 dBi (on-axis)
Preamp noise figure: 1.0 dB
Feed line + misc loss: 1.3 dB
System G/T: −9.8 dB/K
Transmitter power output: 10 W (avg)
Transmit antenna gain: 13.0 dBi (on-axis)
Feed line + misc loss: 1.3 dB
Transmit EIRP: 20.2 dBW (avg) (105 W)

Mode L

Receive antenna: 15.0 dBi (on-axis)
Preamp noise figure: 1.0 dB
Feed line + misc loss: 1.3 dB
System G/T: −9.8 dB/K
Transmitter power output: 10 watts (avg)
Transmit antenna gain: 19.5 dBi (on-axis)
Feedline + misc loss: 0.3 dB
Transmit EIRP: 29.2 dBW (avg) (832 W)

Mode S_1 (General Linear Communications Transponder)

Single dish antenna for TX/RX: 1.5 m (5 feet); dual feed with 50% efficiency.
Receive antenna gain: 28.5 dBi
LNA noise figure: 1.0 dB
Pointing loss: 1.0 dB
Feed line + misc loss: 1.1 dB
System G/T: +4.7 dB/K
Transmit antenna gain: 23.0 dBi
Transmitter power output: 10 W (avg)
Transmit misc losses: 1.3 dB
Transmit EIRP: 30.0 dBW (1000 W)

Mode S_2 (Voice Gateway Interconnect)

Same as S_1 station equipment except:
  Feed line + misc receive loss: 0.6 dB
  Receive noise figure: 0.7 dB
  System G/T: +6.1 dB/K

Mode S_3 (Packet Gateway Interconnect: 19.2 kbits/s)
Same as S_2 station equipment

Mode S_4 (Receive Only Gateway Interconnect-Broadcast Mode)
Same as S_2 station equipment

(Mode S_v and microwave beacon user equipment continue under study at this writing)

Table 4
Link Performance

Mode	Avg Downlink S/N	Peak Downlink S/N	E_b/N_0
J	10.5 dB	21.5 dB	12.0 dB
L	11.3 dB	22.3 dB	12.8 dB
S_1	13.4 dB	24.4 dB	14.9 dB
S_2	15.0 dB	33.0 dB[1]	16.5 dB
S_3	—	—	13.2 dB
S_4	21.4 dB	39.4 dB[1]	12.3 dB[2]
S_v	—	—	12.0 dB[3]

[1] ACSSB use assumed; subjective improvement over unprocessed SSB equal to +8dB.
[2] Result obtained if the S_4 Mode were to be used as a dedicated packet link at 32 kbits/s.
[3] At a data rate 500 kbits/s.
[4] The ratio of energy per bit to the reference noise.

S/N ratio on SSB. Peak S/N (the best measure of signal quality in the short term) would be a very respectable 21.5 dB and 22.3 dB for the J and L links, respectively.

Mode S Transponder

Mode S will also fly on Phase 3C next autumn, but it will be a 70-cm to 13-cm version of Mode S and have only limited bandwidth (25 kHz and power of 1.3 W). On Phase 4, however, Mode S will comprise a special 24-cm-up and 13-cm-down transponder, and will provide some truly stunning performance for both voice and digital users of the transponder. The Phase 4 Mode S transponder is envisioned to comprise four subtransponders, each with its own AGC loops and function. Let's look at the function and performance of each of these subtransponders in more detail (refer to Fig 3).

S_1: General Linear Communications Transponder

The S_1 subtransponder will be used for the traditional type of OSCAR communications most users are currently accustomed to. Essentially, there will be 100 kHz of linear transponder passband for the normal Frequency Division Multiple Access (FDMA) use OSCAR users have been employing since AO-6 days. With 100 kHz, there's ample room for about 25 to 35 QSOs, depending on how well they are "packed" or "stacked." If there are three or four individuals per QSO, as there often are in satellite QSOs, about 100 simultaneous users could be accommodated in this S_1 transponder. S_1 performance would average about as good as AO-10 got at its best: S/N of about 13.4 dB. Moreover, under ideal conditions, S_1 could deliver 24.4-dB S/N, peak (see Table 4). In order to realize the specified user S/N, the Mode S_1 user equipment suite (or better) would be required. As seen in Table 3, it consists of a 1.5-m (5-ft) parabolic dish antenna with a dual 24-cm/13-cm feed. A 10-watt average uplink transmitter would produce 1000-watts EIRP using the recommended 23-dB dish gain at 24 cm.

S_2: Gateway Interconnect

The S_2 subtransponder will potentially provide one of the most important services as well as one of the most dramatic. S_2 will be a gateway interconnect transponder. A gateway is simply a portal from one type of network to another. A terrestrial voice repeater can be viewed as a network—a network of users with radios clustered around and interconnected through the repeater. Similarly, the satellite users can be viewed as a network. Interconnection of these networks is accomplished through a gateway. In this context a gateway could be a repeater equipped with an interface to the satellite. That is an uplink transmitter, a downlink receiver and associated interface and control circuitry. Functionally, the gateway serves to extend the repeater user's telecommunication into the satellite's network of users, and vice versa. Ideally, the interface would be transparent; that is, a user in either domain (terrestrial repeater user community or satellite user community) could be totally unaware of the existence of the facilitating gateway. Furthermore, by extension, a terrestrial repeater user linked to the satellite through a gateway could then be further linked through the satellite to a second gateway and its respective user community. Again, if the links were executed properly, users on either end of the dual gateway circuit could be unaware of the extended circuit supporting their QSO.

But there is much more to this gateway arrangement than novelty. Sure, it's amusing to visualize a pair of 2-meter handheld-radio users half a globe apart enjoying a pleasant chat, describing the radically different scenes before them. But because of the very disposition of equipment within the gateway arrangement, gateway operations using combinations of terrestrial repeaters linked via satellite offer an

January 1987   43

extremely important approach to emergency communications.

A portable gateway established at a major flood or earthquake site could, for example, link the disaster reaction team to major relief organizations. Support and logistics control could be organized on an unprecedented level. On-scene leaders could communicate instantly with virtually any other QTH in the hemisphere 24 hours a day. A single hand-held radio hiked to a mountaintop airline crash site could communicate directly with state or federal authorities using a gateway on a nearby mountaintop. Establishment of DX communications for local or regional emergency centers could be as simple as implementing the gateway to the continuous coverage satellite(s).

Aside from the unprecedented potential for saving lives and property, gateway facilities would be available for more mundane use between selected repeaters on a daily basis. A limited number of repeater gateways would be authorized access for these routine QSOs when there were no emergency operations underway or if adequate spectrum sharing schemes were to be established. So one age-old fantasy many hams have harbored of having freedom of movement (being mobile or even foot-mobile) while engaging in a DX QSO would be realized simultaneously with the penultimate emergency communications resource!

Moreover, because the real communications "work" involved in communicating the 71,400 km (44,400 mi) or so to/from the geosynchronous satellite is accomplished by the gateway, the equipment burden on the gateway user is reduced to absolute minimum—essentially, only what is needed to communicate over the distance to and from the local gateway/repeater. And that could even be done in some cases with one of those new, ultra-miniature 100-mW hand-held rigs now on the market. For a community of terrestrial repeater users who have an interest in linking their repeater to others across the continent, it makes sense to pool their resources to establish a single gateway for the long-haul to/from the satellite, rather than each individual undertaking the cost. Thus, the gateway users sharing the resource would be, in effect, establishing a Time Division Multiple Access (TDMA) system for communicating with the world outside their local repeater community on a given "channel,"-one of several FDMA channels available.

Compare this TDMA access to the FDMA access users of the S_1 transponder enjoy. The S_1 FDMA user undertakes his own uplink/downlink burden. It costs him the equipment required to establish the link. For this investment he obtains time-independent use of the S_1 linear transponder, ie, he can use it whenever he cares to. On the other hand, the gateway TDMA user, having pooled the uplink/downlink resource in the form of the gateway equipment, may have to queue up to use the resource, ie, wait until it is free for his use. Thus, he has reduced his personal equipment burden at the cost of time-independent QSOing; he's time-sharing the resource with others.

To establish a gateway QSO, the user could simply pick up his hand-held and tap out a few numbers on the DTMF pad to instruct the terrestrial repeater to enable gateway mode. When the gateway replied with a signal indicating the satellite's Demand Assignment Multiple Access (DAMA) facility had responded, indicating a vacant channel pair was available, the gateway user would then tap out the code for the other gateway repeater he wanted to link to. The DAMA facility would then assign a channel pair to the originating gateway and the target gateway, and the link would be established for a preset time period. Users of the originating repeater would then be in contact with users of the target repeater.

The technology to achieve this type of circuit is not new. It derives straight from the pages of today's terrestrial cellular mobile telephone systems. Amateur Radio implementation of a similar system could be much simpler, however, since much of the redundancy and protection used in cellular mobile radio (to assure privacy and avoid misconnects) could be eliminated. It's obvious the S_2 subtransponder could spur enormous achievements in emergency as well as routine communications.

S_3: Packet Gateway Interconnect

Packet radio is generally acknowledged to be the area in which Amateur Radio is currently experiencing the fastest growth. Nearly 20,000 packeteers are now active, according to some sources. That's probably 10-15% of all active US amateurs. The proportion is expected to grow significantly in the last years of this decade. Local Area Networks (LAN) established around a digipeater hub have been linked to other LANs through VHF, UHF and even HF links. Coast-to-coast connectivity, albeit noninstantaneous, is now a fact. Messages dropped in specific packet-radio nodes often reach an individual destination addressee in a day or less. And they arrive there error-free.

The growth of the terrestrial networks is progressing in a step-wise, part directed, part random pattern. Interconnection between widely separated digipeaters on the East Coast and West Coast and some places in between is now possible. But what if these LANs and groups of LANs could be linked by satellite into a continental or even multicontinental network? That's exactly what the S_3 Packet Gateway Interconnect transponder is about. It could link dozens, even hundreds, of packet gateways together with a high-speed trunk. While our initial calculations were made based on a 19.2-kbits/s data rate, the trunk bandwidth could even be up to 56 kbits/s or more if projected-use estimates indicate more resource is warranted.

Recreational use of the packet gateway transponder would, of course, be part of its mission statement. But there is much more to it than merely the digital ragchew, even the DX digital ragchew. Just as the essential "justifying" rationale for the S_2 voice gateway interconnect transponder is the facility and capacity to provide unprecedented emergency communications capability, so, too, would the packet gateway interconnect transponder open new modes of public service. Today's Amateur Radio communicators are coming to well appreciate the tremendous benefits packet radio has over more traditional modes such as CW and even RTTY. Packet-radio messages are error-free, high-speed and self-documenting. Traffic handling, routing, sorting, etc, can all be automated. The result is often remarkable improvements in traffic throughput, accuracy and, most important, communications effectiveness. Portable packet terminals installed on jeeps, rescue trucks and the like are now appearing in and among forward-thinking Amateur Radio emergency-communications communities.

The S_3 transponder aims to afford the emergency LAN a port to a wider community. As required, the field operations center and even portables could communicate with regional or even national emergency-management centers to communicate status, request specific support and implement actions directed by headquarters via this channel. As with the S_2 voice gateway interconnect, S_3 would be available for recreational use, but earn its keep in providing unique emergency and general public-service communications resources as required.

S_4: Broadcast Mode Gateway Interconnect

S_4 is not a separate transponder, but rather a different mode of employment of the S_2 voice gateway interconnect subtransponder. By reallocating on-board resources, a broadcast capability of notable proportions could be established. As shown in Table 4, nearly 40-dB peak S/N ratio might be obtained using advanced SSB techniques. (Amplitude-compandored single sideband, ACSSB, is one means of achieving this very high level of S/N ratio performance.) That's as good as, and in some cases better than, commercial telephone circuits.

The S_4 Mode might be used for many routine and public-service activities. In routine use, ARRL W1AW bulletins might be sent to groups of terrestrial gateway repeaters. Listeners would use their VHF or UHF hand-held radios to tune in the bulletins on their local repeater. Groups of repeaters could be addressed selectively, say by time zone, by tone-encoded addressing. When a given repeater heard its address on the S_4 Mode downlink, it would interconnect the gateway's downlink receiver to the repeater transmitter to retransmit the audio to the repeater's coverage area. Local repeater operators could, of course, override the linking signal at will with local, manual intervention.

However, in the event of an emergency, groups of repeater gateways could be called up using the tone-activated alert scheme. In this way, news of regional or more general emergencies could be flashed to hundreds, even thousands, of repeaters in a few seconds. Imagine the improvements in emergency response afforded. When combined with existing emergency communications structures at the regional and state level, the result could be unprecedented effectiveness in response to earthquakes, hurricanes, general tornado activity, sudden flood emergencies, and so forth.

On the more routine side again, the S_4 mode could help unify Amateur Radio by facilitating the teleconference radio net concept, which to this point has relied on terrestrial telephone network linking of a hundred or more repeaters several times per year. Imagine this concept expanded to several thousand repeaters on line. Moreover, the equipment requirements for a S_4 Mode Receive Only (RO) gateway are quite moderate. As shown in Table 3, a 1.5-m dish with a single 2.4-GHz feed, a routine LNA and a mixer to a convenient IF are all that would be required. By the time the S_4 mode flies, one could likely establish an S_4 RO gateway facility for $300 or less!

S_v: The Mode S Video Subtransponder

Advances in digital television and video data-compression techniques suggest to us there may at last be a good mesh between amateur TV (ATV) and OSCAR satellites. Previously, constraints of power and bandwidth have made anything but occasional forays with slow-scan TV (SSTV) impossible on OSCAR. Now, however, using video data compression techniques we believe it possible to include a transponder capable of relaying digital video at the rate of perhaps 500 kbits/s. Commercial and military developments using comparable rates are very encouraging. Thus, we have every reason to believe these leading-edge techniques will be available to advanced amateurs by the time S_v is on line.

A more general view of the S_v transponder is that it is a general-purpose, high-speed transponder and that it could (should) be configured to handle the Amateur Radio equivalent of the Integrated Services Digital Network (ISDN) now being fielded by telecommunications companies throughout the world. If this were done, bulk file transfer could be accomplished at astounding rates. The types of services that could be provided with the S_v transponder beyond these examples are numerous. Distribution of Amateur Radio software, articles and research papers are some examples that come to mind.

Using the S_v transponder as an ISDN facility for digital video, very-high-speed packet, digitized voice, file transfer, some combination of these or some new, presently unforecast mode is a matter for our study teams and the Amateur Radio community to decide. But it seems clear that this area could be as fertile as our collective imagination.

Microwave Experiment

A further module that could be included on board Phase 4 is a microwave-beacon experiment. Much work is being done using narrowband emissions as high as X-band (10 GHz). Imagine having a permanent 10-GHz beacon aboard AMSTAR to align antenna feeds, tweak LNAs and calibrate antenna positioning equipment. Such a field alignment tool might go far in advancing both interest and proficiency in the SHF bands. This experiment continues under study for possible inclusion.

Conclusion

Traditional OSCAR users have been a specialized lot. They have enjoyed many of the occasionally esoteric challenges becoming highly proficient on OSCAR involves. Tracking and figuring access are not bothersome chores but rather part of the fun to this dedicated bunch. But clearly the view of what's fun and what's not depends on one's interest. Certainly, an emergency communicator is less interested in calculating access to a satellite than communicating his emergency traffic! So unless something changes, OSCAR use will remain a special art practiced by a relatively small group of aficionados.

But it is now abundantly clear that the nature of the satellite game is about to change dramatically with the advent of Phase 4. These changes come about from two fundamental causes:

1) Maturation of OSCAR technology and technologists to where the media becomes transparent to the user, whereas previously the medium was in large measure part of the message (or reason for being on OSCAR). Thus, rather than evolve to further refinements of a traditional theme, OSCAR will be revolutionized to become a utility available to virtually anyone who wishes to participate. Acquisition of special equipment and skills will be minimized and, in essence, consolidated in the gateway concept. There, many participants can share the cost burden. The esoteric aspects of satellite communication can be offset and eliminated by more sophisticated engineering than has ever been incorporated. In sum, it is the highest form of the engineering discipline to make the inherently complex seem simple and generally accessible.

2) There is a growing, urgent need to make productive use of our incalculably valuable spectral resources. Where commercial interests see our UHF spectrum quite literally in terms of gigabucks (billions), you must be convinced the pressure to abscond with the heart of our hobby (our frequencies) will become enormous. We simply *must* do better to justify our continued occupancy of the UHF bands, lest we lose them forever. Far from being the sounds of distant cannons, the threat is clear and present. If we don't move now, we could very well face significant challenges for our spectrum at the next World Administrative Radio Conference (WARC)—or even sooner if the FCC opts to change those secondary allocations. An Amateur Radio satellite using key UHF frequencies in providing real, tangible, demonstrable public service on a regular basis is one of the best ways we know to ensure we retain our spectral resources. Building Phase 4 and using it for the general public benefit is not just a further expression of altruism, then, but an element in the preservation of our most valuable resource—spectrum—for decades to come. We *must* make better use of our UHF spectrum soon or it surely *will* be gone!

The challenge of Phase 4 is this: Come to understand the potential for unprecedented levels of public service and technical achievement; develop the plan to implement the system that manifests the potential and wisely manage the powerful resource that results.

Is Amateur Radio up to this challenge? We obviously believe so, or we would not have brought this preliminary vignette to your attention. We sincerely believe Phase 4 will be operational in about five years and that it will forever change the nature of our hobby. To realize its full potential, however, substantial effort must be dedicated to first eliciting suggestions on meshing the strawman system with actual needs of the user community. For example, the operational requirements of the emergency communications community are best known by the emergency communicators. The direction and objectives of the packet-radio activity are best known to the packeteers, etc. Thus, one of AMSAT's main challenges is to "network" (establish working relations with) its system architects and engineers with the user communities.

To that end, AMSAT is briefing leaders in various Amateur Radio communities regarding the nature of the project and progress toward specific goals. Conversely, AMSAT is actively seeking inputs on technical and organizational matters. Would-be participants should understand at the outset, however, that this is a long-term project that will require comparably long-term dedication by the participants. ATVers, microwave experimenters, repeater organizations, emergency communicators, traffic networks, packet-radio users and all those with a long-term interest are invited to share their ideas on Phase 4 and potential applications. Invitations to participate in applications research studies will be issued in 1987 to individuals and groups who may contribute to the program. Expressions of interest may be sent to AMSAT, Phase 4 Program Manager, PO Box 27, Washington, DC 20044. (Please include a business-size SASE if a reply is sought.)[1]

Phase 4 can change Amateur Radio for the better by providing real public service while simultaneously providing space-age telecommunications to a broad cross-section of Amateur Radio. In that sense, it's not something that we would *like* to do, but rather something we simply *must* do!

---

[1]AMSAT membership is open to the public. Members receive the biweekly newsletter, *Amateur Satellite Report*, and other benefits. Inquire about membership and how to get started in OSCAR by writing to AMSAT.

"AMSAT's MICROSAT/PACSAT Program" by Tom Clark, W3IWI

By Jan King, W3GEY and Ward Silver, NØAX

Published in 1988 in the *Proceedings of the 6th AMSAT-NA Space Symposium*, the paper that follows captures well the ground-breaking "small sat" design process and presents an initial overview of the satellite structure. The basic idea began as creating PACSATs that were purely digital, acting as orbiting packet radio bulletin board systems. Packet radio standards and basic TNCs had just been announced in 1981, yet it seemed logical to the initial design group that the packet network could be extended into space.

Creating a reliable packet link between the ground and an orbiting BBS was not as simple as just increasing the turn-around delays on the packet TNC! Numerous advances at all levels of the communication link were required. Karn's paper from the 1983 AMSAT conference (see the References table at the end of this book) covers a wide variety of issues that had to be addressed, especially techniques new to Amateur Radio such as forward error correction (FEC) and dealing with the "hidden transmitter" problems associated with a receiver having a visibility footprint hundreds of miles across!

Nevertheless, the basic design seemed feasible and buildable. Amateurs had more than a dozen successful satellites to their credit and were rapidly building experience and credibility with space programs around the world. During the late 1970s and early 1980s, however, American launch capacity had shifted to the STS (Space Shuttle) system and with the loss of the Challenger in 1986 AMSAT had lost its primary ride to orbit.

A year later, Jan King, W3GEY, had solidified his design, settling on a 9 inch by 9 inch cube with five internal 8 inch by 8 inch trays of electronics and batteries and the outside of the cube covered in solar cell panels to supply power. The idea of standardizing on specific design details, mechanical form factors, electrical and data interfaces, power sources, and so on turned out to be a very useful one for the amateur satellite program, leading directly to the CubeSat form factor that is in widespread use today. Even so, as King describes it, the idea was a tough sell when most satellites tipped the scales at hundreds of kilograms.

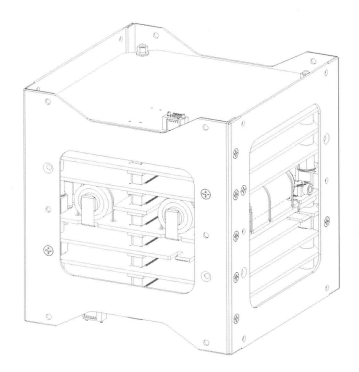

The *Fox 1* satellite, currently under construction by AMSAT-UK and scheduled for launch in 2014. Carrying FM repeater and high-speed digital communications capability in a 10 cm cube weighing approximately 1.33 kg (3 lb), the satellite is typical of the CubeSat satellite family. Illustration Robert Davis, KF4KSS and Tony Monteiro, AA2TX; courtesy AMSAT

"The idea of small satellites fulfilling research roles or operating as a constellation to handle larger missions had not yet evolved. I think, even today, this is a major issue…there is not a full confidence that small satellites can tackle difficult missions.

"By the time 'small satellites' (Lite-sats at that epoch) were born the Amateur Radio community had been building satellites for 19 years and had launched 9 of them in total. So, we'd been at this for a pretty long time already…we didn't see what all the fuss was about. Small satellites were not a new idea to us at all.

"There are some who would ask, 'Have small satellites really succeeded?' But I would now respond resoundingly, yes, they have. You cannot look at the 2.5 meter resolution photos that are now being produced by the *TOPSAT* satellite and not marvel that a 150ish kg spacecraft took those pictures. You can't help but marvel that a small Canadian satellite like *MOST* can, day-in and day-out point at a star with an accuracy of under one arc-second. These accomplishments were vastly more cost effective than their large satellite counterparts and in my option, we have turned the corner. What made this possible really occurred in three broad areas of development:

• Moore's Law: Memory density, processing speed and just sheer circuit complexity have all increased exponentially while power requirements to support these improvements have decreased exponentially. Certainly, computers with 200-400 MIP capability operating on PCBs that are only 10 cm by 10 cm on a side and requiring only a few watts of power can do an awful lot of calculating in a very small volume.

• Major improvements in the efficiencies and radiation hardness of photovoltaic device technology. Solar cells during my professional career (starting in 1968) have increased in efficiency from 8.0% to 28.6%. That's an improvement of 3.6 times in say, 35 years. Such improvements make high power "minisats" a force to be reckoned with and they make CubeSats possible.

• Major technology improvements in RF devices. Their dc-to-RF efficiency and frequency operating range have increased dramatically. These improvements are particularly important to small satellite system designers who must be mindful of power consumption, dissipation and device reliability at all times.

"We haven't yet done a real deep space mission with a proper small sat but AMSAT among others is working on that…our German affiliate organization AMSAT-DL is working on a Mars mission called Phase-5. I believe we can build a small satellite constellation that can "make a difference" and put them into orbit about any of the inner planets or moons of same. But, the 'killer app' — where is she?"

At the conclusion of a book documenting a century of technology advances in Amateur Radio, it seems appropriate to close by referring to a mission to Mars. Amateurs have participated in many state-of-the-art activities, supported science at the frontiers of exploration, and created entirely new systems through a love of experimentation and innovation. When sometime in our upcoming second century, the first weak amateur signals from a transmitter on the Red Planet appear out of the noise, Amateur Radio will have demonstrated that it not only belongs to humanity's relentless technological expansion but it is an essential element. Are you ready?

One of Amateur Radio's great unclaimed prizes, the Elser-Mathes trophy is to be awarded for the first two-way amateur contact with the planet Mars. Perhaps the bicentennial edition of this book will feature the winner and tell the tale of how that QSO was made!

AMSAT's MICROSAT/PACSAT PROGRAM

Tom Clark, W3IWI
6388 Guilford Rd.
Clarksville, MD 21029

ABSTRACT

In 1989 AMSAT-NA plans to launch the first of a series of low-earth orbit (LEO) satellites dedicated to serving digital store-and-forward message handling. These satellites are quite small cubes, approximately 230 cm (9 inches) on a side weighing less than 10 kg; this small size has led to our calling the project MICROSAT. Despite the small size, the satellites are crammed with state-of-the-art electronics. This paper will review the development program leading to this design and some of the technical details as well as describing how the terrestrial user will make use of the resource. We are planning on the launch of 4 satellites using MICROSAT technology into LEO in early 1989, and several more launches over the next 2 years.

A BIT OF HISTORY

In October 1981, the ARRL, AMRAD and AMSAT jointly hosted the first Networking Conference when packet radio was in its earliest period of development. Doug Lockhart (VE7APU) and the VADCG group had put the first TNCs into our hands. Hank Magnuski (KA6M) and the PPRS had the first digipeater on the air. In the D.C. area a few of us (W4MIB, WB4JFI, K8MMO, W3IWI, KE3Z) were on the air making funny sounds. The seed was planted!

On a warm sunny afternoon the following spring, at the AMSAT lab at NASA Goddard, I took Jan King (W3GEY) aside and told him of an idea I had. At the time we were building the AO-10 satellite which was to provide global scale communications from its vantage point in high earth orbit (HEO). My idea was to provide similar communications coverage from LEO using digital store-and-forward techniques, albeit not in real time. The basic idea was for the sender to uplink a message to the LEO satellite; then at a later time when it was in view of the recipient, it would be forwarded to him automatically.

After some more design work, I enlisted the aid of Den Connors (KD2S) who was then spearheading the effort in Tucson which became known as TAPR. Den and I started beating the bushes for support for the program. When the ideas became known to AMSAT, some of the old timers accused us of having lost our minds with statements like "There aren't more than a couple of hundred people on packet. Packet radio will never amount to anything. etcetera etcetera". By the fall of 1982 we were starting to see some ground-swell of support, so Den and I scheduled a special meeting (to be held in conjunction with AMSAT's annual meeting) which was to get inputs from packeteers in several groups on the PACSAT concept. The second purpose was to try to see if we couldn't come up with a national protocol standard; the result was the adoption of AX.25 (for which some people STILL blame me!).

Soon thereafter we found a potential sponsor who needed PACSAT support to aid in disseminating information on technologies appropriate to developing countries and thus was formed a tie between AMSAT and the Volunteers in Technical Assistance (VITA) and Gary Garriot (WA9FMQ). The VITA PACSAT project enlisted the assistance of Harold Price (NK6K), Larry Kayser (VE3QB/WA3ZIA, now VE3PAZ) and a number of others. The VITA/PACSAT team decided to test their messaging concepts on a UoSAT spacecraft resulting in UO-11's Digital Communications Experiment (DCE). The partnership between VITA and the UoSAT group has continued, and the UoSAT-D spacecraft (to be flown at the same time as our Microsats) is the culmination of that effort.

In the meantime I told the Miki Nakayama (JR1SWB) and Harry Yoneda (JA1ANG) of JAMSAT of our design concepts. The JAMSAT/JARL team were able to implement many of these ideas in the mode "JD" hardware on the Japanese JAS-1 (JO-12) satellite. They also developed state-of-the-art reproducable 1200 BPS PSK demodulator designs which have become important for future spacecraft designs. Unfortunately the negative power budget on JO-12 has limited the utility of an otherwise excellent spacecraft.

Figure 1. A photograph of the structural model of the MICROSAT satellite.

For the next couple of years any idea of our building a PACSAT in the USA languished. First we were busy building the AO-13 satellite in consort with AMSAT-DL. The American dependence on the Space Shuttle and the lack of suitable launches on which we could hitchhike made opportunities few and far between. We looked at low-thrust motors using water or Freon propellants to lift us to a suitable LEO if we used the Shuttle's GASCANs. Two groups flew small satellites ejected from GASCANs on the shuttle; one was NUSAT, built by a of students and faculty at Weber State College in Ogden, Utah. Then with the loss of the Challenger, even those hopes for our building a PACSAT were dashed.

THE BIRTH OF MICROSAT

The scene now shifts to November, 1987 in a hotel room in Detroit after the banquet at AMSAT's annual meeting. Jan King, Bob McGwier (N4HY), Phil Karn (KA9Q) and I are sitting around at 1AM. Jan starts telling us of a concept that he and Gordon Hardman (KE3D) have been thinking about. It involves a very small, simple satellite, a 9" cube. He describes how five 8" x 8" x 1.6" module "trays" would be stacked to make up the inner frame of a satellite. Then on the small 9" x 9" solar panels would make up the outside skin. He told us that he believed he had several different potential launches that could carry several of these cubes to LEO and asked us what we could do with the limited space. By 3 AM we had a conceptual design, we had done link margin calculations, we had selected a candidate CPU, and we had estimated size, weight and power requirements for each of the modules. The adrenalin flowing in our veins was at an all-time high!

By early December we had refined the basic design. Dick Jansson (WD4FAB) had done a complete mechanical design. We held a preliminary design review at the AMSAT office and decided we were GO!

While all this was going on, contacts were made with Junior DeCastro (PY2BJO) of the Brazilian BRAMSAT group, Arturo Carou (LU1AHC) of AMSAT-LU and with the NUSAT group at Weber State. Each agreed to join the team and we settled on building four satellites: The AMSAT-NA and AMSAT-LU satellites would be classical PACSATs. The Weber State satellite would be a PACSAT augmented by a TV camera which would send down pictures encoded in normal AX.25 packet frames. The Brazilian satellite would be the DOVE (Digital Orbiting Voice Experiment) which would "talk" voice bulletins which could be copied on a normal HT.

PACSAT AND ALOHA

First we need to review a little packet radio theory. Let us assume that the satellite operates with its transmitter and receiver on different bands so that the communications links are full-duplex. Let us also assume that there are many users, each with similar capabilities, who are spread out over the entire spacecraft "footprint". Let us further assume that traffic is balanced -- whatever goes up to the spacecraft equals what comes down, so the uplink and downlink channel capacity needs to be balanced.

Since the ground-based users are spread out, the cannot hear each other. Each will transmit at random in the hopes that his packets make it thru. This is the classic ALOHA network configuration with "hidden terminals". It can be shown that collisions on the uplink channel will statistically reduce the channel capacity so that only $(1/2e)$ = 18.4% of the packets make it thru. Thus, the downlink (on which there are no collisions) can support about 5 times as much traffic as can a single, collision-limited uplink.

There are two ways out of this dilemma. First, the uplink users could use a data rate about 5 times the downlink; this approach was taken by the AMSAT-DL designers of AO-13's RUDAK experiment where a 2400 bit per second (BPS) uplink is balanced against a 400 BPS downlink.

The second approach is to have multiple, separate uplink receivers. The FO-12 satellite has four 1200 BPS uplink channels balancing one 1200 BPS downlink.

MODEMS AND RADIOS FOR PACSAT

For our PACSATs, we have allowed for both solutions to the ALOHA limit. Like FO-12, there are to be four user uplink channels; however each of which can be commanded to support 1200, 2400, 4800 and possibly 9600 BPS uplinks. The downlink transmitter will start its life at 1200 BPS, but higher rates should be possible.

Our design was heavily influenced by a decision we made early on: we would only use standards which were supported and available "off the shelf". Thus when our PACSAT comes to life, the ground user can use the identical hardware he uses for FO-12 today. The user's uplink will be at 1200 BPS, Manchester-encoded FSK and the downlink will be 1200 BPS binary PSK. These standards are supported by the TAPR and G3RUH modems, by the myriad FO-12 modems available on Akihabara in Japan, and by the DSP modems that N4HY and I have been working on.

These "mo" modulator in these modems plugs into the mike jack on a stock 2M FM radio, which we assume can be tuned in 5 kHz steps. The satellite link margins should be such that 10-25 watts into an omnidirectional antenna should be adequate (providing everyone runs similar power).

The "dem" demodulator plugs into an SSB-capable 70 cm receiver or all-mode transceiver, which needs to be tunable in 100 Hz (or preferably finer) steps. The PSK downlink should be "Q5" even with an omnidirectional antenna, providing the local noise level is low.

The spacecraft's receiver has 15 kHz wide channels, regardless of the bit rate programmed at the spacecraft. The 1200 BPS data rate combined with an FM deviation of < 3 kHz, plus doppler shift, plus 5 kHz steps on a typical FM radio just fit the 15 kHz bandwidth. At some later date we will begin enabling selected uplink receiver channels for higher data rates (like 4800 BPS), but the user will now have to pre-steer the doppler and set his frequency more accurately than 5 kHz. Also most stock FM radios will not pass the 4800 BPS data rates without significant modifications.

5

ONBOARD PACSAT

Let us now discuss some of the features of the satellite's architecture. The electronics is divided into modules, with the space inside each module being about 7.8" x 6.5" x 1.5". The mechanical layout has five of these modules stacked atop each other as shown in Figure 2, which we will describe from top to bottom.

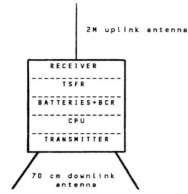

Figure 2. PACSAT LAYOUT

RECEIVER

The core of the receiver is the Motorola MC3362 single-chip FM receiver, couple with a stock NDK crystal filter with 15 kHz bandwidth centered at 10.7 MHz. The filter has very good skirts, with 80-90 dB ultimate rejection. The input to the 3362 is an IF in the 40-50 MHz range. The 1st LO in the 3362 is crystal controlled to mix to 10.7 MHz. Following the filter, the 3362's second mixer is driven from a crystal controlled 8.9 MHz 2nd LO to produce a final IF of 1.8 MHz selected for best linearity of the MC3362's FM detector (discriminator).

The MC3362's FM detector drives two matched data filters, each of which uses one section of a TLC274 CMOS op amp; the 2-pole Butterworth filters are optimized for 1200 and 4800 BPS data rates. A CD4066 analog switch selects the output of one of the two filters to drive the data clipper section of the 3362. The appropriate filter is selected by the CPU.

In addition, one section of the TLC274 produces an analog signal in the 0-2.5v range corresponding to the user's frequency (the "disc meter") and another produces a 0-2.5v analog signal corresponding to the user's signal strength (the "S meter").

All this circuitry takes up 1.5" x 3" on the receiver's circuit board and draws under 20 mW (< 4 ma at 5V). This circuit is replicated five times to provide the 4 user uplink channels plus a command/control channel.

The design of this portion of the receiver was done by W3IWI with invaluable inputs from Eric Gustavson (N7CL).

In front of this bank of five FM IF strips is a fairly conventional GaAsFET preamp with a noise figure < 1 dB. A narrow-band 3-stage helical filter provides selectivity between the GaAsFET preamp and a dual-gate MOSFET mixer which is driven by a crystal-controlled LO at about 100 MHz. The output of the MOSFET (at 40-50 MHz) drives five emitter followers to provide isolation between the five FM IF stages. The design of these stages was done by Jim Vogler (WA7CJO) and W3IWI.

The total power consumption for the entire receiver is about 150 mW.

[As a side note -- the receiver modules designed for PACSAT have been made easily reproducable, with very few "twiddles". All components, including the coils and helical filter are off-the-shelf items purchasable from sources like Digi-Key. It is anticipated that TAPR and/or AMSAT will make single-channel receiver kits available for use in dedicated packet link applications if there is enough interest].

TSFR

For PACSAT, this is a dummy module. TSFR means "this space for rent", and is reserved for future expansion.

POWER SYSTEM

The Battery Charge Regulator (BCR) module contains the NiCd battery pack, the charger that conditions solar panel power to charge the batteries, and the switching regulators that produce the +5 and +10 v power needed by each module. The BCR and regulator design was done by Jon Bloom (KE3Z) with help from Gordon Hardman (KE3D).

The solar panels make use of high-efficiency silicon cells with back-surface reflectors (BSR). BSR technology is new, but it allows for much higher efficiency; if a photon does not produce electricity as it passes thru the silicon on its way in, the reflector allows a second chance to "grab" it. The solar panel electrical and mechanical design was done by Jan King (W3GEY) and Dick Jansson (WD4FAB), and the solar panels are being produced under contract by Solarex.

The price of space qualified NiCd batteries has become prohibitive, so new, low cost approaches have been adopted. Larry Kayser (VE3PAZ) and his group in Ottawa proved with UO-11 that if good, commercial grade batteries were purchased, they could be flight qualified. The qualification procedure involves extensive cycling to characterize the charge-discharge curve and temperature performance, X-raying the batteries to look for internal structural flaws, then selecting only the best cells, and then finally potting the batteries.

While the solar panels produce about 14 watts, when averaged over a whole orbit (some time is spent in eclipse), and after losses in power conditioning about 7-10 watts is available.

CPU

In many ways the flight computer is the key to PACSAT. At the time we were selecting the CPU, the SANDPAC group in San Diego were finishing the first pre-production run of the new PS186 network switch. Based on their experience, we selected a similar architecture. The flight CPU is based on the NEC CMOS V-40 CPU (quite similar to an 80C188). The flight CPU includes EDAC (Error Detection and Correction) memory for storage of critical software, plus bank-switched memory for data storage (i.e. "RAM Disk"). We hope to fly upwards of 10 Mbytes on each PACSAT (limited only by available space and the price of memory chips). The CPU, when running hard draws about 2 watts of power.

A companion paper by Lyle Johnson (WA7GXD) and Chuck Green (N0ADI) describes the CPU's architecture in much more detail. A paper by Bob McGwier (N4HY) and Harold Price (NK6K) describes the multi-tasking software. Jim DeArras (WA4ONG) is converting Lyle and Chuck's wire-wrapped prototype to multi-layer circuit board. The ROM-based bootloader to allow recovery from disasters has been written by Hugh Pett (VE3FLL) whose code had previously saved the day on UoSAT.

TRANSMITTER

At the time of this writing, the transmitter is still in the design phase, so some of these parameters may change. The transmitter will be BPSK modulated, and will have its power output changeable by ground command. The current plans are for two power levels, about 1.5 or 4 watts. The transmitter starts out with a crystal oscillator at 109 MHz, and is followed by two doublers to 436 MHz. This design is being done by Stan Sjol (W0KD). Gordon Hardman (KE3Z) is working on a power amplifier using a Motorola MRF750 driver and a MRF752 output stage. The collector voltage on the driver stage will be command selected to be either the +5 or +10v bus to provide power agility. This collector voltage may be amplitude modulated to provide some time-domain shaping to minimize the transmitted bandwidth. Transmitter development is also being done in Canada by Bob Pepper (VE2AO).

GLUE

The myriad mechanical details were all sorted out before we cut a single piece of metal by Dick Janssen (WD4FAB); Dick made extensive use of modern CAD techniques and all drawings were done with AutoCAD (see Figure 3). In Boulder, Jeff Zerr has been shepherding the detailed mechanical layout and find what pieces don't fit. A "show and tell" model was built by ???? with help from Dick Daniels, and a mechanical mockup for vibration testing has been built by Jeff Zerr.

When we began developing the Microsat concept, we took a look at problems that had been major hassles on earlier satellites. High on the list were problems in building a wiring harness and testing individual modules. We also wanted a design that allowed a "cookie cutter" approach to manufacturing since we anticipate a number of launches in the next few years. We came to the conclusion that we needed to develop a bus-like wiring approach with all modules having similar interfaces, and we needed to minimize the number of wires. I took on the task of solving this problem and defining the electrical "glue" that holds the system together.

After exploring a number of options, the design we adopted was to use hi-rel DB25 25-pin connectors on each module and use a 25-wire bus made like a flexible printed circuit. Of the 25 wires, about 40% are used for power distribution, about 40% to carry packet data from the receiver to the CPU and from the CPU to the transmitter, and the final 5 wires are used to let the CPU control functions in the individual modules and for analog telemetry.

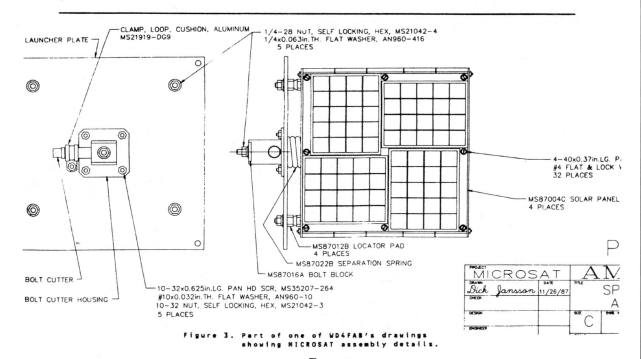

Figure 3. Part of one of WD4FAB's drawings showing MICROSAT assembly details.

AART

In order to squeeze all these command, control and telemetry functions into only five wires, we have built a very small (7 inches long!) LAN with the CPU acting as the network master node and each module being a slave node. Data communications from CPU to module consist of two byte packets; the first byte (with the MSB=1) addresses up to 128 slaves, and the second byte (with MSB=0) is a 7-bit received data field to be passed to the module (RXD). On receipt of a valid address, the module automatically sends back two 8-bit bytes (TXD) of data on another wire. All data is sent with normal asynchronous protocols.

On the CPU side, this async data is generated and received by the UART built into the V40 chip. The protocol is easily simulated on a PC, so testing each module does not require a complete working spacecraft.

In each module, we use a clever IC: the Motorola MC14469F Addressable Asynchronous Receiver/Transmitter (AART). The 14469 is a 44-pin surface mount part (also available as a 40-pin conventional DIP) which implements the protocol just described with very few external parts. It has separate pins for the 7 address bits, the 7 RXD bits and the 16 TXD bits.

The 7 RXD bits are used for a number of functions. The MSB of this word is used to select analog vs. digital functions, with the control data specified by the remaining 6 bits. For digital functions, the 6 bits are treated as two 3-bit nibbles which constitute the address and data for three CD4099 addressable latches, resulting in 24 bits of digital data being available for control functions in the module.

When the MSB selects analog functions, the 6 bits are taken as addresses for CD4052 CMOS analog multiplexer chips which decode 6 discrete analog telemetry samples plus four thermistors. When a module is selected in analog mode, the selected analog signal is switched onto two wires (signal plus return) in the 25-wire bus, and when the module is de-selected the two wires are floated. A single, fast 8-bit 0-2.5v A/D converter in the CPU handles all spacecraft analog telemetry. Each module is responsible for pre-conditioning its analog signals to fit the 0-2.5v range.

All these parts, including some op amps to condition the thermistor signals, plus the DB25 spacecraft bus interface connector and tie-points for all signals needed in the modules are fitted onto a 7.8" x 1.5" board which is mounted against one wall of the module frame. The interface boards in each of the "slave" modules are identical except that the AART chip is strapped to different addresses. This small board has been dubbed the AART board. It was designed by W3IWI and Bob Stricklin (N5BRG). Each board requires 5 mW of power (about 1 ma at 5v).

THE OTHER MICROSATS

DOVE

So far we have described the two Microsat PACSATs: those sponsored by AMSAT-NA and AMSAT-LU. The BRAMSAT DOVE spacecraft is still in the final design phases, but it will be built from many of the same pieces and will have the same general mechanical layout. DOVE will transmit its digitized voice signals in the 2M band with conventional FM modulation. Rather than designing a different receiver system, we have decided to have the command uplinks also on 2M; the DOVE transmitter will turn itself off every few minutes to listen for commands. Only the transmitter module is different for DOVE. As of the time of this writing we are planning to use differentially-encoded voice synthesis (e.g. "delta modulation") with up to 4-bit encoding of the differential data. Preliminary design on the speech synthesizer has been done by Bob McGwier (N4Y) and W3IWI and is being simulated using our DSP hardware.

NUSAT

The Weber State NUSAT MICROSAT is different mechanically from the PACSATs, shown in Figure 4.

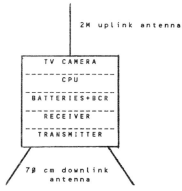

Figure 4. NUSAT LAYOUT

The major difference is that NUSAT has a CCD TV camera in the top module. The TV camera is connected to a high-speed multi-channel "flash" A/D converter which can digitize incoming video signals at 10 MHz sample rate. Its data is stored in memory which can also be accessed by the CPU. The Weber TV camera module and CPU were placed in adjacent modules so that the memory could be easily dual-ported.

The sample rate for the A/D converter and the input signal source can be selected by the CPU. The primary signal source is a CCD TV camera equipped with an electromechanical iris built into its lens. The iris's aperture can also be controlled by the CPU. The camera's field of view allows a 350 km square to be imaged from the satellite's 800 km high orbit.
The camera assembly occupies about 1/4 of the space in the module. It is planned to use video data compression techniques to minimize the downlink data requirements; Weber State and AMSAT-NA plan to have software to support these advanced video techniques available around launch time.

Weber State also plans to try a 1269 MHz video uplink. Video data from this uplink will be digitized by the "flash" A/D converter and loaded into the dual ported memory, just like data from the CCD camera. It is also hoped that the TV camera can be used as an visible and IR spectrometer covering the 400 to 2000 micrometer wavelength band.

The other NUSAT modules are nearly identical to the PACSATs and NUSAT could be also turned into a PACSAT merely by loading different software.

The Weber State team consists of a number of students, staff and faculty members from the Center for Aerospace Technology (CAST) including Bob Twiggs, Bob Summers and Chris Williams.

THE FIRST MICROSAT LAUNCH

AMSAT-NA and the UoSAT group have worked with the European Space Agency and Ariannespace to develop a new launch capability for very small satellites. This will be first tested on the launch of the SPOT-2 Earth Resources Satellite in early 1989. On that flight there will be SIX small satellites -- our four Microsats and two somewhat larger UoSAT spacecraft. The orbit is nearly ideal -- sun synchronous at 800 km altitude, much like the Oscar-8 orbit. At mid-latitudes, passes will occur twice per day at predictable times around 10:30 A.M. and 10:30 P.M. local time.

USING THE MICROSAT SATELLITES

As we mentioned before, our PACSATs and Weber State's NUSAT use ordinary AX.25 packet protocols. To receive any of the three, you merely need to add a PSK demodulator to your 70 cm receiver. The uplink requirements are modest and the same as FO-12. At a later time, when transmitter technology permits and user loading dictates, some of the receiver channels will be reprogrammed to higher speeds. But initially, if you are able to use the FO-12 satellite, then you are all set.

The spacecraft software that you will see will be designed for message handling, and the code is being written by Bob McGwier (N4HY) with inputs from a number of us. The initial software will probably look very much like a W0RLI/WA7MBL BBS system, with a few enhancements. First of all, the prompt that the satellite will send to you will have two telemetry numbers in it -- these are your signal strength and discriminator meter readings. The discriminator meter should be invaluable in helping you center your signal in the receiver's passband and its use will become mandatory as we migrate to higher uplink speeds. The spacecraft software will support multiple, simultaneous users. There may be commands that allow you to request specific telemetry information from the satellite.

I anticipate that much of the utility of these satellites will be as an augmentation of the terrestrial HF long-haul message forwarding networks. If this proves to be true, then fully automated gateway stations will make heavy use of the satellite capabilities.

Therefore it is important that we design both the ground-based and flight software to work together smoothly. We have had ongoing discussions with the writers of BBS code (like W0RLI and WA7MBL) to make sure that both sides of the link will be ready on launch day. In these discussions we have been devising schemes so that the burden of maintaining routing information resides on the ground. New forwarding protocols in which the receiving station tells the sender what message addresses it can handle are being defined. It is likely that these will be coupled with heirarchial domain-oriented addressing schemes like are used by TCP/IP protocols. A user on the W3IWI BBS would have an address like W3XYZ@W3IWI.MD.USA and if I were operating as a gateway for the MD/VA/DE/PA/NJ area, I would be able to inform the spacecraft to send me any messages so addressed.

At the same time that "connected" mode activity is going on, the satellite will be sending UI "broadcast" (i.e. UNPROTO) frames with telemetry and bulletins of interest to all. On NUSAT, digitally encoded pictures of the earth will be sent as UI frames which will be reassembled by the user on the ground.

THE FUTURE

We have reason to believe that there are a number of launch opportunities to LEO for very small satellites. We have designed our Microsats to be easily reproducable. As new capabilities (perhaps 9600 or 19,200 BPS modems? Experiments to fit into the TSFR module?) are developed, we feel there will be opportunities to fly them.

We anticipate non-amateur uses of our technology. Initial discussions with scientists specializing in oceanography and seismology have shown that they have a need for low-cost data collection systems from remote locations. We anticipate a scheme for a commercial licensee to "sell" our technology in these markets. Just like royalties from TAPR's TNC2 project have provided resources for future development activities in packet radio, we hope that Microsat royalties will provide a similar legacy for advancing amateur satellite technology.

We also see that the Microsat technology provides a perfect way for fledgling space groups associated with other AMSAT organizations around the world and with universities to develop their own satellite programs. Don't be surprised to see Microsats being built by people from many nations.

The spacecraft operating software can be uploaded from the ground. As NK6K and N4HY discuss in their companion paper, the software we will be flying is the most complex ever attempted in the amateur satellite program. It probably will crash! We have designed in several safeguards to make this possible. With this flexibility, we also have the ability to try new things. Perhaps we will see new mail-handling protocols developed which use datagrams. Perhaps we will see a PACSAT programmed to be a TCP/IP FTP file server. As the old adage states:

IT'S ONLY SOFTWARE !

PARTING COMMENTS AND ACKNOWLEDGMENTS

The most important "glue" that holds a project like this together is the project manager. We are indeed fortunate to have Jan King (W3GEY), with his wealth of experience, his contacts in the aerospace industry, his mother-hen persistence in reminding us of the rigors of space, and his compulsive personality to make sure everything happens.

Jan's "glue" binds together a team of high-strung, emotional prima donnas who are equally compulsive. Many of the team members have invested a lot of 3AM mornings working on this project! All the team members have had to wear very thick skins to withstand the FLAME ON! communications blasts some of us are prone to emit. Bob Mcgwier, Dick Jansson and Lyle Johnson all deserve special credit for service above and beyond the call of duty.

This project has significant players spread out all over North America, with major activities in NJ, MD, VA, FL, CO, UT, AZ, TX and CA. Unfortunately amateur radio communications are inadequate to keep such a dispersed team working together. We have relied heavily on commercial electronic communication channels, particularly AMSAT's network on GTE TeleMail and TAPR's channels on CompuServe, plus a lot of phone calls. Every few months we get a number of the people in one place and lock the door to make sure everyone REALLY understands what is happening.

We have made heavy use of various CAD tools during the development activities. Mechanical layout was done with AutoCAD. ORCAD was heavily used for developing schematics, wiring lists, parts lists and net lists. CAD PCB layout used Smartwork, ORCAD PCB and Tango. See Figure 5 for an example of some of this use of CAD techniques.

We have done some experimentation using higher-level networking for technical communications to move CAD data using my TOMCAT FTP file server which has a SLIP port in addition to being on the "real" network.

There are two organizations not mentioned earlier that have contributed a lot to this project: TAPR and the ARRL. For many of the volunteers working on this project, the distinction between TAPR and AMSAT is fuzzy since they seem to wear two hats. In addition to the TAPRites working on this project, TAPR has made vital contributions of funds and hardware, without which we couldn't make it. Special thanks to Andy Freeborn (N0CCZ) for helping to make the TAPR/AMSAT interface smooth. At the ARRL labs in Newington, Paul Rinaldo and Jon Bloom have made many vital contributions.

From the AMSAT organization, two people deserve a lot of credit. Vern Riportella (WA2LQQ) was instrumental in arranging the AMSAT-LU and BRAMSAT participation in the project. Martha Saragovitz has acted as mother confessor, paid bills, handled meeting logistics and kept smiling thru it all, despite repeatedly crying out "Where's the money coming from?".

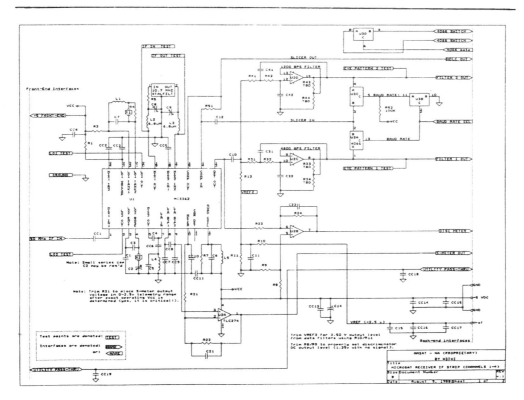

Figure 5. One of W3IWI's ORCAD schematics of the MICROSAT receiver IF strip.

Appendix: Reference Table

This table lists a number of related articles that offer further reading on the topics presented in this book. Some articles, indicated with an X in the last column, are available for download on the ARRL website at **www.arrl.org/history-of-qst**. In the Pages column "ff" means following pages. All *QST* articles are available for download to ARRL members at **www.arrl.org/qst**.

General Historical

Author	Title	Publication or Publisher	Publication Date, Issue or URL	Pages	Avail on Web
C.P Yeang	When Hobbyists were Experts: The U.S. Radio Amateurs' Long Range Short-Wave Experiments Circa 1920	MIT Library	web.mit.edu/sts/pubs/pdfs/ MIT_STS_WorkingPaper_ 37_Yeang.pdf		
C.P Yeang	Characterizing Radio Channels: The Science and Technology of Propagation and Interference, 1900-1935	MIT Library	dspace.mit.edu/bitstream/handle/ 1721.1/39172/60412278.pdf		
C.P Yeang	Probing the Sky with Radio Waves: From Wireless Technology to the Development of Atmospheric Science	University of Chicago Press	2013		
G. C. Southworth	Forty Years of Radio Research	Gordon & Breach	1962		
O. G. Villard, Jr, W6QYT	The ionospheric sounder and its place in the history of radioscience	Radio Science	Nov 1976 Vol. 11, No. 11	pp 847-860	
Kevin McQuiggin, VE7ZD	Amateur Radio and Innovation in Communication Technology	Simon Frasier University	2001		

Amateur Radio in the Spark Era

Author	Title	Publication or Publisher	Publication Date, Issue or URL	Pages	Avail on Web
K. B. Warner, 1BHW	The Story of the Transcontinentals	QST	Mar 1921	p 5ff	X
P. Godley, 2ZE	Official Report on the Second Transatlantic Tests	QST	Feb 1922	p 14ff	
ARRL Staff	The Story of the Transatlantics	QST	Feb 1922	p 17ff	X
K.B. Warner, 1BHW	Direct Contact with Japan	QST	Feb 1913	p 14	
ARRL Staff	Communication with New Zealand	QST	Nov 1924	pp 15, 68	

Amateur Radio's Contributions to Propagation Science

Author	Title	Publication or Publisher	Publication Date, Issue or URL	Pages	Avail on Web
J. Reinartz, 1XAM	A Year's Work Below Forty Meters	Radio News	Apr 1925	pp 1894-95 and 1983-86	
J.O. Smith	Variation of Strength of Amateur Station Signals	QST	Apr 1925	p 17	
A.H. Taylor and E. O. Hulburt	Wave Propagation at High Frequencies	QST	Oct 1925	pp 12-21	X
A.H. Taylor	An Investigation of Transmission on the Higher Radio Frequencies	Proceedings of the IRE	Dec 1925	pp 677-683	
R.A. Heising, J.C. Schelleng & G. C. Southworth	Some Measurements of Short Wave Transmission	Proceedings of the IRE	Vol. 14, No. 5 Oct 1926	pp 613-647	
A.H. Taylor	An Investigation of Transmission on the Higher Radio Frequencies	Proceedings of the IRE	May 1927	p 677	
E. Quaeck	Propagation of Short Waves Around the Earth, Further Communication of the Propagation of Short-Waves	Proceedings of the IRE	Vol 15, 1927	pp 341-345	
A. Russell	The Kennelly-Heaviside Layer	Nature	Oct 1927	p 609ff	
C. Størmer	Short Wave Echoes and the Aurora Borealis	Nature	Nov 1928	p 681ff	
B. Van der Pol	Short Wave Echoes and the Aurora Borealis	Nature	Dec 1928	p 878ff	
J. Millen, W1HRX	Practical Working Data on 3/4 Meter Transmission	Radio News	Dec 1932	pp 348-350, 377	

Author	Title	Publication	Date	Pages	
R. Hull	Extending the Range of Ultra-High-Frequency Amateur Stations	QST	Oct 1934	p 10ff	
R. Hull	Practical Communication on the 224-Mc. Band	QST	Nov 1934	p 8ff	X
Albert W. Friend	A Summary and Interpretation of Ultra-High-Frequency Wave-Propagation Data Collected by the Late Ross A. Hull	*Proceedings of the IRE*	Jun 1945	pp 358-373	
W. Foley, K4FEC	Forecasting Long-Distance Transmission	QST	Feb 1946	pp 36-41	
H. Kauffman, W2OQU	A DX Record: To the Moon and back	QST	May 1946	p 65ff	
O. G. Villard, Jr., W6QYT and A. M. Peterson	Instantaneous Prediction of Radio Transmission Paths	QST	Mar 1952	pp 11-20	
O. G. Villard, Jr., W6QYT and A. M. Peterson	Meteor Scatter	QST	Apr 1953	pp 11-15, 124-126	X
D. Morgan, W2NNT	Trophospheric Scatter Techniques for the Amateur	QST	Mar 1957	p 11ff	X
W. Bain, W4LTU	V.H.F. Meteor Scatter Propagation	QST	Mar 1957	p 20ff	
O. G. Villard, Jr., W6QYT, S. Stein and K. C. Yeh	Studies of Transequatorial Ionospheric Propagation by the Scatter-Sounding Method	*Journal of Geophysical Research*	Sep 1957 Vol. 62, No. 3	pp 399-412	
R. B. Fenwick, K6GX and O. G. Villard, Jr. W6QYT	A Test of the Importance of Ionosphere-Ionosphere Reflections in Long Distance and Around-the-World High Frequency Propagation	*Journal of Geophysical Research*	68 (20), 1963	pp 5659-5666	
R. B. Fenwick, K6GX	Round-the-world high frequency propagation	Stanford Electronics Laboratory, Technical Report No. 71	1963 www.dtic.mil/dtic/tr/ fulltext/u2/404303.pdf		
R. A. Whiting, 5B4WR	How Does TE Work?	QST	Apr 1963	pp 13-14	X
O.G. Villard Jr, W6QYT, et al	Long-Delayed Echoes — Radio's Flying Saucer Effect	QST	May 1969	p 38ff	
O.G. Villard Jr, W6QYT, et al	There Is No Such Thing as a Long-Delayed Echo	QST	Feb 1970	p30ff	
F. Moore, WB9GCC	Homebrew DX Prediction	QST	Aug 1971	pp 52-57	
C. S. Gillmor, W1FK and J. R. Spreiter (Eds.)	Discovery of the Magnetosphere	American Geophysical Union, *History of Geophysics*	Vol. 7 (1987)		
C. Luetzelschwab, K9LA	Transequatorial Propagation	K9LA website		myplace.frontier.com/ ~k9la/Trans-Equatorial_ Propagation.pdf	

Amateur Radio's Collaboration with the Scientific Community

Author	Title	Publication or Publisher	Publication Date, Issue or URL	Pages	Avail on Web
G. Reber, ex-W9GFZ	Cosmic Static	*Astrophysical Journal*	Vol. 100 (1944)	p 279ff	
M. Southworth, W1VLH	ARRL-IGY Propagation Research Project	QST	Sep 1956	p 15ff	X
G. Grammer, W1DF	An Opportunity for Amateur Participation in IGY Satellite Program	QST	Mar 1957	p 32	
K. Bowles, KØCIQ and R. Cohen	N.B.S. Equatorial Region V.H.F. Scatter Research Program for the IGY	QST	Aug 1957	p 11ff	
W. Matthews, G. Ludwig	Scientific Telemetry for USNC-IGY	QST	Jan 1958	p 41ff	
M. Southworth, W1VLH	Another Peek at PRP	QST	Aug 1958	pp 42-44	
M. Southworth, W1VLH	A Look Back and Ahead at PRP	QST	Jun 1959	pp 48-49	
M. Southworth, W1VLH	Night-time equatorial propagation at 50 Mc/s: First results from an IGY amateur observing program	*Journal of Geophysical Research*	Vol. 65, Issue 2, 1960	pp 601-607	

Amateur Radio's Contributions to Antenna Design

Author	Title	Publication or Publisher	Publication Date, Issue or URL	Pages	Avail on Web
J. Kraus, W8JK	The Square-Corner Reflector Beam Antenna for Ultra-High Frequencies	QST	Nov 1940	pp 24-25	X
J. Lawson, W2PV	Simple Arrays of Vertical Elements	QST	May 1971	pp 22-27	
J. Sevick, W2FMI	The W2FMI Ground-Mounted Short Vertical	QST	Mar 1973	pp 13-19	X
J. Sevick, W2FMI	Simple Broadband Matching Networks	QST	Jan 1976	pp 20-23	
J. Lawson, W2PV	Yagi Antennas (Nine-part series)	*Ham Radio*	Jan-Dec 1980		
R. Lewallen, W7EL	Baluns: What They Do and How They Do It	*ARRL Antenna Compendium, Vol 1*	1985		X
R. Lewallen, W7EL	The Simplest Phased Array Feed System — That Works	*ARRL Antenna Compendium, Vol 2*	1989		
D. Straw, N6BV	QST Compares: Antenna-Modeling Software	QST	Oct 1995	p 72ff	

B. Beezley, K6STI	Another Way to Stack VHF/UHF Yagis	QST	Feb 1996	pp 32-34
L.B. Cebik, W4RNL	NEC and MININEC Antenna Modeling Programs: A Guide to Further Information	QEX	Mar 1998	p 47ff
L.B. Cebik, W4RNL	A Beginner's Guide to Modeling with NEC (four part series)	QST	Nov 2000, Dec 2000 Jan 2001, Feb 2011	

Amateur Radio and Radio Circuit Design

Author	Title	Publication or Publisher	Publication Date, Issue or URL	Pages	Avail on Web
J. Lamb, W1CEI	Stabilizing Superheterodyne Performance	QST	Apr 1932	pp 14-17	X
J. Lamb, W1CEI	What's Wrong with Our C.W. Receivers?	QST	Jun 1932	pp 9-16, 90	
J. Millen, W1HRX	A New Approach to Transmitter Design	QST	Mar 1938	p 24ff	
R. Bateman, W4IO and W. Bain, W4LTU	New Thresholds in V.H.F. and U.H.F. Reception	QST	Dec 1958 through Mar 1959		
W. Hayward, W7ZOI	A Competition-Grade CW Receiver	QST	Mar 1974, Apr 1974	p 16ff, p 34ff	
R. Sherwood, WBØJGP (now NCØB)	Present-Day Receivers — Some Problems and Cures	Ham Radio	Dec 1977	p 10ff	
D. Demaw, W1FB and G. Collins, ADØW	Modern Receiver Mixers for High Dynamic Range	QST	Jan 1981	p 19ff	
U. Rohde, KA2WEU (now N1UL)	Testing and Calculating Intermodulation Distortion in Receivers	QEX	Jul 1994	p 3ff	
U. Rohde, KA2WEU (now N1UL)	Theory of Intermodulation and Reciprocal Mixing: Practice, Definitions and Measurements in Devices and Systems, Parts 1 and 2	QEX	Nov 2002, Jan 2003	p 3ff and p 21	X
U. Rohde, KA2WEU (now N1UL)	Performance Capability of Active Mixers	Ham Radio	Mar 1982, Apr 1982	p 30ff and p 38ff	
U. Rohde, N1UL	From Spark Generators to Modern VHF/UHF/SHF Voltage Controlled Oscillators	QEX	Jul 2008	p 42ff	

Amateur Radio, Modes, and Networks

Author	Title	Publication or Publisher	Publication Date, Issue or URL	Pages	Avail on Web
J. Lamb, W1CEI	Background for Single-Side-Band Phone	QST	Oct 1935	pp 33ff	
E. Williams, W2BFD	The Story of Amateur Radio Teletype	QST	Oct 1948	pp 16-20	X
J.P Costas	Poisson, Shannon, and the Radio Amateur	Proc. of the IRE, Vol. 47	Dec 1959	pp 2058-2068	
C. MacDonald, WA2BCW	S.C.F.M. — An Improved System for Slow-Scan Image Transmission	QST	Jan 1961, Feb 1961	pp 28ff, pp 32ff	
I. Hodgson, VE2BEN	Introduction to Packet Radio	Ham Radio	Jun 1979	p 64ff	
P. Martinez, G3PLX	Amtor, An Improved Error-Free RTTY System	QST	Jun 1981	pp 25-27	X
T. Fox, WB4JFI	AX.25 Amateur Packet-Radio Link Layer Protocol, Version 2.0	ARRL	1984		
P. Rinaldo, W4RI	AX.25 Link-Layer Protocol Specification (see www.tapr.org/pub_ax25.html for current spec)	QEX	Feb 1985	p 1	
P. Karn, KA9Q	TCP/IP: A Proposal for Amateur Packet Radio Levels 3 and 4	Proceedings of the 4th ARRL Computer Networking Conference	1985		X
P. Karn, KA9Q	Addressing and Routing Issues in Amateur Packet Radio	Proceedings of the 4th ARRL Computer Networking Conference	1985		
P. Karn, KA9Q	A High Performance, Collision-Free Packet Radio Network	Proceedings of the 6th ARRL Computer Networking Conference	1987	pp 86-89	
P. Karn, KA9Q	MACA — A New Channel Access Method for Packet Radio	Proceedings of the 9th ARRL Computer Networking Conference	1990		X
W. Sinsner, VE4WK	Forward Error Correction for Imperfect Data in Packet Radio	Proceedings of the 9th ARRL Computer Networking Conference	1990		
R. Petit, W7GHM	The "Cloverleaf" Performance-Oriented HF Data Communication System	QEX	Jul 1990	p 9ff	

Author	Title	Publication	Date	Page	X
J. Mortensen, N2HOS	A Beginner's Tour to and Through AMTOR	QST	Nov 1990	pp 53-55	
ARRL Staff	New Packet-Radio Software Available: DX Cluster Monitor Program	QEX	Mar 1991	p 17	
Clas, DL1ZAM and Mack, DL3FCJ	PTC — The PACTOR Controller	QEX	Oct 1991	p 7ff	
R. Bruninga, WB4APR	Automatic AX.25 Position and Status Reporting	Proceedings of the 11th ARRL Computer Networking Conference	1992		
W. Henry, K9GWT	CLOVER Development Continues	QEX	Mar 1992	p 12	
B. Levreault, W1IMM and K. Wickwire, KB1JY	Some recent Amateur Use of Federal Standard Automatic Link Establishment (ALE) Signaling	Proceedings of the 11th ARRL Computer Networking Conference	1992		
G. Reedy, W1BEL	PACTOR: An Overview of a New and Effective HF Data Communication Protocol	Proceedings of the 11th ARRL Computer Networking Conference	1992		
H. Price, NK6K	KA9Q on FEC	QEX	Jun 1993	p 17	
R. Campbell, KK7B	A Binaural I-Q Receiver	QST	Mar 1999	pp 44-48	X
J. Gibbs, KC7YXD	D-STAR: Parts 1-3	QEX	Jul 2003, Sep 2003, Nov 2003		
J. Taylor, K1JT	The JT65 Communications Protocol	QEX	Sep 2005	p 3ff	
R. Meuthing, KN6KB	WINMOR...A Sound Card ARQ Mode for Winlink HF Digital Messaging	Proceedings of the TAPR and ARRL 27th Digital Communications Conference	2008		
R. Bruninga, WB4APR	Universal Ham Radio Text Messaging Initiative	QST	Sep 2009	pp 72-74	
R. Meuthing, KN6KB	WINMOR Phase 2: Demonstration to Deployment	Proceedings of the TAPR and ARRL 29th Digital Communications Conference	2010		
J. Taylor, K1JT	WSPRing Around the World	QST	Nov 2010	p 30ff	X
D. Rowe, VK5DGR	Codec 2 – Open Source Speech Coding at 2400 bit/s and Below	Proceedings of the TAPR and ARRL 30th Digital Communications Conference	2011		

Amateur Radio in Orbit

Author	Title	Publication or Publisher	Publication Date, Issue or URL	Pages	Avail on Web
Various	Oscar III: Technical Description and Operational Guides	QST	Feb 1963 through May 1965	pp 53-56	
W. Orr, W6SAI	Oscar II: A Summation	QST	Apr 1963	p 68ff	
J. King, W3GEY	The Sixth Amateur Satellite	QST	Jul 1973		
K. Meinzer, DJ4ZC	IPS: An Unorthodox High-Level Language	Byte	Jan 1979	pp 152-159	
D. Conners, KD2S and T. Clark, W3IWI	PACSAT — A New AMSAT Satellite Project	QEX	Nov 1982	p 2ff	X
P. Karn, KA9Q	Modulation and Access Techniques for PACSAT	Proceedings of the 2nd ARRL Computer Networking Conference	1983		X
J. King, W3GEY	A Review of the Phase IV Project	Proceedings of the 4th AMSAT Space Symposium	1986	pp 77-81	
D. Jansson, WD4FAB	The Phase IV Project — A Transition to Phase IIID	Proceedings of the 8th AMSAT Space Symposium	1990	pp 3-6	
J. King, W3GEY	The In-Orbit Performance of Four MICROSAT Spacecraft	4th Annual USU/AIAA Small Satellite Conference	1990		
F. Bauer, KA3HDO and L. McFaddin, W5DID	Shuttle Amateur Radio Experiment (SAREX) Hardware Configurations and Flight Operations Support	Proceedings of the 10th AMSAT Space Symposium	1992	pp 100-110	
J. Kasser, W3/G3ZCZ	Amateur Radio in Space: OSCAR at 30 + Years	Proceedings of the 10th AMSAT Space Symposium	1992	pp 240-253	
P. Shuch, N6TX	Introduction to Amateur SETI	Proceedings of the 15th AMSAT Space Symposium	1997	pp 92-102	
F. Bauer, KA3HDO	Amateur Radio On-Board the International Space Station	Proceedings of the 15th AMSAT Space Symposium	1997	pp 205-211	
J. Puig-Suari and R. Twiggs, KE6QMD	CubeSat: The Next Generation of Educational Picosatellites	Proceedings of the 18th AMSAT Space Symposium	2000	pp 21-38	X
A. Friedman, 4X1KX/KK7KK et al	RUDAK DSP — Software Defined Radio in Space	Proceedings of the 20th AMSAT Space Symposium	2002	pp 28-40	
R. Wright, KC9CDL	Remember, We're Pioneers! The First School Contact with the International Space Station	Proceedings of the 22nd AMSAT Space Symposium	2004	pp 118-126	
B. Bruninga, WB4APR et al	PCSAT2 and AX.25 Packet Radio for University Payloads	Proceedings of the 23rd AMSAT Space Symposium	2005	pp 155-163	X
T. Monteiro, AA2TX	AMSAT-FOX Preview	Proceedings of the 28th AMSAT Space Symposium	2010	pp 113-121	